THE Daily Mail BOOK OF
HOUSEHOLD
HINTS & TIPS

Barty·Phillips

DORLING KINDERSLEY·LONDON

Senior editor
Jemima Dunne

Art editor
Philip Lord

Editor
Sandy Shepherd

Designer
Peter Bailey

Managing editor
Daphne Razazan

Published in Great Britain in 1989
by Dorling Kindersley Limited
9 Henrietta Street, London WC2E 8PS
Second impression 1989
Copyright © 1989 Dorling Kindersley Limited, London
Text copyright © 1989 Barty Phillips

British Library Cataloguing in Publication Data

Phillips, Barty
    The Daily Mail book of household hints
    and tips.
    1. Household management
    I. Title
    640

    ISBN 0 86318 3301 Hbk
    ISBN 0 86318 3743 Pbk

Printed and bound in Italy by A. Mondadori, Verona

Contents

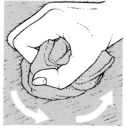

Home Laundry and Clothes Care 113

Household Contents 145

Painting and Decorating 181

Repairs and Maintenance 213

Introduction

Less than a century ago the methods of running a home and the recipes used were long tried and tested, passed down through the generations from mother to daughter. Even so, not everyone in those days was adept at home craft, or Mrs. Beeton would never have had such success with her book Household Management. Today the products and equipment we use in our homes are created by scientists and engineers in laboratories. The extraordinary number of new "wonder" products that they have invented for cleaning the home, the automatic machines which do the work previously done by hand, and the synthetic materials and easy-care fibres, may have made life easier but they have also turned the whole skill of home craft into a much more complicated task.

What you'll find here

This book is full of tried and tested hints and tips aimed at doing a good job in the easiest, quickest and most effective (and least damaging) way. They cover the gamut of home affairs, from organizing your home so that it is easy to run, functional and pleasing, and cleaning it efficiently and safely, to painting and decorating it and keeping it in a good state of repair. All of these tips and ideas are designed to streamline your life so that you have more time to enjoy yourself.

On the whole consumers are still treated with far too much condescension by advertisers and manufacturers, so that where advice is given on products, the reasons for it very often are not. It is obviously better to follow advice if you know the reasons for it. You will find explanations running throughout the book of why particular ways of doing things work best.

There are practical hints on choosing, storing and preparing foods, not only with the health of your family in mind, but also to save you time or to help avert, or rescue, culinary disasters. You are what you eat and modern research has produced some very decided ideas about what is good and what isn't in the way of food and food preparation.

The home repairs section is full of useful tips for decorating your home and protecting it from storm and weather, but it does not assume that you are a D.I.Y. fanatic. The tips cover everything from painting and decorating, laying floor coverings and putting up shelves, to simple electrical and plumbing repairs. Such jobs are enormously expensive if you get someone in to do them and yet they are not difficult to tackle, even for the inexperienced. Here you will find short cuts which won't diminish the finished result, hints on measuring and buying, on choosing the essential tools for the job, and tips to give a professional finish to the first job you attempt.

A large part of the book is devoted to ideas for streamlining the housework, particularly cleaning and home laundry. These cover traditional and effective ways of cleaning the home, trouble-free ways to organize the washing and ironing to avoid a home permanently festooned with washing, guides to removing stains from almost every type of surface, as well as hints on the general care of furniture and valuables.

For parents with young children there are ideas for minimizing the work and mess and streamlining chores, so that you have more time to spend with your children. Having children should be a joy. It should not be clouded by constant worries about not cleaning the house or about whether you are doing the right thing.

There are hints and tips too on choosing and caring for houseplants and pets, which can add warmth to the home and, in the case of pets, provide companionship for adults and children. There is a list of easy-to-care-for plants which the novice indoor gardener might like to start with.

Avoiding pollutants

Many of the new wonder products recommended for use in the home are poisonous to plants and animals, so when we pour them down our drains we pollute the water system and kill living organisms; when we spray some of the aerosols we are doing untold damage to the atmosphere. Even the manufacture of some of these materials creates pollutants in the air.

Advertisements encourage us to use chemicals indiscriminately in the cleaning and polishing of our homes and convince us that there is only one remedy to deal with a problem or household chore. What they won't tell us is that there is no such thing as a completely clean home, and that in fact we need many of the bacteria which live in our environment to protect us against other, more harmful organisms. So, although cleanliness and hygiene are important, obsessive cleanliness, by means of chemicals, is unhealthy and destructive.

It is unfortunate that there is so little information provided by the manufacturers of household products. Few products have a list of ingredients on the label, and if they do, the list is not necessarily comprehensive. However, you can be fairly sure that most household chemicals are harsh, toxic and flammable, and pollute our rivers and waterways to an unacceptable degree. But there are many substances which do the job just as well, without being in any way harmful.

In this book, when household chemicals are mentioned, you will find, where relevant, safer alternatives, or GREEN TIPS, suggested as well. These tips are usually indicated by a 🍃 symbol. Curiously, these are often exactly the same cleaning agents or methods that our grandmothers and great-grandmothers used.

Vinegar, for example, is one of the most versatile substances you could use. It is therefore possible to have a well-run home without polluting the atmosphere.

Waste and recycling

Most products for household use are packaged in materials that are not bio-degradable (that is, they cannot disintegrate into a form that can be absorbed into the environment). This means that it will never be possible to get rid of them. But these containers are so cheap to manufacture and made in such huge quantities that we are encouraged simply to buy items packed in them and throw the packaging away – and join the orgy of waste.

There are products sold in bio-degradable containers, and by recycling as much as possible you will be actively helping the environment: bottle banks collect glass for recycling, paper collection schemes help to reduce the number of trees sacrificed each year; vegetable waste makes excellent compost.

Safety in the home

Homes in general are among the unsafest places. This may be hard to believe, but if you look around your own home critically, you may be surprised to find some classic causes of accidents which you hadn't noticed before. Unguarded fires, old electrical wiring, insufficient or badly placed lighting, loose stair rods, poisonous household chemicals left where children can get at them, flexes trailing over the floor or electric points too near the sink, are all possible causes of accidents. Add to this the sense of familiarity and security the home engenders, which leads a normally sensible person to imagine that he or she can paint a ceiling or put in a new light bulb by balancing an old stool on an armchair, and you can see why there are so many unnecessary accidents in the home every year. In this book you will find safety guidelines and warnings against common unsafe practices, indicated by a ❗❗ symbol. Take heed of them. It is much better to take a little extra care than to end up in hospital with broken bones.

How to use the book

This book is not intended to be "a good read", but to be used as a reference source to keep constantly at hand so that the newest of homemakers and the most experienced can look up anything at a moment's notice. Get into the habit of pulling it out and checking on things you are not quite sure about, but first do read and assimilate the sections on Safety and First Aid so that you never need be caught unawares.

Use the book as a tool. Be as familiar with it as you are with your favourite wooden spoon. And remember, with a house full of lemons and vinegar – who needs chemicals?

Organization

A well-organized home (not an over-organized one) runs smoothly, gives you a neat, clean ordered base to work from and time to enjoy yourself. There is always more work to do in the home; the skill lies in deciding what's necessary and what isn't so that you don't get so involved with the house that you have no time for anything else.

PRIORITIES

Your home should offer harmony, comfort, relaxation, a warm and loving atmosphere.
- It should be orderly but not regimented – it's a house, not an army barracks.
- It should be safe: many homes are highly unsafe with bad lighting, dangerous electrics and things to trip over. Children and old people are particularly at risk.
- It should be maintained and in a good state of repair so that you don't build up trouble and immense bills later on.
- It should be comfortable: not cluttered with too much furniture, and not so formal that you can't lounge back after a hard day.
- It should be tidy but not sterile.
- It should be clean but not obsessively so. Where you can, and should, be insistent is in the correct and hygienic preparation and storage of food.
- It should have a well-stocked store cupboard or larder.
- There should be a carefully thought out budget plan so that you can live comfortably within your income.

Set realistic goals

- If work in the home makes you bad tempered and ratty, you are doing too much.

- Get help from your family but don't expect your high standards from them.
- If you are out at work all day, look into the possibility of a cleaner coming in once or twice a week.
- Do the minimum to keep things under control rather than the maximum: vacuum the main living areas once a week rather than once a day if you can get away with it – some rooms don't even need that.
- Don't attempt too many tasks at once; better to do one or two jobs properly than leave several half done.
- Make sure there's enough food in store for the whole family, but don't feel it necessary to produce two cooked meals a day, especially at weekends. Serve a simple but nutritious lunch of soup, bread and cheese or pâté followed by fruit.
- Let the family do some of their own preparation or buy some convenience foods and encourage them to heat up their own.
- Don't overstretch yourself, financially or physically.
- If you have small children and no help in the house, don't attempt to give large formal dinner parties. If you like entertaining, make it informal.

EFFICIENT HOME MANAGEMENT

This needs, above all, a basic sense of order. There are several tools and techniques to help you achieve this.

Storage

Everything should have its place and should be conveniently sited.

◆ Store kitchen utensils in compartments in drawers or hang them on hooks near the worktop.

◆ Keep plates in a cupboard or on shelves near the sink or in the dining area.

◆ Keep all tools and equipment in a tool box or on hooks on the wall where they can be recognized and reached quickly.

◆ Coats and boots can be kept on hooks and racks in the entrance hall.

◆ Store things off the floor if possible: brooms can be hung between rods or on hooks, shoes can be placed on racks etc.

◆ Toys should be stored in boxes and be graded according to size or type (otherwise the large things damage the small ones).

◆ Keep a toy box in each room so that you can sling the toys in for an instant clear-up.

◆ Spare fuses or fuse wire, a torch and a small electric screwdriver should be kept on a shelf next to the fuse box. Keep spare light bulbs and plugs handy too.

No hoarding

Throw out what you don't need. A house full of old belongings means a house difficult to clean, and things never used because you can't find them.

◆ Discard anything you haven't used for the last 12 months.

◆ Discard anything you or the children have grown out of.

◆ Throw away broken, worn out or redundant belongings, especially those beloved sneakers.

◆ Don't discard toys without asking the children first.

◆ Dispose of all out-of-date medicines by pouring them down the lavatory pan or taking them back to the chemist.

◆ Get rid of all out-of-date brochures and magazines (newspapers can be useful for lighting fires or covering things while painting or cleaning). Take them round to the local charity shop or hospital, but ring first as they may be inundated already.

◆ Remember that charity shops would like your belongings so long as they are in fairly good condition and clean.

Making lists

Making lists is an excellent way of organizing your mind.

◆ Reminder lists on a blackboard on the wall are useful if you want other people as well as yourself to remember things.

◆ A blackboard is specially useful as a "shopping list"; anyone in the house can write on it if they notice things have run out and it saves hunting around the house to check every time you go shopping.

◆ Some people have a "day book" with permanent lists of things to be done and phone calls to be made. These lists are ongoing, dated at the top. When the page becomes full, transfer the uncompleted jobs to the next page and add others as they come up. Tick them off as they are achieved.

Year planners

◆ Offices have year planners – a large wall sheet showing the entire year – so why not homes? Once they are filled in there is no excuse for not knowing who has to be where and when.

◆ Fill in any important date pertaining to the family such as:

◇ Holidays (yours, the children's, the home help's, the company you work for and so on)

◇ Birthdays and name days

◇ Wedding anniversaries

◇ School open days, prize givings, teachers' evenings and other school specials

◇ Visits to or from relations or friends

◇ Medical and dental appointments

◇ Appointments with electrical or gas service engineers and others

THE HOME OFFICE

◆ Set aside some time every day to deal with phone calls, bills and letters. Half an hour to an hour should be enough – you may not always need to use the time but it's better to allow for it just in case.

◆ Make an ongoing list and keep it by the telephone of people you need to get in touch with day by day.

◆ Keep current letters and bills in a box or folder which you go through regularly – once a week or month.

◆ File paperwork that has been dealt with in an indexed file so that you can find it in case of future queries.

USEFUL FILING CATEGORIES

◆ **Pending** Unpaid bills and letters that need to be answered.

◆ **School correspondence** To include correspondence and information.

◆ **Other correspondence** Separate this into "private" and "other".

◆ **Financial** Bank statements; mortgage papers; insurance papers; pension schemes; credit card statements; relevant correspondence.

◆ **Car** Road tax; insurance; registration document; purchase details; hire-purchase details; details on motoring club or association; driving licence; relevant correspondence.

◆ **Home** Details of maintenance and repair work; decorating work, materials used and where you bought them; any other relevant information and correspondence not filed elsewhere.

◆ **Paid invoices** Receipts and relevant correspondence.

◆ **Guarantees and instruction leaflets** Any not in home file.

◆ **Hobbies and interests** This could include catalogues, stockists of materials and tools, cuttings from magazines, the magazines themselves, relevant correspondence, information on clubs you belong to.

FILING SYSTEMS

◆ **Box files** Large A4-sized cardboard boxes, separately labelled, keep different categories of papers separate.

◇ *Variations of these are "cut away" box files which are cheaper and which leave the top half of the papers revealed. You can use an old shoe box instead.*

◆ **Concertina files** These are indexed and particularly useful for filing receipts and paid-up bills.

◆ **Folders** There are cardboard folders or transparent plastic ones, which are useful for papers you want to carry around with you, because they are lightweight and not bulky.

◆ **Filing cabinets** Two-drawer office filing cabinets are available in bright colours, there's no need to be saddled with office green or grey. One should hold enough papers for the most complicated household; two make excellent bases for a desk top.

◆ **Card index files** Useful for addresses or indexed information on particular interests.

◆ Keep filing categories to a minimum or you will forget what you have filed where.

◆ If you have a lot of paperwork – mortgages, budget accounts, school papers, information on hobbies or some aspect of running the home – use a specially designed indexed concertina file, or separate box files on a shelf out of the way of the children. If you have a great deal of paperwork, you may find a small filing cabinet useful.

◆ Keep all documents relating to purchases – bills, receipts and correspondence – at least until the purchase has been finalized and goods received and, even better, until the guarantee runs out.

◆ Most financial papers (bank statements and correspondence about overdrafts and loans; credit card statements; bills and receipts; notifications about budget or long-term payments; tax papers, etc.) and legal papers (e.g. solicitors' letters) should be kept for seven years after they are finished with. After that it is alright to throw them away.

WORKING MOTHERS

◆Rule Number One for the Working Mum: "THE FAMILY COMES BEFORE THE HOUSEWORK".

◆Don't feel guilty. Enjoy your work and make sure the housekeeping doesn't get too complicated. Don't ask too much of yourself.

◆Buy plenty of socks, underwear, shirts, etc. for everyone so that you don't have to do a major wash too often.

◆Do a major wash at night provided the noise doesn't disturb your sleep (or your neighbours'), so that there's one less job to do at the weekend.

◆Shop once a week for the whole week. Try to shop on late night openings during the week so you don't have to compete with the crowds at weekends.

◆Organize meals for the week: frozen to be heated in the microwave; slow-cooked meals to be ready when everyone arrives home; salads which are quick to prepare.

◆Buy ready-made salads and special foods from delicatessens sometimes as a treat for you and the family. Occasional treats are the stuff of life – don't feel guilty about them.

◆Give your young children a good start by getting them up in time so that breakfast is not rushed and there's no panic.

◆For a simple breakfast that can be prepared quickly but that will nourish, try orange juice, milk for the children and tea or coffee for you, cereal with fruit and bread or toast.

◆Encourage other members of the household to do their share of the housework. Don't make it a chore with lists of who does what, but if you are cooking, you can quite well expect somebody else to lay the table and wash up – better still buy a dishwasher.

◆As soon as the children are old enough, encourage them to be responsible for making their own beds and tidying their own rooms.

◆Use duvets and fitted sheets to cut down on bedmaking.

◆Save yourself extra work. Don't do the unnecessary. Don't iron underclothes, tea towels or sheets; do buy drip-dry clothes and machine-washable clothes; do cook potatoes in their jackets instead of peeling them.

◆Equip your house with labour- and time-saving devices to help you. These are essential tools of your trade – as important as a word processor to a writer or a chain saw to a tree surgeon.

◆Always put your children in the picture. Tell them you are going to work, to have a new baby, to meet a friend. Explain that you will see them for lunch/tea or whatever.

◆Get clothes ready the night before and let the children help you choose and prepare their lunch boxes (if any). Allow them to feel involved in whatever's happening.

◆If you are tired and cross when you arrive, last one home, get the children to make you a cup of tea when they hear you arriving. This will give you time to unwind, make them feel good and generally have a relaxing effect on everybody. Or have a bath and do some yoga, then prepare supper, discuss homework, search for the odd sock.

◆Allow small children lots of imaginative play when you are at home – washing up in the sink, for instance. It is absorbing and will keep them quiet for hours. Give them plastic mugs and jugs and a big waterproof apron and let them get on with it.

◆When picking up very young children from playgroup or crèche, give them your full love and attention for at least an hour. They will then be more likely to settle down and give you some time for yourself later.

TIPS FOR THOSE WITH BABIES AND TODDLERS

◆If you don't have much help, simply concentrate on the baby and your partner and let standards slip for a while.

◆If you're exhausted during the week, leave everything. Go to bed as soon as the baby has gone to sleep; you'll probably have more energy to cope with the chores quickly in the morning.

◆Use disposable nappies and make sure that the baby's clothes and bedding are all machine-washable. Buy as many cot sheets and changes of clothing for the baby as you can afford, to minimize washing.

◆A food processor is invaluable for preparing food quickly for a baby.

Food and Drink

SHOPPING GUIDE

The food that you buy can make the difference between your family's present and future health. Include on your shopping list plenty of fresh green vegetables and salad vegetables; fresh fruit; wholemeal bread; whole-grain cereals, wholemeal flour, brown rice and wholemeal pasta; beans and lentils;

porridge oats and muesli base. Buy foods in season – they will be fresh, unadulterated by preservatives and at their cheapest. Avoid processed foods. Unprocessed foods have fewer additives, you will have more control over their preparation and they are richer in protein, vitamins and minerals.

PLANNING

◆ Plan main meals one week ahead and buy all the ingredients at once, so that you don't have to shop every day.

◆ Always keep a store of "staples" in the larder so that you never need go short, even if you can't get to the shops, see overleaf. These should include rice, lentils, pasta, tinned meats and/or fish, herbs and spices, sugar, flour, tinned tomatoes, tubes of tomato paste, mayonnaise and olives. With these you can always provide a meal.

◆ Keep a supply of "fast foods" in the freezer for you or the family should you or they arrive home late and hungry.

Shopping lists

◆ Make a list of foods required for the week and make your list in the order you will visit the shops (and the shelves within the shops); it makes shopping easier.

◆ Keep a list near the fridge or larder and encourage all members of the family to add to the list as they use things.

Tinned food

◆ Look for tinned foods without additives, particularly tinned fruit without sugar; it is much better for you (see UNDERSTANDING FOOD LABELS, page 18).

◆ Dented cans from bargain baskets are safe to buy, but blown cans (bulging outwards) are not. Make sure the dent is not on the seam, it could let air into the can.

Packaged foods

◆ Don't buy food wrapped in cling plastics if the plastic touches the food. The chemicals in the plastic can transfer to the food, especially meats and cheeses.

◆ Avoid foods containing too many artificial additives, especially those with colours and

SHOPPING CHECK LIST

STAPLE FOODS
◇ Breakfast and other cereals
◇ Stock cubes
◇ Cooking oil
◇ Dried beans and lentils, rice, pasta
◇ Wholemeal flour and cornflour
◇ Tins: of soups, tomatoes, ham, tuna, anchovies, fruit
◇ Jams, preserves and sugar
◇ Tea, coffee, chocolate
◇ Root vegetables
◇ Bacon, salami
◇ Sauces, mayonnaise, seasonings, herbs, spices

FRESH FOODS
◇ Milk, butter and other dairy products
◇ Margarine
◇ Eggs
◇ Bread
◇ Fruit juices
◇ Fresh fruit
◇ Green and salad vegetables
◇ Fish and meat

E.E.C. EGG CLASSIFICATIONS

E.E.C. classifications of eggs must be marked on the boxes and are as follows:
◆ **Battery produced** The hens are caged and cannot move. They have no perches; they simply feed and lay.
◆ **Deep litter** The birds are kept in units with litter on the floor. They are not caged and there must be no more than seven hens per square metre/yard.
◆ **Perchery or barn** The hens are kept in similar units to those in deep litter but also have perches.
◆ **Semi-intensive** The hens must have continuous access to open-air runs. The ground should be mainly covered with vegetation and the maximum number of hens per hectare (2.2 acres) is 4,000.
◆ **Free range** Conditions the same as for semi-intensive hens, but the number of hens per hectare (2.2 acres) is only 1,000.

flavours, antioxidizing agents, preservatives and stabilizers.
◆ Avoid processed meats, they tend to have a high saturated-fat content, see page 46.
◆ Healthfood stores and some supermarkets sell excellent polyunsaturated margarines without chemical additives.

Vegetables and fruit

◆ Avoid vegetables and fruit imprisoned in sealed plastic bags. They become bruised and deteriorate without air.
GREEN TIP: Buy organic vegetables and fruit (which have been grown using no chemicals). They are more expensive, may not look as good as the others and don't keep so long but are much better for you.

Eggs

◆ White eggs are normally cheaper, although they have exactly the same protein value as brown eggs.

◆ Eggs vary in price depending on how intensively they are farmed: battery-farmed are the cheapest and free-range the most expensive, see above.

Economy tips

◆ Pulses can be bought in bulk because they store well and are usually comparatively cheaper bought this way.
◆ Skimmed milk powder makes up to a milk equal to the protein value of fresh milk and costs less – don't use it for feeding babies and young children because many of the nutrients contained in milk are removed during the skimming and drying processes.
◆ Cheese spreads and cheese slices are more expensive than hard cheeses and are more likely to contain additives.
◆ Home-made bread is much cheaper than bought bread and free from stabilizers and emulsifiers, therefore better for you.

CHECKING FOR FRESHNESS

Fresh food not only tastes better than food that's been lying about in containers and shops, it is better for you and looks and handles better too. You can quickly learn to recognize it because it looks bright, firm and healthy and smells fresh.

Fish and meat

◆**Fish** Fresh fish have clear, shining, slippery skins, bright, bulging eyes and well-marked colourings.

◆**Shellfish** This should be firm and heavy and smell of the sea.

◆**Meat** Fresh red meat should look silky and red rather than brown. The fat should be white, not yellowing, and it shouldn't smell of old sawdust.

◆**Poultry and game** Legs should be pliable, the breastbone should feel soft and the breast should be plump and light in colour.

Vegetables

◆**Salad vegetables and greens** These should be bright green with no brown edges and no rotting leaves.

◆**Tomatoes and radishes** Both should be bright red and firm; no wrinkles or spots.

◆**Avocados** These should be firm but with a slight "give" when gently squeezed. It doesn't matter if they are beginning to blacken if they are to be eaten straightaway or used to make an avocado dip.

◆**Root vegetables** All root vegetables should be firm.

◆**Artichokes** These should have a good bloom on their leaves. Put the stems in water as soon as you get them home and eat them quickly before they go to seed.

◆**Aubergines** Ripe aubergines should be very shiny, deeply coloured and as firm as a baby's bottom.

◆**Mushrooms and other fungi** All types should be firm and dry – not slimy. Don't buy mushrooms sealed in plastic bags.

Fruit

◆Don't buy fruit with patches of mould. The rot spreads fast and may affect other fruit as well.

◆**Grapes** Choose fruit that is shiny, brightly coloured and firm.

◆**Stone fruit** (cherries, plums, peaches, nectarines) These should be firm and plump, just soft to the touch, brightly coloured, with unbroken skins and without wrinkles.

◆**Berry fruit** (strawberries, raspberries, blueberries) These should be coloured and firm. They are all very perishable so should be eaten as soon as possible after buying. If you see any mould, reject them.

◆**Figs** Ripe figs always have bloom and should be plump but soft.

◆**Mangoes** These should have bloom and a fragrant smell. The skin should be coloured; if it is green the mango will not ripen.

◆**Kiwi fruit** The fruit should be firm and plump; skins should show no sign of damage.

◆**Bananas** These are ripe when the skin is bright yellow with small brown spots on it. They are underripe when green and overripe when going soft and brown.

◆**Melons** Choose plump, firm fruit without scars or bruises and with no "soft spots". They should smell sweet and "melony".

◆**Pineapples** These should be firm, fragrant and show no sign of damage. Pull one of the centre leaves, it should come away easily.

◆**Nuts** The shells should be glossy and should not rattle when shaken. Fresh nuts are easier to shell and taste better than elderly ones, which can be bitter.

Dried and packaged foods

◆Buy packaged and dried foods from shops with a good turnover; they are less likely to be stale.

◆**Pulses** Choose beans that are brightly coloured and plump. Avoid those with wrinkled skins.

◆**Dried fruit** This should be plump and juicy, not hard and leathery. Don't buy fruit that has been artificially plumpened – often labelled "no soak". Some dried fruit, such as Hunza apricots, is always dry-looking.

BUYING IN BULK FOR THE FREEZER

Farmers and gardeners use their freezers for home-grown produce. The rest of us will use the freezer in different ways.

◆Freezing in bulk is often (though not always – do check) cheaper than buying food in small quantities. There are substantial savings to be made on meat, icecream and vegetables and, of course, on freezing vegetables and fruit grown at home. You can make savings by buying food in season, when it is cheapest, then freezing it for use later in the year.

◆ Make sure that pieces of meat or fish are separated with pieces of greaseproof paper, or wrapped into small blocks when you buy or freeze them, or you will have to unfreeze and cook the whole lot at once, which you may not want to do.

◆Buy pizzas in large packets out of which the family can help themselves when hungry.

◆Bread, pastry, cakes and buns all freeze well. You can safely buy all of these in large quantities, though you probably won't save money on this.

◆It is cheaper to buy in bulk from specialist chain stores and from special frozen food departments (in grocery chains). Prices and quality vary hugely. Basically you get what you pay for.

◆Local butchers may offer discount prices for fresh meat bought in bulk and cut up ready for freezing. They may even be able to "blast" freeze it for you, faster and more effectively than you can do it in a domestic deep freeze. Remember that a whole, half or quarter animal will yield many cuts which you might not normally buy, including trotters, tails and ears. You may prefer to buy a packet of joints or chops that you know the family will eat.

UNDERSTANDING FOOD LABELS

When shopping for food ALWAYS read the labels. Once you understand their language you will find they tell you a good deal about the food inside and some of the information is quite shocking.

◆By law, all canned, bottled and other prepacked foodstuffs, with certain exceptions such as confectionery and biscuits, must have the following information stated on the label:

◇ *Name of the food*
◇ *Description of the food if the name is not self-explanatory*
◇ *List of ingredients in descending order of weight, including additives*
◇ *Name and address of the seller, packer or manufacturer*
◇ *Net weight of the entire contents*
◇ *Country of origin, if imported*

◆The use of any food additives, colourings and artificial sweeteners must be declared on the label.

◆Labels will tell you which products are most heavily processed.

◆Learn which additives are known or believed to cause health problems and try not to buy products which contain them. Some supermarkets offer free leaflets telling which additives are which and what their function is so look out for them.

◆When comparing prices, check that the quantities tally. A similar-looking package doesn't necessarily contain the same amount as its neighbour on the shelf.

Date stamping

Packed meats, prepackaged dishes and dairy produce and some bread and cakes are generally date stamped. The "SELL BY" date indicates the date by which the product must be sold (e.g., "Sell by 24 June"). The "BEST BEFORE" date indicates the date by which the product should be used (e.g., "Best before 24 June").

◆NEVER buy outdated goods, you could give yourself food poisoning.

THE STORE CUPBOARD

Store food in a cool place such as a refrigerator to keep it fresh. A larder should be well ventilated and preferably face away from the sun so that it will stay cool. You can use a cool cellar for storing perishable goods for one or two days. Cover cooked joints of meat or cheese in the larder with a wire dish cover to keep flies off.

STORING FOOD

◆ Many foods can be kept twice as long if stored correctly.

◆ Larder shelves should have as cool a surface as possible.

◆ If you don't have a larder, keep packaged and dried food in a cool cupboard and perishables in the refrigerator.

◆ See also MAKING USE OF A REFRIGERATOR, page 21, and MAKING USE OF A FREEZER, pages 22–3.

Canned foods

◆ Canned foods, except rhubarb and prunes which should be eaten in six months, will keep indefinitely.

◆ Once a can is opened, keep the food in a bowl in the refrigerator and eat it within a day or two.

Dried and packaged foods

◆ If well sealed, they should all keep for up to three months, then begin checking everything for weevils.

◆ Coffee beans can be kept in airtight jars for up to three months.

◆ Keep pulses, rice, flour, dried fruit and spices in cool, dry conditions and out of direct sunlight. They will keep up to five times longer in dark jars.

◆ Put a piece of lemon peel in a jar of dried fruit to keep the fruit moist.

◆ Spices are best bought whole; they keep longer that way.

◆ Buy ground spices in small quantities and store in airtight jars. Use them as soon as

DRYING HERBS

1 Pick herbs early in the morning before the sun is up. Wash and pat dry with paper towels.

2 Either spread on a baking sheet and place in a low oven – 130°C/260°F/gas mark ½, see above. Alternatively, tie the herbs into small bunches and hang them up in a warm dry room, see right.

3 Crush the dried herbs and store them in airtight jars in a cool place.

possible after purchasing because they don't keep well.

Herbs

◆ Store herbs in dark airtight containers, or in jars in a cupboard, to keep them fresh.

◆ Pick fresh herbs in the summer and dry them for winter use, see above. Alternatively, wrap them in foil and put them in the freezer; do this in small parcels.

◆ Chop herbs into an ice tray, fill with water and freeze. Use as required.

Meat and fish

◆ Store all meat, unsmoked charcuterie products and fish in the refrigerator.

◆Unless it is frozen, take meat out of its wrapping to allow it to breathe.

◆Keep fish well wrapped, preferably with aluminium foil, to prevent the smell travelling to other foods.

Vegetables

◆Keep all vegetables in a cool, ventilated larder or cupboard or in the vegetable drawer or larder section of a refrigerator.

◆Put a dry sponge in the vegetable drawer of the fridge to absorb extra moisture.

◆Onions and salad vegetables may be stored in well-ventilated baskets or wire racks.

◆Keep potatoes and other root vegetables in the dark.

◆Don't keep vegetables wrapped in polythene bags, they will deteriorate faster.

Dairy produce

◆Milk, cream and yogurt will keep in the fridge for three or four days.

◆Wrap cheese lightly in foil or place it in a cheese dish with a lid and keep it in the larder or refrigerator.

Eggs

◆ Keep eggs in a cool place; you don't need to put them in the refrigerator. Eggs will keep for one or two weeks in a cold larder, three weeks in the refrigerator.

◆ Don't wash eggs; it destroys the protective film on the shells.

Bread, cakes and biscuits

◆Bread should be kept in a bread bin, preferably one that allows a little air in or the bread will go mouldy very quickly. Any mould in the bin will encourage the next lot of bread to go mouldy.

◆Cakes and biscuits will keep for up to four weeks in airtight tins or jars. Always keep them in separate containers.

◆Small cakes keep longer if iced.

◆Fruit cakes keep for six months.

PRESERVING FRUIT AND VEGETABLES

◆Choose only sound and fresh food for preserving; damaged fruit won't last.

◆Sterilize containers before filling them. Rinse jars in very hot, then cold water. Put rubber rings and lids into a pan of cold water, bring to the boil and simmer for 5 minutes. Don't dry the jars.

Pickling

1 Juicy vegetables: slice and sprinkle salt between the layers. Leave overnight to soak. Dry vegetables: soak overnight in salt water. Root vegetables: cook in weak salt water until tender.

2 Pack vegetables into sterilized jars to within 1cm ($\frac{1}{2}$in) of the top and pour on spiced vinegar, leaving 1mm space at the top. Cover juicy vegetables with hot vinegar, dry and root vegetables with cold.

3 Cover jars with waxed paper, parchment paper, glass tops or calico dipped in melted paraffin wax or melted candle wax.

4 Store in a cool, dry, dark but airy place. Leave for two months.

TIPS FOR CONTAINERS

◆You can use ordinary jam jars with special covers but jars with wider necks are easier to pack. Bottling jars have a rubber ring and a glass or metal lid held in place with a spring clip or screw band.

◆Check jars for bottling or preserving before you start; make sure there are no chips in the glass.

◆Buy new rubber rings as soon as the old ones show signs of perishing.

◆Replace metal lids on bottling jars if the lacquer on the inside is worn. The lacquer protects the lids from fruit acids.

MAKING SPICED VINEGAR

1.5 litre (3pt) vinegar 8 cloves
12g (½oz) peppercorns 6g (¼oz) blade of mace
6g (¼oz) red chillies 6g (¼oz) allspice
12g (½oz) whole ginger 1 clove garlic, crushed
6g (¼oz) mustard seed piece of muslin

1 Pour the vinegar into an aluminium or enamel saucepan.

2 Put the spices and garlic in the muslin and tie the top. Add to the pan. Bring slowly to the boil and boil for 5 minutes, remove from heat.

3 Leave for at least 3 hours to steep, then remove the spices. Use the vinegar immediately or bottle it for use later on.

Bottling

1 Stew prepared fruit in a minimum amount of water. No sugar is necessary. Cover vegetables with cold water containing not more than 5ml (1tsp) salt per 425ml (¾pt) water and cook as normal.

◇ You can use a pressure cooker for stewing. Cook fruit for 1–3 minutes at 2.2kg (5lb) pressure and vegetables for 2–7 minutes at 4.5kg (10lb) pressure, or as instructed in the manual.

2 Mash the fruit while still boiling hot. Pour into hot, sterilized jars. Seal jar. Deal with one jar at a time and reheat pulp before filling and sealing next jar.

3 Dip vegetables in cold water before packing them into the container. Cover with brine (very salty water), then seal jar.

4 The day after bottling, remove screw bands or clips. Lift each jar by its lid. If a vacuum has formed, the lid will stay on. If the lid comes off, rebottle the fruit or vegetables or eat within a few days.

MAKING USE OF A REFRIGERATOR

◆ Don't overfill the refrigerator: a choked-up refrigerator is inefficient.

◆ Keep all food covered.

◆ The door of the refrigerator is potentially the weakest part; don't force anything into the storage compartments.

◆ Don't put hot food into the refrigerator; it will cause condensation.

◆ Fresh food can be safely kept in the fridge as follows: salted butter 2–3 weeks; margarine 2–3 months; cheese (hard) 1–2 weeks, (soft) 3–4 weeks; cooking fat 12 months; eggs 3 weeks; milk 3–4 days; yogurt 3–4 days; uncooked meat 2–3 days; bacon (smoked) 5 days; pâtés 2–3 days; pastry (dry mix) 3 months, (dough) 2–3 days; bread dough 1 day; fresh yeast 1 month; green vegetables 2–3 days; berry fruit 1 day.

Covering food

GREEN TIP: Cover food with grease-proof paper or foil rather than plastic cling films.

The plasticizers in some cling films may be carcinogenic and they migrate into some foods, particularly fatty ones. If you do use cling plastic don't let it touch the food.

GREEN TIP: To keep egg yolks fresh for a few days, cover with water or salad oil and refrigerate, or beat them with a little cold water, cover and refrigerate.

Defrosting refrigerators

◆ Defrost your refrigerator regularly – when the ice in the frozen food compartment is about 5mm (¼in) thick. Switch off the appliance, allow the ice in the freezer box to melt, then wipe out both the freezer box and cabinet with a clean cloth rinsed in a mild detergent.

◆ Don't scrape the icy bits off with anything that is sharp; you can damage the lining.

◆ Put a towel in the bottom of the fridge to soak up moisture.

AUTOMATIC DEFROSTING

If the defrosting is automatic, ice is prevented from forming and any moisture is channelled out of the cabinet where it evaporates.

◆ Defrost automatic fridges manually about three times a year to prevent a build-up of ice.

MAKING USE OF A FREEZER

◆ Keep the freezer full; it's more efficient as the frozen food helps keep the interior cold.

◆ Food stored in a freezer will keep its flavour from one month to a year, depending on the type of food, see pages 24–25.

◆ Keep the freezer in a cool dry place. The floor should be firm and the freezer level.

◆ Keep all packages well labelled so that you can tell the difference between mushroom soup and pulped strawberry; you can buy coloured polythene freezer bags to make coding even easier.

◆ Freeze leftover portions as meals for one.

◆ If you are working all week, have a "cook-in" once a week and prepare one-dish meals for the rest of the week.

◆ When cooking casseroles for freezing, line the dish with foil, cook then freeze in the dish. When frozen, remove from dish, then overwrap for storage. Food can then be returned to the same dish for reheating.

Meat and fish

◆ Separate pieces of meat or fish with two pieces of greaseproof paper so that you can take them out one at a time.

◆ Wrap items with sharp edges, such as chicken legs or chops, with foil to prevent damage to outer wrapping.

◆ Cool poultry for 12 hours before freezing.

◆ Adding salt to cooked mince shortens the length of time it can be kept in freezer.

Vegetables

◆ Vegetables should be blanched before freezing to kill enzymes which cause loss of flavour and colour. After blanching rinse in very cold water, drain thoroughly and pack at once.

TIPS FOR HOME FREEZING

◆ Before freezing food, turn the control switch to the lowest setting or switch on the freezing control.

◆ Freeze only foods that are in perfect, fresh condition.

◆ Handle food as little as possible and keep it clean.

◆ Foil punctures easily, so overwrap with heavy-duty polythene.

◆ Introduce fresh food gradually – no more than one tenth of the freezer's capacity a day.

◆ The length of time for food to become frozen varies according to the type of food and the size and density of the packages; it is best to leave all foods overnight.

◆ Once the food is solidly frozen, stack it tightly in the storage zone ready for the next batch of food.

◆ Cool hot food for freezing quickly; put in a cool part of the kitchen or stand it in a basin of cold water.

◆ DON'T put warm foods in the freezer; it creates condensation.

◆ Seal the food in moisture- and vapour-proof materials or the food will go grey and lose its flavour. Wrap so that all air is excluded, otherwise the food can suffer "freezer burn".

◆ When freezing liquids leave 1cm ($\frac{1}{2}$in) space at the top of the container to allow for expansion.

◆ Thickened and semi-liquid foods become thicker as a result of freezing, so make them a bit runnier than usual. If they separate, you can usually cure this by beating well during reheating.

◆Check for blanching times in a freezer handbook: three minutes will be enough for most vegetables. Do not blanch more than 450–900g (1–2lb) produce at a time because you won't be able to freeze it all.

Fruit

◆Freeze soft fruit whole or puréed; hard fruit whole, sliced or puréed.

GREEN TIP: Use crumpled wax or greaseproof paper, not plastic, on top of lightweight fruit to hold it under liquid.

GREEN TIP: Adding lemon juice or citric acid to apricot and cherries prevents darkening and retains flavour.

◆Red cherries freeze better than black.

◆Melons will freeze if cut up first.

Eggs and dairy products

◆Don't freeze eggs in their shells, they become "gluey". Break them and either whisk them lightly or separate them and freeze the yolks and whites individually.

◆Soft cheeses freeze well.

◆Homogenized and skimmed milk freezes for short periods.

WHAT NOT TO FREEZE

◆Fresh milk: it separates and will not reconstitute.

◆Hard cheese crumbles when thawed.

◆Hard-boiled eggs become very leathery if frozen.

◆Yogurt, soured cream and mayonnaise all separate when frozen.

◆Don't freeze highly seasoned foods since the flavourings alter or intensify during storage.

◆Never store carbonated drinks in the freezer or there may be a small explosion.

◆Pasta loses its texture.

◆Be wary of freezing fish and shellfish; it has often been frozen during transport from fishing grounds.

▼▼ Never refreeze anything; you can
◆◆ give yourself food poisoning.

EMERGENCY ACTION FOR FREEZER BREAKDOWN

◆Food will remain in good condition for at least eight hours in the event of a power cut or breakdown. Don't open the freezer to see how the food is faring; it takes 12–14 hours for food in an unopened freezer to thaw out.

◆ You can insure the contents of your freezer against loss due to power failure.

◆ Stick a label with the telephone number of the service company on the freezer door or lid so you know where to contact them quickly.

Bread, cakes and pastries

◆Wrap in heavy foil or polythene bags.

◆Shortcrust pastry takes three hours to thaw out, before it can be rolled. So, shape pastry into pieces, flan cases or tarts first.

◆Any uncooked biscuit mixture with over 25 percent fat to flour will freeze well.

◆Cut biscuit mix takes up a lot of space so freeze it in rolls of the same diameter as the required biscuit.

◆Pipe or spoon soft biscuit mixtures onto a baking tray and freeze uncovered on the tray. When frozen, lift off with a palette knife then pack and seal.

Defrosting freezers

◆Defrost when food stocks are low, say, after the school holidays, or towards the end of the winter.

1 Switch off and unplug the freezer.

2 Remove food and wrap it up in thick layers of newspaper, blankets or a duvet.

3 Allow ice to melt, then absorb water with terry towels. Don't scrape the icy bits with anything sharp or you will damage the freezer lining. Wipe out the inside with warm water and bicarbonate of soda.

4 Switch the power on, turn the freezer to its lowest setting and leave it closed for an hour before returning the food.

FREEZER STORAGE AND THAWING

BREAD AND CAKES

◆ STORAGE TIME: fresh bread, pastry and cakes 4 weeks; crisp and crusty bread 1 week.
◆ Thaw in wrappings for 3–6 hours.

SOUPS, SAUCES, CASSEROLES

SOUP AND STOCK
◆ STORAGE TIME: stock and thin soup 1 month; thick soup 2 months.
◆ Gently heat through in a saucepan.

SAUCES
◆ STORAGE TIME: white and brown sauce 1 month; tomato sauce 3 months.
◆ Reheat from frozen in a double boiler.

CASSEROLES
◆ STORAGE TIME: 1 month.
◆ Cook from frozen in moderate oven.

FISH AND SHELLFISH

FISH
◆ STORAGE TIME: raw 4 months; smoked 12 months.
◆ Thaw in wrappings in fridge for 6 hours or 3 hours at room temperature. Thaw smoked fish in fridge for 3 hours.

SHELLFISH
◆ STORAGE TIME: 1 month.
◆ Thaw in wrappings in fridge for 6 hours per 500 g (1lb) or 3 hours at room temperature.

MEAT

POULTRY
◆ STORAGE TIME: 9 months.
◆ Thaw a 2–2.5kg (4–5lb) bird overnight in the fridge or 4 hours at room temperature. Leave a 4kg (9lb) turkey for 36 hours.

GAME BIRDS, HARES AND RABBITS
◆ STORAGE TIME: 6–8 months.
◆ Thaw in wrappings, allowing 5 hours per 500g (1lb) in refrigerator or 2 hours per 500g (1lb) at room temperature.

BEEF, LAMB AND PORK
◆ STORAGE TIME: beef 10–12 months; veal 6–8 months; lamb 6–8 months; pork 4 months; minced and cubed meat 2 months.

◆ Thaw joints, steaks and chops in wrappings in refrigerator, allowing 5 hours per 500g (1lb).

HAM AND BACON
◆ STORAGE TIME: whole 3 months; sliced 3 weeks.
◆ Thaw in wrappings in the fridge. Allow 5 hours per 500g (1lb) if whole; 3 hours altogether if sliced.

VENISON
◆ STORAGE TIME: 8–10 months.
◆ Thaw in wrappings in refrigerator for 4 hours. Unwrap, cover with a marinade and thaw for a further 5 hours per 500g (1lb).

OFFAL
◆ STORAGE TIME: 2 months.
◆ Thaw in wrappings for 3 hours in refrigerator or $1\frac{1}{2}$ hours at room temperature.

VEGETABLES

ASPARAGUS
◆ STORAGE TIME: 9–12 months.
◆ Cook from frozen – plunge into boiling water and cook for 5 minutes.

BEANS
◆ STORAGE TIME: 12 months.
◆ Cook from frozen – cook whole beans for 7–8 minutes; cook cut beans for up to 5 minutes.

BEETROOT
◆ STORAGE TIME: 6–8 months.
◆ Thaw in refrigerator for 2 hours. Serve cold.

BROCCOLI
◆ STORAGE TIME: 12 months.
◆ Cook from frozen – plunge into boiling water and boil for up to 8 minutes.

BRUSSELS SPROUTS
◆ STORAGE TIME: 12 months.
◆ Cook from frozen – as for broccoli.

CARROTS AND PARSNIPS
◆ STORAGE TIME: 12 months.
◆ Cook from frozen – boil or bake.

CAULIFLOWER
◆ STORAGE TIME: 6 months.
◆ Cook from frozen – plunge into boiling water and cook for up to 10 minutes.

GLOBE ARTICHOKES
◆ STORAGE TIME: 12 months.
◆ Cook from frozen – plunge into boiling water and boil until leaves are tender.

MARROW AND COURGETTE
◆ STORAGE TIME: 6 months.
◆ Cook from frozen – boil or fry sliced marrow; reheat crushed marrow in double boiler.

MUSHROOMS
◆ STORAGE TIME: 3 months.
◆ Thaw in covered container in fridge.

PEAS AND MANGETOUT
◆ STORAGE TIME: 12 months.
◆ Cook from frozen – plunge into boiling water for 5–7 minutes.

POTATOES
◆ STORAGE TIME: new potatoes 12 months; cooked potatoes 3 months.
◆ Cook from frozen. Reheat mashed potato in a double boiler.

SWEETCORN
◆ STORAGE TIME: 12 months.
◆ Cook from frozen. Treat cobs and kernels similarly, but kernels need less cooking.

SPINACH
◆ STORAGE TIME: 12 months.
◆ Cook from frozen: steam or sauté.

TURNIPS
◆ STORAGE TIME: chopped 12 months; mashed 3 months.
◆ Cook from frozen – cook chopped turnips in boiling water; reheat mashed turnips in a double boiler.

FRUIT

BERRIES AND CURRANTS
◆ STORAGE TIME: 12 months.
◆ If frozen in dry sugar, thaw in unopened carton and use just before completely thawed.
◆ If frozen in syrup, thaw slowly in fridge.

GRAPES (WHOLE BUNCH)
◆ STORAGE TIME: 2 weeks.
◆ Thaw for $2\frac{1}{2}$ hours at room temperature.

HARD FRUIT
◆ STORAGE TIME: 12 months.
◆ Thaw in wrappings for $2\frac{1}{2}$–3 hours.

MELONS
◆ STORAGE TIME: 12 months.
◆ Thaw unopened in the refrigerator.

STONE FRUIT
◆ STORAGE TIME: 12 months.
◆ Thaw in pack for $3\frac{1}{2}$ hours.

STORING WINE

◆ All wines, even the cheapest, should be rested before being drunk, so buy wine at least two days before you expect to drink it, preferably longer.
◆ Store wine preferably in the dark because light causes deterioration.
◆ The storage area should be dry, airy, draught free and vibration free. Try to keep a constant temperature of around 12–15°C (54–59°F).
◆ Never store wine in the fridge, particularly sparkling wines, they will get too cold and lose their flavour.
◆ Table wines that are to be stored for any length of time should be stacked horizontally on special racks or shelves so the corks are kept moist and expanded.
◆ Store fortified wines (port, sherry and so on) upright.

Serving temperatures

◆ Serve most red wines at room temperature, at about 18°C (65°F). Burgundy and Beaujolais and some light Italian red wines are at their best when served at about 16°C (61°F).
◆ Bring red wine up to room temperature slowly; it is better to serve it cold than to overheat it. Open the bottle a few hours before you want to drink it to let it breathe and keep in a warm part of the room.
◆ Serve dry white and rosé wines cold – at "cellar temperature", about 10°C (50°F). Chill in the refrigerator for about an hour before you serve them. Serve sweet white wines at a lower temperature than dry ones; chill for about an hour and a half before serving. Exceptions are the high-quality Sauternes and German wines of the "Auslese" grade, which prefer a temperature of 14°C (57°F), so chill for half an hour.
◆ Fortified wines, such as sherry, to be served as an apéritif can be slightly chilled. Put them in the refrigerator for half an hour before serving although you can simply serve them with ice.

CHOOSING KITCHEN EQUIPMENT

One rule applies to all major appliances and smaller labour-saving equipment: shop around – don't buy the first thing you like the look of. There are so many refinements and permutations in cooking and related appliances, you need to do quite a bit of research before buying.

When choosing tools, such as knives and utensils, always buy the best – they will last longer. If you can't afford everything at once, it is better to buy the basic essentials and add to the collection gradually as and when you can afford them, than to make do with cheaper alternatives.

COOKING APPLIANCES

The choice is between free-standing cookers, separate oven and hob, or a range. Fuels include electricity, gas, bottled gas, solid fuel, or oil.

◆ Microwave ovens as separate or combination units can be very useful and save a lot of time, particularly if you are working.

◆ A separate oven and hob are more expensive to buy and install than one cooker unit and they need separate housings. They do enable you to have a combination of fuels, for example, a gas hob and an electric oven. The advantage of a separate oven is that it can be mounted at a convenient height.

◆ Free-standing cookers designed to slot in between worktops to look as though they are built in are easier to clean.

◆ Free-standing cookers are available with a hinged top to cover the hob when not in use.

◆ Kitchen ranges are the most expensive cooking appliances to install.

◆ Elderly or handicapped people may find a separate hob or table-top appliance more convenient for wheelchair use.

Electricity

Electricity probably offers the greatest sophistication in cooking.

◆ An electric fan-assisted oven will cook faster than an ordinary oven because the heat is distributed more evenly.

◆ If you are short of space, get a combined microwave and electric cooker.

POINTS TO LOOK FOR WHEN CHOOSING A COOKER

◇ Height of unit; it will be more convenient if it is the same height as the kitchen units.
◇ Good-quality finish.
◇ Ease of cleaning.
◇ Automatic ignition on gas cookers.
◇ Oven size and shape.
◇ Number of ovens – some units have a main oven and a small economy one.
◇ A bottom-hinged oven can be more convenient for sliding pans onto.
◇ Interior glass door on oven or glass panel in door, and preferably an interior light, to enable you to see the food without opening the door.
◇ Insulated oven door, particularly if you have young children.

◇ Height of grill; eye-level grills are easier to use. Some grills can be folded away when not in use.
◇ Baking racks which slide out.
◇ Economy ring which only heats up at the centre for small pans.
◇ Control knobs on the top of a hob, rather than the front, are safer if you have young children.

USEFUL FEATURES
◇ Self-clean oven.
◇ Digital automatic timing.
◇ Integral food thermometer.
◇ Spit-roasting device.
◇ Foldaway safety panel for children.

◆Ceramic hobs are very easy to clean and neat to look at.

◆If you want a ceramic hob, make sure you buy one with a safety feature that shows when the heat is turned on.

Gas

◆Gas is a cheaper fuel than electricity.

◆Gas burners are easy to control; there is no residual heat when they are turned down.

◆Choose a gas oven if you are likely to want to cook several dishes requiring different cooking temperatures at the same time – the oven is zoned, and is hotter at the top than the bottom.

The kitchen range

◆Traditionally these cookers run on solid fuel. Modern "ranges" can be powered by solid fuel (wood or coal), gas, bottled gas, electricity or oil. They may be convertible from one fuel to another (at some cost).

◆Kitchen ranges can be used for hot water and heating as well as cooking so you don't need a separate boiler. Kitchen ranges are expensive to buy initially but they are warm, friendly and convenient, particularly for large families and people who are at home for most of the day.

◆Points to look for:

◇ *All-night burning*

◇ *Versatility of fuel*

◇ *Number of ovens: should have at least one slow and one fast oven*

◇ *Good insulation*

◇ *Thermostatic control*

◇ *Adjustable heat setting*

◇ *Back boiler*

◇ *Ability to heat radiators*

◇ *Ease of emptying ash tray if range is fired by wood or coal.*

MICROWAVE OVENS

◆Ideal if out at work all day and want meals ready quickly in the evening.

◆A microwave oven is cheaper to run than a conventional electric oven.

◆Microwave ovens can cook more or less anything but can't brown food, although you can get browning dishes (see page 32) or buy a microwave with a grill in the top.

◆Microwave ovens can be portable or free standing.

◆The simplest microwave oven has two power levels: "defrost" and "cook". The most sophisticated microwave ovens cook by temperature and have a sensor probe which will switch off the oven when the correct temperature is reached.

◆Some have a turntable and/or a stirring mechanism; otherwise, with foods that need stirring, you must take out the dishes and stir them by hand.

POINTS TO LOOK FOR:

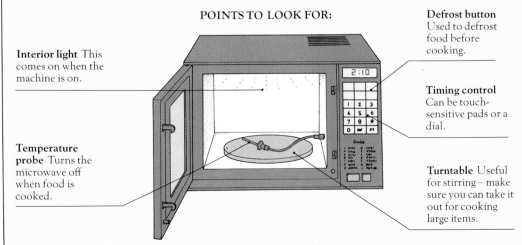

Interior light This comes on when the machine is on.

Temperature probe Turns the microwave off when food is cooked.

Defrost button Used to defrost food before cooking.

Timing control Can be touch-sensitive pads or a dial.

Turntable Useful for stirring – make sure you can take it out for cooking large items.

REFRIGERATORS AND FREEZERS

◆ Make a note of the measurements of the unit and the space in the kitchen before you buy anything. Sizes range enormously from small worktop refrigerators to huge free-standing ones. As an indication of suitable size, an average family of four is supposed to need about 242 litres (8.4 cu ft) of refrigeration. All fridges and freezers require ventilation for the motor. Some have a self-ventilating grille at the front; others must have a space between the back and the wall.

◆ If you don't need or have room for a refrigerator and a freezer, a combined fridge-freezer may be the answer. Find one with the freezer at the bottom and the fridge at the top for greatest convenience.

◆ If you have a freezer, buy a larger refrigerator without a freezer compartment; it will give you more storage space.

◆ Choose a fridge or freezer with a door that opens in the right direction. Some models can have the door hinged on the right or the left; some are adjustable.

◆ Choose a refrigerator with suitable fitments (sometimes simple shelves are more convenient than egg racks and cheese compartments). Adjustable shelves can be useful.

◆ If the fridge is small, make sure the door shelves are deep enough for open bottles.

◆ Automatic defrosting saves time.

◆ Some fridges have cold-water dispensers; these may need plumbing in.

◆ There are two types of freezer: chest freezers, which open from the top, and upright freezers, which are front opening. Upright freezers have drawers to prevent cold escaping; chest freezers are easier to pack because the baskets are removable.

◆ Don't choose a larger freezer than you'll need; a half-empty freezer is much more expensive to run.

◆ If you keep your freezer in an outhouse, invest in a freezer alarm to warn you if the temperature becomes warmer than it should.

STORAGE TIMES

The star rating on fridges with freezer compartments and freezers indicates the temperature of the freezer and therefore the length of time frozen food can be safely stored.

◇ One star (*) indicates approximately $-6°C$ (21°F) and stores frozen food up to a week.

◇ Two stars (**) is approximately $-12°C$ (10°F) and stores frozen food up to one month.

◇ Three stars (***) indicates $-18°C$ (0°F) and stores frozen food for up to three months.

◇ Four stars (****) – the symbol shown on domestic deep freezers and fridge-freezers. Food can be stored for anything up to a year.

KITCHEN TOOLS

Every cook has his or her own particular leanings and will eventually want specialized equipment. However, the list of basic equipment opposite should carry you through until you can add other extras of your choice.

◆ There is one overriding rule: always buy the best. Badly made tools of cheap materials will be frustrating to use and will probably not last very long.

◆ It is better to buy catering equipment with a serviceable look rather than stylish utensils that are difficult to use.

Knives and utensils

◆ Non-stainless steel knives hold their sharpness better than any other type. Blunt knives are potentially more dangerous than sharp ones, because you have to press so hard to get them to cut.

◆ Look for utensils with hooked handles, or handles with holes in the end, so that they can be hung up.

◆ Always make sure that the handles are dishwasher proof.

Chopping boards

◆ Laminated plastic blunts knives; wood is the best material.
◆ Buy a large board: the larger it is, the more convenient it is to work on.
◆ Buy a board that can be used on both sides and keep one side for onions.

Pans and baking tins

◆ Buy non-stick pans and baking tins; they are much easier to wash up.
◆ Cast-iron pans and casseroles are very good for slow cooking but they are heavy.

◆ Check that the handles are secure!
◆ If a saucepan has metal handles, make sure that they are hollow; solid metal handles get very hot.
◆ Ovenproof glass pans or lids allow you to see what's going on.
◆ Buy saucepans with thick bases; thin bases will buckle with use so won't sit flat on the hotplate or burner.
◆ Aluminium spreads heat evenly, though marks easily.
◆ Enamel pans heat up very quickly and food tends to stick.
◆ Stainless steel, although expensive, is long-lasting and easy to clean.
◆ Don't use cast-iron or copper pans for cooking vegetables because both metals destroy vitamin C.

BASIC EQUIPMENT

THE COOK'S MINIMUM

KNIVES AND UTENSILS
◇ 20cm (8in) cook's knife
◇ 8cm (3in) vegetable knife
◇ Kitchen scissors (left- or right-handed)
◇ Fish slice
◇ Carving knife and fork
◇ Stone for sharpening knives
◇ Potato peeler
◇ Grater
◇ Selection of wooden spoons
◇ Ladle
◇ Perforated spoon
◇ Balloon whisk
◇ Potato masher
◇ Pastry brush
◇ Rolling pin
◇ Skewers
◇ Rotary whisk

PANS AND BAKING EQUIPMENT
◇ 2 saucepans with lids
◇ Milk pan, with pouring lip

◇ Frying pan with lid
◇ Casserole dish with lid
◇ Pie dish
◇ Baking and roasting tins and trays
◇ Flan dish
◇ Bread tin and cake tins as required

MISCELLANEOUS
◇ Vegetable scrubbing brush
◇ Sieve
◇ Measuring jug
◇ Kitchen funnel
◇ 2 chopping boards (one for bread)
◇ Mixing bowl
◇ Can opener
◇ Bottle opener (sometimes included on can opener)
◇ Corkscrew
◇ Set of measuring spoons
◇ Citrus squeezer
◇ Garlic crusher
◇ Coffee maker
◇ Kettle

ADDITIONAL EQUIPMENT

Later you can add some labour-saving or specialist items:

KNIVES AND UTENSILS
◇ Larger selection of knives (e.g. serrated tomato knife, boning knife)
◇ Mezzaluna for chopping herbs
◇ Herb mill
◇ Pestle and mortar
◇ Melon baller
◇ Apple corer
◇ Nutmeg grater
◇ Spatula
◇ Meat hammer
◇ Fat spray sieve for frying pan
◇ Flour sieves
◇ Colander
◇ Revolving icing stand
◇ Salad spinner
◇ Jelly moulds
◇ Pastry wheel
◇ Pastry cutters
◇ Scales

PANS AND BAKING EQUIPMENT
◇ Chicken brick
◇ Fish kettle
◇ Larger selection of saucepans, casseroles, oven dishes and cake tins
◇ Vegetable steamer
◇ Wok
◇ Omelette pan
◇ Double boiler
◇ Blanching basket

LABOUR- OR TIME-SAVING GADGETS
◇ Pressure cooker
◇ Slow cooker
◇ Food mixer, blender or combination of the two
◇ Food processor
◇ Juice extractor or pulper
◇ Electric coffee maker
◇ Electric can opener
◇ Toaster
◇ Icecream maker
◇ Pasta maker
◇ Microwave oven and utensils

GADGETS

The three most important points to bear in mind when buying are:
◆ If a gadget will be difficult to clean – DON'T GET IT.
◆ If it will be difficult to assemble or store – DON'T GET IT.
◆ If it looks as though the handles might drop off after washing – DON'T GET IT.

Blender

Can be free-standing, wall-mounted or an optional attachment to a food mixer. Most are good at making breadcrumbs, chopping nuts, pulping raw meat and cooked or raw vegetables and fruit, mixing drinks, liquidizing soups and making mayonnaise.
◆ Check on the number of speeds. Large blenders have two or more speeds; smaller ones have only one. You probably won't be able to run the motor for more than one minute, or two minutes on larger models.
◆ Can be awkward to clean.
◆ Some blenders have a small attachment for grinding coffee beans.
◆ Choose one with a large goblet, especially if you want to use it for soups.
◆ A wall-mounted, hand-held blender next to the cooker can be invaluable for blending soups and making purées in the pan; it saves on a lot of washing up.
◆ Hand-held blenders are easy to clean.

Food processor

This will do nearly every food processing job from mincing meat to slicing vegetables and kneading dough. You can buy attachments for making pasta, grinding coffee, whisking cream and eggs, grating and slicing vegetables. Most food processors are not too good at whipping cream or eggs.
◆ Make sure you can run the motor for long periods without damage.
◆ Choose one with a large bowl, it will be more versatile.
◆ Buy one that is dishwasher proof.

Can opener

◆ Manual ones are cheap. Choose for strength and durability.
◆ A wall-mounted opener is more readily accessible and is often easier to work than a hand-held one.
◆ Electric can openers can be free-standing or wall-mounted. Some have a combined knife sharpener and bottle opener.

Scales

◆ Scales with lipped containers are easier to pour from.
◆ Choose a pair with a metric and an imperial scale to save you converting recipes.

Slow cooker

This casseroles food very slowly. All you do is prepare the dish, set the temperature and forget about it for 12 hours or longer. The food is cooked in a stoneware pot which sits inside an insulated metal casing.
GREEN TIP: Very cheap to run, using about the same amount of power as a light bulb.
◆ Choose a cooker with two heat settings – high and low – they are more versatile.
◆ Capacity varies from 1.5–3 litres (3–6pt) so choose one to suit your needs.

Pressure cooker

A saucepan designed to seal in and control the steam which escapes from a conventional pan, so speeding up cooking time. There are two main types: fixed pressure – this is suitable for all meat and vegetables; and variable pressure – particularly useful for bottling fruit and vegetables.
◆ Choose the most robust you can find, but check the weight, some are very heavy.
◆ Look for a built-in timer.
◆ Choose one with a domed lid if you want to do any bottling.

Wok

The wok is a Chinese high-sided frying pan in which vegetables and small pieces of meat are very quickly stir fried to retain their flavour and nutrients.

◆ All woks are suitable for gas stoves; traditionally woks are used over a fire.

◆ Woks are available for use on electric or solid-fuel cookers.

◆ You can buy electric woks.

◆ A two-handled wok is easiest to carry.

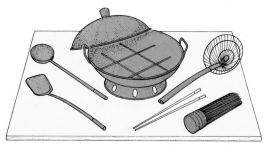

Wok equipment *Spatulas, straining spoons and chopsticks are used for cooking. A lid and inside rack are useful for steaming, a bamboo brush for cleaning the wok afterwards.*

Jug kettle

◆ Available in a variety of sizes; choose one with a good capacity and that can boil as little as one cup of water. Some jug kettles have a water-level indicator.

◆ Automatic switch-off is much safer.

Electric coffee makers

There are three types of electric coffee maker: percolator, drip filter and vacuum (capuccino/espresso) machines. Each has a different method of forcing boiling water through a container of ground coffee.

◆ Filter and vacuum machines use finely ground coffee and are economical.

◆ Check on the number of cups a coffee machine can make. Some can make up to ten cups of coffee at a time; others, such as capuccino and espresso machines, can only make one or, at most, two cups.

◆ Percolators are simplest and keep coffee hotter, but check the capacity before buying one – some can't make less than 600ml (1 pt) of coffee.

◆ Some machines have their own stainless steel filters; others need paper filters.

◆ If you prefer to grind your own beans, buy a machine with a built-in grinder.

◆ Check how long a coffee maker can keep coffee warm without spoiling the taste. Filter machines have an element in the base to keep coffee warm.

Toasters

◆ If you have a large family or always want a lot of toast in one go, buy a toaster that can make up to six slices at once, or buy a catering toaster.

◆ If you like thick pieces of toast or muffins, choose a toaster with a self-adjusting toasting slot.

◆ Buy a toaster with adjustable browning controls, you are less likely to burn the toast. Some have a thermostat that allows you to toast frozen bread.

Yogurt maker

◆ You will need one that makes at least six pots because one has to be kept as a starter for the next batch of yogurt.

Icecream maker

◆ Make sure the mixing bowl will fit inside your freezer.

◆ A stirring device saves having to stop the machine and stir it manually.

◆ The better machines have a built-in fan to control the freezing process.

Pasta maker

◆ Kneads flour and eggs together, then extrudes the dough in the size and shape you want through one of six discs.

◆ Cheaper machines will only roll and cut the pasta dough.

FREEZER AND MICRO-WAVE EQUIPMENT

◆Always use freezer-quality equipment, otherwise food will dry out and suffer from "freezer burn".
◆You do not have to buy new cooking utensils for a microwave oven.

Freezer equipment

◆Use 120–150-gauge polythene bags for wrapping irregular shapes such as chicken legs or cuts of meat. These are not suitable for liquids.
◆Heavy plastic bags are available in a variety of colours for wrapping different groups of food, making identification easier. Specially useful for chest freezers.
◆Freezer paper, ordinary brown paper or mutton cloth (muslin) can be used to over-wrap large items.
◆Greaseproof paper or waxed paper is ideal for separating individual pieces of meat or covering fruit for freezing.
◆Cardboard boxes can be used to store several packages in chest freezers.
◆Polythene boxes are useful for soups and sauces: make sure they have well-fitting lids.
◆Plastic sheeting is available in rolls. Good for wrapping joints of meat, poultry, baked goods and larger items.
◆You'll need wire ties, freezer tape or a heat-sealer for sealing bags and sheet polythene.
◆You can buy freezer-quality self-adhesive plastic film, which is useful for wrapping small items as part of a larger pack.
◆Boil-in-bags made of strong polythene or nylon are useful for food such as stews and vegetables which may be frozen and reheated from frozen by boiling.
◆Use foil for wrapping small quantities of food or for extra protection of food such as chicken or fish; it is unsuitable for acid fruit because it reacts with the acid and discolours the fruit. Use the dull side towards the food. Heavy-duty aluminium foil is more robust than ordinary foil.
GREEN TIP: Shaped aluminium dishes are good for pies, puddings, cakes and

individual meals. They are light, space-saving and reusable.

Microwave equipment

◆Use roasting bags for roasting. They prevent spitting and keep the oven clean; make a few holes in the bag.
◆A ceramic browning dish is worth buying if you do not have a grill. Preheat it in the microwave. Place fish or steaks in it and it will seal and brown the food.
◆You can buy freezer-to-microwave dishes; many can be used in normal ovens up to 200°C/400°F/gas mark 6.
◆Food can be cooked in boil-in-bags, plastic bags that retain moisture. Prick small holes in the plastic.
◆Use foil only to protect parts of food from overcooking (e.g. ends of joints).
▼▼Don't use self-seal cling plastics for
◆ ◆ microwave cooking because the plasticizers may be carcinogenic.

SUITABLE DISHES FOR A MICROWAVE

◆ You can use ovenproof pottery, glass and china dishes. Wood or straw baskets can be used for short periods.
◆Use round dishes in which food cooks evenly, rather than rectangular dishes, in which food tends to burn in the corners.
◆Use soufflé dishes for baking bread.
◆Choose deep dishes for casseroles that need to be stirred during cooking.
◆Food cooks faster in shallow, open dishes because a larger surface area is exposed to the microwaves.
◆Food cooks fastest in microwave-quality plastic.
◆DON'T use metal or foil dishes; the microwaves will not pass through metal. This disturbs the magnetic field and causes sparks.
◆DON'T use gold-rimmed china.
◆DON'T use poor-quality plastic; it tends to melt.
◆DON'T use dishes that have been re-paired with glue; the glue melts.

CROCKERY, GLASS AND CUTLERY

You don't need elaborate sets of crockery and glass. Here is a basis for a range which you could add to later.

Crockery

◆ Choose a design that is not likely to be withdrawn from the market for a while so that you will be able to replace breakages and add to your set.
◆ Every piece should be dishwasher proof.
◆ You will need:
◇ *Dinner plates*
◇ *Side (or tea) plates*
◇ *Dessert plates*
◇ *Soup bowls (choose a shape that can be used for cereal too)*
◇ *Cups and saucers (these can be used for both tea and coffee)*

Serving dishes

◆ You will also need serving dishes; these do not need to be the same pattern as the china. Ideally you should have:
◇ *Vegetable dishes*
◇ *Casserole dish*
◇ *Large platter for meat or fish*
◇ *Gravy boat or sauce jug*
◇ *Salad bowl*
◆ Ovenproof dishes save on washing up.

Cutlery

◆ Silver cutlery is expensive and needs regular polishing.
◆ Stainless steel is available in a wealth of different designs, often with wooden or plastic handles.
◆ Make sure handles are dishwasher proof.
◆ Before you buy, hold the cutlery as though you were using it. Check on its weight, balance and sharpness, size and shape. A badly balanced knife will be difficult to manipulate, a badly shaped spoon won't fit

in your mouth and forks with sharp prongs can be very painful.
◆ Ideally you should have:
◇ *Table knives (if they are not very sharp, you may need steak knives too)*
◇ *Table forks*
◇ *Dessert spoons*
◇ *Dessert forks*
◇ *Soup spoons (optional – you can use dessert spoons)*
◇ *Serving spoons*
◇ *Large serving forks*
◇ *Soup ladle*
◇ *Salad servers*
◇ *Carving knife and fork*
◇ *Teaspoons (or pointed fruit spoons)*

Glass

Glasses should add to the pleasure of drinking wine, or any other beverage.
◆ Plain long-stemmed glasses are elegant and will do for any occasion, though they may be difficult to fit into the dishwasher. A shorter, sturdier stem can still look good and is less likely to get broken. Glasses with a thin rim are nicer to drink out of.
◆ Don't be seduced by price: some of the cheapest glasses are among the best looking.
◆ Choose heavy bases so the glass can't be knocked over easily.
◆ Ideally you should have:
◇ *Tumblers for water, juice or spirits* (**A**)
◇ *Red wine glasses with plenty of room in the bowl. Curved lips are best for burgundy and claret* (**B**)
◇ *White wine glasses with a smaller bowl* (**C**)
◇ *Sherry glasses (which can be used for port or Madeira as well)* (**D**)
◇ *Balloon glasses for brandy (optional)* (**E**)
◇ *Liqueur glasses* (**F**)

COOKING AND SERVING

Organization is all-important in the preparation of meals. This doesn't mean such regimentation that all inventiveness goes out of the window. It means thought going into a meal so that you are not left with half an hour to cook something that is still frozen or that calls for an overnight soak. Work out a balanced menu. This doesn't have to be elaborate. A baked . potato, salad and cold meat makes a good meal and doesn't require much forward planning. Check that you have all the necessary ingredients and check the length of time a dish takes to cook before you start. Cookery books are often over-optimistic about timing, not allowing for the fact that they know the recipe off by heart and you may not.

Don't plan elaborate meals if you are busy with hundreds of other chores, and don't plan two complicated dishes at the same meal unless you have the time or you enjoy cooking. If you are a reluctant or new cook, work out a schedule for cooking before you start work:

10.30 peel potatoes
11.00 prepare ingredients for casserole and start cooking
11.30 prepare ingredients for pudding
12.00 prepare salad and dressing
12.20 cook pudding and potatoes
1.00 eat!

QUICK PREPARATION AND COOKING

◆Keep canned emergency rations in the store cupboard in case fresh ones take too long to prepare, or are ruined in preparation.

◆Use the food processor as much as possible to cut vegetables; it's quicker.

🍃GREEN TIP: Cook vegetables with their skins on, preparation is much quicker and it's much better for you as there are valuable nutrients just under the skin.

◆Crush nuts between sheets of waxed paper with a rolling pin – it's much quicker than blending and requires less washing up.

◆To get hazelnuts out whole, toast them under the grill to break down the shells; to get walnuts out whole, soak overnight in cold water.

◆To peel tomatoes, peaches, grapes and cherries, first place them in boiling water for a couple of minutes; the skin will come off easily. Soak oranges in boiling water for 5 minutes before peeling – you can then remove the skin and pith together.

◆Put peeled apples in water with lemon juice to stop them turning brown.

◆For baked potatoes in a hurry: parboil the potatoes for 5 minutes before putting them into the oven, or put an aluminium skewer through them. Either speeds up the baking time by 15–20 minutes.

◆For roast potatoes in a hurry: cut them up to smallish size and parboil them for 5 minutes. Put them in the oven as usual and they'll be done in half an hour.

◆Make a quick stock flavouring for stews by combining onion, garlic and carrots in a blender with a small amount of water.

◆Cooking pulses in a hurry: instead of an overnight soak, boil hard for 3–4 minutes, leave to stand in water for an hour. Prepare and cook as normal.

◆Add a tablespoon of oil or mayonnaise to water when cooking pasta to stop it boiling over and prevent the pasta sticking.

CANNED SUBSTITUTES FOR FRESH FOODS

◇Carrots and new potatoes
◇Tomatoes
◇Pulses
◇Consommé (to use as stock)
◇Fruit, unsweetened in natural juice
◇Fish, such as tuna, sardines or anchovies

ENERGY-SAVING COOKING

◆Prepare casserole meals a day in advance and slow cook them overnight.
◆Cook very quickly to seal in flavour.

Stir frying

A cooking technique using a wok, where food is cooked very quickly in a minimum amount of very hot oil, so that it retains its flavour, crispness and nutrients.
◆Add seasoning at the last moment, then add liquid to give food a burst of steam.

Using a wok *Cut all the ingredients into even-sized pieces, cook items requiring the longest cooking time first, then add the rest.*

Pressure cooking

◆A pressure cooker is both economical and quick. Ideal for cooking stews, stocks, vegetables, soups and pulses that normally take quite a long time.
◆Produces fewer cooking smells and less steam in the kitchen as well as retaining nutrients and flavour.
◆Don't fill the cooker more than two-thirds full of solid food to leave room for the steam to circulate.
◆To reduce pressure quickly, stand the pressure cooker in a basin of cold water.
◆To reduce pressure slowly, turn off heat and remove the cooker to a cold part of the hob or stand it on a heat-resistant surface.

Electric slow cooking

◆Ideal for casseroles or stocks if you are at work or busy with children all day.
◆Leave the lid on throughout cooking; if you take it off it takes 15 minutes to regain lost heat.
◆Shorten cooking time by covering cooking pot with foil then the lid.
◆Use fewer strongly flavoured vegetables; their flavour will dominate the dish.
◆Frozen meat must be completely thawed.
◆You need less liquid than normal.
◆Do not use milk or cream during cooking as they will curdle.
◆Use whole fresh herbs and spices if possible. Dried ones tend to develop a stale taste.

Hay box cooking

GREEN TIP: This is a traditional method of cooking soup, porridge or casseroles very slowly in a highly insulated box. You can make a hay box out of a wooden box filled with straw, hay or polystyrene granules.

1 Put the filling in small sacks and pack them tightly around the inside of the box.

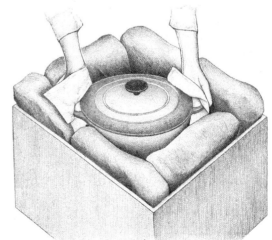

2 Start the dish in the usual way, and simmer for about 20 minutes, then place in the box. Cover with more filling and leave overnight.
◇*The initial cooking is essential to kill any organisms in the food.*

SOUPS

◆The first priority is a good stock. Failing that a stock cube, or a tin of consommé, is better than nothing. Use the water from cooking vegetables in the stock.

◆Use the remains of beef, lamb, pork, poultry, game or fish to make a stock.

◆Use vegetable peelings and the cooking water from vegetables or pulses to make a vegetarian stock.

◆Add wine dregs as a fillip if you wish; use slightly more if making for game stock – otherwise sherry or Marsala is best.

◆Freeze some of the stock so that you always have some.

Soup garnishes

◆Fried croutons, cubes of bread, yogurt, sour cream or smetana liven up any soup. Use crumbled bacon in vegetable soups.

◆Chopped herbs: sage for fish and cream soups; tarragon for consommé or mushroom, chicken, tomato and turtle soups; thyme for fish, meat and beetroot soups; watercress for fish soup; rosemary for cauliflower, chicken, pea and spinach soups.

◆Diablotins can be served with soup. Grate Gruyère and Parmesan and mix with egg yolks to make a paste. Season well with salt, cayenne and paprika; spread onto small rounds of bread. Brown quickly in the oven.

THREE BASIC STOCKS

MEAT STOCK

◆Get your butcher to chop the bones for you. You can use poultry bones instead of beef bones.

◆To save time, use a pressure cooker. You could make this stock in about 45 minutes.

1.5kg (3lb) shin of beef with bones cut into large pieces	5 litres (8pt) cold water
1 hambone, chopped (optional)	2 leeks, halved and chopped
500g (1lb) knuckle of veal	2 celery stalks, chopped
2 carrots, chopped	2 onions, chopped
1 turnip, chopped	12 peppercorns
bouquet garni	salt to taste

1 *Brown bones and root vegetables in a hot oven for half an hour.*

2 *Transfer to a large saucepan and add the remaining ingredients, except salt and peppercorns. Bring slowly to the boil, cover and simmer gently for at least four hours. Add the salt and peppercorns after two hours.*

3 *Strain and leave overnight in a cool place.*

4 *Skim off the layer of fat and pour off liquid; discard the sediment. Keep in the refrigerator for a couple of days or freeze.*

FISH STOCK

1–1.5kg (2–3lb) fish heads and trimmings	3 sprigs parsley bouquet garni
1 stalk celery, chopped	275ml ($\frac{1}{2}$pt) white wine
1–2 spring onions or small onions, peeled and chopped	2.5 litres (4 pt) water
5–6 bacon rinds	12 peppercorns
sprig of thyme	salt to taste
1 bay leaf	

1 *Put all ingredients into a saucepan and bring to the boil. Skim, cover and simmer the stock for half an hour.*

2 *Strain. Keep in the refrigerator for two days or freeze for use another time.*

VEGETABLE STOCK

Any combination of vegetables, such as outside leaves of cabbage, cauliflower stalks, outside celery stalks and leaves, green tops of leeks, watercress stalks, mushroom	stalks and peelings. bouquet garni peppercorns 1–2 cloves

1 *Chop or shred all vegetables and put them in a saucepan. Add boiling water to come three-quarters of the way up the vegetables.*

2 *Add remaining ingredients, cover and boil for 20–30 minutes. Strain.*

COOKING FISH AND MEAT

◆ Fish or meat should be completely thawed before it is cooked, otherwise there is a risk of food poisoning. All parts of the meat or poultry will feel soft when thoroughly thawed.

◆ Fresh fish and meat putrefy quickly so should be eaten as soon as possible.

◆ A little goes a long way in a casserole. Both fish and meat are digested slowly so you won't feel hungry half an hour later.

Fish and shellfish

◆ Never overcook fish; it'll disintegrate.

◆ Thin fillets will take 5–6 minutes to deep fry and 6–9 minutes to shallow fry; thicker ones take 6–10 and 8–12 minutes.

◆ Poached or steamed whole fish are cooked when the flesh comes away easily from the bone; fillets when a creamy white fluid oozes between the flakes.

◆ Bake fish at 180–190°C/350–370°F/gas mark 4–5. Allow 15–30 minutes for fillets and 20–30 minutes for a trout-sized fish.

◆ Add shellfish to a sauce or fish stew just before it is ready to eat; 5 minutes is long enough for them to cook.

Poultry and game birds

◆ Hang fresh game birds up by the neck for a few days to let them mature. Two days is long enough if the weather is mild, up to a week if weather is cold. They are ready to eat when you can pull a feather out of the tail easily.

◆ If you are plucking your own bird, dip it in boiling water first to loosen the feathers. This may not work for ducks and geese.

◆ Game that has hung for too long but is not off may be better served as a casserole because the flavour can be very strong.

◆ Start cooking frozen game as soon as it has thawed, while it is still cold, to prevent any loss of juices.

◆ Stuff with fruit to make the meat juicier.

TIPS FOR TENDERIZING MEAT

◆ Tough stewing steak can be tenderized and sweetened by adding a few drops of lemon juice.

◆ Use 800ml ($1\frac{1}{4}$pt) tea as the cooking liquid for casseroles.

◆ To tenderize steak pierce all round the sides with a skewer – this helps to break down the fibres.

◆ Beat with a rolling pin or meat mallet before cooking.

◆ Roast duck or goose on a rack in an oven dish to drain the fat.

Beef, lamb, pork, venison

◆ Neck, knuckles and tail have large muscle fibres and are naturally coarse. They require slow and moist methods of cooking such as stewing and braising. Fillet, rump and loin can be roasted, grilled or fried.

◆ When grilling meat, brush with soy sauce for a rich brown colour.

◆ When mincing meat, put any other ingredients, such as herbs, onions, garlic and breadcrumbs, through the mincer or food processor with the meat; it saves time and improves flavour.

◆ If meat has been left in the wrapping too long and smells stale but has not yet gone off, rub it with diluted vinegar before cooking.

◆ Pork must always be well cooked – never underdone – to make it more digestible.

◆ Loin of pork produces the best crackling. Make cuts in the skin, then rub with salt and olive oil before putting in the oven.

◆ When cooking pork, add a spoonful or two of water to the roasting tin to stop fat from burning. This will also make better gravy.

◆ Make oxtail soup or stew in advance, allow to cool. Skim off the fat, then reheat.

◆ For a low-fat alternative to beef or pork, try venison.

◆ Marinate venison while it is thawing and roast with strips of bacon over it to make it juicier.

COOKING VEGETABLES

◆Steaming takes half as long again as boiling but is a healthier way to cook, see right.
◆Don't leave vegetables sitting in cold water because water leaches out the enzymes.
◆To cook vegetables throw them into the water when it is boiling to preserve the nutrients.
◆Flavour with lemon juice instead of salt; it is better for you.

Root vegetables

◆Cook fast until the fibres have been softened; the older the vegetables, the longer this will take.
◆Don't boil old potatoes too fast or they will fall to pieces. Put them unpeeled in cold water and cook them with the lid on.
◆Boiled potatoes will stay white if you add 5ml (1tsp) lemon juice or vinegar to the cooking water.
◆Beetroot peels easily if you dip it in cold water as soon as it is cooked.
◆Onions to be fried can have boiling water poured over them. Then pat dry and fry them; they fry faster this way.

Green vegetables

◆Cook vegetables in one layer so that they are all ready at the same time; don't pile everything up in a small pan.
◆If you can't steam, blanch (cook for a very short time in rapidly boiling water). After blanching, refresh the vegetables by running cold tap water over them for no more than a second or two.
◆Spinach should be cooked only in the water which sticks to it after washing or it will be soggy.
◆Two lumps of sugar in the water with a cauliflower and other vegetables will help them stay white.
◆Fresh peas can be cooked without water. Instead line the pan with lettuce leaves and lay the peas on top. The moisture in the lettuce will steam the peas.

STEAMING VEGETABLES

◆Steaming is better than boiling; the vegetables don't touch the water so retain their flavour and vitamins.

Tiered steaming pan

Steaming basket

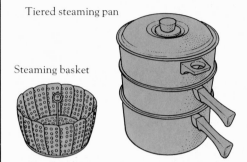

Equipment *You can buy an adjustable steaming basket that fits into most saucepans. Alternatively, buy a tiered pan which allows you to steam one or more different vegetables together. The water sits in the bottom and each layer has holes in the base for steam to pass through.*

COOKING EGGS AND DAIRY PRODUCTS

◆ If adding milk, cream or yogurt to soups or stews, always do so near the end of cooking time; they are less likely to curdle.

Eggs

◆ Raw egg has been found to be the source of infection in some cases of salmonella poisoning. Current advice is that pregnant women, young children, the elderly and people weakened by poor health should avoid raw egg and not use recipes containing it.
◆ Remove eggs from the fridge a few hours before use; they are less likely to burst.
◆To peel shells from hard-boiled eggs, salt the cooking water. When the eggs are cooked, rinse them quickly in cold water and crack the shell at the ends.
◆If you are not sure if an egg is hard boiled, spin it on its side on a flat, hard surface. A fresh egg will spin unevenly, a hard-boiled egg will spin evenly.

◆To make scrambled eggs fluffy, add a little carbonated water. Watery and hard eggs are the result of over-cooking.

◆Never use the omelette pan for anything but omelettes; you may damage the surface.

◆Never make an omelette with more than six eggs, it won't cook evenly.

◆Eggs will curdle in cooked liquid mixtures, such as custards, soups or sauces, if the two threads attaching the yolk to the white have not been broken. Break the threads off with a sharp piece of eggshell or strain the eggs first.

◆If making a soufflé, don't open the oven before the time stated in the recipe, it'll sink.

Fresh and bad eggs *A fresh egg should sink at once in a bowl of salted water and lie on the bottom, see left; a bad egg will float, see right.*

Cheese

◆Quickly heated dishes containing cheese should be eaten as soon as ready, while the cheese is soft; cooked cheese can be leathery.

◆Cook cheese dishes requiring long-term cooking slowly or the cheese will curdle.

◆Light, soft cheese, such as quark, curd cheese and ricotta, is best for fillings.

◆Grated hard cheeses, such as Cheddar, Parmesan, Cantal, Emmenthal and Gruyère, are ideal for toppings and making sauces.

◆Most hard cheeses keep well, and can be grated and used even when dried up.

◆Grated Parmesan is convenient bought in pots, but it costs more and doesn't taste very good. Buy a block and grate off as much as you need; the block will last longer as well.

Dairy products

◆Whip cream straight from the fridge. Add two or three drops of lemon juice to make it whip faster.

◆Use yogurt, *fromage fais* or smetana as low-fat alternatives to cream.

PASTRY, CAKES AND BREAD

◆The proportions of pastry ingredients must be correct or the pastry won't work: the rule is half as much fat as flour.

◆Too much liquid makes pastry hard and tough. Add it slowly and carefully. The liquid should be cold; always use it straight from the refrigerator.

◆Pastry to be served cold will be crisper if you make it with milk rather than water.

◆For rich shortcrust pastry, add the yolk of one egg to the water.

◆Handle pastry as little as possible.

◆Keep all pastry cool: before rolling out, place dough in a plastic bag in a cool place for about half an hour to harden the fat and cool the ingredients. The cold air expands during baking, making a light pastry.

◆Don't use too much flour on the pastry board and rolling pin – you might alter the proportions in the mixture.

◆Roll forward and backward – side-to-side rolling makes pastry rise unevenly.

◆Bake in a hot oven – the richer the mixture the hotter the oven should be.

◆Put a shallow dish of water in the bottom of the oven to prevent cakes from burning.

◆If you are short of eggs for a rich fruit cake, one egg can be replaced with 5ml (1tsp) vinegar.

◆Add 15ml (3tsp) boiling water to cake mix just before putting it into the tin to make it rise. Don't open the oven during cooking.

◆Use fruit concentrate instead of sugar for healthier cakes – 30ml (2tbsp) to every 25g (1oz) sugar.

◆Use the food processor for kneading bread dough or making pastry.

◆If making bread dough for freezing, use about 50 percent more yeast than normal.

◆Flour varies in absorbency; add more if the dough is slack.

◆Fresh compressed baker's yeast is easier to work than dried yeast.

◆Don't use dried yeast for fancy pastries, it has a strong "beery" flavour.

◆Put very fresh unsliceable bread in the freezer for half an hour to make it firm enough for you to cut.

FLAVOURING FOOD

Sauces can add to flavour or hold different ingredients together and improve the look of a dish.

Marinating is a way to introduce a variety of tastes into meat and fish before cooking and helps to soften fibres.

Marinades

◆Basic ingredients for a marinade: red or white wine, wine vinegar, lemon or orange juice, peppercorns, juniper berries, coriander seeds, cumin seeds, rosemary, thyme, bay leaf, parsley, shallots, celery, garlic, onions, root vegetables, olive oil, sunflower or maize oil.

RECIPE FOR LIGHT MARINADE

◆ The following combination is suitable for game, fish and meat.

1 lemon, thinly sliced	2 bay leaves
1 carrot, thinly sliced	3 whole cloves
15ml (1tbsp) vinegar	1 sprig parsley
15ml (1tbsp) olive oil	12 peppercorns,
1 sprig thyme	crushed

1 Place the meat or fish in a flat-bottomed dish and add the marinade ingredients. The marinade must completely cover the meat or fish or air will decompose the exposed parts.

2 Stir the mixture gently once in a while and turn often.

3 Keep in a cool place. In winter a piece of meat can be left five to six days. In summer 24 – 48 hours is the maximum.

Making sauces

◆Use a sauce to combine leftovers and make a meal.

◆For a thin sauce use 25g (1oz) butter and 25g (1oz) flour to each 600ml (1pt) liquid.

◆For a medium sauce allow 50g (2oz) each butter and flour to 600ml (1pt) liquid.

LAZY WHITE SAUCE

1 Measure the cold liquid, butter and flour and put them all in the saucepan.

2 Set over a low heat, whisking as the butter melts. Continue whisking until the mixture reaches boiling point and thickens.

3 Lower the heat and simmer until all trace of the raw flour taste has vanished. Season.

◆White wine, a pinch of nutmeg, pepper and/or herbs can be used to season a white sauce.

◆For a thick sauce allow 75g (3oz) butter and flour to 600ml (1pt) liquid.

◆For a healthy low-fat sauce make it with margarine or sunflower oil, wholemeal flour and skimmed milk.

◆If the sauce is too thin, make a cornflour paste and gradually add it to the mixture.

◆If the sauce is too thick, add more liquid.

Herbs

◆Herbs can be used to reduce intake of salt. For instance, lovage, thyme and marjoram can replace salt almost completely.

◆Some herbs can replace condiments which may not be good for some people. Basil, thyme, marjoram and nasturtium can replace pepper, which is difficult for people with digestive problems to digest.

◆Sprinkle a variety of chopped herbs over salads for extra flavour. Mint, fennel and marjoram are particularly good.

◆Fresh herbs can be dried or frozen for winter use, see page 19.

Lemon balm, fresh

Lemon balm, dried

Angelica

Herbs to replace sugar *Lemon balm, above left, and angelica, above right, can be used in cooking instead of sugar. They are particularly good with tart fruits such as rhubarb, currants or apples.*

USE OF OILS IN COOKING

◆ Use oils containing polyunsaturated fats rather than saturated fats for cooking because they actually break down cholesterol, see page 45.

◆ Use cold-pressed oils; the heat used in other extraction processes can turn an unsaturated fat into a saturated one. Cold-pressed oils are also free from artificial preservatives.

◆ Good oils for cooking are: corn, sesame, olive, cottonseed, peanut, safflower, sunflower and soya bean.

◆ Olive oil is a monounsaturated fat – it doesn't do any harm, but it doesn't break down cholesterol. It is the most easily digested oil.

◆ Avoid coconut and palm oil because they contain saturated fats.

◆ Peanut oil is good for frying at high temperatures. It can be re-used about ten times and should then be thrown away.

◆ When oil begins to smoke, lower the temperature. At this stage it may burst into flames and cause a fire.

▼▼ Never put water on a fat fire: remove
◆ ◆ pan from the heat and cover with a lid or damp towel (see EMERGENCY ACTION, page 356).

FOOD PRESENTATION

◆ Keep a bunch of mixed fresh herbs in a jar of water in the kitchen so that you can chop up a handful for garnishing dishes.

◆ Fresh peppers are available in red, green, and even black. Use them to add a touch of colour to salads and rice dishes.

◆ Decorate fish or pieces of chicken with slices or twists of lemon.

◆ A topping of grated cheese or breadcrumbs, browned for a few seconds under the grill, can make all the difference to a basic casserole. Alternatively, a swirl of sour cream or yogurt can lift a dish.

◆ Cold meats can be turned into works of art by careful arrangement of different kinds together with sliced vegetables.

◆ Make cuts in the top of radishes and dip them in cold water to make radish flowers.

◆ Plan your menu so that everything is not the same colour.

◆ Use dishes of one colour to set off the food. White bowls for tomato soup or bortsch; salad in glass bowls and so on.

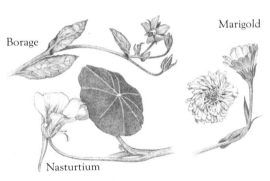

Flowers in food *Scatter edible flowers over salads: nasturtium, marigolds and the blue flowers of borage are all spectacular.*

Keeping food hot

◆ Put hot food into heated dishes with the lid on (except vegetables, which should be eaten as soon as cooked).

◆ Keep casseroles in a low oven. Don't turn the oven off; the residual heat can encourage bacteria.

Making lemon twists *Cut lemon slices. Make a cut from the centre of each slice to the edge, then twist.*

Table-top food warmer *Trays with nightlight burners as found in Indian restaurants are cheap and highly effective for keeping dishes hot at table.*

SERVING WINE

◆Uncork or decant red wine an hour or two before serving to allow it to breathe and bring it up to room temperature.

◆If you want to check white wine, open it an hour or so before serving. Replace the cork lightly before chilling the wine in the refrigerator.

◆Don't open champagne or sparkling wines until just before serving; they will go flat.

◆If the cork breaks, take a sharp pointed knife or a skewer and stab it into the cork against the side of the bottle and try levering the cork out. If the cork breaks up into the wine, decant it through a tea strainer, see below.

◆Smell the cork after it is drawn to check that it smells only of wine and isn't tainted by mould. There usually is a slight smell of cork in newly opened wine, which should disappear after a short time.

◆Before serving, wipe the mouth of the bottle with a clean cloth.

DECANTING WINE

◆The decanter should be at room temperature. Pour wine slowly and steadily into the decanter, until the sediment begins to flow. Most wines have very little sediment, however, so you can save most of the wine.

◆Decant young red wine, such as Beaujolais Nouveau, three or four hours before being served.

◆Never decant champagne, sparkling wines and white wine.

Filtering wine *You can decant wine which is full of cork bits through a tea strainer, set on a funnel, into a decanter.*

RESCUING DISASTERS

◆Soup can be livened up with a dollop of cream, sour cream, yogurt, fromage frais, quark or smetana.

◆If a dish lacks flavour, add a good tablespoon of mustard or some paprika or cayenne pepper. A spoonful of curry powder or paste, say, or yeast extract will improve bland soups, sauces or mayonnaise.

◆Breadcrumbs, yogurt, cream and parsley can all help absorb saltiness.

◆If a dish won't stand more salt or pepper, try fresh herbs or lemon juice.

Soups, sauces and dressings

◆Grease on soups or sauces can be soaked up with a kitchen towel laid on the top. If you have time, chill the soup then remove the congealed fat from the top.

◆Thicken thin stocks, soups or sauces by boiling with the lid off the saucepan.

◆If these go lumpy, put them in the blender or food processor briefly.

◆Curdled mayonnaise: start with a clean bowl and a new egg and gradually add the curdled mixture, or start again with a different oil. Most vegetable oils make good mayonnaise but olive oil, nut oil and sunflower oil are almost foolproof.

◆To rescue a curdled sauce, take the pan off the heat and plunge it into cold water, or take it off the heat and add a teaspoonful of cold water or cream to the sauce.

◆If custard curdles, whip in 10ml (2tsp) cornflour per 600ml (1pt) liquid.

◆Improve a sickly sweet sauce by adding a squeeze of lemon juice.

Meat, poultry or vegetables

◆Crumbling pâtés can be served as a soft pâté from the bowl or, if there's time, put them back into a food processor with a bit of added butter and re-pot.

◆Don't stir a burned stew; you will ruin the unburned part. Pour the unburned part into another pot and add a raw potato or a slice of stale bread to absorb the burned taste. After

10 minutes take the potato or bread out and put a good dollop of pepper and Worcestershire sauce into the stew. If there is not enough left, add a tin of tomatoes and/or sour cream or yogurt.

◆ If poultry is overcooked, break it up and serve it on a bed of rice. Alternatively, mix with a white sauce and use it to fill pancakes or vol-au-vents.

◆ Rice which has formed heavy wet lumps can be put in a ring mould then baked in the oven for about 10 minutes. Turn out and serve with sauce or stir-fried vegetables in the middle of the ring.

◆ To crisp celery, put it in a bowl of water and add a slice of raw potato. Let it stand in the fridge for a few hours.

◆ To crisp lettuce, put it in a bowl of cold water, add the juice of half a lemon per head of lettuce and stand in a cool place for about half an hour.

Eggs and dairy products

◆ Cut overcooked omelette into squares and use to garnish a clear soup.

◆ A soufflé which has not risen or has sunk can be served on toast with lots of parsley.

◆ Eggs that you accidentally cracked can be cooked without bursting if you add a teaspoonful of salt to the cooking water and cook the egg thoroughly. Don't cook eggs that were cracked before you bought them.

◆ Cream that has gone off can be used in goulashes or watercress or sorrel soups instead of yogurt.

Burned milk *If milk boils over onto an electric hotplate, sprinkle it with salt at once to stop it smelling.*

Pastry and cakes

◆ If pastry starts to shrink over the pie dish you can add new pastry to patch the holes even half way through cooking.

◆ Sticky pastry will never quite recover because the proportions were wrong. However, if you put it in the fridge for half an hour, then roll it out between two pieces of lightly floured greaseproof paper, it will at least cover a pie.

◆ If rich fruit cake turns out dry, break it up. Add some butter or margarine and a measure of brandy, leave it to soak for 24 hours, then squash it into a pudding bowl, steam it and eat as a pudding.

◆ If glacé icing goes wrong, cover it with some chocolate buttons.

◆ If royal icing is so hard you can't cut it, break it all off and make a new batch, this time adding a drop or two of glycerine.

Moistening dry cakes *If a cake is slightly dry, skewer it all over and pour brandy or fruit juice into it.*

Miscellaneous

◆ If your coffee tastes bitter, put two or three cardamom pods into the pot while it is brewing and call it Jordanian coffee.

◆ To unstick dried dates, figs or raisins, place them in a low oven for a few minutes.

◆ Marmalade which doesn't set may have been cooked beyond the setting point. You will have to add more pectin or save the day with gelatine; use about a quarter the amount of gelatine that you would use to make jelly.

◆ If jam crystallizes, the sugar didn't dissolve properly; reheat in the oven until the crystals melt, then re-pot.

HEALTHY EATING

The nutrients in food are the chemicals needed to build, repair and maintain our bodies and to provide energy. For energy we need protein, carbohydrates, fats and oils.

For building and maintenance we need protein and minerals. For protection, control and regulation of the body processes we need vitamins and minerals.

NUTRIENTS AND WHAT SUPPLIES THEM

Oxygen, carbon and hydrogen are the basic elements from which all of our body protein and fat are built. They are found in protein, carbohydrate and fat.

PROTEIN
◇ Poultry, beef, lamb, pork and game
◇ Fish
◇ Eggs
◇ Milk and dairy products
◇ Pulses
◇ Nuts
◇ Wholemeal bread and pasta
◇ Potatoes

CARBOHYDRATES
◇ Starches and sugars
◇ Cereal grains and wholemeal flour
◇ Potatoes
◇ Other vegetables

FATS AND OILS
◇ Margarine
◇ Butter
◇ Cooking fats and oils
◇ Cheese and milk
◇ Fish oils
◇ Nuts
◇ Animal fat

VITAMINS AND MINERALS
◇ A great many foods of plant and animal origin, particularly fresh fruit and vegetables.

CALORIES

These are the units by which body energy is measured. Your food should provide exactly the amount of energy you use in a day.

Requirements vary according to age, sex, height, weight, environment and activity: a small 50-year-old woman with servants, living in a warm climate, would need fewer calories than most other people, whereas a working mother or a teenage, football-playing boy in mid winter would need a lot of energy-producing foods.

Daily needs

◆ On average these are the number of calories which should be consumed daily: men 2,700–3,000; women 2,200–2,500; teenage boys 2,800–3,000; teenage girls 2,300; children 1,200–2,500 depending on age; babies 800. If you stick to the guidelines, you should not need to count the calories.

◆ As a general rule, ten percent of our calorie intake should come from protein. Proteins are made of amino acids, which act like building blocks for the body. Eight of these acids, essential to health, cannot be manufactured by the body so must be included in your diet. Protein from animal sources contains all the essential amino acids in the correct proportions.

◆ Don't forget you may be taking protein in the form of sweets too: custards, cheesecakes and pancakes are all protein-rich foods.

◆ Two examples of a satisfactory protein intake for one day are given below. Young children would probably need to take all the milk and less meat; adults might take less milk and slightly more white meat or fish.

EXAMPLE ONE
◇ 300ml ($\frac{1}{2}$pt) milk adults/600ml (1pt) children
◇ 1 egg
◇ 90g (3oz) cooked lean white meat or fish
◇ 4 slices wholemeal bread
◇ A portion of porridge or wholemeal breakfast cereal.

EXAMPLE TWO
◇ 300ml ($\frac{1}{2}$pt) milk
◇ 60g (2oz) meat
◇ 60g (2oz) beans or lentils (weight before cooking)
◇ 170g (6oz) potatoes
◇ 2 slices of wholemeal bread

BALANCED DIET

In general, everyone would benefit if they followed these general rules:

◆ Eat more fruit, vegetables, and whole grains.
◆ Eat less meat.
◆ Eat fewer animal (saturated) fats.
◆ Eat more vegetable (polyunsaturated) fats.
◆ Drink more skimmed, or non-fat, milk instead of whole milk.
◆ Eat low-fat dairy products.
◆ Eat less butter and eggs.
◆ Eat less sugar and sugary foods.
◆ Eat less salt and salty foods.
◆ Eat a minimum amount of processed foods; many contain hidden sugar and salt as well as artificial additives. Read the labels.

TIPS FOR VEGETARIANS

◆ Tofu (otherwise known as soya bean curd) is a good source of protein.
◆ Nuts and peanut butter are a good protein source.
◆ Eat yeast extract for its vitamin E content.
◆ Eat a wider variety of vegetables, especially dark green leafy ones.

Generally - - ➤   Sometimes •••▷
complementary   complementary

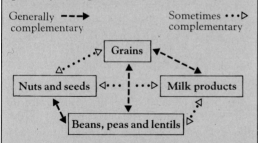

Complementary proteins *No single vegetable protein contains all the essential amino acids in the proportions required by the body. You need to combine complementary protein foods to get them in right proportions in your diet.*

Carbohydrate and fibre

◆ For good health, a diet should contain 40 to 45 percent carbohydrate and not more than 15 percent of that should be sugar.

WHERE TO FIND FIBRE

HIGH-FIBRE FOODS	MEDIUM-FIBRE FOODS
◇ Bananas	◇ Apples,
◇ Bran	◇ Oranges
◇ Brown rice	◇ Green vegetables
◇ Muesli	◇ Nuts
◇ Pulses	**LOW-FIBRE FOODS**
◇ Wholemeal bread or pasta	◇ Peeled potatoes
◇ Jacket potatoes	◇ Cucumber
◇ Leafy vegetables	◇ Grapefruit
◇ Sweetcorn	◇ Lettuce
◇ Rhubarb	◇ White rice and pasta
◇ Dried fruit	

◆ Carbohydrate foods, such as whole-grain cereals, fresh vegetables and fruit, also contain fibre, which aids digestion, so they should form an important part of your diet. Fibre in diet prevents digestive problems such as diverticular disease, haemorrhoids and hernias.
◆ Fibre comes from fibrous parts of vegetables and fruits.
◆ To boost your fibre intake, eat wholemeal bread. It contains more than three times as much fibre as white bread.
◆ Peas and beans which have not been refined are rich in fibre.
▼▼ Avoid processed carbohydrates, which
•• have been robbed of much of their fibre. They fill you up temporarily, then you want to eat more. These include: white bread; potato chips or crisps; pastries; light sponge cakes with cream or icing; chocolate biscuits.

Fats and oils

Fats are necessary for flavour and for supplying energy. A little fat under the skin protects the body from injury, but on the whole people in Western countries eat twice as much fat as they need.

There are three types of fat: saturated fat, which encourages the body's production of cholesterol, which in turn builds up inside the blood vessels and causes circulatory problems; polyunsaturated fats, which break

HOW TO EAT LESS FAT

◆ Choose white meat, game and fish.
▼▼ Watch out for shellfish because it
◆ ◆ contains saturated fats.
◆ If you eat red meat, trim away all the
fat and buy lean mince or, better still,
mince your own.
◆ Buy skimmed milk.
◆ Eat fewer eggs; egg yolk in particular is
high in saturated fat.
◆ Eat more wholewheat cereals, including bread, pasta and rice.
◆ Increase vegetable intake.
◆ Use margarine rich in polyunsaturated
fats for spreading on bread.
◆ Grill don't fry.
◆ Make cakes and pastries with vegetable oil or polyunsaturated margarine.
◆ Substitute oil for butter when cooking
soups and stews, scrambled eggs,
omelettes and sauces.
◆ Don't buy foods containing hydrogen-
ated fats; the heat used in the hydrogen-
ation process can turn a polyunsaturated
fat into a saturated one.

TIPS FOR PRESERVING VITAMINS AND MINERALS

Vitamins can be destroyed during
cooking and preparation. Water-soluble
vitamins, such as C, are damaged by heat;
others such as the B group vitamins are
destroyed by light. Vitamins A, D and E
are not water-soluble so are not destroyed by cooking.
◆ Vegetable water contains vitamins and
minerals. Don't throw it away, use it in
soups or sauces. Don't keep spinach
water; it contains oxalic acid, which prevents absorption of calcium.
◆ Eat foods containing vitamins A and E
at the same meal, for example, put margarine on carrots (the vitamin E in margarine helps the absorption of vitamin A
in the carrots).
◆ Green vegetables will lose more
vitamin C if kept in a warm dish; eat as
soon as cooked.
◆ Prepare salads at the last minute, particularly if ingredients are grated, because
cutting exposes the vitamins to light.
◆ Lemon juice in salads helps preserve
vitamin C (use it instead of vinegar in
dressing).

down the cholesterol in the body; and
monounsaturated fats, which don't cause a
build-up of cholesterol, but don't break it
down either.
◆ Choose vegetable fats because they are
polyunsaturated fats.
▼▼ Avocado pears, coconut and palm oil all
◆ ◆ contain saturated fat.
▼▼ Animal products and shellfish contain
◆ ◆ saturated fats.
◆ Even lean meat is marbled with plenty of
fat, so don't eat too much.
◆ Avoid offal, such as liver and kidneys,
because they contain saturated fat.
◆ See also USING OILS, page 41.

Vitamins and minerals

◆ Children, pregnant and lactating women,
the elderly and people recovering from illness or injury need more vitamins.
◆ Different minerals often work together so
correct balance of each is vital, see above
right and opposite.

PLANNING BALANCED MEALS

If your diet includes a good variety of foods
you will automatically be eating well and
giving your body the things it needs.
◆ Food doesn't have to take hours to prepare
in order to be good. In fact many foods are at
their best raw because some cooking
methods can destroy the nutrients. Salads
are excellent nutritionally and there's no end
to the variety.

Breakfast

◆ The meal should contain some good-
quality protein, which will slowly release
nutrients during the morning.

SOURCES OF VITAMINS AND MINERALS

VITAMIN	Needed for	Source
A	Healthy eyes, tissue, skin and mucous membranes.	Liver, fish, shellfish, butter, margarine, carrots, tomatoes, all green vegetables.
B group Includes B1, B2, B3, B6, B12, folic acid	Important for metabolism of carbohydrates. Needed for brain functioning, healthy skin and hair, and production of red blood cells.	Meat (especially liver and kidneys), fish, milk, cheese, eggs, yeast, whole-grain or enriched cereals and bread, oatmeal, pulses, leafy green vegetables.
C	Maintains healthy muscles, ligaments and tendons, promotes healing and helps fight against infection; facilitates absorption of iron.	Green vegetables, potatoes, citrus fruit, summer berry fruits, and to a certain extent other vegetables.
D	Helps the body absorb calcium from the intestine, and regulates the amount of calcium entering the bones from the blood. Needed for bone development, especially in the very young and the elderly.	Oily fish, shellfish, margarine, milk, cheese, eggs, butter.
E	Thought to regulate fat metabolism and helps to prevent circulatory problems.	Vegetable oils from seeds or cereal grains, other cereal products, eggs, nuts, yeast extract, margarine.
K	Necessary for normal blood clotting.	Cabbage, cauliflower, spinach, peas, foods from cereal grains.
MINERAL	**Needed for**	**Source**
Calcium	Works with phosphorus and magnesium for construction of bones and teeth. The main constituent of blood and important for many metabolic processes.	Milk, cheese, fish and green vegetables.
Phosphorus	As for calcium.	Most foods.
Magnesium	As calcium. Also, deficiency can cause weakness and depression.	Most foods.
Sodium	Keeps body fluids regulated, inside and outside body cells. Needed in very small amounts. Too much inhibits the action of potassium.	Fruit, vegetables, meats and cereals.
Potassium	Regulates state of fluids in body cells, in particular the muscle cells and blood cells.	Bananas, beetroot, potatoes, cabbage, butter beans, dried fruit, nuts, milk, meat.
Iron	Essential for formation of red blood cells and muscle cells.	Liver, kidney, eggs, bread, flour, oats, figs, dried apricots, prunes, black treacle, molasses, cocoa.
Trace elements	Zinc, copper, manganese, selenium, chromium, iodine, fluorine, molybdenum are needed in minute quantities.	Most foods.

WHAT'S IN MANUFACTURED SOFT DRINKS

◇ Squash or cordial must have 25 percent fruit juice before you dilute it.

◇ Crush is ready-to-drink and must contain at least five percent fruit juice.

◇ Fruit barley water must have 15 percent fruit juice before it is diluted.

◇ A fruit drink is made with at least 4.5kg (9lb) whole fruit per 4.5 litres (1gal) and includes flesh and peel pulped and is therefore about 50 percent fruit.

◇ Fruit-ade or fruit-flavoured drinks have practically no fruit at all.

◇ Cola drinks are made with sugar and saccharin or other artificial sweetener and added phosphoric acid, which counteracts the excessive sweetness. They have no nutritional value and are very bad for teeth. Most contain small amounts of caffeine which is not good for children.

▼ ▼ Read the labels of fruit drinks care-
♦ ♦ fully because many contain artificial additives such as the sweeteners saccharin and aspartame, as well as colourings and flavourings.

♦ Eating a good breakfast will give you more energy and better powers of concentration during the day.

♦ Fruit is the best appetizer. (One orange will provide about half the daily requirement of vitamin C.)

♦ Porridge, cereals, bread, croissants and toast are energy foods and provide protein and iron too. Wholemeal foods are digested slowly, last longer and provide more fibre.

♦ Milk with the cereal, or a boiled or poached egg, provides protein.

Main meals

♦ Ideally all meals should contain some green leafy vegetables for vitamins and fibre.

♦ Substantial home-made soups can form the main part of a meal if they contain lentils, fish, beans or peas.

♦ Soups and casseroles are good for families who come home at different times, because they won't spoil by being kept hot.

♦ Fish is an excellent source of protein and makes a change from meat.

♦ Jacket potatoes with different fillings and a salad are excellent nutritionally. Nutritious fillings include: curd cheese and herbs, baked beans (not tinned because they contain sugar), tuna fish, sweetcorn, cheese.

♦ Offer a piece of fresh fruit or fruit salad instead of sticky puddings.

♦ Put less sugar in fruit puddings and pies or use fruit concentrates.

♦ Use fromage blanc or yogurt instead of cream on puddings.

Light meals

♦ Serve egg and cheese dishes and a side salad.

♦ Sandwiches with imaginative fillings can be a complete meal in themselves.

♦ Eat salads containing vegetables, nuts and pulses, and a slice of wholemeal bread.

Drinks

♦ If you are changing to a low-fat, high-fibre diet, drink plenty of water to help digestion.

♦ Coffee and tea both contain caffeine, which is a stimulant – although there is far less caffeine in tea. If you find yourself drinking a great deal of either, give it up for a week. It may make you feel better.

♦ Decaffeinated coffee is better for people with heart conditions or who have bladder problems.

♦ Drink herb teas and cereal coffees.

♦ Cocoa (and chocolate) may contribute to migraines. Use carob powder instead.

♦ Vegetable juices are not as good for you as eating the whole vegetable; chewing is good for you and so is the fibre which you don't get from the juice on its own.

♦ Fruit juices are excellent foods: pops, colas and other fizzy drinks are NOT.

♦ Make yogurt drinks, mixing fruit juice, yogurt and water in a blender or food processor. You can add herbs as well.

♦ Watch out for mixer drinks, most of them contain sugar as well as other additives.

ENTERTAINING

The secret of success is in forward planning. If you have everything organized beforehand, you will be able to enjoy your guests. Don't be over-ambitious: if you are new to cooking, don't try to produce the kind of meal you might eat in a restaurant. If you have young children and no help, make the meal informal; you'll enjoy it a great deal more. Plan the menu so that you don't have lots of things to do at the last moment. If you are out at work all day, prepare as much as possible the evening before, so that it is less of a rush on the day.

If you are inviting only a few people make sure they all have a common interest; it's easier to get the conversation going.

PREPARATION

◆Several days before, write down a menu which is seasonal, using the best fresh ingredients you can afford.

◆Try to plan a menu in which one or two courses can be made ahead and frozen, made the night before or in the morning. Check up on the store cupboard and make a list of everything you need to buy.

◆Don't attempt anything you haven't done before or aren't sure about. Better to have one main dish with salads and a good cheese board than attempt four or five complicated courses which need your constant attention and, more importantly, which might go wrong at the last moment.

◆Make sure there's a relaxed atmosphere.

Don't feel that everything must be tidied away; things are what make your home interesting to others. It's better to have guests chatting in a relaxed way in the kitchen with you than sitting formally in another room on their own.

◆Always provide soft drinks for the drivers.

Menus

◆Combine dishes which are varied in taste, colour and texture as well as appearance and calorie value in each course. Try not to follow one course with another using the same ingredients or one that is the same colour.

◆Balance a rich, heavy dish by something light, such as a salad or fruit.

TIPS FOR BEING PREPARED WHEN GUESTS ARRIVE

◆The main dish should be ready and keeping warm.

◆Vegetables should be prepared with pans of water simmering ready to receive them; alternatively, you can par-boil vegetables earlier on (not green ones), put them in the serving dish and warm them in the microwave at the last minute.

◆Salads should be prepared and ready for dressing and the dressing made.

◆Hot puddings should be ready to put in the oven.

◆Cold sweets should be in the fridge.

◆Bread should be warming.

◆Plates should be warming in a bottom oven if the meal is hot.

◆Cheeses should be out in a warm room.

◆Red wine should be open and sitting in a warm room; white wine or champagne cooling in the refrigerator.

◆The table should be set.

◆Coffee should be measured out, ready to make; the coffee tray laid with cups, spoons, sugar, cream.

◆Drinks, glasses, ice cubes, snacks should be laid out in the living room.

◆Soap and hand towels should be laid out in the bathroom.

Laying the table

◆ Don't have any extras on the table. All you need are: condiments, wine, water, serving spoons and forks, place settings and a centrepiece (flowers or a small plant). Keep everything else ready but on a separate table or in the fridge.

◆ Lay out cutlery so that the items you use first are on the outside of the arrangement and, as the courses proceed, work through from the outside in.

◆ A tablecloth looks better than table mats, which can look cluttered. Put some mats under the cloth to protect the table.

◆ Beautifully laundered linen is making a comeback, but it must be beautifully laundered, and that is hard work. You may be better off choosing an easy-care material.

◆ Patterned china looks best on a plain cloth and vice versa.

◆ There is tremendous scope for colour with food; try serving colourful food on white or contrasting plates.

Lighting

◆ Candles are important for lending atmosphere and are definitely the most flattering light you can have.

◆ Candle flames must be below eye level or those trying to talk to each other across the table will be dazzled.

◆ If candles are not enough, have dimmed background lighting, nothing too brash.

Flowers and foliage

◆ Fresh flowers always look good unless the table is very full, although they can always be removed after the first course.

◆ Make sure the vase is low and small. Use several along the length of the table if you like. One or two flower heads floating in a bowl can look very pretty.

◆ Green foliage such as ivy can be draped all round a table, and perhaps tied with small satin bows for formal occasions.

FOLDING NAPKINS

◆ Napkins neatly folded into triangles are all a dinner table actually needs, but if you have the time and the inclination you can fold napkins into all sorts of intricate shapes.

◆ Most folding methods require a square napkin. Complicated folds need a large well-starched napkin.

◆ Linen napkins must be beautifully ironed.

◆ Your hands and the working surfaces must be clean.

The fan *Lay the napkin out flat. Working away from you, make a series of narrow pleats* (1). *Fold the pleated napkin in half. Set the bottom of the fold into a wine glass and open out the pleats* (2).

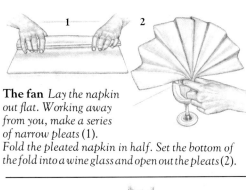

French fold *Fold the napkin in three lengthways, then make staggered folds to form steps or pockets.*

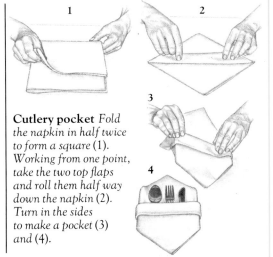

Cutlery pocket *Fold the napkin in half twice to form a square* (1). *Working from one point, take the two top flaps and roll them half way down the napkin* (2). *Turn in the sides to make a pocket* (3) *and* (4).

OLD-FASHIONED BUT USEFUL TABLE ETIQUETTE

◆ Put plates down in front of a guest from the right and take them away, when empty, from the left.
◆ Offer food in dishes from the right for guests to help themselves.
◆ Serve wine and water from a person's right.
◆ After the main course, remove salt, pepper and sauces from the table.
◆ Cheese and biscuits may be left on the table while coffee is served.

Seating arrangements

You may not need to be very formal at dinner parties but the rules are useful to know:
◆ The host sits at one end of the table and the hostess at the other.
◆ The male guest of honour sits on the right of the hostess and the female guest of honour on the left of the host.
◆ Couples do not sit together.
◆ In reality, nowadays, there may be only one person giving a dinner party and there may not be an equal number of men and women, in which case put people next to each other who you think will have something to say to each other.

BUFFET PARTIES

◆ These are a practical way of entertaining a lot of people at home or a few people where seating is limited.
◆ One conspicuous flower arrangement should be enough, or you can make the food itself decorative in its own right.
◆ To ease congestion at the food table, put drinks and glasses on a separate table.

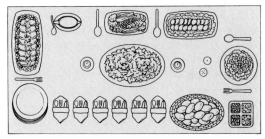

Arranging a buffet table *Arrange the food around the table in menu order to prevent "traffic jams" at one end of the table.*

Hiring crockery and glass

◆ You can often hire glasses when you order wine in quantity from a wine merchant.
◆ Always phone around because there may be a large variation in price as well as quality. Catering companies sometimes hire out crockery more cheaply than hire companies.

ESTIMATING QUANTITIES

◆ Meat or fish in made-up dishes goes further, theoretically, but people often have second helpings.
◆ The following are approximate quantities:
◇ 300ml ($\frac{1}{2}$pt) soup per person
◇ 175–250g (6–8oz) fish per person
◇ 175–250g (6–8oz) meat on the bone per person
◇ 125–175g (4–6oz) meat off the bone per person
◇ 50g (2oz) rice, weight uncooked, per person

◇ 125g (4oz) pasta, weight uncooked, per person
◇ 175g (6oz) vegetables per person
◇ 2 rolls per person
◇ 1 large lettuce will make a base for a salad for 6
◇ 1 large fruit pie for 10 people
◇ 4 litres (6$\frac{1}{2}$pt) fruit salad for 50 people
◇ 3 litres (5pt) cream for 50 people
◇ 2 litres (2$\frac{1}{2}$pt) icecream for 50 people

DRINKS
◇ 1 bottle sherry should yield about 16 glasses
◇ 1 bottle spirits gives 32 measures
◇ 1 bottle wine or champagne about 6 glasses
◇ If serving wine at a party allow an average of $\frac{1}{2}$bottle per person
◇ 600ml (1pt) water is enough for 6 small cups of tea or coffee

CHILDREN'S PARTIES

◆ Keep the party as small as possible; don't invite more children than you can cope with – five children is perfect if they are under three, very young children will be perfectly happy with a party for two.

◆ Keep the party as short as possible: an hour is about right for toddlers; two hours is ideal for 7–10 year olds.

◆ Very young children prefer very small bits of food such as crisps and small biscuits, tiny sandwiches, iced cakes, icecream and jelly.

◆ Bake cakes in sweet papers rather than cake papers.

◆ Make the cake in the shape of an engine or a house and they will enjoy looking at it; don't worry if they don't eat it.

◆ Don't make a rich cake. Sponge or Victoria sandwich are ideal.

◆ As children grow older, you can cut out the jelly and add more filling foods such as flapjacks, larger sandwiches, pancakes, chicken legs and so on.

◆ If you think they'd prefer hamburgers and chips, take them to a McDonalds.

◆ A low table saves having to help very young children on and off chairs. Put the top of a trestle table on the floor propped up on some books or bricks and sit the children on cushions around the edge.

◆ All children make a mess at parties. The best thing is to buy disposable plates, beakers and cutlery which you can sweep into a large plastic bag and put straight in the dustbin, together with the enormous amounts of un-eaten food.

◆ Cover the table with a plastic tablecloth taped to the underside of the table so that no one can pull it off accidentally.

Games

◆ For babies just have lots of toys lying about. For toddlers, you can play nursery records or tapes to jump and clap to. Don't worry if they don't play with each other.

◆ Under fives enjoy musical games, hunt the thimble or cotton reel and follow my leader. They will probably need plenty of adult attention to keep them going.

◆ Older children enjoy team games. For example, each team tries to find the hidden objects on a list first, or a person has to act out the title of a book, play or programme to his or her own team and the first team to finish wins.

◆ Games of skill like the tray game are good for older children. Everyone is given one minute to look at, say, 12 objects on a tray and then has to remember as many of them as possible.

◆ Sardines is a good game. One person hides, the others try to find him or her and, when they do, creep into the hiding place and keep very quiet.

◆ Dressing up is a winner at any age. Give them hats and scarves if you haven't got a dressing up box.

◆ Shopping list is a good quietening game before everyone goes home: first child says "I went shopping and I bought a ... pig"; second child "I went shopping and I bought a pig and a chocolate cake"; third child "I went shopping and I bought a pig, a chocolate cake and a skipping rope ..." and so on. When a child forgets what's been bought, he or she is out of the game, until there is only one left – the winner.

◆ The jigsaw game: cut old Christmas cards into four pieces and hide three of the pieces. Give each child one of the pieces left and send them off to find the other three pieces of their cards.

Presents

Children do love getting little presents all through the party and when they go home.

◆ Buy lots of little items, for example, key rings, pencils, pencil sharpeners, note books, tiny toys.

◆ Make sure every child gets a present or two. A little cheating may be necessary on your part.

◆ Give a small parting present for children to take home: a balloon, and a tiny home-made bag with some transfers and a mini packet of sweets, for instance.

Cleaning

ORGANIZING YOUR CLEANING

Keeping a home clean should be a matter of prevention rather than cure. Cleanliness is not all and an immaculately clean home is not automatically a happy one. Never let the housework rule you and never become a martyr to it.

Cleanliness is necessary in some aspects of home care, the kitchen and bathroom for instance, and a clean home will probably make you feel better. Your aim should be to find a way of cleaning efficiently and with as little extra work as possible. Be disciplined about your cleaning. Have a routine, but don't let your life be dominated by it.

Don't get depressed if your home is not perfect. Nobody else achieves perfection either and it's boring anyway. The secret is: don't allow any unnecessary items to hang about for long, especially if you live in a small apartment, and don't hoard things, you'll end up with no room in the cupboards and everything that would otherwise be put away will be on the floor or table, making the home impossible to clean.

When moving home, bear in mind that new houses are nearly always easier to keep clean than old ones, where dust has made itself at home in nooks and crannies for years.

TIPS TO MINIMIZE CLEANING

◆ Tidiness leads to cleanliness so tidy up as you go along. A tidy home looks cleaner.
◆ Wipe up immediately anything spilled, including crumbs; you will prevent stains, which are difficult to remove.
◆ Get a good door mat, preferably one that fits, like a carpet, over the width of the hall; less dirt will be carried into the rest of the house.
◆ Encourage everyone to take their shoes off, or at least change their shoes, when they come in from outside; the carpet will stay clean for longer.
GREEN TIP: Wipe all surfaces often so that they never get so dirty that you have to use dangerous household chemicals to get rid of the dirt.
◆ Some parts of the house need cleaning frequently, others don't. Don't exhaust yourself unnecessarily.
◆ Varnished wooden floors are easier to keep clean; polishing is very hard work.
◆ See that everybody in the house takes their fair share of the cleaning burden: children should be encouraged to look after their own rooms from an early age. Unless your children are very young, everyone should contribute to the vacuuming and washing up, especially if most people in the house are out all day.

PRIORITIES

◆ Vacuum the floors only when they need it – valuable carpets may suffer with too much vacuuming anyway.

◆ The kitchen and bathroom are the two rooms where hygiene is paramount. Wipe down the toilet and bathroom basin every day. Clean the kitchen sink every day and mop the kitchen floor as often as you can.

Parents with small children

◆ Let your standards lapse a bit without feeling guilty. It's better to spend time with your children than be forever chasing after their crumbs and scattered toys.

◆ At their bedtime collect up all toys in a basket and carry them to the toy boxes. Then vacuum if it really needs it. In the morning you start off with a clean base. Don't attempt to vacuum again until evening. Just sweep up breakfast and lunch crumbs, the mess from under the baby's chin and wipe sticky fingers immediately after a meal.

◆ Keep the floor or place where children play relatively clean, but don't try for perfection, which will be impossible and make you frustrated and bad-tempered.

◆ When you are tidying up, carry a basket round to collect up everything that's in the wrong room, then put it away when you arrive at its correct home.

◆ Make a house rule: always eat in the kitchen or dining room, never in the living room or bedrooms. That way any mess will be concentrated in one part of the house.

◆ Keep larger jobs, such as cleaning windows or the fridge, for weekends when your partner can take the children off your hands (or you can take them off his). Don't worry about the curtain and upholstery cleaning, fit it in when you can.

◆ Wash and sterilize baby bottles straight after use to prevent bacteria developing; don't leave cups and plates of older children too long before they are washed, especially if there are animals in the house.

◆ Wash the children's bed and nightclothes at least once a week and preferably more often. For bed-wetters, every day.

CLEANING TACTICS

◆ Make your life easier by dividing the chores up into things you must do every day and things that can be left for a few months or that only need to be done once a year.

◆ When you clean the house, do the hall first because dust from here gets trailed through the house to the main living areas.

◆ Always vacuum before dusting because the action of the vacuum cleaner can beat more dust out of the carpet.

◆ Always dust or polish furniture from the top down.

At home all day

◆ Just because you are at home all day it does not mean there is merit in housekeeping all day. Cultivate your own interests and use your time creatively. Organize your day so that you only do housework in, say, the morning. Keep the afternoon for your own interests, visiting the library, preparing an evening meal, the garden, any homework for your courses.

◆ Plan your morning so that every morning you:

◇ *Vacuum the main living areas*
◇ *Make your bed (the children should have made their own)*
◇ *Tidy and dust all round the house*
◇ *Pause for a cup of coffee or some stretching exercises, half an hour of yoga or a quick jog round the block*
◇ *Slot in extra tasks each day, for example:*
MONDAY Thoroughly clean bedrooms
TUESDAY Do the laundry
WEDNESDAY Iron and air the clothes
THURSDAY Clean the bathroom
FRIDAY Clean the kitchen and do the weekend shopping.

Out at work all day

Your standards may have to drop a little. You want to create harmony and efficiency without spoiling your life.

◆ Keep major tasks for the weekend when you will probably have more energy.

FREQUENT, REGULAR AND OCCASIONAL JOBS

FREQUENT (daily)

◇ Tidy up all round the house
◇ Wipe down surfaces
◇ Clean pet dishes and the floor around them. Clean out cat litter trays
◇ Empty ash trays, or better still, don't smoke
◇ Make beds and put clothes away
◇ Wash dishes or load or un-load dishwasher
◇ Vacuum if you have to
◇ Clean toilet, basin and kit-chen sink

FREQUENT (weekly)

◇ Vacuum the living areas
◇ Wipe out the refrigerator
◇ Dust everywhere
◇ Shake the door mat
◇ Clean out fire grate, if using coal
◇ Do the laundry
◇ Sweep back yard, front steps and entryway etc.
◇ Shake out pets' bedding and clean cages

REGULAR (monthly)

◇ Give individual rooms a thorough clean in rotation, including hall, stairs and landings
◇ Clean out food cupboards
◇ Clean mirrors, telephone, stereo and other electric or electronic equipment
◇ Polish silver and metalware
◇ Clean the cooker
◇ Clean and disinfect dustbin
◇ Clean filters in washing ma-chine and spin and/or tumble dryer
◇ In winter, clean central heat-ing radiators

OCCASIONAL (two or three times a year)

◇ Clean heaters
◇ Clean out fireplace if burn-ing wood
◇ Clean windows thoroughly, all together or in rotation
◇ Defrost fridge
◇ De-scale kettle, coffee ma-chine and steam iron

◇ Clean out drains and gut-ters, particularly in the autumn
◇ Polish floors
◇ Polish furniture
◇ Clear out cupboards

RARELY (once a year)

◇ Move heavy furniture and clean behind/under it
◇ Wash down walls
◇ Shampoo carpets, uphol-stered furniture and curtains, or get them cleaned
◇ Get chimneys swept (if any)
◇ Take out books and dust them and the shelves
◇ Get gas appliances serviced
◇ Get electric blankets serviced
◇ Clean filter on cooker hood
◇ Get scissors, knives, shears, secateurs etc. sharpened
◇ Oil metal curtain rails and sliding door tracks
◇ Remove and clean light fittings

◆ Before you leave the house, make sure it is tidy and trim: no dirty dishes left by the sink, no dirty clothes flung down on the floor. This is for your own benefit when you come home. Get up half an hour earlier if this will help you to get organized in the morning.

◆ Before you go to work, or last thing at night if you need time for other things in the morning, plump up cushions, put away stray newspapers; it's much nicer to come home to, or down to in the morning.

◆ Brush round the loo and wipe the basin every day; they are breeding grounds for germs.

◆ Vacuum only if it's necessary: if you can manage this in the morning so much the better. The sound of vacuuming in the even-ing can be very invasive.

◆ Evening blitzes are not very sensible, since one is usually tired after dinner. However, some things may be fairly soothing, such as: cleaning the silver; spot dry-cleaning uphols-tery; furniture polishing.

◆ If you must do something energetic in the evening, take one job and do it thoroughly. Don't take on too much – you probably won't finish it. For example:

◇ MONDAY Vacuum floors, curtains or upholstery
◇ TUESDAY Clean bedrooms, or do laundry and/or any spot cleaning
◇ WEDNESDAY Vacuum or iron and air clothes
◇ THURSDAY Clean kitchen
◇ FRIDAY Clean bathroom
◇ SATURDAY Clean some of the windows and/or the refrigerator
◇ SUNDAY Day of rest!

◆ If you are not too exhausted in the evening, occasionally take one room and give it a thorough clean. If you have been keeping things vaguely under control, it shouldn't involve too much time and effort. If you are exhausted, go to bed with a book and leave it for another day.

ORDER OF WORK FOR THOROUGH CLEANING OF A ROOM

1 *Open all of the windows to air the room.*

2 *Remove old flowers, empty ashtrays and waste-paper baskets, put away kicked-off shoes and any other bits and pieces. Pick up any rugs.*
◇ *If cleaning a sitting room or bedroom, move all the small pieces of furniture out of the room.*
◇ *If cleaning the hall, move wellingtons, coats, umbrellas and stands, prams or pushchairs out.*

3 *Clean out fireplace, if any. Oust spiders and webs and brush out cupboards.*

4 *Vacuum the floor, curtains and the upholstery.*

5 *Dust everywhere. Mop and polish floor surrounds. Clean paintwork and windows.*

6 *Shake rugs outside before putting them back in the room.*

7 *Replace all furniture, give it a polish if necessary.*

For cleaning a bedroom In addition to the instructions left, you should also:
◇ *Strip and air the bed*
◇ *Tidy away clothing, towels, shoes, toys etc.*
◇ *Put all ornaments, hair grips and jewellery in a large scarf and lay it on a chair*
◇ *Vacuum the mattress and turn it over (from head to foot); this makes it wear evenly*
◇ *Dust and polish ornaments and jewellery and put them back in their places*
◇ *Remake the bed.*

SPRING CLEANING

Even a room that is cleaned regularly will benefit from a good spring clean when the time comes. The first rays of spring sun show up all the splatters, smears and dust that have accumulated on the windows over the winter.

♦ It's a good discipline in spring to cope with the freezer, if you haven't already done it, the cupboards and reorganization of the home in general. Turn out those parts of the home which normally don't get the full treatment: the basement, the attic, the space under the stairs, cupboards, medicine chest, kitchen cupboards and so on.

♦ Do one task at a time, or you'll be overwhelmed by the whole thing, and you may end up completely exhausted with several half-finished rooms.

♦ Get rid of non-helpful members of the household – to the golf course, playgroup, aunts, grandmothers, neighbours.

♦ If you can't get rid of the children, it may be easier to let them help you. Small children are usually very happy to "help" with the dusting or to swill water about in the kitchen sink, even if they don't actually do any cleaning – at least it keeps them occupied.

THINGS TO REMEMBER WHEN SPRING CLEANING

♦ Take down pictures and clean them, and the wall behind them.

♦ Take down all the ornaments and clean them (and the shelf or wall behind them).

♦ Get at areas behind doors, above door frames and under tables, behind and under chests of drawers and large pieces of furniture, which have been forgotten or skimmed over throughout the year.

♦ Oust cobwebs; they are dust traps.

♦ Wash down paintwork thoroughly; remember the sides of the stairs next to the stair carpet if you are doing the hall.

♦ Polish all the furniture.

♦ Clean lamps and shades. Don't forget light fittings as well; take them off to clean them, if necessary.

♦ Shampoo the carpets and upholstery and get curtains washed or dry cleaned.

♦ Vacuum thoroughly and replace everything.

♦ Clean out all the kitchen cupboards.

♦ Take the opportunity to throw away all those things that you never use; you'll have less to put away.

CHOOSING EQUIPMENT

◆ Shop around when buying major equipment; price and quality vary enormously.

◆ Disposable cloths and dusters can be expensive but save time and effort. If you don't buy disposable cloths, always buy machine-washable ones.

Brushes and mops

◆ Soft brushes are best for smooth hard surfaces, hard bristles for carpets and rough surfaces such as concrete.

◆ Bristles should be close together in tufts. The brush should not look thin on top.

◆ Choose brushes with holes in the end of the handles, or rings, so that they can be hung up out of the way.

◆ Dustpan and brushes sometimes clip together for storage, which can make finding them a great deal easier.

◆ Nylon brushes are easier to wash than bristle brushes. They won't rot or go mouldy and they are often softer.

◆ Sponge mops are useful if you have smooth floors; cotton mops are better for very large or slightly rough floors.

◆ Sponge mops with a squeegee on the end are good for scraping off hardened dirt, especially in the kitchen.

CLEANING KIT

◆ If your home is on more than one floor, keep a basic set of cleaning equipment upstairs as well as the main kit downstairs to save you running up and down stairs.

◆ If your hardware store doesn't stock what you need, try a janitorial supplier.

WHAT YOU NEED
◇ Vacuum cleaner
◇ Broom
◇ Dustpan and brush (or two brushes, one hard bristled, one soft bristled)
◇ Sponge mop (and spare sponges) or a cotton mop
◇ Floor dusting mop
◇ Squeegee (a rubber blade on a handle for washing windows)
◇ Bucket (better still, two)
◇ Scrubbing brush
◇ Cloths: for floors, for wiping kitchen and bathroom surfaces, for dusting, for window cleaning, for polishing
◇ Tea towels

◇ Lavatory brush (one for every toilet)
◇ Sponge for cleaning the bath
◇ Washing-up brush – or better still, three: one for general dishwashing, one kept for pets' plates and bowls and one for getting around awkward corners when cleaning the sink
◇ Pot scourers
◇ Cleaning agents: cream cleaner, furniture polish, silver polish, washing, or household, soda, bleach, vinegar

ADDITIONAL EQUIPMENT
◇ Bottle brush for cleaning vases or sink overflows

◇ Cobweb brush
◇ Carpet shampooer (non-electric)
◇ Floor polisher
◇ Plastic tool box for carrying cloths and cleaning agents round the house.
◇ Carpet sweeper (optional). Useful if you live in a small flat and can't afford a vacuum cleaner. Buy one with a good capacity.
◇ If you prefer to use a cotton mop, it is worth buying a mop bucket in which to wring it out. It'll save your muscles from overwork and your fingers from splinters.

ECONOMY TIPS
◆ A polishing mitt can be made from an old woollen sock.

◆ Good floor cloths can be made from old terry towels. Don't use old vests and other pieces of linty material, they won't absorb moisture or dirt very well.

◆ Keep old toothbrushes – they are ideal for cleaning awkward corners.

◆ If you haven't got a cobweb brush, tie a duster round the top of a broom.

◆ It is almost never worth while to buy your own electric carpet shampooing equipment. It is expensive and bulky and needs a lot of maintenance. It is better to hire it, use a non-electric one, or get your carpet cleaned professionally.

◆ Larger machinery, such as floor polishers and large wet/dry vacuums (useful if you have a flood), can all be hired.

Vacuum cleaners

There are three basic types: upright, cylinder and wet/dry.

◆**Upright vacuum** Less work than other types as you don't have to bend, though can be awkward for cleaning the stairs. Most uprights suck and brush, some even beat gently to raise the dust for sucking up. They can be rough on valuable carpets.

◆**Cylinder vacuum** This is light and portable, though still quite cumbersome to carry upstairs. Cylinder vacuums are the best for smooth floors but not as good on carpet as the upright.

◆**Wet/Dry vacuum** More efficient and flexible than an ordinary vacuum cleaner. It sucks up water or other liquid until the tank is full, at which point a float will shut off the suction and it is time to empty the tank and start again. For dry vacuuming, you simply attach a cloth filter. A wet/dry vacuum will:

◇ *Pick up spare water from floor washing*
◇ *Clean up food and drink spills before they dry and stain*
◇ *Pick up vomit, cat and dog messes*
◇ *Pick up sink, bath and rain floods and overflows inside and outside the house.*

Floor polishers

◆Choose one with two or three motor brushes on the head and make sure you can replace worn bushes.

◆The more sophisticated types will suck up dirt and excess polish, saving you work, but they are expensive.

POINTS TO LOOK FOR WHEN CHOOSING A VACUUM

◆Check how noisy it is; a noisy vacuum can be very invasive.

◆A long flex saves you having to unplug it all the time.

◆Automatic flex rewinding makes storage easier. Some models also store accessories inside the body.

◆Check the weight: a heavy machine is difficult to carry about.

◆Check how near the wall it will go and how low under furniture.

◆Make sure the bags are easy to replace.

◆Buy one with a large bag; small bags need emptying all the time.

◆For wet/dry cleaners, a 23 litre (5 gall) capacity stainless or polyplastic tank is recommended, but you can get a smaller one if you wish.

◆Some cylinder vacuums blow as well as suck; this can be useful for unblocking the hose, or cleaning behind radiators.

◆Variable speed can be useful if you have valuable carpets, which need to be treated gently, as well as carpets that get a lot of use, which need stronger suction.

◆Upright vacuums should have attachments such as expanding tubes and upholstery brushes for stairs and corners.

MAINTAINING EQUIPMENT

All good tools deserve correct treatment and will last longer if kept in good repair.

Vacuum cleaner

◆Remove bits of fluff and cotton threads from the brushes and rollers every time you use the machine.

◆Check the flexes occasionally, especially where they enter the machine and the plug, and change them at once, if frayed. Check the hose and make sure it has no holes in it; a damaged hose won't suck properly.

◆Empty the bag before it gets overfull. Clean permanent vacuum cleaner bags by brushing them lightly. Do not wash them as this may open the weave of the fabric, enabling dust to get into the motor.

◆Renew filter on cylinder vacuums regularly – about every six months.

◆Replace worn vacuum brushes because they don't pick up all of the dust.

Mops and brushes

◆Rinse mops thoroughly after use: they will not need extra washing if you use very little all-purpose household cleaner in the water when cleaning non-wood floors.

◆Wash brooms and short-handled brushes in warm, soapy water from time to time; they'll last longer. Beat the head up and down on the water surface so that the water reaches well into the bristle tufts. Rinse well. Shake and dry in a warm place.

◆New bristle brooms should last longer if dipped in salted water before use. Don't do this to nylon or plastic brooms.

◆Don't leave brooms standing on their bristles; the bristles will bend.

Carpet sweeper

◆Empty the dust box after every use and run your hands along the brushes to remove threads and fluff.

◆Unclip the brush occasionally, wash it in detergenty water and wipe out the inside of the sweeper; it'll sweep more efficiently.

Electric floor polisher

◆Clean the polishing heads from time to time and fit new ones when they get too dirty. To clean them, stand the bristles in a shallow bowl of white spirit until the polish has softened. Then rub the brushes clean with an old rag and leave to dry.

Carpet shampooer

◆Empty and rinse the tank after use.
◆Clean fluff from brushes and rollers.

Cloths and leathers

◆Always rinse and wring washing cloths well after use. Wash all cloths and dusters regularly; wash chamois leather with pure soap, see page 90.

STORAGE

◆There are two basic rules worth observing for storing cleaning equipment, both from the practical and safety points of view.

◇ *Make sure everything has a place and is kept in its place. A jumble of equipment is depressing and will not be used to best advantage because you'll never find anything.*

◇ *Get everything off the floor if you can. This makes sweeping underneath easier and is generally more practical.*

◆Hang carpet sweepers by the handle. The working part twists up, flush with the wall.

◆Keep all household cleaners, and other chemicals, out of reach of children and preferably in a lockable cupboard.

◆Put up hooks or shelves for all attachments and accessories of all cleaners, such as floor polish pads, vacuum cleaner bags, dusting attachments, as well as for vacuum cleaners, brooms and floor mops.

◆Clean the broom cupboard occasionally with a solution of mild detergent. Leave the door open until the cupboard is dry again. Then put the equipment back.

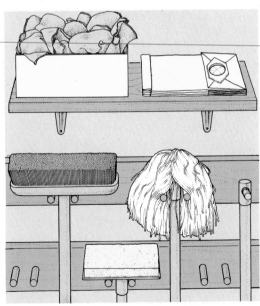

Organizing the cleaning cupboard *Hang brooms and mops head-up between wooden dowel rods. If you stagger rows of hooks or rods, you will get more in the cupboard. Keep spare cloths and vacuum bags in boxes or neat piles on a shelf.*

CLEANING THE KITCHEN

The kitchen is the room that gets most obviously and intractably dirty because of the grease and condensation caused by cooking.

Hygiene, therefore daily cleaning, is of paramount importance to prevent giving yourself and your family food poisoning.

PREVENTING CONDENSATION IN THE KITCHEN

Condensation can be bad in the kitchen because so much moisture is created in cooking. Ventilation, heating and insulation are ALL necessary to combat condensation.

◆ Make sure there is sufficient ventilation – turn on the extractor fan, open the windows, particularly when cooking.

◆ Make sure the room is adequately and constantly heated.

◆ Insulate the walls so they don't provide a cold surface for the moisture to collect on. For example, cover walls with emulsion paint rather than gloss paint, or with warmer materials, such as thick wallpaper, polystyrene covered with paper, cork or hessian (except behind the cooker because they could catch fire).

◆ Don't boil anything in pans with the lids off; it creates excess steam.

◆ Don't use a tumble dryer in the room, or if you do, have it vented to the outside.

◆ Pressure cook rather than boil, and wait until the pan has cooled down before taking off the lid.

◆ Use a slow cooker more often.

◆ Cook casseroles in a low oven and not on top of the stove.

"WET" AREAS

◆ Clean the sink and draining area with a proprietary cream cleaner.

◆ Clean stainless steel occasionally with a proprietary stainless steel cleaner if it is tarnished, looks cloudy, or is badly marked by water spots. These stains can be difficult to clean with cream cleaner.

GREEN TIP: Rub stains with a damp cloth dipped in bicarbonate of soda.

◆ Don't leave acid foods such as vinegar, salad dressing and fruit juices on stove enamel sinks because they will mark them.

◆ To whiten a ceramic sink, fill with hot water and a little bleach and leave to soak for an hour or so.

▼▼ Bleach makes things white, but not necessarily clean. Use it very sparingly and only if you must. It damages plastic laminates and many other surfaces as well as skin and eyes and the water system.

Overflows and drains

GREEN TIP: An occasional handful of household soda down a drain, with boiling water poured over it, will keep the drain clear and fresh.

GREEN TIP: A strong but non-caustic drain cleaner can be made with 255g (8oz) salt, 150g (5oz) baking soda, 30g (1½oz) cream of tartar. Put three or four tablespoons of the mixture down the drain, let it stand for at least 20 minutes, then flush thoroughly with hot water.

Removing rust stains *Rub the surface of the sink with a cut lemon. If the stain is stubborn, persevere; it will go eventually.*

◆ Clean sink overflows and plugholes with a small toothbrush or a bottle brush.

Preventing blockages *Keep a sink trap over the plughole all the time to prevent solid waste accidentally blocking the drain.*

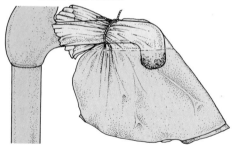

Taps

◆ Use an angled washing-up brush to clean awkward taps and corners of sinks.

◆ Clean taps with warm, soapy water or mild cream cleaner.

◆ Hard-water deposits can be tackled with a little cream cleaner on an old toothbrush.

🍃 GREEN TIP: Hard-water deposits on a tap can be rubbed with vinegar or half a lemon. Push the cut surface of the lemon onto the spout and press it round, or soak a piece of paper towel with vinegar and leave it on the mark for a while.

🍃 **Removing hard-water deposits** *Break down heavy deposits around the spout by filling a small plastic bag with dissolved water softener and tying it onto the tap. Leave for about two hours.*

KITCHEN UNITS

◆ Wipe up spills, particularly berry juices, as they occur; otherwise they'll stain. Keep a clean cloth beside you while preparing food for just this purpose.

◆ Wipe the worktop immediately after preparing food to minimize germs.

Worktops

Before cleaning the worktop remove everything, much of which can be put away elsewhere or thrown out.

▼▼ Don't clean worktops with harsh abras-
◆ ◆ ives or cleaners containing bleaches; they are extremely poisonous.

◆ Clean laminated worktops with a damp cloth dipped in bicarbonate of soda or cream cleaners. Rinse thoroughly.

◆ Rub teak, maple or mahogany worktops with teak or linseed oil about twice a year. Always rub along the grain.

◆ Rub heat marks or stubborn stains on wooden worktops, with equal parts of linseed oil and cleaning fluid and wipe off. Or try lemon juice or a proprietary wood bleach, following instructions.

🍃 GREEN TIP: Wipe down slate work-tops with milk to give a semi-shine.

◆ Marble worktops should be wiped regularly with a cloth wrung out in water and a mild detergent; marble is porous, so don't let it get wet (see also MARBLE FURNITURE, page 98).

🍃 GREEN TIP: Stains on marble can be removed with lemon juice or vinegar, but with great caution, making sure that the acid does not affect the marble. Leave the lemon on for no more than one or two minutes, repeat if necessary.

▼▼ Don't chop on a laminated worktop: it
◆ ◆ will damage the surface and the knife.

Cupboards

◆ Clean out food cupboards about once a month because flour, crumbs and sticky bottles attract insects and mice. Crockery or glass cupboards need cleaning out only about once a year.

◆ Take everything off shelves and clean thoroughly inside, especially in the corners. Leave the doors open while the surfaces dry.

◆ Wipe greasy and sticky bottles and jars with warm detergent solution before putting them back. Check that all the food is fresh, and throw out anything that is doubtful.

◆ Wash the crockery and glass before returning it to the cupboard.

KITCHEN EQUIPMENT

Clean any equipment used to prepare food as soon as possible after use to prevent bacteria breeding in the corners. For the same reason, wipe all of the outer surfaces regularly with a damp cloth.

Cooking appliances

Follow the instructions in the manufacturers' booklet. If the cooker is secondhand, or you've lost the booklet follow these tips.
◆ Wipe the cooker frequently – in fact, every time you do any cooking. Keep a damp sponge or cloth next to the cooker whilst you work, so that you can wipe up as you go along.
◆ Ovens and hobs are easier to clean if they are warm.
◆ After a major cooking session, or once a month, take off all removable parts, such as gas burners and metal surrounds, and wash them in hot, detergenty water. Give the whole surface of the hob a thorough clean. Use a cream cleaner on the hob and outside of the cooker. Use a nylon scourer for stubborn spots. Never scrape the surface with a knife or sharp implement; you'll damage the surface.
◆ If a hob is very dirty with burned-on food, clean it with caustic jelly applied with an old toothbrush. Follow manufacturer's instructions carefully and wear rubber gloves.
◆ Keep solid electric hot-plates clean by brushing them with a stiff wire brush.
◆ Ceramic hobs only need to be wiped with a damp cloth, or at most a cream cleaner.
◆ Kitchen ranges have very flat hot-plates, which must be kept very clean, since it is the contact of the whole of the surface with the base of the pan which heats the pan – even a tiny crumb on the hot-plate will make cooking much slower.
◆ Clean vitreous enamel stoves with liquid detergent and hot water. You can occasionally rub with very fine wire wool, but don't do this too often or too vigorously or you'll damage the enamel.
◆ Self-cleaning ovens should burn themselves clean and just need brushing down

TIPS TO MINIMIZE CLEANING

◆ Line the tray beneath the electric ring with foil, then if something boils over, all you have to do is change the foil.
◆ To prevent food spitting in the oven, cover the dish with foil, cook in a casserole with a lid or in a roasting bag.

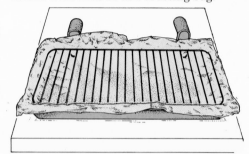

Keeping the grill pan clean *Line the bottom of the grill pan with aluminium foil. Then if you grill something fatty, you need only to throw away the foil.*

after use with a stiff bristle brush.
◆ For self-cleaning ovens, or ones with detachable non-stick walls, always follow manufacturers' instructions. You'll damage the surface if you use a proprietary oven cleaner.
◆ There are various oven-cleaning preparations on the market for ovens which are not self-cleaning. Follow the manufacturers' instructions and wear rubber gloves because most of them are caustic.
GREEN TIP: To clean an oven safely, sprinkle baking soda on the walls and floor of a warm oven and leave for an hour, then wipe clean.
GREEN TIP: Glass doors can be cleaned with a damp cloth dipped in dry bicarbonate of soda; if necessary, rub stubborn marks with fine wire wool.
◆ Before cleaning an electric oven, switch it off at the mains; you could give yourself an electric shock.
◆ You don't need to clean the ovens of kitchen ranges, they are virtually self-cleaning; since they are so hot, they burn away all deposits.

Extractor fans and cooker hoods

◆Clean the outside regularly to prevent a build-up of grease.
◆The filters that collect the grease must be cleaned or replaced regularly (some models indicate by a light when this is necessary) or they may catch fire. Check every six months, or more often if you do a lot of frying. Change replaceable charcoal or mesh filters about once a year or as recommended.
◆To clean the extractor, switch off the fan and unplug. (If there is no plug, remove the fuse from the spur socket or turn off at the mains.) Remove outer cover and wash in warm water and detergent. Wipe fan blades with a just damp cloth: don't get them wet. Dry and replace the cover.

Refrigerator

◆Wipe the refrigerator out about once a week. Use a cloth which has been wrung out in warm water. Wipe bottles, jars and containers before replacing them.
◆If you spill something in the fridge, clean it up straightaway; if left it will probably start to smell or go mouldy.
◆Defrost when ice in the frozen food compartment is about 6mm ($\frac{1}{4}$ inch) thick. Defrost automatic-defrosting refrigerators about three times a year, see page 21.
◆From time to time unplug the refrigerator and dust the grille at the back to keep it running efficiently.
◆If the refrigerator is covered with the dark brown, greasy deposit of ages, spray with a heavy-duty all-purpose cleaner, which has some ammonia in it. Leave for a while to allow the greasy film to dissolve, then wipe it off; use paper kitchen towels which you can throw away.

Freezer

◆Defrost the freezer once a year, when stocks are low, see page 23.
◆If the food has thawed by accident and been left in the freezer for some days, throw it away. Then defrost and wash out, using sterilizing solution for babies' bottles. Wipe round all surfaces, avoiding any metal. Fill the bottom of the freezer with screwed-up newspaper and leave for a day or so, with the door ajar, before switching it on again.

Dishwasher

◆Leave the door ajar when the machine is not in use so that air can circulate.
▼▼ Don't leave the dishwasher open if you
◆◆ have young children.
◆Clean regularly, particularly around the door seal where food particles get caught. Clean the filter after each wash or the particles will be recirculated in the next wash.
◆Before going on holiday, rinse the machine and make sure it's clean. Dry the inside with a soft cloth and leave the door ajar. Switch it off at the socket.

MICROWAVE OVENS

◆Wipe out the inside with a damp cloth after use.
◆Clean the outside with cream cleaner if it gets very dirty.

Cleaning a dirty microwave *Stand a dish of hot water in the cooker. Add a slice of lemon and boil the water in the oven until plenty of steam is produced. Then wipe over the interior with a damp cloth.*

ELECTRIC GADGETS

▼▼ Do not put any electrical equipment in
◆◆ water; you can electrocute yourself.
Likewise, switch off and disconnect appliances from the mains before cleaning.

Food mixer/processor

◆ When you've finished blending, leave the sharp blades and discs on the worktop until you are ready to wash them. Clean them, one at a time, under running water, using a small brush so that you don't cut yourself.
◆ Clean the bowl in a dishwasher or with detergenty water; use a toothbrush to remove oily deposits on the base.
◆ To clean a hand-held, wall-mounted mixer, fill its bowl with warm water and spin the mixer in it, then hang it up to drip dry.

Toaster

◆ Turn the toaster upside down gently to let the crumbs fall out; if possible, unscrew the bottom to get at the crumbs.
◆ Wipe the exterior with a damp cloth from time to time.

Kettle

◆ Wipe enamelled or painted finishes with a damp cloth.
◆ Clean stainless steel or chrome kettles with a cream cleaner then buff up with a clean dry cloth.
▼▼ In hard-water areas kettles build up
◆◆ mineral deposits (furring) on the element. These should be removed, as they slow down the heating element, increasing the running costs. Various proprietary products are available, all of which are very strong and should be used with care.
🍃 GREEN TIP: Instead of a proprietary defurring product, cover the element with vinegar. Bring just to the boil, switch off and allow to cool. Empty and rinse several times. Boil the kettle at least once and pour water away before using it again.

🍃 GREEN TIP: To prevent your kettle furring up, keep a marble or piece of sponge loofah inside it; the "fur" will collect on that instead of the element.

Coffee machines

◆ Wipe over an electric coffee machine but don't immerse it in water.
◆ If plastic, take care not to scratch it. Don't use scouring pads or abrasive cleaners and don't put the parts in the dishwasher.
◆ De-scale drip machines two or three times a year to prevent the pipes clogging up.
▼▼ Proprietary de-scalers are very toxic, so
◆◆ it is important to rinse thoroughly after use. Or use the vinegar method for kettles.

Coffee grinder

◆ Wipe out the bowl with the cutting blades with a clean damp cloth.
◆ Wash the top in warm water.

Carving knife

◆ Unplug the knife, remove the blades and wash them separately. Wipe any greasy parts with a just-damp (not wet) cloth.

Slow cooker

◆ You can take the earthenware pot out and wash it, but the outer casing must never be immersed in water.
◆ To clean the pot, empty out contents, fill it with warm, soapy water and clean with a soft sponge, brush or cloth. Rinse well and wipe dry. If food is burned on, leave to soak for a few minutes.
▼▼ Don't use abrasive pads to clean the
◆◆ earthenware pot and never fill the outer casing with water.
◆ In hard-water areas a whitish deposit may appear on the inside of the pot. Remove this with a mild liquid abrasive cleaner. Wipe the earthenware with a little vegetable oil to restore its sparkling look.
▼▼ Avoid subjecting the pot to sudden
◆◆ temperature changes or it may crack.

WASHING UP BY HAND

◆Stack all dirty dishes and utensils systematically: plates together, glasses together, serving dishes together.

◆Clear the plate rack and draining board to give yourself a clear run.

GREEN TIP: You can wash up with washing-soda crystals and pure soap dissolved in very hot water; this is far less harmful to the environment and you. In soft-water areas you can leave out the soda or the soap, except for very greasy items.

GREEN TIP: A tablespoon of vinegar instead of liquid detergent in washing-up water helps to remove grease.

GREEN TIP: Some healthfood stores sell ecologically safe washing-up liquids.

◆Use hot water and only just enough detergent to dissolve any grease. This is much less than most people use. Rinse everything in a bowl of clean hot water, which is less wasteful than running it under the tap.

◆The hotter the water, the better. The water will evaporate quickly, and the dishes will dry faster.

◆Wash the cleaner items first so you don't make the water unusable for the next items.

◆Save drying by putting cutlery into a drainer and plates into a rack.

◆If you only have a small draining board and no plate rack, pull up a trolley or small table to put the washed china on.

◆If you have run out of drying space, spread a tea towel or paper towels on any surface to catch the bulk of the drips.

◆Clean the sink outlet, empty the sink basket and wash it, wipe the sink, taps and surrounds; to prevent water deposits and stains on the sink or draining board.

DISHWASHERS

◆If you are a working mother, an automatic dishwasher is indispensable.

◆Rejoice in the thought that a modern dishwasher can be cheaper to run than washing up by hand.

◆If you have a dishwasher, choose crockery and glass with a flat base so water won't collect in them.

Using and maintaining a dishwasher

◆Dishwashers require very alkaline detergents so other detergents should never be used in them. Different machines also need different detergents. Always follow the manufacturer's instructions. Use a detergent and rinse aid from the same manufacturer for best results.

◆Don't use too much detergent; it makes too many suds and prevents the machine from cleaning properly. Sometimes it builds up on china and glass to an ugly chalky deposit that is difficult to remove.

◆In soft-water areas use much less detergent. The same applies if your machine has a built-in water softener.

◆Check the water softener level and refill regularly. If you don't, a film will start to appear on the crockery and glass.

◆If hard water causes a build-up of white deposits on crockery, try a different detergent or you may have to install a water softener or exchange your machine for one that has a built-in water softener.

◆Dishwashers should be serviced regularly.

TIPS FOR WASHING UP BY HAND

◆Wood, bone and ivory handles fixed by glue should be kept dry.

◆Lift stemmed glasses by the stem.

◆Use a plastic washing-up bowl in the sink, to prevent breaking china and glass against the side of the sink.

◆Don't jumble glass in the washing-up bowl; dip each piece carefully.

◆To remove stuck or burned on food, let the pan soak in cold water containing a little salt overnight, or until food is soft. Boil water in the pan if stuck food is intractable.

◆You can buy wall-mounted drainers that can double as a plate storage area to save drying up and putting away.

CHOOSING A DISHWASHER

◆ Measure the dishwasher and the space in the kitchen before you buy one.

◆ Do plenty of market research: prices and quality vary.

◆ Some dishwashers are designed to take more plates than cups or glasses; others have interchangeable or adjustable baskets, which can be more useful.

◆ A machine with no central column is the most spacious.

◆ Trays that slide in and out make loading and unloading easier.

◆ A removable lower basket allows you to get at the filters more easily to clean them.

◆ A filter with a grinder that automatically disposes of any food particles means you don't have to scrape the food off the plates before loading.

◆ An anti-flood device is essential if your kitchen is not on a ground floor.

◆ Most machines fill with cold water but some have a hot fill option.

◆ Many dishwashers have a built-in water softener, which prevents hard-water deposits building up on glasses.

◆ Dishwashers may have as many as 11 different programmes: a rapid programme may be useful for some households constantly using cups or mugs; an economy programme is good for not-very-dirty items. A pre-rinse cycle eliminates stale food smells if dirty dishes are kept in the machine for any length of time.

◆ Some machines have three spray levels, which means that hot spray will get to all the items.

◆ If you haven't got any under-the-counter space, you can buy small machines that sit on the worktop and connect to the taps.

Loading and unloading a dishwasher

◆ Remove large scraps from plates and pans before putting them in a dishwasher; otherwise they may block the filters.

◆ See how the water is dispersed and, when loading, make sure that one item doesn't shield another from the spray.

◆ Stack glasses, cups, bowls, saucepans and oven dishes with rim downwards so that they don't fill up with water.

◆ Never put stainless steel in the same basket as silver or silver-plated cutlery; it will cause pitting or staining of the silver.

◆ Don't block the outlet of the detergent dispenser, or the action of the jets.

▼▼ Don't put any plastic items near the
◆ ◆ heating element; they'll melt.

◆ Anchor lightweight items firmly between other items to stop them falling into the bottom, or becoming caught in the runners.

◆ Always unload the bottom basket first, otherwise drips from the top may land on the items at the bottom.

TIPS FOR USING A DISHWASHER

◆ Don't put anything in the dishwasher that isn't dishwasher-proof.

◆ Don't put crystal in a dishwasher without a water softener; it will become opaque.

◆ Everyday glass and cutlery with wood or plastic handles should be washed in the low temperature programme.

◆ Never leave cutlery in the machine once the wash cycle is completed or eventually the blades may become pitted through too long contact with the water.

◆ The following are not suitable for dishwashers:
◇ *Thin or heat-sensitive plastics*
◇ *Wooden ware*
◇ *Insulated mugs and glasses*
◇ *Valuable glassware*
◇ *Glassware with metal trim*
◇ *Fine or delicate china*
◇ *Hand-painted antique china*
◇ *Ironware*
◇ *Lacquered metals*
◇ *High-gloss aluminium.*

SPECIAL PROBLEMS

◆If you use a chopping board for onions or garlic, wash it thoroughly with a hard-bristled brush and wipe dry immediately. Wipe with a little vegetable oil after washing.

◆Wash vacuum flasks with hot water and detergent or baking soda. Always store with cap off to prevent mould. Use a bottle brush to get the neck of a vacuum clean. Don't immerse a vacuum flask in water.

◆Don't immerse wooden salad bowls in water; the wood will dry and split. Wipe them out with a paper towel.

China and porcelain

◆Rinse china used for egg dishes promptly with cold water, then wash. (Hot water will congeal the egg onto the plate.)

🍃 GREEN TIP: Rub tea and coffee stains on cups or mugs with a wet cloth dipped in dry bicarbonate of soda.

◆Modern dishwasher-proof crockery or oven dishes will not be harmed by very hot water or prolonged soaking.

◆Wash very old china by hand in warm, not hot water. Wash it straightaway; it can be damaged by foods such as gravies and salad dressings that leave it wet for some time.

▼▼Don't soak gold glazes or trimmings; ◆ ◆ soaking can lift the glaze.

◆Don't wash or rinse china or glazed pottery in very hot water; it can cause crazing (very small cracks all over the piece).

◆Always stack china carefully because the footing is often unglazed and may scratch the piece underneath it.

◆Glazed pottery can be hand washed in warm water with a mild detergent or soap.

Glass

◆Avoid extreme changes in temperature with all glass, i.e., don't put cold glasses into very hot water – they will break.

◆Wash valuable glass with a synthetic detergent. Rinse in clear hot water and allow to drain dry on a soft cloth or polish with a linen cloth. Don't wash very old glass.

CLEANING DECANTERS

◆Never use detergent to clean a decanter; it is difficult to rinse.

◆Crushed egg shell swirled round in water will remove deposits you can't get at. Also effective are:

◇ *Grated raw potato with a little vinegar*
◇ *Lead shot*
◇ *Sand*
◇ *Mustard seed.*

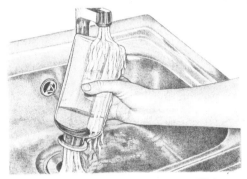

Drying a decanter *After rinsing out, fill the decanter to the brim with cold water. Then turn it quickly upside down and allow it to empty while the cold tap, turned full on, runs over the base. This seems to get rid of nearly all the water and the rest will evaporate.*

▼▼Gilt and silver ornamentation will come ◆ ◆ off if the water is too hot, or if you leave the glass to soak.

◆Clean the crevices in cut glass with a soft bristled brush. Then rinse carefully with warm water.

◆Glass oven-to-tableware can be cleaned with any cleaner you like. You can even rub it with steel wool without damaging it.

◆To get rid of stains or cloudiness in glass vases, carafes, cruets or decanters, fill them with water containing a teaspoon or two of household ammonia. Leave them to stand for a few hours and then wash and rinse them with clear water.

◆Mineral deposits will also yield to the ammonia treatment, above.

🍃 GREEN TIP: Instead of using ammonia to remove stains, try shaking tea leaves and vinegar around in the glass.

◆Rinse milk bottles in cold water as soon as they are empty to stop milk congealing.

Knives and cutlery

◆Clean silver cutlery from time to time with proprietary silver cleaner. Wash it afterwards. If working on your stainless steel sink, cover it with newspaper first because silver cleaner will mark stainless steel.

◆Remove egg stains from silver spoons by rubbing them with salt before washing them.

◆Carbon steel knives should be washed as soon as they are finished with and dried at once or hung in a warm atmosphere to prevent the blades rusting.

◆Don't leave stainless steel cutlery in contact with salt in very hot water or with rhubarb, lemon juice and vinegar; they all corrode it. Stainless steel cutlery is not affected by the salt used in water softeners. (The salt in the dishwasher is there to activate the water softener and shouldn't damage stainless steel cutlery either.)

SHARPENING KNIVES

◆When sharpening knives on a steel or stone, hold the blade at a shallow angle (about 15°). It's holding a blade at the wrong angle that makes so many knife sharpenings failures.

◆If using a rotary grinder with little wheels, pull the blades through several times in the same direction.

▼▼ Don't sharpen knives with serrated
◆ ◆ edges; you'll ruin the blade.

Using a mug *You can sharpen knives on the unglazed footing of a mug. Hold the blade at a slight angle and slide it in one direction.*

◆Remove any corrosion on carbon steel knives by rubbing with a cork dipped in scouring powder, steel wool or salt and greaseproof paper. Rinse well, then polish with a cotton cloth.

Cast-iron and iron pans

◆These must be looked after correctly or they will rust. Wash in warm soapy water, dry immediately, then coat with vegetable oil and keep in a dry place. Avoid harsh abrasives and metal scrapers. Don't run cold water into a hot pan ; it'll crack. Don't store cast iron with its lid on; it will rust.

PREPARING IRON AND CAST IRON

◆Buy pre-seasoned cast-iron pans if you can. If you don't, you will have to "season" the pan with oil to prevent food sticking to the sides and to prevent it rusting, see below.

◆Before using a pre-seasoned pan, scour the pan to remove lacquer, rinse it, dry it and grease the inside lightly with an unsalted fat. Grease it again before using it.

SEASONING CAST IRON

1 *Remove the protective coat of lacquer by rubbing the pan with scouring powder and a stiff brush. Wash the pan in hot detergenty water and dry thoroughly.*

2 *Coat the pan with vegetable oil and heat in a slow oven (or over a low heat if the pan has wooden handles) for several hours. Apply more fat from time to time. Wipe off any excess fat at the end. Grease it before and after using it for the first few weeks.*

Aluminium pans

◆Wash in mild detergent and water. Rinse with very hot water. If you must scrape, use steel wool pads impregnated with soap.
◆Remove dark stains by simmering a strong solution of vinegar and water or cream of tartar and water in the pan.
◆Brighten aluminium by cooking acid foods such as apples, rhubarb or lemon in it.

Stainless steel pans

◆Stainless steel is rustproof, but salt and acids in food can cause pitmarks. Remove these marks with fine steel wool or steel wool and scouring powder. You can also buy proprietary stainless steel cleaners.
◆Marks that result from stainless steel getting too hot can't be removed.

Tinware

◆Clean badly discoloured baking tins by boiling in washing soda and water.
◆Soften rust marks with cooking oil, then rub gently with a cloth. Don't use abrasives.
🍃 GREEN TIP: To make a tin rustproof, wipe all over with buttered paper and place in a moderate oven for 15 minutes.

Non-stick pans

◆Wash in warm soapy water.
◆If black non-stick finish is wearing out, condition pans by rubbing around the inside surface with oil on a piece of kitchen paper.

Copper pans

◆Remove protective lacquer on new pans before use, see right, or you will get lacquer all over the cooker and in the food.
◆Copper must be kept scrupulously clean to avoid "green-rust", which is poisonous.
◆Copper pans are sometimes lined with a tin or chromium plating, which prevents copper reacting with food. If the lining

CLEANING A PRESSURE COOKER

◆Wash after each use but don't immerse the cover or you may damage the gauge and clog the vents.
◆Wipe the cover with a soapy cloth and rinse with a clean, damp one.
◆Wash the gasket with care, replace it if it gets worn or stretched because it won't seal in the steam.

Cleaning the openings in the cover *Draw a pipe cleaner through the holes several times; the dirt should collect on the fibres.*

becomes worn, get the pan replated.
🍃 GREEN TIP: Corrosion spots can be cured with vinegar and salt, lemon juice and salt, or buttermilk. Rinse and dry.
◆Corrosion can also be cleaned off with proprietary copper cleaner. For the green patina, use soapsuds and ammonia.
◆Burned on food can be removed with mild scouring powder.
◆Always wash copper in hot soapy water after using acids or it will tarnish.
🍃 GREEN TIP: Make your own copper polish with equal parts salt, vinegar and flour. Rub the copper with this mixture until clean, then wash in hot water, rinse and dry.

Removing lacquer *Cover the pan with boiling water, let it stand until the water has cooled, above left. Then peel off the lacquer, above right.*

CLEANING BATHROOMS

The bathroom, like the kitchen, should be kept clean, not just cleaned up from time to time, because it is a breeding ground for germs. This isn't difficult to manage if you do a little cleaning every time you go into the bathroom. Regular cleaning can help to prevent unpleasant smells, as can opening the window periodically. By keeping the

bathroom well-aired at all times you will also prevent condensation and damp.

If you are fitting a new bathroom and you hanker after coloured fittings, be warned: if you live in a hard water area, you will have to clean the fittings every time they are used because soap and lime-scale leave their grey coating over them every time.

PREVENTING CONDENSATION

To prevent condensation you need adequate ventilation, and continuous background heat and insulation.

◆ You can ventilate by putting in a fan or by having a window that opens.

◆ You can heat with a radiator; a heated towel rail; a heater/light; or a fan heater fitted to the ceiling.

◆ You can insulate windows by double glazing and the walls using polystyrene covered with wallpaper or by covering them with cork tiles.

◆ Paint walls with special anti-condensation paint.

◆ Run cold water into the bath before adding the hot to minimize steam.

BATHROOM FITTINGS

◆ Frequent wiping down with a mild detergent solution will prevent a build-up of dirt or scale and makes the use of strong cleaners unnecessary. Wipe the toilet and basin down every day to prevent germs multiplying.

◆ Try to persuade members of your household to wipe down the bath or shower tray every time they use them, and certainly no less than once a day. This will prevent the bath or shower cubicle from getting very dirty and save time and trouble later.

◆ Keep the bath cleaning equipment in an obvious place, which leaves the family no excuse for not using it.

Baths and showers

◆ Clean vitreous enamel baths and ceramic shower trays with a cream cleaner. For stubborn marks use a very smooth cream cleaner.

▼▼ Bath salts make the water soft but since
◆ ◆ they are made of coloured and scented

washing soda they may damage enamel baths and are bad for the skin too.

◆ If you live in a hard-water area, use water softener (sodium sesquicarbonate) in the bath to minimize lime-scale.

◆ Rust marks can sometimes be removed with a proprietary rust remover.

◆ If the bath has been damaged by rough treatment or stains from long neglect, you can have it professionally cleaned chemically or resprayed. The finish won't be as tough as the original.

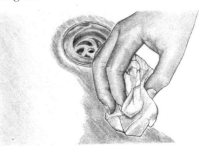

Cleaning hard-water marks *Rub vinegar onto the brownish stain that forms where a tap drips or the water drains away. If the stain persists, put some paper towel soaked in vinegar on the mark.*

TIPS FOR LOOKING AFTER BATHS AND SHOWERS

▼▼ Never clean the bath or shower with
♦ ♦ anything abrasive, with lavatory cleaners or bleach; you will damage the finish. Likewise, don't use the bath for developing photographs.
♦ Don't wash sharp-edged objects such as Venetian blinds in the bath.
♦ Don't leave non-slip mats sitting in the bath or shower tray – they may stain it permanently.

♦ Wipe acrylic baths with washing-up liquid using a soft cloth or wad of cotton wool. Rub resistant stains with half a lemon. Rub scratches with a little silver polish, then buff up. Acrylic baths are easy to look after; they are not affected by bath salts and are non-porous.
♦ You can safely use diluted chlorine bleach or hydrogen peroxide on coloured acrylic, but don't leave it on.
♦ Buy a hair trap for the shower plughole to prevent blockages.
▼▼ Too much use of acid (i.e., very strong
♦ ♦ bathroom cleaner) and abrasive pads will damage baths, basins and shower.

Taps

♦ Clean around the taps with an old toothbrush dipped in cream cleaner.
♦ Gold-plated taps scratch easily so just use a soft cloth and warm water.
♦ Hard-water deposits under the taps and round the plughole can be cleaned with proprietary cleaners which use acid to eat away the stain.
🍃 GREEN TIP: Use vinegar or a half a lemon to remove hard-water deposits. Leave it on the stain as long as possible. Repeat until the stain has dissolved.
🍃 GREEN TIP: If there is a heavy build-up of hard-water deposits, hang a plastic bag full of dissolved water softener from the tap, see page 61.
♦ Don't allow taps to drip – get the washers replaced if you can't turn the tap off.

Shower heads

♦ Shower heads clog up very quickly with lime-scale in hard-water areas unless you have a strong jet. Take the shower head apart and clean it from the inside, see below. The harder your water, the more often you will have to do this.
♦ Soak plastic washers in warm water and vinegar (15ml/1tbsp vinegar to 600ml/1pt of water) or rub them with a cut lemon to remove lime-scale.

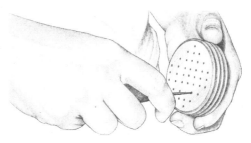

Cleaning the shower head *Unscrew the head and scrub with an old toothbrush or nail brush. Then poke a bodkin through the holes to clear them.*

Shower curtains and doors

♦ Leave the curtain opened out after having a shower to allow the air to circulate and thus prevent mildew.
♦ Canvas or cotton shower curtains should be washed in hot, soapy water like any other cotton fabric, and then ironed if necessary. Most should drip dry satisfactorily.
♦ Spots of mildew are difficult to remove. Try washing with a mild bleach solution, using 15ml (1tbsp) bleach to 600ml (1pt) warm water and then wipe dry.
▼▼ Bleach will get rid of mildew stains but
♦ ♦ won't prevent them from coming back.
♦ You can use silica gel (from chemists) to retard mildew. Just hang a packet of the crystals in the cubicle to absorb moisture.
♦ If stains won't come out, buy new curtains; they're not very expensive. You can buy canvas curtains that are mildew-proof and water-resistant.
♦ Waterproof silk curtains should be placed on a flat surface and sponged with lukewarm suds. Suitable flat surfaces are not so easy to

find, but you could use a decorator's trestle table or the kitchen worktop.

◆ Clean out water and dirt in shower door tracks with an old toothbrush or cotton bud.

◆ Wash down shower doors regularly with detergenty water or a cloth soaked in vinegar, to prevent lime-scale.

Basins and bidets

◆ Wipe basins frequently with a cream cleaner, rinse and dry; never use abrasive cleaners, which may damage the surface.

◆ Clean bidets with a mild disinfectant or vinegar and wipe dry. Don't forget the taps and the plughole.

◆ Clean inside the overflow with an old toothbrush or bottle brush.

Toilets

◆ Briskly scrub inside the bowl every day with a toilet brush for a few seconds, using the cleaner of your choice to remove deposits, discoloration and tide lines. Be particularly careful to clean under the rim. Rinse the toilet brush in a fresh flush of water after cleaning and occasionally give it a wash in hot water and disinfectant.

GREEN TIP: You can use vinegar instead of a proprietary toilet cleaner. Leave it on for an hour or so and then flush. You may need to use several applications.

◆ Wash the seat, handle, cistern and all the surrounds every day. Many a man's or child's aim is less than precise and even the flushing of the loo releases millions of droplets into the air and from there onto the floor and walls, which are not entirely germ-free.

◆ If your bathroom is carpeted, use a toilet mat and wash it frequently.

◆ If you need to remove old encrustations of dirt, empty the lavatory bowl first by tying a cloth round the lavatory brush so that it fits the drain hole and pushing it quickly up and down. This will push the water out and leave you a bare bowl to work on. Give the cloth-covered brush a coating of cleaner and coat the inside of the toilet bowl. Leave this for as long as you can, then flush. If after cleaning there's still a ring, rub very gently with a pumice stone or wet-and-dry paper.

◆ Don't waste money on toilet cistern capsules. They are only coloured bleaches with air freshener. They don't actually keep the lavatory clean.

THE DANGERS OF TOILET CLEANERS

▼▼ Do not be tempted to double the ◆ ◆ effectiveness of a toilet cleaner by using two different ones together. Different chemicals combine to form explosive and toxic gases.

▼▼ Bleach is not a cleaning agent, it just ◆ ◆ makes things white. It will eventually damage chrome, laminates and other plastic materials as well as the environment. Vinegar, lemon juice and mild disinfectant are equally good and safer.

▼▼ Most toilet cleaners are poisonous. ◆ ◆ Buy ones with childproof tops and store out of reach of children.

BATH SURROUNDS AND TILES

◆ A coat of paste wax on chrome, plastic, fibreglass, marble and other surrounds helps to repel dirt and lime-scale, saving you a lot of work.

Tiles

◆ Wipe over with a cream cleaner on a damp cloth, then rinse.

◆ In hard-water areas tiles often show water splashes even when they are clean. Rinse the tiles with equal amounts of warm water and vinegar or rub with a cut lemon and leave it to soak in. Wipe dry and buff up.

◆ When the grouting becomes blackened with mildew, as even waterproof grouting generally does after a time, this can be cleaned with an old toothbrush and a specially formulated bathroom cleaner or a half-and-half domestic bleach and water solution. Don't let the bleach get into the bath or basin. If you can't remove the stains, it may be easier to regrout.

FURNITURE AND ACCESSORIES

◆ Treat chrome bathrails as you would the taps.
◆ If you have a linen cupboard in the bathroom, take everything out from time to time, wipe down shelves and leave to dry before replacing linen.

Wastebins and laundry baskets

◆ Don't use metal bins in the bathroom; they will quickly become rusty.
◆ Line wastebins with a bin liner or plastic carrier bag.
◆ If you are using disposable nappies, keep a bin specially for them and empty it daily.
◆ Wicker benefits from being scrubbed out once in a while. Do this out of doors with warm, soapy water and salt. Leave to dry.

Medicine chest

◆ Regularly clear out the medicine chest and throw away used razor blades and other out-of-date items. Old medicines should ideally be returned to the chemist. It is not always safe to flush them down the lavatory or throw them in the dustbin. Wipe out the cupboard with a cream cleaner if it is very dirty, otherwise a damp cloth will do. Rinse and leave to dry.
◆ Check the lock regularly. Then put back the usable items.

Mirrors

🍃 GREEN TIP: Wipe with a weak vinegar and water solution.
◆ Remove hairspray with a little white spirit on cotton wool; the room should be well-ventilated when you do this.
◆ Prevent steaming up by rubbing with a little neat washing-up liquid or an anti-misting product.
◆ Plastic mirrors are less likely to mist as their surfaces are warmer than glass.

Bath mats

◆ Wipe cork bath mats with a damp cloth.
◆ Wash small plastic mats in the sink or basin with warm soapy water. Large mats need to be scrubbed out of doors.
◆ Put fabric mats in the washing machine.

Sponges, face flannels

◆ Rinse thoroughly after use to prevent them going slimy. Wash occasionally in weak vinegar solution or put flannels in the washing machine. Allow to dry naturally, outside if possible.

Light fittings

◆ Switch the electricity off at the mains before cleaning any bathroom light fittings and make sure your hands are dry, otherwise you could get an electric shock.
◆ Wipe the bulb with a damp cloth. Don't replace it until you're sure it's dry.

BATHROOM CHECKLIST

Check that everything that should be in the bathroom is there and that nothing needs to be replaced.
◇ *Toothbrushes in good condition for the entire family*
◇ *Toothpaste, mouth wash and dental floss*
◇ *Nail brush and nail scissors or clippers*
◇ *Face cloths or sponges*

◇ *Soap (and bath oil and talcum powder if you use them)*
◇ *Clean towels*
◇ *Toilet paper*
◇ *Lavatory brush and cleaner*
◇ *Bath cleaning equipment*
◇ *Wastebin and nappy bucket*
◇ *Laundry basket*

CLEANING FLOORS

If you can manage to keep your floors clean, the rest of the house will look clean and will certainly be easier to keep clean, because less dirt is being carried through the home. Concentrate particularly on the hall and any door leading to the outside because that's where most of the dirt comes from. Sweep or sponge mop the kitchen and bathroom floors frequently, preferably every day; they are both breeding grounds for germs.

Occasionally, when spring cleaning, say, move the furniture out of each room, roll up the carpet or any rugs so that you have elbow room, and get down on your hands and knees and clean out any dirt in the corners and along the skirting boards.

TREATING HARD FLOORS

Most floors need only a damp mop every so often to keep them clean, some floors, such as stone or tile floors, benefit from a heavy-duty wash from time to time.
◆ A sealer and/or water- or wax-based polish will help to protect most hard floors.

Wooden floors

◆ Sanded and sealed floors only need to be damp mopped.
▼▼ Never soak wooden floors and don't use
◆◆ very hot water, which softens the wood and can cause it to splinter.

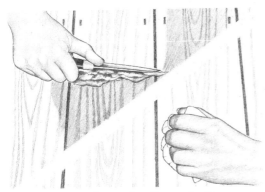

Removing trodden-in dirt *Scrape the dirty area gently with an old knife, working along the grain, above left. Then rub with white spirit. Apply polish, give it time to soak in, then buff up, above right.*

◆ Polished wood floors shouldn't need washing at all. Sweep regularly and polish occasionally with a wax polish.
◆ Use liquid wax polish, it's easier to apply.

Cork floors

◆ If sealed, just mop from time to time.
◆ If polished, give a coating of wax polish sparingly about twice a year – no more. Buff up occasionally.
◆ Vinyl-coated tiles just need to be damp mopped with detergent solution when dirty.
◆ Sealed cork that is in bad condition can be sanded and re-sealed.
▼▼ Never let cork get too wet, it may crack.
◆◆ Dry thoroughly after washing.

Linoleum floors

◆ Wash floor with warm, soapy water.
◆ Remove marks by rubbing gently with medium-grade steel wool dipped in turpentine or white spirit (don't scrub). Then seal.
◆ Can be protected with an oil-based sealer.

Rubber floors

◆ Damp mop with mild detergent solution.
◆ Polish with water-based emulsion polish or special rubber polish.
◆ Don't use wax polishes, turpentine, paraffin or solvent-based cleaners or polishes.
◆ Protect with water-based sealer.

Painted floors

◆Damp mop with mild detergent solution, using as little water as possible.
◆Painted floors can be wax polished, which makes them easier to clean.
◆Glossy enamel paint can be washed with hot water. Rub gently. Rub stubborn spots gently with a very mild scouring powder or fine wire wool.

Varnished floors

◆Wash waterproof varnish with warm, soapy water.
◆For non-waterproof varnish, wipe with a damp detergenty mop.

Vinyl and thermoplastic floors

◆Damp mop with detergent.
◆Polish with water-based emulsion polish.
◆Never use solvent-based cleaners or polishes – they will damage the tiles and then the dirt will become ingrained.
◆Wax polish if you must, but it can make the tiles slippery and surely you have better things to do?

Asphalt floors

◆Mop with a sponge mop, squeezed out in mild detergent. Rinse and dry.
◆Don't use abrasives or cleaning powders.
◆Polish with a water-based emulsion polish. Don't use oil- or wax-based polishes, as they tend to soften the surface.

Concrete floors

◆Clean with a damp mop. Don't use soap on unsealed floors it's difficult to rinse off.
◆May be sealed to make cleaning easier (this will also make it non-slip).
◆Sealed floors can be wax polished.

Marble floors

◆Need little maintenance but get professional advice if the floor becomes stained or blistered. Don't use abrasives.
◆Oils, fats and acids are harmful because marble is porous.
◆Wipe with diluted washing-up liquid, using a just damp soft mop or cloth. Don't let the floor get wet.

Quarry tile floors

◆Treat a newly laid tile floor with linseed oil. Don't wash it for at least two weeks.
◆Damp mop with warm, soapy water and scrub if necessary.
◆White patches on newly laid tiles can be wiped with a weak solution of vinegar and water. Rinse with clear water. (The patches are caused by the lime in the cement.)
◆Use a silicone polish if you want to but it's not necessary.

Slate and stone floors

◆Wash with household detergent or washing soda dissolved in water.
▼▼ Do not wash the floor with soap, it will
◆ ◆ form a scum not to be got rid of.
GREEN TIP: Apply a little lemon oil to slate after it has been washed and dried to give it a lustrous finish. Remove all excess with a clean cloth.
GREEN TIP: You can also shine slate with milk, but use only a little if you don't want the house to smell like a dairy.
◆Protect stone floors with a cement sealer and wax polish.

Terrazzo floors

◆Sweep and damp mop as necessary. Use detergent such as washing-up liquid, not alkaline cleaners such as washing soda, ammonia or borax.
▼▼ Don't use abrasive cleaners; you'll
◆ ◆ damage the surface.

HEAVY DUTY WASH FOR VERY DIRTY FLOORS

This method is suitable for terrazzo, ceramic or quarry tiles, stone, marble, concrete and vinyl floors. Do not treat wooden, linoleum or cork floors in this way; they should be damp mopped.

1 *Sweep and/or vacuum. Apply the floor cleaner of your choice, made up as directed on the packet, with a wet mop (cotton or sponge).*
2 *Leave it to soak for 10–15 minutes. Don't allow the floor to dry out but do check that the water doesn't run under the skirting boards, where it may get into the electric wires and sockets. Scrub any very dirty bits (usually by the walls and in the corners).*
3 *Wipe over with a barely damp cloth, rinsed frequently in clean water. Rinse thoroughly in order not to leave a film of detergent on the floor, which will prevent any polish from being absorbed and will make the floor slippery.*
4 *Dry with a dry cloth or mop.*

POLISHING FLOORS

A good shine will conceal all sorts of blemishes in any floor. Too much polish leads to a build-up of dirty polish, which will be difficult to buff up. The only alternative is to remove it and start again, see opposite.

Types of floor polish

◆ **Solid paste polish** Generally wax, this type of polish is suitable for unvarnished wooden floors, lino and cork. Quite hard work to apply and has to be done by hand. The shine lasts a long time.
◆ **Liquid solvent polish** This type spreads easily and can be applied with an electric floor polisher. Can be wax or oil. The solvent evaporates, leaving the polish. Suitable for the same floors as solid paste. You will probably have to apply it slightly more often than solid paste.
◆ **Water-based emulsion polishes** Generally silicone polishes, they are easy to apply and long-lasting. These can be used on all floors except unsealed wood, cork or lino.
◆ You can thin some solid wax polishes with turpentine but it is easier to use a liquid wax in the first place.

Applying wax polishes

1 Apply the polish evenly and lightly with a soft cloth (paste) or a polisher (liquid solvent) and allow to soak in.

2 Buff up with a floor polisher, a broom whose head has been tied up in a soft terry towel or a hand-operated "dumper" (a heavily padded weight on a stick), or you can get down on your hands and knees and use elbow grease.
◇ *You should not have to apply more polish for two or three months or more.*

Applying water-based polishes

1 Use a very clean cotton or sponge mop. Wet the mop head and leave it damp.
2 Pour polish onto the mophead and lay it on the floor, spreading it until there are no bubbles left. Buff up the floor as for wax polish, above.
◇ *Apply polish sparingly, it's better to apply too little than too much.*
3 Build up the surface with two or three thin coats, buffing up between coats – more is not better.
◇ *The first coat should cover the whole floor. The second and third coats should only cover the "traffic areas". You shouldn't have to polish again for several months.*
▼▼ Don't splash the walls and skirting
◆◆ boards with polish; it is difficult to get polish off paint work and it can stain wallcoverings.

TAKING OFF OLD WAX

If you have been polishing too much, there will be a big build-up of polish so you will have to remove the wax and start again.

1 *Mix a bucket of floor cleaner, preferably with a little ammonia in it, or use a proprietary wax remover.*

2 *Apply plenty of this with a mop over a small-ish area at a time and let it soak in (don't let it dry out).*

3 *As soon as the wax and dirt begin to dissolve, wipe them off. Use old crumpled newspaper, or, better still, a sponge mop, above left. Scrub obstinate parts by hand or with a polisher, using the bristle pads. Scrape the floor with your fingernail to see if you've removed all the old wax, above right.*

4 *Damp mop with a clean mop. Then start on another patch.*

5 *Do the whole floor again until you are sure it's quite wax-free. Let the floor dry thoroughly before you apply new wax.*

CARPET CARE

All carpets get dirty. No matter how careful you may be, dust from outside, smut from the street, or food crumbs will land on the best cared for carpets.

◆ Regular maintenance will help carpets stay cleaner and last longer.

◆ All carpets should be kept free of things spilled, dust, litter, crumbs, pieces of thread and hob-nail boots.

◆ Vacuum the main living areas, hall and stairs daily, and certainly weekly, if you can; don't wait until the carpet looks dirty. Although this is a counsel of perfection, regular vacuuming will mean fewer

shampooing sessions, easier vacuuming sessions and better-looking carpets. Bedroom carpets need vacuuming less often than carpets in other rooms.

Stair cleaning

◆ Always start from the bottom of the stairs and work upwards so that you don't tread the dirt into the carpet.

Protecting stair carpet *If polishing stair rods, place pieces of paper under the rods to protect the carpet.*

Vacuuming techniques

Vacuuming is the most efficient way of cleaning carpets and the most effective vacuum cleaners for carpets are those which beat as well as suck.

◆ Before you begin to vacuum, pick up by hand all buttons, pins, toys, dead leaves and sticks, coins and as many stray threads as possible. The vacuum will choke on the larger metal objects and the threads will get caught up in the rollers.

◆ Move the cleaner with slow, even strokes. Officially, thorough vacuuming means going over the area 10 to 12 times. Unofficially, it's enough when the carpet seems clean.

◆ Don't wear yourself out, vacuum one room at a time, then have a break.

◆ If the vacuum hose gets blocked, unblock it with a coat hanger, see below. If your vacuum can blow as well as suck (which makes unblocking the hose easier), do this into a bag, preferably out of doors.

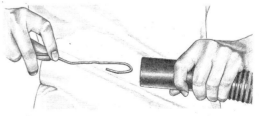

Unblocking a vacuum hose *If the hose becomes blocked, unwind a metal coat hanger and use the "hook" to remove the blockage.*

CLEANING A CARPET

◆ To keep a carpet in good condition, shampoo about once a year. You may want to shampoo the traffic areas more often, particularly if you have children or dogs.

◆ Shampoo before the carpet gets too dirty; left too long the dirt can be impossible to shift. You have left it too long when there are obvious dark patches.

◆ Call in a professional carpet cleaner if the carpet is old and/or valuable, or if you are a working woman with other pressures.

◆ Small cotton rugs can be washed in a washing machine.

◆ Carpet tiles can be vacuumed and individual tiles lifted and replaced or shampooed with carpet shampoo to remove stains.

▼▼ Get Oriental carpets shampooed pro-
◆ ◆ fessionally, because they are sometimes touched up by hand painting after they are made and these colours often run.

Raising flattened carpet pile *Rub up the pile with the edge of a small coin.*

◆ If the pile has been pressed flat by furniture feet, raise it before shampooing. Try rubbing the area with a coin, see left. Alternatively, lay a wet terry towel, folded twice, over the flattened bit. Then steam it gently with a hottish iron to lift the pile.

Shampooing a carpet yourself

◆ Shampooing large areas of carpet is much quicker if you use a mechanical shampooer. Share the cost of hiring one with a relative, friend or neighbour who also wants to clean a carpet. (Don't share the cost of buying. The cleaner will always be in the other person's house when you need it.)

◆ Take all the furniture out of the room.

◆ Drape your curtains over a coat hanger and hang it over the curtain rail to get them out of the way.

1 Vacuum thoroughly (12 strokes over each section, overlapping each stroke). If possible, vacuum underneath as well.

2 To make sure the colours won't run, do a test run on a hidden piece of carpet using your chosen carpet shampoo, see opposite.

3 If the test is satisfactory, dilute the shampoo, following the manufacturers' instructions. Apply the shampoo.

◇ *If using wet shampoo, be very careful not to let the backing get wet. If using dry foam shampoo, wait until the crystals have formed, then sweep or vacuum them up.*

TIPS FOR SHAMPOOING CARPETS

◆ Use a dry foam carpet shampoo which crystallizes – absorbing the dirt particles – as it dries and you won't get the carpet saturated. The colours will be less likely to run, too. Other detergents can contain bleaches and other alkalis which damage some carpets.

◆ Don't walk on wet carpets, you can damage them.

◆ Don't let carpets get too wet because the carpet backing will get wet and the carpet will be difficult to dry and the colours more likely to run. Wool carpets are the easiest to clean because they absorb more moisture before becoming saturated and are more resistant to fungus if they get wet: a 100 kg (220lb) carpet will absorb about 16kg (35lb) water before the backing becomes saturated and liable to damage, whereas 100kg man-made fibre will absorb only about 2.5kg (6lb) water before the backing is affected. Don't brush too hard on synthetic carpets because the fibres may crack.

4 If any areas are really filthy, give them another dose of shampoo.

5 Vacuum again to remove any left over foam and dirt and to raise the pile.

6 When the carpet is dry, replace the furniture. Vacuum the carpet again.

Protecting the wet carpet *If you have to return furniture to the room before the carpet is completely dry, place a piece of greaseproof paper or foil under the legs.*

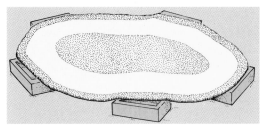

Drying a rug or unfitted carpet *You can help an unfitted carpet to dry quicker by raising it on bricks or draping it over chairs to let the air circulate underneath.*

Testing colour-fastness

◆ Many carpet dyes run when they get wet so testing is important.

◆ Test colours on a patch under a piece of furniture where it won't be visible.

1 Vacuum or beat the carpet. Dampen a piece of carpet with the shampoo.

2 Leave for an hour or so, then rub with a white cloth, or put several layers of white kitchen tissue on the damp patch with a weight on top. The longer you leave it, the surer the test.

3 If there's no bleeding of colour, go ahead and shampoo the whole carpet.

4 If there is slight bleeding, try the test again but this time add acetic acid, vinegar, or household ammonia to the mixture.

Professional cleaning

◆ Get an estimate, or preferably two or three estimates. Always ask whether the

---

CARPET FINISHES

◆ Choose carpets that have been treated with soil retardant; they are much easier to keep clean.

◆ Synthetic carpets sometimes give mild electric shocks, especially in centrally heated homes, in frosty weather and where there is double glazing. Look for synthetic carpets sold as anti-static, they contain a small amount of stainless steel fibre which earths the electricity and prevents shocks.

◆ You can apply special chemical finishes to minimize static or to stop the carpet getting dirty and prevent things spilled from soaking into the fibres.

SOIL RETARDANTS

◆ Soil retardants can be applied to old or new carpets but the carpets must be clean. They have to be applied by licensed agents and can be expensive to have done. Soil retardants will not affect the colour of your carpets and should last three years.

◆ You will still have to vacuum your carpets but not shampoo them.

ANTI-STATIC AGENTS

◆ If your carpet produces a lot of electricity, treat with anti-static spray about once a year.

---

price includes moving the furniture. Some cleaning companies offer a discount if they don't have to move the furniture out of the room. Most firms also offer silicone treatments (soil retardants) to prevent the carpet from getting dirty again. These are worth while if you can afford it.

▼▼ For Oriental wool carpets, be wary of ◆ ◆ chemical cleaning methods, in which chlorine bleaches are used to dissolve part of the rough surface fibres and make them smoother and brighter looking. Sometimes the dyes are affected and will have to be retouched professionally by hand painting, which is expensive.

◆ If you have old carpets, look for a carpet specialist who will clean them with detergent using hand brushes.

PROBLEM CARPETS

▼▼ Beater/brush upright vacuum cleaners
◆ ◆ are, although adjustable, too rough for
old Persian carpets and Numdah rugs. For
these use a cylinder suction vacuum or sweep
by hand with a bristle brush.
◆Handmade carpets, particularly Oriental
ones, should be professionally cleaned.

Coconut, sisal, rush matting

◆Take the whole lot up and shake or beat it
out of doors from time to time and vacuum
up dust trapped underneath. Scrub occasionally with soapy water (no soda) and dry flat.
◆If the matting has been tacked down,
vacuum regularly.
◆Door matting, which you can buy in rolls,
has a rubber backing which traps dirt. Take
the mat outside and beat the dust out.

Fur and sheepskin rugs

◆If the rug has a backing, it can be cleaned
with French chalk, unscented talcum powder
or fuller's earth. Shake the powder over the
fur, leave it for several hours and then brush
and shake it out. You may need to do this
several times.
◆Wipe unbacked fur rugs with a cloth
wrung out in lukewarm mild detergent solution. Don't let the water go more than fur
deep. It must not wet the skin.

Numdah rugs

Made of matted goats' hair with hand embroidered designs.
◆Never wash them. They shrink and the
colour runs. Dry clean if necessary.
◆Do not shake them. Vacuum very gently.

Hooked rugs

◆Vacuum but don't beat or shake.
◆Dry clean if necessary.

REMOVING STAINS

◆Treat any spill as soon as it occurs. Marks
that will disappear like magic if treated at
once are almost impossible to remove once
they have dried out.
◆Always work from the outside edge to the
centre of the stain. Always blot, do not rub
or brush, and don't let the carpet get too wet.
◆Wools and polyesters prefer acid stain
removers (lemon juice and vinegar) to alkalis.
◆Cellulose, cotton, jute, viscose, rayon, silk
and nylon prefer alkali stain removers
(borax, ammonia) to acids.
◆If there is a mark on the carpet, use acid
stain removers to remove alkali stains and
vice versa.

EMERGENCY ACTION FOR SPILLS

1 *Absorb or scrape up the spill immediately,
before it dries.*

For liquids *Pour on a generous amount of salt
and leave for at least an hour, then vacuum, or
blot up with a wad of tissues. Change tissues as
they become saturated.*

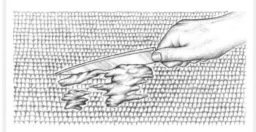

For solids *Scrape them up carefully with the
back of a knife; don't rub them into the carpet.*
2 *If the spill leaves a mark, apply appropriate
stain remover, see opposite and overleaf.*

Stain removal kit

Keep everything in a small plastic tool or cutlery box or basket, out of reach of children. Label the box clearly so that others can find it easily.

◇ *Neutral detergent (one advertized as safe for fine fabrics) and dry foam carpet shampoo*
◇ *White spirit, methylated spirit or turpentine*
◇ *Household ammonia (always dilute with 10 parts water)*
◇ *Dry-cleaning fluid containing perchloroethylene. Use straight from the bottle. DO NOT use lighter fluid, petrol, paraffin or carbon tetrachloride; the fumes are harmful.*
◇ *Distilled white vinegar*
◇ *Clean white terry towelling cloths*
◇ *Soft bristled brush*
◇ *White kitchen tissues*

TREATING SPECIFIC CARPET STAINS

◆ When applying stain removers, work with small amounts.
◆ If you start removing a stain with one formula, leave to dry completely before trying another. You can't tell whether the stain has gone until the carpet is dry.
◆ If you are worried about the colours running, add a teaspoonful of vinegar, acetic acid or household ammonia to the detergent or shampoo.
◆ When you have finished the treatment, rinse with cold water, then blot dry with a clean piece of towelling.
◆ See pages 142–44 for any stains not listed.

DRINK STAINS

ALCOHOL AND SOFT DRINKS
Apply diluted liquid detergent solution and blot dry. Apply white vinegar and water (half and half), then blot. Rinse and blot dry.

COFFEE, BLACK
Squirt stain with soda siphon, rinse and blot. Shampoo with dry foam carpet shampoo.

COFFEE, WHITE
Squirt stain with soda siphon, rinse and blot. Shampoo with dry foam carpet shampoo. Use dry-cleaning solvent to remove any remaining milky stain. Shampoo if necessary.

CREAM, ICECREAM, MILK
Apply a little liquid detergent solution. Rinse with cold water. Treat remaining grease stains with dry-cleaning solvent. Shampoo with dry foam shampoo.

FRUIT JUICE
Blot with a cloth dipped in diluted mild detergent. Shampoo.

TEA, BLACK
See COFFEE, BLACK

TEA, WHITE
See COFFEE, WHITE

WINE
Blot as much as possible with water or tissues. Shampoo. See also ALCOHOL AND SOFT DRINKS.

BIOLOGICAL STAINS

BLOOD
Apply cold water then blot. Repeat as many times as necessary. Rinse and blot.

FAECES
Remove deposit and sponge with clear, warm water or flush with soda water syphon. Use pet stain remover to soften the deposit if necessary. Disinfect, and shampoo if necessary.

URINE
Treat quickly. Rub with a cloth wrung out in clear water. Mop up immediately with a clean cloth. Repeat several times. Shampoo.

VOMIT
Remove deposit with knife or crumpled newspaper. Sponge with made-up carpet shampoo, adding one eggcupful of white vinegar to each 500ml (1pt), or spot clean with dry-cleaning fluid.

Continued ▷

TREATING SPECIFIC CARPET STAINS (Continued)

 HOUSEHOLD STAINS

BALLPOINT PEN
Rub with white spirit on a clean cloth. Keep turning the cloth so that you are using a clean piece all the time. When you have finished, treat with a dry foam carpet shampoo.

CANDLEWAX
Cover the wax with blotting paper, kitchen tissue or brown paper. Iron with a warm iron so that the wax melts and is absorbed. Continue with clean paper until all the wax is removed.
◆ Coloured candlewax may leave a stain. Treat this with a little white spirit on a piece of white cotton wool. Don't soak. Vacuum when dry.

CHEWING GUM
Pick off what you can, treat the remainder with white spirit or methylated spirit. You may have to repeat this several times.

FELT PEN
Try rubbing with white spirit using a clean cloth. Shampoo afterwards.

FOUNTAIN PEN INK
Treat with carpet shampoo, work slowly, applying a little of the shampoo and blotting immediately. Then do some more. The chances are, you will not be able to remove the stain completely.

FURNITURE POLISH
Treat as for GREASE AND OIL.

GREASE AND OIL
Dab with white spirit on cotton wool. Shampoo. Bad stains may have to be professionally cleaned.

MUD
Leave to dry, then brush or vacuum. Treat residual stain with methylated spirit, then liquid detergent solution.

PAINT
Most paint stains cannot be removed once they are dry.
Acrylic paint Wash out with diluted detergent, then dab with methylated spirit.
Cellulose paints Treat with cellulose thinners.
Emulsion paint Wash it out with cold water while still wet.
Gloss paint Sponge with white spirit if wet; if dry try a proprietary stain remover.

SHOE POLISH
Very carefully scrape off as much as you can. Dab with white spirit. Shampoo.

SOOT
Cover with dry salt. Vacuum up. Dab with detergent solution. Rinse and dry. Shampoo.

TAR
Scrape off as much as you can. Dab with white spirit on cotton wool. Shampoo.

CLEANING WALLS AND CEILINGS

As with all cleaning, the more often you wipe over, or dust, the surface the better. If you let a wall or ceiling become really dirty, you will have to work very hard to get it clean again; this can mean re-decorating.

Light colours require far more maintenance than dark ones since every fingermark shows up, every coffee splash and every fly spot. If you are much troubled by marks that cannot be removed (children's fingermarks and artistic attempts, dog tide lines, scuffed skirtings), then give up all idea of having a gracious home and cover the walls with something washable, at least until the children are older, see page 195.

GENERAL CARE

◆ If you have tall ceilings, dust them with a clean long-handled broom. Don't use water until you are ready to do a proper wall wash.
◆ A quick way of dusting is to blow along the wall with a pair of bellows. Alternatively, use a cobweb brush, a clean duster tied over a broom head or a clean soft broom.
◆ Keep a copy of the symbols supplied with the hanging instructions for your wallcovering; they include care instructions.
◆ Protect fabric or paper wallcoverings in vulnerable places (the hall, for example) with a special finish so that grease and dirt spots

---

WALLCOVERING CARE SYMBOLS

These are the cleaning, or care, symbols. There are other symbols relating to hanging coverings listed on page 195.

 Can be sponged

 Easily washed

 Can be washed

Can be scrubbed

---

on these can be wiped off with a damp cloth. Test the wall for colour fastness, then apply the finish using a large distemper brush.

Cobwebs

◆ Tackle cobwebs while they are fresh. Once covered with grease and dust, they are much more difficult to remove.

◆ You can try to tackle the whole spider problem by spraying with insecticide if you really want to. But new spiders will always find their way in and are neither dirty, nor dangerous. They act as small fly catchers, so why bother to attack them so ferociously?

Clearing cobwebs
Cobwebs cling to damp surfaces so you can pick them off by using an only-just-damp mop or a broom covered with a damp towel.

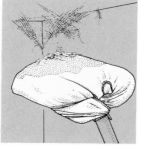

WASHING WALLS AND CEILINGS

◆ Dust walls or ceilings and remove cobwebs before washing them.

◆ Gather together detergent and water in one bucket and rinsing water in another, two or three sponges or absorbent cloths, a thick cloth and/or a long-handled sponge mop and squeegee, which helps to get into corners and

angles. A long-handled sponge mop is useful if you have no stepladder; the squeegee can be useful for getting into the corners.

GREEN TIP: Rather than detergent, use pure soap and water, adding about 50g (2oz) borax per 1 litre (2pt) water to both soapy and rinsing water.

◆ Do not use scouring powders to clean paintwork, unless you are preparing to paint.

◆ Instead of household detergent you can make up a washing solution for paintwork and washable wallcoverings: 125ml (4fl oz) turpentine, 250ml (8fl oz) milk and 30ml (3tbsp) of jellied soap (use the bits that are left in the bathroom, soaked in water until they turn to jelly) mixed up in 2 litres (4pt) hot water. Add this to the washing water.

◆ Change washing or rinsing water when it gets dirty or you'll smear the walls.

◆ Rinse well after washing because any leftover detergent will attract more dust.

SAFETY TIPS

◆ Get yourself into comfortable old clothes, which should not be too baggy or they will catch in ladder projections or prevent you seeing the rungs and buckets beneath you.

◆ Cover your wrists with sweat bands or bits of old terry towel to catch the drips before they reach your eyes.

◆ If you are reaching high, use a stepladder or at least make sure your support is firm. A dining chair balanced on a card table, perched on a stool, will not do.

◆ Wear plimsolls or rubber-soled shoes; they are safer for climbing around on ladders or chairs.

◆ Wear rubber gloves if you are allergic to any household chemicals.

Keep water away from electrical wall fittings, such as wall lights; you could give yourself an electric shock. Likewise, make sure electrical appliances are disconnected before you begin and do not pull out electrical cords with wet hands.

◆ Don't leave the bucket at the foot of the ladder where you will step right into it on your way down and always move the bucket before the ladder.

WALLS

◆ Wash with household detergent solution.
◆ Against all advice to wash from the bottom of the wall up, it is usually easier and just as effective to start at the top and work down.
◆ For stains on different wall surfaces, see pages 88–9.

Emulsion paint

◆ Clean small areas around light switches with cream cleaner.
◆ Most marks can be washed off with detergent or soap solution, see also page 88. On particularly dirty walls, for instance in the kitchen where greasy splatters get dried on, it won't hurt to use a plastic scouring pad. Alternatively, add a spoonful of ammonia to your washing solution.

Gloss paint

◆ Wash with warm water and soapless detergent, starting at the top and working down.
◆ When washing gloss paints, use a dryer cloth than for emulsion paints.
◆ If cleaning textured paints, add a little borax to the water (50g/2oz borax to 1 litre/2pt water). Rinse with clean water.
◆ Remove stains with a paste cleaner, mild scouring powder or a little whiting or a paste made with fuller's earth, see page 87.

Whitewash

◆ You can't wash walls finished with distemper (whitewash) and similar washes. You have to brush all the distemper off and apply another coat. Luckily, these finishes are seldom used now, since emulsion paints are so easy to apply.

Washable wallcoverings

◆ Textured vinyl wallcovering can be cleaned with a solution of detergent in warm water, applied with a thick absorbent cloth or a very soft nail brush. Wait a little then rinse thoroughly with clean water.
◆ Vinyl wallpaper must be dusted and/or damp mopped frequently – dirt tends to make it brittle if left. Proprietary drycleaning fluids can be used on vinyls. Don't use lacquer solvents; they melt the surface of the wallcovering.
◆ Embossed wallcoverings get thickly encrusted dirt in the folds. Use a smaller brush such as a soft toothbrush to get the dirt out – make sure you get all the detergent out as well as all the dirt.
◆ Lacquered wallpapers can be washed with warm suds. Rinse and wipe dry.

Non-washable papers

◆ Ordinary wallpaper, made of paper without a protective finish, is not washable. Brush it from time to time with a cobweb brush or broom head covered with a duster.
◆ Marks can be rubbed lightly with a damp cloth. Then gently pat the paper dry. Do not rub the paper dry or the surface will come off in tiny rolls.
◆ Non-washable papers can be cleaned with a commercial cleaner that looks rather like a lump of dough, or use a soft eraser or lumps of bread, see below. None of these works well on very dirty walls; they tend to leave streaky marks. So don't let the walls get too dirty before cleaning them.

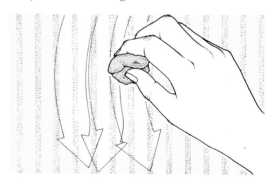

Cleaning non-washable wallpaper *Using bread rolled into balls, a soft rubber or wallpaper cleaning dough, rub the wall with a series of wide sweeping downward movements, overlapping each stroke. Don't rub too hard and don't rub upwards or sideways. As the dough or rubber picks up dirt, turn it so that a clean bit is always on the outside. Work patiently and carefully so that you don't get streaky results.*

◆ Another bread technique is to cut a two-day-old loaf into eight chunks. Work as described below left. Cut the dirty part of the bread away from time to time and take a new piece whenever necessary.

◆ Heavier non-vinyl "washable" papers are not really washable, but can be sponged with mild white soap suds on a soft sponge and squeezed very dry. Use a light touch, very little liquid, and pat dry with a clean cloth.

Fabric and cork wallcoverings

◆ Dust the wall then vacuum with the vacuum cleaner dusting attachment.

◆ You can, very gingerly, try a damp cloth wrung out in warm water. Check that any colours won't run on a small hidden piece of covering before tackling the whole wall.

◆ Don't use felt in places where it is likely to get particularly grubby because it "felts up" when rubbed.

◆ If you are worried about cork becoming dirty, you can seal it with a matt seal – the same sort of thing you'd use for wood – then you can treat it as a washable wallcovering.

Ceramic tiles

◆ Treat as for gloss paints, see opposite.

🍃 GREEN TIP: You can save a lot of time and expense by rubbing the splattered tiles with a cut lemon. Leave for a quarter of an hour, then polish with a soft cloth.

Cleaning discoloured tile grouting *Rub with a toothbrush using a proprietary bathroom cleaner, or a half-and-half solution of household bleach or liquid antiseptic and water. If it won't clean up, it's better and easier to regrout.*

Wood panelling

◆ Waxed or sealed wood panels require very little cleaning except dusting. If they do become dirty, give them a wipe with a sponge rinsed out in diluted detergent, or give them a polish with a liquid wax.

◆ Varnished or lacquered wood panelling can be cleaned with furniture polish.

◆ Clean painted panelling with a detergent solution. Don't use abrasive cleaners.

◆ Rub fine scratches on untreated panelling with fine steel wool dipped in white spirit, working in the direction of the grain. Polish then buff up.

◆ Clean waxed panelling as for wooden furniture, see pages 93–5.

Touching up discoloured panelling *Apply a small amount of shoe polish, dark wax polish, or proprietary wood stain to the affected area.*

Brick walls

◆ Brush and vacuum the entire surface occasionally, pulling out all loose grit.

◆ Untreated brick attracts dirt. There's nothing to stop things sticking to it, and nothing to help you get marks off again. Ignore the small marks, other people will think they are part of the charm of the brickwork. You can try washing them off with warm water containing a little washing soda and rinse thoroughly. Wash very gently if the bricks are soft and very porous, and don't get them too wet.

◆ Seal the bricks with a matt-surfaced seal, then you can wash them with a detergent solution.

MOULDINGS

◆Dust with anything you can lay your hands on that will get into the nooks and crannies of cornices, dado rails, ceiling roses and so on. You can use a cobweb brush, a feather duster on a long handle or a clean soft broom head.

◆If you feel you must wash the moulding, check that it is washable and that any chips and cracks won't be damaged by water. The best way to wash is with a spray, since nothing else will get into all the nooks and crannies, see below.

◆Use a thick terry towel for drying; the loops get into the crevices.

◆Don't attempt to wash plaster mouldings. You will only make a dirty moulding look worse, whereas the likelihood of anyone noticing a slightly dusty corner or strip is very small. Paint it when the time comes to paint the rest of the ceiling.

Spray-cleaning mouldings *Using a plant spray, squirt detergent solution into the crevices. Wait for the liquid to penetrate, then wipe off as best you can and spray again with clear water. Wipe again.*

Cleaning in awkward corners *Use a paint brush, an old toothbrush or a bottle brush to get at the dirt in corners or crevices in the moulding.*

CEILINGS

◆Avoid washing a ceiling. It's tiring on the arms and neck and, unless you do a thorough job, you will get exhausted half way through and find you've left a mess of streaks of not-quite-perfectly cleaned ceiling. It is better to keep the ceiling regularly dusted until it needs painting again.

◆Cover up small marks on a white ceiling with a dab of white shoe polish.

◆Acoustic tile ceilings don't show the dirt badly, because they usually start off a greyish colour and their texture conceals marks. Keep dusting them though, or eventually you will have to paint and that ruins the acoustics, let alone the tiles.

◆If you must wash the ceiling, work on a 1m/yd square section at a time. Cover the area with detergent solution. By the time you've reached the end of your patch the dirt will be loosened and you can go back and wipe it off. Repeat across the entire ceiling.

▼▼Don't press hard or squeeze the cloth
◆◆ while working; you will get detergent all over your hair and face.

◆Cover the floor with polythene sheeting or several layers of newspaper.

◆If a ceiling is badly marked by smoke from a solid fuel fire, cigarette smoke or fluorescent tubes, don't attempt to wash it, the marks are difficult to remove. It's much easier to repaint it.

◆While you are dusting the ceiling, take the opportunity to clean the light fittings (bulbs and shades) and to check the fixings (wires, chains etc.).

REMOVING STAINS

Small marks are much more noticeable to you than to anyone else. Don't think they are the end of the world. You can always hang a poster or child's painting over a dirty mark to cover it up.

◆ Some marks on paintwork (fingermarks, for instance) will respond to a bit of diluted washing-up liquid rubbed in gently and then rinsed off thoroughly. Rub the mark only, not the surrounding area. If only a vague patch remains (stand back and try to look at it objectively), leave it and concentrate on something more vital.

◆ If the mark is in a natural untreated wood, wallpaper (as opposed to vinyl wallcovering) or other porous surface, it may be impossible to remove. Too much scrubbing will simply damage the wall surface around it. So leave it, enjoy it as a work of art, then repaper or cover the surface later.

◆ If a spot on paintwork doesn't appear to be cleanable, you can try to retouch the area with the tiniest dab of left-over paint. Put on

a very thin coat and don't leave a hard edge. This will look very obvious at first but will soon blend in.

◆ Very bad spots on wallpapers, which you have made worse by trying to remove, can be covered with a patch of the same paper cut to fit, see page 202. (That's why you always buy an extra roll.)

Cleaning grease marks from wallcoverings
Make a thick paste from fuller's earth, French chalk or talcum powder and dry-cleaning fluid. Smooth the mixture onto the wall like a poultice, starting well outside the stain and rubbing gently over and round it, as you would on fabric, above left. Allow it to dry out then brush it off with a soft brush, above right. Two or three applications may be necessary.

REMOVING ADHESIVE TAPE

If you use masking tape to protect woodwork while painting the walls, peel it off while it is still fresh; it should come off easily if you are careful.

◆ Ancient masking tape, which has been draughtproofing the windows, or tape on the walls holding up posters, can be difficult to remove. Peel off carefully to avoid leaving glue and tape behind or tearing the wallcovering, see below. Use acetone or non-oily nail varnish remover to soften the glue base before you start.

▼▼ Acetone and non-oily nail varnish
◆ ◆ remover are safe to use on glass, but will damage some paint and some plastic surfaces (and acetate fabrics), so don't leave them on too long. These solvents are highly flammable and must be used in a well-ventilated room.

◆ **From paint** If the tape lifts any paint, touch up with new paint.

◆ **From wallpaper** If the tape leaves a mark where the dust has stuck to the glue, draw this off with acetone and absorb it with a warm iron over kitchen tissues. Or patch it with a new piece of paper.

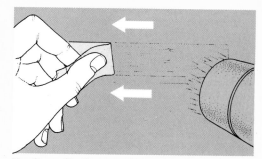

Peeling off adhesive tape *The safest way to remove tape is to lift the top edge and then pull it back on itself, keeping it parallel with the wall, pulling slowly and evenly. This way you lift the minimum amount of paint or paper with it. It sometimes helps to play a hair dryer along it – the warmth softens the glue.*

TREATING WALL STAINS

◆ When using water or other liquids, always test a hidden piece of wallcovering first to make sure the colours won't run.

PAINT

UNIDENTIFIED STAIN
◆ **Water-based paints** Dust then wash with weak detergent solution. Clean small areas at a time. Rinse and dry before doing the next bit.
◆ **Oil-based paints** Dust and wash with detergent solution. Rub residual stain with cut lemon or fine wire wool.

GRAFFITI
◆ Some felt tip pens respond to detergent.
◆ Methylated spirit or white spirit may get rid of ballpoint.
◆ Wax crayon can sometimes be removed with an eraser.
◆ If you can't remove the graffiti, cover it with a new coat of paint.

GREASE
Rub with strong detergent solution containing a little white spirit, or use a kitchen cleaner.

WALLCOVERINGS

UNIDENTIFIED STAIN
◆ **Washable and unwashable wall coverings** Rub over with stale bread. Don't use water.
◆ **Vinyl wallcoverings** As for painted walls.
◆ **Textured wallcoverings** Sponge with mild detergent solution.
◆ **Embossed wallcoverings** Rub with a bread ball or soft eraser, see page 84.

GRAFFITI
◆ For wax crayon, first draw out the wax with a warm iron over blotting paper, or kitchen tissues, which will absorb it. You may still be left with a colour stain which may respond to white spirit, or rub gently with moistened bicarbonate of soda on a damp cloth.
◆ Another method for crayon is to sponge with dry-cleaning fluid. Follow with a soap-and-water rinse on washable coverings, or a just-damp cloth on non-washable ones.
◆ Blot ink immediately and try not to smear it while doing so. Then use ink eradicator. Unfortunately, this may eradicate the colours on your paper. Retouch or patch.
◆ Pencil marks can be removed with an eraser or a bread ball, see page 84.

◆ If dry-cleaning fluid leaves a ring mark, try the fuller's earth pack described for grease stains, see page 87.

GREASE
◆ **Washable and unwashable wallcoverings** Draw out the grease with blotting paper or kitchen tissues under a warm iron. Alternatively, apply a paste of fuller's earth and dry-cleaning fluid and brush it off when it has dried, see page 87. It may help to dab the residue with moistened borax.
◆ **Embossed wallcoverings** Dab with talcum powder, leave for a couple of hours then brush it off gently.
◆ **Vinyl wallcoverings** Dab with white spirit or dry-cleaning fluid, then detergenty water.

CORK

UNIDENTIFIED STAIN
Sponge gently with warm water and detergent. DO NOT get it very wet.

GRAFFITI
As for WALLCOVERINGS, below left; anything more drastic will damage the cork. You may have to live with the marks.

GREASE
Dab with water containing borax or a mild detergent solution containing a few drops of household ammonia.

GRASSCLOTH AND HESSIAN WALLCOVERING

UNIDENTIFIED STAIN
Dab with talcum powder. Leave for a couple of hours and then brush off gently. Don't use dry-cleaning fluids or upholstery cleaners.

GREASE
Use a dry-cleaning fluid or white spirit, but test colour first – some fabrics won't take kindly to this treatment. If you can, get professional advice.

GRAFFITI
Try dry-cleaning fluid. If that doesn't work, recover the wall.

SILK WALLCOVERING

Call professional dry cleaners for all stains.

WOOD PANELLING

▼▼ Any treatment will discolour the wood. Use
♦♦ wood stain or shoe polish to bring the wood
back to its correct colour.

UNIDENTIFIED STAIN
◆ If wax finished, use furniture polish.
◆ If sealed, wash with mild detergent solution,
rinse and buff up.

GRAFFITI
Try mild detergent solution, followed by white
spirit on cotton wool.

EXPANDED POLYSTYRENE

◆ Don't use solvents, you'll melt the tiles.

UNIDENTIFIED STAIN
◆ Sponge with warm mild detergent solution.
Rinse. DO NOT press hard or the polystyrene
will come off in your hands or at the very least
get dented.

GRAFFITI
◆ Recover the wall.

BRICK/NEW PLASTER

EFFLORESCENCE *(white crystals or furry
deposit)*
Brushing with a dry paint brush should get rid
of it. If not, wipe with pure warm water. Repeat
if necessary, allowing the wall to dry between
washings.

UNIDENTIFIED STAIN
Wash with warm detergent solution with a
handful of washing soda crystals dissolved in
it. Rinse thoroughly.

GRAFFITI
Use paint remover and give it time to work on
the marks before you scrape it off. Wash with
detergent solution. If the worst comes to the
worst, sandpaper off the marks.

GREASE
Sponge with white spirit.

CLEANING WINDOWS

*Keep your windows clean, don't wait until
they are really dirty: slightly dirty windows
need only to be wiped with tepid water; very
dirty windows need to be scrubbed with detergent or stronger cleaner. Very dirty
windows also cut down the amount of light
in a room.*

*Always clean the window frames before
you clean the glass, otherwise you will dirty
the glass again.*

WASHING THE GLASS

◆ When cleaning the inside, take down
blinds, curtains and so on, and all objects on
the window sill, so that you won't be in-
hibited and they won't get broken or
damaged by the cleaning mixture or dirt
from the window.
◆ Use tepid, not hot water, although it is not
quite so pleasant to work with.
◆ Take two buckets of tepid water and two
cloths or chamois leathers, or a squeegee (a
rubber blade on a handle, sometimes with a
sponge as well) and a cloth; one lot is for the
cleaning and the other for rinsing.
◆ A chamois leather is best for cleaning
windows, but if you haven't got one, choose
a cloth which leaves no fluff – a linen tea
towel or an all-purpose kitchen cloth.
Crumpled newspaper is particularly good for
drying the window after washing.
◆ Squeegees on extendable handles make
cleaning large windows much easier.

GREEN TIP: Vinegar in the water instead of proprietary window cleaners and crumpled newspaper instead of a cloth are both effective and cheap.

◆**Small windows** Squeeze out the cloth or leather in the first bucket of water, wringing it out well. Work round the edges of the pane and into the middle. Wipe with the clean cloth squeezed out in the clean water immediately – don't wait for it to dry.

◆If you use anything other than clear water, rinse thoroughly with clear water or the residue could run down and ruin the paintwork.

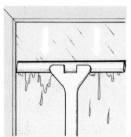 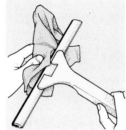

Cleaning large areas of glass *Use a rubber squeegee instead of a cloth. Work downwards from the top of the pane,* above left, *wiping the blade on a cloth after each stroke,* above right; *you are less likely to get streaky windows. Repeat for rinsing.*

CARE OF YOUR CHAMOIS LEATHER

Chamois leathers may be more expensive than other cloths, but looked after well, they should last for years.

◆Don't use powder or liquid detergents to clean the window if using a chamois leather. The detergents react with the natural oils in the skin and destroy them. Stick to methylated spirits, vinegar or clear tepid water.

◆Wash the chamois after use in warm soapy water; rinse it out well in clean water. Do not wring out the water but squeeze the chamois gently and shake it out flat. Allow it to dry slowly away from direct heat and never in sunlight as heat and sunshine will destroy the natural oils in the skin.

◆Crumple and rub the leather when it is dry to bring back the softness.

TIPS FOR WASHING WINDOWS

◆NEVER scrub dirty windows with a dry cloth, you'll scratch the glass.

▼▼ Don't clean windows on a frosty
◆ ◆ day, the glass will be brittle.

◆Don't clean them when the sun is shining (which is when you really want to); the water will dry too quickly, leaving streaks on the glass.

◆Change the water frequently, especially the rinsing water.

◆If the weather is very cold, you can add a small amount of methylated spirits or white spirit to the water to stop it from freezing on the glass. (You have been warned, though, it is better not to wash the windows when the weather is as cold as that.)

◆Use all detergents, chemicals etc. sparingly. There is always a temptation to use too much and that causes streaks and leaves layers of residue. Never use soap because it is very difficult to rinse off.

GREEN TIP: Wash off hard specks, such as fly spots, with warm tea.

◆If you are cleaning the window inside and out, use crossways strokes for inside and vertical strokes for outside, then it will be obvious where the smears are.

Using proprietary window cleaners

◆These are convenient to use but they are expensive. They are available as aerosols, sprays or liquid emulsions. Use liquid sprays because they evaporate quickly without leaving any build-up. The emulsions leave a white smear on the surface which is more difficult to wipe off. Don't use aerosols, they damage the environment.

◆Wipe spray cleaner off with a soft clean absorbent cloth (not paper kitchen towels, as they disintegrate too quickly when wet).

◆If the window is dirty, rinse off the worst of the dirt before applying a proprietary window cleaner.

Cleaning the outside

◆If you have fly screens on the outside of the windows, remove them before cleaning the outside. Brush them with one of the vacuum cleaner brushes, or a stiff bristled brush.

◆For windows that are difficult to reach or higher than the first floor, get a professional window cleaner.

▼▼Don't sit on the window ledge and lean ◆◆ out to clean upstairs windows. Don't lean ladders against guttering and never use a ladder in a high wind.

◆Hang the washing bucket onto the ladder using an "S" hook, available from any hardware store, or use a ladder with a platform. Don't carry the bucket or perch it on a narrow window ledge.

◆You may be able to clean the outside from the inside by using a squeegee with an extending and angled handle.

◆Don't bother with magnetic window cleaners which go over the outside while you clean the inside. They sound fantastic but are not easy to use effectively.

Preventing a ladder slipping *On soft ground, place the ladder on a piece of strong board. Nail a piece of wood to the board to wedge the ladder against, so that it won't slip.*

Removing paint, putty and other marks

◆You can get rid of fresh paint marks with turpentine, dry-cleaning fluid or nail varnish remover on a non-linty cloth.

◆Dried paint can be softened with turpentine and scraped off.

▼▼If you use the time-honoured way of ◆◆ slipping a very sharp knife under the paint and prising it off, make sure you don't scratch the window.

◆There is a special tool available from DIY shops which will scrape hardened paint splashes off the window.

◆Use ammonia to remove putty marks or soften with turpentine as for paint.

◆Don't use nylon pads, wire wool or abrasive cleaners on window glass because they will scratch it.

◆Labels from new windows can be removed with difficulty. Wet the surface of the glass and keep it wet. When the water has soaked in, the label usually slides or floats off.

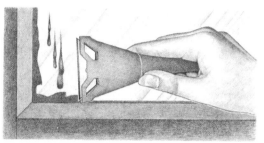

Scraping paint or dirt off the window *Use only razor-sharp blades or a flat razor-type paint scraper. Always work in one direction. Make one forward stroke, lift the tool off the glass, then make another forward stroke. Never scrape backwards and forwards; you risk scratching the glass.*

VERY DIRTY WINDOWS

◆If windows are very dirty, add a small amount of washing-up liquid or borax to the washing water.

🍃 GREEN TIP: Make up a strong vinegar and water solution.

◆Make a strong cleaning mixture by using 125ml (4fl oz) ammonia and 125ml (4fl oz) white vinegar in a bucketful of water. Alternatively, make up a solution of equal parts paraffin, 300ml (8fl oz) water and a cup of methylated spirits, all shaken up well together in a bottle. Wipe the window with the solution, allow to dry, then polish it off.

SPECIAL PROBLEMS

◆If the panes of glass on a piece of furniture such as a glazed bookcase are very dirty, dust them and then wipe the glass over with methylated spirits on cotton-wool swabs. Dip the swabs in the methylated spirits so that they are almost dry and wipe with a circular motion so as to avoid leaving streaks. Change swabs as soon as they are dirty.

Small paned windows

These include window lights and jalousies, or louvred windows.

◆Don't use the squeegee method; unless you have your squeegee cut down to fit, it's pure frustration when dealing with lots of little panes. Wash them with a chamois leather or non-linty cloth.

◆Unlike larger windows, you can leave these little windows for longer periods without cleaning them because they do not show up the dirt like large expanses of plate glass.

◆This is one instance where it probably is worth using a proprietary spray cleaner because it saves time and effort. (Don't use a glass "wax" or polish.) You can use the same cleaner to wipe the little window ledges as you go along.

Stained glass and leaded windows

The term stained glass applies to two main types of coloured glass: that made by adding pigment to the glass during manufacture and that produced by painting the surface of clear glass before firing.

◆Examine the window once a year for signs of weakness in the lead, which is shown by the window bowing out of its true vertical shape. If you notice bowing or cracks, get them repaired by a professional.

◆Most modern stained glass is pretty robust and can be cleaned as for window panes.

◆If you have glass that you think is valuable or vulnerable, just take a little extra care. Wipe occasionally with a damp cloth, but do it very gently. Don't use any commercial detergent or window cleaning product.

◆Never wash painted "stained" glass, because the paint is often loose on old glass, particularly heraldic glass, and this can very easily be dislodged and lost by washing. Dust with a very soft paint brush.

ULTRA-VIOLET FILTERS

It is possible to treat windows with an ultra-violet filter, to protect valuable items and fabrics, for example, from being damaged by sunlight. There are many different types of filter available. Follow the manufacturers' instructions for cleaning because they vary. There are a few general tips:

◆Don't touch the windows for at least a month after treatment with a UV absorbent varnish; you may damage it.

◆Don't use any detergent, cleaning agent, alcohol or methylated spirits on the windows because they can all remove the varnish. Similarly, don't use brushes, a chamois leather or paper towels for cleaning.

◆Don't put adhesive tape on the treated glass; it will destroy the coating.

Wooden window frames

◆Use very little water when cleaning painted window frames and change water often.

◆A rough cloth (terry towelling, say) takes off fly specks better than a smooth one.

GREEN TIP: Remove fly specks from painted frames with cold tea or use a soft cloth dipped in a mixture of equal parts of skimmed milk and cold water.

◆Rub sealed or varnished wood with cold tea or use a liquid abrasive cleaner.

◆Clean waxed wood with a mild detergent solution or fine steel wool dipped in liquid floor or furniture wax. Then polish.

Aluminium window frames

◆Wash with a hot solution of household detergent.

◆Don't use abrasive cleaners as they scratch the surface, but you can use a soap-impregnated pad of finest steel wool for any really dirty patches.

CLEANING FURNITURE

The idea when dusting is to collect up the dust, not just move it on elsewhere. So always use a clean duster, and shake it out after use, preferably outside. It is worth while moving every piece of furniture at least once a year and cleaning each side, as well as the floor behind it; otherwise dust collects, providing a haven for moths and *beetles and making more work for you. To minimize cleaning and prevent marks, stand flower vases, glasses or hot cups on mats, even on marble surfaces, so that the heat or liquid doesn't damage the surface, and put a piece of dark felt or chamois leather underneath ornaments to prevent them scratching the surface.*

WOODEN FURNITURE

Polish does not penetrate the surface and feed the wood, as people tend to think. All it does is fill some of the fine scratches and other blemishes and protect the surface, leaving a finish which is easier to dust.

◆ Never use dusters with raw edges and dangling threads, particularly if the furniture has inlays or veneers – the threads can catch on the furniture, leaving tufts and even pulling pieces off.

◆ Polish, wax and oil finishes need cleaning regularly to keep them in good condition.

◆ A lot of modern wooden furniture is protected with hard-wearing lacquers which need very little special cleaning; just wipe over them with a damp cloth.

◆ Use a soft, old toothbrush to remove dirt stuck in corners. Polish carved furniture with a clean, soft shoe brush; dust with a feather duster.

Dusting carved furniture *Clean modern carved furniture with a feather duster or a dusting brush, which are good at getting into the crevices. Do this fairly frequently or the dust will cling to corners and be very difficult to remove.*

French polished furniture

◆ Rub the surface with a clean, soft cloth.

◆ Polish occasionally with furniture cream applied sparingly. Too much is difficult to remove and looks awful.

◆ Remove sticky marks with a cloth wrung out in warm, soapy water, then dry thoroughly and polish as above.

◆ If a child runs a tyreless toy car over the surface, rub with furniture renovator, working in the direction of the grain. You can try using D.I.Y. French polish, but you must follow the instructions exactly.

◆ If in doubt about your treatment of the piece of furniture, get professional advice.

Alcohol spills on French polish *Wipe up liquid immediately and rub the area with your hand. The oil in your hand will help to restore some of that taken out of the wood by the alcohol.*

Waxed furniture

◆ Treat as for French polish. Don't use the first rag you can find; it's important to use clean dusters and uncoloured polish, or the wood will lose its characteristic lightness.

Painted, varnished or sealed wood

◆ Wash with warm water and detergent. Rinse and wipe dry.
◆ For bad marks use a cleaning paste, but don't use abrasive powders or cleaners because they damage the finish.

Lacquered or japanned finish

◆ Wipe down with a damp cloth when it needs it.
◆ Remove fingermarks with a damp chamois leather and rub with a soft duster.
◆ Polish the surface with furniture cream or spray polish occasionally.

Gilded furniture

◆ Dust gently with a feather duster.
◆ Clean with a soft cloth, lightly dipped in warm turpentine or white spirit. (Warm either by standing the bottle in hot water.)
◆ If any piece of gilt or gesso seems to be flaking, the object should not be cleaned. Get professional advice.
▼▼ Never rub gilding. If necessary, brush
◆ ◆ the dust off with a soft water-colour paint brush. Never let water get onto a gilded surface, or you'll ruin the surface.
◆ Never re-touch the gilding with any form of gold paint because it gives a completely different effect and will discolour.

🍃 **Stained gilding** *Remove stains by dabbing the surface gently with a cut raw onion.*

Veneer

◆ Treat according to the type of wood.
◆ Mop up water spills at once to prevent them marking the surface.
◆ Check veneered surfaces for bubbling when you clean them. Small bubbles in veneer can be re-glued, see page 250; get larger ones repaired professionally.

Marquetry

◆ Dust gently and buff up occasionally. Never wash it; you will damage it.
◆ Lightly polish with a wax paste.
▼▼ Try not to catch the edges of the strips
◆ ◆ with your duster when cleaning.

Plastic laminates

◆ Melamine is easily scratched so don't use scouring powders or pads.
🍃 GREEN TIP: Remove light stains by rubbing with a damp cloth dipped in bicarbonate of soda.
◆ Mop up anything spilled, particularly berry juices, at once with hot, soapy water.
◆ For an ink stain, rub in neat washing-up liquid. For stubborn stains, you can use toothpaste, see below, or apply a paste of bicarbonate of soda and water and rub off after a couple of minutes.

Stubborn stains *Rub a little toothpaste onto the stain with your finger to remove it.*

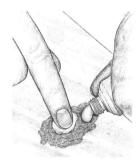

Untreated wood

◆ Unpolished or unsealed wood tables can be washed after use, then dried thoroughly. Don't leave the surface wet.

◆Scrub deal kitchen tables with a clean scrubbing brush and detergenty suds.

◆Rub hardwood worktops or chopping boards along the grain with linseed oil or a fast-drying oil, such as teak oil. Do this about twice a year.

▼▼ Linseed oil is highly flammable so take
◆ ◆ care. Throw away any oily rags – they are flammable too.

Reducing the shine *If linseed oil has made the wood too shiny, rub with a cloth moistened with white spirit. Then apply a little teak oil, gently rubbing it along the grain with fine sandpaper or steel wool, above left. Wipe off the excess, then rub with a soft cloth, using a circular movement to get the oil into the wood, above right.*

Antique furniture

Regular dusting, so that every surface that can be reached is free of dust, is the greatest aid to conservation.

◆Most antiques need only a light dusting. Occasionally, buff up the polished surface with a clean, dry duster or chamois leather.

◆Never use feather dusters as the feathers break and scratch the surface.

◆Be particularly careful when dusting furniture which has pieces of moulding or veneer missing because the pieces next to the gap are nearly always loose.

🍃 GREEN TIP: Remove greasy marks with a chamois wrung out in vinegar and water – 15ml (1tbsp) vinegar to 300ml (½pt) water. Dry well.

◆Polish only once or at most twice a year. Use a wax paste or old-fashioned furniture cream. Apply sparingly and evenly and rub in well until a good shine has been built up. If you put it on too thickly, it will dry before you have finished polishing, leaving the surface smeary and making it difficult to buff up.

◆Never polish near pieces of wood that are cracking or lifting. If wax gets under them, it will make it more difficult to glue back the bits later on.

◆If the dye in the polish is darker than the wood, it will darken it. If using lighter coloured polish on dark wood, take care that no residue is left in the crevices, because it will show up when the wax dries out.

▼▼ Modern furniture cream is not recom-
◆ ◆ mended for antiques because, in order to keep the wax and solvent in suspension, an emulsifying agent has to be used. Although many of these agents are harmless, it is impossible to check all the polishes.

▼▼ Don't use furniture polishes with added
◆ ◆ silicones or aerosol polishes. These give an instant shine but the film does not fill scratches and other surface blemishes, as wax does. With aerosol sprays the solvent comes out with such force that it can damage the polished surface; where they have been used a lot, the surface may acquire a milky look. There is no cure for this short of stripping and resurfacing the object.

◆Don't waste time trying to cure any difficult problem yourself, you will probably worsen it; go to a professional.

◆When cleaning a desk or chest of drawers, check that the drawers run smoothly; if they don't loosen them with wax or talcum powder as described below.

◆Always pull on both drawer handles at the same time and don't knock the drawer to get it in if it sticks.

Sticky drawer runners *If drawers are not running smoothly, take them out and rub a white candle along the runners or sprinkle talcum powder on them.*

Treating specific woods

◆**Fumed or limed oak** Clean with a chamois leather wrung out in vinegar and water. Dry and polish with furniture cream.

TREATING STAINS OR MARKS ON WOOD FURNITURE

◆ Don't use oiled or treated dusters on waxed surfaces; they'll damage them.

◆ Wipe up spills immediately.
◆ Don't use much water on wood.

DRINK STAINS

ALCOHOL
Soak up immediately. Rub any mark with the palm of your hand to replace some of the grease the alcohol will have removed. Wipe with a little teak oil, furniture polish or linseed oil, depending on the type of wood.

 GREEN TIP: Rub with a paste of olive or vegetable oil plus salt or cigarette ash. Then remove the paste and give the piece a coat of wax polish.

COFFEE OR TEA
Wipe up immediately. Treat heat stain as opposite.

MILK
See ALCOHOL

SOFT DRINKS
See ALCOHOL

BIOLOGICAL STAINS

BLOOD
Mop up at once. If natural wood, sandpaper the surface lightly and swab with hydrogen peroxide. Blood is unlikely to mark treated wood.

URINE
Mop up quickly. Apply a little furniture polish or oil, then some scratch cover or boot polish to restore the colour.

HOUSEHOLD STAINS AND MARKS

ADHESIVES
Remove adhesive before it dries, then rub mark with cold cream, smooth peanut butter or salad oil.

CANDLE WAX, GREASE, FATS AND OILS
Veneered and inlaid wood Cover mark thickly with talcum powder, cover that with a few layers of tissues. Iron with a warm dry iron.

Most furniture Remove mark with lighter fuel.

◆ **Waxed oak, mahogany, pine, walnut, beech, elm** Dust and rub frequently. Polish occasionally with a light-coloured wax polish.
 GREEN TIP: A cheap and traditional method for cleaning oak and mahogany is to wipe with a cloth dipped in warm beer.
◆ **Teak and afrormosia** From time to time rub in teak oil or cream – never wax polish.
◆ **Cedar and hardwoods** (usually garden furniture) Remove marks with steel wool, rubbing along the grain. Treat with exterior-grade wood preservative.

Whitewood and plywood

◆ Wipe with a chamois wrung out in warm water. Rinse with cold water and dry.
◆ Remove stains by rubbing gently with fine wire wool along the grain; don't scrub too vigorously or use harsh abrasives.

LEATHER FURNITURE

◆ Dust or vacuum leather upholstery, then clean with saddle soap when necessary. Use as little water as possible. When dry, buff up with a soft cloth.
◆ Rub dark leather once or twice a year with castor oil or neat's foot oil (oil obtained from cow's hooves) to prevent cracking. On pale leather, use white petroleum jelly. Don't wax leather furniture, it won't absorb it. You can clean it with a little shoe cream.
◆ If hide leather furniture begins to look parched, sparingly apply a proprietary hide food with swabs of cotton wool; leave for 24 hours so that it will be absorbed, then polish with a soft clean duster. Alternatively, sponge with a solution of 5ml (1tsp) household ammonia and 20ml (4tsps) vinegar and 600ml (1 pt) water. Then apply castor oil on a

HOUSEHOLD STAINS AND MARKS (Continued)

CIGARETTE BURNS
Treat as HEAT MARKS, see below. If necessary, lightly sandpaper area, then build up again with coloured beeswax, see page 250.

COSMETICS
See ALCOHOL, left.

GRAFFITI
See WOOD PANELLING, page 89.

HEAT MARKS, WHITE
Remove finish with methylated or white spirit. When dry, re-colour wood with proprietary wood stain, scratch cover or boot polish. Repolish the whole surface.
Cellulose and lacquered finishes Rub with brass polish. Wipe off polish before it dries, then rub with a very hot duster (heated in the oven or under the iron). Re-polish.
Oiled wood Rub with teak oil, furniture polish or linseed oil.

HEAT MARKS, BLACK
As for HEAT MARKS, WHITE.

Rub with a cut lemon to bleach the mark, repeating it until you get a result.

INK
Absorb as much as you can into a damp cloth, then rub with a cut lemon.

PAINT
You won't be able to remove dry old stains, so tackle the mark as fast as you can.
Oil-based stains Wipe with liquid furniture polish or turpentine, then polish.
Water-based stains Wipe with soap solution.

SCRATCHES
Rub with a waxy substance of a suitable colour.
Ebony Use black shoe polish, wax crayon, eyebrow pencil.
Mahogany Use dark brown shoe polish, wax crayon, eyebrow pencil.
Maple Use iodine diluted with white spirit. Dry and rewax.
Oak Use white or pale brown shoe polish and rewax.

Pine As for OAK.
Red mahogany Brush iodine over surface with a fine brush. Leave to dry and rewax.
Teak Sandpaper gently before rubbing with a half-and-half solution of linseed oil and turpentine. (Remember that these substances are flammable.)
Walnut Rub with the broken kernel of a fresh walnut.

WATER MARKS, WHITE
Rub with very fine steel wool and oil in the direction of the grain. Apply a paste of mayonnaise or olive oil and cigarette ash (or oil and salt). Buff with a damp cloth. Or apply a half-and-half solution of linseed oil and turpentine, leave for two hours and remove with vinegar.

WATER MARKS, BLACK
Rub surface gently with fine steel wool until fresh wood is reached. Re-colour or stain wood. Re-polish or oil wood as necessary.

---

rag. When the leather is dry, polish with furniture cream.
◆ If the upholstery is badly damaged, do not treat it yourself, but get advice from a professional conservator.

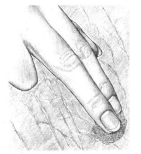 

Seasoning leather upholstery *Rub neat's foot oil (for dark leather) or petroleum jelly (light leather) into the surface of the leather with your fingertips, above left. Then wipe it all off with a soft absorbent cloth, above right.*

Plastic or fake leather

◆ Wipe sticky marks with a cloth squeezed out in warm, detergent solution (not soap) and polish with a soft cloth.
◆ Don't use wax or cream polish, it tends to leave the surface tacky.

Desk and table tops

◆ Wash with a just-damp cloth wrung out in detergenty suds.
◆ Rub with leather renovator or hide food.
▼▼ When using leather renovator, avoid
◆ ◆ any embossed gilding and take care not to touch any surrounding wood.
◆ Rub ink stains very gently with cotton wool dipped in white spirit. Apply white spirit sparingly, it can remove the colour.

OTHER MATERIALS

▼▼ If you are going to take a marble or glass
◆ ◆ top off a table to clean it, don't carry it
flat, as both marble and glass can break under
their own weight. Hold it vertically instead.

Metal furniture

◆Most modern tubular metal furniture
needs only an occasional wipe with warm
soapy water.
◆Check about the cleaning when you are
buying the furniture, because metal parts
may have been given a special non-tarnish
(lacquer) finish. If you damage the lacquer,
the metal will tarnish.
◆Generally, a thin film of silicone-wax polish will be enough to protect the surface.
◆See also CLEANING METALWORK,
pages 102–105.

Cleaning wrought iron *Remove loose dirt on*
wrought iron with a bristle brush. Use a wire brush
if the metal is rusty.

Glass table tops

GREEN TIP: Rub with lemon juice or
vinegar and dry with paper kitchen
towels. Buff up with newspaper.
◆ You can use ammonia or proprietary glass
or window cleaner instead.

Marble furniture

▼▼ Marble is porous so stains easily. Don't
◆ ◆ use any more water than you absolutely
have to when cleaning it.

◆Wipe regularly with a cloth wrung out in
water and mild detergent. Then wipe dry and
polish with a clean, soft duster.
◆Marble that is much the worse for wear is
difficult to deal with. You can rub it with wire
wool and then polish it with an electric
polishing pad to bring back its dull shine or
rub carefully with a liquid abrasive cleaner.
GREEN TIP: You can clean marks with
lemon juice or vinegar, but take great
care. It is best to leave the lemon for no more
than a minute or two. Repeat if necessary;
don't leave it to soak. Then rinse and dry.
◆Proprietary marble cleaners and conditioners can be used for light scratches.
◆Get antique or valuable marble dealt with
professionally.
◆Marble that has been painted may have to
be treated with a paint stripper. Follow the
manufacturer's instructions; several coats
may be necessary. When all the paint is
removed, rub with wire wool and polish with
an electric polisher. This method is frowned
on by perfectionists, but it does work.
◆For cosmetics, tea and tobacco stains,
apply a hydrogen peroxide solution containing a few drops of ammonia. Leave for two
hours and then rinse dry.
◆For grease or oil stains, rub with alcohol,
acetone or lighter fuel, rinse and dry.
◆If anyone has spilled wine, coffee or alcohol, or burned the marble with a cigarette
stub, consult a professional.

Basketware, bamboo, cane and wicker

◆Brush or vacuum regularly to prevent dust
accumulating.
◆If a piece is dirty, scrub with warm, soapy
water and borax or a soapless cleanser and
rinse well. Never use detergent. For a slightly
more drastic clean, use soapsuds plus a little
ammonia, rinse and leave to dry.
◆Rinse unpainted wicker and bamboo with
a salt water rinse to stiffen and bleach them
again.
◆All such furniture will benefit from being
left to dry out of doors on a sunny day (never
in front of a fire).
◆Polish, if you wish, with furniture cream.

CLEANING SOFT FURNISHINGS

As with everything else in the home, the more often you give your upholstered furniture and curtains the once over, the less effort you will have to put into spring cleaning them. If you prevent surface dirt, dust, *sweat, food, etc. landing on the surface, or at least staying there, the fabric is less likely to be marked or damaged and it will last longer. The easiest way to clean soft furnishings is to vacuum them.*

TIPS FOR VACUUMING TEXTILES

◆ Never vacuum fringes or embroideries which have beads or sequins on them, you will pull them off.

◆ Never use brush attachments when cleaning textiles, as brushes of any description can rough up loose threads. Use the general-purpose head.

◆ Never use a vacuum cleaner with extra strong suction on textiles; it can pull out loose threads.

◆ A small, hand-held vacuum cleaner is ideal for most textiles. If you have many curtains and much upholstery, it would be worth investing in one of these as they are light to carry around and far less cumbersome than any other type of vacuum.

UPHOLSTERED FURNITURE

◆ Vacuum the sofa, chairs and any cushions regularly – preferably once a week but certainly once a month when you do your thorough room clean. Clean arm rests, backs and crevices with the upholstery attachment.

◆ Regular dusting and cleaning does prolong the life of a sofa or chair and prevents sharp objects tearing the cushions or somebody's trouser seat.

◆ Before vacuuming, check in the crevices for small toys or buttons and so on; they could block the vacuum.

◆ Shampoo chairs and seats at least once a year – before they look dirty.

◆ Remember that cleaned upholstery gets dirty faster if you don't rinse off all the detergent or shampoo properly.

◆ Silicone sprays can be sprayed onto upholstered furniture to prevent dirt settling. Re-treat every couple of months since people's bottoms are constantly rubbing against the fabric so the finishes wear off.

◆ Use proprietary cleaning products that contain a soil-retarding ingredient.

Loose covers

◆ Removable covers are usually washable and are better if you have young children. Follow care label if there is one or see A–Z of FABRICS, pages 114–18.

◇ *Stretch covers can be satisfactorily washed at home in a machine.*

◇ *Larger cotton and linen loose covers may fit into a domestic washing machine, but it might be easier to wash them in the larger machines in a launderette.*

◆ Ironing may be difficult because of the bulk. Iron on the wrong side so that the fabric does not become shiny, unless it is glazed chintz, which should not be ironed.

◆ Many stretch fabrics are drip dry and don't need ironing.

Ironing loose covers
Iron cotton and linen loose covers on the wrong side, while still damp. Put the cover on the sofa straight away so that it dries to the shape of the sofa.

Cushions

◆Don't overwet fillings when cleaning as this can cause foam and feather fillings to break down or lump together. Some dry-cleaning fluids can have the same effect.

◆Dry clean kapok fillings (a fibre from the seed pods of the kapok tree) but not too often. Kapok can go very lumpy if allowed to get wet, making it uncomfortable to sit on.

◆Cover cushions with removable covers.

Stains

◆Mop up anything spilled at once, before it sinks in far enough to damage the fabric.

◆Blot liquids with salt or tissues and scrape off anything thick with a blunt knife. If the spill leaves a mark, apply appropriate stain remover; treat non-removable covers as for carpets, see pages 81–2, and loose covers according to fabric concerned, see pages 114–18 and 142–44.

CLEANING FURNISHING FABRICS

◆Fitted covers can be cleaned in situ using a dry foam upholstery shampoo. The basic rules are: don't let the furniture get too wet, brush all of the shampoo off the upholstery thoroughly and don't let anyone sit on it until it is completely dry.

◆Test a hidden area before cleaning to make sure the colours don't run.

CANVAS AND SAILCLOTH

◆Scrub with warm sudsy water; rinse in clear water. Dry in the open air.

◆Use a soft eraser for small dirty marks.

GLAZED CHINTZ

◆By rights it should be dry cleaned, but you can wash it in the machine on a gentle wash and a cool rinse.

◆Don't rub, twist, wring or bleach it and, if the glaze is permanent (as most modern glazes are), you should not have to starch it.

DRALON

◆For non-removable covers, use dry foam upholstery shampoo, don't rub vigorously.

◆For removable Dralon covers and curtains, wash in warm water, with a cold rinse and short spin.

◇ The cold water rinse is to cool the fibre so it won't crease and applies to all man-made fibres.

◆Pile fabrics may be brushed lightly when dry.

◆You can iron with a cool iron if necessary, after the fabric is dry. Most of these fabrics are drip dry.

BROCADE

◆Dry clean all brocades because they are so heavy to handle when wet.

COTTON AND LINEN

◆Can be laundered, but remove stains beforehand. If very dirty, soak in detergent or soapy suds in warm water. Wash in hot water and rinse thoroughly.

◆Iron on the wrong side with a hot iron while still damp.

◆Starch cottons before ironing them, they will look better.

◆Replace loose covers with piping while they are still very slightly damp; otherwise the piping may tighten, or even shrink.

REPP

◆Wash as for the weakest fibre, see A–Z OF FABRICS, pages 114–18.

SILK

Used on its own or with cotton for upholstery and curtain fabrics.

◆Dry clean silk taffetas and brocades.

◆Other silks and mixtures may be very carefully washed, see page 117.

◆Iron while still damp with a cool or a steam iron.

◆Clean non-removable covers with dry foam upholstery shampoo.

TWEED

◆Dry clean woollen tweeds.

◆Tweeds made with polyester or acrylic can be washed according to their fibre, see A–Z OF FABRICS, pages 114–18.

◆Clean non-removable upholstery covers with dry foam shampoo. Don't rub wool fabric while it is wet.

VELVET

◆Can be cotton or acrylic. If in doubt as to which fibre your velvet is made of, have it dry cleaned. Many velvets are uncrushable, spot proof and easily washed.

◆To remove creases on loose covers, hang up the cover over a boiling kettle.

VELVETEEN

◆May be cotton or viscose, so wash as appropriate for the fibre, see A–Z OF FABRICS pages 114–18. Shake occasionally while drying and smooth the pile with a soft cloth.

◆May be dry cleaned.

CURTAINS

Remove dust and dirt from curtains by vacuuming, but don't use the brush attachments as you may damage the fabric; use the upholstery ones.

◆Clean curtains, or get them cleaned, at least once a year; they'll last longer. Follow the manufacturer's care instructions. Always test colours before washing; some of them will run.

◆Small curtains can be washed in the washing machine, provided the curtain material and the lining (if any) are the same; if not, one or other may shrink.

◆Large curtains other than sheers become very heavy when wet. Either take them to a launderette which has large machines or have the curtains professionally cleaned.

◆Remove curtain hooks, curtain weights etc. before washing.

◆Wash delicate fabrics by hand.

◆If the curtains are lined, wash as for the weakest fibre.

◆Stretch cotton curtains gently before hanging out to dry so that linings and curtains still hang correctly.

◆Never machine wash, twist or iron fibreglass curtains, or have them dry cleaned; the fibres can break. Always wear gloves when washing them.

◆Never iron plastic curtains; they'll melt.

◆Never soak rayon or silk curtains.

Net curtains

Soak in plenty of warm sudsy water with enough room so they can be gently moved around. Try the bath or the sink if it's large; a small bowl may crease the nets.

◆Do not rub, twist or wring, just move the fabric gently around in the water.

◆Whiten "grey" nylon curtains with a nylon whitener sold specially for net curtains. Rinse and drain them well.

◆Dip freshly washed net curtains in starch to give them a bit of added crispness.

🍃 GREEN TIP: You can stiffen net curtains in a solution of sugar and water – 15g (½oz) sugar to 600ml (1pt) water.

VENETIAN BLINDS

◆Dry dust them from day to day with a clean duster.

◆When the time comes to wipe off the fly spots and unidentifiable marks, about once a year, close the louvres so that you get one flat surface instead of rows of narrow fiddly ones. Brush the mechanism bits using a soft bristle brush. Then wipe the slats down with a cloth dipped in a detergenty solution (add a little ammonia if the blinds are very dirty), or use the glove method with ammonia and cold water, see below. You can take the blinds down completely, lug them to the pavement or driveway and clean them there, but this is difficult, gets in other peoples' way, and you still have to find somewhere to hang them up to dry, so why bother to take them down.

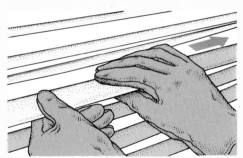

Quick way to clean Venetian blinds *Put on a pair of old fabric gloves (not leather or rubber ones) and dip your gloved fingers into a cold water and ammonia solution – 5ml (1tsp) ammonia per litre (2pt) water. Now run your fingers and thumb along each slat in turn.*

◆Re-hang net curtains while still slightly damp to allow the creases to drop, then you won't have to iron them.

◆Faded areas where the fabric has been bleached by the sun can't be washed out or covered over by dyeing.

◆You can sometimes get mould spots out of net curtains by bleaching, see page 141.

CLEANING METALWORK

Metal surfaces are not infinitely durable, they scratch easily and can wear away. Too much polishing is not good for metal and will eventually disfigure a metal object; so save yourself the work. If you think a piece is valuable, don't polish it with patent cleaners – you could do irreparable damage – take it to a jeweller.

Keep metal in dry conditions to prevent it tarnishing (tarnish is caused by gases and moisture in the air acting on the surface of the metal). Don't use elastic bands to secure wrappings around metals that tarnish; they can corrode it.

Silver

◆ If you use and wash your silver regularly, you won't have to polish it so often, which is easier for you and better for the silver.
◆ Wash as soon as possible after use in hot water and washing-up liquid.
◆ Dust ornamental pieces regularly and wash them once a week to keep them bright.
◆ You can remove small scratches with jeweller's rouge.
▼▼ Don't wrap silver with self-stick plastic
◆◆ film or plastic bags because condensation can form inside the covering and tarnish the silver.

TIPS FOR CLEANING METALS

◆ Wear cotton gloves when cleaning metal, otherwise the acid in your skin will tarnish the metal.
◆ Badly tarnished or dirty antique metals should be cleaned professionally.
◆ Never use silver cleaner on metals other than silver, gold or platinum, unless specified.
◆ Impregnated wadding cleaners are useful for flat objects, but not very good at getting into crevices.

◆ Rub tarnished silver with proprietary silver cleaner. Don't leave any polish on the silver – it will encourage it to tarnish again more quickly.
▼▼ Clean tarnished silver near an open
◆◆ window because it gives off a sulphurous gas when it is cleaned.
◆ A drop of white spirit on a piece of cotton wool will brighten up silver in a hurry before a dinner party. Rinse well.
▼▼ Never clean silver with scouring pow-
◆◆ der; you will scratch it.
▼▼ Never clean silver with bleach as it leaves
◆◆ a permanent stain on silver.
▼▼ Don't dry silver with new linen tea
◆◆ cloths, which still have their "dressing" on, because they are too abrasive.
◆ Use long-term silver polish; it lasts several months in most atmospheres (though only weeks by the sea).
◆ Use dip cleaners for cutlery in daily use for etched and embossed pieces.
◆ Dip cleaners should not be re-used indefinitely because they become over-charged

LACQUERING METAL

◆ Precious metal objects can be lacquered (coated with a special varnish) to prevent tarnishing.
◆ Metalwork that has been lacquered need not be touched again for up to ten years, except for an occasional light dusting.
◆ Lacquering should only be done by experts because the preparation is complicated.
◆ Once metalwork has been lacquered, don't touch it with your bare hands because the acidity in the skin will still tarnish the metal.
◆ Handle lacquered metal carefully because if the lacquer is damaged, moisture can creep in under the lacquer and tarnish the metal, making it impossible to clean. Lacquer is difficult to remove.

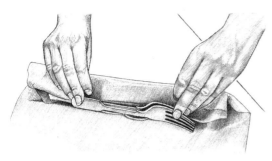

Protecting silver from tarnish *Silver will tarnish more quickly in a damp or salty atmosphere. Wrap it up in special bags or rolls of cloth impregnated with a tarnish preventer, which you can get from jewellers, or with acid-free tissue paper.*

with silver, which is deposited back on the surface as matt silver. Pour some cleaner into a jar and keep that for regular use; never dip anything into your main supply because it will become over-charged and stop working.

🍃 GREEN TIP: Make your own silver dip. Mix up a solution of one part washing soda to 20 parts water and pour it into an aluminium pan. (Don't be alarmed when you see this bubbling like a witches' brew.) Dip the silver into the mixture, then rinse in hot water and dry.

◇ *Don't use this homemade dip for silver settings with stones; you may loosen the setting.*

◆ Make your own silver cleaning cloths by mixing a soaking solution from 10 parts cold water to 2 parts household ammonia and 1 part long-term silver polish. Cut up several squares of cotton and saturate them in the mixture. Leave them to drip dry.

🍃 **Cleaning silver** *Immerse the silver in a bowl containing a handful of washing soda and a handful of foil bottle tops or kitchen foil. Add enough water to cover the silver. (The tarnish collects on the milk bottle tops – but it will also collect on any silver sticking out of the water.) Rinse in hot water and dry. Wipe with a long-term silver cloth.*

CLEANING TOOLED SILVER

◆ Use special silver cleaning brushes, and ONLY use them for silver. For once don't use a toothbrush or a paint brush because the bristles will scratch the surface.

◆ Use a special plate-brush, which you can get from a jeweller, or soft childrens' toothbrush, to get into the grooves on large objects.

Cleaning deep "valleys" *Wrap cotton wool around the end of a wooden cuticle-stick. Dip the stick in a dip polish and work it into the crevices to remove the tarnish. Rinse well.*

◆**Silver plate** Treat as for silver but, since the silver is just a coating, items should be cleaned more gently.

◆**Silver gilt** Never polish it or you will remove the gold completely, revealing the silver underneath, which will then tarnish. Dust occasionally.

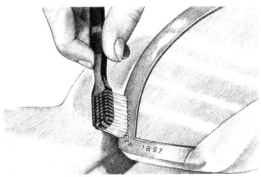

Cleaning engraved surfaces *Using a soft toothbrush, rub each piece with straight strokes, not in circles. Finish off with a soft cloth or chamois leather.*

Gold and platinum

◆Platinum doesn't tarnish and is not affected by acids. Clean with detergent or soap and water solution and dab dry.

◆Never touch the surface of a precious gold

item except to dust it lightly with a clean, dry duster or chamois leather – ordinary cloths may harbour tiny particles of grit, which could damage the metal.

◆ Clean tarnished low-carat gold with a long-term silver polish. When not in use, wrap in chamois leather or acid-free tissue.

◆ For a precious piece, go to a jeweller.

Chrome

◆ Wipe with a soft damp cloth and polish up with a dry one. Very sticky chrome can be washed with a mild soap or detergent.

🍃 GREEN TIP: Polish the surface with a cloth dipped in cider apple vinegar.

◆ A little paraffin on a damp cloth, or bicarbonate of soda on a dry one, will clean greasy deposits.

◆ A thin film of silicone furniture polish protects chrome furniture.

◆ Rub burned on grease with silver polish, whiting or bicarbonate of soda.

▼▼ Don't use washing soda or salt on ◆ ◆ chrome; salt will scratch it and washing soda damages the shine. Never use harsh cleaners – they will wear off the plating.

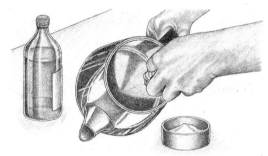

🍃 **Cleaning the inside of a teapot** *Chrome teapots can be cleaned inside with a cloth moistened with vinegar and dipped in salt.*

Stainless steel

◆ Wash in hot soapy water. Don't use metal scourers or scouring powders. If a piece is very dirty, soak in warm soapy water.

◆ You can use a proprietary stainless steel cleaner on the outside of a pan.

🍃 GREEN TIP: Shine the inside and outside of a stainless steel pan by rubbing with lemon juice or vinegar on a cloth.

Brass

◆ Lacquered brass does not need cleaning. Wash occasionally in detergenty water.

◆ If a brass object is very dirty, wash it in a solution of household ammonia.

🍃 GREEN TIP: Clean very dirty brass with a lemon dipped in salt, a paste of equal quantities of vinegar, flour and salt or a paste of vinegar or lemon and salt. Rinse off thoroughly, then clean with brass polish.

◆ Polish with brass polish. Use a soft brush to get into engraved surfaces; a stiff brush could scratch the surface.

🍃 GREEN TIP: Instead of brass polish you can use an essential oil on a soft cloth, but such oils can be expensive.

◆ Ingrained dirt on brass objects such as fire tongs should be rubbed with steel wool or very fine emery cloth, unless they are antiques, in which case get expert advice.

🍃 GREEN TIP: Clean the inside of brass preserving pans with a solution or paste made of vinegar and salt.

◆ Wash and rinse brass pans thoroughly after cooking, and dry before storing to prevent any corrosion.

▼▼ Don't use metal polish on the inside of a ◆ ◆ brass pan you use for cooking; any residue could get into the food.

◆ For antique brass handles Britain's National Trust says that "... as a matter of policy brass fittings on furniture such as handles or knobs should not be polished. The brass should look cared for but not gleaming or shiny. To get this effect brass on furniture needs no special polishing." So why give yourself extra work?

🍃 **Cleaning small brass ornaments** *Small objects can be boiled in water containing salt and vinegar. Rinse thoroughly and dry.*

Copper

Copper's way of tarnishing is to form a greenish surface film (green rust) which can cause nausea and vomiting if eaten.

◆Protective lacquer on new pans must be removed before the pan is used, see page 69.

◆Clean the outside of a pan with a proprietary copper polish.

🍃GREEN TIP: Make a copper polish from equal parts salt, vinegar and flour.

◆Treat stubborn stains with a strong solution of household ammonia.

🍃GREEN TIP: Buttermilk, or vinegar or lemon juice and salt, as for brass, will all remove corrosion. Rinse and dry well.

Bronze

◆Don't touch the surface except once or twice a year, to dust it lightly with a soft clean duster. Don't use a wire brush or harsh abrasives, they will damage the surfaces.

◆Lacquered bronze only needs dusting and the occasional wipe with a damp cloth.

◆Antique bronzes must be cleaned professionally. Don't attempt it yourself.

▼▼Never wash antique or valuable bronze –
◆◆it can cause rapid corrosion, which leads to "bronze disease" when the metal starts flaking away. And never use methylated spirit on antique or valuable bronze.

◆Remove verdigris by scraping lightly with a knife or rubbing with a toothbrush. Heavy incrustations which won't scrape off should be washed with water containing 10 per cent acetic acid. Rinse.

Cleaning bronze *For not very valuable, but very dirty, pieces, wash with a soft brush in very hot water and mild detergent. Rinse, dry and buff up.*

Pewter (Britannia metal)

◆Keep it dry or it will develop a "hume", a sort of grey film, and tarnish.

◆Don't disturb the heavy oxide scale found on antique pieces, the piece may disintegrate.

◆Polish with a suitable metal polish or with whiting and a little household ammonia.

◆Rub badly stained pewter with fine wire wool and olive oil.

🍃**Cleaning pewter** *Rub the surface with a raw cabbage leaf or the green part of a leek leaf. Rinse and dry.*

Lead

◆Scrub with turpentine or white spirit.

🍃GREEN TIP: Remove white deposits by boiling in several changes of water.

🍃GREEN TIP: Place a very dirty object in a solution of 1 part vinegar to 9 parts water with a little bicarbonate of soda. Rinse in several changes of distilled water.

Iron

◆Remove rust by rubbing with steel wool dipped in paraffin. If the item is small enough, soak it in paraffin for a couple of hours, then rub with steel wool. Polish with liquid wax or paint it to prevent it becoming rusty again.

◆Rub large objects (gates, table legs) with a bristle or wire brush. Wipe over the surface with white spirit on cotton wool swabs; don't use water, the iron will rust again.

◆Paint iron furniture for out of doors, otherwise you'll be out in all weathers with your wire brush trying to keep the rust under control. Remove all rust first. Then apply two or three coats of suitable outdoor-quality paint.

CLEANING FIRES AND RADIATORS

An open fire is one of the most primitive pleasures, but having one does involve a fair amount of time and trouble. Even if you don't want a real fire, a fireplace with a well polished or painted grate can provide a focal point to a room.

FIREPLACES AND STOVES

◆ Use blacking or a proprietary cleaner to clean metal parts and free-standing stoves.
◆ Brush the hearth while the damper is closed, to prevent dust from flying about.
◆ If it is an old fireplace and you want to admire it, not use it, you can give it a thin coat of a matt black paint. (A thick coat would hide the decoration.) Thin the paint, if necessary, with white spirit.
◆ Old steel and cast-iron fenders, grates, hearths and irons can be burnished by a professional metal renovator. Your local ironmonger should be able to help you.
◆ Remove old paint with chemical paint stripper, then "blacken" or paint as soon as possible to prevent rust.

The grate

◆ Wood ashes may be left in the grate and will build up a good base for your fire throughout the winter; coal ashes should be cleared out more often, perhaps once a week.
◆ Always put the ash into a metal container to take it to the rubbish bin. There may be hot embers in it which will burn through paper and plastic.
◆ Use a plate brush for cleaning a metal grate, and keep it just for the grate.

Brick surrounds

◆ Clean brick fireplaces with water or a proprietary cleaner, never use soap, which leaves a scum.
◆ For bad marks, apply neat vinegar, then rinse thoroughly.

Stone fireplaces

◆ Wipe with clean water only.
◆ If stained, use a bleach solution, rinse with clean water and dry. Or use proprietary stone cleaner.
◆ Soot stains can be removed with a soap, water and pumice stone solution. Put 1 litre (2pt) hot water to 120g (4oz) yellow laundry soap into a pan and heat until the soap has dissolved. Let the mixture cool, then add 225g (8oz) powdered pumice and 120ml (4fl oz) household ammonia. Mix well and rub the stone with this. Rinse well.

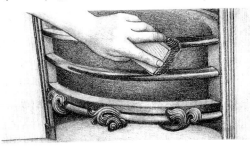

Polishing the grate *Apply the blacking (or metal polish for stainless steel), then, using a plate brush, polish backwards and forwards along the bars.*

Removing bad stains *Scrape these off the stone with a pumice stone or with powdered carborundum and water.*

Tile surrounds

◆ Wash ceramic tile fire surrounds in hot water and detergent.

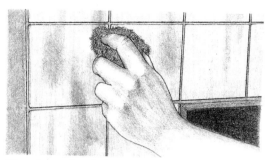

Cleaning stained tiles *Rub stains very gently with steel wool or scouring powder.*

Marble fireplaces

◆ Wipe regularly with a cloth wrung out in water and mild detergent. Wipe dry and polish with a soft duster.
◆ Stains on mantelpieces from coffee cups or wine glasses are almost impossible to remove since the marble will have absorbed them. If they upset you, find a professional stone cleaner who may be able to help.
◆ At a pinch you can rub stained marble with wire wool and then polish it with an electric polishing pad.
◆ If your marble fireplace has been painted, you will have to use paint stripper to remove the paint, see page 98.

Fireguard and irons

◆ Dust the fireguard with a brush.
◆ If very dirty, wash with hot water and detergent or a cloth dipped in paraffin.
◆ Clean brass fireguards and fenders as for brass, see page 104.
◆ Use a toothbrush to clean between wires of the fireguard mesh.
◆ Rub ends of fire-irons with a cloth moistened with paraffin to stop rusting. Clean the handles with metal polish.
▼▼ Most metal polishes are flammable so
◆ ◆ work away from the fire and wipe off all the polish before using the irons again.

Chimneys

The drier the wood you burn, the more efficient the combustion, and the fewer tar deposits you will get in your chimney.
◆ Get all chimneys in use swept at least once a year by a chimney sweep. If you burn wood, get the chimney swept twice a year, as the resin from the wood settles in the chimney and can catch fire.
◆ Modern flues on wood-burning stoves are insulated with a double "skin", which does not give the resin a chance to stick in the same way, but they should still be swept.
◆ If you have a box stove fitted into a closed fireplace by a short flue pipe, it is a good idea to cut a soot cleaning hole with a well-fitted door above the fireplace, for the sweep to gain access with a vacuum cleaner. You can hang a picture over this door when it is not being used.

CHECKING A CHIMNEY

◆ To check whether or not a chimney is clear, hold a piece of smouldering newspaper close to the fireplace while it is cold. The smoke should be drawn up quite briskly.
◆ If the house is old, the next check involves lighting a good fire in the grate and covering it with damp newspaper. Now go round upstairs sniffing for any smoke in the bedrooms.

HEATERS AND RADIATORS

◆ Most heaters need only the occasional wipe over with a damp sudsy cloth.

Central heating radiators

Heat from radiators carries the dust up the wall and spreads over the surface. Cleaning is difficult but worth the bother.
◆ Clean radiators at least once a week during

winter, less often when they are not in use.

◆If the vacuum cleaner has a device for cleaning radiators, use it. You can usually either suck or blow the dust out from behind the radiator. If it hasn't got an attachment, use a good radiator brush. A feather duster will also work quite well, or you can make your own tool, see below.

◆Always cover the floor below the radiator with an old towel or piece of polythene when cleaning, for obvious reasons.

Making a radiator cleaner *Find a stick, rake or broom handle that fits down the back of the radiator. Tie a sponge on the end and cover the sponge with an old sock. Change the sock when it gets dirty.*

Electric heaters

◆**Radiant heaters** These need no particular maintenance other than the normal dusting and occasional wipe with a sudsy cloth.

◆**Convector heaters and radiant convector heaters** Dust regularly to keep the inlet and outlet grilles clean and free of dust and fluff.

◆**Oil-filled radiators** Dust regularly and occasionally wipe with a damp sudsy cloth.

◆**Fan heaters** Need occasional cleaning to remove dust and fluff that may clog the mechanism, see below.

▼▼ Always handle fan heaters gently, especi-
◆ ◆ ally when moving them about the house, because once the fan is out of true, they begin

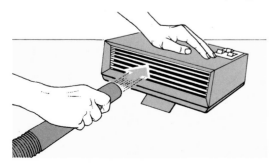

Cleaning a fan heater *Unplug the heater and use your vacuum cleaner to blow through the grille, holding the nozzle about 10cm (4in) away from the fan.*

to make a terrible racket and clatter and become less efficient.

◆**Tubular heaters** Keep the perforations clean by regular dusting. Don't cover with cloths or clothes, or the heater will overheat, which could cause a fire.

Gas heaters

◆Dust and wipe over bottled gas heaters occasionally with a damp cloth.

◆Keep grilles free of fluff.

▼▼ Don't block the inlet grilles of radiant
◆ ◆ convector heaters with nappies, socks or anything else; you will prevent the air from flowing and the elements will overheat. Some models have thermal cut-out devices.

◆Replace the ignition battery occasionally and get the jets cleaned by a qualified gas fitter; don't do it yourself.

◆Put wire fireguards around radiant elements to keep children away.

Paraffin heaters

◆Wipe occasionally with a sudsy cloth.

◆Trim the wicks regularly or the fire will smoke. Most heaters have a wick-trimmer, which is the best thing to use. If that is lost, use a pair of scissors to trim off any rough bits at the top and get a new trimmer as soon as you can.

SAFETY TIPS FOR PORTABLE HEATERS

◆Both paraffin and gas heaters should be burned in a well-ventilated room.

◆Never move a paraffin or gas heater while it is alight; your clothes could catch fire.

▼▼ Never clean an electric heater while
◆ ◆ it is still plugged in; you could get an electric shock.

◆Don't clean a paraffin or gas heater until it has cooled down.

◆Never leave children in a room where there is a portable heater.

◆Never store paraffin in the house and always mark the container clearly.

CLEANING ORNAMENTS

Ornaments need careful dusting to prevent breakages, and an occasional wash, unless they are valuable, in which case take them to a specialist. If you are taking objects into *another room to wash them, carry them in a basket lined wih plenty of tissue paper.*

For cleaning jewellery, pictures and other specialist items, see pages 168–80.

CHINA AND GLASS

◆ Decorative china, ceramics and glass just need careful dusting every so often. If they get very grimy, wipe with a damp sudsy cloth, then with a clean dry one.

China and ceramics

◆ Wipe very fine china kept for display occasionally with a damp cloth, then dry with a linen tea towel.

▼▼ NEVER use detergents or bleaches on
◆ ◆ ceramics to try to remove stains.

▼▼ Don't use cleaning powders or scouring
◆ ◆ powders on china or ceramics, you will damage both the glaze and the pattern.

Cleaning a raised pattern *Brush with a soft brush to clean into the grooves.*

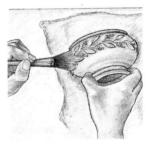

Glass

▼▼ Don't touch glass with painted or gilded
◆ ◆ decoration or early glass (pre 1700); the decoration may not be firmly fixed and could come off in your hand. Very delicately brush with a soft water-colour paint brush or photographer's lens brush.

◆ Glass with metal mounts should only be dusted. If the glass is very dirty, clean it with slightly damp swabs of cotton wool and dry at once. Don't let the metal get wet.

CLEANING CRACKS IN PORCELAIN

◆ Cracks in fine porcelain can often be made less obvious by cleaning.

1 *Cover the crack with a cotton wool pad squeezed out in warm water then dipped in bicarbonate of soda. Leave for several days, wetting the pad occasionally.*

2 *Scrub gently with a fine bristle brush dipped in ammonia solution (5ml / 1tsp ammonia to a cup of water). Rinse and dry.*

Handling a delicate glass *Support the glass while cleaning or drying by cupping your hand under the bowl. Don't hold it by the stem, which can snap very easily.*

TIPS FOR HANDLING CHINA AND GLASS

◆ Handle as little as possible.
◆ Use both hands to pick up an object.
◆ Make sure you have plenty of elbow room and are not likely to knock anything else over.
◆ Never pick up a decorative object by its handle or a delicate plate or bowl by its rim. They are often not strong enough to support the weight of the piece.
◆ Pick up objects with "bocage", or pieces sticking out, by supporting the base with both hands.

◆ Don't grip figurines that have small decorations, such as flowers or leaves on them. The decoration is very vulnerable and pieces can snap off.
◆ If washing china and glass, use a plastic bowl so that you don't chip the object. Don't put more than one item in the bowl at a time.
◆ Put glasses and cups down on a cloth or piece of paper towel to dry, never on a wet, smooth draining board – they slide about easily when wet.

Cleaning vases

◆ Remove the whitish film that is left at the waterline of glass vases with vinegar. Soak a piece of cotton wool or kitchen towel with vinegar and leave it on the ring for five minutes or so, to soften the scale before you remove it.
◆ To get rid of plant and flower verdigris there are proprietary cleaners that you leave to soak in the vase, then rinse out. Alternatively try one of the following:
◇ Fill the base with ball bearings or lead shot and rattle these around in it.
◇ Fill the vase with water into which you put 10ml (2tsp) household ammonia. Stand overnight, then wash and rinse.
◇ Put a little clean sand into the vase with a squeeze of washing-up liquid and a little warm water. Shake well, leave to soak overnight, shake again, then rinse.
◇ Use a good dentifrice powder – a heaped tablespoon to half a tumbler of warm water. Leave it to soak overnight, then rinse.

Removing plant stains from a vase *Put a handful of tea leaves into the vase, cover with vinegar and shake them in the vase.*

LAMPS AND LIGHT FITTINGS

◆ When cleaning any lamp or light fittings, check that all wires are secure, unfrayed and undamaged; replace if necessary.
◆ Clean lamps and shades in the kitchen, bathroom and workroom often, they are more likely to get dusty and greasy than those in other parts of the house.

Table lamps

◆ Take off the bulb(s) and shade. Dust or vacuum the shade and wipe the bulb.
◆ Wash glass or plastic globes and reflectors in warm detergenty suds. Rinse and dry carefully. Or wipe with a chamois leather dampened with methylated spirits or white spirit, then buff up with a non-linty cloth.
◆ Clean glass bases with a cloth wrung out in clear or sudsy water. You can use a toothbrush on cut glass to get into the crevices, but dry the glass well afterwards with kitchen paper or a lint-free cloth.
◆ Porcelain bases, glazed earthenware and china can be cleaned with a cloth wrung out in mild suds. Rinse and wipe dry with kitchen paper or a lint-free cloth.
◆ Wipe marble and alabaster with a damp cloth. They shouldn't need any more attention, but if they do, follow the instructions for marble, see page 98.
◆ Metal lamp bases may be polished if they

have not been lacquered. But you shouldn't do this too often.

◆Lacquered surfaces only need dusting. In fact you can damage the lacquer by cleaning them, see page 102.

Ceiling or wall fittings

◆Clean pendant fittings regularly: bowl shades, in particular, soon become full of dead flies and moths.
◆BE WARNED: some fittings, once together, are not easy to remove, and once dismantled are not so easy to put back together again.

Dusting a ceiling light *Dust with a feather duster, it's much easier on your arms than a cloth.*

Lampshades

◆ Wash kitchen shades with a strong detergent – even carpet detergent in a strong solution – because they get dirtier and greasier than others. Rinse well afterwards or the dirt will be attracted back more rapidly.

Cleaning raffia and straw shades *Vacuum often with the upholstery attachment. If they get really dirty, it is difficult to clean them. You can wipe with a damp cloth, but this is more likely to smear the marks than get rid of them.*

◆**Fabric shades** Vacuum lightly every so often to remove dust. Fabric shades are not normally washable.
◆**Glass and metal shades** Dust with a duster or a feather duster.
◆**Plastic and glass shades** Take down, wash in detergent solution, rinse, dry.
◆**Acrylic shades** Wash in warm soapy water and drain them on a terry towel.
◆**Paper shades** Brush often with a feather duster. Do not attempt to wash. If they get very dirty, buy replacements.
◆**Parchment shades** Wipe with a cloth wrung out in vinegar and water. Leave to dry before you touch them.
◇*Vegetable parchment should be dusted only.*
◇*Imitation parchment can be cleaned with a pencil eraser.*
◆**Silk shades** Get these cleaned professionally before they begin to look dirty.
◆**Fibreglass shades** Wipe carefully with a damp cloth.

SAFETY TIPS FOR CLEANING LIGHTS

◆Unplug lamps and switch off light fittings at the mains before you begin cleaning them.
▼▼ Never touch a live switch or light
◆ ◆ with wet hands.
◆If you are cleaning wall fittings or ceiling lights, make sure you have a steady stool or ladder and somewhere to rest new lightbulbs, mop, cloth, or whatever you are cleaning with.

TIPS FOR CLEANING LAMPSHADES

◆Always remove removable lampshades for cleaning.
◆Some washable fabrics may be stuck together with unwashable glues, so don't plunge a lampshade into water unless you know it is safe.
▼▼ Washable fabrics may not have
◆ ◆ washable linings.
▼▼ Don't let metal lampshade frames
◆ ◆ get wet, they can rust.

LIGHTBULBS

◆ Clean the lightbulbs when you are cleaning the fittings. Take bulbs out of their sockets about once a month and wipe with a damp cloth. (This makes quite a difference to how much light you will get from the lamp – you can lose 20 per cent with a very dirty bulb.)

◆ Make sure a bulb is dry before you put it back to prevent electric shocks.

◆ Fluorescent tubes should be wiped with a damp cloth.

◆ Change fluorescent tubes when they start to flicker; don't wait for the tube to give up altogether.

◆ Keep a supply of all the bulbs in use in your home so that you can change blown bulbs when cleaning the light fittings.

◆**Metallic paper shades** Rub with a solution of paraffin and white spirit or turpentine – 15ml (1tbsp) turpentine or white spirit to 150ml ($\frac{1}{4}$pt) paraffin – and wipe off.

◆**Nylon and rayon shades** Detachable shades should be repeatedly dipped in warm sudsy water. Rinse in warm water. Dry quickly. Do not pull or stretch while wet.

◆ Reflectors of sun lamps should be brightly polished to reflect as much heat as possible. Use a proprietary impregnated wadding which you cannot spill.

▼▼ Don't rub acrylic or any plastics or you
◆ ◆ will increase the static which attracts dust. Rub with an anti-static cloth if they seem to attract a lot of dust.

Chandeliers

◆ Dust them when you clean the room. More thorough cleaning should be done according to the material they are made of.

◆ Spray cleaners are available which allow the chandelier to be cleaned in situ.

◆ Wipe over all parts of the chandelier with a cloth wrung out in sudsy water.

◆ Unscrew and clean every light bulb (no matter how many).

◆ While cleaning, take the opportunity to check the condition of the main chain and the ceiling fixture.

Paraffin oil lamps

◆ Clean paraffin lamps after every use. Wipe the chimney with a damp cloth or wash with sudsy water.

◆ Wash old brass lamps that have yellowed in gentle detergent and water. Then use a spray polish and buff with a soft cloth.

◆ Clean brass lamps as for brass, see page 104, and glass ones as for glass, page 109.

◆ Lacquered brass will just need wiping over with a damp cloth.

◆ Wash the chimneys in mild detergent and warm water and clean with a special chimney brush (slightly larger than a bottle brush).

Trimming wicks *Trim the wick with a pair of sharp scissors, or a wick cutter. Keeping the wick trimmed prevents the lamp from smoking.*

CANDLESTICKS

▼▼ Tempting though it may be, do not
◆ ◆ use a knife to scrape off wax.

◆ Wash china and crystal candlesticks in warm soapy water, rinse and dry. Clean metal ones according to the metal they are made of, see pages 102–5.

◆ Wipe lacquered metal candlesticks with a damp cloth.

◆ Don't immerse weighted or hollow candlesticks in hot water.

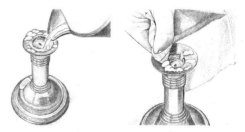

Removing old wax *Pour warm water into the candleholder to soften and remove old wax, above left. To remove wax from outer surfaces cover your finger with a soft cloth and push the wax off gently with your nail, above right.*

Home Laundry & Clothes Care

FABRICS GUIDE

All fabrics need to be looked after correctly if you want them to last. However, some fabrics need special care, which can be time-consuming, so always check the care label *when buying them. If possible, buy machine-washable items, particularly bed linen and children's clothes, and buy drip-dry clothes to save ironing.*

CARE LABELS

All garments made nowadays must have a label on them with details of how to care for them in symbols and words.

◇ The number in the symbols indicates ideal wash temperature. NEW OLD

Normal wash cycle
For cotton and other fabrics which can stand maximum washing conditions.

Reduced wash cycle
For synthetics and other fabrics – bar indicates medium washing conditions.

Minimum wash cycle
For machine-washable wool and wool blends, which need a gentle wash (broken bar).

Hand wash only

Chlorine bleach suitable

Can be tumble dried

Cool iron

Warm iron

Hot iron

DO NOT

DRY CLEANING
Ⓟ A letter inside a circle indicates the types of dry-cleaning fluid that should be used for that garment.

A Any type of fluid can be used; can be cleaned in a coin-operated dry-cleaning machine.

P Many fluids may be used. Any dry cleaner can clean this garment.

P Certain precautions have to be taken. The dry cleaner should be made aware of this.

F Only solvent 113 should be used.

A–Z OF FABRICS

ACETATE
Cellulose acetate fibre usually made from wood pulp.
◆ Acetate is colourfast and doesn't shrink.
◆ Machine-washable: warm wash, gentle action, cold rinse, short spin (but only if care label says so).
◆ Do not wring or twist. Roll in a towel to absorb excess moisture.
◆ Hang on a hanger; don't use clothes pegs, they leave marks.
◆ Iron on the wrong side, with a cool iron. Air on hanger.
◆ Use ordinary dry-cleaning fluids. Don't use acetone, alcohol or acetic acid; they melt it.

ACRYLIC
Fabric made with a by-product of oil.
◆ Machine-washable: warm wash, cold rinse, short spin.
◆ Chlorine bleach won't damage it.
◆ Drip dry pleated garments.
◆ Lightweight acrylics can be drip dried, or dried in a cool tumble dryer.
◆ Heavy jerseys should be pulled into shape and dried flat on a towel.
◆ Brush pile fabrics with a soft brush when completely dry.
◆ Iron, if necessary, with a cool iron when quite dry, on the wrong side.

ALPACA See WOOL

ANGORA
Rabbit hair, often mixed with wool or nylon.
◆ Hand wash and dry as for wool.

ASTRAKHAN
Lamb's skin or imitated skin.
◆ Treat as sheepskin: hand wash as for wool, or dry clean.
◆ No need to iron.

BONDED FIBRES
Man-made fibres.
◆ Machine-washable: warm wash, cool rinse.
◆ Don't rub, spin or wring; they'll crease.
◆ Drip dry, iron with a cool iron if necessary.

BROCADE
May be acetate, cotton, silk, viscose or a mixture.
◆ All brocades should be dry cleaned.

BUCKRAM See COTTON

CALICO See COTTON

CAMBRIC See COTTON

CAMEL HAIR See WOOL

CANDLEWICK
Made of cotton, nylon, polyester, triacetate or viscose.
◆ Treat as for fibre, see care label.

CANVAS
Made from linen, cotton, or man-made fibres.
◆ Wash and iron as for the weakest fibre, see care label.

CASHMERE See WOOL

CHENILLE
May be cotton, silk, wool or viscose.
◆ Wash old chenille with great care, by hand in warm water.
◆ Don't iron. Stretch the fabric gently before hanging it to dry. Brush lightly to raise the pile.

CHIFFON
May be silk, or a man-made fibre, such as nylon or viscose.
◆ Wash as for fibre, see care label.
◆ Do not wring.
◆ Cool iron when nearly dry, stretching gently in all directions and then into correct shape. Don't hurry.

CHINTZ See COTTON

CORDUROY
Can be cotton, viscose or cotton/polyester.
◆ Machine-washable: turn inside out for washing and wash as for most delicate fibre in the fabric, see care label.
◆ Do not rub; you'll damage the pile.
◆ Smooth and shake the pile as it dries.
◆ No ironing needed but you may press gently while still damp, with several thicknesses of cloth between the corduroy and the iron.

COTTON
Natural fibre, sometimes used on its own, or combined with other fibres to strengthen them.
◆ Machine-washable: white cottons are tough and can have a hot wash, hot rinse and long spin, although you can also use a cold wash.
◆ Test coloured cottons for colour-fastness, see page 122, or follow care label. Wash like colours with like.

◆ Wash combined fibres as for weakest fibre, see care label.

◆ **Voile, organdie, and other delicate fabrics, and cottons with drip-dry or water-repellent finishes** Treat according to the care label.

◆**Muslin and chintz** Can be starched.

◆**Buckram** Dry clean.

◆**Chintz** Dry clean or wash as for cotton, but don't rub, twist or bleach. Don't iron chintz because this destroys the glaze.

◆ Iron cotton on the right side while damp, with a hot iron.

CRÊPE

Can be silk, polyester or viscose.

◆ Hand wash in hand-hot water. Roll in a towel to absorb moisture.

◆ Iron on the wrong side with a warm iron while still damp, or use a steam iron.

CRIMPLENE See POLYESTER

DAMASK

Made from cotton, linen, silk, wool, viscose, or a mixture.

◆ Treat as for weakest fibre, see care label.

DENIM

Can be pure cotton or cotton/rayon mixture.

◆ Wash new denim separately as it is usually not colour-fast.

◆**Cotton denim** Machine-washable, but check care label and wash as for weakest fibre.

◆ Choose pre-shrunk denim, otherwise it will shrink.

◆ Iron as for cotton or as care label.

DRALON See ACRYLIC

DRILL See COTTON

ELASTOMERS

Synthetic fibres mostly based on polyurethane, also known as elastomeric fibres or elastofibres.

◆ Follow the care label or hand wash in warm water, or give a gentle machine wash.

◆ Rinse, short spin or roll in a towel, drip dry.

◆ Don't iron.

FAILLE

Made of silk, cotton or man-made fibres.

◆ Treat as for weakest fibre, see care label.

FELT See WOOL

FLANNEL See WOOL

FLOCK FABRIC

Can be of various materials.

◆ Wash according to fibre, see care label.

◆ Don't spin or wring, just roll in a towel to remove excess moisture.

◆ Drip dry.

◆ Iron on the wrong side with a warm iron.

FOULARD

Usually acetate, may be silk.

◆ Treat as for fibre, see care label.

FUR FABRIC

Can be nylon, viscose, cotton, acrylic or polyester.

◆**Cotton and viscose** Dry clean.

◆ If in doubt, wash as nylon, or lightly sponge, rinse and dry with a towel.

◆ Don't iron.

GABARDINE

Made from cotton, worsted or man-made fibres.

◆ Dry clean only.

GEORGETTE

Made from wool, cotton, silk or man-made fibres.

◆**Silk or wool** Dry clean.

◆ Treat man-made fibres according to the weakest fibre, see care label.

◆ Test for colour-fastness, see page 122.

GLASS FIBRE

Fine glass filaments.

▼▼ Hand wash only: wear rubber gloves and
◆ ◆ handle with care, moving the fabric round gently in warm suds.

▼▼ Don't wash with other items and don't
◆ ◆ spin, wring, dry clean or iron.

◆ Don't peg on a washing line; hang over a rail or line, then pull hem straight.

▼▼ Rinse the sink out well in case bits of
◆ ◆ glass fibre remain in it.

GROSGRAIN

Made from various fibres.

◆ Treat according to care label.

JERSEY

Can be cotton, silk, wool, nylon or acrylic.

◆ Treat according to care label.

◆ If there is no label, dry clean.

Continued ▷

A–Z OF FABRICS

LACE

Can be cotton, polyester, nylon or a mixture.
◆ Hand wash with powder or liquid specially formulated for delicate fabrics.
◆ Old or delicate lace can be washed and rinsed inside a pillow case.
◆ Use biological detergents for short soaks only. Take lace out as soon as it looks clean.
◆ Use borax as a water softener, whitener and stiffener.
◆ Squeeze, don't wring. Pull into shape while hanging to dry.
◆ Don't have delicate lace dry cleaned.
◆ **Cotton lace** Starch, and iron with a hot iron on the wrong side.
◆ Man-made fibres shouldn't need ironing.
▼▼ Never spin or tumble dry old lace, you
◆◆ will ruin it.

LAMÉ See METALLIC YARNS

LAWN

Fine fabric of cotton, cotton/polyester or cotton/viscose.
◆ Hand wash in hand-hot water, or give a short machine wash.
◆ Rinse thoroughly, wring or spin.
◆ Iron while damp, according to care label.

LINEN

◆ Machine-washable: hot wash, rinse thoroughly, spin and hang to dry.
◆ Can be starched.
◆ Iron with a hot iron while still damp or spray steam on the wrong side of the fabric, to prevent shiny patches.

LUREX See METALLIC YARNS

LYCRA See ELASTOMERS

MERINO See WOOL

METALLIC YARNS

Aluminium threads coated with plastic and woven with other yarns.
◆ Dry clean only.

MILIUM

Metallic-finished fabric with good insulation.
◆ Dry clean only.

MODACRYLIC

Similar to acrylic but weaker.
◆ Machine-washable: warm wash, thorough rinse, drip dry.
◆ Iron with a cool iron, only if necessary.

MOHAIR See WOOL

MOIRÉ See SILK

MUNGO See WOOL

MUSLIN See COTTON

NET

Made from cotton, nylon or polyester.
◆ **Cotton net** May shrink when washed for the first time, so tack a deep hem which you can let down after washing.
◆ Wash often; once net is grey it is grey for good, although proprietary whiteners can help to restore whiteness.
◆ Rinse, drip dry, and iron on the right side with a warm iron.
◆ Wash net on dresses by hand in warm sudsy water. Rinse well.

NYLON

A man-made fibre used on its own or mixed with natural fibres. Paper nylon is nylon which has been resin-treated.
◆ Machine-washable: wash often in warm wash and rinse in cold water.
◆ **Paper nylon** Spread it out in a bath and dip it up and down. Any dirty marks can be rubbed lightly with a soft nailbrush. Add a starch solution of 50 per cent, if necessary.
◆ Don't use bleach; white nylon may be re-whitened with a proprietary whitener.
◆ Wash delicate and pleated garments after every wearing to keep the pleats in.
◆ Dip pleated garments quickly up and down in the water. Don't twist or wring; short spin and drip dry, hanging on plastic hangers.
◆ If you send nylon for dry cleaning, mark it clearly "NYLON".
▼▼ Don't expose to direct heat or sunlight;
◆◆ the fabric will "yellow" permanently.
◆ Don't iron, although paper nylon can be pressed with a warm iron.

ORGANDIE

Often made of nylon, but sometimes cotton.
◆ **Cotton organdie** Hand wash by squeezing gently in warm water and mild detergent.
◆ Revive limp organdie with 50g (2oz) borax in a litre (2pt) of warm water.
◆ **Nylon organdie** Wash as for nylon.
◆ Iron on the right side while still damp, with a medium iron.

ORGANZA
May be of various fibres.
◆ Treat as for fibre, and handle gently.

PVC
Strong, man-made plastic material.
◆ Hand wash only.
◆ Drip dry only. Do not iron; it'll melt.

PIQUÉ
Cotton or viscose fabric.
◆ Treat as for weakest fibre, see care label.

POLYESTER
Very strong by-product of petroleum. Won't shrink or stretch.
◆ Machine-washable: hot wash, cold rinse, short spin and/or tumble dry.
◆ Don't boil; it'll crease.
◆ Wash pleated garments by hand; drip dry.
◆ Use a cool iron, only if necessary.

POPLIN
Can be silk, wool, viscose or (traditionally) cotton.
◆ Hand wash, and iron according to fibre.

RAYON See VISCOSE

REPP
Can be cotton or a mixture of cotton and man-made fibres.
◆ Treat as for weakest fibre, see care label.

SATEEN
Can be cotton or viscose.
◆ Treat as for weakest fibre, see care label.

SATIN
Can be silk, cotton, polyester, nylon or acetate.
◆ Lightweight satins may be washed as for the fibre, see care label.
◆ Heavy furnishing satins should be dry cleaned.
◆ Press satin on the wrong side while still slightly damp, using a hottish iron.
◆ **Acetate satin** Iron on the wrong side with a cool iron while evenly damp. Don't sprinkle water on it or it may leave marks.

SEERSUCKER
Cotton, silk, nylon or polyester.
◆ Wash as for fibre, see care label.
▼▼ Don't iron seersucker, you will ruin the
◆ ◆ surface. Drip dry.

SERGE
Blends of wool and viscose or other fibres.
◆ Hand wash quickly in warm water; squeeze out water.
◆ Dry away from direct heat.
◆ Can be dry cleaned.
◆ Warm iron under a damp cloth.

SHANTUNG
Silk fabric but may also be acetate or nylon.
◆ Treat as for the fibre, see care label.

SHARKSKIN
Nearly always acetate.
◆ Wash as for fibre, see care label.
◆ Iron on the wrong side with a cool iron when evenly dry.

SHEEPSKIN
Wool from sheep, or may be acrylic.
◆ Machine-washable in the wool programme.
◆ Can be shampooed in hand-hot water with a mild detergent. Rinse in warm water, squeeze, and dry away from direct heat.
◆ Can be dry cleaned. Best taken to a specialist cleaner.

SILK
◆ Weakened by sunlight and perspiration.
◆ Check care label to see if washable; if so, hand wash every time the garment is worn, to remove perspiration.
◆ Don't soak in biological detergent.
◆ White silk may be bleached with hydrogen peroxide solution or sodium perborate, but not chlorine bleaches.
◆ Renovate silk by sponging with a weak solution of household ammonia.
◆ Coloured silks should be given a final rinse in 10ml (2tsp) strong (30 per cent) acetic acid in 3 litres (6pt) water. Dry without rinsing again.
◆ Never rub silk while it is wet.
◆ Stains should be removed by dry cleaning. Tell the dry cleaner what the stain is.
◆ **Brocade, taffeta, silk ties and moiré** Dry clean only.
◆ Cool iron while still damp.

TAFFETA
Made from silk, wool, acetate, viscose, polyester or nylon.
◆ **Nylon taffeta** May be washed by hand.
◆ All others should be dry cleaned.

Continued ▷

A–Z OF FABRICS

TERYLENE See POLYESTER

TREVIRA See POLYESTER

TRIACETATE

Made from wood pulp and cotton. Often blended with other fibres. Won't crease easily, stretch or shrink, and dries quickly.
◆ Machine-washable: short warm wash, cold rinse, short spin.
◆ Dry clean in perchloroethylene. (Care label should have a **P** symbol.)
◆ Don't attempt to remove stains with acetone, acetic acid or alcohol; they will melt the fabric.
◆ Cool iron if necessary, on the wrong side.

TRICOT

Made of viscose, nylon or polyester.
◆ Treat as for weakest fibre, see care label.

TULLE

Fine net of cotton, viscose, nylon or mixture of other fibres.
◆ Treat as for fibre, see care label.
◆ **Limp cotton tulle** Dip in weak starch.
◆ **Limp nylon or rayon tulle** Dip in a gum arabic solution to stiffen it.

TUSSORE (tusser, tussah) See SILK

TWEED

Usually wool, but occasionally made in polyester or acrylic.
◆ Wash and iron man-made tweeds according to the fibre, see care label.
◆ Dry clean woollen tweeds.

VELOUR

Made from silk, cotton or man-made fibres.
◆ Dry clean.

VELVET

Silk, cotton, wool or man-made fabric.
◆ **Cotton velvet** Hand or machine wash in warm water. Short spin.
◆ If in doubt, dry clean.
◆ Steam over kettle spout to remove creases, or iron on the wrong side and brush pile gently.

VELVETEEN

Made in cotton or viscose.
◆ Dry clean only.

VICUÑA See WOOL

VILENE See BONDED FIBRES

VISCOSE

Man-made fibre made of wood pulp. Weak when wet, strong when dry. Can look like silk, wool, linen or cotton, but should be treated much more gently. Rayon is a viscose product.
◆ Hand wash frequently in cool water.
◆ Don't twist, wring or pull while washing.
◆ Iron with steam iron, or while still damp.
◆ Shiny fabrics should be ironed on the right side, matt fabrics on the wrong side.
◆ Don't press over seams.

VIYELLA

Brand name for a fabric that is woven from wool and cotton.
◆ Hand wash in hot water.
◆ Iron with a cool iron on the wrong side of the fabric while damp.

VOILE See COTTON

WOOL

Natural fibre from sheep, lamb or goat. Special wools from alpaca, camel, llama, rabbit and vicuña (now nearly extinct).
▼▼ Don't soak it for long periods; wool felts
◆◆ and shrinks easily when wet.
◆ Use a special cold water wool detergent and hand wash by squeezing water gently through, never rub.
◆ Machine-washable wools are available. Consult the care label.
◆ To whiten wool which has yellowed soak in a weak solution of hydrogen peroxide. Rinse in warm water.
◆ Wash oiled wool in warm water and soap-flakes (not detergent).
◆ Either dry flat on a towel, or give a short spin and hang over a towel rail.
◆ If the wool has shrunk after washing, stretch the garment while drying, first in one direction, then the other.
◆ **Camel hair, heavy flannel, felt and worsted** Dry clean only.
◆ Make sure your dry cleaner knows the garment is made from wool and not a man-made fibre, since so many knitted garments are made of man-made fibres these days.
◆ Iron inside out with a damp cloth and a cool iron.

WORSTED See WOOL

LAUNDRY EQUIPMENT

Do plenty of market research before you buy any piece of equipment and talk to people who have recently bought the make you are interested in, to find out whether they have had any problems. Find out how easy it is to get the engineers to service your machine. Don't forget to measure the space for the machine, before you buy it. If you have a narrow space, the machine that you have chosen may not fit. It is a good idea when buying large equipment, such as washing machines, to choose machines with castors so that they can be moved easily. Make sure that filters can be easily cleaned.

WASHING MACHINES

◆ Combined washing machine/tumble dryers can wash 4·5kg (10lb) but can dry only half that amount at a time.

◆ Check that the hoses are long enough. Some machines have very short hoses and it is a nuisance having to extend them.

◆ If the machine uses cold water only, check that it can actually take hot and/or cold and that a small attachment can be fitted to adapt it to either.

◆ Check the range of programmes on a washing machine – particularly useful programmes include one for an economy load and a separate spin for hand-washed articles.

◆ Make sure that you can use any detergent you wish in the machine.

Automatic front-loading washing machines

These are the most expensive washing machines, but they will wash, rinse and extract most of the water by themselves once you have selected the programme.

Features include capacities from 3–5.5kg (6–12lb) dry weight of clothes, up to 20 different wash programmes, a memory which will run programmes in sequence, and a tumble dryer within the machine to boost the spin-drying operation.

◆ Look for a machine to fit under your worktop. Most are designed to fit under a standard 90cm (35½in) high worktop, and most are 60cm (23½in) wide.

◆ Some machines can be connected to the kitchen taps by a length of hose.

◆ Find out how long the washing cycle is; it can last from 75 to 90 minutes or longer.

◆ Choose one with a "half wash" or economy cycle for small loads.

◆ The faster the spin programme the better, particularly if you have no way of drying clothes outside. Spin programmes range from 500 to 1100 revolutions per minute.

◆ Avoid machines which need to be bolted to the floor; they are awkward to repair.

Semi-automatic top-loading machines

These are very similar to front loaders in that the control of temperature and washing times is automatic but you have to adjust the controls from one cycle to the next.

◆ They can be stored out of the way under a work surface after use.

Twin-tub machines

These machines are also top loading and incorporate a separate washing machine and spin dryer in one unit. They have a capacity varying from 2.75–3kg (5½–7lb) dry weight of clothes.

◆ Choose one that fits beneath the worktop so that you can put it out of the way when it is not in use.

◆ They are much cheaper and just as good as the automatic and semi-automatic machines but involve a lot of work on your part.

Wringer machines

This type consists of a washing machine with a wringer. The disadvantage is that, although you have control over the amount of water you use and number of rinses etc., you have to operate the machine yourself.
◆ Wringer machines are much cheaper than the automatic types.

ELECTRIC DRYERS

◆ If you have limited drying space, a tumble dryer or drying rack will speed things up, but they are expensive to run.
◆ A spin dryer will spin excess water out of clothes and speed up drying. It takes up very little space and is relatively cheap to run.

SPIN DRYER
◆ **Gravity outlet spin dryer** Useful if you only want to spin water out of the clothes prior to drying.
◆ **Pump action spin dryer** Buy this type if you want to rinse as well as spin clothes. Needs to be attached to a tap for the rinsing.
◆ Choose one with a good capacity; most take 4kg (9½lb) dry weight of clothes.
◆ Good for quick spinning: maximum extraction takes about 4 minutes.

TUMBLE DRYER
◆ Don't install a tumble dryer where you have a condensation problem because it will generate a lot of moisture.
◆ Choose one that collects moisture in the cabinet, reducing condensation.
◆ They can be difficult to install because most models must be vented to the outside.
◆ Choose one with programmes for different kinds of fabric.

DRYING RACK
Electric racks are suspended in a bathroom or enclosed in a cabinet.
◆ Useful if you have no outdoor clothes line, or for wet weather.
◆ Not suitable for clothes that must be dried away from a direct heat source.

MAINTAINING LAUNDRY EQUIPMENT

◆ Don't overload washing or drying machines, you can damage the motor.
◆ Unplug machines after use and wipe down with a damp cloth.
◆ Check the filters once a month.
◆ Keep the machine door open to let the air circulate, except when children are about.

Washing machines

◆ Use the right amount of the correct powder. Using more than specified will only make rinsing more difficult.
◆ Don't use abrasive powders to clean the outside of the machine.
◆ Grease only the parts the instruction book tells you to, but don't touch any others.

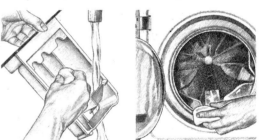

Keeping a washing machine clean *Wipe out the soap powder compartment regularly*, above left. *Wipe the rubber door gasket where water often collects in the folds*, above right; *if left it can rot the rubber.*

Spin dryers

◆ Be careful not to drop things down between the casing and the drum. They may block the outlet or get caught in the mechanism, resulting in an expensive repair.

Tumble dryers

◆ Take off the filter from time to time and remove the blanket of fluff that will have accumulated there.
◆ Don't run them for longer than necessary.

WASHING AGENTS

◆Use a low-lathering "automatic" soap powder or detergent in front-loading machines or you will have soapy water all over the floor. These soap powders can be used for other machines.

🍃 GREEN TIP: Cold water detergents are just as good as hot water detergents, and save on energy.

🍃 GREEN TIP: Use enzyme-free detergents, with as few additives as possible and no perfumes – they are better for your skin, especially if you are prone to allergies.

🍃 GREEN TIP: Use phosphate-free washing powders to minimize water pollution. Synthetic detergents pollute water.

Soap powders

◆Use on their own in soft-water areas. In hard-water areas add water softener as well.
◆Use for normal machine or hand wash, in hot or cold water.

Biological detergents

▼▼ The enzymes in these detergents can
◆ ◆ cause allergies.
◆Use biological "enzyme" powders to break down protein-based dirt in clothes.
◆Most effective at hand-hot temperatures (around 55°C/132°F), but can be used for cold washes. Biological detergents won't work at temperatures above 60°C (140°F).
◆Use in machines with a pre-wash programme or for soaking clothes in a basin.

Soap powder and detergent mixture

◆Low foaming, good for automatic front-loading machines.
◆If washing by hand, make sure the powder has dissolved thoroughly before putting clothes into the soapy water; soap particles may get caught between the fibres.
◆Can be used in hot or cold water.

Soap flakes

◆Good for hand washing.
◆High foaming, so don't use for machine-washing.
◆Best for soft-water areas; use with added water softener in hard-water areas.
◆Use for delicate woollens, articles which are not very dirty, or man-made fibres.
◆Can be used in hand-hot or cold water.

Pre-wash detergents

These consist of a mixture of detergents and dry-cleaning solvents.
◆Use with cold water to soak clothes in, or in a machine with a pre-soak programme.

Laundry soaps

These are bar soaps which can only be used for hand washing.
◆If you live in a soft-water area, they are a better alternative to detergents.
◆In hard-water areas add a few tablespoons of washing soda (except when washing flame-resistant garments).

Fabric conditioners

These are used for soft garments and towels.
◆Add to the final rinse water in a machine or hand wash, to hot or hand-hot water. They make ironing easier by reducing the friction between fabric and iron and prevent static electricity from man-made fibres.
▼▼ Fabric conditioners coat clothes with oil
◆ ◆ or metal and contain enzymes; never use them for babies' nappies or clothes worn by people with sensitive skins.

Fabric whiteners

◆Get the right one for the fabric: some are for treating nylon and wool, others for curtain net, etc.
◆Add a whitener when washing or rinsing whites that have gone yellow or grey.

WASHING AND DRYING

Sort the wash out into suitable piles, reds and browns together, whites together, hot wash items together, hand wash items together, etc. Never mix them, the results are often disastrous. Before washing anything: make sure the pockets are empty; close zippers – open ones can damage other items as well as pull the clothes out of shape – and do up buttons; and mend any tears, however small – even hand washing will make them bigger. Don't wash more than you can dry easily or your home will look like a laundry.

SOAKING

Soaking before washing is the best way to get rid of stubborn dirt.

◆ Search for stains and, if necessary, soak the garment for 12 hours in detergent solution or treat with a proprietary pre-wash treatment.

◆ Use the pre-soak programme on your washing machine if space is limited.

◆ Start the soak with warm water to loosen the dirt; hot water sets it.

◆ Don't soak clothes in an enamel or a metal container; it may rust. Use a plastic bucket that's large enough to enable the clothes to wallow in the water.

◆ Make sure the powder is thoroughly dissolved before putting clothes in.

◆ For particularly obstinate stains, rub neat detergent into the mark before putting the item in to soak.

◆ Be patient. A long soak is more effective than a thorough wash.

◆ Never soak silks, woollens, leather, fabrics with flame-resistant finishes, non-colourfast or drip-dry fabrics.

◆ Never soak coloureds and whites together; colours may run.

◆ Never soak metal zip fasteners in biological detergent; they will rust.

TESTING FOR COLOUR-FASTNESS

◆ Test colour-fastness on any fabric you are not sure about. Test on a hidden area such as the hem.

1 Dampen a pad of cotton wool and leave it on the fabric for five minutes.

2 If any dye comes off on the cotton wool, do not wash the fabric but get it cleaned professionally.

MACHINE WASHING

◆ If you have only a few garments of various types of fabric to wash, you can put them all in the machine together (provided the colours won't run), but you must then wash them as for the most delicate fibre.

◆ Use less powder. Most manufacturers recommend more than necessary and you can usually use half as much, if not less.

◆ If there are suds left in the water after the last rinse, put the things back in for one more rinse and put a teacupful of vinegar into the washing machine.

◆ If your wash turns pink or blue because you've added a garment of the wrong colour by mistake, remove the offending article, then put all the affected garments straight back into the machine and put them through another complete wash cycle. Quick action may be enough to wash all the colour out.

BLEACHING

▼▼ Never use undiluted hypochlorite
◆ ◆ (chlorine) bleaches; they'll burn holes in the fabric.

▼▼ Never use chlorine bleach on wool,
◆ ◆ silk, rayon, drip-dry or deep-coloured cottons, or cottons with finishes.

▼▼ Check the care label to see if bleach is
◆ ◆ safe on a fabric. If in doubt, try a weak solution on a hidden part of the fabric.

◆ Don't bleach damaged or discoloured materials; they won't bleach evenly.

◆ Rinse fabric thoroughly after bleaching.

◆ Don't wash unbleached fabrics with garments that have been soaking in bleach; the bleach from the latter may bleach the other in patches.

◆ Don't use metal containers for bleaching fabrics in – they will rust – and test the container first with a little bleach to make sure that it is colour-fast.

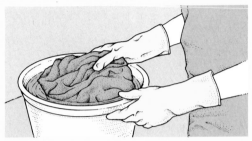

Protecting your hands *Always wear rubber or plastic gloves when bleaching fabrics.*

HAND WASHING

Sort the wash according to the hand wash part of the care label: cool (30°C/80°F) feels cool to the hands; warm (40°C/104°F) feels comfortably warm; hand hot (50°C/122°F) is as hot as the hand can bear.

◆ Before putting clothes in the water, make sure the detergent has dissolved.

GREEN TIP: Instead of detergent, bar soap and some washing soda dissolved in hot water make a good soft soap which is just as effective for cleaning clothes.

◆ Soak clothes (except for woollens) for about two hours before hand washing to loosen the dirt.

◆ Some fabrics, including wool, can be given a short spin in the machine to remove most of the water.

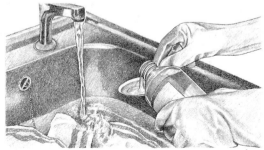

Getting rid of soap scum *Add a tablespoon of vinegar to the rinsing water.*

SPECIAL PROBLEMS

◆ Wash often-used garments and fabrics frequently. This will prevent them from greying and will make stains easier to remove if spills occur.

◆ Air dry-cleaned blankets, duvets and pillows thoroughly before use because the fumes are extremely toxic. Never use coin-operated dry-cleaning machines for these articles because the fumes remain in them.

Collars, cuffs, hems, turn-ups

◆ Dampen them and rub a bar of soap along the grimy mark. Leave for five minutes, then scrub with a nailbrush or old toothbrush. Then wash as usual. Alternatively, use a stain remover, see page 140.

Elastic and elasticized garments

◆ Never boil or wash in hot water – they'll shrink. Don't wring or pull – they'll stretch.

◆ Give a very short spin or roll in a towel to remove excess moisture.

Knitted clothes

◆ To wash knitted items, use a liquid detergent or special wool detergent and gently squeeze the water through the garment. Never rub wool while wet – it will shrink.

◆ Don't spin or pull knitted man-made fibres while they are still wet and warm.

▼▼ Don't hang knitted garments up while
♦♦ heavy with water; they will stretch.

Washing knitted garments *Wash by hand, then roll them carefully in a towel to remove excess water. Then lay flat on a dry towel. Pull gently into shape and leave to dry away from direct heat.*

Lace

◆ Pre-soak in warm water.

◆ Hand wash in warm or hand-hot water.

◆ Don't use bleaches on delicate lace.

◆ Wash lace seldom if you don't want it to end up looking like an old rag.

◆ Never mix lace of different colours; the colours often run.

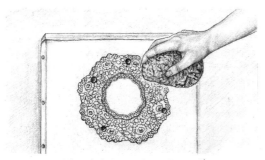

Washing old and delicate lace *Pin it flat on a linen-covered board, using pins that won't rust. Sponge it clean with soapy water and then leave to dry on the board.*

Pleated skirts

◆ Get them dry cleaned professionally unless the care label is very clear about how to wash them yourself.

Nappies

◆ If using fabric nappies, scrape off any faeces as soon as you've changed the baby, and put the nappy to soak straightaway in a bucket full of detergent solution or proprietary soaking liquid, preferably with a lid.

◇ *If you leave the nappy lying about it will begin to smell of ammonia and attract flies.*

◆ Use soap flakes instead of washing powders to prevent rashes.

◆ Wash nappies in the hottest wash or, if you have to hand wash them, boil them from time to time.

◆ Rinse thoroughly after washing – any remaining soap may irritate the baby's skin.

Blankets

◆ If wool, have them dry cleaned. Other fibres may be washed but if they are bulky and heavy they may not fit into your machine. Take them to the launderette or have them dry cleaned too.

◆ If you machine-wash blankets, use the wool programme with a very short spin.

Duvets

◆ To keep a duvet as clean as possible, always use a cover, and wash it frequently.

◆ Check the care label to see if the duvet can be washed; most synthetic fibre duvets can be washed by hand or machine.

◆ Have feather and down duvets cleaned by specialist firms.

◆ Washable children's duvets will fit into an ordinary washing machine; double duvets may need to go to the launderette.

Pillows

◆ Pillows take ages to dry, so always use a pillow case and wash it frequently.
◆ Foam and feather pillows can be hand or machine washed. Polyester pillows should be washed on a cool wash, then drip dried.

1 To hand wash, immerse the pillow in tepid water with 30g (1oz) of washing soda or soap suds, and squeeze the water through.

2 Rinse by lifting up and allowing to drain and then immersing again. Repeat the process, two or three times if necessary.

◇ *If you used soapsuds, soften the first rinsing water with a little ammonia to get rid of the soap.*

3 While drying, turn the pillow over several times until completely dry. This could take several days. Finish it off by drying in the airing cupboard.

◇ *If you can get a pillow into a spin dryer, give it a short spin before drying.*

Sheets

◆ When these become discoloured try rubbing liquid detergent on and leave for an hour or two before rinsing. Alternatively, try a slightly hotter wash than usual, though this may cause creases, especially in polyester/cotton sheets so the sheets may need ironing thereafter. They may also lose some of their colour.

Towels

◆ Wash frequently, using a hot wash.
◆ Greying, but still good, towels can be dyed. Use colourfast dyes and trim the ends with bias binding, if they need it.

Tablecloths

◆ Soak tablecloths before washing to remove food and wine stains.
◆ Wash and rinse linen that is to be stored to prevent moths.
◆ Intractable stains on white linen may be removed with a little neat dye remover.

STARCHING

◆ Don't use starch on anything except cotton or linen.
◆ It is easier to starch clothes in a basin than in a washing machine.
◆ Starch the clothes after washing and spin them after starching. Rinse the machine afterwards to get rid of starch deposits.
◆ Spray starches are expensive but convenient. They last for one wash only but are good for collars and cuffs, and for freshening garments between washes.

DRYING CLOTHES

Care labels usually indicate whether a fabric is suitable for tumble drying, drip drying, line drying, or drying flat. Before following the suggested method, check the label to see if the fabric can be given a short or long spin to remove excess water.

◆ A tumble dryer is the most efficient but most expensive system. Most fabrics can be dried in a tumble dryer with variable heat, except for woollens, other knitted fabrics, delicate fabrics and elastomers.
◆ Man-made fibres must be given a cool tumble so that they do not shrink or take on permanent creases. Cool tumbles can also reduce creasing in natural fabrics.
◆ Drying fabrics in the open air keeps them fresh and is particularly good for white cottons, which are whitened by the sun.
◆ Do not dry nylon, wool or silk in the sun; nylon discolours and wool and silk are weakened.
◆ Drip dry lightweight acrylics, elastomers, nylon and pleated garments. Hang them on hangers if possible.
◆ Roll delicate fabrics, such as acetates, silks, chiffon and crêpe, in a towel or sandwich them between two towels to absorb excess moisture. Then hang them on a hanger indoors to dry.
◆ Knitted fabrics should be laid flat on a towel to dry, away from a direct heat source, and pulled gently into shape.
◆ Almost dry fabrics can be left in a warm cupboard or airing cupboard.

IRONING

*Buy drip-dry or easy-to-care-for polyester/
cotton clothes and wash them correctly in
order to minimize the amount of ironing
you have to do.*

*Most fabrics are easier to iron if they are
damp: either tumble dry them to the right
dampness, bring them in from the garden at
the correct moment, or dampen them as you*

*iron them. If you don't have time to do all
the ironing, put the damp clothes in a plastic bag and keep them in the deep freeze
until you have a chance to finish them off;
that way they won't go mouldy.*

*Ironing can be less of a chore if you listen
to the radio or watch television at the same
time, and you can sit down to do it.*

TYPES OF IRON

There are basically three types of hand iron:
dry irons, steam irons and combined
steam/spray irons. All electric irons have
heat settings marked either with the names of
the fabrics they are suitable for, or with the
dots corresponding to the care labels code,
or (as in older irons) numbered heat settings:
1 = cool, 2 = warm, 3 = hot and 4 = very hot.
There is usually only one heat setting for
steam ironing; fabrics that need a cool iron
cannot be steam ironed.

◇**Dry irons** These can be set to the heat
required for the fabric you are ironing, but
cannot dampen it as you iron.

◇**Steam irons** These have a chamber for
water which is turned to steam and automatically dampens the clothes as you iron.

◇**Steam-spray irons** The same as steam
irons but can shoot out a jet of steam when
you operate a thumb control, which is good
for quick dampening and for certain fabrics,
such as linen, which crease heavily.

◆ Steam irons can be used as dry irons.

Choosing an iron

◆ Make sure the iron has a label saying that it
meets the safety standards in its country of
manufacture and/or sale.

◆ A closed handle gives a better grip and
better balance, but an open handle (with a
gap in the front) makes it easier to iron folds
and pockets.

◆ Irons vary in weight from less than 1kg

(2lb) to more than 1.5kg (3½lb). Steam irons
are usually larger and heavier and may weigh
up to 1.8kg (4lb) when filled. Choose an iron
that feels right for you, although a very light
iron may not be as effective at smoothing out
creases as a heavier one.

◆ See where the cable is fixed. It may be on
the left or the right or on top of the heel of the
handle. Choose an iron where the flex will be
least in the way; a top-fitting flex is better for
left-handed people.

◆ Cordless irons can be easier to use because
no flex gets in the way.

◆ An iron with a button groove is useful.

◆ Look for an iron with a pilot light that
comes on when the iron is heating and goes
off when it reaches the chosen temperature.

◆ Non-stick sole plates are easier to keep
clean.

◆ Run your finger over the sole plate to
check that the design of vent holes or screws
and openings has not got in the way of its
smoothness.

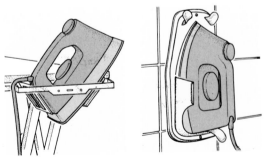

Storing the iron *A heel rest stops the iron tipping
over when upright, above left. A wall bracket is
invaluable for storing the iron when not in use, above
right; you can put it inside a cupboard.*

IRONING BOARDS

Most ironing boards are adjustable. Find one which you can set up and put down easily and which does not weigh too much; some are very cumbersome.

◆ There are various widths: choose one which suits the ironing that you do.

◆ Make sure there is a secure heat-proof plate to stand the iron on.

◆ Tie covers for boards are available in cotton, siliconized cotton, or stain- and scorch-resistant material. They are often lined with milium to retain the heat and make the ironing smoother.

◆ A flex holder is useful, attached to the board or to the iron, to keep the flex out of the way of the clothes.

◆ A sleeve board, either loose or attachable, is useful for ironing sleeves and children's clothes.

◆ Steam irons are easier to fill, or top up, if there's a water-level gauge or if the water container is made of clear plastic.

◆ Choose an iron that can be switched directly from steam to dry so that you can iron different fabrics easily.

◆ Choose a steam iron that can be filled with tap water; it'll save hunting for distilled water.

Rotary irons

A rotary iron has a large padded roller and a curved, heated metal ironing plate which presses against it.

◆ Ideal for ironing large items, such as sheets, tablecloths or other large, flat pieces of fabric, because it has such a large ironing area. With practice, even shirts can be ironed much more quickly than with a hand iron.

◆ Rotary irons are expensive and take up a lot of room.

MAINTAINING IRONS

◆ Rub persistent stains gently with a piece of fine wire wool when the iron is cold.

◆ If you run out of distilled water, use the defrosted water from your fridge or freezer or water that has been boiled in the kettle; don't use tap water unless your iron has a special valve.

◆ Buy distilled water from a hardware shop. Distilled water obtained from a garage may be for batteries, in which case it may contain acid, so it's better not to risk it.

◆ You must have the iron at the "steam" setting if you are using it with steam.

◆ Irons and non-stick sole plates are best cleaned with a sponge dipped in warm water and detergent. Never use an abrasive.

◆ Sticky sole plates often result from ironing man-made fibres with a very hot iron.

◆ Starch marks can be cleaned from the sole plate by rubbing them with olive oil while the iron is warm.

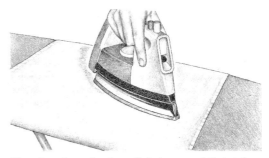

Cleaning the sole plate *Rub the iron while it is hot over a piece of coarse damp cloth held tight over the ironing board.*

SAFETY TIPS

◆ Do not wrap the flex round and round the iron while it is hot; you may damage the flex.

◆ Always replace worn flexes.

◆ Don't leave the iron on while answering the door/telephone/baby's cry.

◆ Never fill a steam iron while it is on; you could electrocute yourself.

◆ Never leave a hot iron where a child can get hold of it.

IRONING TECHNIQUES

◆ Use a plant spray for dampening clothes. After spraying, roll them up so that the dampness becomes evenly distributed.

◆ Leave the iron for five minutes after you turn it on before you start ironing. The thermostat takes time to settle and the initial temperature may be higher than you've set it.

◆ Start with the items that require cool ironing first. Adjust the setting upwards as you come to the more robust fabrics, like cotton and linen.

◆ Always iron at the temperature given on the care label. When there is no label, iron clothes on the lowest setting, unless you are sure they are cotton or linen.

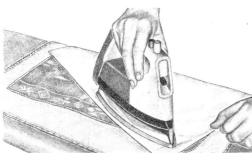

Ironing an embroidered pattern *Lay a clean cloth on a folded blanket. Place the embroidery face down on this. Put a thin dampened cloth on the back of the embroidery and quickly apply a hot iron.*

Ironing a shirt

This technique can be used for dresses as well. Always start at the top and work down.

1 Iron the collar starting at the points and working towards the centre back, on both sides. Then iron the cuffs.

2 Iron the sleeves, starting at the under-arm seams. Run the point of the iron into the gathers at the cuff and then work up towards the shoulder.

3 Iron the body, starting at one front and working round. Hang the shirt to air.

Ironing trousers

This technique is for trousers with a centre crease down the legs. If you don't want creases, don't iron right over the inner and outer edges of the legs.

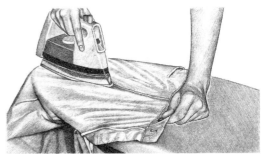

1 Iron the pockets. Then fit the top part of the trousers over the end of the ironing board, and iron.

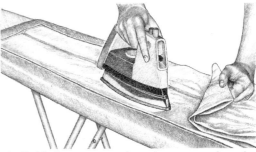

2 Fold the trousers lengthways so that the seams are in the middle and the creases at the outside edges. Iron the inside and then the outside of one leg. Turn the trousers over and repeat on the other leg.

TIPS FOR IRONING

◆ Pull flat articles (tea towels, napkins, scarves) into shape before ironing to get them quite square.
◆ Tack pleats into place before ironing them; they will be easier to iron.
◆ Iron sheets folded. Fold each sheet lengthways twice with the right side inwards, then reverse the top flap.
◆ Embossed cottons should be pressed rather than ironed, on the wrong side. Don't slide the iron over the surface or you will flatten the pattern.
◆ Iron acetate, acrylic, crêpe, flock fabric, cotton lace, linen, satin, silk, triacetate, matt viscose, viyella and wool garments inside out.
◆ Iron cotton (except for chintz), net and silky viscose right side out, while damp.
◆ Iron polyester and polyester/cotton mixtures either way.

PRESSING

This is for garments you can't iron.
◆ Use a hot iron and a clean, damp, lint-free cloth (a tea cloth is good).
◆ You can buy trouser presses, which press trousers overnight.

1 *Place the garment on the ironing board with the tea cloth on top.*

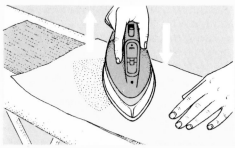

2 *Press the iron down, then lift it, then press it again, etc. all over the cloth until it is dry.*

CARING FOR SPECIAL ITEMS

Take special fabrics such as leather, suede and fur, to specialist cleaners for regular overall cleaning. There are, however, things you can do yourself that will prolong their life and reduce the need for dry cleaning or repair: clean marks as soon as possible to prevent staining – apply fuller's earth or unperfumed talcum powder to the skin, leave it for an hour then brush it off; apply scent before putting on a fur or leather garment, and wear a scarf around your neck because perfume stiffens the skin; avoid wearing brooches on leather, suede or fur because they can tear the skin.

DRY CLEANING

◆ Check the care label first, to make sure that the garment can be dry cleaned (indicated by a circle, see page 117).
◆ Dry clean any garments which have a fabric you are unsure about.
◆ Dry clean garments as soon as any dirt shows around the collar and cuffs. The dirtier the garment, the more difficult it will be to get really clean again.
◆ For leather and fur, choose a specialist dry cleaner; you can normally tell by the rows of suede and leather dyes on the shelves.
◆ The best cleaners will touch up faded colours, repair damaged cuffs, collars and pockets and match any replacement buttons at the same time.
◆ Always remove buckles and trimmings on clothes.
◆ Explain the cause of any stain on a garment so that the cleaner will know how to deal with it.

LEATHER AND SUEDE

◆ Use warm water with detergent and a soft cloth to wipe muddy or dirty leather boots, coats or bags.

◆ To stop the collar of a suede or leather garment getting dirty, wear a scarf or a shirt with a high collar between your neck and the collar of the garment.

◆ Condition new or newly cleaned leather to prevent it from drying out.

◇ *For ordinary leather use neat's foot oil, lanolin or castor oil. Rub the oil in with your fingers or a soft cloth pad, allowing it to soak in until the leather is soft.*

◇ *For shiny and patent leather use a half-and-half mixture of lanolin and castor oil. Don't use neat's foot oil – it makes patent leather very difficult to polish.*

◇ *On white or pale-coloured leather use white petroleum jelly.*

◆ Clean suede regularly to keep it in good condition. Always clean it before putting it in storage.

◆ Oil or grease stains are very difficult to remove from suede. Try making a thick paste with fuller's earth and a little dry-cleaning fluid and rub it into the stain. Leave it for several hours or overnight if possible, then brush it all off.

◆ Use a suede-cleaning cloth to remove the greasy marks round the neck of a garment.

◆ If the suede looks a little flat and tired, use a proprietary suede cleaner to liven it up.

▼▼ Never use chemical fluid or spot cleaner
◆ ◆ on a suede garment; the colour will run and you will get ugly rings round the stain.

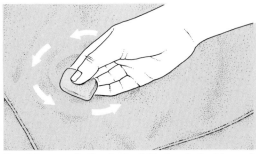

Brushing suede *Suede should be brushed with a soft rubber or bristle brush, or a wire suede brush. Do not rub too hard and do it in a gentle circular motion, eventually covering the whole of the leather.*

◆ Proprietary stain repellents that protect suede against food and water marks are available, but these should be used only on clean garments.

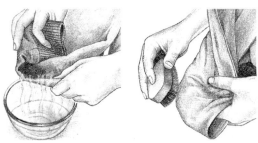

Reviving flattened suede *Hold the article over a bowl of boiling water or a kettle spout,* above left, *let the steam get well into the nap, then brush it up with a soft bristle brush,* above right.

Leather gloves

◆ Wash pale-coloured gloves every time you wear them.

◆ If you'd rather dry clean your pale gloves, rub any marks with dry pipeclay, which will not discolour them.

1 Wash gloves while wearing them, with warm water and soap flakes. Leave a little soap in the gloves after washing.

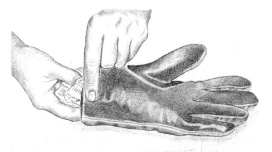

2 Dry the gloves on a wooden or wire "hand", or stuff with newspaper.

3 When dry, soften them by rubbing them between your fingers. Finish by giving them a good shake.

Boots, shoes and bags

◆ Stuff leather shoes, boots and bags with newspaper when wet, to keep their shape. Allow them to dry naturally, in a warm place but away from direct heat.

◆Always use shoe trees in shoes, or rolled up newspapers or magazines in boots, to keep the shape of footwear while you are not wearing it.

◆Stuff leather bags with crushed newspaper while you are not using them to help them keep their shape.

◆Rub soles and uppers of wet shoes, and the leather of bags, with leather conditioner or castor oil to soften the leather. The same goes for hard, dry shoes which have been tucked away at the back of the wardrobe for months.

◆Clean leather handles, which get dirtier quicker than the rest of the bag, with saddle soap and then rub with leather conditioner. Buff up the leather well.

◆Dry clean the lining of leather bags with fuller's earth or non-perfumed talcum powder. Brush or vacuum it out well. Alternatively, rub the lining with a damp cloth soaked in soapy water and then clean water. Allow to dry away from direct heat.

Artificial leather

◆Wipe after use with a soapy cloth. Treat any remaining marks with a paste of French chalk and water, spread over the stain. Leave until dry and then brush off.

POLISHING BOOTS AND SHOES

◆Polish leather boots and shoes regularly with shoe cream or polish, choosing the colour carefully.

◆Apply shoe cream with a soft cloth.

◆If applying polish, use three different brushes; a stiff one for taking off mud and surface dirt; a soft one for applying the polish all over; a medium one for buffing up.

◆For best results use a "buffer" for getting a brilliant shine. This can be a small pad covered in velvet, about 12 × 8cm (5 × 3in).

◆Clean patent leather with a soft damp cloth and detergent. Buff up with a soft cloth. Wax will crack the leather.

CLEANING SPECIFIC LEATHERS

◆**Buckskin** Brush well to remove dust. Rub off difficult marks with sandpaper or use a proprietary cleaner.

◆**Calf** Can become stiff if dried too quickly or near heat. Soften it by rubbing a mixture of milk and water into the surface of the leather.

◆**Crocodile** Buff up frequently with a soft cloth after wearing. You will only occasionally need a shoe cream.

◆**Pigskin** This is very difficult to clean. Try to keep the pigskin from getting too grubby, and try a dry-cleaning powder such as fuller's earth to absorb grime. Brush it off gently with a soft brush.

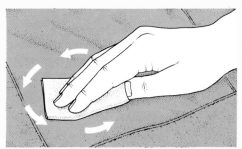

Removing obstinate marks from buckskin
Rub the skin gently in a circular movement with a piece of very fine sandpaper.

FURS

◆Get good furs professionally cleaned once every year.

◆If an old fur coat has a "do not dry clean" label, use fuller's earth. Brush it well into the fur, leave for a couple of hours and carefully brush out again.

◆Fur fabric will have washing instructions on the care label. Cotton and viscose should be dry cleaned. Other fibres can be washed as for nylon. Alternatively, sponge the garment with a solution of warm detergent and rinse. Pat gently with a towel to dry.

▼▼Do not dry wet fur near direct heat ◆◆ because it will become stiff. Shake it well and then hang it up to dry on a tailor's hanger, in a well-ventilated place.

DYEING FABRICS

Dyeing fabrics at home is easy and cheap, and is a good way of rejuvenating old or faded clothes, linen or curtains.

Wash articles before dyeing them to remove any starches or other dressings and remove stains, see pages 142–43, so that the fabric will take colour evenly; you may even need to remove the colour before you start if the article is blotchy. Bleach and fade marks cannot be cured by dyeing, nor can scorch marks. Patterns will not be obliterated by *dyeing, though they may be less obvious, and will produce a two-tone effect as colours are combined, see page 134. You can't make a dark colour paler by dyeing it.*

A word or two of warning though: don't dye wool in a washing machine unless it is machine-washable – it will shrink; and polyester fabrics can only be dyed to a very pale colour, whereas polyester/cotton mixtures can be dyed – the more cotton there is, the stronger the effect you will get.

DYES AND HOW TO USE THEM

There are four main types of fabric dye: cold-water dyes, hot-water liquid dyes, multi-purpose dyes and wash-and-dye mixtures.

◆ Make sure the dyeing vessel is large enough for the fabric to be completely covered with water and stirred round easily.

◆ Wet the fabric thoroughly before putting it in the dye.

◆ Heavy woollen jumpers, dresses, coats and so on should be steeped in cold water for about 20 minutes before being put into the dye bath, otherwise there may be some dry patches and you will get an uneven result.

◆ Don't use more than 7 litres (12pt) of water to each tin of dye or the colour will not match the shade card.

◆ Don't dye more than half the washing machine's wash load.

◆ After removing the dyed fabrics, put the washing machine through a hot-wash cycle with washing powder and a cupful of bleach.

Using cold-water dyes

These are powder dyes which must be mixed with water and a special "cold fix" preparation or washing soda.

◆ Can be washed in by hand or machine.

REMOVING COLOUR

If the base colour on a garment is blotchy, remove it before dyeing or it will not take the colour evenly.

◆ Garments can be washed in colour remover by hand or machine.

◆ Use colour removers on nylon, cotton, wool, velvet, linen, candlewick, viscose and acetate. Don't use removers on polyesters, triacetate or materials with special finishes.

▼▼ Ventilate the room when using
◆ ◆ colour removers, because the fumes are not pleasant.

DYEING IN FRONT-LOADING AUTOMATICS

◆ Soak the fabrics thoroughly in cold water before putting them into the washing machine.

◆ Pour the dye solution over the clothes or fabrics in the machine, and then immediately run hot or cold water (according to the dye) into the machine.

◆ If using hot-water liquid or powder dyes, or wash and dye mixtures, use the hottest cycle.

◆ Always put fabrics through a rinse to remove excess colour.

◆Colourfast, so suitable for things you are likely to wash often.

◆Best for natural fibres but can be used on polyester/cotton mixtures and viscose.

◆Use these dyes for batik and tie dyeing.

For hand dyeing or top-loading machines:

1 Dissolve each tin of dye in 600ml (1pt) hot water and stir well. Pour it into a bowl, basin or machine. Add cold water. Mix in 50g (2oz) salt per tin of dye and 15ml (1tbsp) washing soda or one sachet "colour fix". (If dyeing wool, use 350ml/12floz vinegar instead.)

2 Put fabric into solution and top up with water to cover it. Stir continually for 10 minutes if dyeing by hand, or agitate in the machine for 20 minutes. Rinse, and then wash in hot water and detergent.

Using hot-water liquid dyes

These are ready-mixed dyes which come in bottles and are easy to use.

◆Can be washed in by hand or machine.

◆Good for most washable fabrics and man-made fibres but not for polyester.

◆These dyes are not colourfast, so wash dyed fabrics separately.

For hand dyeing or top-loading machines:

1 Fill the basin, bowl or machine with very hot water.

2 Add dye with 25g (1oz) salt for each half bottle of dye, and stir.

3 Add fabrics and top up with hot water if the fabric is not covered.

4 Stir or agitate for 20 minutes (stir wool gently for 10 minutes). Rinse thoroughly.

Using multi-purpose dyes

Sold in powder form; must be mixed according to instructions.

◆Can be washed in by hand or machine.

◆Good for natural fibres and nylon, acetate and some rayons.

◆These dyes are not colourfast.

◆If dyeing by hand, use a container that can be heated on top of a cooker.

For hand dyeing or top-loading machines:

1 Dissolve each tin of dye in 600ml (1pt) boiling water.

2 Fill container or machine with very hot water and add dye plus 15ml (1tbsp) salt. Stir well.

3 Add fabric. If dyeing by hand, simmer for 20 minutes (10 minutes if dyeing wool), stirring continually, or agitate in the machine for 20 minutes. Rinse thoroughly.

Using wash-and-dye mixtures

These are a mixture of dye and detergent to be used in the washing machine only.

◆Good for large articles.

◆These dyes are not colourfast.

For top-loading machines:

1 Run very hot water into the machine, and add dye.

2 Add fabric and agitate for about 10 minutes. Rinse thoroughly.

COLOUR COMBINATIONS

A dye of one colour applied to a fabric of another colour will produce a different and often unexpected shade.

◇ *Red and yellow will make orange or red.*
◇ *Blue and yellow will make green.*
◇ *Yellow and pink will make coral.*
◇ *Green and yellow will make lime.*
◇ *Light brown and medium red will make a rust colour.*
◇ *Red and blue will make purple.*
◇ *Pale blue and pink will make lilac.*
◇ *Dark brown and light red will make a dark red-brown colour.*

SPECIAL PROBLEMS

◆ When dyeing articles the same colour but in batches make sure that:
◇ *The amount of dye and weight of fabric are always in the same proportion*
◇ *You follow the same procedure exactly*
◇ *The water temperature is the same.*

Large articles

◆ If pairs of curtains are so large they have to be dyed separately, use fresh dye liquid for each one to get them to match.
◆ Use a wash-and-dye product for dyeing any large particles.
◆ Do not dye acrylic blankets or those made from polyester or polyester mixtures because they won't take up the colour.

Lace

◆ If you want to dye lace to an ecru colour, use cold tea instead of dye. In varying amounts this will give a permanent colour ranging from beige to old ivory, depending on how long you leave the lace in.

Feathers

Feathers are fragile and have to be treated with great care if they are to last.

◆ Use a multi-purpose dye.
1 Hand-wash feathers with care in warm water, and then rinse.

2 Immerse the feathers in the dye bath while still soaking wet.
3 Raise the temperature of the dye by adding boiling water and maintain a constant temperature for 10 minutes exactly, moving the feathers gently but constantly.
4 Rinse the feathers until the water runs clear and then leave to dry.

Leather and shoes

◆ Like everything else, leather must be clean before you try to dye it. Wipe clean with warm water and detergent.
◆ Satin shoes should be dyed with multi-purpose dye.
◆ Leather coats, suede and so on should always be dyed by professionals.

Dyeing canvas shoes *Wash the shoes in hot water and detergent. Stuff them with newspaper and allow them to dry in a warm place out of direct heat. Then dye with an appropriate dye.*

GUIDE TO DYEING FABRICS

◆ Always test the dye first on a hidden part of the fabric to see if it will take the dye and to check that the colour is what you were expecting it to be.

SUITABLE FABRICS

ACETATE
Good results with hot-water and multi-purpose dyes. Don't use cold-water dyes.

COTTON
Good results on all cotton fabrics with all dyes.

LEATHER
Use a brush-on leather dye.

LINEN
Good results with all dyes.

NYLON
Good results with hot-water and multi-purpose dyes. Don't use cold-water dyes.

NYLON/POLYESTER
Quite good results but only with hot-water dyes.

POLYESTER
Paler shades with hot-water dyes only.

POLYESTER/COTTON MIXTURE
Pale shades only with hot- and cold-water dyes.

SILK
Good results with hot-water dyes, multi-purpose dyes and reduced shades with cold-water dyes.

SUEDE
Use a brush-on suede dye.

TRIACETATE
Reduced shades with hot-water dyes. (Special instructions may be included.)

VISCOSE
Good results with hot- or cold-water dyes.

WOOL
Good results with hot-water dyes, quite good with cold. Don't rub wool.

UNSUITABLE FABRICS

◇ Acrylic
◇ Angora
◇ Camel hair

◇ Cashmere
◇ "Finished" fabrics (e.g. drip-dry or rain-repellent finishes)

◇ Glass fibre
◇ Mohair
◇ Polyester/wool mixture

STORING CLOTHES AND LINEN

Fabric needs room to "breathe", so it should never be so tightly packed that it becomes creased. Always clean clothing and linen before storing it to help prevent moths laying their eggs in it.

Cover hanging garments that are to be put away for any length of time, or that are seldom used, with a plastic bag, to prevent dust collecting on the fabric. Keep linen in a cool place on slatted shelves so that air can circulate around it. Put hats in boxes, stuffed with tissue if necessary; never leave them lying on a flat surface – it may damage the brim permanently.

CLOTHING

◆ Hang clothes in groups in a wardrobe so that often-used and outdoor clothes do not rub against your less-used or more delicate dresses and suits.

◆ To make the best use of space, create two tiers by putting up an extra rail above or below the main one. Hang shirts and blouses on the lower one.

◆ Cover full-sleeved garments with short plastic covers so that the sleeves are not pulled in and creased.

Hanging ties *Hang them over expanded curtain wire fixed to the inside of the wardrobe door.*

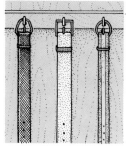

Hanging belts *Hang them by their buckles from hooks on the inside of the wardrobe door or in the wardrobe itself.*

◆Don't hang knitted or jersey clothes because they will stretch. Fold them carefully and store them in a drawer or on a shelf where they won't be too squashed.

Coat hangers

◆Keep a plentiful supply of good sturdy coat hangers. Thin, wire hangers are not good for clothes as a permanent arrangement. Ideally hangers should be padded or covered with cardboard or foam rubber so that they don't pull the clothes out of shape.

Ideal hangers *Make sure that the hanger fits the garment exactly. It should span the width of the shoulders and the back should support the neck of the garment.*

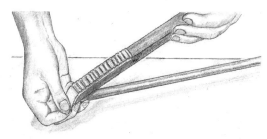

Keeping garments on hangers *Stick strips of rubber at each end of a hanger to help prevent a garment from slipping off.*

DRAWERS AND SHELVES

◆Divide shelves up into areas to take jerseys, scarves, socks, underwear, or table and bed linen. This will keep them tidy and make it easier to find things when you need them.

▼▼Don't keep anything in polythene ◆◆ bags if you have young children; polythene can cause suffocation.

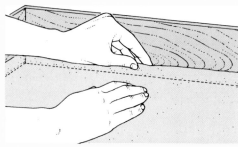

Lining drawers and shelves *Keep drawers and shelves clean by lining them with wallpaper or self-sticking plastic. Cut the lining 5cm (2in) larger than the drawer all round and turn it up at the sides.*

◆Use wooden tailor's hangers to hold tailored and weighty clothes such as suits, coats and furs; they provide more support.
◆Never hang clothes from a loop at the back of the neck. The shoulders and the neck of the garment should be well supported.
◆Make sure you hang garments centrally on hangers. If you don't, your clothes will look lopsided the next time you wear them.
◆Cover garments with purpose-made plastic covers or make covers out of dustbin bags and coat hangers to protect them.

Knitwear and shirts

◆Store light-coloured jumpers in plastic bags to prevent them from fading and gathering dust.
◆Don't squash sweaters into a drawer because you will damage the fibres, which may result in permanent creases.
◆Shirts are probably best stored on hangers if you have enough cupboard space, but you can fold them and store them in drawers or on shelves.

FOLDING CLOTHES

FOLDING KNITWEAR

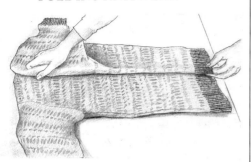

1 Lay the sweater face down. Fold one side and arm to the middle.
2 Fold the arm back down on itself. Do the same with the other side.

3 Fold the sweater in two taking the top down to the bottom, with the sleeves inside the fold.

FOLDING A SHIRT

1 Button the shirt to the top to prevent it from creasing and to stop the collar from becoming distorted and sitting wrongly.

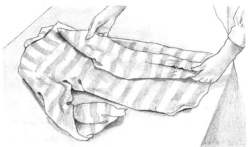

2 Lay the shirt face down. Turn both sides into the middle, with the sleeves lying flat down the back in line with the collar band.

3 Turn the tail up, then fold the bottom fold up to the collar.

Trousers and suits

◆ Fold trousers along the crease and store on hangers. Tape a piece of folded card or foam rubber to the hanger to prevent a crease mark developing across the middle of the legs.
◆ Press trousers and suits in regular use in a trouser or suit press before putting away; they'll keep their shape for longer.

Dresses and skirts

◆ Hang long dresses and evening dresses inside out to keep them clean.
◆ Sew loops into the waist of long dresses to stop the hem trailing on the floor. Skirts are also best hung from loops sewn into the inside of the waistband.

Keeping pleats in Cut the foot off a stocking or half a pair of tights and draw pleated skirts and dresses through it. Store flat.

Boots and shoes

◆Don't pile shoes and boots on top of each other. Build or buy a rack where they can be stored tidily and where they will not rub together and mark each other. A shoe rack can be fixed to the inside of the wardrobe door or on a rail at the back of the wardrobe, but make sure the shoes don't rub against the clothes.

◆Buy a pair of shoe trees for each set of shoes, and put rolled up newspaper or magazines in boots, to make them last longer.

◆Smart boots can be kept upside down over long wooden pegs set at an angle, or simply clip them together with a large clothes peg or bulldog clip on the insides of each boot.

Hanging wellington boots *Punch a hole in the top of the rubber of each boot and put a piece of string through. Hang from a nail or hook.*

LONG-TERM STORAGE FOR CLOTHES

◆Always wash or clean clothes before you put them away for the summer or winter.

◆Pleats should be tacked together and all buttons and fasteners done up.

◆Put tissue paper between the layers.

◆Don't starch summer dresses before putting them away because creases will set.

PRECIOUS LACE

◆ Wrap garments, veils and tablecloths made of valuable lace in blue paper to protect them (white paper will let in the light). The item must be completely covered.

◆ Make sure the colour of the paper won't rub off onto the lace.

BED AND TABLE LINEN

◆The airing cupboard is not necessarily the best place to store bed and table linen, because the constant warmth discolours the fabric and weakens the fibres.

◆Place clean linen at the bottom of the pile so that you use it in rotation. This will make everything last longer.

◆Cover the bed linen pile with a blanket to keep it fresh and clean.

◆Treat linen for moths before storing it for any length of time, see opposite.

◆Store duvets and eiderdowns in large plastic bags on top of the wardrobe or in drawers under the bed so that they don't become squashed.

Leather and suede

◆Shake the leather well before putting it away so that creases don't set into it and so that it maintains its shape.

◆Condition leather shoes, boots and bags with dubbin before storing them.

Storing leather and suede garments *Hang them in a hanging "wardrobe" made from heavy plastic, to keep them clean.*

Fur

◆Beat fur gently with a cane out of doors. Then shake it well before you put it away.

◆Store it in a well-ventilated place (the coldest you can find), or keep it in a sealed container with paradichlorobenzene crystals ("para" crystals) to prevent moths.

◆Better still, have the fur professionally cleaned at the end of the winter and store it with a specialist furrier.

MOTHPROOFING

All man-made fibres are mothproof, but when blended with natural fibre, the fabric is still liable to be damaged by moths and needs to be protected when it is put into storage.

◆ Pack clothes in airtight chests, or boxes or hampers with plastic linings, or hang them in mothproof bags.

◆ Sprinkle moth repellent between the layers of material.

◆ There are several types of moth repellent, some of which are available from chemists:

◇ *Paradichlorobenzene ("para") crystals*
◇ *Aerosols, but these are not recommended because they smell, can damage some fabrics (such as fur), and some of the propellants used can damage the environment.*

GREEN TIP: Lavender and plants of the Artemisia genus, such as southernwood and wormwood, make good moth repellents. Place them in gauze sachets between the layers and folds of clothing.

GREEN TIP: You can place muslin bags, each containing 50g (2oz) of ground cloves, cinnamon, black pepper and orris root, among the clothes.

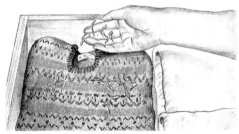

Traditional mothproofing *Scatter dried orange peel through the clothing.*

PACKING CLOTHES

◆ When packing clothes to travel, make a list of the clothes and accessories so that you don't leave something vital behind.

◆ If you are packing for children as well as yourself, make separate lists for them.

◆ Collect up everything you want to pack and lay it out on a bed, so you can see what you've got; you may find that you need only half of it.

◆ Do up all fastenings before folding and pack everything face down; it is less likely to crease.

◆ Put tissue paper between the folds to prevent knife-edge creases from forming.

◆ Never squeeze too many things into the case. This will crease the clothes.

◆ Use a sturdy suitcase; clothes are less likely to be squashed.

1 First pack heavy things, such as shoes and books. Pad out the spaces with rolled up socks, gloves, underwear, etc.

2 Heavy garments and suits go in next. Fold each garment to the size of the case and keep each layer as level as possible.

3 Pack underwear and woollens. Lay breakable items on this layer.

4 Pack wool dresses, then pleated skirts by pulling them through an old stocking and laying them along one side of the case.

5 The top layer should be thin dresses, shirts and blouses. Cover them with a cloth or large piece of tissue paper and make sure everything is packed fairly tightly so that it will not move about.

◇ *Small nylon bags with clothes for a week or weekend don't need this elaborate packing, but the same principles apply: heavy things at the bottom, pad out the spaces, light things and overnight things at the top.*

STAIN REMOVAL

Remove spills on fabric immediately, because once anything has soaked into the fabric, it is much harder to get out. Absorb or scrape up as much as possible – be very careful not to work more of the substance into the fabric; dab or lightly scrape it off, don't rub.

Apply a stain remover as a secondary treatment only if the spill leaves a mark. If the stain is not greasy, and the garment is washable, put it straight into cold water;

this can be just as effective as any biological detergent and is better for the skin. Don't use hot water because it "cooks" the substance, fixing it for good.

A stain will come out more easily if it is removed the way it went into the fabric, so work from the back of the fabric rather than pushing the mark through from the front. Work in a circle around the mark then in towards the middle to prevent a permanent "ring" developing around the mark.

EMERGENCY ACTION FOR SPILLS

◆ **For solid matter** Scrape off the substance as soon as you can, using the back of a blunt knife, or a spatula.

◆ **For acids** Hold the fabric under cold running water immediately. Then sponge with household ammonia or bicarbonate of soda in a little cold water. Rinse well.

◆ **For grease marks** Apply liquid detergent to the stain and rub it in, then wash at a high temperature. For unwashable fabrics apply dry-cleaning solvent.

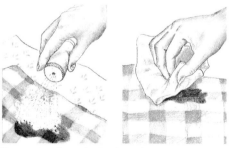

Removing liquids *For liquids such as urine, fruit juices and wine, scatter salt liberally to absorb the substance, above left. Dab other liquids with clean absorbent paper tissues or a clean cloth, above right. Then soak the fabric in cold water, if possible. Do not soak dyed silk, moiré fabrics or wool.*

◆ **For liquids on unwashable fabrics** Use fuller's earth or talcum powder to absorb liquid. Treat residual stain.

STAIN REMOVAL KIT

Have a stain removal kit ready to hand for emergencies and keep it in a box, next to your carpet stain removal kit (see page 81). You will need the following things:

◇ *A clothes brush*
◇ *Fine sandpaper for cleaning suede*
◇ *Bicarbonate of soda, household ammonia, methylated spirits, surgical spirit, white spirit, borax, acetone, amyl acetate, dry-cleaning solvent, white vinegar, and a bleach such as hydrogen peroxide, sodium perborate or chlorine bleach. Label all these substances clearly*
◇ *A collection of small sponges*
◇ *Some white absorbent cotton material and paper tissues to place behind a stain while removing it and to absorb any surface liquid*
◇ *Some cotton wool for applying solvents, detergent, etc.*
◇ *A medicine dropper or syringe for controlled application of powerful solvents. Don't store solvents in them. Rinse thoroughly after use*
◇ *A plant spray (available from garden centres) to squirt water onto a stain.*

BLEACHING

This is a secondary treatment for residual stains left after absorbing, scraping or washing. See page 123 for guidelines on bleaching.

Hydrogen peroxide

◆ Can be safely used on wool or silk.
◆ Use one part hydrogen peroxide to four parts cold water.
◆ Soak the garment for up to 12 hours, rinse thoroughly, then wash.

Sodium perborate

◆ Can be used on wool and silk.
1 Dissolve 15–30g (1–2tbsp) of crystals in 600ml (1pt) water as hot as the material will allow.
2 Soak for several hours because this is a slow-working bleach.
◇ *Only leave silk or wool or other delicate fabrics in the solution for a short time. Don't soak these fabrics; they start to deteriorate.*
◇ *If the fabric yellows, sponge with white vinegar and rinse.*

Chlorine (sodium hypochlorite) bleach

◆ Can be used for small stains or spots on cotton and linen.
▼▼ Do not use on silk or wool or any
◆ ◆ garment with a strong colour or pattern; it may affect the colour.
1 Test for colour-fastness on an inconspicuous part of the garment.
2 Mix 10ml (2tsp) bleach with 800ml (1¼pt) cold water.
3 Put a clean tissue under the stain. Then dab the stain with another cloth moistened with the bleach solution. Rinse thoroughly, then wash.
◇ *For larger stains, immerse the whole garment in a solution of 475ml (16fl oz) bleach and 8 litres (14pt) of cold water for about 15 minutes, then rinse thoroughly and wash.*

USING SOLVENTS

This is a secondary treatment for residual grease or oil stains. Solvents are used by professional dry cleaners. They can be bought as spot removers under various trade names, in liquid, aerosol or paste form. Shop-bought solvents will have full instructions which you should follow meticulously.
◆ You can use white spirit, surgical spirit, acetone or alkalis (household ammonia, used with caution, or borax).
GREEN TIP: Useful substitutes for proprietary products are: acetic acid (white vinegar, straight from the bottle); citric acid (lemon juice, straight from the lemon); and mayonnaise or butter, which can be used to soften tar and oil.

1 Place a clean tissue under the stain to absorb extra moisture and the solvent.

2 Soak a clean cloth in the solvent and dab the stain, working in a circle outside the stain and moving into the centre.
3 Rinse thoroughly and wash, if the fabric is washable. Otherwise air it well.
◇ *If you can't wash the garment, dry any remaining solvent with a hair dryer. Use a circular motion following the way you applied the solvent to prevent marks.*

TREATING SPECIFIC STAINS

◆ When using solvents, bleaches or proprietary stain removers, always work with small quantities.

◆ Always work near an open window and far from a naked flame.

◆ Always test fabric for colour-fastness

before applying stain remover.

◆ Never use acetone on acetate fibres – it will dissolve the fabric.

◆ Never mix solvents. Let the fabric dry after applying one solvent and rinse before applying another.

COSMETIC STAINS

ANTIPERSPIRANTS
Treat with dry-cleaning solvent, then household ammonia, and rinse.

FOUNDATION CREAM
Rub in liquid detergent and flush it out with water. Greasy foundation may respond to dry-cleaning solvent.

LACQUER
Treat with amyl acetate, then flush with dry-cleaning solvent.

LIPSTICK
Treat with dry-cleaning solvent or methylated spirits, then wash in liquid detergent and ammonia solution.

NAIL VARNISH
Treat with amyl acetate or acetone but don't use oily nail varnish remover. Flush with white spirit and wash.

PERFUME
Treat with household ammonia straight from the bottle. Wash in liquid detergent.

BIOLOGICAL STAINS

BLOOD
Wash at once in cold water with salt added to it. Don't use warm water.
◆ Hardened blood should be brushed off and soaked in cold water with biological detergent or hydrogen peroxide solution.

FAECES
Absorb matter or scrape it off. Soak in a borax solution for

half an hour. Then wash as normal, preferably with a biological detergent.

URINE
Apply salt liberally until urine is absorbed and then rinse in cold water. Treat residual stain with household ammonia straight from the bottle, then rinse and apply white vinegar. Alternatively, treat remaining stain with

diluted hydrogen peroxide. Wash as normal, preferably with a biological detergent.

VOMIT
Absorb or scrape off. Squirt with a soda siphon and then sponge with a borax solution. Wash as normal, preferably with a biological detergent.

FOOD AND DRINK STAINS

BEER
Soak in white vinegar and, if necessary, biological detergent. Rinse. Wash at a high temperature, if possible.

BEETROOT
Sponge at once with cold water and soak in cold water overnight. Work neat liquid detergent into stain and rinse.

Sprinkle borax on the dampened stain and pour boiling water over it.

BUTTER
Wash fabric at a high temperature. Alternatively, treat with solvent and dry with a hair dryer.

CARAMEL
Rinse with cold water, liquid detergent and then, if necessary, apply diluted hydrogen peroxide.

CHEWING GUM
Put the article in the freezer or ice box, or dab it with ice cubes to freeze the gum, and

then break it off. Treat the residue with methylated spirits or white spirit.

CHOCOLATE
Scrape it off, rinse with cold water, and soak in biological detergent. For residual stains, try a solvent.

COFFEE
Soak in hand-hot detergent solution. Then treat with methylated spirits. Use diluted hydrogen peroxide for residual stains.
◆ Wash off milky coffee in warm water using a biological detergent.

CREAM
Rinse in cold water and wash with biological detergent.

EGG
Rinse in cold water and then wash with biological detergent. Soak stubborn stains in hydrogen peroxide to which you have added five drops of ammonia.

FAT
Cold fat Treat as for BUTTER.
Hot fat Rub in liquid detergent and rinse.

FRUIT AND FRUIT JUICES
Rub the stain with salt before washing. Rinse in cold water and soak in liquid detergent.

Then wash at a high temperature, if possible. Treat the residue with household ammonia, diluted hydrogen peroxide or borax.

GRAVY
Soak in cold water or detergent, or try a dry-cleaning solvent.

ICE CREAM
Remove with a spoon or knife and soak in warm detergent. Treat greasy residue with solvent.

JAM
Rinse in cold water and soak in liquid detergent. Apply diluted hydrogen peroxide if necessary.

KETCHUP
Rinse in cold water and soak in liquid detergent. If necessary, treat with methylated spirits.

LIQUEURS
Rinse with cold water and wash with liquid detergent.

MEAT JUICE
Rinse in cold water and soak in a biological detergent. Treat with dry-cleaning solvent if necessary.

MILK
Rinse in cold water and soak in a biological detergent.

MUSTARD
Rinse in cold water and soak in liquid detergent.

SOFT DRINKS
Rinse in cold water and soak in liquid detergent. For stubborn stains, flush with methylated spirits diluted with a little white vinegar.

TEA
Treat as for COFFEE.

TOBACCO
Rinse in cold water and then in white vinegar. Wash in liquid detergent with a little methylated spirits. Treat residual stain with diluted hydrogen peroxide.

TURMERIC AND CURRY POWDER
Soak in diluted household ammonia or white spirit. Bleach if the fabric will take it.

VEGETABLE OIL
Saturate fabric with water and treat with methylated spirits with a little white vinegar added. Treat residual stain with several applications of dry-cleaning solvent.

WINE
Cover with salt immediately, to absorb the liquid. Then soak in cold water or a borax solution for half an hour. Wash as usual.

 # HOUSEHOLD STAINS

ACIDS
Plunge immediately into cold water. Dab on household ammonia or bicarbonate of soda dissolved in cold water and rinse thoroughly.

ADHESIVES
Cellulose-based adhesive
Wash out in cold water, or wet and treat with diluted household ammonia or biological detergent, and rinse.

Epoxy adhesive Remove with methylated spirits before the glue sets.
Model aircraft cement Treat with acetone or amyl acetate.
◇ *Some manufacturers supply a solvent for their cements.*
PVA Clean off with methylated spirits.

Synthetic rubber adhesive
Remove with non-oily nail varnish remover, acetone or amyl acetate, then flush with dry-cleaning solvent.

Sticky labels and tape Soak or leave covered with a wet cloth, then rub with methylated spirits or white spirit.

Continued ▷

TREATING SPECIFIC STAINS

BALLPOINT PEN
Flush repeatedly with methylated spirits. Then air or rinse the garment thoroughly.
◆ On suede, rub marks with fine sandpaper.

CANDLEWAX
Freeze the wax with ice cubes or by putting the garment into the freezer or ice box, then break off the frozen pieces. Sandwich the material between blotting or brown paper and melt the wax off with a warm iron. Treat the residual stain with dry-cleaning solvent, then flush with methylated spirits.

COUGH MEDICINES
Flush with detergent and water. Follow with diluted household ammonia, then methylated spirits or amyl acetate.
◆ Tar-based cough medicines should be softened with lard or white spirit. Then treat with dry-cleaning solvent or wash with detergent.

CRAYON
Dab with dry-cleaning solvent and flush with methylated spirits.

CRUDE OIL
Soften with white spirit or butter, then scrape off. Flush with dry-cleaning solvent.

DYES
Cleaning marks caused by dyes is difficult. Rinse with cold water and treat with liquid detergent. If the stain persists, apply household ammonia, methylated spirits or amyl acetate.
◆ For residual stains of leather dye, use diluted hydrogen peroxide.

ENGINE OIL
Rub undiluted liquid detergent into the stain or flush it out with dry-cleaning solvent.

FELT TIP PEN
Lubricate with household soap or glycerine and wash as usual. Sponge the residue with methylated spirits.

FLOWER STAINS
Saturate the fabric with water and treat it with liquid detergent while wet. For residual stains try dry-cleaning solvent, amyl acetate or methylated spirits.

FURNITURE POLISH
Treat with dry-cleaning solvent.

GRASS STAINS
Treat with methylated spirits. Dry the fabric and then wash it with liquid detergent or use a stain remover.

GREASE
Scrape it off and wash at a high temperature if possible, using washing soda and borax to emulsify the grease and release the dirt. Hydrogen peroxide and paraffin oil also dissolve grease. Use dry-cleaning solvent for residual stains and dry with a hair dryer.

INK
Flush with cold water while wet, then rub in liquid detergent and rinse, or sponge with lemon juice and rinse with ammonia.
Duplicating ink Flush with white spirit, then soak in liquid detergent.
Duplicating powder Brush it out, never wet it.

IODINE
Moisten with water and place in the sun or flush with methylated spirits.

IRON MOULD
Cover with salt, squeeze lemon juice over the stain and leave for an hour.
◆ On white fabrics use a proprietary rust remover.

◆ Get specialist treatment for woollens and silks.

MILDEW
Flush with diluted bleach.
◆ Wipe mildewed leather with antiseptic mouthwash.

MINERAL OIL
Saturate fabric with water and treat with lemon juice while wet. Apply dry-cleaning solvent to residual stains.

MUD
Wait till dry and brush off. Treat remaining stain with methylated spirits followed by liquid detergent.

PAINT
Acrylic Blot with tissues and wash in detergent. Alternatively, use solvent or methylated spirits.
Cellulose Use cellulose thinners (but not on viscose).
Emulsion Wash while still wet; when dry it is not removable.
Oil Apply white spirit, then soak in liquid detergent.

SCORCH MARKS
Dampen the stain with one part glycerine to two parts water and rub it in with your fingertips. Then soak in a solution of 50g (2oz) borax to 600ml (1pt) warm water. Leave for 15 minutes.

SHOE POLISH
Treat with dry-cleaning solvent, then wash with liquid detergent, or flush with methylated spirits.

TAR
See CRUDE OIL

TARNISH
Sponge with diluted ammonia or bicarbonate of soda. Flush with some white vinegar or lemon juice.

WAX POLISH
Treat with dry-cleaning solvent, then liquid detergent.

Household Contents

STORAGE

Never underestimate the amount of storage you need: everything needs to be stored somewhere, whether you use it every day or only once a year. Putting things away, *however, does not have to mean hiding them; you can make a display, particularly of some of the more decorative or colourful items, on open shelves and room dividers.*

ASSESSING YOUR REQUIREMENTS

◆ When planning your storage, try to imagine how your needs will change over the coming year, or years, and plan accordingly. For instance, if you are expecting a baby, allow space for everything from nappies to bathing equipment and pushchairs.

◆ Make a list of all your possessions, just like an inventory but in categories: books, music centre, records, tapes, "collections" (be they of cigarette cards, netsuke, teapots, lead soldiers or masks), kitchen equipment, clothes, shoes, paintings, bedlinen, papers, toys, jewellery and so on. Then, working logically, room-by-room, assess the potential in your home for storage space. Then decide what sort of storage/display would suit each category of possession: for example, a glass-fronted cabinet for china, open shelves or specially designed cabinets for books, bureau or desk for papers, fitted cupboards or free-standing wardrobes and chests of drawers for clothes.

◆ Have cupboards or shelves built in to a small space; searching for a free-standing cupboard or shelf unit to fit the space can be very time-consuming.

◆ Make sure that storage is in a convenient place – books near where you will want to read or refer to them, any kitchen equipment where it can be taken out and used with ease, clothes where you can reach them.

Storage for small rooms

◆ Use open storage in a small room; closed storage can make a room look smaller. Make a display of your belongings rather than cramming them into the cupboards.

◆ Don't take shelves right up to the ceiling, because this makes a room feel small.

ODD SPACES THAT CAN BE USED FOR STORAGE

There are many wasted spaces with a lot of potential in most homes; for example, the space under the stairs or on the landings, alcoves in passages, basements or attics can all be used.

UNDER THE STAIRS

◆ If the space is tall enough, use it to house a wall-hung telephone with a message board and a small table or shelf unit for telephone books, pads and pencil. (Make sure the telephone has a light shining on it so that you can read the numbers.)

◆ Store the cleaning equipment under the stairs, but organize the space so that everything hangs neatly on the wall, like a well-ordered workshop.

◆ Put a small cupboard and stool in the space and use it for storing shoes and shoe-polishing equipment. You could arrange boot trees or hooks for boot storage.

◆ Close it in and use it as a cleaning cupboard or as a spare cupboard for tinned food or gloves, woolly hats and scarves, but don't let it become a depository for unused stamps, unwashed handkerchiefs, unwanted gifts, and damaged tennis balls.

◆ If the space is large, fit a shower and basin. Make sure you can provide adequate ventilation to prevent condensation.

LANDING

◆ Build shelves for books or records, for example. A large draught-proof landing with shelves and an armchair can even make a good library corner or a music listening corner (but only if the listener wears earphones).

◆ Use the space to make a hobbies corner with a bench and shelves for all the equipment or papers.

◆ Put a spare wardrobe in the space for winter clothes during summer, or summer clothes during winter, or a collection of fashion clothes from past eras.

BASEMENTS AND ATTICS

◆ Use these as playrooms for young children, provided they are not damp. They're ideal places to keep a model railway, as the carefully designed construction doesn't have to be dismantled at bedtime.

FITTED CUPBOARDS AND FURNITURE

The choice includes fitted cupboards (either bought as units or built in) or free-standing pieces of furniture.

◆ Cupboards with folding or sliding doors are best in a small space, where a standard door might not be able to open fully if, for example, a bed is in the way.

◆ Buy cupboard units with adjustable shelves to make planning the interior easier. Some storage systems have shoe racks and/or drawers already fitted.

Fitted unit furniture

◆ Use this type when you need storage flexibility and plenty of space. It consists of pre-fabricated parts of a particular width, or multiples of that width, linked together along a wall, most commonly used as kitchen or bedroom storage.

◆ Avoid taking the cupboards right up to the ceiling because they can make a room look much smaller.

◆ Tall unit storage can be useful in the hall, landing or passages for extra storage.

Modular storage

This is free-standing storage built up from cubes, shelves, drawers and cabinets.

◆ Buy boxes or cubes – either square or rectangular – that can be ranged alongside each other or stacked on top of each other. Use them to cover a whole wall, or to make a pyramid, or staggered storage. Commonly made from plastic, hardboard, melamine-faced board or medium-density fibreboard, they are available in a variety of colours.

◆ Choose cubes or boxes with drawers or

small shelves for a more versatile system.

◆ Single cubes make very good bedside tables, particularly for children.

◆ If you buy kits for home assembly, work out the number of pieces and connecting pieces you will need very carefully beforehand. Beware: some of these kits are very difficult to assemble.

Free-standing furniture

◆ If you are likely to move house a number of times, opt for free-standing pieces of furniture so that you can take them with you.

◆ Make your own racks or buy wire baskets if the interior isn't adjustable.

◆ Use pieces of furniture to give your rooms a more interesting appearance; this is not always the most economical use of space but furniture can provide sculptural decoration.

◆ For an unusual effect, paint junk shop furniture to match your decorating scheme.

◆ When buying old furniture, check for woodworm and don't buy it if it is infested. (Signs are pin-sized holes with bits of sawdust seeping out.)

◇ *You can treat very small areas of woodworm but it must be done as soon as you get the piece home, see page 256.*

ORGANIZING THE INSIDE OF A CUPBOARD

To maximize space in a fitted wardrobe, plan it to accommodate adjustable shelves or drawers, hanging rails, pull-out wire baskets and shoe racks.

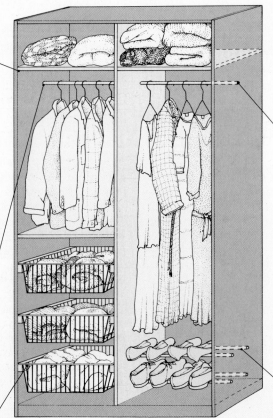

Top shelf Put up a shelf at the top of the cupboard to store pullovers or out-of-season clothes.

Shirt rails Group short short clothes, such as jackets and shirts, on one side of the cupboard so that you can use the space below for shelving.

Basket racks Use wire baskets on runners to store underclothes and pullovers.

Hanging rail Run the rail parallel to the wall, about 30 cm (12in) away from both sides so that coat hangers hang at right angles, and 1.6–1.8m (4ft 6in–5ft) from the base so that it is high enough to take long dresses.

Shoe racks Make shoe shoe racks out of two parallel rods 10cm (5in) apart and about 7.5cm (3in) off the floor.

SHELVING

◆Fix shelves for books where there is no damp in the walls and where there is no direct heat; heat and damp damage books.

Permanent shelving

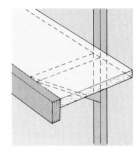

Making a shelf look more substantial *Fix a strip of hardwood along the front of a shelf to form a "lip" to make a thin shelf look stronger. If the end of the shelf is visible, continue the strip around the end so that the shelf looks neat.*

The load your shelves will be able to carry depends on: the strength of the wall; the strength of the supports; the distance between the supports; the strength and thickness of the shelving material. The simplest shelving is individual metal or wooden brackets fixed to the wall with a shelf laid or screwed on top.

◆For flexible shelving use metal or wood uprights with slots for shelf brackets at intervals up their length. You can vary the heights between shelves, so providing space for very large books and even the television and record player, as well as paperbacks and small ornaments. Robust systems, originally intended for offices and commercial use, are ideal for books or other heavy items. Prettier, but less robust, shelving is available for ordinary domestic use. But remember, once the shelves are up and filled, you will probably not notice the uprights and brackets, so you would do better to get the stronger type anyway.

◆For display purposes, buy an adjustable shelving system that consists of wooden side panelling with slots in it to take brackets for the shelves.

◆The best shelving materials are 15mm ($\frac{5}{8}$in) timber, melamine-covered chipboard (now available in a selection of bright primary colours), blockboard, plywood, medium-density fibreboard (though this is heavy and not always easy to get hold of) or 10mm ($\frac{3}{8}$in) glass. Plywood can vary a lot in strength and in cost, according to the number of plies and the quality of the timber used. It can be stronger than solid wood, though it will never look quite as good. Melamine-covered chipboard, although cheap to buy, can work out more expensive in the long run for heavy items because you need to use more uprights and brackets.

◆Use a batten at the front of a thin shelf to give it a more substantial look.

◆Make existing shelves in cupboards in your home more flexible by fitting dowels or specially designed strips to take shelf supports. You can get these strips in do-it-yourself shops.

Shelving units

◆You can buy free-standing shelving either as individual pieces of furniture or as a modular system; buy the latter if you are likely to want to extend it later.

◆Place free-standing units against a wall where they are out of the way, or across the room to divide it.

◆The cheapest free-standing shelving is metal office shelving, which is usually in a hideous gunmetal grey but which you can spray any colour you like.

◆Small pine shelving units consisting of three shelves with sides can be useful in the kitchen (with cup hooks and hooks at the side for baskets or oven gloves), in the living room for ornaments, or in a bedroom for odd trinkets. Antique or second-hand oak or mahogany shelves are sometimes to be found but don't spoil them by screwing cup hooks into them.

Plate supports *If you want to display decorative plates on a shelf, nail a thin batten along the shelf near the back edge, to prevent them slipping.*

MAXIMUM DISTANCES BETWEEN SHELF SUPPORTS

The heavier the load, or the thinner the shelving material, the closer together the brackets should be. Use the chart below as a guide to the reccommended distances.

Material	Thickness of shelving	Distance between uprights
Hardwood	15mm ($\frac{5}{8}$in)	50cm (20in)
	22mm ($\frac{7}{8}$in)	90cm (36in)
	28mm (1$\frac{1}{8}$in)	105cm (3ft 6in)
Plywood	18mm ($\frac{3}{4}$in)	80cm (30in)
	25mm (1in)	1m (3ft 3in)
Blockboard	12mm ($\frac{1}{2}$in)	45cm (1·8in)
Medium density fibreboard	18mm ($\frac{3}{4}$in)	70cm (27in)
Melamine-covered chipboard	15mm ($\frac{5}{8}$in)	40cm (16in)
	18mm ($\frac{3}{4}$in)	50cm (20in)
	32mm (1$\frac{1}{4}$in)	90cm (36in)
Glass	10mm ($\frac{3}{8}$in)	70cm (27in)

TYPES OF SHELVING

Metal brackets
Angled metal brackets are the cheapest strong shelf brackets.

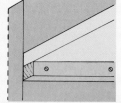

Wooden supports
Use these as side supports for a permanent shelf and along the back of a long shelf.

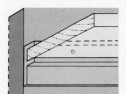

Metal clip shelf
Use this angled metal strip to support the back edge of a shelf.

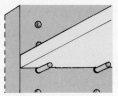

Wooden adustable shelving *Use for display shelving; you can't see the supports.*

PUTTING UP SHELVES

◆Draw a plan to scale on paper before you start putting any shelves up. Then mark the positions on the wall with a pencil.
◇*Make a note of light switches and power points and be careful not to hammer or screw into any wires or you may get an electric shock.*
◆Fix shelf supports to a load-bearing wall, or part of the wall, if they are to support heavy items such as books.

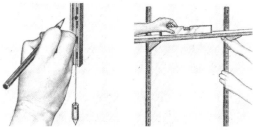

Putting up adjustable shelving *Fix the top of the first upright loosely to the wall. Hang a plumb line (or use a weight on the end of a piece of string) from the top to align it vertically,* above left, *and mark the point for the bottom screw. Get someone to hold the second upright in position while you lay a shelf between the two and place a spirit level on it,* above right. *Mark the screw positions.*

Partition, or hollow, walls

The load-bearing points of partition walls are the timber uprights (called "studs"). They are usually 40–45cm (16–18in) apart, covered with plasterboard.

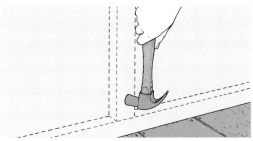

Finding the wall studs *Tap along the wall lightly with a hammer and listen for a change in sound between the hollow board and the solid stud. Or stick a bradawl into the wall at intervals.*

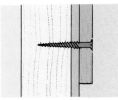 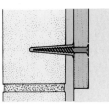

Securing the brackets or uprights *Fix them with screws that are long enough to go through plasterboard into the stud to a depth of at least 15–20mm ($\frac{5}{8}$–1in), above left, or into the brick and plaster to the same depth, above right.*

◆ Span the studs with crosspieces. If you need to fix extra brackets between the studs.
◆ To fix shelves to plasterboard, use special wallplugs, or toggles, see below; don't use the shelves for anything heavy because they will pull away, bringing the plasterboard too.

Solid walls

◆ Make sure that the wall isn't damp or crumbling before you start to fix the shelves, or the shelves will come away as soon as you put anything on them. To check, bore a hole with a bradawl or small masonry drill in an inconspicuous spot at the base of the wall.
◆ If fixing brackets or uprights to a brick and plaster wall, plug the holes with fibre or nylon wallplugs; these give the best grip.
◆ **Breeze block walls** Test as for brick and plaster. If the drill goes in easily, the wall is load bearing. Use fixings as for brick walls.

WALLPLUGS AND TOGGLES

Use anchors for board thicknesses of up to 20mm ($\frac{4}{8}$ in) and toggles for board up to about 7.5cm (3in).
◇ **Nylon wallplug** Plug that expands to grip the inside of the wall when the screw reaches the end.
◇ **Gravity toggle** A bolt with an arm that drops down when the bolt gets through the hole in the plasterboard. The toggle will fall off if you remove the bolt.
◇ **Rubber anchor** Inserted in the wall, this bulges when the screw is tightened.
◇ **Spring toggle** A screw with "arms" that fly apart when they get through the hole in the plasterboard.

IDEAS FOR STORAGE AROUND THE HOUSE

◆ Use baskets to store toys. Choose baskets that are big and roomy with wide mouths and strong handles. They can also be used to carry toys when visiting.
◆ Store large items such as skis or surfboards under beds if you haven't got a spare cupboard, an attic or a basement.
◆ Use insulating cork to make a noticeboard or samples board for the kitchen, workroom or children's bedroom; it is thicker than other types of cork.
◆ Make a wall panel with lots of different sized pockets – out of striped deckchair canvas, for example – and hang it in the kitchen, or on the back of a child's bedroom door. Sew large paper clips and/or hooks into the bottom for gloves or notes.
◆ If you have a tall hallway, erect a pulley system and hang bicycles upside down, near the ceiling.

Kitchens

◆ Run a narrow shelf right round the kitchen or along one wall for herb and spice jars, sauce bottles, salt and pepper mills and all the little things which so often get lost behind large packets in a cupboard.
◆ Fix wire baskets to the insides of cupboard doors to hold miscellaneous items like spare washing-up brushes, washing-up liquid and shoe-polishing equipment.
◆ Use glass jars and metal boxes for dry food. They can look very decorative in a row on a shelf. The glass is specially good as you can see how much you have left. Use coloured glass, otherwise the food will deteriorate too quickly.
◆ Hang stemmed glasses upside down from slots in a piece of wood or shelves.
◆ Hang cups and mugs from cup hooks under the high cupboard units or a shelf, where they will be decorative and out of the way at the same time.
◆ Use wicker baskets as vegetable racks; they let the air in and look attractive.

MAKING LADDER WALL STORAGE

1 Measure the height and width of the space. Cut (or get cut for you) two battens of 5 × 1cm (2 × ½in) wood in the length you require for the uprights. For the crossbars, get several lengths of wood cut, enough to leave gaps of 12mm (½in) between the bars.

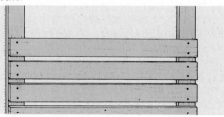

2 Fix the uprights to the wall, then nail the crossbars to them at right angles, leaving a 12mm (½in) gap between each bar.

3 Make hooks from old wire coat hangers, using a pair of pliers. Alternatively, buy some butcher's hooks from your kitchen supplier.

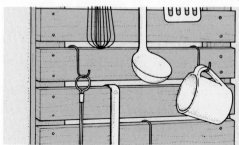

4 Hang the wire hooks on the slats and your implements on the hooks. Hang implements with hooked handles from them as well.

◆If drawer and cupboard space is limited, buy wire mesh panels or make your own ladder rack storage panels, see opposite, or screw hooks into a pegboard, and hang implements from them.

◆Run a metal bar across the room and hang baskets and pans from it.

◆Pottery mugs or jugs are useful for keeping wooden spoons tidy on the worktop.

◆Use a filing cabinet to hold large kitchen equipment such as saucepans or large little-used items.

◆Store plates in a wall-mounted wooden plate rack that will drain them as well.

◆Keep a shelf for cookery books, a note pad and correspondence so that they are within easy reach when you need them.

Making handy storage pockets Edge shelves with strong carpet binding, tacked firmly at intervals, leaving gaps wide enough for scissors, spoons and pens.

Children's rooms

◆Bottle crates make good stacking storage for rolled-up posters, in fact rolls of anything. Take out some of the plastic divisions so that the crate will also do as a shelf unit for shoes, books or torches.

◆For toy boxes that are easy to move from room to room use coloured plastic stacking boxes.

◆A cane mirror with a shelf or a set of shelves (or several all over the wall) can hold tiny books, dolls' house furniture or toy models in an older child's room.

Bedrooms

◆Draw a curtain across a fitted cupboard front; it takes up less space than a standard door. A roller blind (or several next to each other) can look even neater.

◆When buying a bed, buy one with large drawers underneath to increase storage space.

◆Make "fitted" cupboards by installing floor-to-ceiling sliding doors, or a curtain across an alcove, or sliding doors and an end panel against a wall.

◆Use an old-fashioned wicker laundry hamper to store clothes out of season.

Bathrooms

◆If you don't have space for a separate cupboard in the bathroom, build a cupboard around the basin. If you use it to store detergents and cleaning equipment and there are small children in the house, it must be lockable. Hide the key as well.

◆Put the children's bath toys in a string bag and hang it from the wall over the bath, or over the taps, so that they are out of the way when you have a bath.

Workrooms

◆Hang work tools on a pegboard. Paint the profile of each item on the board so that you can see where everything should go (and if anything is not where it should be).

◆Look at office suppliers' catalogues for colourful and useful storage ideas.

◆Use two filing cabinets to make "desk legs" and give you extra storage as well.

Hall

◆Large wicker baskets or old chimney pots make good umbrella stands. Put a plant saucer in the bottom to catch the drips.

◆Place a bentwood hat stand in a small hall for coats and hats. Alternatively, put up a Victorian mirror incorporating narrow shelves and hooks. These are useful because they provide somewhere for gloves and hats or for letters and notes.

Wall baskets *Hang wicker bicycle baskets on the wall—one for each member of the household—and put letters, telephone messages, gloves and scarves in them.*

KITCHEN PLANNING

◆When designing a kitchen, make sure that the three main areas – storage (refrigerator and larder), food preparation (sink, work surface, chopping block, pastry marble, etc.) and cooking (oven and hob) – are fairly close to each other but with sufficient space between them to put things down before washing up, take them off the stove in a hurry and so on.

◆The kitchen is not the best place for the laundry, but if you have no alternative, make sure the space for the washing machine is near the sink because washing machine hoses are normally fairly short.

◆Don't put the cooker next to a door or under the window, particularly if it is gas; the draught can blow out the flame and the light from the window can prevent you from seeing whether or not it is on.

◆Don't put cupboards so high that you will have to stand on a chair or steps to reach things in everyday use.

◆Use a wide shelf (about 22cm/8¾in) as a worktop if space is very limited.

◆Store pots and pans near the oven and hob where you can reach them easily.

◆Allow space for the wastebin where you need it most – under or close to the sink or near the dishwasher.

KITCHEN UNITS

◆When deciding what kitchen units to install, remember that it is easy to have too many. Badly positioned head-height units are inclined to open and hit you on the temple when you least expect it.

Worktop height
Ideally the worktop should be 5–7cm (2–3in) lower than your elbow when you stand at it. Mount units on plinths if they are too low.

◆ Make sure that your units have a flush worktop; they will be much easier to keep clean if they do.

◆ If your kitchen units have no backs, you must fit them, otherwise mice can get in. Cut a piece of hardboard to fit, and fix it to the back. Then paint with gloss paint; gloss paint is easier to clean.

FREE-STANDING FURNITURE

◆ Measure free-standing furniture carefully before you buy it or you may find yourself with a piece of furniture you can't get into the kitchen, or into the space. Suitable furniture includes dressers, washstands with marble tops for rolling pastry, and glass-fronted cupboards.

LARGE KITCHEN

By having units along two walls there is plenty of storage room as well as an eating area in this 4m (14ft) square kitchen.

Shelf Put up a narrow shelf near the cooker for herbs and spices.

Built-in oven and hob These can look neater and are easier to clean than free-standing appliances.

Extractor fan Get an extractor ducted to the outside to minimize cooking smells.

Dishwasher Install it near the sink because it needs to be near the water supply.

GALLEY KITCHEN

By careful planning you can pack a great deal into a very small space. This kitchen is approximately 2 × 2.4m (6 × 7ft).

Wall plate rack Useful for plate storage. Make sure the wall can take the weight.

Rubbish Keep a bin under the sink so that you don't trip over it – mount it inside the sink cupboard door.

Washing machine Keep it near the sink where it is close to a water outlet.

Fridge/freezer A combined unit is better if space is limited.

Saucepan rack Pots and pans make a good wall display and are instantly accessible.

Wall-mounted oven This is useful if you want more low-level cupboards.

Shelf A shelf running the length of the wall is best; things fall off short shelves.

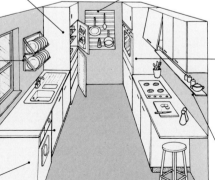

LIGHTING

Plan your lighting and install fittings and switches before you decorate a room because plaster may need to be removed to run wires up inside the wall. Work out all the lighting for a particular room before buying the fittings; you may need less than you think.

TYPES OF LIGHTING

There are four different types of lighting: general overall lighting, task lighting, display or accent lighting and lighting that is primarily decorative.

◆**General overall lighting** Use this for background or ambient lighting in a room. The most familiar type is the pendant that hangs from the ceiling. You can almost double the amount of light by reflecting it off a white wall or ceiling.

◆**Task lighting** Use it to light an area where someone is reading or working. To prevent glare, conceal the light source from the person working and position it so that his or her shadow doesn't fall across the work.

◆**Display or accent lighting** Use this to highlight features in the room, such as plant leaf patterns, architectural arches or alcoves, or to shine onto displays.

◆**Decorative lighting** To add to the room decoration, use lamps which are decorative in their own right, such as Tiffany lamps with their stained glass shades, or lamps in the form of sculptures.

Downlighters

◆Use for both general and task lighting. Place them high (on a wall or in the ceiling) for general lighting. Use table and standard lamps with shades directing light downwards as task lights.

Uplighters

Uplighters send their beam upwards so that the lighting effect is created mainly by reflecting light off the ceiling.

◆Use them to complement general lighting when all the lights are on or to give soft, reflected light in the evening, for example, when you don't want the main lights on.

◆You can use wall lights, free-standing tall spot lights, standard lamps or discreet floor spot lights as uplighters.

BULB SHAPES

◆Globe bulbs are good for lantern, or coolie, shades where you can see the bulb. Normally white.

◆Use mushroom bulbs for shallow light fittings.

◆Use candle-shaped bulbs in some wall lights or chandelier fittings; can be clear, white or twisted.

◆Choose an internally silvered bulb if you want a narrow, concentrated beam of light, or a floodlight or spotlight for a broader flood of light.

Standard pear bulbs

Clear   Pearl finish   Silver crown   **Globe bulb**

Spot reflector bulb (ISL)   **Mushroom bulb**   **Candle bulbs**

Filament tube

Fluorescent strip

GLOSSARY OF COMMON LIGHTING TERMS

A-lamp Standard lightbulb (USA)

Architectural strip or tube See Filament tube

Baffle Shield to prevent glare

Ballast A device fitted to fluorescent tubes to prevent them consuming more and more electricity

Bayonet fitting Type of bulb fitting

Cold beam bulb A spotbulb with a special reflector that reduces the heat of the beam

Crown silvered bulb An internally silvered bulb which gives a sharply defined beam

Diffused light Light filtered evenly through a translucent material

Direct light Light coming directly from a fitting to a surface

Edison screw fitting Standard screw-type bulb fitting

Filament tube Tube-shaped filament bulb

Fluorescent tube Glass tube coated with phosphor powders and containing an inert gas and mercury vapour at low pressure (available in different whites as well as colours)

GLS bulb Standard lightbulb (UK)

Incandescent bulb Lightbulb that gives off a yellowish light (standard bulbs all do this). Pearl-finished bulbs give more diffused light than clear ones

Indirect light Light bounced off another surface before it reaches its destination

ISL bulb Internally silvered reflector bulb which reflects light forwards

Low-voltage bulb A mini bulb running on 12 or 24 volts rather than mains voltage (needs a transformer)

Lux An internationally agreed unit used to measure the amount of light falling on a particular surface

Metal-halide bulb Produces white light (commonly used for outdoor floodlighting)

Multi-mirror bulb Mini low-voltage bulb with integral multi-faceted reflector (used in many modern standard and table lamps)

Neon bulb Coloured bulb used for decoration only

PAR bulb A bulb which incorporates its own reflector to direct a powerful narrowish beam. Heat-resistant

Pendant light Hanging ceiling light

Reflector bulb Bulb which incorporates its own reflector

Spotlight A single light source producing a directed beam

Track An insulated fitting in various lengths into which light fittings can be clipped

Transformer Device to lower or raise the domestic electricity supply from mains voltage to that suitable for low-voltage or neon lighting

Tungsten bulb See Incandescent bulb

Tungsten halogen bulb Incandescent light with halogen gas which gives a brighter light and lasts longer

Volt Unit expressing the potential of an electric circuit

Watt Unit of power describing the electrical output of a bulb

LIGHT FITTINGS

◆For versatility choose portable lamps, since they can be moved around easily if you change your lighting plan.

◆Buy extra lamps if you find that you need to move lamps around regularly; you probably have not got enough.

◆Use lights with low-voltage bulbs if you want more precise control than you can achieve with conventional bulbs. They are very useful for lighting sculptures or pictures on a wall, because they produce less heat than other bulbs. You can buy low-voltage track fittings with a built-in power reducer (they must be professionally installed) or special table and floor lamps with transformers.

▼▼ Don't aim spotlights directly at valuable
◆ ◆ furniture or paintings (or sit table lamps directly under pictures), the lights produce too much heat, which may damage them.

Pendant lights

◆Use for overall lighting, but don't rely on one light because the light it distributes is generally rather bland. You can vary the effects by altering the length of the flex and the careful choice of fitting, bulb and shade. Pendant lights nearly always need other supporting lights.

◆For more light (and a more interesting light), install a chandelier-type fitting which has several bulbs on one stalk.

◆ECONOMY TIP: Chinese paper globes are very useful if you want to hide the bare bulbs in a new home before deciding on the final lighting scheme. They give an efficient and pleasant light, which doesn't glare into the eyes, and are extremely cheap.

◆For maximum versatility, install a pendant light on an adjustable "rise and fall" mechanism, which can be pulled low over an eating area or a coffee table, and pushed up again for general lighting. This is effective in the kitchen if you turn out the task lights so that the working area doesn't intrude on the eating area when you are entertaining, for example.

Ceiling lights

◆Use recessed or semi-recessed ceiling lights to provide discreet lighting; you can't see the light source.

◆If you want to be able to direct the light at an angle, install "eyeball" downlighters which can be swivelled in their sockets.

◆Use one recessed ceiling light to light a space above a coffee table for instance; use several for general lighting for a whole room. If you use several downlighters, arrange the

---

LIGHTING TIPS

◆Lamps with their own reflectors are more expensive to buy than lights that need reflector bulbs, but replacement bulbs for the former are cheap, whereas replacement reflector bulbs are not.

◆Site light switches within easy reach of doors so that as you go out of or enter a room you can switch the light on or off.

◆Install separate switches for groups of lights or individual spotlights, and dimmer switches to enable you to vary the lighting.

◆You need about 20 watts of lighting per square metre/yard of space.

◆Use wall lights to make a room look smaller and pendant lights to make a room look lower.

◆Several table or floor lamps scattered about the room will give a softer effect than one central one. They won't be any more expensive to run if you use low-wattage bulbs.

◆Make a room look broader by directing ceiling lights towards a wall to flood it with an even amount of light – especially effective against pale walls.

---

switching so that you don't have to have all the lights on together.

◆Place a ceiling downlighter close to a wall to effectively light the wall space; the reflection will then provide unobtrusive general room lighting.

Wall lights

◆Use wall-mounted fittings to provide general light in place of a pendant ceiling light in a hall where there is no place to put a table lamp, or where a standard lamp might be tripped over, or on the stairs when a ceiling light is too far away to provide adequate light for you to see the stairs.

◆For background lighting try a pair of wall lights with uplighting shades. The light reflected from the ceiling can be made discreet or quite bright depending on how pale the ceiling is, and the strength of the bulb.

◆A wall light with a glass or acrylic cone will diffuse light gently into a room, adding to the general light level.

◆For an unusual effect, use a ship's bulkhead light vertically instead of horizontally.

Spotlights

◆Use spotlights for accent lighting, of pictures or plants, for example. They are very flexible because the beam can be directed wherever you choose. If you change your picture display, all you need to do is turn the spots to the new focal point. You can also vary the effect by changing the type of bulb.

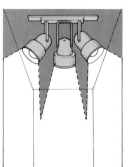 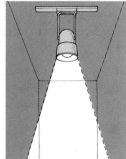

Using spotlights *Use a cluster of spotlights on one light fitting for good general lighting,* above left, *and a single spotlight to light a particular part of a room,* above right.

◆ For maximum light from one electrical source, fix spotlights to a lighting track or cluster fixed to a wall or ceiling.

◆ Fit single spotlights directly to walls, ceilings or floors for accent lighting of plants or groups of paintings.

Standard and table lamps

◆ Use these lamps as uplighters, downlighters or task lights.

◆ If you want a lamp to stand behind an armchair for reading, make sure that the light shines on the book and does not cast a shadow between book and reader. A "coolie" type shade, which is narrow at the top and wide at the bottom, will cast a good light if the lamp is high enough.

◆ Direct a free-standing uplighter at a low, white ceiling to give good reflected light for reading and also for background light. For more control buy a shade that is completely closed at the top.

◆ Use a traditional table lamp to produce enough light for reading and writing and also to give a relaxed feel to the room.

◆ Scatter small ceramic "bowl" lamps about on desks, windowsills and tables to add warmth and softness to a room.

Desk lamps

◆ Use strong uplighters for lighting office space where you need a good light.

◆ Buy an adjustable desk lamp to give you the advantage of flexibility with a direct beam of concentrated light where you need it. With two lamps, you could have one directed upwards, giving general reflected light bounced off the ceiling, and the other directed onto your work.

◆ Look for desk lamps with miniature fluorescent bulbs; they give efficient, longer-lasting and cheaper light.

◆ If space is limited, buy desk lamps that clamp or screw down or that fit into wall brackets. Some even stand on the floor.

Positioning a desk lamp for writing *Place a desk lamp on the left of a right-handed person and vice versa for a left-handed person, so that there is no glare and no shadow falls across the paper.*

Strip lighting

Traditionally used to light work areas where bright, even light is needed, but it can also be used as concealed lighting.

◆ Use concealed small fluorescent tubes and filament tubes to light the space under kitchen cupboards above the worktop, the top of alcoves with shelves and display cabinets.

◆ Fit fluorescent strip lights inside wardrobes, with a sprung switch on the door frame so that the light goes on and off as you open and shut the door.

▼▼ Fit an ultraviolet absorbent jacket
◆◆ around a fluorescent tube because the ultraviolet radiation it produces is harmful to wood, particularly antiques.

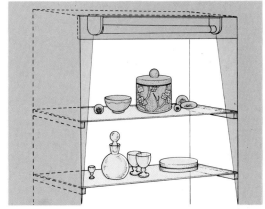

Accent lighting with strip lights *Fit a strip light behind a pelmet above shelving to create effective accent lighting on displayed objects.*

LIGHTING FOR SPECIFIC PURPOSES

◆ Do not position the light sources so that they dazzle.

◆ Make sure no shadows are cast where they might cause people to fall.

▼▼ Do not overload sockets already ◆◆ occupied by electrical appliances because the circuit fuse will blow. Keep water and electrics firmly apart.

▼▼ Do not allow flexes of portable lamps ◆◆ to trail across worktops or anywhere near the sink.

◆ If you have children, use safe connections, childproof safety sockets and fit plugs with partly sheathed pins.

◆ Keep the main switches for outside lights on the inside of the house.

HALL, LIVING ROOM AND KITCHEN

HALL AND STAIRS

◆ Make sure that these are always well lit to prevent accidents, as well as looking "warm" and welcoming.

◆ Use spotlights on a track or in a cluster for good general lighting.

◆ Fit a bright bulb if there is only one pendant light so that there is enough light.

◆ Use wall-mounted lights on the stairs.

◆ Install two-way switches on the stairs, particularly if you have more than one flight of stairs, to make switching on and off easier.

◆ Decorate dark halls with pale colours so that light is reflected off the walls.

LIVING ROOM

◆ Use accent lighting to pick out specific areas, pictures and sculptures, arches, alcoves, or plants.

◆ Use task lighting, such as a standard lamp or table lamp, for reading areas, tables where board games are played and for the music centre.

◆ One pendant with a simple, modern shade can look good hung low over a low coffee table, or group several small pendant lights together.

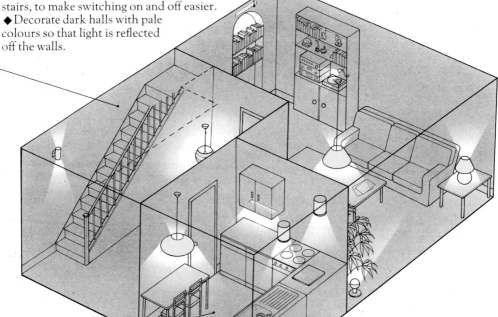

KITCHEN LIGHTING

◆ Good general lighting and task lighting are important in the kitchen. It is essential to have your work space well lit.

◆ Install separate switches for general lights, task lights and lights above an eating area so that you don't have to have them all on.

BEDROOMS AND BATHROOMS

BEDROOM LIGHTING
◆ In a bedroom fit good general lighting for dressing by, bedside lights to read by and a light which shines into the wardrobe.
◆ Reading lights by the bed should be high enough to shine onto the book and not cast a shadow but not so high that they shine directly into your eyes.

◆ If your bedside table is usually cluttered with alarm clocks, books, radio alarm etc., mount your bedside lamp on the wall.
◆ If yours is a double bed, make sure the light doesn't shine into your partner's eyes or is so bright as to keep him (or her) awake if he doesn't want to read.

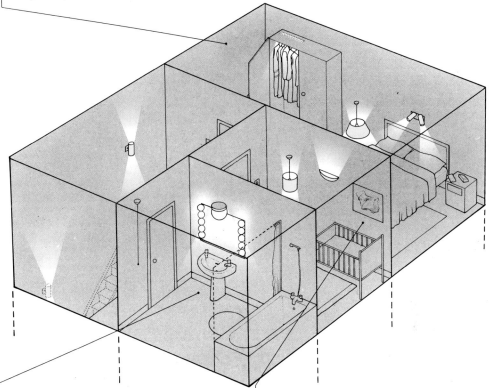

BATHROOM LIGHTING
◆ Line the sides of the mirror with a strip of bare bulbs. Light then falls above, below and to each side of your face, making shaving and making up easier.
◆ Put a small strip light inside the bathroom cupboard where razor blades and medicines are kept so that you can find them easily.
◆ Seal all fittings with glass or plastic covers specially designed for wet areas. Don't take portable lights into the bathroom – water and electricity don't mix.
◆ Use only a pull cord switch inside the bathroom. If you want a wall switch, fit it on the wall outside the bathroom. A dimmer switch is good for late night visits.

CHILD'S ROOM
◆ Use wall-mounted lights in a child's room instead of free-standing fittings, adjustable or fragile lamps which can be broken. Use robust fittings with an authorized safety symbol and which can be fixed to a wall or ceiling, away from small fingers.
◆ Install a dimmer switch if your child is frightened of the dark.
◆ Leave a glowing nightlight in a baby's room.

HOUSEPLANTS

Houseplants can immediately transform a stark room into a warm and welcoming one. Choose evergreen plants that stay green permanently under the correct growing conditions. Most perennials (plants that die back each winter when outside and flower again the following year) will keep their leaves if kept inside through the winter.

Read the care label or ask the nurseryman about growing conditions before you buy a plant: some are as indestructible as plastic; others need carefully controlled conditions.

KEEPING PLANTS HEALTHY

◆ If you have a garden or balcony, put the plants outside in the summer to give them fresh air and sunshine. If you have no garden, open the window to ventilate the room but guard against strong draughts.

Encouraging bushy growth *If a plant starts to get "leggy", i.e. has long stems with few leaves, pinch out the growing tips to encourage more growth from the base of the stem or plant.*

Watering

◆ Water plants only when they need it. Let them almost dry out before watering. For most plants this means watering once to three times a week between spring and autumn and only once to three times a month in winter. Start "summer" watering again when the weather begins to warm up.

◆ Rain water is the best water for plants, so collect it if you have the facilities. Otherwise, tap water is fine for most plants. Before you water more delicate plants, let the water stand overnight in a bucket so that it reaches room temperature and some of the chlorine evaporates.

◆ Don't water cacti and succulents in winter unless there are signs of shrivelling, in which case, water sparingly.

◆ Check plant trays about half an hour after watering and pour away any water.

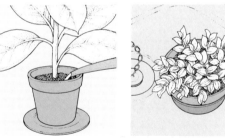

The best way to water *Either water with a long-spouted watering can directly under the leaves into the soil, above left, or immerse the pot in water to just below the compost level and leave it to soak until the soil glistens, above right. Leave to drain.*

TIPS FOR WATERING

◆ Don't water routinely (every Monday, Wednesday and Saturday, for instance), or you may overwater. Too much water means that the roots get waterlogged, leaving them cold and deprived of air.

◆ The larger the leaf surface of a plant, the more water it will need.

◆ Be particularly careful not to overwater in winter.

◆ Never leave a plant standing in pools of water; it may rot.

Feeding

◆ Feed houseplants every two weeks in the growth period (spring and summer). Healthy growth depends on an adequate supply of plant nutrients – nitrogen (for leaf growth), phosphates (for root development) and potash (for fruit or flowers), together with small amounts of trace elements. The amount of each nutrient contained in fertilizer should be on the label.

◆ Don't fertilize a newly repotted plant; fresh potting compost contains about two months' worth of plant nutrients. If you feed the plant, the roots will not spread into the new soil.

◆ Liquid fertilizer is the best way to feed a pot plant. Put five drops or so into 600ml (1pt) water, then water the plants with the solution. This way you can be sure to get fertilizer into the soil, and not to put neat fertilizer on young roots or leaves, which can burn them.

◆ Reduce or stop feeding during resting periods (usually winter). Start again when new growth appears.

▼▼ Don't overfeed, you will encourage
◆ ◆ weak growth. Too little food encourages disease or pest attack.

Light

◆ The majority of plants like to be kept in semi-shade, filtered sunlight or under bright house lights, but out of direct sun, which can burn the leaves.

◆ Plants with variegated leaves need more sunlight than other plants, because the sunlight brings out the colour.

◆ Flowering plants will need some sunlight to get them to flower.

◆ Cacti and succulents need more light than other plants and can stand direct sunlight.

Temperature

◆ Keep most plants in a moderate temperature of 10–15°C (50–60°F) during the spring/summer growing period and a slightly cooler temperature 7–10°C (45–50°F) during the resting season. Some hardy plants will do well at temperatures as low as 4°C (40°F) – so they can be left on the windowsill, even behind the curtains, all year round.

◆ Keep tender tropical varieties in temperatures above 15°C (60°F); don't leave them on the windowsill behind the curtains in winter, it can get very cold.

◆ Provide extra humidity if the room temperature goes above 24°C (75°F), see below.

◆ Keep the temperature constant; avoid sudden changes. Put a maximum/minimum thermometer in a shady part of the room.

Humidity

◆ Group plants together in centrally heated rooms so that they reap the benefits of increased moisture from the damp compost and foliage of the surrounding plants.

◆ If the room is very dry, spray your plants all over with a mister in the morning and again at midday if you can. Do not mist while the foliage is exposed to direct sunlight; the combination of sunlight and water can burn the leaves.

Increasing moisture levels *If the weather is very dry, "double-pot" by burying plants and their pots in a waterproof container filled with moist peat, above left. Or stand pots in a dish of absorbent pebbles and keep the pebbles wet almost to the top, above right.*

Plant pests and diseases

◆ If you see trouble, act at once. You might save an expensive plant that you would otherwise have to throw out.

◆ Keep affected plants away from other plants while you treat the problem to prevent it spreading.

REMEDIES FOR COMMON PESTS AND DISEASES

APHIDS
(Greenfly, blackfly, grey or orange fly)

◆ Remove these because they suck sap in shoot tips and flower buds, distorting growth. They also secrete a sticky substance, which attracts mould, and carry virus disease.

GREEN TIP: Wipe them off with your fingers and thumb if there are not too many of them, alternatively spray with insecticidal, or potassium, soap.

◆ Spray with a systemic insecticide.

CATERPILLARS
GREEN TIP: Pick off and destroy individual caterpillars.

RED SPIDER MITE
Look out for the signs in hot dry weather. The spiders are almost invisible to the naked eye. You'll notice their webs on the underside of leaves.

◆ Spray an infested plant with a systemic insecticide. Mist plants daily in dry weather to prevent a recurrence.

MEALY BUG
These are about 5mm ($\frac{1}{4}$in) long and resemble woodlice. On the leaves, they protect themselves with a white water- and insecticide-proof "wool".

GREEN TIP: Wipe small infestations off with a damp cloth or cotton bud.

◆ Spray more severe infestations weekly with a systemic insecticide.

◆ For root mealy bugs, immerse potting compost in a systemic insecticide two or three times at fortnightly intervals.

SCALE INSECTS
Seen as small brown waxy discs, which attach themselves to veins on the underside of leaves. They suck sap and secrete a sticky honeydew substance that attracts mould.

GREEN TIP: Wipe off with a damp cloth or cotton bud.

◆ If badly infested, the leaves will turn sticky and yellow; throw the plant and pot away to prevent the insects spreading.

BOTRYTIS (grey mould)
◆ Cut away and destroy all affected parts and take out mouldy compost. Destroy a badly affected plant.

◆ Spray with a systemic fungicide.

◆ Improve ventilation and reduce watering to prevent a recurrence.

CROWN AND STEM ROT
The crown and stem may become soft and rotten as a result of overwatering or of keeping the plant too cool.

◆ If you catch it early enough, you could try cutting away the rotten areas and reviving the rest of the plant in the proper conditions. If the plant does not respond quickly, throw the plant and pot away.

VIRUS
Normally shows as yellow or pale green patches or white streaks on leaves, and causes distortion or stunting of the plant.

◆ Throw the plant and pot away. There is no cure and it can spread to other plants.

◆ Treat any aphid infestation; aphids carry virus disease.

Repotting

◆ Repot plants into a larger pot when the potting mixture dries out very quickly and the plant needs more frequent watering and feeding than usual. Do this in the spring just before the plant starts into its main growth period. If you do it in winter when the plant is dormant, the roots won't spread into the new soil.

◆ Repot into a pot that is only slightly larger than the old one, otherwise you encourage too much root growth instead of leaf growth.

◆ If your plant is already in a large pot and you don't want the plant to grow much taller, "top-dress". Remove the top soil and replace it with new potting compost.

Repotting a plant *Line the base of the new pot with drainage material so that the plant will sit at the same level, above left. Place the old pot inside the new one, and fill the gap with potting mixture, above right. Remove the pot and insert the plant, fill gaps with potting mixture and firm in well.*

PLANT CARE WHILE YOU GO ON HOLIDAY

◆If there's no one available to water your plants, use one of the automatic watering methods. The length of time that you can leave plants depends on the weather and the thirst of the plants. Test your chosen watering method for a time while you are at home to give yourself an idea of how long the water will last.

◆"Double-pot" your plants in a container of moist peat, see page 161. This way they will last for a couple of weeks.

◆Buy self-watering containers, which will keep a supply of water for a limited period. These are available from garden centres. Some self-watering containers store enough water for up to a month.

THE PLASTIC BAG METHOD

◆You can "bag" your plants for periods of up to a week – no longer because the plant may begin to rot.

◆Don't leave "bagged" plants in direct sunlight; they will produce too much condensation and are more likely to rot.

1 Water the plant well. Push four bamboo stakes taller than the plant into the compost at equal intervals around the rim of the pot and angled outwards, so that the bag won't touch the leaves.

2 Put the plant and pot into a clear airtight plastic bag, big enough to enclose the plant completely. Seal the top of the bag with adhesive tape. This way the water is recycled back into the compost after evaporating from the leaves.

Capillary matting

Capillary matting is suitable only for plants in plastic pots with drainage holes. Clay pots tend to absorb the water rather than pass it to the plant.

◆Use capillary matting if you have quantities of plants to leave. Some plants can be left for two to three weeks and the matting can be reused several times.

◆If you have left it too late and have no time to buy capillary matting, try using sodden newspapers instead.

Using a capillary mat *Place one end of the mat in a basin, sink or bath filled with water and the other end on the draining board or a shelf behind the bath; the end that is in the water should be lower than the level of plants. The mat absorbs the water and the plants take up the water as they need it.*

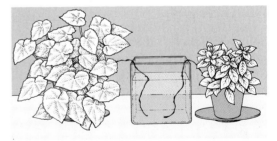

Making a watering wick *For individual plants, or plants in clay pots, make a wick, using any water-absorbent material, such as cotton laces, oil lamp wicks, old ties or tights. Plant one end firmly in the compost and the other trailing in a container of water.*

GUIDE TO EASY-CARE VARIETIES

Mother of thousands, or Strawberry geranium

Painted nettle

Asparagus fern

Grape ivy

Bromeliad

CISSUS spp.
◆ Perfect plants for beginners. *C. antarctica* (kangaroo vine) has light green leaves and the *C. rhombifolia* (grape ivy) has darker leaves. Use as a room divider or to cover a wall.
Position Needs warm filtered sun. Likes good ventilation in very hot weather. *C. antarctica* can stand draughts.
Size Can grow to a height of 2m (6ft) with a spread of 60cm (2ft) in 2 years.
Watering Needs plenty of water in summer, less in winter. Spray if the foliage becomes dry.

PAINTED NETTLE
Coleus blumei
◆ Coleus plants have a great variety of brilliantly coloured leaves. Group several plants together to get the full effect of their colours.
Position Plenty of sunlight to bring out the colour. Keep them somewhere that is usually quite warm.
Size Grows to a spread of up to 45cm (18in) in one year.

Watering Keep the soil moist. Spray occasionally.

ASPARAGUS FERN
Asparagus setacus
◆ A vigorous fern related to the vegetable asparagus.
Position Stand it on a windowsill where it will get plenty of light, in a warm temperature.
Size Produces stems up to 1.2m (3ft 6in) long.
Watering Water enough to keep the potting mixture slightly moist, but no more.

BROMELIADS
◆ Some of the easiest plants to grow, bromeliads have brilliantly coloured leaves.
Position Keep in a warm temperature, with filtered sun.
Size Grows to about 30cm (1ft).
Watering Water when the compost looks dry, pouring the water into the centre "cup" of the plant with a narrow-spouted watering can.

MOTHER OF THOUSANDS, STRAWBERRY GERANIUM
Saxifraga stolonifera
◆ Compact plant with veined leaves and little plantlets hanging from red, thread-like stems. Ideal for a hanging basket or high on a shelf.
Position Needs plenty of light and an hour or two of morning sun to help it keep its leaf colouring.
Size The main plant reaches about 20cm (8in).
Watering Keep the root-ball moist but not too wet.

SWISS CHEESE PLANT
Monstera deliciosa
◆ Ideal for "decorating" an empty corner because of its stylish sculptural shape.
Position Likes a warm shady position.
Watering Water thoroughly, but allow the compost to become quite dry before watering again.
Other care Use a moss stick to provide a support for the plant and to supply moisture

Swiss cheese plant   Rubber plant   Kentia palm   Cast-iron plant

Silk oak

through the aerial roots to the upper leaves. Clean old leaves regularly.

SILK OAK
Grevillea robusta
◆ A good indoor tree-like shrub with evergreen, fern-like leaves.
Position Keep in a cool sunny place.
Size Can grow to 11.5m (5ft) in two years.
Watering Water liberally from spring to autumn, sparingly in winter.
Other care Encourage bushy growth by stopping the main shoot when it is young.

RUBBER PLANT
Ficus elastica decora
◆ Use it in a group of plants or on its own as a decorative feature.
Position Likes a warm shady position.
Size Can grow to 2m (6ft) tall.
Watering Water when not quite dry. Stand in a bucket of water to let it soak up as much as it wants.

Other care Clean the old leaves occasionally, not the new ones.

KENTIA PALM
Howia belmoreana
PARLOUR PALM
Chamaedorea elegans
◆ The Kentia palm is a tall elegant plant. Ideal for the corner of a room. Buy young Parlour palms, as the leaves become coarse with age.
Position Warm filtered sun.
Size A Kentia palm reaches heights of up to 2.5m (8ft); Parlour palms take several years to reach 90cm (3ft).
Watering Water regularly, but keep well drained so that the roots don't stay wet.
Other care Avoid sudden temperature changes.

CAST-IRON PLANT
Aspidistra elatior
Position Use it in a shaded corner where other plants won't grow. Likes cool filtered sun.
Size Grows to a height/spread of 1m (3ft).

Watering Water it well, especially in summer, every time it dries out. Don't keep it waterlogged. Feed every two weeks in the growing season.
Other care Polish the old leaves from time to time with a proprietary product.

SUCCULENTS AND CACTI
◆ Good plants for beginners as they can stand a great deal of neglect and bad treatment.
◆ Succulents and cacti need sunshine and good ventilation. They all like warmth in the summer growing period and a cooler, dry, winter rest period. For best results, keep them on a very sunny windowsill and, if possible, give them a period out of doors in the summer.
◆ Give little or no water in the autumn and winter.

CUT FLOWERS

Cut garden flowers early in the morning, before the sun reaches full strength, because the heat of the sun draws moisture from the petals, or in the evening so that they may regain moisture overnight.

▼▼ Don't cut flowers on a hot day because
♦ ♦ they won't last as long.

▼▼ Don't buy flowers if: the ends of the
♦ ♦ stems are dark or slimy; the pollen is falling off; the petals (of daffodils and tulips particularly) are becoming transparent or looking brown.

♦ Ask the shop to wrap them so that their heads are well protected, especially from wind and heat.

♦ Look for buds that are just opening, very tightly closed buds may not open. Daffodils are the exception; they are nearly always sold in bud and will open well and last a long time bought like that.

Making flowers last longer

♦ Cut flowers will last much longer if their stems are treated so that they can take up water quickly, see below.

♦ Keep the water topped up all the time; water with a proprietary cut-flower food.

♦ Keep the vase out of direct sun, direct heat and draughts.

♦ Remove dying heads immediately because they emit ethylene gas, which can affect the healthy flowers.

PREPARING STEMS

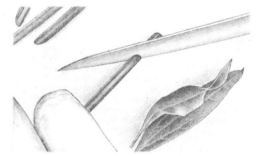

1 *Remove the bottom leaves. Cut about 1cm (½in) off the end of the stem in case it was sealed while out of water. Cut on the slant.*

For woody stems *Peel the leathery outer skin off the bottom 1.5cm (¾in) or crush it with a mallet.*

2 *Split all except woody or small hollow stems to about 1cm(½in) from the bottom.*
For large hollow stems *Turn the flower upside down, fill the stem with water, then plug it with cotton wool.*

Hellebores and tulips *Pierce right through the stem at regular intervals, or score from the head to the stem end with a needle, to prevent an airlock in the stem, which will stop water getting to the flower.*

3 *Place the stems in deep water and leave them there for a few hours or overnight.*

DRYING FLOWERS

◆Gather the plants on a dry day. Choose flowers which are not quite fully developed; they will keep their colour better. Don't pick damaged or badly formed flowers.

Hanging flowers to dry

Suitable plants for hanging include: hydrangeas, early summer grasses, which still have their seeds, and everlasting flowers or "immortelles", such as helichrysum, statice, rhodanthe and ammobium.

◆Dry the flowers, heads down, in a warm, dry, well-ventilated space out of direct sunlight, for example, near a boiler.

◆Remove the lower leaves on the stems because they shrivel and slow down the dehydration process.

◆Wire the heads of flowers that are on weak stems, before you dry them, so that they are supported, see below left.

◆Tie the flowers in small bunches so that the inner stems can dry.

Using a drying agent

◆Use this method if you want dried flower heads that look like the fresh plant. The agents used remove moisture, but preserve colour and shape. Suitable flowers include: daffodils and narcissi, hellebores, mimosa, primroses, tulips, carnations and pinks, clematis, paeonies, marigolds, roses, dahlias and zinnias.

◆Use alum or borax powders for the more delicate flowers, silica gel or prepared sand for robust ones. Silica gel dries flowers in two or three days; the other agents take two to three weeks.

◆If you use sand, you must prepare it first. Place the sand in a bucket, fill the bucket with water, stir well and pour off the water. Repeat several times. Spread the sand on trays and dry in the sun.

◆You can use the drying agents again. Dry them after use in baking trays in a very cool oven (no more than 120°C/250°F/gas mark ½) for an hour and store in containers.

1 Remove stems from flowers and wire the heads, see below.

2 Cover the bottom of an airtight tin with a 6mm (¼in) layer of drying agent. Place the flowers in the tin.

3 Gently sprinkle more of the agent over the petals through a sieve. When the flowers are covered by at least 6mm (¼in), seal the container.

4 Peer into the tin every two or three days to check whether the petals have become papery and dry.

WIRING FLOWER HEADS

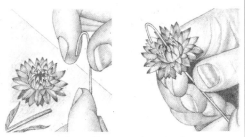

1 Remove the stalks. Cut a length of narrow wire and make a tiny hook in one end, above left. Push the straight end of the wire through the flower face, pull the wire through and embed the hook in the flower face, above right.

2 When the flower has dried, slip a corn stalk over the wire, or attach the wire to a twig.

ANTIQUES AND VALUABLES

Treat your antique furniture with respect but don't be afraid to use it. Furniture was made to be sat on, eaten off, and generally used. Avoid subjecting furniture and valuables to *extremes of anything – light, dampness and dry heat can all do irreparable damage. Get valuable pieces repaired as soon as possible if they are damaged.*

HARMFUL CONDITIONS

◆Don't use any sort of paraffin or bottled gas heaters in a room where you have valuable furniture or paintings because they produce a lot of moisture. They also produce gases containing tiny amounts of sulphuric acid, which can harm furniture.

▼▼ Don't put valuables – antique furniture,
◆ ◆ paintings or books – against a newly plastered wall; it will be damp.

◆Try to avoid any sudden changes in temperature and humidity. A sudden move from an unsuitable atmosphere to a suitable one can be as bad for furniture (and especially a piano) as leaving it where it was.

Light

Any light can affect the colour of wood to a surprising degree; it makes light wood become darker and dark wood lighter.

◆Protect furniture with shutters, blinds and sun curtains: sunlight is damaging.

▼▼ Don't leave a piece of furniture under a
◆ ◆ window, particularly if the surface is inlaid with dark and light wood, because light can destroy the effect completely. Damage caused by light can't be reversed without removing some of the surface.

Heat

Heat dries wood out, causing it to split. It also dries out fabric and paper, making it very fragile.

▼▼ Don't place portable heaters near a piece
◆ ◆ of antique furniture, or put furniture, books or paintings near a fire or radiator.

◆If you have a weekend home that is closed all week and opened up at weekends, leave your heating on very low in winter if possible, so that you don't subject the furniture to sudden changes of temperature.

◆Get the central heating thermostat checked regularly to make sure that it works.

◆Use low-voltage spotlights, see page 155. Don't direct ordinary spotlamps or other lamps directly onto furniture or pictures because they can become very hot and damage wood, frames and pictures.

Damp

Damp in the form of condensation or rising damp can cause mould to develop, warp furniture, damage polished surfaces and will rot fabric.

▼▼ Don't keep any pieces on a bare stone or
◆ ◆ brick floor or too near any outside walls because they can be cold and often very slightly damp. Don't put furniture or paintings against a damp wall.

▼▼ Don't keep good furniture or paintings
◆ ◆ in the bathroom.

Humidity

◆Ideally, keep valuables at a humidity level of 50–60 percent. It is safer for a room to be too humid rather than too dry. Above 70 percent, moulds might form. Below 40 percent paper and water-absorbent materials become brittle and wood shrinks, and may then warp and crack. Buy a hydrometer to keep a constant check on humidity levels.

◆If your house is very dry, install a humidifier that fans vaporized water into the air to raise the humidity level.

LOOKING AFTER FURNITURE

◆ Make sure the legs of any antique furniture share an even weight. If a piece of furniture sits wrongly for some time, it may warp slightly and this can be difficult, or even impossible, to mend. If the floor is uneven, put wedges under the legs to compensate.

◆ Inspect your antiques for any signs of damage or deterioration at least once a year, whether they are actually in use or being stored in a separate room.

◆ Don't overload old furniture because this weakens the joints. Drawers particularly can fall apart if too many things are stuffed into them.

◆ Keep any pieces that fall off the furniture. Simple repairs can sometimes be done at home; difficult repairs, or repairs to very valuable pieces, should be done by a professional repairer.

▼▼ Never put a new seat cover over an old
◆ ◆ one because this will make the seat too big and you can break the seat rail joints trying to force the seat into the frame.

◆ If a drawer is sticking, ease it out and rub a candle along the runners, or sprinkle talcum powder on them, see page 95.

◆ On bookcases and wardrobes, make sure that the interior catches are locked before you close the second door. Otherwise the doors can open and this may split the wood around the lock.

◆ Polish the brass only when you are polishing the wood, and use the same wax furniture polish on it. Never use a patent brass cleaner on brass furniture fittings. It will not only make the brass too bright, but often smears and leaves white marks on the wood round the brass. These smears must be removed by an expert, which is expensive.

◆ Don't write at polished tables without a writing pad or block under the piece of paper; don't scratch the surface of the wood with sharp implements or stand on furniture with shoes on.

MOVING ANTIQUE FURNITURE

◆ Move and handle as little as possible to avoid damaging it.

▼▼ Don't move a heavy piece of furniture
◆ ◆ on your own, even if it's small; carry it by the lowest load-bearing part.

◆ Before you move furniture, remove any drawers and other removable parts so that they don't fall out during the move. Shut all doors firmly and lock them if possible to prevent them from swinging open. If they won't lock, secure them with tape and/or adhesive putty, see below.

▼▼ Never tip a piece of furniture back on
◆ ◆ its legs or turn it without lifting it because you will weaken the legs. Lift it right off its legs, then move or turn it.

◆ Carry stools and chairs by the legs to avoid weakening the seat joints.

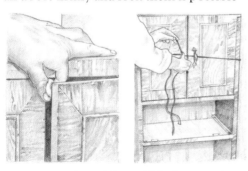

Securing cupboard doors *If the doors won't stay shut, tack the corners with a bit of reusable adhesive putty, above left. Then tie a length of binding tape or string right around the piece, above right.*

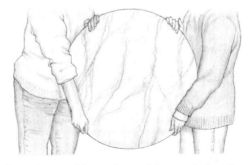

Carrying marble or glass table tops *Lift and carry them in a vertical position. Carried horizontally they can break under their own weight.*

Care of various surfaces

◆Clean the surface of boulle (marquetry using thin sheets of brass or pewter and tortoiseshell, mother of pearl and ivory) with a soft brush or a hair dryer set on cool. Never use a duster or chamois leather because the surface may be loose or the metal proud of the inlaid material; the cloth or leather could catch in the metal and pull pieces out.

◆Leave flaking lacquer well alone, because treatment is difficult.

▼▼Don't rub gilded furniture and never let
◆ ◆ water get onto gilt; it will damage it permanently.

◆Never try to repair or touch up gilded furniture with any form of gold paint because it gives a completely different effect and will soon discolour, leaving the gilding in a worse state than before.

Storing antique furniture

◆Keep the storeroom clean, well ventilated and dry because wood and upholstery are very susceptible to attack by woodworm, moth and mould.

◆Don't store your valuable pieces in a damp basement because the wood may warp or become mouldy.

◆Cover furniture with a clean dust sheet or a special cover to protect it from light and dirt while it is in store. Never put dirty dust sheets onto clean furniture.

◆Dust sheets must be made from a light, closely woven cotton. Make fitted covers with French seams because loose threads can stick to upholstery or catch and pull off pieces of veneer and metal decorations.

◆Wash dust sheets at least once a year.

◆Be very careful how you put on and remove dust sheets and covers – don't whisk them away with a flourish or you may damage the furniture.

CARING FOR VALUABLES

◆If in any doubt, get the advice of a professional.

▼▼Don't attempt to repair anything valu-
◆ ◆ able yourself; you will probably ruin it.

Books

◆The temperature of a room in which books are kept should ideally not be higher than 15°C (60°F); never put them above a radiator, the heat can seriously damage them.

◆Make sure the room is not too dry. If books get too dry, the paper and the binding will become brittle and the adhesives will deteriorate.

◆Don't pack books tightly in the shelf; you can damage the bindings. Put similar-sized books together for support.

◆Lay very large books on their sides as they may be too thick or heavy to support their own weight. Don't stack too many books on top of each other though, because you can damage the bindings.

◆When moving valuable books, wrap each one in clean paper and pack it on its side in tough cardboard boxes padded with blankets so the books can't slide around.

▼▼Never put books loose on the back seat
◆ ◆ of a car; they will slide around and get damaged and sunlight will dry them out.

◆Dust all your books about once a year. Work on one shelf at a time and start with the top shelf. Have a strong table next to you to put the books on.

◆If dust has got inside a book, open up the book, blow the dust very gently, page by

Taking a book down from the shelf *Push the books on either side forward so that you can get a firm grip. Never pull a book out of a bookcase by the top of its spine or by gripping it with your finger-nails; you will damage the binding.*

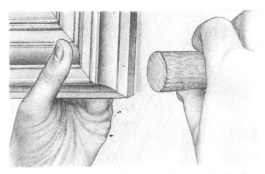

Dusting a book *Hold the book by its front edge to keep it closed so that you don't transfer the dust to the inside of the book. Gently brush along the top edge with a clean, dry, soft brush. A shaving brush is ideal.*

Protecting paintings *Fix two corks to the back of a painting on an outside wall, to allow a passage of air to flow between the back of the painting and the wall and prevent condensation damage.*

page, or brush it out with a soft water-colour paint brush.

▼▼ Don't bang books together to get rid of
♦ ♦ the dust; you will damage the bindings.

Paper

♦ Keep paper flat to prevent it from warping. Store it in an airtight box interleaved with acid-free tissue. Pick it up by the margins and support it with the palm of your hand, or use the acid-free tissue.

▼▼ Don't keep trying to unfold paper, it will
♦ ♦ eventually crack along the fold.

♦ Dust very gently with a soft brush. Don't brush very brittle paper.

▼▼ Handle paper as little as possible. Mod-
♦ ♦ ern papers are made from poor-quality materials and are apt to yellow and disintegrate. Older paper made from linen fibre is much stronger and stays white.

Paintings

♦ Hang paintings where they are free from direct sunlight, draughts and damp and keep artificial light on the paintings low. Do not hang pictures on freshly plastered walls, above radiators or on sections of wall which have hot pipes or internal flues.

▼▼ Don't put picture lights on valuable
♦ ♦ paintings or paintings on wood, metal, paper or vellum because the light and heat can damage the picture. For the same reason don't place a standard or table lamp immediately beneath a picture.

♦ Support large, heavy frames underneath to prevent the mitres from opening under the strain. Either hang the picture so that the base is resting on a sideboard or fix small blocks of wood to the wall for the frame to rest on.

♦ Choose varnished or sealed wood frames because they are easier to clean.

♦ When taking down a painting with a carved or fragile plaster frame, lower it onto a pillow or other padded surface to avoid damaging the frame.

♦ Keep works of art on paper (water-colours, drawings and prints) framed under glass to prevent the surface getting dirty.

♦ If a drawing or print gets damp, dry it between layers of blotting paper to stop it buckling as it dries, see below.

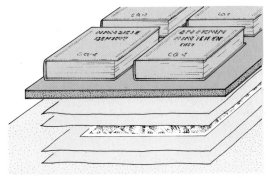

Drying a damp drawing or print *Take it out of its frame and place it between several pieces of thick blotting paper under a gentle, even weight (a piece of melamine-covered board and a few books are ideal). Change the blotting paper nearest to the surface of the drawing after an hour, then again after another hour, then two hours. Change the paper again every 12 hours for a couple of days.*

CLEANING PICTURES

OIL PAINTINGS

◆Dust pictures with a very clean duster or brush. If you use anything that is even slightly greasy it will grind the dust in. Even a speck of dust can act as a focus for condensation.

▼▼ Don't clean a valuable painting yourself
◆◆ because you may ruin it; take it to a restorer instead.

◆Brush mould off the surface of a painting with a soft brush. Move the painting to a warm dry place for several weeks to dry it out.

◆Apply a very thin film of cream furniture polish after dusting to brighten the surface. All advice from now on is: don't do any more to a painting. However, if the painting has been in a very smoky atmosphere and you are adamant about cleaning it, there are patent cleaners on the market which are effective. Alternatively, moisten a piece of cotton wool in an ammonia solution (3ml/$\frac{1}{2}$ tsp ammonia to a cup of cold water) and wipe the painting. Then apply a thin layer of wax polish and rub gently.

WATER-COLOURS, PRINTS AND DRAWINGS

▼▼ Don't touch the water-colours with water;
◆◆ the paint will run. Water-colours are almost impossible to clean, especially by an amateur.

◆Remove surface dust by rubbing very gently with a bread ball. This will absorb a little dust without damaging the paper or the paint. Real erasers are too rough.

Cleaning an oil painting *Dust the painting lightly with a cotton rag or a clean soft brush. Don't use soap, water, bread-crumbs or an eraser because the smallest speck left on the paint-ing will attract moisture.*

Cleaning works of art on paper *Very gently stroke the sur-face of the paper with a bread ball. Don't drag the bread ball across it. Brush any crumbs away gently with a water-colour paint brush.*

PICTURE FRAMES

◆Wipe wooden frames with a cloth squeezed out in warm detergenty water, then polish with a little cream furniture polish.

◆Gilt frames that are not valuable can be cleaned with a dry-cleaning solvent. Alternatively, use a cloth dipped in a little warmed turpentine or white spirit. Warm white spirit or turpentine by standing the bottle in a bowl of hot water. Don't touch valuable frames.

▼▼ Don't touch the picture while cleaning or
◆◆ touching up the frame; you may damage it.

◆Dust ornate frames lightly. The beading comes off very quickly if it gets wet, or if it gets knocked in any way.

Touching up scratches *Touch up modern gilt frames with gilt paint; you can buy small pots from art suppliers. These paints are poisonous, so don't lick your fingers while working with them.*

Cleaning the glass *Wipe the glass with a piece of cotton wool dipped in a solution of vinegar and water or just warm water.*

Enamels

◆ Handle enamel with great care; it is actually multi-layered glass fired onto a metal base and it is easily chipped. Enamel can't be repaired without reheating, which will probably do more damage.
◆ Dust very occasionally with a water-colour paint brush. Never use water, it can work its way between the layers and lead to corrosion.

Ivory, bone and horn

◆ Keep out of direct sunlight and away from any form of heat such as radiators, radiant heaters and spotlights. Heat and sunlight dry them out, causing cracking.
◆ Keep ivory and bone in a light place but away from direct sunlight; light keeps them white. Keeping them in the dark accelerates the yellowing caused by ageing.
◆ If you need to put ivory, bone or horn away for a while, wrap it in acid-free tissue paper. Don't use cotton wool, soft paper or cloth as they all retain moisture, which will work its way into the ivory, bone or horn. Don't use coloured paper or cloth whose colour may be transferred to the object.
◆ Dust frequently with a soft cloth to avoid scratching the surface. Dust carved ivory with a water-colour paint brush. Never wash ivory or allow it to come into contact with liquid because it absorbs liquid, which can cause it to swell.
◆ Polish ivory with a cloth dipped in whiting, followed by a wax polish.
🍃 GREEN TIP: Protect ivory, bone and horn with a coat of almond oil.
◆ Remove yellow stains by rubbing with a piece of cotton wool dipped in 20 volume hydrogen peroxide; leave in the sun to dry.
▼▼ Don't bleach old ivory – the yellowing
◆◆ (patina) is valued.

Tortoiseshell

◆ Keep it out of sunlight or strong artificial light. Even a small amount of light can cause tortoiseshell to lose its lustre and even turn it white and milky-looking.

Polishing whitened tortoiseshell *Remove the top layer with very fine wet-and-dry abrasive paper, working as gently and evenly as possible. When the white layer is removed, polish the surface with jeweller's rouge or wax polish on a soft cloth.*

◆ Rub dried tortoiseshell with repeated coats of linseed oil or wax polish. If this doesn't work and the piece is valuable, take it to an expert. If the piece isn't valuable, remove the dead layer and repolish the layer beneath, see above.
◆ Clean tortoiseshell in bad condition with a paste made by moistening jeweller's rouge with a couple of drops of olive oil. Rub in gently with a soft cloth, leave for a few minutes, then polish with a clean duster. Tortoiseshell in good condition can be cleaned with furniture cream.
◆ Wash imitation tortoiseshell in warm soapy water.
◆ Repair broken bits with an epoxy resin adhesive. You can use another piece of tortoiseshell to patch the first piece. Boil the new piece to soften it enough for cutting, cut it to shape, then flatten it by putting a heavy weight on it. Glue it into place.

Lacquer

◆ Keep lacquer in a balanced temperature; it's particularly prone to damage from damp.
◆ You can repair mass-produced 19th-century lacquer with model aircraft paints or nail varnish. For a good deep red, mix nail varnishes together.
▼▼ Don't attempt to retouch valuable old
◆◆ lacquer or flaking lacquer; it will just deteriorate faster.

Wooden boxes and ornaments

▼▼ Keep these well away from water. Wood
♦ ♦ absorbs water and will crack, warp or go
soft if left wet for any length of time.

♦ If a box has a missing hinge, look out for a
similar, more battered box you could take
the hinges off; alternatively, find a jeweller
who can make one.

♦ Use household glue to repair or replace
worn baize or leather.

▼▼ Keep old cylinder musical boxes out of
♦ ♦ direct sunlight or away from any form of
heat, because the shellac cement used to
secure the mechanism slowly melts and sinks
to the bottom of the cylinder.

▼▼ Don't clean, oil or touch the mechanism
♦ ♦ of a musical box yourself; take it to a
professional repairer.

♦ Run the mainspring of a musical box down
before moving it, to reduce the risk of an
accident. If the box is stopped or runs down
in mid tune, the teeth of the comb will be
leaning on the cylinder and could break if
you jolt the box.

Clocks

▼▼ Never try to repair, clean or oil clock or
♦ ♦ watch mechanisms, dials or brass case
mounts because you may damage them.

♦ Keep clocks and watches in good working
order. Take clockwork watches and pendulum clocks to a clockmender about once a
year to be cleaned and oiled; modern clocks
and watches will probably need to be sent
back to the manufacturer. Tiny wrist watches
– worn like pieces of jewellery – work harder
than others and should be cleaned and oiled
every eight months.

♦ You don't need to clean electric clocks
because the mechanism is sealed, and therefore protected from dust.

♦ If a watch gets wet, take it to a jeweller
immediately or it will become rusty and stop
working.

♦ Get cracks in wooden clocks sealed by a
jeweller to keep the dust out of the workings,
particularly if the clock is valuable or old.

WINDING WATCHES AND CLOCKS

♦ Always turn the hands clockwise,
never anti-clockwise or you will damage
the workings.

♦ Wind a clock with its own key. If you
have lost the key, get another one made.
Memorize the number of turns needed.

♦ Wind pocket watches once a day, preferably at the same time each day to keep
them running smoothly. Wind small
wrist watches twice a day.

♦ To wind an old watch without damaging the spring, place your thumbnail and
middle fingernail just below the winder
and press them together. This forces the
winder out just far enough for you to be
able to set the hands; pull it a little further to wind it up, never pull it right out.
Wind the winder backwards and forwards between your finger and thumb. If
you keep winding it forwards, you are
more likely to overwind it.

Setting the time on a striking clock *Turn the hands clockwise and wait for the clock to finish striking before moving them on. For example, if the clock is quarter striking, wait at each quarter hour until it has completed striking. If you don't do this, the clock will strike the wrong time.*

♦ If the weights in a pendulum clock are
suspended from ropes, try to get them replaced with chains because ropes create fluff,
which can get into the mechanism.

♦ If you drop your watch in seawater, put it
in ordinary water in an airtight container, so
that the salt doesn't oxidize and start to rust
the mechanism. Take it to a jeweller as soon
as possible.

Dolls

Most collector's dolls have unglazed porcelain (bisque) heads and limbs and wooden or fabric bodies. Some have wax heads and limbs and fabric bodies.

◆If the head is badly damaged, don't try to salvage the doll – it will be almost impossible to repair.

◆Look in specialist antique shops for replacement eyes.

◆Repair damage round the leg sockets with the hardest kind of plastic padding. You can get this is in modelling shops, or use plastic padding used to repair cars. Repair damage to the main part of the body with plastic padding or tiling cement.

◆Repair fingers and toes of porcelain dolls with barbola paste (from a modelling shop) or cold-set modelling clay.

◆If the hair is matted, comb it from the bottom up, or you will pull the hair out.

◆Wash the hair with a very weak solution of shampoo or washing-up liquid and water. Gently squeeze the hair in the solution; don't get it too wet and don't rub it, or the tangles will get worse.

▼▼Don't wash doll's hair if it is on a gauze
◆◆ mount. The water can damage the gauze and the glue.

◆Clean wax dolls with cold cream on a piece of cotton wool. Clean bisque dolls with cotton wool dipped in a weak liquid detergent solution.

◆Never throw away a doll's clothes, no matter how dirty or raggedy they may be. They may indicate the age of the doll.

Combing out a doll's hair *Separate a small strand of hair at the bottom (around the neck) and gently tease the tangles out; work through the wig this way.*

Mending small cracks in wax dolls *Wipe a piece of cotton wool dipped in turpentine or white spirit over the crack. Apply the liquid sparingly because these substances soften the wax and remove paint.*

Weapons

◆If you want to use an old gun, get a gunsmith to restore it and test it in a special chamber. Be warned: if the gun is very old, there is a good likelihood that it will blow itself up in this process.

▼▼Never, under any circumstances, try to
◆◆ fire an old gun that has not been checked, even if it is empty of ammunition.

◆Don't force any mechanical part on an old gun; you'll probably break it.

◆Don't replace any parts if the gun is valuable because the repairs will affect its value. It is difficult to tighten old ivory and horn valves enough for the gun to be used because they absorb damp and dirt, so keep the gun for display only.

◆Keep display guns high up on the wall where prying fingers won't be able to reach them easily.

◆Treat other weapons, such as swords or daggers, according to the material they are made from. See CLEANING, pages 53–112.

JEWELLERY

*Inspect your jewellery regularly and get loose
pieces mended if necessary; don't wait until
they break, you may lose the vital stone.
Check any valuable necklaces every time you
want to wear them. If there is any sign of
weakness, don't wear them, get them re-
strung as soon as possible.*

*Don't wear gold and silver rings for ener-
getic activities; even very slight knocks can
bend them out of shape. Keep a saucer near
the kitchen or bathroom sink so that you
always take your rings off in the same
place when washing up or washing your
hands; that way you won't lose them.*

CLEANING AND STORING JEWELLERY

◆Keep all jewellery in separate boxes or
compartments of your jewellery case, or
hang it up. If there is the slightest chance of
anything becoming scratched, wrap each
piece individually in tissue or cotton wool.
Gold and platinum scratch particularly easily
and a diamond will wreak havoc on jewellery
made from soft gold.

◆Prevent tarnish on cheap costume jewellery by covering it with clear cellulose lacquer (from art shops) or even clear nail
varnish. Cover the whole surface carefully so
that air will not get in. Let it dry properly
before you wear it. Remove old lacquer from
time to time with varnish remover or lacquer
thinners and repaint the object.

▼▼Don't lacquer a valuable piece yourself,
◆ ◆ take it to a jeweller.

◆See also CLEANING, pages 102–5 and
109–12.

Gold and platinum

◆Rub gently with a piece of chamois; don't
use an old cloth or rag as it may harbour bits
of grit and damage the metal.

◆Treat gold-plated items with great care –
true gold will rub off eventually.

◆Keep gold jewellery in separate boxes or
wrapped in tissue because it scratches easily.

TIPS FOR CLEANING JEWELLERY

◆Wash jewellery (without stones) with
mild detergent and hot water. For intricate bits use a soft bristled toothbrush.
To loosen very stubborn dirt, add a little
household ammonia to the washing
water. Rinse in hot water and dry.

◆Use a proprietary jewellery cleaning
fluid as a dip for cleaning jewellery with
stones. Read the manufacturer's instructions carefully first. Don't use hot water
because this may expand the settings (especially claw settings) and clasps, and the
stones may fall out.

▼▼Don't use ammonia or proprietary
◆ ◆ cleaner for jewellery with pearls or
coral; acids dissolve them. Never use
silver cleaner on anything except silver,
gold or platinum, it may damage it.

◆Clean stones and beads on a necklace
with a brush dipped into dry bicarbonate
of soda; don't use water because it may
rot the string.

Silver

◆Wrap sterling silver in jeweller's bags and
wraps, which are impregnated with a tarnish
preventer.

◆Clean with a proprietary silver polish specially formulated for jewellery. Do not leave
polish on the silver as it will tarnish again
more quickly and almost certainly leave
marks on your clothes.

◆ Don't let silver jewellery come into contact with egg, fruit juices, olives, perfumes, salad dressing, salt, vinegar and so on; they all tarnish silver.

◆ Make your own silver dip with washing soda and hot water in an aluminium pan, see page 103. Don't use this dip for silver jewellery with stones in it because you can damage the setting.

Cleaning pearl necklaces *Rub gently with a clean, soft chamois leather. Work carefully between the beads to remove the film of dirt which pearls pick up from their wearers and from the atmosphere.*

Diamonds

◆ Rub occasionally with a clean soft cloth to maintain their sparkle.
◆ Use a soft toothbrush or a soft eyebrow brush to loosen dirt in the back of the setting.
◆ Boil diamonds (but no other stones) very briefly in a solution of soap, water and ammonia, see below.

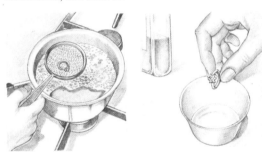

Cleaning a diamond *Place the piece of jewellery in a tea strainer or a piece of muslin, above right. Prepare a weak solution of soapsuds and water, containing one or two drops of ammonia, in a saucepan and bring it to the boil. Dip the diamond into the boiling liquid just for a moment, let it cool, then dip it into an eggcupful of white spirit, above left. Then lay the diamond on paper tissues and let it dry.*

Pearls

◆ Wash pearl rings, bracelets or earrings with a cloth dipped in warm water and mild detergent. Don't add ammonia; the pearls will start to disintegrate.
▼▼ Don't let pearls come into contact with
◆ ◆ any acid – it will destroy them.
◆ Remove dirty marks by brushing with powdered magnesia. Don't wash pearl necklaces as the water can rot the thread.
◆ Wear pearls as much as possible; contact with skin keeps them white. They lose their lustre and discolour if left in a box.

Coral

◆ Clean coral jewellery as you would pearls. All the same rules apply.

Glass

◆ Wash in warm water and detergent. Use a soft brush to get at crevices or patterns.
▼▼ Don't wash glass with very hot water as
◆ ◆ it may crack the stones. Don't leave it in the water for too long because the stones may become loose.
◆ Polish glass objects, a bracelet for example, with a silver cloth or stainless-steel cleaner.
◆ Rub scratches with a chamois leather and jeweller's rouge, pressing lightly.
🍃 GREEN TIP: Polish a glass stone with vinegar and water.

Jet

◆ Clean with a soft brush dipped in warm, soapy water. Rinse in cold water and dry.
▼▼ Don't wash decorated jet. Washing it
◆ ◆ can damage the decoration.
🍃 GREEN TIP: Remove greasy marks with bread rolled into a ball.
◆ Dust carved jet with a soft paint brush.

Amber

◆ Wipe amber with warm soapy water and dry immediately. Don't leave it soaking because water makes amber cloudy. Buff up with a chamois leather.
🍃 GREEN TIP: Clean greasy marks on amber with a bread ball or by wiping it over with almond oil.

▼▼ Don't touch amber with alcohol or any
◆ ◆ solvent; they will leave it with a matt
surface. Be careful with perfume or hair
spray because they contain alcohol and solvents, which damage amber.

Opals

◆ Dry wash them in powdered magnesia. Put
them in a jar of powder, shake gently, then
leave overnight. Brush the powder away with
a soft brush.
◆ Don't subject opals to extreme changes of
temperature, and handle carefully because
they are very brittle.

Jade

◆ Wash with warm soapy water. Use a soft
toothbrush to get at the dirt in crevices or at
the back of the setting. Dry with a soft cloth.
◆ Clean grease marks with cotton wool
dipped in methylated spirits.
▼▼ Don't leave a glued setting to soak in
◆ ◆ water; it will loosen the glue.

Ivory

◆ Keep ivory in the light if you don't want it
to yellow too quickly. Ivory will turn yellow
with age, but this process is accelerated by
keeping it in the dark.
◆ If you do want to store ivory, wrap it in
acid-free tissue; don't use cotton wool
because it absorbs moisture and this can
damage the ivory.
🍃 GREEN TIP: Rub with a soft cloth
dipped in almond oil to give it a good
protective coating.
◆ Take old ivory to a professional to clean –
don't try to do it yourself because you may
ruin its patina.
◆ Bleach yellowed ivory by rubbing it with a
cloth dipped in 20 volume hydrogen peroxide, then leave it in the sun to dry. (Don't
embark on this exercise if it's raining.)
◆ Clean dirty or stained ivory with a cotton
wool bud dipped in some whiting and
methylated spirits.
◆ Don't use water to clean ivory – it absorbs
liquid and swells up, and may crack.

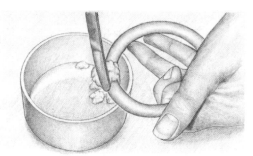

Removing stubborn stains from ivory *Smear a
stiff paste of whiting and a few drops of 20 volume
hydrogen peroxide onto the mark. The paste must not
be too runny because the ivory will absorb the liquid.
Leave the piece out in the sun until the paste is dry.
Then wash it off with methylated spirits and dry
thoroughly with a tea cloth.*

Wood

◆ Wipe wooden bangles, necklaces, pend-
ants and brooches with a barely damp cloth.
Do not wash them with water because this
may stain or warp the wood.
◆ Polish with some wax polish or rub in a
little olive oil. Always apply oil or polish
sparingly or you will get grease marks on
your clothes.

Plaster and paste

◆ Don't wash plaster or paste jewellery
because water dissolves it. Wipe dirty marks
with a clean cloth dipped in alcohol or
diluted ammonia.

Acrylic

◆ Sponge with lukewarm detergenty water.
Then wipe dry with a damp clean cloth.
◆ Polish scratches out with a silver polish.
Wash the polish off thoroughly or it will
come off on your clothes.

REPAIRING JEWELLERY

◆Tighten loose claws in claw mounts immediately to prevent the stone from falling out. If the jewellery is made of very soft metal, bend the claws down by pressing with your thumb. Otherwise press very gently with a knife handle or use a pair of pliers.

◆When replacing an old stone, pick off the old glue. Clean both the stone and the setting, then roughen the surfaces to be stuck with a pin or a piece of emery cloth. Replace the stone using an epoxy resin adhesive and leave for the full drying time given in the instructions before wearing the piece again to be certain the glue has set.

▼▼ If the jewellery is valuable, don't try to ◆◆ mend it yourself. Take it to a professional jeweller and get it done properly or you may ruin it completely.

◆Repair broken clasps on costume jewellery with an epoxy resin adhesive.

RE-STRINGING BEADS

◆Use nylon stringing thread; it doesn't fray as quickly as cotton.

◆Tie a knot between each bead or group of beads, particularly if they are valuable. Then if the thread breaks, only a couple of beads will drop off and there will be less chance of losing them. Also the stringing is more flexible and the beads will not rub against each other.

◆Check the clasp before restringing. If it's losing its flexibility, get a new one. If it is valuable, get it repaired.

1 Collect the beads together in a fold of newspaper or around the edge of a solitaire board. If they are graded in size or colour, lay them out in the right order.

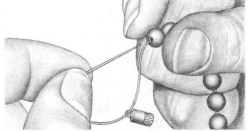

3 When you have made the final knot, pass the thread through the clasp, then back through the last bead.

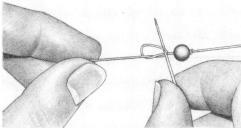

2 Tie a knot 7cm (3in) from the end of the thread and feed the first bead onto it. Make a second loop, stick a needle into it and use the needle to pull the loop as close to the bead as you can.

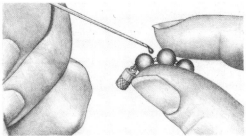

4 Tie a knot between the last two beads. Put a tiny drop of adhesive to keep it there. Put a little glue on the ends of the thread to stop it fraying before you put the clasp on.

5 Tie the other side of the clasp onto the other end and put a drop of adhesive onto the knot.

VALUATION AND INSURANCE

For valuation purposes, jewellery is divided into: ornaments made of precious metal and stones; and costume jewellery, which is made of non-precious metal and stones.

◆Check to see if jewellery is hallmarked. The hallmark is a row of small letters and pictures stamped into the article. Together they will tell you how old the object is, where it was made and who made it. Jewellery made of silver, gold or platinum will be hall-marked. A "lion passant" (a lion walking to the left and holding up one paw) on a piece of silver means that it was made in England and that it is sterling silver – sterling silver must be at least 92.5 percent pure silver. If you see the letters EPNS on the back or base, the item is silver plated.

◆Check the carat value of gold, which should be stamped on it. Pure gold is 24 carat. The purer the gold, the softer it is, so hardly anything is made of pure gold and most jewellery is made of 18 and 9 carat gold.

◆Buy precious jewellery from reputable and well-established firms or crafts people. Jewellery by designer craftsmen may have a high value if the craftsman has a good reputation for his or her work.

◆Antique jewellery, found in antique shops and junk shops, may have a high value because of age but beware of old costume jewellery which might be worth very little.

Insurance

◆Take out an "all risks" policy if you have valuable jewellery. This can be taken out either as an extension to the policy for house contents or as a separate policy to provide further cover. "All risks" policies are designed to cover your more valuable possessions against loss or damage by any cause; this includes fire, theft and accident, inside or outside the home.

◆Keep receipts for all expensive pieces of jewellery. If an item is old, get a valuation statement from an expert or a shop which specializes in the field. Get valuation certificates updated every year.

◆Read the small print carefully. In spite of the title "all risks" there are always exclusion clauses such as limits to the amount you take out of the country or no cover for radio-active contamination or riots. You can often overcome limits or exclusions in a policy by paying an additional premium. This is not likely to be very large and is usually worth the extra cost.

TYPES OF PEARL

◆To check whether pearls are natural or artificial, draw them through your teeth. Natural and cultured pearls feel rough when drawn across the teeth, artificial ones will feel absolutely smooth.

NATURAL PEARLS
Pearls consist of layers of calcium carbonate, which is produced by oysters and clams as protection against pieces of grit or a particular parasitic worm in their shells. These are the most expensive type of pearl.

CULTURED PEARLS
Cultivated by placing a tiny bit of mother-of-pearl (lining of a shell) in the oyster shell. The oyster immediately starts to cover it with calcium carbonate. These are normally slightly cheaper than natural pearls.

ARTIFICIAL PEARLS
Made from hollow glass lined with fish scales in order to achieve a pearl-like effect.

Painting and Decorating

ORGANIZATION

Measure and mark up accurately all of the surfaces to be decorated so that you can estimate how much paper or paint you need. You will also need to treat any damp before you start decorating, see pages 224–25.

Be disciplined about your sequence of work, your home will be easier to live in while the work is going on and you'll finish each job more quickly. Make sure you have all the tools you need before you start; don't just make do with what you have in the

house – you could ruin hours of work, or worse still have an accident. You will need:
◇ *A sturdy ladder (aluminium ladders are lighter and cheaper than other types)*
◇ *Dust sheets, newspaper and polythene for covering floors and furniture*
◇ *Stripping and sanding tools*
◇ *Filling knife and filler*
◇ *A bucket for mixing wallpaper paste, sugar soap, etc., a paint kettle or paint tray and a selection of brushes, rollers and cloths.*

THE WORK SEQUENCE

◆ Work on one room at a time so that you get each job finished and can use the rooms that are not being decorated.
◆ Clear the room first. If possible, take out all the furniture and store it somewhere for the duration. If not, take anything you may need from drawers and cupboards. Move the furniture into the middle of the room and cover it with dust sheets. Remove loose floor covers, curtains and pictures.
◆ Remove door and window furniture (handles, door plates, hooks, snibs, locks,

bolts and catches), and light fittings to prevent them from being covered in splashes of paint or stripper.
◆ Tape polythene around wall sockets and light fittings to stop water getting into them.

Covering light fittings *Cut a piece of polythene to fit, and tape it over the fitting, using masking tape. Make sure that no water can get under the polythene.*

ORDER OF WORK

◆Prepare all the surfaces, then decorate in the following order:

◇ *Ceiling*
◇ *Walls and alcoves (if painting them)*
◇ *Doors*
◇ *Windows*
◇ *Skirtings*
◇ *Radiators*
◇ *Walls and alcoves (if wallpapering them)*

◆ Wait until the wallpaper paste or paint is dry before you put back all the furniture so that you don't accidentally touch and ruin the surface.

◆ Paint the stairs and stairwell when you have finished moving furniture about – you are less likely to damage the newly decorated surface.

Protecting floor coverings *Fix polythene firmly to the skirting and corners, using double-sided tape.*

◆Roll up carpets and cover them with polythene or an old cotton sheet. If you can't roll up carpets, cover the floor completely with a sheet of polythene or a number of old sheets, bedcovers or even newspaper.

◆Make sure the polythene or dust sheets are flat on the floor and not rucked up, or you will trip over them.

◆Assemble all the equipment you will need so that you have everything to hand.

MEASURING A ROOM

◆ You need a good, retractable measuring tape, a calculator (unless your mental arithmetic is very good), a piece of paper and a pencil.

Walls Measure the floor-to-ceiling height of each wall, leaving out any skirting or frieze. Then measure the width of each wall, without deducting window and door areas, and multiply the width by the height for the total wall area. For example, a wall measuring 3m (10ft) high by 3.5m (11½ft) wide has a total area of 10.5sq m (115sq ft). To measure the surface area of a room, multiply the circumference by the height.

Ceilings Multiply the widths of two adjacent walls together. Calculate the ceiling area of the alcoves in the same way and add this to the ceiling measurement.

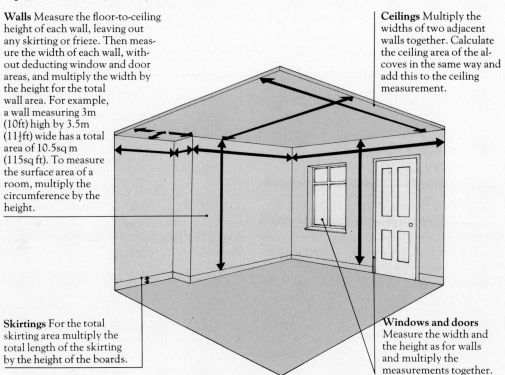

Skirtings For the total skirting area multiply the total length of the skirting by the height of the boards.

Windows and doors Measure the width and the height as for walls and multiply the measurements together.

PREPARATION

Every surface to be painted or decorated must be absolutely smooth, clean and dry and the cracks filled. Untreated cracks and flaws will quickly show through new paintwork or wallcoverings. They may even get worse, and you may have to strip everything off completely in order to redecorate properly. Prepare ceilings and walls before woodwork because they generate more dust and mess.

Prime bare patches of wood or plaster before painting or papering to seal them – that way they'll soak up less paint. Wash walls to be painted with sugar-soap solution and leave it to dry. This cleans grease

patches off the walls and provides a key for the paint to adhere to. Small areas can be washed with detergenty water or rubbed with wet-and-dry paper. You can buy specially prepared tacky cloths for removing specks of dust, grit and fluff from walls before decorating and between each coat of paint.

Walls that have been painted with distemper or whitewash cannot be washed or painted with another type of paint because the distemper or whitewash leaves a chalky layer on the wall. Instead either paint over it with the same type of paint or scrape it off with a scouring pad or scraper and water.

WALLS AND CEILINGS

◆Don't try to paper over old wallpaper. Strip it off first. You can strip small areas by hand with a scraper. If you have a lot to do, hire a steam stripper.

◆Seal bare walls or ceilings that are to be papered with size or wallpaper adhesive. This stops the surface from absorbing the paste and helps the paper slide into place.

◆Let new plaster dry out before you paint it. Leave newly plastered walls for about 12 months before applying gloss paint, so that they can dry out completely. You can apply emulsion paint to new plaster within two or three weeks, because the moisture can still evaporate through the paint.

◆Seal a hardboard wall or ceiling with primer before decorating so that it doesn't absorb the paste or paint.

◆If a wall is still rough or uneven after filling and sanding, cover it with lining paper, see Hanging lining paper, page 197.

Stripping wallpaper by hand

1 Soak the paper well with water, using a sponge mop or a wet cloth.
◇ *Add a wallpaper stripper to the water if the paper is reluctant to come off.*

2 Strip the paper, using a special wallpaper stripping knife or a flat scraper. Hold the implement at an angle to the wall and don't dig it into the plaster.

Washable wallpapers *Score the surface with a serrated scraper, then soak the paper and scrape it off with a wallpaper stripping knife or a flat scraper.*

Vinyl wallcoverings *Lift the top layer from the backing paper at the bottom corners of each strip, and peel upwards. Remove the backing as for ordinary wallpaper.*

3 Sand lightly over the wall with glass paper to remove any remaining bits and pieces of wallpaper.

Filling plaster

◆Fill fine cracks and small holes with a surface filler, available in tubes or in powder form to be mixed with water. Smooth it over with your finger or a knife.

◆Cover wide cracks between the ceiling and walls with a fabric-based self-adhesive tape and paint over them.

◆If you have a badly cracked ceiling which you cannot fill satisfactorily, cover it with textured paint or embossed paper instead of filling it.

◆Fill large cracks in walls with a suitable cellulose filler, see over.

1 Rake out crumbling plaster, *above left* and dampen each crack, *above right*.

2 Fill cracks by degrees: put in the filler a little at a time and let each layer dry before adding the next. A thin layer of filler should dry in about 10 minutes.

3 Smooth down the final layer with wet-and-dry glass paper but leave it just proud of the plasterwork next to it.

4 When the filling has dried hard, rub it down with a fine abrasive paper, making it flush with the surrounding plasterwork.

5 Seal the filler and the area around it with two coats of a universal primer or emulsion paint before painting the wall.

SANDING AND SANDING EQUIPMENT

Sanding, whether by hand or machine, is the best method for smoothing wood or plaster surfaces, or making surfaces slightly rough to provide a key for paint or varnish.

◆ Mechanical sanders are quicker for large areas but are not effective in corners or difficult spaces, which need to be sanded by hand instead. Mechanical sanders can generally be hired.

◆ To achieve a smooth finish, start with fairly coarse paper and work through the grades to finish with fine paper.

◆ When sanding wood, always work with the grain to get the smoothest finish.

◆ To prevent wet-and-dry paper from clogging, dip it often in water and rub it on a piece of soap to lubricate it. (This applies only if you are sanding by hand.) Don't dampen any other type of abrasive paper or you won't be able to use it.

◆ To clear clogged sandpaper, slap the back of the paper hard against the edge of a table; alternatively, run the back of the sheet up and down over the edge of a table or workbench.

◆ When using a disc sander, make sure that only the outer edge of the disc is in contact with the wall surface or you may damage the machine.

ABRASIVE PAPERS
These can be applied by hand or machine. There are several types, normally sold in 275×225mm ($10\frac{1}{2} \times 8\frac{1}{2}$in) sheets with the grade (from fine through to coarse) marked on the back:
◇ *Glass paper (sandpaper)*
◇ *Aluminium oxide (open- or dense-coated)*
◇ *Waterproof silicon carbide (wet-and-dry)*
◆ Sandpaper is cheapest, but clogs more easily than other types do.

MECHANICAL SANDERS
Disc sanders These are suitable for removing a substantial layer of material but don't provide a perfectly smooth finish. They are supplied as attachments to electric drills. Use with sanding discs or sandpaper cut to fit, and place over a special rubber backing on the drill.

Orbital sanders (finishing sanders) Use these sanders for a good finish; they are not suitable for heavy sanding. They can be bought as an accessory for an electric drill or to be used on their own. Don't use with glass paper, because it tends to tear, and if using aluminium oxide paper, choose the densely coated type.

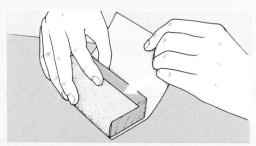

Sanding by hand *Wrap a sheet of sandpaper round a sanding block or a block of cork, wood or rubber. This makes sanding by hand easier and also helps you to apply pressure evenly.*

WOODWORK

◆Before priming, rub down bare woods with glass paper to make them smooth.

◆For bare softwoods, apply knotting over knots and areas of resin, see FILLING KNOTS IN WOOD, page 186, to stop the resin from oozing out.

◆Wipe bare hardwoods that are oily with a rag soaked in white spirit, so that the paint will stick to the wood's surface.

STRIPPING EQUIPMENT

SCRAPERS
◆Use scrapers to lift paint off woodwork and walls.

Flat scrapers *These are good for stripping paint off large surfaces.*

Flat scraper

Shavehook *This is particularly useful for mouldings around doors and windows.*

Shavehook

HEAT STRIPPERS
Paraffin blowlamps These are the most economical heat strippers, but they are messy and tedious to light and you have to keep them pressurized by pumping them from time to time.

Gas blowtorches They are easier to light and use than paraffin blowlamps but are less economical. Use one with a pressure regulator if possible.

Hot air guns These have special nozzle attachments which allow you to strip places that are awkward to get to, or, for instance, to shield glass round windows. They work off electricity. Try them out before buying or hiring one because some are noisy and heavy.

CHEMICAL STRIPPERS
Dichloromethane strippers Use on cellulose, emulsion or oil-based paints.
Caustic strippers Use only on emulsion and oil-based paints. You may have to use a bleach afterwards because they darken natural wood.

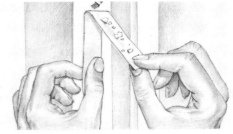

Testing for unsound paint *Apply a strip of masking tape to the paint. If, when you lift it off, it pulls paint away, the paint is unsound. Strip the affected area and then prime it before painting.*

◆Sound paint can be left, just sand it lightly with a fine abrasive paper to provide a key for the new paint.

◆If the paint is blistered, cut the blisters with a knife and rub down with glass paper. Then apply knotting, fill any holes, and prime the bare area.

◆When stripping a door, strip all of the mouldings before stripping the rest of the door. The paint on the panels will protect the wood should your shavehook slip while you are stripping the mouldings.

Heat stripping

This is the quickest method of stripping paint off woodwork.

▼▼ Don't use heat strippers on wood that is
◆ ◆ to be left unpainted because it may scorch it.

◆You will need a shavehook for mouldings and a scraper for flat surfaces.

◆Wear gloves to protect your hands (cotton is better than rubber, which gets hot under the heat of the heat stripper).

1 Hold the blowtorch 15–20cm (6–8in) from the surface. Pass the flame over the surface, keeping it moving all the time. Be careful not to burn the wood underneath.

SAFETY TIPS FOR HEAT STRIPPING

▼▼ Don't use a blowtorch or blowlamp
◆ ◆ on plaster walls, asbestos sheeting, around panes of glass, or on softwood boards because you will set fire to them.

▼▼ Never use a blowlamp or blowtorch
◆ ◆ on old paint unless the room is well ventilated; the paint may contain lead, which gives off dangerous fumes.

▼▼ Never use a blowlamp or blowtorch
◆ ◆ near a thatched roof or anything that could catch light.

▼▼ Always keep a bucket of water
◆ ◆ handy.

SAFETY TIPS FOR USING CHEMICAL STRIPPERS

▼▼ Wear rubber gloves and old clothes,
◆ ◆ and move anything likely to get splashed because many strippers are caustic. Protect your eyes by wearing goggles.

▼▼ Don't smoke, because these strip-
◆ ◆ pers are highly inflammable.

▼▼ If any stripper gets onto your skin or
◆ ◆ into your eyes, bathe the affected area immediately in cold water.

2 Scrape the paint as it shrivels, starting at the top and working down but scraping upwards or away from you. (Hold your hand out of the way of dripping burning paint.) Remove all softened paint before it hardens again. Play the flame over any remaining paint, until it can be scraped off.

▼▼ Catch burning scrapings before they
◆ ◆ reach the floor, and use a tin tray, never newspaper or anything flammable.

3 Rub the surface down with medium-grade glass paper. Rub away any scorch marks because paint will not stick to them.

Dry scraping

🍃 GREEN TIP: This method is the cheapest and safest way of stripping paint, but is slow work and is therefore suitable for small areas only.

◆ Use a two-bladed scraper, with a serrated and a plain blade, to make things quicker.

1 Score the surface lightly using the blade with the serrated edge.

2 Remove the paint with the plain edge. Try not to scratch or score the wood.

Chemical paint strippers

◆ Use these on wood that you don't want to paint, or near glass and on moulded surfaces. They don't leave scorch marks and can be brushed into corners and crevices.

◆ Make sure you use the correct stripper for the job, with a solvent that is suitable for the original paint – cellulose thinners for cellulose paint, for example. Follow the directions to the letter.

1 Apply a thick layer of the stripper and leave it to work through the paint as the manufacturer instructs.

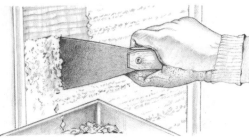

2 When the paint shrivels, remove it with a scraper and a shavehook. Put the scrapings in an old tin; don't let them fall onto the floor – they can burn it.

3 Clean the stripped surface with white spirit, and when it is dry rub it down with glass paper.

Filling knots in wood

1 First paint over the knot with knotting and then fill any gaps with a rigid general-purpose filler. Apply the filler in layers of about 12mm ($\frac{1}{2}$in) thick and allow two or three days' drying time between each layer.

2 Leave the final layer of filler slightly proud of the wood and rub it down flat with glass paper when dry. Prime the wood before painting it.

PAINTING

Use the best-quality paint – it lasts much longer, is easier to apply and therefore saves money in the long run. Always use an under-coat – one coat of undercoat and one of top coat lasts much longer than four coats of top coat. If you then look after the paintwork (wipe it regularly), and there are no open fires or smokers in the house, it should last five to eight years.

If you are using paint manufactured before 1986, check the lead level with the manufacturers. Lead paints are toxic, and give off toxic fumes if you are heat stripping them. Household paints produced after 1986 are lead-free.

You can remove the smell of paint in a room by leaving a cut onion in the room overnight; throw the onion away afterwards.

CHOOSING PAINTS

◆ Decide on the type of paint you want before you choose the colour; the finish that is suitable for your walls or woodwork may not be available in every colour.

◆ Calculate the quantity as accurately as you can and make sure you buy all the paint you need if you are using a blended colour. You may not be able to match the colour later.

◆ Buy a colour test pot and try it on the wall or door before buying the full amount so that you know what the colour will look like.

◆ Use non-drip (thixotropic) paints where possible; they are easier to smooth out and have better covering power than ordinary paints, so you need fewer coats. Don't stir them, even if they look lumpy, or you will make them become liquid and they will form drips. Non-drip emulsions are particularly good for ceilings, and non-drip gloss is very good for woodwork.

Primer

◆ Use primers before painting to seal porous surfaces such as new or bare plaster and wood, and to provide a key on smooth surfaces such as bare metal.

◆ Use all-purpose primer for any surface; use wood primer on softwood and chipboard; aluminium wood primer on hardwood and oily woods; plaster primer on plasterboard; hardboard primer on hardboard; alkali-resistant primer on plaster and brick; multi-purpose primer on concrete and stone; and zinc chromate primer on metals.

Undercoat

◆ Use on primed surfaces before applying a top coat, and on dark surfaces where the top coat is to be a paler colour. These paints contain more pigment than top coats and so reduce the amount of top coat you have to paint on.

◆ To clean tools used to apply undercoat, wash with white spirit.

◆ Use an undercoat which is compatible with the top coat.

Emulsion paints

◆ Use these paints to speed up the painting process – they are quick-drying.

◆ Use matt emulsion paints rather than silk where there is liable to be condensation, because they resist water well. Alternatively, use anti-condensation emulsion if you have a problem with condensation. It cannot stop it altogether but it often contains a fungicide, which deters mould.

◆ If you object to the smell of paint, use emulsion paints; because they are water-based, they do not smell as strongly as oil-based paints.

◆ Use for walls but not for metal, because being water-based they will rust the metal.

◆ If you need to thin emulsion, do so with water only.

Oil-based paints

◆ Useful for woodwork because they are tough and hard-wearing.

◆ Make sure the room is well ventilated when using these paints because they are slow-drying and have a very strong smell.

◆ You must apply an undercoat if painting wood, because wood is absorbent; it is not necessary for metalwork.

◆ To make oil-based paints go further, thin them with white spirit.

Textured paints

◆ Use these paints for hiding cracks and irregularities in walls and ceilings; they are thick and leave a rough finish.

◆ Apply with a roller, which helps to leave a stippled finish.

◆ Some textured paints cannot be left uncovered and must be painted with emulsion once they are dry, so check when you buy.

Polyurethane paints

◆ Use these tough, hard-wearing paints for radiators, pipes and metal windows – they resist moisture and hard knocks well.

◆ Apply these paints as you would oil-based ones. To make them spread further, thin with white spirit.

Flame-retardant paints

◆ These paints are particularly suitable for expanded polystyrene tiles, which are highly flammable if left unpainted.

ESTIMATING PAINT QUANTITIES

◆ Measure the walls and ceiling and add up their totals to arrive at the surface areas, see page 182.

◆ Remember to allow for any extra space taken up by alcoves and chimneys.

◆ Include windows and doors as part of the surface unless they are very large.

◆ When estimating for windows, in general allow 2 sq m ($2\frac{1}{2}$ sq yd) for a small window, 4 sq m ($4\frac{3}{4}$ sq yd) for a medium-sized window, and 5 sq m (6 sq yd) for a large window.

◆ Check with the paint covering capacity chart to see how much of a particular paint you will need.

◆ If the surface is very porous, you will need two or even three undercoats, even after sealing.

◆ On a textured surface you will need more paint, or add water to the first coat.

◆ You will need fewer coats for non-drip paints because they are thicker.

◆ You will need extra coats if painting a light colour on top of a dark colour.

◆ Silk emulsions may need more coats than matt ones.

COVERING CAPACITIES OF PAINTS

◆ For a total area of 6.3 sq m ($7\frac{1}{2}$ sq yd) to be covered in a paint with a covering capacity of 15 sq m (18 sq yd), divide 6.3 by 15 (or $7\frac{1}{2}$ by 18) to find the amount of paint needed per coat: 0.4 litres (14 fl oz).

PAINT TYPE	Sq m per litre	Sq yd per $\frac{1}{4}$ gal
All-purpose and other primers	5–9	6–$10\frac{3}{4}$
Undercoat	15	18
Emulsion	15	18
Non-drip emulsion	14	$16\frac{3}{4}$
Oil-based silk finish	12	$14\frac{1}{4}$
Gloss	17	$20\frac{1}{4}$
Non-drip gloss	12	$14\frac{1}{4}$

PAINTING TOOLS

◆Use good-quality tools – they last longer and provide a better finish.

Brushes

◆Buy brushes with natural bristles rather than synthetic ones, even though they are more expensive – they have a longer life, and the bristles don't fall out as easily. Even so, always expect a brush to lose some of its bristles when you first use it.

◆Don't buy brushes with short bristles or with large filler strips – their paint-holding capacity is low.

◆You will need:
◇*A 100mm (4in) brush for applying paint to walls and ceilings*
◇*A 50mm (2in) brush for painting skirting boards and doors*
◇*A 25mm (1in) brush for painting windows and other narrow areas*
◇*A cutting-in brush with angled bristles for painting around windows*
◇*A radiator brush with a long handle and angled head for painting behind radiators.*

Rollers

◆Use rollers if you want to cover the area quickly. However, they can be messy as they tend to splash paint about. They are not suitable for small areas, corners or around sockets etc., you'll have to use a brush.

◆Rollers are the best tools for painting textured walls and ceilings.

◆Buy a paint tray if you are using a roller; this allows you to distribute the paint evenly.

◆Attach an extension handle to the roller for painting high walls and ceilings. (Make sure your roller has a hole in the handle to take the extension.) You can buy one or make your own from a broom, mop or long window squeegee handle.

◆Choose sturdy rollers without raised seams on the sleeve; less robust ones will deteriorate quickly.

◆Use sheepskin rollers where possible; they have the longest pile and can hold more paint than nylon pile rollers – enough to cover a square metre/yard of non-absorbent wall surface. They are not suitable for gloss paints, however, because they leave a slightly textured finish.

◆Avoid foam (sponge) rollers; they are cheap but they hold too much paint, and so spatter a fine spray of paint while you work. They also leave bubbles in the paint surface, which dry out into small craters.

◆Use narrow rollers for painting skirtings and door panels but not for corners because they can't get into them easily.

Foam pads

Pads are inexpensive, light, faster to use than brushes, and are more or less splash free, but they often leave a disappointing finish. As with rollers, you can use them for large areas but not for corners.

◆Buy a paint tray for flat pads with a handle on the back. For pads shaped like a paint brush, a paint kettle will do.

◆Use edging pads, which have small wheels, for cutting in between a wall and a ceiling (they won't get into corners). Keep the wheels paint-free and be careful not to get too much paint on the pad.

◆Sash and crevice pads are useful for reaching awkward places.

◆Long-handled pads are good for radiators and other places that are hard to reach.

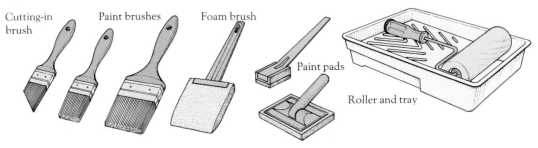

Cutting-in brush   Paint brushes   Foam brush

Paint pads

Roller and tray

CLEANING AND STORING PAINTING EQUIPMENT

BRUSHES

◆ If you've been using emulsion paint, wash the brushes in water and detergent as soon as you have finished painting to keep the bristles supple and ready to use again.

◆ Clean brushes used for lacquers and oil-based and polyurethane paints with white spirit, paraffin, turpentine substitute or a proprietary paint brush cleaner. Then wash out the brushes with soap and water.

◆ Dry brushes with the bristles held together in the right shape with a rubber band to keep them in good condition.

Storing brushes in water *Drill a hole through the handle of the brush and thread a piece of wire or a thin stick through it. Place this over the rim of a jar. This ensures that the bristles do not touch the bottom of the jar and lose their shape.*

◆ As a temporary measure, store brushes used for oil-based paints with their bristles just immersed in clean water. Before using them again, brush out the water on an old piece of hardboard.

◆ To store brushes overnight, put them in a polythene bag or wrap in self-seal plastic film or foil, with a few drops of white spirit or turpentine substitute on their bristles. Brush this out properly before you use the brush or it will thin the next load of paint.

ROLLERS

◆ Before washing rollers, roll them out on newspaper to remove excess paint.

◆ Most rollers should be taken apart for cleaning. You may need a spanner.

◆ Use plenty of water to clean off emulsion paint.

◆ If you are using gloss paint, it's best to buy replacement sleeves and throw the old ones away. Cleaning off gloss paint is messy and time-consuming.

PAINTING A ROOM

◆ Try to set aside three or four uninterrupted hours for painting, preferably so that you are working in the same light, and so that you can finish painting at least one coat.

◆ Keep a damp cloth by you to remove dust, drips and blobs.

Ceilings and walls

◆ Dab nail heads, and anything else that might rust, with oil paint and allow it to dry before you apply emulsion.

◆ If using a roller, first coat the corners of the room, and where the ceiling meets the walls, with a narrow brush; the roller will not reach these areas.

◆ Small bubbles may appear if you are painting with water-based paint over wallpaper. They should all disappear of their own accord as the paint and the paper dry. If they don't, remove them (see right).

◆ Use a roller with a long pile for textured surfaces. Very heavily textured surfaces may need to have the paint stippled into the texture with a brush.

◆ Paint a ceiling systematically from wall to wall in 60cm (2ft) wide strips, keeping the edges ragged. Make sure the edges are wet when joined.

◆ Paint around windows and door frames with an angled "cutting-in" brush; it's easier to control where you are putting the paint.

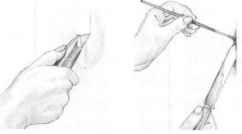

Removing paint bubbles on wallpaper *Slit bubbles with a craft knife or razor blade, above left, dab the slit with wallpaper paste and flatten to the wall, above right. Leave to dry out and then repaint.*

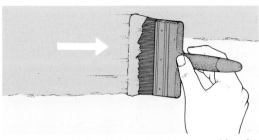

Painting walls *Apply the paint in horizontal bands – it is less tiring and you are less likely to get paint drips. To make overlaps less noticeable, keep the bottom edge (or top edge if you are starting on the ground) of each band fairly ragged.*

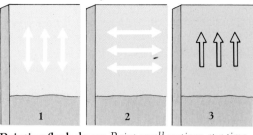

Painting flush doors *Paint small sections at a time. Begin with vertical strokes (1), brush across them with horizontal strokes (2), and end with light upward strokes (3).*

WOODWORK

◆Use gloss or silk-finish paint to protect wood from wear and tear.

◆ You must use an undercoat for gloss paint even if the existing paintwork is sound; sand between coats to give the gloss paint a surface it can stick to.

◆Don't overload the brush with paint or you will get drips down the surface.

◆Don't allow the paint to build up in ridges at the edges; these will spoil the smoothness of the surface.

◆Don't apply too much paint to the top and not enough at the sides – this is a common mistake and causes drips.

◆ You need not paint the top edge of a door unless it can be seen from the stairs or landing, but it will be more difficult to clean if left unpainted.

Flush doors

◆To paint flush doors use a 7.5cm (3in) brush for the door and a 5cm (2in) brush for the edges; these give the best finish. Start at

Painting door edges *Jam the door open by tapping a wedge under it to expose its hinge and handle edges for painting. Don't close the door until the paint has dried thoroughly.*

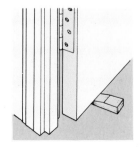

the top corner on the hinge side and work in 25 sq cm (10 sq in) sections until you reach the bottom corner on the handle side.

Panelled doors

◆Use a 2.5cm (1in) brush for the framework and a 5cm (2in) or 7.5cm (3in) brush for the panels; these are the best sizes for the areas you are painting.

◆If painting panels and framework in contrasting colours, paint one colour first, leave it to dry for three days and mask it with masking tape before applying the second colour; this way you prevent one colour from bleeding into the other.

▼▼ Be wary of masking tape. Don't put it on ◆ ◆ until the paint is very dry and don't leave it in place for more than a day in case it pulls the paint off with it. Pull it off very slowly and carefully, see page 87.

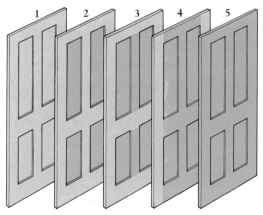

Painting panelled doors *Paint in this order: mouldings (1), panels (2), central verticals (3), horizontals (4) and edges (5).*

PAINTING WINDOWS

SASH WINDOWS

1 Push the bottom sash up and the top sash down until there is a 20cm (8in) overlap. Paint the meeting rail of the top sash and then the accessible vertical sections.

2 Almost close both windows and insert matchsticks between the frame and the window to prevent them from sticking. Then paint the rest of the top sash.

3 Paint the bottom sash, catching any drips from the vertical sections.

4 Paint the frame. Close the windows and paint the runners (but not the cords).

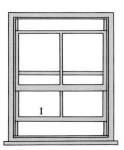   

CASEMENT WINDOWS

◆ If one window is fixed, start with the one that opens – it will dry fastest.

1 If your windows have crossbars, paint the rebates of these bars first and then the crossbars themselves, see below. Use a cutting-in brush.

2 Paint the crossrails. If your windows don't have crossbars, paint the crossrails first.

3 Painting the side verticals and edges.

4 Paint the frame and then the sill. Paint the stay last so that you can open or close the window while you are painting it.

◇ If paint gets onto the hinges, wipe it off before it dries or it will be hard to remove.

Painting around glass Protect glass with a paint shield or strips of masking tape before painting the woodwork. Remove masking tape before the final coat of paint is dry.

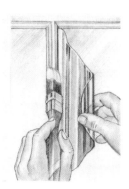

Painting crossbars Place the brush on the bar about 3mm ($\frac{1}{8}$in) from the edge of the glass and carefully push it towards the edge. Press down lightly and draw the brush along quickly to make a long, clean line.

Skirtings

◆Use a 50mm (2in) brush; this is the best size for the average width of skirtings.
◆Dab a cutting-in brush into the corners and crevices to draw away excess paint.
◆Prevent paint from smudging onto the walls and carpets by using masking tape, card or a carpet shield, see below.

Using a carpet shield *Place the shield against the skirting so that the edge tucks under the skirting and covers the edge of the carpet. Leave until the paint is completely dry.*

Stairs and stairwells

◆It is most important to set up a safe working platform so that you can reach even the least accessible parts without danger.
◆The best sequence of work is as follows:
◇ *The landing ceiling*
◇ *The walls of the stairwell from the top down*
◇ *The stairs, banisters, handrail.*
◆Try to keep people off the stairs and stop them from coming in and out of the front

PERFECTING PAINTED WOODWORK

Teardrops and wrinkles in the paint, specks and pimples, flaking, brushmarks and loss of gloss or the previous coat showing under the new one are caused by not cleaning and abrading the surfaces properly, overloading the brush, and overthinning the paint.
◆Allow the paint to harden for a week, then rub it down with glass paper, clean the surface, and apply a fresh coat of paint more carefully.

SETTING UP A SAFE WORK STATION

◆Wrap cloth round the top of the straight ladder to prevent it from slipping or damaging the wall.

1 *Put up a sturdy step ladder on the top landing. Lean a long ladder against the wall opposite the landing, with its foot lodged against a stair riser.*
2 *Link the ladders with boards. For gaps longer than 1.5m (5ft) use two planks one on top of the other, secured with nails and strong tape.*

door until the paint has dried, because this spreads dust, which sticks to wet paint.

Pipes and radiators

◆For difficult areas and for a panelled radiator, use a 25mm (1in) brush and a crevice or radiator roller or brush.
◆Paint when cold and allow to dry thoroughly before you turn the heating on again. Otherwise the paint may blister or not stick to the metal.
◆Check old pipes and radiators for rust; they may need to be treated and primed before you paint them.
◆Never paint threads or joints on radiators or pipes; you may not be able to undo them.
◆When painting pipework, start at the top and work downwards so that you can catch any paint drips.
◆Copper pipes don't need primer; just give them a coat of undercoat and gloss.
◆When pipes are close to the wall, hold a card to shield the wall from the paint.

WALLPAPERING

Buy good-quality wallcoverings because they are easier to put up and last longer. Cheap wallcoverings usually tear or stretch when handled, especially when wet. Check the numbers on rolls when you buy them; the numbers will be the same on rolls from the same batch. If they are not the same, order all the rolls from another batch; colours always vary slightly from one batch to another. Always buy an extra roll. This will come in useful for patching later, or making up for a mistake when hanging.

Check whether the paper needs trimming before you take it home; if it does, get the retailer to do it for you – it's very difficult to do it yourself.

CHOOSING WALLCOVERINGS

◆Before buying wallpaper, check the symbols on the packaging to see how easy the paper will be to care for.

◆Buy washable papers; they are cheaper than most vinyls and easily looked after.

◆Ready-pasted wallcoverings are much easier to hang than those that you have to paste yourself.

◆Choose easy-strip wallcoverings if you think you will want to change the covering at a later date. You peel off the front part and leave the backing as a lining for the next covering.

◆Read the instructions to see if the manufacturer recommends using lining paper.

Estimating wallpaper quantities

Standard wallpapers come in rolls of about 10m × 53cm (11yd × 21in). Lining paper rolls are usually slightly wider and come in both standard and economical large rolls.

◆Measure the floor-to-ceiling height of the room (not counting skirtings and friezes), and add 10cm (4in) to the total to allow for trimming after hanging.

◆Find out the distance between the repeats in the pattern – this will affect the quantity you need. Add 10 percent for wastage when choosing a large pattern.

WALLCOVERINGS QUANTITY CHART

Check this chart to estimate the number of rolls you will need.

HEIGHT OF ROOM	CIRCUMFERENCE OF ROOM								
	9m 30ft	12m 38ft	14m 46ft	16m 54ft	18m 62ft	21m 70ft	23m 78ft	26m 86ft	28m 94ft
2.14m/7ft	4	5	6	7	8	9	10	12	13
2.45m/8ft	5	6	7	9	10	11	12	14	15
2.75m/9ft	6	7	8	9	10	12	13	14	15
3m/10ft	6	8	9	10	12	13	15	16	18

TYPES OF WALLCOVERING

LINING PAPER
◆ Makes hanging wallcoverings easier because it gives a smoother surface.
◆ Always line walls if you want to hang heavy wallpapers or wallcoverings with a special finish.
◆ Use if you are going to paint the wall rather than paper it, because it provides a smoother finish than a bare wall.
◆ Buy the heaviest lining paper you can find – it is less likely to tear when you are hanging it.

STANDARD WALLPAPERS
◆ Buy the thicker papers – they are better at hiding cracked, rough or otherwise defective walls, do not tear easily and do not stretch.
◆ These papers are not washable and are therefore unsuitable for kitchens, children's rooms or hallways.

WASHABLE PAPERS
◆ Good for bathrooms and kitchens because they are protected by a transparent film. However, this film may make them very difficult to remove later on.

EMBOSSED PAPERS
◆ High-relief papers, good for cracked walls and ceilings.
◆ Easy to use because they don't stretch when pasted.
◆ Can be painted with emulsion paints.

WOODCHIP
◆ Good for hiding cracks and imperfections in walls and ceilings.
◆ Most can be painted with emulsion paint.
◆ Beware: they are difficult to get off surfaces once stuck on.

VINYL
◆ Good for children's rooms, kitchens and bathrooms because they are easy to clean and resist steam and water.
◆ Easy to clean – they can be scrubbed with a soft brush.
◆ To save time and mess, buy them ready-pasted.
◆ If pasting, use a vinyl adhesive which contains a fungicide.

LINCRUSTA
◆ High-relief wallcoverings, good for badly cracked ceilings.
◆ More hard-wearing than other relief coverings.

FLOCK
◆ Good for hiding cracks and bumps in walls, but it is expensive.

HESSIAN
◆ Useful for hiding imperfections in walls and good for areas of condensation.
◆ Can be painted with oil-based paints or emulsion.
◆ Do not use where they may get dirty, unless painted.

GRASSCLOTH
◆ Good decorative effect but expensive and difficult to put up without the joins showing. Get a professional to hang them.

FOIL
◆ Use these only on walls with a very smooth surface because they reveal every underlying bump.
◆ Good decorative effect.

FABRIC
◆ Use for a luxurious effect, either pasted to the wall or stapled to a framework around the wall. Choose a lightfast and colourfast material which will not shrink or stretch.
◆ Get them hung by a professional as mistakes can be very expensive.

CORK
◆ Useful where there is condensation, because of its warm surface.
◆ Provides good insulation against sound and cold.

WALLPAPER CARE SYMBOLS

Wallpaper manufacturers are now using these international symbols to indicate the type of wallpaper and how it should be used.

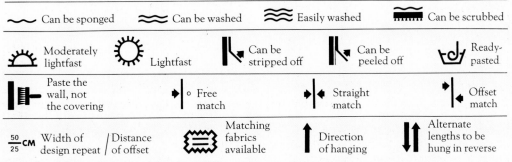

EQUIPMENT

◆A platform step ladder is essential so that you can reach the ceiling level safely.

◆If the wallpaper is not ready-pasted, you need a long table to lay it on while you paste it. Folding pasting tables are quite cheap, or use a flat door or board on two supports.

◆For ready-pasted wallcoverings you don't need a long table, just a cardboard soaking tray, which is usually given to you when you buy the paper. But a table will come in useful anyway for laying out and marking up the lengths of wallcovering.

Wallpapering tools

You will need:

◇**Measuring tools** A steel tape measure and a pencil.

◇**Cutting tools** A pair of sharp scissors with long blades and a sharp knife or pair of small scissors for trimming around light switches, sockets, etc.

◇**Straightedge or steel rule** For cutting textured wallcoverings.

◇**Boxwood seam roller** To make sure seams are well stuck down and for patching wallcoverings. Don't use it on embossed wallcoverings because it will flatten them.

◇**Plastic bucket** To mix paste in.

◇**Pasting brush** Use a 100mm (4in) paint brush or a paint roller with a foam sleeve.

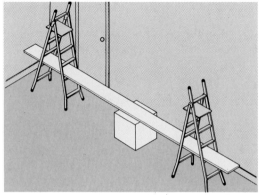

Constructing a platform *When papering ceilings you need a scaffold board and two step ladders to create a platform on which you can walk the length of the room. Support the planks in the middle.*

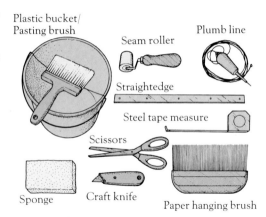

Plastic bucket/Pasting brush · Seam roller · Plumb line · Straightedge · Steel tape measure · Scissors · Sponge · Craft knife · Paper hanging brush

◇**Cloth or sponge** To wipe the table clean for the next piece of wallpaper.

◇**Size** For sealing bare plaster. Alternatively, use a diluted solution of wallpaper paste.

◇**Wallpaper paste** See below.

◇**Plumb line** To enable you to hang the paper vertically. You can improvise a plumb line by using a small flat weight and a length of fine cord.

◇**Paper hanging brush** For smoothing the wallcovering into place, fitting it into angles and getting rid of bubbles. Choose one with soft flexible bristles. You can smooth down vinyls with a sponge instead of a brush because it doesn't matter if you get paste or water on the surface, provided you wipe it off fairly quickly.

Wallpaper pastes

◆Allow between 0.5 and 0.7 litres (1–$1\frac{1}{4}$ pt) of paste for each roll (more if it is heavily embossed because paste collects in the hollows of the surface).

◆Choose the correct paste for the wallcovering you are about to hang so that it adheres properly. There are several types:

◇*Cold water powders – for standard wallpapers.*

◇*Ready-mixed pastes – for standard wallpapers and special wallcoverings (vinyls, hessian, grasscloth, metallized foils, etc).*

◇*Heavy-duty pastes – for standard wallpapers, heavy wallpapers, high-relief and embossed wallpapers.*

◇*Fungicidal pastes – for standard wallpapers, washable and vinyl wallcoverings, vinyl relief and foamed polyethylene.*

HANGING WALLPAPER

◆Paper the ceiling before the walls so that paste can't drip onto a newly papered wall.

◆Start papering on the wall adjacent to the wall with the main window so that cut strips end up on the darkest wall in the room.

◆Hang lining paper on previously painted surfaces or on new plasterwork. This will prevent the top layer of wallpaper from creasing and stretching. The paste also dries faster on lining paper.

◆Leave lining paper for 48 hours before hanging the top covering so that it can dry.

◆Apply a coat of size or diluted wallpaper paste to the wall or lining paper to create a slippery surface, which makes it easier to position the wallpaper.

Putting up lining paper *Hang lining paper horizontally for walls, and at right angles to the final covering for ceilings (indicated by the dotted lines). This ensures that the seams of both layers do not meet, which would make them bulky.*

Hanging lining paper

◆Each length should be the full length of the wall or ceiling; don't join pieces – it's difficult to get a perfect join.

◆Butt the pieces against each other; don't overlap them or the joins will be visible.

CUTTING OUT WALLPAPER

1 Measure the height of the wall at the point where the first length will be hung.

2 Cut the first length about 10cm (4in) longer than this measurement to allow for trimming. If the pattern is bold, decide where you want the first motif to go and cut the paper accordingly. Mark the top of the length on the back of the paper, so you hang it the right way up, and number the piece.

3 Measure and cut further lengths as required until you get to the end of the roll. (A roll should give four lengths unless the repeat is very large or your ceilings are especially high.) If the paper is patterned, watch the pattern match carefully, especially if the pattern is stepped. Use leftovers to paper above doors and above and below window openings.

4 When cutting stepped patterns, mark the back of the first length "cut 1" and the back of the second length "2". The third length will be an exact match for 1 and the fourth a match for 2 and so on.

Pasting and folding wallcoverings

◆Keep the brush well coated with paste and brush it along the centre of each length, then out to the edges. This will prevent the paper coming away from the wall in patches or along the edges.

◆Put each length aside after you have pasted it, to absorb moisture and become supple, while you paste the next length or hang the previous one.

◇Leave mediumweight papers for about five minutes and heavyweight papers for about 10 or 12 minutes. If there are no instructions, leave the paper until it is supple. Keep the soaking time constant between lengths.

◇Don't prepare so many lengths that you no longer have any room to move around in.

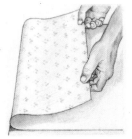 

Folding wallpaper *Fold one end to the middle, pasted sides together above left. Fold the other length over to meet the first in the middle above right. Don't crease the fold.*

HANGING PAPER IN TRICKY AREAS

RADIATORS

◆ Tilt the radiator forward to paper behind it. If you can't tilt the radiator, tuck enough paper down behind it to give the impression that the wall is completely papered. Use a long-handled roller or pad to smooth the paper onto the wall.

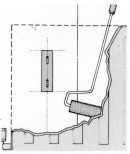

Papering behind a radiator *Cut slits in the paper before pushing it down behind the radiator, so that it will go round the brackets which hold the radiator in place. Use a long-handled roller or paint pad to smooth paper.*

CORNERS

◆ Hang full lengths until you are less than a full width away from a corner. When you reach the corner, measure between the edge of the covering and the corner of the room in several places (the distances may differ – very few homes have perfectly straight walls).

Papering a corner *Cut a length of paper about 10mm ($\frac{1}{2}$in) wider than the widest measured distance between the corner and the wall-covering, paste it and hang it. Turn the overlap neatly onto the other wall and brush it down. Paste the edge of the next length over it.*

DOORS

◆ When you reach the door, measure the distance between the edge of the covering and the door frame in several places. Cut an L-shape out of a full length piece, about 5cm (2in) less than the height of the door and 5cm wider than the distance between the paper and door to allow for trimming. Hang the paper from the ceiling to the top of the door frame. Make a diagonal cut in the paper in the corner of the door frame, see below. Crease the paper along the top of the frame and cut it. Crease the paper along the vertical, and trim. Smooth the paper into place.

Trimming paper around a door frame *Make a diagonal cut in the extra trimming, about 2.5cm (1in) long, in the angle between the top of the door frame and the vertical.*

ARCHES

1 *Paper the outer walls first. Trim to leave a 2.5cm (1in) margin of wallpaper to be turned into the arch.*

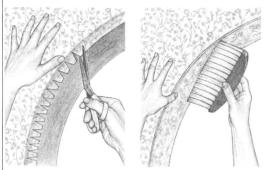

2 *Make small V-shaped cuts in the edge of the paper to allow for the curve of the arch, above left. Fold the flaps around the corner and smooth them down. Paper the inside of the arch in two pieces cut to the exact width of the arch, and butt the joint neatly at the top. Smooth the paper down, above right.*

WINDOWS

Papering dormer windows *Leave a 2.5cm (1in) margin of extra paper on the paper from the outer wall into the reveal. Cut accurate triangular pieces to cover the reveal walls and overlap the margin.*

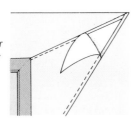

Papering window reveals *Paper the inside walls first, cutting the paper to align exactly with the edge of the outer wall. Then hang a length on the outer wall, with a small margin overlapping the papered reveal. Match the pattern carefully (if there is one).*

LIGHT FITTINGS

◆ Switch off the electricity at the mains before touching anything.
◆ To paper round a removable ceiling rose, detach the light fitting and the rose, make a hole in the wallcovering and pass the flex through the hole. Replace the rose and the light fitting. For a fixed rose, paper as for chunky sockets and switches, see below.

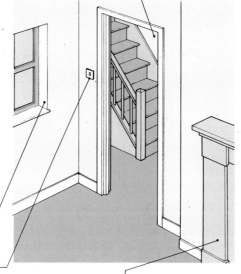

STAIRWELLS

◆ Set up a safe work station, see page 193.
◆ It is easiest to hang the longest length first and work away from it in both directions.
◆ Make sure each piece is long enough to allow for the slope of the stairs.

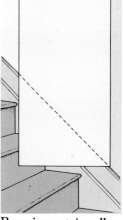

Papering a stairwell *Hang the paper as normal, then crease it along the skirting, and trim off the excess.*

FIREPLACES

◆ With very wide mantelpieces, treat the wall above and below the shelf as two separate areas. Hang the top half first and then the bottom. Match the pattern carefully and make a neat butt joint where the two pieces meet. Chimney breasts look best if the joins and overlaps are on the recessed walls.
◆ If the mantelpiece spans only part of a wall, hang the length of wallpaper as one piece.

Papering around a fireplace *Brush on the top half of the paper and cut it along the rear edge of the mantelshelf. Brush on the bottom half of the paper and mark the contours of the fireplace surround with the back of a pair of scissors. Cut out the shapes and smooth the paper into place with a brush.*

Papering around cover plates *Remove the cover plate, then hang the paper as normal until you reach the fitting. Cut a hole in the paper about 5cm (2in) smaller than the plate. Smooth the paper onto the wall. Replace the plate.*

Papering around chunky sockets and switches *Make small cuts in the paper radiating from the centre of the fitting to about 10mm ($\frac{1}{2}$in) beyond its edges. Brush the paper around the block and trim off the flaps.*

Folding ceiling paper *Fold this alternately back on itself and forward so that you concertina the length.*

3 Unfold the rest gradually, brushing it into place against the guideline, walking along the platform as you go. Crease and trim the ends.

Papering ceilings

◆Get someone to help you if you can. Papering ceilings is very tiring.

◆Keep the paper parallel to the main window in the room, otherwise the seams will be visible.

1 Make a guideline on the ceiling for the first length of paper, see below.

2 Position the top flap of the folded paper in the corner, in the angle between the wall and ceiling. Brush it into position.

MAKING A CHALK GUIDELINE

1 *Pin a string coated with coloured chalk to the wall adjacent to the wall with the main window, slightly less than a full width of the wallcovering away from the window wall.*

2 *Hold the other end of the string against the wall on the opposite side of the room and the same distance away from the window wall. Pin it as above.*

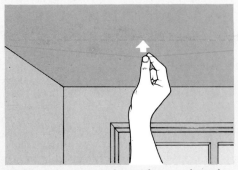

3 *Pluck the string with your finger so that it hits the ceiling. It will leave a chalk line which will be your guide.*

Covering walls

1 Use a plumb line to mark a true vertical on the wall in pencil before hanging the first length (or use a chalk-covered string as for ceilings).

2 Hold the length exactly against this line and brush it with firm strokes from the middle outwards.

3 Push the paper into the angles of the wall with the bristles on your brush.

4 Use the back of the scissors blade to mark the angles on the wallcovering, *above left*. Pull the paper away from the wall and trim it along the marked lines, *above right*.

HANGING WALLPAPER BORDERS

◆Use borders and friezes to make a room look taller, lower, or simply more "finished". They can also be used to co-ordinate colours in a room or add a bit to accent colour.

◆Put them up at the level of picture rails, or use them as a vertical wall surround or as the trim to a sloping ceiling, to finish off an area of wall tiles in the bathroom or to outline a door.

◆Don't apply a border or frieze until at least 48 hours after hanging the wallpaper, to allow the paper to dry.

◆Hang both borders and friezes with ordinary adhesive.

OTHER WALLCOVERINGS

◆ Textured wallcoverings can give a room a warm feeling and also ward off condensation. Many act as heat or sound insulators.

◆ For thin or shiny materials, put up lining paper first, otherwise every small flaw will show. Lining paper helps heavy and textured coverings to adhere better. If the covering is semi-transparent, paint the lining paper with a coat of a neutral-coloured emulsion.

◆ Paste coverings with a paper backing like an ordinary wallpaper; they are easier to hang than unbacked fabrics.

◆ Take great care not to stretch or stain fabric coverings. Modern wallcoverings can usually be spotcleaned but silks have to be cleaned professionally, and even then may be impossible to get clean again.

Silk

◆ Paste the wall, not the fabric, and make sure there are no lumps in the paste, because they will show through.

◆ Check your measurements carefully before you cut; silk is very expensive.

◆ Cut and trim the fabric with a sharp knife against a straightedge to prevent fraying.

◆ Smooth the fabric to the wall with a clean soft roller.

Grasscloth

◆ Paste this as you would any other wallpaper but cover the face of the pasting table with a strip of lining paper to protect the face of the fabric, which is vulnerable to adhesive and scratching.

◆ Don't fold the cloth – this will leave permanent, hard crease lines on it.

◆ Apply the lengths directly to the wall and smooth them down with a paint roller.

◆ Make a crease line for trimming at the corner of the wall and ceiling and at the skirting. Wait until the adhesive is quite dry before trimming each length with a sharp knife against a steel rule.

Hessian

◆ Treat paper-backed hessian like any other wallpaper. For unbacked hessian, paste the wall and not the hessian. Flatten each strip in place with a roller.

◆ Get someone to help you – hessian is easily stretched. Try to line it up right first time.

◆ Overlap strips and finish all the walls before you trim.

Trimming hessian *Cut through each overlap with a very sharp craft knife held against a steel rule. Remove the offcut and press the join. Trim the top and bottom with a sharp knife against a wide-bladed scraper.*

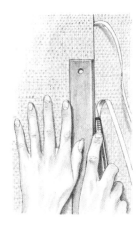

Fabric

◆ Choose an easily matched pattern.

◆ Paste the wall and then smooth the fabric into place with a paint roller, overlapping the edges. When dry, trim the edges with a sharp knife against a steel rule.

◆ Alternatively, staple fabric to battens or a wooden framework round the wall. Fold the fabric under at its edges first, to stop it from fraying. This is a good method for a pleated or gathered wallcovering.

Foil

◆ Paste foil with a foam roller. Immerse ready-pasted foil in a trough of water to activate the paste. Hang each length of foil from the top down and smooth onto the wall with a clean sponge.

◆ Make sure you match the pattern carefully because foil attracts the eye.

◆ Trim the top and bottom edges, butt the lengths and flatten the joins with a roller.

PATCHING WALLCOVERINGS

If a piece of wallcovering gets torn, you may be able to stick it back on again using a dab of latex adhesive. Rub off surplus adhesive with your fingers. A badly torn or marked piece of wallcovering will need a patch.

WALLPAPER

1 *Raggedly tear a piece of paper to fit entirely over the damaged area. (Torn edges are less noticeable than cut ones.)*

2 *Paste the patch and stick it over the area, taking care to match the pattern accurately.*

3 *Leave it to dry for a few minutes and then roll with a seam roller (or a rolling pin).*

VINYL, HESSIAN OR GRASSCLOTH

1 *Cut a piece of the wallcovering to match the pattern, and make sure that it is slightly larger than the damaged part.*

2 *Hold the piece against the wall and cut a square through both layers with a very sharp knife. Take out the old patch. Paste the new one and fit it into the gap.*

3 *Roll it lightly with a seam roller to get rid of any creases.*

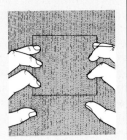

TILING

Buy self-adhesive tiles – they are easier and much less messy to lay than those that need adhesive. For large areas of tiles, buy mosaic or other tiles that are bonded in large sections; it is less time-consuming than laying individual tiles. If you are in any doubt about your ability to tile, get a professional in, it may be cheaper.

PREPARING THE SURFACE

◆ Lay your tiles on a dry, firm foundation. It is difficult to lay tiles on a poor surface: an unevenness will show through soft tiles and eventually crack or damage hard tiles.

◆ If necessary, reline uneven walls with plaster or plasterboard, and floors with hardboard, chipboard or plywood, to provide a level surface to tile on.

◆ Never tile over wallpaper or similar wallcoverings because if the wallcovering comes away, the tiles will fall off.

◆ If tiling over paint, make sure that the paint is sound, see page 185.

◆ Sand the wall with a coarse-grade abrasive paper to provide a key, or rough surface, for the adhesive to grip on.

◆ Leave old tiles on the surface where possible. It is easier to tile over them, or just replace a few damaged ones than to remove them and start again. If you do remove tiles, remove the old adhesive.

◆ To remove old ceramic tiles, use a bolster chisel and club hammer, or a small kango hammer with a chasing tool.

◆ To remove old vinyl, cork or polystyrene tiles, use a wide scraper. Use a hot air gun to strip the adhesive. If the tiles seem stuck for good, you will have to tile over them. Brush on a coat of special primer and then a coat of latex-based self-levelling compound. Make sure that the adhesive for the new tiles you use is compatible with the compound. (Ask at your D.I.Y. shop for a suitable adhesive.)

◆ Brush very powdery cement floors with a stabilizing agent and fill any cracks with mortar. If necessary, prime the floor with diluted PVA adhesive and then apply a self-levelling compound according to the manufacturers' instructions. Work in small sections because it sets quickly. Allow the compound to dry out for two weeks before laying the tiles.

◆ Scrub floor boards with warm detergenty water before laying new tiles, and make sure all boards are firmly nailed and secure, otherwise the adhesive may not stick.

◆ If the boards are old or uneven, coat them with a latex compound to fill the gaps and cover all nail heads. Then put down a layer of water-resistant hardboard (shiny side up), chipboard or plywood. Use exterior grade chipboard or plywood so that you don't have to seal it. Make sure there is enough under-floor ventilation to prevent moisture from collecting and rotting the floor. If there are no air bricks, get a builder to fit some.

◆ If you plan to lay ceramic or quarry tiles on floor boards, get someone to check that the floor can take the weight.

TILING WALLS AND CEILINGS

◆ Make a plan of the wall on graph paper to work out where to put the tiles, especially if they are patterned or you want to insert a patterned tile randomly among plain ones.

◆ When you have finished tiling a bathroom or kitchen wall, spread a silicone sealant

Cutting tiles *Score along the surface with a tile cutter, and then hold the tile in pincers, squeeze the handle and break the tile in two (above left). If you do not have pincers, score the surface of the tile, and then place the tile face up on top of two matchsticks lined up under the scored line (above right). Press your fingers lightly on the edges of the tile either side of the line and it should break along the line.*

TILING EQUIPMENT

◇ **Tile cutter** There are many types, but the most commonly used ones have a cutting wheel and a pair of snappers to break the tile along the scored line.

◇ **Sharp knife and a straight edge** For cutting soft tiles.

◇ **Clippers, pincers, tile saw** For cutting ceramic tiles.

◇ **Vice** For holding tiles while you saw cut curved edges.

◇ **Tenon saw** For cutting wood tiles.

◇ **Tile file** For smoothing rough edges.

◇ **Card** For making templates for awkward spaces.

◇ **Battens, string and a T-square** For positioning wall and ceiling tiles.

◇ **Hammer, nails, screws, screwdriver and spirit level** For fixing battens.

◇ **Staple gun** For fixing soft tiles to battens.

◇ **Adhesive** Use a thin-bed adhesive for smooth surfaces, and a thick-bed adhesive for uneven floors. Choose a waterproof adhesive for bathrooms, shower rooms and other places likely to get damp or wet.

◇ **Trowel or spatula** For applying adhesive; for polystyrene tiles you need an old paint brush.

◇ **Notched plastic spreader** To distribute the adhesive evenly.

◇ **Grout** Ready-mixed grout is the easiest to use and it is available in many colours. If you can't get the right colour, buy powdered grout and add powdered pigment.

◇ **Rubber grouter, squeegee or spatula, or a sponge** For filling the joints.

◇ **Tile spacers, or a box of matches** For spacing tiles. Choose the type of spacers that are shallower than the tiles; they don't have to be removed – you just grout over them.

◇ **Thin stick with a rounded end, or an orange stick** To run along the grouting between the tiles.

◇ **Large sponge** For wiping the tiles clean.

along the line where the tiles meet the bath or the kitchen surface, to stop water from seeping down behind it. A more expensive, but better-looking alternative is to fit curved edging tiles or a curved plastic strip along the joining edges. In a kitchen you can also fit wooden beading where the tiles meet the work surface.

Ceramic tiles

◆ Lay straight-edged tiles with spaces between them, but universal tiles (with angled edges) must butt against each other.

1 Nail a horizontal batten lightly to the wall where you want the base of the bottom row of tiles to begin, to support the tiles until the adhesive has dried.

2 Start in the bottom left-hand corner, or in the middle of the wall if the pattern is a large one, so that the cut tiles will be at the edges. Smooth a layer of adhesive over about 1 sq m/yd of wall with a trowel.

3 Draw a notched spreader horizontally over the area so that its teeth touch the wall surface.

4 Place the first tile on the batten and press it into the adhesive with a slight twist, so that it is in full contact with the adhesive.

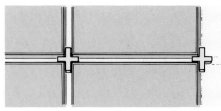

5 Lay the tiles in horizontal strips. If using straight-edged tiles, place matchsticks or spacers between each tile and each row of tiles to make an even gap for grouting. With very thick tiles you can leave wider gaps.

6 Leave the tiles to dry for at least 12 hours before grouting them. Remove the batten and spacers (unless they are the type that remain), and then grout.

CUTTING CERAMIC TILES

◆ For angles score the surface and then nibble away the excess tile with pincers or pliers.
◆ File rough edges with a tile file, working away from the glaze so that you do not damage it.
◆ Some tile breakers are a bit flimsy. If you have many tiles to cut, or they are difficult, hire a robust floor tile cutter, which is much quicker and less frustrating.

Cutting curves *Make a template of the curve on card and trace the outline onto the upper surface of the tile. Fix the tile in a vice and use a tile saw to cut the shape out of the tile.*

GROUTING

◆ Use grouting to prevent dirt and water from getting under the tiles.
◆ Use waterproof grout to prevent damp in areas where there is heavy condensation or running water, and on surfaces which you wash regularly, otherwise the adhesive may not stick.

1 *Spread the grout onto the surface of the tiles, around the gaps.*
2 *Use a rubber spatula or a piece of damp sponge to work it well into the gaps between the tiles. Wipe the tiles clean with a sponge.*

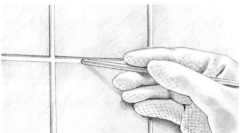

3 *When you have covered the whole area, draw a thin stick with a rounded end, such as an orange stick, along each joint to press the grouting home lightly. Wipe clean again.*

Mirror tiles

◆ If the walls are cold, heat the room first, so that the self-stick tabs on the tiles adhere.

◆ Fix a sheet of chipboard to the wall if it is not absolutely true. If you stick mirror tiles to an uneven surface, they will produce very distorted images.

◆ Mirror tiles do not need grouting; you can butt them up against each other.

Cork tiles

◆ Leave cork tiles unwrapped in the room for 24 hours before laying them, so that the cork can become acclimatized.

◆ Use a straightedge and a very sharp knife to cut cork, or it may crumble. Always cut cork tiles with the smooth side up.

◆ Apply these tiles as for ceramic tiles but use a special cork wall tile adhesive and butt them closely together.

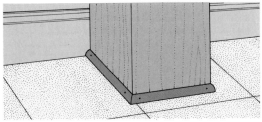

Finishing cork tiling *Where cork tiling is taken up to exposed edges, such as the corner of a buttress, protect the edge with wooden beading.*

Polystyrene ceiling tiles

1 Make sure the surface is clean and dry. Mark the ceiling with chalk lines as for the floor, see over.

2 Spread polystyrene adhesive all over the tile, from edge to edge. Working from the middle outwards, fix the first tile so that it lines up with your crossing chalklines in the middle. Butt the tiles up to each other.

CUTTING A POLYSTYRENE EDGE TILE

1 *Place the tile to be cut exactly over the last full tile in the row. Put another tile on top and butt it against the wall.*

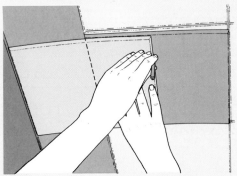

2 *Trace the edge of the top tile (the edge away from the wall) onto the tile beneath it, which is the tile to be cut.*

3 *Score along the line with a sharp knife. The cut tile should fit into the gap.*

TILING FLOORS

◆ Draw a room plan on graph paper, marking all doors, alcoves, chimney breasts, etc., to work out how many tiles you'll need and roughly where to start laying them.

◆ Lay cork, linoleum and vinyl tiles from the centre of the room outwards; it looks better if the tile shapes are centred.

◆ Lay wood flooring and ceramic and quarry tiles from a corner farthest from the door, working back to the door so that you can get out of the room when you have finished.

◆ Take all inward-opening doors off their hinges before you start. Floor tiles raise the floor by at least 12mm ($\frac{1}{2}$in) and if the doors are shut you may not be able to get out of the room once the tiles are laid.

Vinyl and cork tiles

◆ Peel off the backing paper, or spread the glue, check that any pattern is placed in the right direction, and place the tiles down, starting from the centre.

◆Unfinished cork tiles should be sanded by hand and then wiped carefully to get rid of all the dust. Seal with a polyurethane seal.

Fitting a threshold bar *If the tiles start at a doorway, fit a wooden or metal threshold bar over the edge of the tiles to prevent them from becoming scuffed.*

◆In a bathroom apply a bead of silicone sealant between the floor tiles and the wall to stop water seeping down the gap.

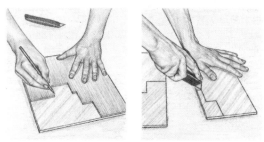

Fitting tiles around awkward spaces *Make a cardboard template of the shape and trace the outline onto the tile (above left). Cut the tile into several pieces and then cut out the shapes with a sharp knife. Fit them around the space (above right).*

MARKING A FLOOR OR CEILING FOR TILING

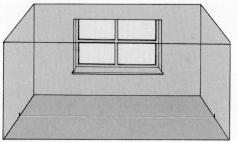

1 Chalk a length of string, stretch it between the centres of the two shortest sides of the room and fix it to the base of the walls, see page 198.

2 Pluck the string with your finger so that it snaps back onto the floor and leaves a chalk line. Measure the line to find its middle point.

3 Using a T-square, mark a short line at right angles to the line.

4 Stretch the chalk string along the short line and fix it to the base of the walls. Snap it to mark a line which runs between the walls.

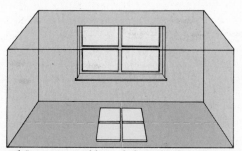

5 Lay out a trial line of tiles either butted together or with a grouting space between them, from the centre to all four walls. Adjust them so that the border tiles will be more or less equal in size, they'll look better.

Wood tiles

◆Unpack the tiles and leave them in the room for a few days before fitting them so that they can adjust to the temperature and humidity level in the room.

◆Spread enough bitumen adhesive on the floor to cover one tile and lay the tile straight down into its place. Don't slide it about to adjust it or adhesive will ooze through the joins between the tiles.

◆Lay all the complete tiles and allow the adhesive to set before cutting and laying down the shaped ones. This takes 15 minutes to half an hour.

◇Woodblocks can be arranged in a variety of patterns, and basketweave mosaic panels can be laid square or diagonally across the room.

Fitting wood tiles *Allow for a 12mm ($\frac{1}{2}$in) gap between the cut tile and the skirting because the wood may expand a little after you have laid it. Cut shapes as for vinyl or cork, in bits, but use a tenon saw or electric jigsaw to do the cutting with.*

▼▼ Wear really old clothes and try not to get
◆ ◆ any of the adhesive on your hands or
face or on the wood. If you do, wipe it off
straight away with a damp cloth.
◆ Sand and seal wood mosaic after the adhesive has dried, to protect it. Parquet does not
need to be sanded or sealed.

Ceramic, clay and quarry tiles

◆ Lay as for ceramic wall tiles, see page 204.
◆ Lay the tiles with a thin-bed adhesive
rather than mortar; it is easier to apply and
dries faster.
◆ Adjust the amount of grout or adhesive
you use while you are laying the tile – quarry
tiles are not always even.
▼▼ Don't walk on the tiles for 24 hours after
◆ ◆ laying or you may dislodge them or
make the surface uneven.
◆ Lay border tiles after the main ones have
dried. Butt the tiles right up to the skirting or
fit special skirting tiles.
◆ Seal unglazed ceramic tiles and quarry tiles
with polyurethane sealant or wax.

CUTTING CLAY AND QUARRY TILES

1 *Mark the desired shape and size on the tile
with a pencil.*
2 *Hold it on top of a brick and tap a row of
chips along the pencil marks with a hammer
and a cold chisel.*
3 *Hold the tile in both hands, and hit the
chipped line smartly against the corner of the
brick; the tile should break along the line.*

**For corners and
narrow pieces** *Nibble
at the marks with a
pair of pincers, until
you reach the chiselled
marks.*

REPAIRING TILES

◆ **For vinyl tiles** Prise off the old tile and
clean the area thoroughly. Take care not
to damage the surrounding tiles. Apply
adhesive to the floor. A new tile will
soon fade to match the rest.
◆ **For polystyrene tiles** Scrape off the
old tile. Spread polystyrene adhesive
over the whole of the back of the new
tile, to about 12mm ($\frac{1}{2}$in) from each edge,
and stick the tile in place.
◆ **For ceramic or quarry tiles** If a tile has
a small crack or chip, it's better to leave
it alone; you may do more damage to the
wall or surrounding tiles. If you do replace one, make sure the replacement tile
is the same size, colour and thickness as
the old one.

Replacing a ceramic tile *Work from the
middle outwards, cracking the damaged tile
into small pieces with a hammer and chisel and
chipping out the bits. Clean out the area, apply
adhesive and position the new tile.*

Replacing a wooden floor tile *Chisel out the
central block and lift out the surrounding pieces.
Scrape the floor surface clean and vacuum
thoroughly. Stick the new blocks in place with
flooring adhesive. If the new blocks are slightly
proud of the rest, plane them down when the
adhesive has dried.*

FLOOR COVERINGS

Buy top-quality floor coverings – they last and keep their appearance for longer than cheaper ones. If you have to buy strips of carpet, bear in mind that the pile of each piece must face the same way or they may look as if they are different colours. Don't join strips across a door; they will fray and can cause an accident.

ESTIMATING QUANTITIES

◆ Many retailers have a free estimating service; take advantage of this. If you decide to work out the quantities yourself, follow this sequence:

1 Sketch an outline of the room including doors and windows.

2 Measure the room's length and width from the base of the skirting to the deepest part of the door threshold, allowing for alcoves, doorways and other protrusions, and mark the maximum measurements on the plan. Include the interiors of cupboards in your plan.

3 Add 7.5cm (3in) for trimming in each direction and allow for any wastage that will be caused by pattern matching.

4 Choose a width of flooring that will waste the least amount of floor covering. Ask the retailer whether or not you can buy a length plus a narrow strip, or if you have to buy a wider roll and waste a strip at the edge.

Estimating for stairs

◆ Add enough to the measurement of the landing carpet for it to overlap the top stair riser and be tacked down.

1 Working from the top tread down, measure each tread and riser and add the height of a riser to the overall length. This is so that the carpet can be tucked under at the bottom and allows for moving it up and down every so often to even out the wear.

2 Add 4cm (1¾in) to the length of each tread to allow for the bulk of the underlay and for tucking into the grippers.

3 Measure the width of the treads. If they have open sides, allow 12mm (½in) for turning under at each edge.

◇ *On winding staircases, measure along the outer edge for the longest length. Allow for tucking in and moving the carpet up and down, as for straight stairs.*

EQUIPMENT

◆ The equipment you need depends on the type of floor covering: for example, foam-backed carpet needs cutting and fixing equipment, whereas carpet tiles need trimming equipment only.

◇ *Trimming knife with curved and straight heavy-duty blades*
◇ *Large, sharp scissors*
◇ *1m (3ft) steel rule*
◇ *Knee kicker*
◇ *Double-sided carpet tape*
◇ *Adhesive spreader*
◇ *Binder bar for edge of floor covering*
◇ *Binder bar for joining floor coverings*
◇ *Flat bolster chisel*
◇ *19mm (¾in) and 25mm (1in) carpet tacks*
◇ *Heavy-duty stapler (with rust-proof staples)*
◇ *Angled and standard grippers*

CHOOSING FLOOR COVERINGS

Choose a carpet grade which is suitable for the "traffic" through the room. Many carpets are classified into "wear factor" categories, see right. Hessian-backed carpet is hardwearing but expensive. Foam-backed carpet is cheaper and easier to lay but is not as hardwearing; it is not suitable for areas such as stairs. Hair, wool and twisted yarn carpets are hardwearing.

◆ If you are buying sheet flooring for a kitchen or bathroom, make sure that it is not slippery when wet.

◆ Don't use carpet in a bathroom. It is very difficult to dry, and wet carpets fade, smell musty, attract mildew and germs and are hard to clean.

◆ For stairs, choose a carpet that won't show the backing at its edges, such as a carpet with bound edges, for example.

◆ Use carpet remnants and carpet squares which have unbound edges for small rooms; butted against the wall the edges won't fray.

CARPET QUALITY

Grade	Situation
1	Rooms with very light "traffic", e.g. study
2	Lightly used rooms
3	Lightly used living rooms
L	High-quality carpets with a long pile, for lightly used areas
4	Rooms in heavy use
5	Very heavily used areas

UNDERLAYS

◆ All carpets need a separate underlay. Newspapers will not do. Good-quality underlay will improve a carpet's heat- and sound-insulating properties and make it last longer.

◆ Hessian- or paper-backed rubber underlay is best for most carpets.

◆ If you have underfloor heating, use a heavy felt underlay.

◆ Plastic foam underlay can be used in bedrooms and other rooms which don't get much heavy traffic, but it flattens easily and needs felt paper underneath it to prevent the backing from sticking to the floorboards.

◆ Use felt paper underlay under foam-backed carpet and rubber underlay. Use felt paper underlay also when there are gaps between the floorboards not wide enough to warrant a complete layer of hardboard.

◆ Use individual stair pads for underlay on stairs – they are much easier to put down than a length of underlay.

CARPETS

◆ Broadloom is the easiest to lay in square or rectangular rooms because it is made in generous widths, which means that there is much less cutting and tacking to do.

◆ Body carpet is useful for oddly shaped rooms and for stairs because its narrow width is easier to cut; it is also cheaper because you are less likely to waste carpet. It can be professionally joined to make wider widths if necessary.

◆ Carpet tiles are easy to lay and trim, and can be lifted and washed, or replaced, individually. They are a reasonably cheap form of carpeting.

MATTING

◆ Rush and split cane matting are usually sold in 30cm (1ft) squares, which can be sewn together to cover larger areas. They are very hardwearing, need no underlay, and can be loose laid onto wood or concrete.

◆ Coconut, coir and sisal matting need no underlay; some may have a non-slip

backing. Good as "door matting" or for a hallway.

◆ Plastic matting is cheap, available in bright colours and easily washable, and is suitable for kitchens and bathrooms.

SHEET FLOORING

◆ Sheet vinyl comes in roll widths of up to 4m (13ft) and unlimited lengths. Most rooms can be covered with one sheet. "Lay-flat" vinyls are the easiest to lay, don't tear, and need no adhesive. Also, unlike other vinyls, they don't shrink. Use cushioned vinyl to hide slight irregularities in the floor. It is also more comfortable and quieter to walk on than other vinyl floor coverings.

◆ Sheet rubber is slightly more difficult to lay than vinyl but is hardwearing, quiet and waterproof. It is available with various raised designs, which make it non-slip.

◆ Linoleum is generally very hardwearing, but is difficult to handle and lay, and breaks easily if it gets bent. It is not waterproof.

LAYING FLOOR COVERINGS

◆ Allow floors treated with wood preservative or anti-woodworm fluid to lie uncovered for several months before covering them; the treatment may damage the covering.

◆ For large areas of carpet and stairs, use a professional carpet layer.

◆ If possible, mark up the new flooring out of doors or in a larger room than the one you are dealing with, to make the task easier.

◆ Put vinyl and linoleum in the room 24 hours before laying, to let them acclimatize.

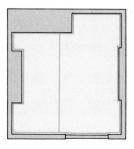

Making a template for the floor covering *Cut a template of the floor using lengths of carpet underlay, which can be taped together to form the room shape. If replacing vinyl, use the old floor covering as a template for the new one.*

Preparation

◆ The floor must be smooth, dry, clean and firm. If you are covering floorboards, secure loose boards first and hammer in any protruding nails.

◆ Take up any vinyl sheeting and scrape away sections that are stuck to the floor.

◆ If a cement floor is slightly uneven, coat it with diluted PVA bonding agent before filling with cement mortar.

◆ If the floor is very uneven, lay hardboard or chipboard to give a smooth base for the floor covering.

◆ Vacuum thoroughly before putting down any floor covering to remove dust and grit.

Laying underlay

◆ Lay the carpet roughly in position before fitting the underlay, otherwise you may damage the underlay by dragging the carpet over it. Roll half the carpet back and lay half the underlay at a time.

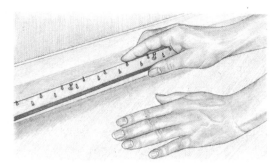

1 Fix grippers in a continuous line around the edges of the room, 6mm ($\frac{1}{4}$in) away from the wall, angling the pins towards the wall. Nail the grippers onto timber floors or use hardened pins or an adhesive recommended by the manufacturer for solid floors.

◇ *If you are not using grippers, stick double-sided tape to the edge of the floor to secure the carpet.*

2 Anchor the underlay 5cm (2in) from the skirting. Secure underlay to a wooden floor with rust-proof staples; use dabs of adhesive on a solid floor.

◇ *Don't put extra thicknesses of underlay on well-worn areas of flooring: this will only cause a lump in the carpet which will wear out quickly.*

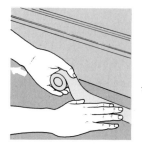

Laying felt paper underlay *Join the strips of underlay before you secure it. Lay strips of double-sided adhesive tape along the edges of the room 5cm (2in) from the skirting, and secure the underlay to the tape.*

Laying hessian-backed carpet

1 Position the carpet so that about 12mm ($\frac{1}{2}$in) of material turns up against two adjoining walls.

2 Hook the carpet to the grippers or tack it down, on one side.

3 Stretch the carpet across the room, see opposite, and hook it onto the rest of the grippers or tack it.

4 Trim the edges and tuck them under the skirting using a bolster chisel or a spatula.

STRETCHING HESSIAN-BACKED CARPET

◆ Use a knee kicker – it makes the job of stretching the carpet much easier (you can hire one). Use the muscle just above your knee to operate the tool.

1 *Hook the carpet onto the grippers in one corner so that it is secured for 30cm (1ft) along the wall on each side of the corner.*

2 *Attach the carpet to the grippers at an adjacent corner. Then fix it firmly along the wall between the two corners.*

3 *Smooth the carpet over to the corner opposite the last and secure it onto the grippers along the wall connecting it and the first corner.*

4 *Kneel on the carpet with your back to one of the completed sides, press the teeth on the knee kicker into the carpet and knock the padded end forward with your knee. Continue until you reach the wall facing you. Hook the carpet onto the gripper. Repeat this along one edge and then do the same for the last unattached edge. Trim the excess carpeting to about 12mm ($\frac{1}{2}$in), and push it under the skirting.*

Laying foam-backed carpet

◆ You can get gripper strips with extra large pins for foam-backed carpet, but it may be easier to use double-sided carpet tape.

◆ Lay the carpet on the floor and make sure there is 12mm ($\frac{1}{2}$in) extra all round to allow for trimming.

◆ Roll the carpet back and stick down the tape. Roll the carpet back down and press it onto the tape. Roll back the other half and then repeat.

◆ Foam-backed carpet needs no stretching.

Trimming foam-backed carpet *Hold a sharp trimming knife at an angle with the handle pointing away from the wall so that you don't cut away too much.*

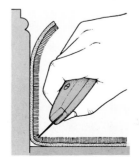

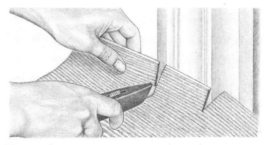

Fitting floor coverings into awkward places *Trim the covering so that 5cm (2in) rests against the wall. Make a series of "release" cuts in the covering until it lies flat. Then trim the "tongues" and slip them under the skirting or onto the grippers.*

Laying carpet tiles

◆ Follow the same planning and laying sequence as for floor tiles, see pages 205–6.

◆ Secure the first tile with double-sided carpet tape and loose lay the rest.

◆ Secure them in doorways with a carpet tile binder bar, to prevent the edges from getting scuffed and fraying.

PATCHING FLOOR COVERINGS

CARPET

1 *Buy a piece of carpet exactly like the one being patched, or take a piece of carpet from somewhere where it won't be missed. Lay the new piece on top of the damaged area and cut through both layers with a sharp knife.*

2 *Cut a piece of hessian slightly larger than the patch. Lay double-sided carpet tape on the floor under the hole and stick the hessian down.*

3 *Apply latex adhesive along the edges of the hole and patch to about halfway up the pile. Leave to dry (until the adhesive is semi-transparent).*

4 *Fit the patch into the hole and tap lightly around the edges to make a good bond.*

VINYL AND LINOLEUM

◆ Use an offcut to patch large tears.

1 *Lay the offcut over the tear and match up the pattern with the rest of the covering.*

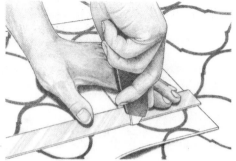

2 *Using a sharp knife, cut through both pieces to make a patch larger than the tear, cutting through both pieces of the floor covering.*

3 *Remove the damaged piece, coat the new piece with adhesive and press it into place.*

Laying sheet vinyl and linoleum

◆ Put sheet vinyl into the room two or three days before you want to lay it to get it to room temperature. This makes it easier to lay. Switch the heating on if you are laying vinyl in winter.

◆ Loose lay it, leaving it overlapping up the wall all round by about 10cm (4in), because it will probably shrink.

◆ Don't bother to stick down the very cheap vinyls, nor those that are intended to be loose laid.

◆ If you are sticking the covering down use the recommended adhesive. Glue cushioned vinyls around the edges, but other types under the whole surface.

◆ Roll back half the sheet and apply the adhesive to the floor. Roll the sheet back down and press it down onto the floor. Sweep it with a broom to get it absolutely flat. Repeat with the other half.

◆ If you have to lay two sheets, overlap the edges and cut through both thicknesses as they overlap, using a sharp knife against a steel rule. Peel away the excess. The cut edges should fit together perfectly.

Cutting around corners and awkward shapes
Trace around the shapes on card with a pencil held against a batten 2.5cm (1in) wide (above left). Re-trace the shape 2.5cm (1in) inside the template outline onto the covering (above right).

Repairs and Maintenance

BASIC TOOL KIT

When buying tools, get the very best you can afford. Good tools are well balanced and well designed, so they are much easier to use than poorer quality tools. They are also more robust, so they will last for much longer, and work out cheaper in the end.

ESSENTIAL TOOL KIT

◆ Keep a very basic tool kit handy for emergency household repairs.

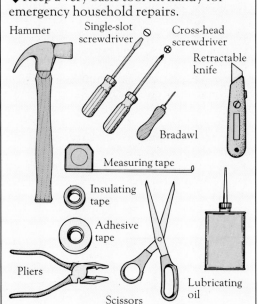

Hammer Single-slot screwdriver Cross-head screwdriver

Retractable knife

Bradawl

Measuring tape

Insulating tape

Adhesive tape

Pliers

Scissors

Lubricating oil

Hammers

◇ **Claw hammer** Good for knocking in nails and pulling them out. This is probably the most useful hammer for the home tool kit.

DESIRABLE EXTRAS
◇ **Cross-pein hammer** Has a tapered head, or pein, which is useful for tapping nails in awkward corners, or establishing small panel pins securely in position before hammering them in properly.
◇ **Mallets** Use a rubber mallet with chisels and a wooden mallet for wood, usually with a towel wrapped round it to prevent the wood from being damaged. Useful also for driving in stakes and tent pegs.

Screwdrivers

◆ It is worth buying a screwdriver set, a handle and a variety of blades, because it's more compact.

◇**Single-slot screwdrivers** Buy these screwdrivers in two or three different tip widths, for greater versatility.

◇**Cross-head screwdrivers** Available in three sizes; you need at least two because unless the tip fits into the screw properly it will slip. Cross-head screws are commonly found on electric appliances.

◇**Short-bladed screwdrivers** Can be operated in confined spaces. You can get them in single-slot and cross-head forms.

◇**Electrical screwdriver** Use this for dealing with plugs and other electrical equipment because the handle is well insulated in heavy-duty plastic. For safety, choose the type with a blade insulated in a plastic sleeve and with a gauge which registers an electric current.

DESIRABLE EXTRAS
◇**Ratchet screwdriver** This is worked simply by turning your wrist rather than by adjusting your grip for each turn. The blade is fixed, so you cannot alter the size.

◇**Pump-action screwdriver** This is worked by applying pressure to the handle rather than turning your wrist, and has a very fast action. You can buy different-sized bits to fit into this type.

Bradawl and gimlet

◆Essential for making small starter holes for screws in walls or woodwork before drilling, so that the drill doesn't slip.

Pliers

◇**General-purpose pliers** Use to bend, stretch, straighten, grip and tug all sorts of metal things, and to cut wire.

◇**Carpenter's pincers** For pulling out nails and tacks.

DESIRABLE EXTRAS
◇**Long-nosed pliers** Useful for small awkward places; you can hold small nails or bolts with them while hammering or twisting the nails or bolts into place.

◆If you do a lot of home repairs, buy specialist pliers to lift tacks, strip electric wires, cut and clip tiles, etc.

Spanners

◇**Open-ended spanners** Use these to adjust nuts or bolts from the side and for pipe joints. Make sure you have various sizes.

◇**Adjustable spanner** Particularly useful in plumbing work but can also be used for any nut or bolt that comes loose.

DESIRABLE EXTRAS
◇**Large, heavy wrenches (monkey wrenches)** Used for gripping pipes and rods, flat or circular metal objects, etc.

Saws

◇**Panel or crosscut saw** For planks, boards, panels of timber, chipboard, and hardboard. The more teeth it has, the finer it will cut.

◇**Hacksaw** For cutting through cables, wires, pipes or small pieces of wood. It has thin, removable blades, which should be renewed often.

DESIRABLE EXTRAS
◇**Tenon saw** For accurate cutting of wood, especially for joints.

◇**Coping saw** To make curved cuts in wood and plastic.

◇**Fret saw** For cutting tight curves in wood, plastic and glass fibre.

◇**Tile saw** For cutting ceramic tiles.

◇**Pad saw** To cut small holes (key holes, for instance).

◇**Electric jig saw** For cutting straight, curved or scroll cuts quickly in timber, man-made boards, metals, plastics and various other materials.

◇**Electric circular saw** For straight cutting of timber, man-made boards, plastics and laminated boards, sheet metals, thicker soft metals, masonry and ceramic tiles. These saws cut with greater accuracy and safety than smaller saws. The 18cm (7$\frac{1}{4}$in) model is the most useful.

◆You can hire a circular saw; buy one only if you are likely to do a lot of DIY. Get one with at least a half horsepower motor, and make sure there is a spring-loaded guard which comes down automatically as soon as you move the saw away from the work.

NAILS AND OTHER FIXING PINS

◇ Round wire nails for strong support.
◇ Oval wire nails are useful where you want them to be hidden.
◇ Tacks for securing carpets and upholstery.
◇ Hardboard nails for joining hardboard and other thin materials.
◇ Masonry nails and steel pins for hanging pictures, and nailing directly into brick or block walls.
◇ Single-slot countersunk head screws for joining pieces of wood and for fittings such as hinges.
◇ Round head screws for attaching metal fittings to wood.
◇ Plastic wallplugs for solid walls.
◇ Toggles and anchors for fixing to cavity walls, see page 150.

DESIRABLE EXTRAS
◇ Wire staples, electrician's staples, aluminium and fibre wallplugs, self-tapping screws, chrome-topped mirror screws, wood-thread dowel screws.

Scissors

◇ **General-purpose scissors** For paper and other "blunting" materials. Don't use good ones for paper, it'll blunt them.

Planes

◇ **Smoothing plane** For smoothing wood for small jobs.
◇ **Jack plane** Useful all-round tool for planing small or large pieces of wood.
◇ **Block plane** Small plane particularly good for smoothing end grain. Can be used with one hand.

DESIRABLE EXTRA
◇ **Bench rebate plane** Has a broad cutting blade which can be used for smoothing open-sided rebates and large joints, when repairing furniture, for example.

Knives

◇ **Trimming knife** Buy one with replaceable blades because this type is cheaper in the end, and for safety buy one with retractable blades. Good for laying floors, cutting paper, fabrics and leather, and stripping wire.
◇ **Craft knife** Necessary if you want to do any delicate work, such as mending china etc.

Chisels

◇ **Bevel-edge chisel** Useful for cutting in small spaces because it has tapering edges. Several sizes are available, which are designed for lightweight work.
◇ **Cold chisel** For chipping off ceramic tiles, removing mortar from brickwork, and lifting wood floor blocks, etc. The most useful width is 12mm ($\frac{1}{2}$in).
◇ **Bolster chisel** For levering up heavy objects, such as floorboards.

Sharpening tools

◇ **Oilstone** For honing chisel and plane blades, and knives.

Drills

◇ **Electric drill** Use a one-speed drill for simple jobs only, like drilling holes in wood or soft walls; use a two- or three-speed drill for drilling through brick or stonework. Buy a drill with a hammer action, so that it can be used for tough jobs. For greater versatility, choose one that can be fitted with sanding or other attachments.

Sanding equipment

◇ **Sanding block** To wrap abrasive paper round and make sanding easier, see page 184.
◇ **Abrasive papers** You will need a selection for a variety of jobs, see SANDING EQUIPMENT page 184.
◇ **Mechanical sanders** Hire one when you need it; it is not worth buying one. Orbital

sanders give a very fine finish on wood, by sanding in circles. Belt sanders can sand metal and wood quickly but do not give a very smooth finish.

Measuring tools

◇**Flexible retractable steel tape** For measuring long lengths.
◇**Steel rule or straightedge** For measuring and for cutting against with a sharp knife.
◇**Spirit level** For determining a straight horizontal line.
◇**Plumb line** For determining a straight vertical line. You can use a weight tied onto a piece of string instead.
◇**Try square** For establishing right angles.

Tapes and adhesives

◇**Clear adhesive tape** For innumerable household jobs.
◇**Masking tape** For protecting glass or surrounding areas when painting and for sealing windows in the winter.
◇**Carpet tape** For carpet repairs and laying floor coverings.
◇**Wide plastic adhesive tape** For sealing packages, boxes, etc.
◇**Insulating tape** For temporary repairs to electrical flex.
◇**Rubber contact adhesives** Sometimes known as latex adhesives, these are used for repairing and binding carpets, rugs, fabrics, upholstery, sticky paper, rubber, wood, and some metals. They are sold ready-mixed, in a pot or tube. The heavy-duty type, which dries black, will join rubber, metal, glass, wood, cork, linoleum, roofing felt, asbestos, concrete, stone, plaster. These adhesives resist water, oil, steam and heat and provide a flexible bond.
◇**Epoxy resin adhesives** Made of resin and hardener which you mix. Use to mend glass, china, wood, metal, rigid plastics, fabrics, cracked lead pipes, and many other materials. Some are white when dry, others are a transparent yellow. Some are heat-resistant; all resist acids, oils and water.
◇**Cellulose-based general-purpose glues** Sold in tubes. Use to fix ivory, plastics, metal inlays, wood, Bakelite, canvas, card. It is water-resistant, and won't stain. Transparent when dry. Remove surplus glue with non-oily nail varnish remover or acetone.
◇**Emergency hose and pipe seal** For leaking pipes. Sold ready-mixed in a tube.
◇**Epoxy filler** For filling large gaps in rusted metal pipes or ceramic tiles, for example. Must be mixed with a hardener.
◇**Synthetic resins (wood glues)** Usually sold in two parts which you have to mix together: the glue and its hardener. Use for general joinery and cabinet work. These glues are waterproof, resist acid, and are very strong – often stronger than the wood that they join. Joints must be clamped while the adhesive is setting to stop them moving.
◇**Polyvinyl chloride (PVC) adhesive** Use for plastic raincoats, tablecloths, shower curtains, vinyls, leather, rubber and fabrics. White when dry. Sold ready-mixed in a tube.
▼▼ Certain materials may not withstand the
◆ ◆ solvent in these adhesives. Test them on a small piece of the material first.
◇**Polyvinyl acetate adhesive** Also known as PVA or filled PVA adhesive, this is sold ready to use in a fairly thick liquid form. Use to stick wood, polyurethane foam, paper, fabrics, card, carpets, leather; not suitable for most plastics. Use filled PVA to stick expanded polystyrene and ceramic tiles and mosaics to plaster, glazed bricks and painted surfaces. These adhesives are water-soluble and can be diluted with water to make a sealant and to make size for priming walls. They are transparent when dry.
◆PVA glues may eventually "creep", so don't use them for a heavy vertical object; the object may begin to move.
◇**Contact adhesives** Use to glue wood, books and their bindings, braid and brocade, canvas, copper, dolls, picture frames, leather, marquetry, paper, parchment, photographs, PVC, carpets, plasters and laminates. This adhesive is strong, heat-resistant and easy to use. Sold ready-mixed and has the consistency of thick cream.
◇**Cyanoacrylate adhesive** Use this glue on flat metal only and not on glass or crockery because it is water-soluble. Sold ready-mixed in a tube.
▼▼ Cyanoacrylate glues bond immediately,
◆ ◆ so don't get them on your fingers. If you do, soak your fingers in warm soapy water until the glue dissolves.

STORAGE

◆ Do not throw tools together in a heap, because you'll never be able to find what you need later.

◆ Make sure that the storage system you choose will not damage blades, or any other working part of the tool. If tools are kept together, they can easily damage or blunt each other.

◆ Make sure that tools are always put back in the right place so that you can find them next time.

◆ For ready access to tools construct a storage system from wooden racks, or use plastic or wire tool-hanging clips fixed to the wall or to pegboard (perforated hardboard) and hang tools on it.

Pegboard Paint the outline of the tool that belongs in each space so that you can see exactly where it should go.

Paint brushes Hang them on a pegboard to make sure their bristles stay in shape.

Shelf A small shelf is useful for storing tins with harmless or non-flammable liquids, or reference books.

Transparent jars Nail the lids of transparent screw-top jars to the underside of a shelf, and use the jars for small items such as nuts and bolts and rolls of sticky tape.

Vice If possible, have a simple vice or a small work bench with one to help you with odd jobs such as gluing wood or holding ceramic tiles while you chip them into shape.

Canvas pocket This is useful for a number of small items such as spanners and drill bits; it will protect these items as well as store them, and can be carried round in a tool bag. You can make one, or buy one from medical suppliers.

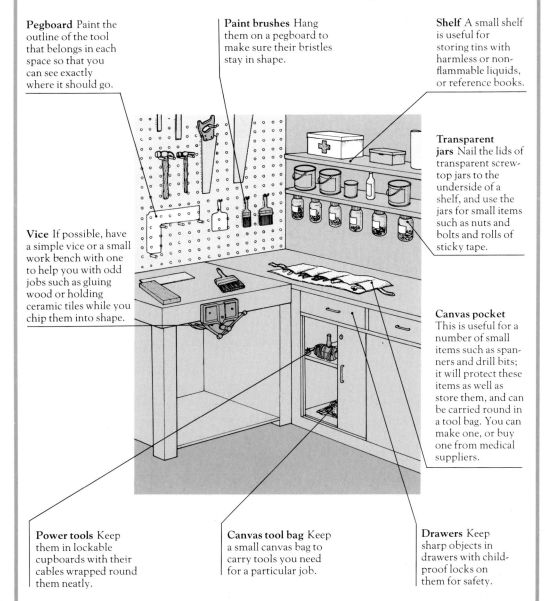

Power tools Keep them in lockable cupboards with their cables wrapped round them neatly.

Canvas tool bag Keep a small canvas bag to carry tools you need for a particular job.

Drawers Keep sharp objects in drawers with child-proof locks on them for safety.

HOUSEHOLD REPAIRS

Repair interior and exterior cracks in walls and woodwork as soon as possible. They are unsightly and, if left, may encourage damp or let cold draughts into the house. Don't leave cracks in the exterior until you next paint the house; fill them at the next opportunity when the weather is dry.

Keep gutters cleared (inspect them about twice a year) and attend to any roof fault as soon as you know about it, otherwise what may have been minor damage will soon need major and expensive repair. Call in professionals to do any repairs on the roof. A damp patch inside the house may be a sign of some roof damage, but it will not necessarily tell you where the source of the leak is. Water can travel quite a long way along roofing felt or a rafter before finding its way in.

Tighten any loose screws inside the house as soon as you notice them; they will eventually drop out and get lost, and you will only have to spend extra time and money replacing them.

Fix doors or windows that stick as soon as possible, otherwise they will be a source of annoyance to you and you may damage them each time you try to open them.

SAFETY GUIDELINES

Always think first about the safety of the job you are about to do. A large proportion of accidents in the home occur because people are not careful enough with the tools and equipment they use. Most of these accidents are easily preventable; they can be avoided by bearing the following guidelines in mind.

Ladders

◆ Check that your ladder is sound and firm.
◆ If you use a ladder extension, check that it is firmly fixed and won't slip.
◆ Make sure the ladder reaches at least 1m (3ft) above the highest level you are likely to want to stand at.
▼▼ Never stand above the third highest
◆ ◆ rung; the ladder may slip.
◆ Face the ladder as you climb so that you can see where you are going, and don't lean over the side as you work.
◆ Use a working platform for large areas. To make one, place a plank between two stepladders. If you are spanning more than 1.5m (5ft), put an extra support (say a box) beneath the plank in the middle, see page 193 for putting up a safe work station.

◆ In stairwells, always lean a long ladder into a stair so that it lodges firmly against a riser.
◆ Out of doors, stand the ladder on a piece of hardboard or chipboard so that it won't sink into the ground, see page 91.
◆ Wear soft, rubber-soled shoes which are comfortable and have a good grip.

Glass and glass fibre

◆ When dealing with broken glass or glass fibre, always wear thick gardening gloves to protect your hands, stout shoes to protect your feet, and goggles or sunglasses to protect your eyes from flying fragments or from strands of glass fibre.

Removing glass from a frame *Put strips of adhesive tape over the glass to hold the fragments together,* above left, *and cover the glass with a cloth as you break it,* above right.

◆Lay a whole newspaper on the floor and wrap pieces of glass in this, then seal it with adhesive tape before you put it in the bin so that nobody can get cut by it.

Flammable materials

Many adhesives, paints, varnishes and solvents are flammable and/or toxic.
◆Don't work near a naked flame, and turn off pilot lights.
◆Work with a window open or make sure there is plenty of ventilation to clear the fumes away quickly.
◆Keep fire extinguishers in the house and in your workshop – one type for electric fires, the second for all other fires, see page 320. Keep a fire blanket handy as well.

Sharp instruments

◆Never leave sharp instruments lying around unattended, even for a second, particularly if you have children.
◆Follow instructions to the letter for the use of all cutting tools and don't allow young or inexperienced people to try them out without supervision.

Electrics

◆Take great care, when hammering into walls and floors, that you are nowhere near an electric cable or water pipe.
◆Always turn the electricity off at the mains if you are working on or anywhere near electric cables. Double check that the circuit is dead by plugging in an electrical appliance (which you know is working) and trying to switch it on.
◆Always switch power tools off at the wall before leaving them unattended.
◆Check the flexes of all power tools before you use them; don't try to patch up a damaged flex – get it replaced.
◆Keep flexes away from your work; you could cut through them.
◆Use a residual current device (RCD) when working with a long flex – it protects you from electric shock should the flex or appliance be damaged.

Gas

◆Find out where your mains gas tap is so that you can turn it off in an emergency. It is switched off when the notch on the valve is at right angles to the pipe.
◆Keep flues and chimneys used for gas and other fuel-burning appliances clear of soot and debris because they could catch fire.
◆If you smell gas, check that no gas jets have been left on accidentally, or that no pilot lights have blown out. Never try to find a gas leak in the dark by using a match – always use a torch. Never turn on a light; the spark could ignite the gas.
◆If you can't find an obvious source of a leak, turn off the mains gas tap. Open all doors and windows to clear the smell, and call the gas region's emergency service.
▼▼ Never attempt to repair a gas fault your-
◆◆ self; you could cause an explosion.

Testing a pipe or gas hose for a leak *Smear a fairly strong solution of concentrated washing up liquid over the hose; it will bubble where the gas is leaking.*

FLOORS AND FLOOR COVERINGS

◆Cover gaps between the floor and the skirting board with beading (a wooden strip nailed into the floor to cover unsightly joins), see below. A cheaper, temporary, way is to squeeze some rubber sealant along the gap.
◆Fill wide gaps between floorboards with wooden strips. Glue the strips at the sides

Covering floor cracks with beading *Press the strip flat on the floor, and nail it to the skirting only, so that as the gap expands and contracts with varying temperatures, the strip can move.*

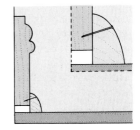

MAKING PAPIER MÂCHÉ

1 *Tear up newspapers into small pieces. Mix a solution of wallpaper paste to a slightly stronger consistency than the manufacturer suggests for use when papering.*

2 *Work the paste and paper together, keeping the mixture fairly dry.*

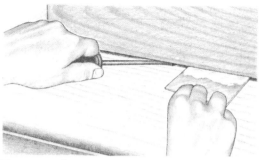

Fixing creaking stairs *Prise the tread and riser apart slightly with an old screwdriver and push a woodworking (PVA) adhesive into the crack on a piece of thin cardboard.*

Filling gaps with papier mâché *Squeeze the papier mâché or fill into the cracks with an old knife or filler knife, above left. Let is set completely and then sand it flush with the boards, above right.*

with PVA adhesive and then tap them gently into the gap with a hammer. Leave the glue to dry for 24 hours and then plane the strips so that they are level with the floorboards.

◆ Fill small gaps between boards with plastic wood or, for a cheaper solution, use papier mâché, see above.

◆ For loose boards, locate the floor joists by finding the existing nail heads. Hammer 2.5cm (1in) long floor nails, or brads, through the boards and into the joists.

◆ Stop floorboards from squeaking either by securing loose boards or by blowing a little talcum powder between the edges of the affected boards to act as a lubricant.

Stairs

◆ Treat creaking stairs by brushing French chalk into the cracks between the tread and riser or by gluing the riser with PVA adhesive, see above right.

◆ If you can get behind the staircase easily, nail triangular blocks of wood or metal brackets behind the tread and riser joints to make them more rigid.

◆ If a stair rod works loose, take it out and squeeze PVA adhesive into the slot at the top

and bottom. Put back the rod and tie it up securely with tape or string until it has set. This is quicker and easier than adjusting the stair rod fastening.

Binding floor coverings

◆ To stop carpeting, rugs and sisal, cord and coconut matting from fraying at the edges, bind them in the following way:

1 Make sure that the floor covering and tape are quite clean.

2 Trim the edges of the floor covering with a pair of large, sharp scissors.

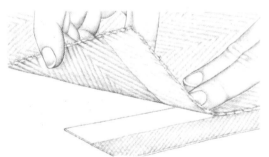

3 Cut a piece of 7.5cm (3in) binding tape to the right length and apply a rubber contact adhesive to half the width of the tape. Apply adhesive to the same width on one edge of the matting. When both are nearly dry, stick the two coated sides together, which should give an immediate bond.

4 Turn the matting over and do the same with the other half of the tape.

5 Tap along both sides with a hammer to make sure the tape bonds well.

WINDOWS AND DOORS

◆Seal gaps round window frames with a rubber sealant or a wood filler with some elasticity to allow for movement. A general-purpose filler should be satisfactory for gaps in wood joints indoors. Clean all surfaces thoroughly before applying filler, otherwise it will not adhere.

◆Repair cracked window panes temporarily by sticking clear waterproofing tape over the crack on both sides. You can even use the tape to cover a hole in the glass temporarily. Use polythene sheeting as a temporary pane for a broken window.

◆If handles and stays begin to work loose, tighten the screws.

◆To repair rattling windows, fix an insulating strip between the frame and the window; this will also stop draughts, see page 238.

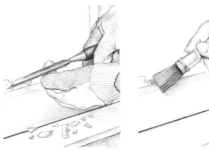

Replacing damaged putty *If putty has fallen off a window, scrape away the old putty, above left, and brush a little linseed oil where the new putty is going to go, above right. (This will prevent wet from getting in and rotting the inside of the window frame.) Apply new putty with a knife or spatula.*

Metal windows

◆If handles on metal windows become hard to move, it may be because they have too many layers of paint on them. Strip off the

REPLACING A WINDOW PANE

1 *Put on a pair of tough gloves. Remove the broken pane of glass, see page 218. Scrape out the putty with an old chisel or screwdriver and tap out any remaining fragments of glass with the handle of a hammer.*

2 *Measure the size of the opening and get a piece of glass cut 1.5mm ($\frac{1}{16}$in) smaller than the opening on all four sides.*

3 *Pull out the glazier's nails with a pair of pincers and clean the window recess where the glass fits with glasspaper.*

4 *Paint the recess with primer and leave it to dry for a couple of hours.*

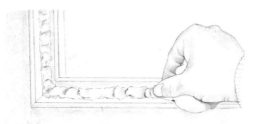

5 *Apply some linseed oil to the glass recess. Roll a thin sausage of putty between your palms and squeeze it into the recess with your thumb and forefinger. Press the glass firmly into place but don't apply pressure at the centre of the pane.*

6 *Gently tap glazier's nails into the recess, flush with the glass, using the edge of a wide chisel as a hammer. When mending glass in a metal frame, use special glazing clips instead of glazier's nails.*

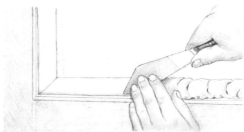

7 *Spread putty around the edges of the glass with a putty knife to form a neat surface. Look at the other windows to get the angles right, and mitre the corners using a putty knife or a special mitre box.*

8 *Scrape off excess putty from inside the window and clean off any fingerprints with cotton wool dipped in methylated spirits.*

9 *Don't paint the putty for seven to fourteen days after applying it, but don't leave it unpainted for much longer or the rain will get in to it and it will start to deteriorate.*

SOLVING COMMON DOOR PROBLEMS

STICKING DOOR

◆ If the door is tight on the hinge side, there is probably too much paint on this edge of the door. Strip it off and re-paint the area.

◆ If the door is tight on the jamb side, pare off some wood from the hinge recesses in the frame with a chisel.

◆ If a door scrapes the floor when it is opened and shut, place a sheet of abrasive paper on the floor under the door and pull the door over it back-wards and forwards several times until it moves easily.

◆ If the door actually sticks on the floor, remove it and plane as much as necessary from the bottom.

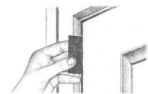

Finding out where a door sticks *Close the door onto a strip of carbon paper. The carbon will rub off onto the door at the point of contact.*

HINGES

◆ For loose door hinges, tighten the screws.

◆ To fix a squeaking door, oil all hinges and work the oil into them. Lubricate exterior hinges with grease rather than oil.

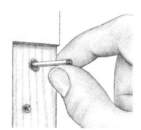

Packing screw holes *If the holes are too big for the screws, remove the hinges and plug them with match-sticks or dowels. Replace the hinges.*

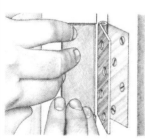

Fixing a loose door *If the door is loose on the hinge side, first support the bottom of the door with wedges, and unscrew and remove one hinge at a time, Pack each recess with card-board and replace the hinge.*

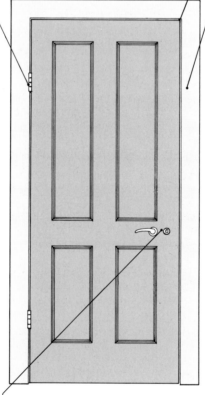

STICKING LOCK

◆ To loosen a sticking lock, try ap-plying a light lubricating oil and operate the lock vigorously a few times, or put a little powdered graphite onto the key by rubbing a pencil along it, and work it into the lock that way.

RATTLING DOOR

◆ Stop a door from rattling either by fitting a strip of draught excluder inside the frame (if the door has shrunk), or by moving the lock plate closer to the catch on the door.

1 *Close the door and mea-sure the gap between the door frame and the door.*

2 *Unscrew the lock plate and move it forwards by the same amount as the gap you have just measured. Extend the recess with a chisel. Fill the old screw holes with wood plugs, and replace the lock plate.*

paint, and treat the handles with a rust inhibitor, then repaint.

1 For rusted metal window frames, clean off all the rust, dirt and grease with a wire brush, then sand the rusted area.

2 Apply a combined primer/rust inhibitor straight away. Give all the edges a second coat because it will run off them and they are more vulnerable.

3 Let the primer dry thoroughly and then apply a finishing coat of oil-based paint.

Cleaning out the drip groove *This groove lies under the projecting edge of each windowsill. It prevents water from dripping back into the window frame and causing rot. Use an old screwdriver or wire coat hanger to dig out any debris.*

WALLS

Most cracks are due to the shrinkage and settlement which takes place after a house is built. Once they have been filled, they are unlikely to occur again.

◆ Fill large holes and cracks with papier mâché, see page 220, or a proprietary filler. If you are using papier mâché, first brush out any loose crumbs of plaster, then press the papier mâché into the crack with a knife or spatula. Let it dry and then cover it with a thin coat of plaster.

◆ Use a cellulose filler to fill small chips and surface blemishes in paintwork and plaster and holes left by old screws and nails. Mix it on an old plate and don't make more than you can use in an hour because it will start to harden. Apply it liberally with a special filling knife and scrape off any extra filler. When it has set quite hard, sand it down.

Filling plasterboard

Vertical cracks may appear in the finishing plaster when individual plasterboard panels move slightly.

◆ Fill cracks in plasterboard with plaster rather than a filler because the filler soon cracks again. It is difficult to fill plasterboard

cracks well and it is therefore probably best to cover the wall with textured wallpaper or textured paint.

To fill a hole in plasterboard:

1 Use a sharp knife to trim the edges of the hole so that they are clean.

2 Cut a piece of plasterboard so that it is 2.5cm (1in) wider than the hole all round.

3 Make a hole in the centre of the piece and thread string through it. Attach a nail to the string on the white side of the board and tie a knot in the string on the grey side.

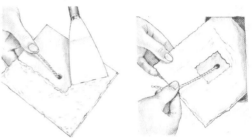

4 Spread filler on the grey side, *above left*. Holding the string, put the plasterboard through the hole, then guide it forward using the string, *above right*, until you are holding it tight against the back of the hole.

5 Fill the hole with filler, leaving enough room for a finishing coat. When the filler is almost dry, cut off the string and apply a finishing coat of plaster.

Exterior walls

Loose rendering on a wall or damaged pointing (the edge of the mortar between bricks) must be repaired to prevent moisture getting into the walls.

◆ Check cracks in concrete rendering because they may be an early warning that the rendering is beginning to come loose. Tap the rendering around the crack, and if this produces a hollow sound, the rendering has come away from the wall. Remove the loose rendering. If the damaged area is small, patch over it with concrete rendering; if it is large, get a builder to repair it.

◆ To repair bad pointing, scrape out the old mortar to a depth of about 12mm ($\frac{1}{2}$in). Replace it with a mixture of one part lime, one part cement and six parts sand.

DAMP

◆ If damp appears on the walls of rooms on the top floor, have the roof inspected because broken tiles in the eaves may be allowing water to come through.

◆ Repair or unblock any gutters which may be causing the damp.

◆ If you suspect fungal rot, get a professional in to examine the extent of the damage and to treat it, see page 226.

◆ If you discover damp on a ground floor, get someone in to look at it; you may need a damp-proof course installed.

◆ After you have checked and repaired any sources of damp, wait until the wall dries out (the person who repaired the damp should advise on how long this should be) and then paint the outside with a silicone water repellent before redecorating. Remove any peeling paint or paper inside and paint the wall with an internal complete seal. Redecorate over the seal.

Roofing, gutters and drains

◆ At least once a year, look at the roof through the attic and scan it through binoculars from the garden to check for broken tiles and a faulty chimney stack or flashing. If you have a flat roof, go up and have a look at it if possible.

◆ Clear gutters of debris in the autumn and in the spring to prevent blockages. If the gutters are low enough for you to reach easily, scrape everything out with a trowel, otherwise get someone else to do it.

◆ To mend a cracked gutter, clean the inside of the gutter with a wire brush, and then seal any cracks by binding waterproof tape around the damaged area and 5cm (2in) beyond it.

◆ If you have to replace gutters, buy plastic ones; they are cheaper than metal gutters, easy to join and won't rust.

◆ If your plastic gutters leak at the joints, remove the remains of the old seal with paraffin or petrol, and replace it with a new rubber seal or waterproof or mastic tape. Wind it in a spiral round the pipe, overlapping each layer.

◆ If the gutter sags in the middle, it won't be able to drain properly and will overflow and cause damp. Clear out the debris at the sag and secure the gutter at the correct height but angle it to slope steadily to the downpipe.

◆ For blocked surface gulleys, lift the grating and bale out as much water and debris as you can, then hose it down and rinse with washing soda and hot water.

◆ Get very long downpipes cleared by a professional; short ones, say on a single-storey building, can be done yourself.

◆ If a downpipe blocks up constantly, fit a little wire cage over the top to prevent leaves and seeds from blowing down it and birds from making their nests there.

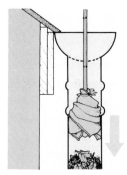

Clearing a downpipe *Tie a rag round a stone and secure it to the end of a long cane. Push the cane down the pipe and push the debris down, into a bowl or bucket at the bottom of the pipe.*

TIPS ON USING ROOFING CONTRACTORS

◆ Get a surveyor to look at the roof first to establish what has to be done.

◆ Before choosing a contractor, make sure he is a member of a reputable professional organization, in case of problems arising from the work done.

◆ Get estimates from two or three builders to compare them. Look for items which may have been left out.

◆ An estimate should specify:

◇ *All materials needed*

◇ *Whether making good and clearing away debris, rubble and old materials are included (as they should be)*

◇ *Whether the job is simply to replace tiles or to make the roof waterproof*

◇ *Statement that the work will conform to a satisfactory standard building code of practice*

◇ *Guarantee of work.*

TESTING FOR DAMP

◆ Use aluminium foil, see below, to test for damp. If moisture appears on the surface, the damp is caused by condensation; this can be cured by improving ventilation and making sure the room is warm, see TIPS FOR MINIMIZING CONDENSATION, page 226. If the surface stays dry and the back of the foil becomes damp, the moisture is coming through from the outside wall and must be treated, see PENETRATING DAMP, below, and RISING DAMP, right.

◆ Another test is to tape a square of polythene over the damp area. If small droplets of moisture form on the undersurface of the polythene, you have condensation. If larger droplets form, you have rising or penetrating damp.

Checking for damp *Tape a piece of aluminium foil over the damp patch and seal the edges well. Leave it for a day or so, then peel away a corner of the foil.*

Penetrating damp

The symptoms of penetrating damp are damp patches with well-defined edges that appear during periods of heavy rainfall but which disappear in dry weather. They may leave a stain or a deposit of white powder on the wall. Check for:
◇ *Defective brickwork*
◇ *Cracked rendering*
◇ *Broken or blocked gutters and downpipes*
◇ *Window sills with blocked or damaged drip channels*
◇ *Cavity wall ties or collected mortar droppings inside the cavity, which draw damp inside. (This is a job for a professional.)*

◆ Once you have checked and repaired any sources of damp, wait until the wall dries out, then treat outside walls (but not windows and woodwork) with a generous application of silicone water-repellent. This treatment should last up to ten years.

◆ If the bricks are porous and the house is very exposed to bad weather, protect the walls by covering them with some form of weatherboarding, tiles, or rendering.

Rising damp

The symptom of rising damp is a "tide mark" which fluctuates some way above the ground floor level.

◆ Check for the same causes as for penetrating damp, see below left.

◆ Check that the house has a damp-proof course. This should be visible as a black or grey line above the bottom row of bricks. If you cannot see one, call in an expert and have one installed.

◆ If there is a damp-proof course, make sure that it is not bridged anywhere, either outside or inside. Outside earth may have been heaped up above the level of the damp-proof course or someone may have built a patio above it. Clear any earth to at least 15cm (6in) below the damp-proof course or remove the patio and rebuild a lower one.

◆ Check that there is no gulley built over the damp-proof course, which may be allowing water to soak into the wall. If there is, buy a "shoe" to direct water away from the wall.

◆ If you are having a patio built, make sure that it is below the level of the damp-proof course, otherwise damp will occur in the wall above the waterproof level.

Condensation

The symptoms of condensation are constantly damp surfaces and misted windows.

◆ To prevent condensation, make sure the walls and windows are well insulated and the rooms well ventilated. Use warm wall coverings on walls, see page 195, and double glazing for windows if you can afford it, see page 241. Where large amounts of moisture are produced, install extractor fans and window ventilators.

◆Try to keep a steady heat throughout the house and avoid "quick response" heating such as sudden bursts of intermittent warm air, or gas cylinder or paraffin heaters, because they produce moisture.
◆Fit controlled ventilators into window glass so that you can improve ventilation in winter without having to open windows.
◆Place a tray of water-absorbing crystals in a room with heavy condensation.

Treating wet rot

◆If damp conditions are likely to persist, as in cellars and basements, get the affected wood replaced with treated timber, concrete or some other inert material.
◆To prevent wet rot in timber which is exposed to damp, apply creosote to the wood; it is the cheapest and most effective wood preservative. Make sure the wood is thoroughly dry before you apply it, because creosote will not penetrate wet wood.
◆If ground floor timber has been so badly damaged by wet rot that you have to renew the floor, have a damp-proof layer installed at the same time. Remove any rubbish under the floor, and see that existing good timber is treated with preservative at the same time.

For repairing windows:
◆Get badly damaged window frames replaced; it's easier than repairing them.
1 Find the source of the damp and treat it so that the woodwork dries out.
2 Scrape out the rotten wood and treat it with a suitable fungicide. Alternatively, if

you catch the rot early enough, drill holes near the joints at the bottom and sides of the frames, insert plastic valves into the holes and inject the fungicide.
3 Use filler to reshape the wood. If a load-bearing piece of timber is affected, use epoxy filler and hammer in some nails to act as a reinforcement.

IDENTIFYING FUNGAL ROT

Dry rot and large areas of wet rot should be dealt with professionally.

DRY ROT
This fungus can penetrate brickwork and plaster, and will cause serious decay if not checked. Unless you are good at DIY, don't tackle dry rot yourself but get in an expert.

Signs
◇*Wood that crumbles when you probe it with a sharp knife.*
◇*Wood that breaks up into rectangular cubes and has a grey, felty fungus growing on its surface.*
◇*White root-like strands or fluffy growths like wool, with lilac or yellow tinges on the wood. These soon become a bright, rusty red, and look like dust – a sign of developing seeds; this may be the first thing you see.*
◇*Bulging, warped or cracked plaster.*

WET ROT
Less serious than dry rot because the fungus spreads only as far as moisture has penetrated, and the root-like strands will not grow into brickwork. Wet rot is common in basement floors and windows with damaged paintwork. You can treat small areas yourself fairly easily.

Signs
◇*Darkened wood, cracks along the grain of the wood, flaking paintwork.*
◇*Dark brown, narrow strands of fungus.*

PLUMBING

Don't neglect leaky plumbing, even if it is leaking only a small amount of water. Dripping water is liable to rot woodwork, and water leaking into electrical fittings can cause fatal electric shocks.

If the methods described below don't solve your problem, or you don't feel very confident about tackling the job yourself, call in a plumber to do it. A little bit of water goes a long way.

TAPS AND PIPES

Don't let a tap drip: although a dripping tap doesn't pose any dangers, it is wasteful of water and, if it's a hot-water tap, energy and money. Repair it as soon as possible.

Cracked pipes must be replaced eventually, but as a temporary measure, seal them using one of the methods described overleaf.

Dripping taps

◆If a tap drips, it almost certainly needs a new washer unless it is a modern tap with ceramic discs. (If ceramic disc taps drip, it probably means that grit has got between the discs, and it will need a plumber to fix it.) Use black synthetic washers, which are suitable for hot and cold taps. Buy a range of sizes because you will not be able to tell immediately what size washer you need. Cut rubber washers to fit if you don't have any of the right size.

1 To change a tap washer, turn off the stopcock controlling the flow of water to the tap you are working on (this could be the main indoor stopcock, the gate valves near the water tank or a gate valve near the tap you are fixing). Turn on the tap and wait until no more water comes out.

2 Unscrew the retaining screw on the top part of the tap to loosen the tap head. If the tap has a plastic shroud, lever off the coloured bit in the middle, to get at the retaining screw.

3 Unscrew the bell-shaped cover or lift the shroud head. If it sticks, pour hot water over it and try again or wrap a cloth around the cover and try to turn it with a monkey wrench. Hold the rest of the tap with another wrench so that you don't turn the whole tap. Then unscrew the headgear nut with an adjustable spanner.

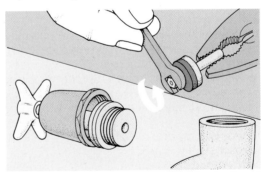

4 Remove the headgear from the body of the tap and lift out the valve. Unscrew the nut that holds the washer in position, remove the washer and put in the new one.

5 Replace all the parts and turn the stopcock on. Leave the tap "open" until water starts coming through, to prevent an airlock from forming in the pipes.

◆If you are having new taps installed, get Supataps; you don't need to turn the mains water off to repair them.

Retaining screw
Capstan screw
Bell-shaped cover
Headgear nut
Washer
Top plate
Shroud head
Headgear nut
Washer

Dripping pipes

A dripping pipe usually indicates that it is cracked. Turn off the water at the mains, turn on all the taps to drain the water system and let the boiler go out.

◆ To repair a small crack temporarily, rub petroleum jelly into the crack and tie a rag round it, or wrap plumber's waterproof tape around the crack.

◆ For a more permanent repair use an epoxy resin adhesive or epoxy putty to seal a crack.

1 Rub the surface of the pipe with an abrasive paper to give the resin something to adhere to. Mix the resin and hardener according to the manufacturer's instructions and smear it over the crack.

2 Bind fibreglass tape or plumber's waterproof tape around the damaged area and smear more resin over it.

3 Leave the resin to set hard before turning the water on again. This may take from 10 minutes to 24 hours, depending on the brand you use. Leave all the taps open until water starts coming through them, to prevent an air lock from forming.

Making a temporary repair to a cracked copper pipe *Get a length of plastic hose 5cm (2in) longer than the crack at either end, slit the hose and wrap it round the pipe. Secure it with hose clips.*

Air locks

If no water is coming out of a tap or comes out only in spurts, the most likely cause is an air lock in the pipes.

◆ To shift an air lock, tap along the pipe with a mallet wrapped in a cloth. The air bubble will probably be at a bend in the pipe, or where the pipe is not perfectly horizontal. If this doesn't work, use the following method.

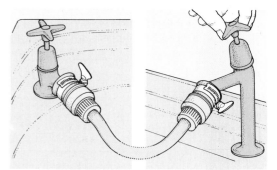

1 Using hose clips, attach one end of a hose to the tap that is affected (it is usually a hot-water tap). Then attach the other end of the hose to a mains cold-water tap (the kitchen cold tap is usually the best).

◇ *If the faulty tap is the bath tap and the hose clip will not fit round it, attach the hose to the washbasin hot tap instead.*

◇ *For a Supatap, remove the nozzle from the tap with the air lock, and then connect up the hose.*

2 Turn on the hot-water tap and then open up the mains cold-water tap. The mains pressure will push the air out of the pipe and back into the cistern.

◇ *For a mixer tap, remove the spout, press a cloth tightly against the spout hole and turn on the hot tap and then the cold tap.*

"Hammering" pipes

◆ If the pipes start hammering and banging when you turn a tap on, the pipework may not be properly supported, especially where it comes down through a ceiling. Secure it to stop all vibration, by fixing a wooden batten from the floor to the rafters; secure the pipe to the batten at intervals with pipe brackets. If the pipes are not loose, the noise may indicate that you have an air lock in the system, the ball valve in the cistern is damaged, or a tap washer needs replacing (check whether a tap is dripping).

BLOCKAGES

◆If a sink is already blocked, bail out the contents into a bucket and try the soda crystal method, see below.

▼▼Don't use caustic soda for unblocking
◆ ◆ the kitchen sink. It will combine with any grease to form a hard soap and block the drain completely.

◆If a blockage is difficult to shift, use a sink plunger, see right.

◇*If you have a double sink and/or a separate sink drainer, plug both of them while "plunging" or you won't get a satisfactory vacuum and the contents of one sink may come through into the second sink.*

TIPS FOR PREVENTING BLOCKAGES

◆Squirt greasy pans with washing-up liquid, fill them with hot water and allow them to soak for a little while so that the fat breaks up into smaller particles before you wash them.

◆Flush out the waste disposal unit regularly (about once a week).

🍃GREEN TIP: Sprinkle washing soda crystals over the sink outlets regularly and pour boiling or very hot water over them to keep the sink clear and clean. Use about one cup of soda to a kettleful of water. Alternatively, pour a cup of salt and a cup of bicarbonate of soda down each sink, followed by a kettleful of boiling water down the sink, or one cup of vinegar, then a thorough rinse with hot water.

◆Don't put the following substances down your drain, kitchen sink or toilet – not only will they block up the drains but they will also make them smell very unpleasant.

◇*Melted fat, it will congeal in the pipes*
◇*Congealed fat or grease*
◇*Coffee grounds*
◇*Tea leaves*
◇*Hair*
◇*Disposable nappies*
◇*Disposable tissues*

Clearing a blocked sink with a plunger
Block the sink overflow by covering it with a cloth or taping over it. Fit the rubber cup over the sink outlet and pump it up and down to create a vacuum which will release the blockage.

Clearing a blocked sink *If washing soda or a plunger do not free the blockage, use a wire coat hanger. Undo the nut under the U bend and poke around in the pipe with the coat hanger until you have found the blockage. Scrape out the blockage into a bucket, then replace the nut. Pour washing soda crystals and boiling water down the sink to flush it clean. If this doesn't work, call the plumber.*

Cleaning a waste disposal unit

🍃GREEN TIP: Put a slice of lemon into the waste disposal unit to make it smell sweeter and help to neutralize smells.

▼▼Don't use drain-cleaning chemicals
◆ ◆ down a waste disposal unit because they are caustic and may damage the unit.

HOW TO AVOID BLOCKING A WASTE DISPOSAL UNIT

All the following will block a waste disposal unit:

◇Metal	◇*Large cartons*
◇*Plastic*	◇*China, glass or cutlery*
◇*Rags*	◇*Large bones*
◇*String*	◇*Hot or cold fat*
◇*Cotton wool*	

1 Run cold water into the sink and turn the unit to the "on" position.

2 If the machine gets clogged up, use the unclogging mechanism to free it. If the machine does not have an unclogging mechanism, switch the machine off at the mains (or take its fuse out). Then fit the "release" tool which comes with the unit through the sink outlet onto the hexagonal nut on the blades and turn this backwards and forwards; the motor should free itself. If you have lost the tool, try to clear the obstruction by hand.

3 Remove the release tool, or withdraw your hand, turn on the mains switch, then the cold tap and switch the machine on.

Blocked toilet

▼▼ Don't keep flushing a blocked toilet – it
◆ ◆ will overflow, causing a flood.
◆ Clean it with a toilet plunger, which is similar to a sink plunger but has a metal plate

above the rubber cup, or tie an old towel around a toilet brush. Move it up and down vigorously until the suction moves the blockage and the toilet can drain as usual.
◆ If you can't solve the problem easily, call in a specialist plumber.

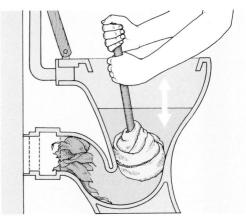

Clearing a blocked toilet *Tie an old towel round a toilet brush so that the brush is large enough to fit the drainage hole tightly. Then pump the brush up and down in the hole, creating enough suction to enable the toilet to drain.*

CENTRAL HEATING SYSTEMS

◆ Have your central heating system flushed out once a year by a heating engineer or plumber, to get rid of any rust or sludge that could damage the pump or cause "cold spots" in the radiators.
◆ Bleed your radiators if they have not been used for a while, at the beginning of winter, for example, see below. If a radiator is warm at the bottom but cold at the top, or if there is a constant gurgling sound from it, there is probably an air lock in the system. Bleed the radiator to get rid of it.
◆ If air locks occur frequently, get a plumber to replace the vent valve with a special air eliminator, which has a valve in it through which air can escape.

BLEEDING A RADIATOR

1 *Turn off the radiator. When the water is warm, not hot, bleed the radiator by turning the vent valve at the top anti-clockwise with a radiator key. When air starts to escape, stop turning; if you turn too far, the valve may come out.*

2 *As soon as air stops escaping and water starts to flow, tighten the valve again.*

EMERGENCY PLUMBING

◆ Turn off the electricity if the water is near any wiring; water conducts electricity. Mop up as much as possible and get the fault repaired as quickly as you can.
▼▼ Don't turn the electricity back on until
◆ ◆ you are sure that the wiring is dry, or you will get an electric shock when you touch the switch.

Overflowing cistern

◆ Stop the overflow by closing the inlet valve, see above right. This will give you time to investigate the problem.
◆ Check the ball float. If it is damaged, buy a new one. Unscrew the old ball and fit the new one onto the arm. Make sure you get one the right size for your cistern: the smaller ones are for lavatory cisterns, larger ones for the cold-water cistern. If you fit the wrong size, you could cause another flood.

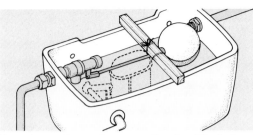

Stopping a cistern from overflowing *Tie the lever arm to a clothes hanger or wooden batten and lay it across the top of the cistern.*

◆ If the ball is not damaged, the float arm that supports the ball may be angled wrongly so that the ball sits too high and won't shut off the inlet valve. If the float arm is plastic, loosen the nut on the arm and lower the ball; if the arm is metal, bend the ball end down with a spanner so that the ball sits lower and the water pushes it up earlier.

◆ Check the washer in the inlet valve, because if it is worn, the valve will drip. To replace it, switch off the water supply to the cistern, remove the forked pin that attaches the arm to the valve then remove the washer and replace it with a new one.

Overflowing washing machine/dishwasher

◆ If your machine empties into a sink or basin, you may simply have left the plug in. Unplug it to drain the water away, and then deal with the flood.

◆ If an automatic machine starts to overflow, turn the dial until the machine begins to empty. Then spread as many towels as you can all over the floor, to sop up the excess water, especially if the flooring is carpet or if there are electric points at ground level.

◆ If the overflowing is caused by the wrong soap powder, put the wash (or the crockery, if the machine is a dishwasher) through several rinse cycles to clean the soap off. Make sure that you always put the right amount of detergent in the machine and that you always use the right sort of detergent for the type of machine.

◆ Check that the filter and the soap powder compartment have been put back properly in the washing machine.

◆ If the flooding is due to some fault in the machine, drain it as above, switch it off, unplug it and call in the service engineer before using it again.

Thawing a frozen pipe

▼▼ Unfreeze a pipe slowly because the ice
♦ ♦ may have already cracked the pipe and you may end up with a flood.

◆ If the frozen pipe is in the loft, play a fan heater at medium heat into the loft space to raise the temperature.

◆ If the frozen pipe is later in the system, turn all the taps on to drain the system and work along the frozen pipe from the tap outlet back to the tank, applying hot cloths or a hot-water bottle, or playing a hair dryer along it bit by bit until the water runs again.

Burst pipe

1 Turn the water off at the mains stopcock (which is probably under the kitchen sink) and turn on all the taps to drain the system. Then turn off the heating.

▼▼ Don't keep the heating system working
♦ ♦ if there is no water for it to heat. You may overheat the metal, which may crack.

2 If the damaged pipe is fed from the water tank, close the gate valves connecting the tank and pipe.

3 Place a bucket under the leak and keep emptying and replacing it as it fills.

◆ If the pipe has burst but the ice has not yet melted, you may be able to detect the damaged area – the ice may glisten through the crack; this often occurs at a join. Wrap a rag tightly round the crack and put a bucket under it to catch the drips, or wind emergency pipe and hose seal tightly round the split to about 7.5cm (3in) each side of it and call the plumber.

◆ If the burst is in the mains pipe leading to the house, turn off the outdoor stopcock. This is situated about 1m (3ft) underground, under a metal cover near the boundary of your property. Use a stopcock key to turn off the valve, or make one from a 1m (3ft) long wooden T-bar with a notch cut out of the end. If you cannot turn it off, call the regional water authority.

ELECTRICITY

If your mains fuse box has fuse holders that contain fuse wire, consider having your house rewired soon, because this means that the wiring in your home is very old and probably unsafe. If you are having your home rewired, ask the electrician to install a fuse box that will take miniature circuit breakers (MCBs). They are safer than fuse wire carriers and easier to deal with than cartridge fuse holders when a fuse blows. All you have to do is press the button to reset them.

GLOSSARY OF ELECTRICAL TERMS

Amp Unit measuring the amount of current in a circuit.
Circuit Complete path around which an electric current flows.
Conductor Anything which carries an electric current, e.g. the metal core in a flex.
Core The wires contained in a flex. A two-core flex will have a live wire and a neutral wire; a three-core flex will have an earth as well.
Earth The pathway along which a current flows to the ground safely, if a fault occurs.

Fuse A weak connection which acts as a protection by cutting off the current when the circuit overloads or if a fault develops in the system.
Live Refers to a circuit or an object through which a current is flowing.
Neutral The core of a flex which carries the current back to its source or the terminal to which the neutral core is connected.
Short circuit A circuit which deviates from its normal pathway, passing through wires or

objects which may not be earthed and which therefore cannot cope with the great amount of heat generated, and may melt or catch fire.
Volt Unit measuring the pressure that drives the current round a circuit.
Watt Unit measuring the amount of power consumed by an appliance.

SAFETY WITH ELECTRICITY

▼▼ Always work on a circuit which is
◆ ◆ "dead". Switch off the mains switch, remove the fuse which protects the circuit you are working on and put the fuse in your pocket so that you know where it is. Plug in an appliance you know to be working to double check that the circuit is dead.

▼▼ Unplug an appliance from the mains
◆ ◆ before working on it because if it is faulty it may give you an electric shock.

◆ Always use wiring, screwdrivers and other equipment which conform to the specifications of the country you live in, to avoid using unsafe equipment; appropriate equipment will be marked as such.

◆ Ensure that cables, flexes and plugs are of the correct amp rating for the circuits and

appliances you use them for. Look in the instruction leaflet to see what kind of plug to use and check on the appliance itself. Use a 3 amp fuse for appliances of up to 700 watts (electric blankets, power tools, record players, clocks and standard or table lamps); use a 13 amp fuse for all other appliances.

▼▼ Never use a fuse with a higher amperage
◆ ◆ than you need, because the circuit will overload, overheat and start a fire.

◆ Make sure all appliances with metal bodies are earthed to prevent shocks. Make sure that all appliances have plugs with double insulation, particularly those without an earth core.

▼▼ Don't ignore a fishy smell; have a look at
◆ ◆ the plug of any electrical equipment that's switched on. If there's a fault, the plug may be overheating and melting the plastic.

◆ If a plug feels warm to the touch, switch it off, switch off at the mains, take the plug out of the socket, remove the fuse for that circuit, and check the wiring in the plug and socket. They may be overheating because of a fault and will eventually catch fire if left.

▼▼ Never touch electrical equipment with
♦ ♦ wet hands, feet or cloths because water is a conductor of electricity and you will get a shock if it touches a live surface.

▼▼ Don't use electrical equipment in the
♦ ♦ bathroom because water may come into contact with the electric current and cause it to short circuit. The only safe exceptions are a razor with a two-pin plug working from a "razor only" socket, a pull cord switch, and a switch outside the bathroom door. If you have to use a drill in the bathroom, make sure you use an extension lead which is plugged in outside the bathroom.

♦ Check plugs and flexes regularly for wear or damage and fix loose connections immediately or they may become dangerous. Never allow a flex to become frayed or worn. If it does, repair it with insulating tape as a temporary measure only – it is not safe as a permanent repair; replace it with new flex as soon as possible.

♦ Keep flexes as short as possible, or you may trip over them.

♦ Don't run flexes under carpets; they may get worn, which will expose the wires, and if the bare wires touch each other they will short the circuit. You will probably forget to check whether flexes are worn if they are hidden under carpets, as well.

▼▼ Don't hammer nails into walls near
♦ ♦ switches or sockets or through floors where there may be electric cables (and water or gas pipes); you may electrocute yourself, flood the house or cause a gas leak.

▼▼ Never use water to put out a fire in an
♦ ♦ electrical appliance unless the mains switch is off, because it will cause a short circuit and make everything the water touches live. Use a fire extinguisher designed specifically for electrical fires, or a multipurpose one.

♦ Always use a residual current device (RCD) when working outdoors or using an extension lead. It protects you from being electrocuted should the flex be damaged.

▼▼ Never improvise when replacing a fuse.
♦ ♦ The fuse is there to protect you and cut off the electricity supply to an area with a fault, preventing a fire or electric shock.

BASIC TOOL KIT

♦ Keep a selection of basic tools together for everyday electrical repairs or emergencies. The best place for them is in a box of their own near the fuse box where you can reach them easily in case you are suddenly plunged into darkness. The essential items are:

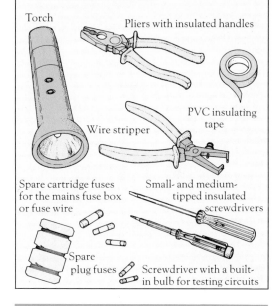

Torch
Pliers with insulated handles
Wire stripper
PVC insulating tape
Spare cartridge fuses for the mains fuse box or fuse wire
Small- and medium-tipped insulated screwdrivers
Spare plug fuses
Screwdriver with a built-in bulb for testing circuits

BASIC ELECTRICAL JOBS

♦ Label the fuse carriers in your mains fuse box according to the circuits they monitor. This will make it easier for you to identify the faulty circuit quickly when a fuse blows.

♦ Always replace broken or cracked plugs because moisture may get into them or the wires may get damaged. Use strong rubber plugs for portable appliances which you use a lot because they won't crack if dropped.

Wiring a plug

♦ If you are buying new plugs, get a push-fit type of plug – these are the easiest plugs to wire because you just push the wires into a slot or clip, and some versions don't need a screwdriver even to open them.

◆To wire an ordinary plug have everything you need ready before you start, and use the following method:

1 Unscrew the cover of the plug and the clamp that holds the flex in place.

2 Undo the screws that hold the conductor wires in place, remove the fuse and detach old wires if necessary.

◇*Keep all bits and pieces, fuses, screws, etc. in a small cup next to you.*

3 Cut away 5cm (2in) of the outer covering of the new flex with wire strippers, taking care not to cut through the individual wires.

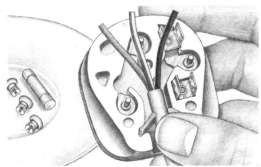

4 Thread the wires through the gate clamp (or under it if it is a flex clamp) and lay them roughly in position.

5 Cut each wire to reach about 12mm ($\frac{1}{2}$in) beyond its correct terminal. Then strip away about 6mm ($\frac{1}{4}$in) of the coloured plastic. You can do this with a sharp knife, but wire strippers make it easier. Some plugs come with a paper template to help you measure the right length.

6 Twist the wires together so that there are no stray strands.

7 Connect the wires to their respective terminals. In some plugs they should be pushed through a small hole in the terminal and then screwed down securely, *above left*, in others, they should be twisted anti-clockwise round a screw terminal, *above right*.

8 Screw down the flex grip tightly, if there is one, or push the flex securely into the gate clamp. Tug the flex gently to make sure that it will stay in place. Put the back of the plug on and screw it together.

CONNECTING WIRES

▼▼ Always attach the correct wires to
◆ ◆ the correct terminals.

◆In modern plugs connect green-and-yellow to Earth (marked E or ⏚), blue to Neutral (marked N), and brown to Live (marked L), *below left*. With old wiring connect green to E or ⏚, black to N, red to L, *below right*.

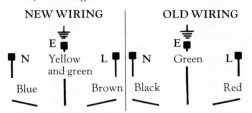

NEW WIRING	OLD WIRING
N — E (Yellow and green) — L / Blue — Brown	N — E (Green) — L / Black — Red

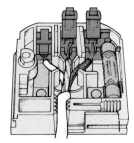

Wiring a push-fit plug *Unclip the terminal covers. Place each wire in the groove of the appropriate terminal, and clip the covers back into place. Slide the plug cover into position to close up the plug.*

Replacing a plug fuse

◆Use plugs which allow you to remove the fuse from the outside, without having to unscrew the plug and open it up. These are easier to handle than plugs which have to be opened up.

1 Take the top of the plug off, if necessary, and lever out the old fuse with a screwdriver.

◇*If you don't need a screwdriver, the clips are probably too weak for safety – throw out the plug and get a new one.*

2 Push a new fuse in, making sure it is the right amperage for the appliance.

Replacing a mains fuse

When a fuse blows or an MCB (miniature circuit breaker) trips, the cause is usually a faulty appliance, although it could also be due to a fault in the wiring.

1 Switch off the mains switch. Then check the fuse in each fuse holder, and put each one back before removing the next, to see which fuse has blown and thereby identify the affected circuit. If you have MCBs, the button or switch on the fused one will be in the "OFF" position.

2 Switch off all appliances and switches on the faulty circuit.

3 Put in a new fuse wire or replace the fuse, see below, or reset the MCB.

4 One by one turn each appliance or switch on the circuit on and off to isolate the fault. If the fuse blows when one of these appliances is turned on, the fault is in the appliance. If the fuse blows when everything is switched on, you are probably overloading the circuit. If you cannot find the fault easily, call in an electrician.

Extending a flex

◆ Use an enclosed connector to extend a flex permanently. Fitting one is as simple as changing a plug but there are two sets of connections to make instead of one, see CONNECTING WIRES, opposite.

◆ Make sure that the additional flex you use has the same number of cores as the flex to be extended and that you connect the conductor wires of the new flex to the corresponding wires of the original flex in the connector.

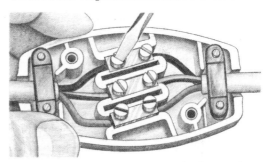

Connecting up an extension *Fit the flexes under the flex clamps. Thread the wires through the holes of the correct terminals, matching up the colours on each side. Tighten the terminal screws and fit the cover.*

REPAIRING FUSES

◆ For a blown cartridge fuse, remove the fuse carrier, take out the blown cartridge, and replace it with another of the correct rating. These fuses are marked with their rating and are usually colour-coded. Some are made in different sizes for the different ratings.

▼▼ Don't join a new piece of fuse wire
◆ ◆ to a piece of old wire and take care when fitting new wire to keep it straight: if the wire becomes kinked, it will fuse more quickly.

BRIDGED FUSE

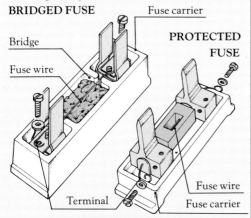

Mending a fuse wire *Take out the fuse holder and remove the two ends of the old wire. Take note of the positioning of the wire because you will have to repeat it. Replace it with wire of the right thickness, or amperage. Wind one end clockwise round a screw. Run the wire over the bridge, above left, or through the holder, above right, and wind it around the second screw.*

Making an extension lead

◆ For safety, always use three-core flex, rated at 13 or 15 amps or more, for an extension lead. You need three-core flex to provide an earth, and it should be rated at at least 13 amps to carry the extra current needed. Use heavy, sheathed flex to protect the wires from damage.

◆ Fit the appropriate plug on one end and the socket device on the other. You can get a socket device for one to four plugs, and some have an indicator light.

◆ To prevent accidents, use the plug connection code, see opposite.

▼▼ Never connect two plugs to an extension
◆ ◆ lead: one plug will have live exposed pins when the other is plugged in.

Fluorescent lighting

◆ Test a tube that won't light properly, or flickers, by turning it on late at night to see whether the fault is due to a temporary reduction in the mains voltage during the early evening, or whether it is in the mechanism of the light itself.

◆ Put in a new motor if a new tube glows white at each end when you switch the light on, but won't light properly. If the tube keeps flickering in a maddening way, or keeps switching on and off, that may be due to a faulty motor too.

◆ Replace a tube that glows red at each end, any old tubes that flicker, and ones that start to go black near the end.

◆ If a new tube lights with a shimmery effect (new tubes often do this), switch it on and off at fairly frequent intervals until it settles down to give a steady light.

DIAGNOSING PROBLEMS

Some electrical problems can be dealt with yourself. Call an electrician when:
◇ You are unable to find a fault after fuses have blown
◇ You are not sure how to tackle a particular electrical job
◇ There are problems with the wiring of the house
◇ The wiring system is old and looks as though it could be dangerous.

◆ Don't fit a new tube if you think the circuit or any components are faulty, because you could damage the tube. If you are unsure, get the circuit checked by an electrician. Always make sure you have the correct motor, choke, tube, etc. for the fitting.

ELECTRICAL FAULTS IN APPLIANCES

SYMPTOMS	PROBLEM	CURE
◇ The flex is hot and the appliance stops working. ◇ A fuse blows either in the plug or in the mains fuse box. ◇ There is a peculiar rubbery or hot smell and the plug or socket becomes a biscuity singed colour.	Poorly insulated live and neutral wires, which cause a short circuit.	Check the wiring in the plug and then check the flex. If either is old or damaged, replace it.
◇ The appliance gives a shock to anyone who touches it, or the fuse blows in the plug or in the mains fuse box.	A poorly insulated live part of the plug or flex is touching a metal part.	Check the wiring to the appliance especially where the flex is connected, and repair or replace any damaged sections.
◇ The appliance or plug starts a fire. ◇ The fuse blows as soon as the plug is re-fused and switched on.	A live part of wiring is poorly insulated, causing the current to flow to earth.	Check the flex and the plug, and repair any damaged wires.
◇ The appliance stops working. ◇ The plug is hot and may catch fire.	Broken wires or loose connection within an appliance.	Check the wiring and the connections in the plug and in the appliance and repair any damaged or loose wires or connections.

INSULATION AND ENERGY SAVING

Before installing any heating system, insulate your home. A well-insulated home will need a far smaller and cheaper heating system than an uninsulated one. In a house that is badly insulated, as soon as heat is generated, it disappears through the roof, *walls and floors, up chimneys, out of doors and windows, and then dissipates into the atmosphere. If you keep your home well insulated, your fuel bills will be lower, the rooms will heat up more quickly and cool down more slowly and you will be warmer.*

HEAT LOSS FROM YOUR HOME

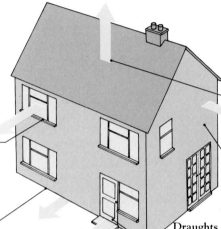

Windows From 10 to 30 percent of heat in your home is lost through single glazing. There are temporary forms of double glazing you can put up yourself, but have permanent double glazing installed professionally.

Floors Around 16 percent of the heat lost goes through ground floors. Floor insulation is best done by a professional.

Roof The roof accounts for about 25 percent of the heat lost in an average home – much more if it is a bungalow, and proportionately less for a flat in a high-rise block. Loft insulation and lagging reduce this loss.

Walls About a third of heat lost from a home goes through the walls. Cavity walls are easily insulated by an expert; solid walls are less easy to insulate.

Draughts A home can lose between 10 and 20 percent of its heat through draughts. You can draughtproof your home quite easily.

DRAUGHTPROOFING

Draughtproofing is one of the easiest, fastest and cheapest forms of insulation. It will normally pay for itself in less than a year.
◆ Don't overlook unexpected sources of draughts – airbricks, for instance, or bath and sink overflows. Airbricks can be papered over temporarily in winter, and although you cannot block up overflows, keeping the bathroom door closed will prevent draughts from reaching other rooms.

Doors and windows

◆ As a temporary measure, use masking tape (not clear adhesive tape because it leaves a mark) to seal hinged windows and doors that you will not want to open during the winter.

Floors

◆ Fill narrow gaps in floorboards with papier mâché, see page 220. Fill wide gaps with narrow wood strips glued into position, see page 219. Fill gaps between the floor and skirting with beading, see page 219.

Fireplaces

◆ If you don't intend to use a fireplace, block off the chimney at the top, or down-draughts through the chimney will lower the temperature of the room. Install an airbrick on the outside wall to allow enough ventilation to prevent condensation on the inside wall.
◆ Don't block up the flue permanently in case someone living in the home after you wants to use the fireplace.

DRAUGHTPROOFING DOORS AND WINDOWS

EXTERNAL DOORS

◆ Choose draught excluders that are designed for external doors because they are more durable.

◆ Cat flaps are also a source of draughts – choose one which closes on a magnet or is radio-controlled by the cat's collar. If you already have a cat flap, try to persuade the cat to use a litter during the winter, and tape up the flap.

◆ Don't seal the tops of doors – the gap there is necessary to allow some fresh air in.

◆ Hang a heavy, lined curtain on a rail fixed to the back of the front door as an additional form of draughtproofing. Don't fix the rail to the door frame or the curtain will get caught continually and become a source of annoyance.

◆ Stop draughts coming through the letter-box by fitting a flap to the back of it, see below left.

INTERNAL DOORS

◆ Fit brush or rubber door strips that reach the floor. A hinged type is available, which will last longer; the sealing strip swings clear of the floor when the door is opened and locks back into place as the door closes. Parallel bar draught excluders are good because they allow the sealing strip to stay clear of the floor when the door is opened. They do take some time to fit though, because they need to be inserted carefully.

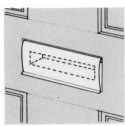

Draughtproofing a letter-box *Fit a close fitting flap to the inner side of the letter-box so that the flap swings inwards only when something is pushed through the letter-box.*

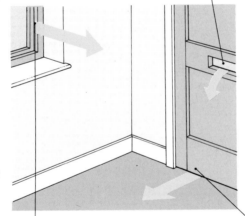

Making a draught "dog" *Cut the arm off an old coat or jersey, stuff it to give it some weight and volume, and lay it along the bottom of the front door.*

FILLING GAPS

◆ For narrow gaps fit self-adhesive foam strip draught-excluders to the sides of the frame of hinged doors and windows; these are the cheapest and easiest to fix but will not last more than about two years.

◆ For wide gaps and for greater durability, fit plastic strip in the form of a flexible tube to the door or window frame; when the door or window is swung shut, the tube is squashed flat and the gap is sealed. Alternatively, use a plastic strip with a flange or a V-shaped strip that closes as the door or window is shut,

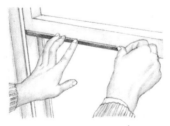

Draughtproofing sash windows *Fit nylon pile strips. Tack the strip around the frame so that the pile presses against the sliding sash.*

preventing draughts, see right. The bronze and copper V-shaped strips are the most expensive but very durable, so can work out cheaper.

Securing plastic draught-proofing strips *These strips are often sold in rolls so it can be difficult to get them to stay in position, even though they have double-sided tape on one side. Position each length on the frame, then secure each length top and bottom with a panel pin.*

LOFT INSULATION AND LAGGING

Loft insulation need not be prohibitively expensive and should pay for itself in reduced heating bills in about three years.
◆ Look for discounts on rolls of insulating material in builder's merchants and DIY shops. There are often good deals to be had in spring and summer.

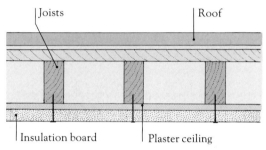

Insulating a flat roof *The easiest way is to pin insulation board through the plaster ceiling into the roof joists. You can paper over the board and decorate. This job is best done by a builder.*

Lofts

◆ If the loft is used just as storage space, put a layer of insulation material on top of or between the joists.
◆ If the roof space is used as an extra room, fix the insulation to the underside of the roof itself. This is a time-consuming business and is probably best left to a professional.
◆ Use rolls of glass fibre or spun mineral wool in mat or quilt form to pack the spaces between ceiling joists or for flat roofs. You will need at least 7.5cm (3in) thickness for adequate insulation. This type is the easiest to handle and lay yourself. Wear gloves, a face mask and goggles because glass fibres can irritate the skin and nose.
◆ Use reflective aluminium foil only as a backing for other types of insulation. It is cheap, but is not adequate on its own.
◆ If you want to insulate the loft permanently with blown material (mineral or cellulose fibres), get a professional contractor in to do the job.

Insulating with loose fill *Use loose fill for insulating awkward spaces, such as the odd shapes around chimneys or between unevenly spaced joists. Lay it at least 10cm (4in) deep. Loose fill is made from grains of cork or polystyrene, or pellets of mineral wool or glass fibre (in which case wear gloves and face mask).*

Insulating with matting *Wearing thick gloves, goggles and a face mask, unroll the matting in the loft and cut it so that it fits the spaces between the joists above left. Press the strips down so that they fit snugly, above right.*

◆ Lay insulation over the pipes – this will save you from having to lag them individually later, which can be very fiddly.
◆ Have the trap door insulated with a box frame filled with loose fill. Make sure it has a draughtproof seal.

Tanks and pipes

It is very important to lag tanks and pipes, because apart from reducing heat loss, it will also stop them from freezing in the winter.
◆ Don't lay insulation under a water tank. Warmth coming up under it will reduce the possibility of it freezing in winter.
◆ As a temporary measure, tie blankets or an old quilt around the water tanks.

◆For permanent insulation buy purpose-made tank jackets or pipe lagging – they are cheap and easy to install. Alternatively, use any suitable material left over from the loft insulation to cover the cold and hot water tanks and pipes. If you have loose fill material left over from insulating the loft, fill plastic rubbish bags with insulation material, see below, or have a box made around the tank and fill that up with the material. The top should be like a tray so that you can take it off easily. Don't get pieces of fibre in the tank itself since they will pollute your water.

◆ You can use felt bandage for lagging pipes, but you must overlap it as you go, because felt is not thick enough to provide sufficient insulation on its own.

◆If you are thinking of replacing your existing hot-water tank, get a factory-insulated tank with a built-in polyurethane layer; this type is only slightly more expensive than an uninsulated tank and a separate tank jacket, but is much better insulated.

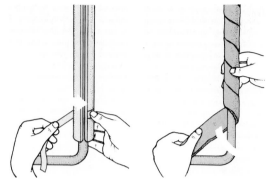

Lagging pipes *The easiest and cheapest method of lagging pipes is to buy lengths of polyurethane foam tubing, which are available in sizes that fit standard pipes, above left. Alternatively, use strips of left-over mineral wool matting to lag pipes from the cistern to the bathroom and hot-water tank. Wind the strips round the pipes in a spiral, above right.*

INSULATING WALLS AND FLOORS

The amount of heat lost through the walls depends on the type of house. A detached house, for example, will lose more than a terraced house because it has a greater outside wall area. The amount of heat lost through floors also varies with the type of the floor. For example, solid concrete is usually warmer than a suspended timber floor, but it may be damper.

Walls

It is best to leave wall insulation to professionals because the plaster has to be hacked off and the walls have to be injected (if they are cavity walls), or covered with some weatherproof material.

◆Have cavity walls insulated by high-pressure injection. This is the best form of insulation, but it is expensive.

◆To insulate solid walls, have them clad in tiles, weatherboarding or rendering. This is the only form of insulation that really works on these walls.

◆Walls can be insulated from the inside by erecting a timber frame in front of them and padding it with insulation, but again this is best done by an expert.

Using insulation matting *Wrap matting around the tank and secure it in place by winding string or sticky tape around it.*

Insulating with left-overs *Fill plastic rubbish bags with left-over pieces of insulation matting or loose fill, above left. Use two bags together so that the mineral or glass fibre cannot escape. Tape or tie them to the tank, above right.*

◆Polystyrene wall tiles are cheap, and can help to solve condensation problems because they provide a warm surface.

Floors

◆Insulate floor surfaces by covering them with carpeting (particularly foam-backed carpeting) and underlay, cork or wood floor tiles, or vinyl floor coverings. However, these coverings will not provide such effective insulation if there are gaps in the floor boards, so make sure you seal the gaps before you cover the floor, see page 220.

◆Get a professional to insulate below the floor. Floor insulation is worth doing but is messy because it involves pulling up floor boards, if it is a timber floor, or digging out concrete if it is a concrete floor. The costs vary greatly but the insulation should pay for itself within about six years.

DOUBLE GLAZING

Heat loss through windows can be reduced by various means. Effective double glazing is too expensive to be worth while for most situations and will take a long time to pay for itself. It is probably only worth considering if the windows are very large and in rooms that are in use all the time, or if you are replacing the windows anyway. But there are cheaper forms of double glazing which, although not quite as effective, may be worth while for comfort's sake. Plastic or polythene sheeting is one of the cheapest forms of glazing and, if you choose the "heat-shrink" type, is not visible. Self-seal plastic film can be used but it is more visible. Perspex panels can be fitted onto a frame for the winter, then removed. They are reusable, whereas polythene, plastic and self-seal film are not, and last for one winter only.

◆Place trays of water-absorbing crystals between glazing and the window pane, to reduce condensation. Choose the reusable ones because they are more economical. Every two or three months put them in a warm oven to dry out.

FITTING HEAT-SHRINK PLASTIC SHEETS

1 Make sure the window frames are clean and dry, then stick 12mm ($\frac{1}{2}$in) wide double-sided tape around the edges of the frame. Cut a piece of plastic sheeting 6mm ($\frac{1}{4}$in) larger on all sides than the whole window area.

2 Stick the sheeting to the top edge of the frame and stretch it. Pulling the sheet down by the bottom corners, press the corners into position on the bottom edge of the frame. Press the edges to secure them, and trim.

3 Play a hairdryer over the sheeting to shrink it and remove any wrinkles.

EFFICIENT HEATING

Your heating system will be more efficient if you can store your fuel energy in some way and control its generation and consumption, see also SAVING ENERGY, opposite.

Storage heating

Night storage heaters store heat that they accumulate during the night, when general electricity consumption is low and cheaper; they run on a special off-peak meter.
◆ If you are buying this type of heater, make sure it has a control which regulates the flow of heat during the day and the charging up time overnight, as well as a day booster. Otherwise, it will lose all its heat in the morning and the room won't be warm enough in the evening.

Central heating

◆ If possible, get the system serviced once a year to keep it running efficiently.
◆ If you have a wet central heating system, get the engineer to flush it out when he is servicing it, and to add a special anti-corrosive to the water. This will remove any rust that may have accumulated and allow the water to move easily.
◆ If some radiators do not get warm, while others get very hot, your system is not well balanced. Get your heating installer to have a look at the whole system.
◆ Fit a sheet of aluminium foil behind your radiators, particularly if they are on outside walls, or fit radiator wall panels to the back of the radiators. These will reflect the heat back into the room instead of allowing it to escape immediately through the wall.
◆ When you have radiators installed, don't place them under windows because the heat will just go straight through the glass and out of the window. If your radiators are already in front of windows, put up a shelf over them to deflect the heat away from the windows and into the centre of the room.
◆ Don't draw curtains over radiators, because you prevent the heat from coming into the room. Instead, fix a small shelf above the radiators to deflect the heat into the room and hang curtains so that their bottom edge sits on the shelf.

Controls

By controlling both the temperature and the timing of central heating, you can save a lot of money on fuel bills.
◆ Choose the most sophisticated controls when you have any heating system installed.

SOLAR POWER

GREEN TIP: Unlike almost every other energy source we use, solar energy is clean, safe and renewable, and there is no waste. However, installing an active solar heating system is liable to be expensive and will take about ten years to pay for itself. In many countries it can only contribute to the hot-water system, rather than provide all your hot water.
◆ Get a guarantee for at least ten years (the average time it will take to pay for itself) if you have solar heating installed.

Passive solar heating You need large expanses of glass facing the hottest sun. Replace roof tiles with special glass panels or build a conservatory sun space. The temperature inside rises higher than outside as the glass lets in the rays of the sun which become trapped inside as heat. The glass does not let the heat out again.

Active solar heating Install a flat plate collector which absorbs the heat and heats water circulating inside the plate. Once the water is heated it can be stored in a tank for "on-tap" hot water, or you can use it to supplement an existing hot-water supply.
◆ To get the highest efficiency, plan on one square metre/yard of collector per person. Any more will reduce the amount you save.
◆ Make sure the collectors are tough enough to withstand all weather conditions since they will be placed in the most exposed part of the house.

It's cheaper than fitting improved controls later. Make sure that the controls enable you to have two separate on-off switchings a day and a manual override so that you can have the heat on twice a day or turn it on all day if you wish.

◆Control the temperature of the whole house by a thermostat mounted on the wall of an easily accessible room such as the living room. Make sure that each radiator has its own valve so that you can turn it off completely and don't have to heat up rooms that aren't in use. Individual radiator thermostat valves which can be set to maintain a particular temperature are a good idea because they enable you to keep each room at a constant temperature.

◆Get the main thermostat checked once a year, when the system is serviced, for example, to make sure it is regulating temperature accurately.

Boilers

◆Have an old, inefficient boiler replaced, particularly after insulating your home; it will consume much more energy than is necessary. Remember that if your house is well insulated, it will require a smaller boiler, which will consume less energy.

◆Choose a boiler with sufficient capacity for your needs – one that is too big for your needs is expensive to run. Make sure that it is big enough to run the radiator system as well as supply hot water to the taps. Modern boilers are compact and can be fitted on a wall or inside a cupboard.

◆Site oil and gas boilers with balanced flues on an outside wall.

◆Have the boiler serviced once a year to make sure that it is running efficiently.

LAYING A FIRE

1 Remove the soot and coal ashes from the old fire (you can leave wood ash as it makes a good basis for fires through the winter). Keep large cinders and half-burned logs.

2 Place a few cinders or coals at the bottom of the grate to create enough ventilation for the fire to draw well when you first light it.

3 Spread a few pieces of bunched up newspaper over the coals or make some paper "crackers". Roll a sheet of newspaper diagonally until you have a long, thin spill. Fold it into a "V" and continue folding each arm until you have a short concertina shape. This will burn slowly but surely so that the fuel catches well.

4 Next, place over the paper some short dry kindling sticks, criss crossed or laid side by side and not too tightly packed.

5 Place firelighters under the kindling to help you start a fire if the fuel you are using is not quite dry or a bit "green" (unripe).

6 Place a few pieces of coal or wood on top, using smaller rather than larger pieces so the fire does not collapse before it has caught.

ECONOMY TIPS: To get more heat for your money, put potato peelings or a piece of chalk on the fire. Alternatively, start the fire with a mixture of green and dry wood. Once it is under way, use only green wood, which will last longer.

SAVING ENERGY

Gas is the cheapest fuel to use, whereas electricity is one of the least efficient fuels to produce and is therefore expensive.

◆With gas, consider having a credit meter installed if you have a pre-payment meter and if you use a lot of gas – the savings could be quite considerable.

◆If you have electricity, consider installing night storage heaters timed to use cheaper, off-peak electricity, and store heat until it is needed. Immersion heaters can be wired into the same system, although you should get an override switch in case you need extra hot water at other times.

◆If you have access to large supplies of cheap or free wood, which you can collect and chop yourself, use a wood-burning stove, because it will be very economical.

◆Use newspaper logs in a wood-burning stove. Roll up old newspapers and magazines as tightly as possible and tie them with bits of old wire. Place them in a container with a few inches of waste oil and leave for a few days. The absorbed oil will make make them last for a couple of hours.

Heating and water

◆Set thermostatic valves on radiators at their lowest comfortable room temperature. Most heating systems are set at 21°C (70°F) in the living room, 18°C (64°F) in the hall and 15°C (60°F) in the bedrooms. However, few of us need to be as warm as that and reducing the thermostat by 2°C (4°F) can lower energy consumption by 10 percent.

◆Close radiator valves and warm air grilles when rooms are not in use, so that you don't waste heat.

◆Keep the doors of warm rooms closed to contain their heat.

◆If your house is conventionally heated and has underfloor access, consider having heat recycling pumps installed. They use little power and reduce the energy required to keep the house warm.

◆Repair dripping hot-water taps, see page 227; they waste a surprising amount of fuel.

◆Get a shower installed and take showers rather than baths because they use much less hot water, and the savings built up over a year can be quite considerable. The cheapest form of shower is a push-on rubber hose – you simply push the ends of the shower over your existing bath taps. However, it is not always very convenient, particularly if you have unusually shaped taps, and the pressure is not always very good. Most other forms of shower should be installed professionally.

◆If you are at home all day think about having a kitchen range installed. This can be used not only for cooking, but also to run hot water and central heating. Kitchen ranges run on coal, electricity, gas, oil and solid fuel.

Windows and doors

◆Fit heavy, lined curtains in front of windows; make sure that they have many folds to trap the warm air in and that they provide a seal down the sides and at the bottom. Put up a pelmet if necessary to create a seal at the top of the curtains. Similarly, when putting up blinds, make sure the base lies on the sill or floor.

◆Don't open windows when you get too hot; turn down the heating instead.

Lighting

◆Switch off the lights when you are not using a room.

◆Install dimmer switches, because they save energy.

◆Use several low-wattage bulbs in a room rather than a single high-wattage bulb.

◆Consider using fluorescent bulbs – they consume less electricity than other bulbs.

Kitchen equipment

◆Make sure that the seals on fridge and freezer doors are sound and that no cold air is escaping from them. Replace or repair them if necessary.

◆Place fridges and freezers in a cold place or against an outside wall; their fans will not have to work so hard to keep them cool and will therefore use less energy.

◆Buy a tumble dryer only if you really think you need it. The combination of a fast spin-drying programme and a dry warm cupboard is cheaper than a tumble dryer.

◆When cooking, keep the lids on saucepans because you will contain the heat inside them better and the food will cook faster.

◆Use a pressure cooker where possible; it cooks food faster than an ordinary pot, and therefore uses less fuel. Alternatively, use a slow cooker because it consumes very little electricity, see page 35.

🍃GREEN TIP: Use haybox cooking whenever possible – the pot is heated up to boiling point then removed from the cooker and placed in the haybox overnight to cook, see page 35.

◆When cooking, cover the flame with the saucepan to maximize your use of the heat generated. With electric rings and solid hot-plates, use flat-bottomed saucepans and keep the pans and the ring or hotplate clean so that the pan is in full contact with the heat source.

◆Use a microwave oven; it uses less electricity than an ordinary oven because the cooking time is shorter.

CROCKERY, GLASS AND FURNITURE

Getting crockery, glass and furniture mended can be extremely expensive and may take a long time, if you are lucky enough to find anybody to do it. With a bit of experience and confidence, you could do a great *deal of your own restoring. It's best to mend broken china and glass as soon as possible; make sure that the edges of the pieces are clean when you stick them and that they don't get damaged any further.*

TOOL KIT

FOR CROCKERY AND GLASS

◇ A small craft knife or scalpel for scraping off glues, and a knife for pressing putty
◇ Fine wet-and-dry paper for smoothing down filler
◇ Glass paper for making rough edges to provide a key for glues
◇ Kaolin powder or titanium dioxide, and pigment, for filling in china; buy from an art shop
◇ Clamps, sticky paper, modelling clay and a box or bowl containing sand for holding the article together or supporting it while the glue sets. Glued brown paper tape makes a good clamp because it shrinks very slightly as it dries

A foam rubber sponge

Adhesives

A soft brush, such as a shaving brush

A hard brush, such as a toothbrush

Pipe cleaners, for cleaning awkward corners

Magnifying glass for inspecting edges for dirt

FOR FURNITURE

◇ Methylated spirits, white spirit and turpentine for cleaning surfaces, removing varnish and as thinners
◇ Paint remover
◇ Lacquer thinners
◇ French polish
◇ Beeswax for polishing
◇ Aniline dye for disguising filler
◇ Adhesives for gluing loose joints
◇ A claw hammer for removing nails and screws
◇ Screws of various sizes
◇ Lubricating oil for loosening nuts and bolts
◇ Domestic chlorine bleach, and ammonia for removing stains
◇ Cod liver oil or scratch cover polish for hiding scratches

Abrasive papers and wire wool to rub surfaces smooth and to remove the surface finish

Cottonwool, and oil for lubrication when French polishing

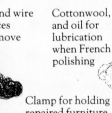

Clamp for holding repaired furniture secure while waiting for the glue to dry

Long-nosed pliers for drawing out nails

CROCKERY AND GLASS

◆ If you can't do the repair at once, place the pieces carefully in a plastic bag and seal it to keep out dust and grease.
◆ Before you start gluing, clean the broken edges so that the glue will stick. Wipe the edges with a bit of silk; don't use cotton, because it will leave bits of fluff behind.
◆ If you think there is any dirt on the broken edges, and certainly if the break is an old one, wash them gently in mild detergent and water and leave them to dry.
◆ Don't touch the broken edges with your fingers or you will leave grease on them, which the glue won't adhere to.
◆ To remove old glue, boil it off slowly in

detergenty water, or try to rub it off with acetone on a clean cloth.

◆Don't boil cracked china; it will weaken the cracks.

Mending broken china

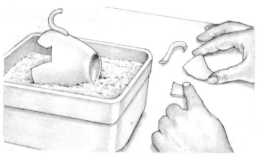

1 Clean the edges of the broken pieces, then lay them out in the order you want to put them together. Use a box filled with sand to hold one large piece to which a broken piece will be fitted.

2 Fit the pieces together dry, to see how they go.

3 Glue the edges of two pieces and stick them together. For extra support stick masking tape along the join until the glue sets. Allow each piece to set slightly before fitting further pieces. Remove surplus adhesive from the joins as you fit each piece, according to the manufacturer's instructions.

Repairing a rounded object *Glue the object together and wrap rubber bands around it to hold it until the glue dries. This must be done carefully to prevent the band pulling the repair apart.*

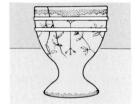

Repairing chipped crockery

◆Use epoxy putty to fill the gaps in chipped crockery; it has the same texture as china when dry and won't be visible.

ADHESIVES

Most adhesives set faster in a warm atmosphere. To speed the process up, lay repaired pieces by a warm stove or radiator or play a hair-dryer on the repair.

◆Follow the instructions faithfully for the type of glue you use, see page 216. Different types of glue have to be applied in different ways. With epoxy resin adhesives, for instance, you apply the minutest amount to each surface and then join them at once. The less you use, the stronger the bond will be.

EPOXY RESIN ADHESIVES

◆Apply epoxy resin to any household china or pottery which you intend to use, provided it is not antique because once the resin has dried you cannot dissolve it should you make a mistake.

◆Remove surplus epoxy resin when the glue is beginning to set and you can get the point of a sharp knife underneath it to peel it off. If you try sooner than that it will smear, and if you leave it too long you won't be able to remove it at all.

◆Be careful to get the join right the first time; once an epoxy resin has set, it is permanent. Quick-setting epoxy resins give you about five minutes to work with and set to full strength within eight hours. The slower-setting varieties give you more time to work on the joins but need to be held in place for 24 hours while the glue sets.

◆Leave repairs made with epoxy resin adhesive for at least three days to ensure a proper set.

OTHER GLUES

◆Use other glues such as acrylic or cyanoacrylate glues for valuable china and glass, because the glue can be dissolved and the piece taken apart and mended again, if necessary. Check the manufacturer's instructions to see that the glue is suitable for the material you are mending.

▼▼ Don't use these glues for everyday
◆ ◆ china, because they won't stand up to a lot of washing, particularly dishwashing.

1 Make your own mixture out of epoxy glue and kaolin powder or titanium dioxide. Colour the filler with the appropriate pigment before making the repair.

2 Press the putty well into the crack with a knife blade or the tip of your finger.

3 Make sure the gap is completely filled, and leave the filler slightly proud of the surrounding area.

4 When the filler has hardened, rub it down with the finest grade of wet-and-dry paper so that it is flush with the rest of the surface. Paint over the repair if necessary and varnish it.

Mending glass

◆Take very old glass to a professional restorer because a repair can easily go wrong; ordinary glass is easy to mend yourself.

◆Before you attempt any mending, make sure the edges of the glass are thoroughly clean by washing them in warm water and washing-up liquid. Then rinse them in clear water and polish them with a silver cleaning cloth – this will not leave any fibres.

◆To break down any grease on cut glass, leave it for a few hours in detergenty water with a few drops of ammonia added.

◆Mend the glass as if it were china, but roughen the edges of the broken pieces with glass paper so that the adhesive has something to cling to.

◆Remove the surplus glue before it sets – but not too soon or it may smear.

▼▼Don't use cyanoacrylate glues on glass ◆ ◆ because they are water soluble and the bond will not last long.

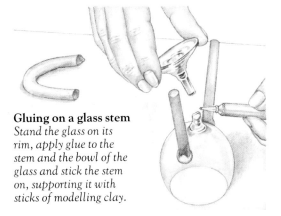

Gluing on a glass stem
Stand the glass on its rim, apply glue to the stem and the bowl of the glass and stick the stem on, supporting it with sticks of modelling clay.

RESTORING FURNITURE

◆Revive old and fading varnished wood with a fresh coat of varnish, but first remove the old finish to get a smooth surface.

◆Repair broken furniture as soon as possible to minimize damage.

Gluing wooden furniture

◆Before regluing, remove all traces of the old glue and dust extremely thoroughly.

◆If the wood was previously glued with Scotch glue, which dries in brown crystals, you will probably have to use the same kind of glue again, because most modern adhesives won't work where this has been used.

◆Glue furniture that gets rough treatment well, or it will soon fall apart.

◆Use a wood glue which is impervious to moisture. In the past, moisture was the downfall of glues because it dissolved them, rendering them useless.

◆Work in a warm room; the glue will dry faster, speeding up the repairing process.

◆Apply the glue to both surfaces and allow it to soak in for two or three minutes before sticking them together; this will make them stick better.

Clamping joints *Cover or bind the wood with a cloth to protect it. Use clamps, brackets or string to hold the joints under pressure while the glue is drying.*

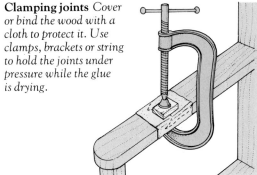

Metal fixings

◆Tighten loose screws or remove and replace, see below, otherwise the joint will be weakened, which could split the wood.

VARNISHING, STAINING AND POLISHING

◆ To find out what kind of finish is on a piece of wood, rub a drop of turpentine onto it: if the wood comes out bare, the surface is coated in oil or wax, which can be removed with turpentine. If the sheen remains, it has been stained or varnished.

◆ To remove varnish, apply a water-washable paint remover to the surface with a cloth. Don't scrape the varnish off with a sharp object, because you may mark the wood.

◆ Use a lacquer thinner to remove lacquer and apply it with a cloth. The thinner liquefies the lacquer and evaporates, leaving a hard, smooth finish.

◆ Clean the room you are going to work in before you start, to avoid getting specks of dust caught in the varnish.

APPLYING VARNISH

1 Thin the first coat with 10 percent white spirit and apply. Leave to dry for 6–12 hours.

2 Apply another three coats with a good-quality, clean paint brush, using a flowing action, leaving each coat to dry for 6–12 hours before painting on the next.

3 When the last coat is dry, sand the surface lightly with fine-grade sandpaper. Remove any dust with a clean rag moistened with white spirit.

APPLYING STAINS, OILS AND WAXES

1 Use a clean, soft lint-free rag to spread a first coat sparingly, working along the grain to get the best, most even, finish.

2 If a stain is too light, add extra layers, but only when the previous coats are dry. If it is too dark, sand it down lightly. With wax stains, apply two coats for a good finish. If you are applying teak oil, make the second coat thinner with a few drops of turpentine and leave it to dry for 24 hours. For a good finish, rub it down with fine wire wool and then polish.

FRENCH POLISHING

1 Remove any wax from the surface with fine wire wool, white spirit and fine glass paper, or remove dirty polish with a proprietary brass polish which is mildly abrasive and will not harm the surface underneath. Do this with care.

2 Pour French polish onto a wad of cotton-wool until it is soaked, right, and then wrap it in a clean lint-free cloth to form a smooth pad. Press the pad gently onto a spare piece of wood to get rid of excess polish.

3 Pour a few drops of linseed oil onto the wood surface for lubrication, above left, and then sweep the pad over the surface in figures of eight, making sure you take in all the edges, above right. Increase the pressure as the polish fades, and when the polish is dry, re-fill the pad and apply another coat. Apply several coats, allowing each one to dry before applying the next.

◇ Keep the pad in an airtight jar while waiting for each coat to dry, to keep it moist and clean.

4 Six hours after the last coat, make a new pad with double thickness linen and wet it with methylated spirits. Work it gently along the grain to achieve a good finish.

◆To remove a tight screw, nut or bolt, loosen it with a little lubricating oil. Put a few drops at the join and allow it to sink in before trying again. Use the correct size of screwdriver so that you don't damage the slit in the head of a screw while trying to remove it, or you will find it almost impossible to remove. If you have no oil, try vinegar instead.

◇ *Try turning an obstinate screw clockwise a fraction while pressing down hard. This may loosen it just enough to get it undone.*

◆If nails are tightly embedded, you may be able to remove them by tapping them through from the other side.

◆Remove protruding nails with a claw hammer. Alternatively, use pliers, but first wrap a piece of cardboard round the nail to protect the wood from the pliers.

◆Take loose wooden knobs off doors and drawers, saturate strips of old sheet or handkerchiefs in wood adhesive, and stuff them tightly into the hole. Then work the screw of the knob into the hole until it is held firmly, and leave until dry.

Working with small nails *Hold very tiny nails in position with a piece of plastic putty while working on furniture. This will make it easier to handle them.*

FILLING SCREW HOLES

Screws sometimes work loose and won't tighten because they have worked away too big a hole in the wood.

1 *Remove the screw and line the hole or coat the split with wood adhesive. Allow it to dry.*

2 *Plug the hole with plastic wood or a broken matchstick.*

3 *Replace the screw or use a new one the same size as the old screw.*

Legs

◆If a wobbly leg has a butterfly nut holding it together, it probably only needs tightening up. If it has screws, you may have to remove the old screws and replace them with slightly thicker (but not longer) ones.

◆It is easier to add to uneven legs rather than make them shorter, because if you get the calculation of the extra bit wrong, you can easily correct it. Only tiny differences are usually involved, so use very thin slivers of wood to build up the leg until you've got the balance right. Cut a piece as near as you can to the diameter of the leg and glue it on with a PVA adhesive.

◆To stop chair or table legs from scratching a polished floor, hammer nail-on studs into the base of the legs. These are slightly adjustable, since you hammer them in only as far as you need, and so are also useful for levelling uneven legs.

Reinforcing legs *When gluing legs, wait until the glue is quite dry and reinforce each leg by gluing a small block of wood inside the back corner.*

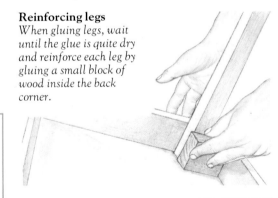

Woodworm

◆Paint a preservative, varnish or seal on bare wood, the underside of furniture, and plywood, to keep woodworm out.

◆Buy a woodworm eradication kit to deal with small areas of infestation. Follow the manufacturer's instructions and wear protective clothing. See also page 256.

◆If valuable antiques are affected, get professional help.

SCRATCHES AND STAINS

▼▼ Never treat a piece of furniture your-
♦♦ self if you think it may be valuable;
you will probably ruin it. Rather, have it
repaired professionally.

RENOVATING SCRATCHES

A scratched surface can be dis-
guised with varnish, cod liver oil
and polish, or beeswax.

Using varnish

1 *First thin the varnish with a
little methylated spirits. Then
apply several coats of the thinned
varnish to the scratched surface with
a small paint brush. Allow each
coat to dry before applying the next
one so that you get a smooth finish.*

2 *When the repair stands
proud of the surface, allow
it to dry before rubbing it flush
with fine wet and dry paper.*

3 *To restore the shine, apply a
thin coat of polish with a soft
cloth.*

Hiding scratches *Pour cod
liver oil into the scratch and
leave it to soak in. Then polish as
usual. Alternatively, rub the
scratch with a proprietary
scratch cover polish.*

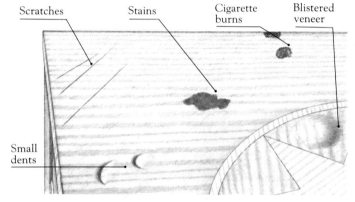

Scratches   Stains   Cigarette burns   Blistered veneer

Small dents

REMOVING SMALL DENTS IN WOOD

1 *Remove the finish with white
spirit and a soft cloth. Then
place a new, damp cloth over the
dent in the surface.*

3 *Repeat this process as often
as necessary until the wood
has risen sufficiently (this may
take a few hours).*

Filling in scratches *Melt beeswax, stain it with an aniline dye
so that it is darker than the wood,
and press it into the scratch with
a spatula or knife.*

2 *Run a hot iron over the cloth,
keeping it on the move, until
the wood absorbs the water and
swells to fill the dent.*

4 *Allow the wood to dry
thoroughly. Sand it down
with fine glass paper, re-stain it
and give it a good polish.*

REMOVING CIGARETTE BURNS
◆ Rub them with very fine glass paper and colour the wood with matching artists' paint. Polish it when dry.

REMOVING STAINS

1 Take off the top coating of dust and wax with a paint stripper.
2 Use diluted domestic chlorine bleach to loosen the varnish (this will also get rid of surplus paint stripper). Don't mix chlorine with any other cleaner or you may produce a chlorine gas, which is highly poisonous. For deep stains, use ammonia.
3 Rub with fine-grade steel wool. Revarnish, see page 248.

RESTORING BLISTERED VENEER
Repair small areas yourself but leave larger ones to a professional.

1 Cut the blister along the wood grain with a sharp knife.
2 Using the knife blade, ease some PVA adhesive into the cut.

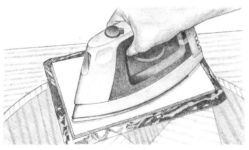

3 Cover the blister with aluminium foil, several layers of blotting paper or brown paper, or a folded sheet, and iron with a hot, dry iron.
4 Turn the iron off after a minute or so, but leave the weight on the blister until the glue has set.

REPAIRING CANE
◆ Glue broken bits of cane in place with a contact adhesive.
◆ For badly damaged pieces in baskets and basket chairs, buy new canes and weave them into the original.

Reviving sagging cane *Apply two cloths soaked in a solution of hot water and bicarbonate of soda, or half vinegar and half water, one on each side of the cane, pressing the cane upwards from below. Go over the whole surface. Rub with a dry cloth and leave to dry, preferably in the sun.*

LEATHER FURNITURE

◆ Treat leather on desks regularly with warm petroleum jelly or castor oil, rubbed in with a soft cloth. Wipe treated leather furniture with a soft cloth only.
◆ Patching leather upholstery is tricky. Get a professional to do it.

Renewing leather desk tops

1 Cut the sheet of new leather about 12mm ($\frac{1}{2}$in) bigger all round than you need.
2 Get the base for the new leather absolutely smooth and clean, otherwise every grain of grit will show through it.
3 Coat the wood and the new leather with wallpaper paste, position the leather on the wood, and press it into place.
4 Smooth the leather with a soft cloth to get rid of any bubbles and creases. Leave it to dry for an hour and then use a metal ruler and craft knife to cut off the excess leather around the edges. Be careful not to scratch the wood.

HOUSEHOLD PESTS

You can prevent your home being overrun by many pests by taking certain measures: for example, don't leave crumbs or food lying about, and keep kitchen, table and floor surfaces clean; don't keep stagnant water near the house; keep your rubbish bins clean and disinfected; and clean drains weekly with washing soda crystals. If you keep pests away, you won't have to use insecticides, which are harmful to the environment.

If, in spite of all you do, you suffer from a real plague of anything from fleas to rats, contact the local council, who may be able to send out a pest control officer to deal with the problem, or get in a professional pest exterminator.

ANIMAL PESTS

◆ Make sure that pets and children can't get hold of poisoned bait. Lock cupboard doors if poisoned bait is inside.
◆ Remove dead mice and rats immediately, particularly if you have used a poisoned bait, so that pets don't eat them and get poisoned.

Mice

◆ Keep all food packed in metal or glass containers so that mice cannot get at them.
◆ Keep all rubbish tightly covered to deter scavenging mice.
◆ Block up all possible entry holes, especially in the larder or in the cupboards under the sink.
◆ Keep a cat. A catty smell alone is enough to discourage mice and keep them away.

Discouraging mice
Hang sprigs of mint and tansy in your kitchen cupboards, or place them on the shelves. Rub the plants often to release their smell.

◆ Set traps and bait them carefully. Peanut butter, bacon and cake are good baits. Put the traps at right angles to the walls in places where you know the mice will go. Check the traps regularly, throw away dead mice, re-bait and re-set the traps.
◆ Alternatively, use poisoned bait. Follow the directions carefully. You may have to persevere for several weeks. Other mouse poisons are very dangerous and should only be used by trained professionals.

Rats

◆ If you see a rat near your home, call the local authority immediately. They will deal with the problem quickly. It is important that you do this because rats carry particularly nasty diseases, as they tend to live in sewers and around rubbish tips.
◆ Don't leave anything lying around which rats could use as a nest, such as old rags or cushions in a shed, household waste in a dustbin without a cover, or uncovered garden compost.
◆ Buy proprietary poison baits for rats. However, some rats have developed an immunity to poisons and it may be wise to use two different kinds. Check with your local pest control officer if necessary. Some poisons are ready to use, others have to be mixed with bait.

INSECT PESTS

◆ For a bad infestation which you find difficult to get rid of, call your local authority.

◆ To keep many insect pests away, vacuum the house thoroughly and regularly, and keep all surfaces clean.

◆ Apply insecticides around skirtings and stairs, and under sinks and windowsills and anywhere else that dust can gather.

Making an ant killer *Mix one part of borax with one part of icing sugar,* above left. *Scatter it over a piece of stone or wood near the entrance to the nest,* above right. *The ants are attracted by the icing sugar and poisoned by the borax, which is not poisonous to humans or animals.*

Ants

Ants are fairly harmless and don't become a nuisance until they come into the house. You can usually keep them away by keeping all surfaces clean. If they still persist, use one of the following methods.

◆ Follow the ants' path as they carry away crumbs to where they leave the house and from there to the nest. Destroy the nest with a suitable insecticide, following the instructions on the packet very carefully.

◆ If you don't want to use an insecticide, block the entrance hole to the nest with a piece of cotton wool soaked in paraffin, which ants don't like. They will probably leave the nest and go elsewhere.

🍃 GREEN TIP: Put pennyroyal, rue or tansy in your kitchen cupboards or on the shelves to keep ants away.

SAFETY WITH INSECTICIDES

▼▼ Don't spray insecticides near pets,
♦ ♦ children or old people or in rooms where they spend much time because the chemicals will make them ill.

▼▼ Don't spray insecticides near food
♦ ♦ because they are poisonous.

◆ When spraying insecticide, follow the instructions carefully. If you get any on your skin, wash it off at once, and on no account let any get near your mouth. Don't inhale insecticide because it can affect your lungs.

◆ Avoid aerosol insecticides containing chlorofluorocarbons because they harm the environment.

Bedbugs

Bedbugs may be found in old and new homes, in mattresses, crevices in furniture, window and door frames, skirtings, loose wallpaper and cracks in plasterwork.

◆ Spray bed and upholstery springs, webbing, slats and frames liberally with an insecticide containing malathion, lindane or pyrethrum, wetting them thoroughly with the insecticide. Pay particular attention to the seams and tufts of mattresses. Spray skirtings, as well as cracks in walls and floor boards.

◆ Don't sleep in the room or on the bed while the insecticide is still wet, and air the room thoroughly before sleeping in it; the insecticide is dangerous to humans.

◆ If the bedbugs persist, get the room fumigated.

◆ At any sign of more bedbugs, spray the whole lot again with equal thoroughness. Better still, burn infested mattresses and furniture and then treat the walls, floorboards and ceilings with insecticide.

Cockroaches

Cockroaches are large brown beetles which feed on food, fabrics and paper, and congregate in inaccessible places.

🍃 GREEN TIP: Sprinkle these areas with pyrethrum powder, a powder derived from the pyrethrum plant.

◆ Spray the cockroaches with an insecticide. Wear a face mask while you sprinkle the powder or apply the spray, because if you breathe them in they will make you ill.

◆ If you have a bad infestation, spray first and then sprinkle insecticide powder, fanning it into cracks and openings.

Fleas

◆ Treat pets regularly with flea powder, because infestation with fleas may lead to dermatitis or tapeworm. Also, although animal fleas can't live on humans, they can and will bite them.

▼▼ Never use a flea powder intended for one
◆ ◆ sort of animal on another: never use dog flea powder on cats, for instance, because the formulae are different and cats can absorb toxic substances through their skin. Also, dogs and cats may be made ill by preparations which are applied incorrectly.

▼▼ Never let flea powder come into contact
◆ ◆ with an animal's eyes or mouth because it will cause irritation.

◆ Take your pet to a vet if it won't take the treatment, or if you are unsure about how to treat the animal correctly. Tell the vet what you've been using; some insecticides react badly when combined with others.

◆ While treating your pet, make sure you clean the whole house out: vacuum carpets, under rugs, crevices, skirting boards, cushions, upholstery and anything soft and warm. Burn the contents of the vacuum bag. Flea eggs can hatch in two to twelve days in warm conditions, but in cool temperatures may remain dormant for months.

◆ Wash, burn or throw away the animal's bedding and replace it with cotton sheeting or paper, or use disposable bed and bedding (a cardboard box will do very well) until you are sure the fleas have gone. Burn or replace the box every few days to make sure that you get rid of the fleas properly.

Protecting pets against fleas *Anti-flea grooming brushes, collars and discs are available in pet shops, and an anti-flea insecticide is available in powder, aerosol, and tablet form.*

Treating your pet for fleas *Soak walnut leaves overnight or mix pyrethrum, derris or wormwood with water, above left, and wash your pet's fur with the mixture, above right. Leave the mixture to dry and then brush and comb the fur vigorously.*

GREEN TIP: Burn the leaves of common fleabane (*Pulicaria dysenterica*), greater fleabane (*Inula conyza*), mugwort or wormwood to fumigate fleas. Try not to breathe in the fumes yourself because they will make you feel ill.

Mites

These are miniscule spider-like insects which live where dust and general debris collect. They attack the warm, soft folds of the body and bite, causing itching, swelling and sometimes fever.

◆ Dust and hoover thoroughly and spray insecticide in all areas where dust can gather.

◆ Clean up any bird cages in your home and spray with a suitable insecticide.

Flies

Flies can spread at least thirty different diseases to people and animals. They lay their eggs in rotting meat and other rubbish and in hot weather multiply quickly.

◆ Keep all food and garbage tightly covered and clean the rubbish bin with disinfectant regularly, particularly in summer.

◆ Don't keep piles of compost or manure near the house because they attract flies.

◆ If you wish to use an insecticide, use contact poisons, which can be sprays or sticky strips and are absorbed through the skin, or use internal systems poisons (systemic poisons), which the flies eat.

◆ Put up fly screens at your windows and

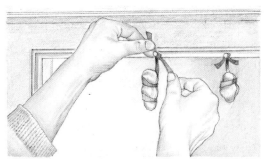

Making a fly strip *Hang a small piece of elecampane root in a window or doorway; it makes a very effective sticky fly strip and doesn't release the poisons that chemical flypapers do.*

doors. These are made of a fine mesh which lets air in and allows you to see through them but prevents flies from coming in.

GREEN TIP: Put sprigs of elder, lavender, mint, pennyroyal, rue or southernwood in vases, or hang them up, to keep flies away. Rub the leaves frequently so that the smell is released.

Wasps and hornets

◆ If there's a nest in the garden or on the wall of the house, contact the local authority, who will destroy the nest for you.
◆ If you destroy the nest yourself, use a suitable insecticide, and follow the manufacturer's instructions carefully. Store the insecticide out of reach of small prying fingers; don't smoke while spraying, wear rubber gloves and remember that the insecticide is probably poisonous to you as well as the wasps.

Mosquitoes

◆ Cover all water butts and rain gutters, and try to eliminate all puddles and any other standing water near the house. Mosquitoes breed in water and multiply fast.
▼▼ GREEN TIP: Spray with pyrethrum (a
◆ ◆ pesticide derived from the pyrethrum plant) but don't use it near fish ponds and pools, because it harms fish and pond plants.
◆ To get rid of mosquitoes in the bedroom at night, give the room a sharp squirt of insecticide before you go to bed.

Keeping mosquitoes away *Use mosquito "rings" (often made of pyrethrum) which burn down slowly. The rings must be used with the windows closed.*

◆ To keep mosquitoes away, use an electrical device which plugs into the wall and dissolves a special tablet. This device can be used with the window open.
GREEN TIP: Put up mosquito screens at all windows and doors and hang nets above beds to keep mosquitoes out. Alternatively, install air conditioning.

Moths

Before they die in early autumn, the little silvery moths that fly around the house lay their eggs in cotton and woollen materials, and furs, which provide food for the larvae when they appear, see also MOTHPROOFING, page 139.
◆ Clean all clothes, bedding and furnishing fabrics before you store them, because moths breed in dust and dirt.
◆ Turn out drawers, wardrobes and chests periodically, and check the clothes for signs of moths; clothes which are in use fairly often are not likely to be at risk.
◆ Clean the storage chest as well; tip out all the dusty debris lying at the bottom and then vacuum the chest.
◆ If you use moth-proofing aerosols, air fabrics after spraying, before you fold them or hang them away because aerosols smell, although the smell does eventually wear off. Don't use aerosol moth-repellants on furs because they damage them.

Keeping materials moth-free *Store blankets, eiderdowns, furs, curtains, and clothes in airtight containers. Wrap them in sealed polythene bags for extra protection.*

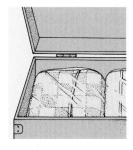

Keeping moths away *Place sachets or balls of moth deterrent (see page 139) between fabrics in drawers, chests or wardrobes. Renew them every six months or so.*

Weevils and food moths

◆Check the dried foods in your cupboards regularly for signs of little maggoty worms, and beetles. Also, if small moths fly out when you open your kitchen cupboards, they are a sign of weevils or food moths. Throw out all dried food in the cupboard – the moths may have laid eggs in any of the containers.

Keeping weevils out *To deter weevils and food moths from laying eggs in flour, rice and pulses, place a bay leaf in each of the containers.*

Woodworm

This is a general term given to several wood-boring beetles which attack furniture and structural woodwork in the home. By far the most common is *Anobium punctatum*, the common furniture beetle. The holes that the furniture beetle makes are small and round, about the size of small pinheads. Recently bored holes will have tiny bits of sawdust falling out of them. Other wood-eating beetles to watch for are deathwatch beetle and powder post beetle.

◆To discourage woodworm, never store wicker baskets or chairs, plywood boxes or old furniture in attics or cellars, especially anything with traces of woodworm.

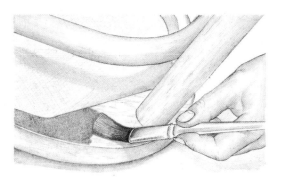

Keeping woodworm at bay *Apply a preservative, varnish or seal to bare wood on the underside of chairs and other furniture and to any plywood backing to furniture.*

◆Apply preservative or varnish to the surface of floors in attics and other rooms in which bare timbers are exposed.
◆Treat a small infestation yourself with a DIY woodworm eradication kit. Follow the instructions carefully, wear protective clothes, don't breathe in the spray or get it on your skin or clothes, and if possible, work outside.
◆If the infestation is extensive, get a professional woodworm expert (who will guarantee the work done) to treat it.

Silver fish

Silver fish live on starch and glue and so can damage fabrics and books.
◆Treat doors, windows, skirtings, cupboards and pipes with a household insecticide in either spray or powder form. Repeat the treatment if necessary.

HOME SECURITY

To identify the vulnerable points in your home ask for the help of your local crime prevention officer. He or she will know the area you live in, the weak points in your home that need securing, the best types of locks, and the habits of burglars.

Most burglaries are opportunist rather than planned, so even if you go to great lengths to secure your home, it will not be safe if you then leave doors or windows open. Keep external doors and fully opening windows closed even when you are at home.

VULNERABLE AREAS OF A HOME

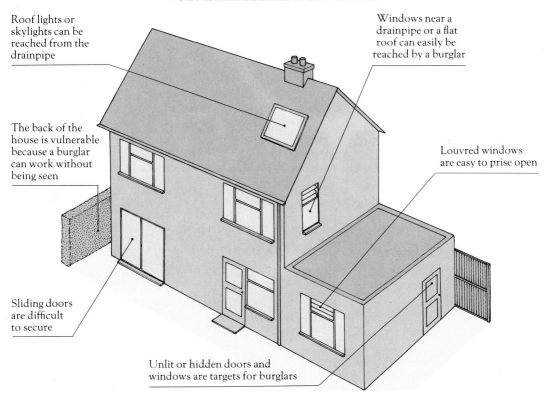

Roof lights or skylights can be reached from the drainpipe

Windows near a drainpipe or a flat roof can easily be reached by a burglar

The back of the house is vulnerable because a burglar can work without being seen

Louvred windows are easy to prise open

Sliding doors are difficult to secure

Unlit or hidden doors and windows are targets for burglars

MAKING YOUR HOME SECURE

◆ Restrict access between adjoining balconies as much as you can, and keep balcony doors locked and protected.
◆ Windows are the most vulnerable points of any house. Make sure that the act of locking windows becomes as habitual to you as locking the front door.

◆ Make sure that windows near a flat roof on an extension or a garage are fitted with locks – they are particularly vulnerable.
◆ Never leave windows near a drainpipe or a flat roof open, even if they are on the second floor, because they are still accessible to intrepid burglars.
◆ Fit iron bars over roof lights that have external fasteners; they are very easy to open and can be more vulnerable than ground-floor windows because a burglar may work on them without fear of being seen.

SECURITY DO'S AND DON'TS

GENERAL TIPS

◆Change the locks when you move into a new home – someone may have copied the estate agent's key.

◆Keep hedges in the front and along the side of your home trimmed low, and cut back trees and shrubs at the front of the house. Doors and windows screened by shrubbery or shade are an invitation to burglars but highly visible doors and windows tend to put them off.

◆Climbable shrubs are invitations to nimble burglars. If you must have a tall plant right next to the house, choose something prickly.

◆Store bicycles and tools in a garage or shed and make sure that the door is securely locked; never leave the tool shed door open because the tools could be useful for a burglar.

◆Keep ladders locked away safely in a garage; don't leave them lying around outside because they will very likely be used by an opportunist burglar.

◆Don't label keys in case they find their way into the wrong hands: visible identification tags and addresses are open invitations to burglars.

◆Don't leave your phone number on the telephone – if you are burgled, the burglar may take your number down so that next time he can ring to check that you are out.

◆Don't leave a window open for the cat – install a cat flap instead.

◆Don't lock internal doors. To a burglar, a locked door indicates that there are valuables in the room and he will kick or jemmy his way in.

◆Get a small safe installed in your home, in a discreet place.

◆Don't put your stereo, TV, video, etc., where they can be seen easily from the street – the sight of them will encourage the opportunist burglar.

◆Get a dog, if possible. Most burglars are put off by them, particularly if they bark.

SECURING YOUR HOME WHILE YOU ARE AWAY

◆Lock all external doors and windows even when leaving the house for a short while.

◆Don't leave curtains drawn during the day – it is a sign that you are not at home and if burglars get in they can work without being seen.

◆Close curtains when you are going out at night so that would-be burglars cannot see that you are not in.

◆Close the garage door when going out in the car – an empty garage is a sign of an empty house.

◆Don't leave any signs that no one is at home, such as newspapers in the letterbox or full milk bottles on the doorstep.

◆Don't leave door keys under a mat, on a string in the letterbox, in a plant pot or anywhere near the door. If you can think

of good places, so can a burglar, and burglars know all the hiding places. Leave your keys with a neighbour or a friend who lives nearby.

◆Don't leave notes on the front door cancelling orders or for someone you expect to call; this is a sure sign that you are out.

◆If you are going to be away for a while, cancel all deliveries, unless a neighbour can take them for you regularly.

◆Get a friend or neighbour to watch your home, switch the lights on and draw the curtains at night, remove post from your letterbox and, if possible, to leave a car on the driveway, while you're away. Alternatively, get someone to stay in your home until you return.

◆Put valuables in a bank if you are going to be away for some time.

◆ Make the back of your house as inaccessible as possible, particularly from adjoining houses; more than 60 percent of break-ins take place at the back of the house.

◆ Paint anti-climb paint on the upper part of your house and on drainpipes. It stays greasy, making climbing virtually impossible. This paint comes in black, dark grey, red or green.

◆ Buy locks from a reputable locksmith, not from a chain of hardware stores or a door-to-door salesman; copies of the keys may have been made. Make sure the packet is sealed. The best type are those with registered keys, which can be copied only on the authority of the owner or leaseholder of the property.

◆ Always buy locks that conform to the standards laid down by the standards authority or trade association of your country.

Alarms

◆ Have an alarm fitted to deter intruders and make it easier to catch them. Experienced house-breakers know how most systems work so they may not be deterred, but opportunist burglars or gangs of boys might be dissuaded.

◆ Have a warning device installed which dials an emergency service when the alarm is set off, and reads out a pre-recorded message to the operator, or alerts the headquarters of the alarm manufacturers who can inform your local police in seconds. The pre-recorded message should operate even when the telephone line is engaged (burglars have been known to phone a victim's house from a call box and leave the receiver off the hook) and the system ought to be fitted with a delayed action audible alarm in case the police are slow to act (which they often are).

◆ If you cannot afford an alarm system, try to get hold of an alarm box that fits onto an outside wall. It may fool burglars and deter them from trying to break in.

Lighting

◆ If you don't want to leave lights on at night, fit a light that contains an infrared detector: when someone walks past the detector, the light is activated and is switched on. These lights can be fitted inside and outside your home.

◆ Leave lights on in living rooms and kitchens when you are out in the evening, to suggest that someone is in. Buy a timer switch which switches on lights at a pre-set time, to simulate activity.

Lighting up your home *Install efficient lighting at the back door and don't block out any street-lighting. The more the door is hidden from view, the more vulnerable it is.*

DOORS

◆ If you are buying an aluminium door, get one with a good durable lock; you will find it difficult to replace a lock without buying a new door.

◆ If you do a lot of DIY, you will find fitting locks easy; if not, get a locksmith to fit them for you.

External doors

◆ To each external door, fit a five-levered mortise deadlock in which the bolt that locks the door can be retracted only by turning the key. This is the strongest lock and can't be manipulated and levered open with a credit card, for example.

◆ Make sure external doors are at least 45mm (1¾in) thick, and solid, so that they cannot be kicked in easily and so that the wood will not be weakened when a mortise lock is fitted. This applies to main entrance doors that are internal as well. If the door is particularly thin, buy a narrow-stile mortise lock, which is designed for this purpose.

◆ For internal entrance doors, fit steel plating to the outside of the door in addition to locks and bolts. Once a burglar is inside the building, he can take his time and make as much noise as he likes getting through your door, but a steel plate will thwart him.

◆ For front doors use a door chain together

with locks and bolts, not as an alternative. Slip the chain on only when someone calls (it's a fire risk). It will give you time to shut and lock the door again or to phone for help. Make sure the links are forged, that the chain is heavy and that it is fixed to the chain plate with strong screws for maximum strength.

◆ Have a door phone or entryphone installed, even in a house, and use it wisely. Don't let strangers in for other residents in the building.

◆ When arranging with other occupants to install an entryphone system, don't skimp on the cost. Don't use the standard locks that are often sold with these systems – they are usually inadequate.

◆ Fit a peep-hole with a one-way lens to the front door, which gives an angle of vision of about 170 degrees, so that you can see who is on the other side.

◆ For an external door with glass panels, fit a rim lock which is key-operated only, on both sides of the door; if a burglar smashes the glass he will not be able to undo the lock.

▼▼ Don't use rim locks with latches on their
• • own, because they are totally inadequate. A good kick will splinter the staple that holds the bolt, and a steel ruler or even a credit card can be used to slip the latch.

◆ If you are attaching bolts to your doors, use bolts that lock and can only be opened by a key, for extra security.

SECURING A DOOR

◆ Make sure each external door has enough hinges to make it secure – three is best – and prevent the door being levered off its hinges if one of them is removed.

◆ Fit appropriate locks to all external doors to make them secure. A mortise deadlock and a rim lock and two locking bolts are ideal.

BACK DOOR

FRONT DOOR

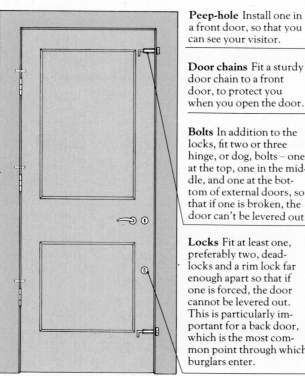

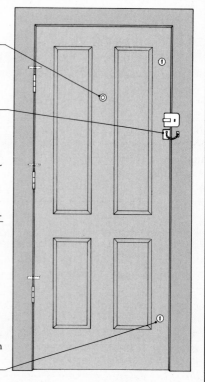

Peep-hole Install one in a front door, so that you can see your visitor.

Door chains Fit a sturdy door chain to a front door, to protect you when you open the door.

Bolts In addition to the locks, fit two or three hinge, or dog, bolts – one at the top, one in the middle, and one at the bottom of external doors, so that if one is broken, the door can't be levered out.

Locks Fit at least one, preferably two, deadlocks and a rim lock far enough apart so that if one is forced, the door cannot be levered out. This is particularly important for a back door, which is the most common point through which burglars enter.

Fitting hinge (dog) bolts *Fit these to doors with vulnerable hinges (doors which open outwards for instance). They lock the door at the hinged side, which is often the weakest part of an old door.*

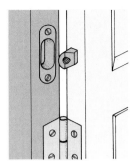

Fitting a striker plate *Fit a steel striker plate to the door frame to hold the bolt of a mortise deadlock; this provides extra protection against crow bars. To give adequate protection for the door frame, the striker plate should be 18–25.5cm (7–10in) long and secured by at least four staggered screws.*

♦♦ Avoid mortise rack bolts; they are operated by a cylindrical key which is widely distributed, so the locks have reduced security value.

♦ Traditional barrel bolts or tower bolts might be enough for a solid door, but you should ensure that the staple into which the bolt passes is strong. A weak piece of metal held in with a couple of wood screws will not be adequate.

♦ Don't use padlocks on an external door because they are exposed to direct attack.

Patio doors, sliding doors and French windows

♦ Patio doors which slide open are very vulnerable and difficult to fit locks to if they are made of metal. If you are thinking of installing such doors, consult your local crime prevention officer first.

♦ Use laminated safety glass or burglarproof glass, which cannot be smashed.

♦ Fit key-operated locking bolts in addition to the main lock.

♦ Fit a hook bolt mortise lock to sliding doors and to doors with a lock that runs up the length of the door to lock into the frame at the top and the bottom. If the door frame is wood, you can probably fit these locks yourself quite easily, but not if it is plastic or aluminium.

Garage doors

♦ If there is access to the house through the garage, keep the garage door and access door securely locked.

♦ Use the strongest sort of padlock on a garage or tool shed door; it should have at least five levers or six pins so that it cannot be unpicked.

♦ Use two padlocks on a garage door which lifts up – one at the top and one at the bottom – so that the door cannot be used as a lever against them.

Securing a padlock
Use a padlock together with a padbar or padbolt to give extra security; an ordinary bolt with a padlock can be levered off.

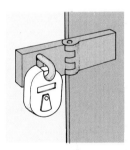

WINDOWS

There is a wide range of window locks available, so shop around. Measure the window frames before you buy locks to make sure the locks will fit.

♦ Fit locks to all ground-floor and any easily accessible upper-floor windows.

♦ Make sure that the fixing screws of window locks are not accessible should the glass be broken.

♦ Whatever lock you put on your windows, make sure that keys are close to hand or that everyone in the house knows where they are, so they can get out if there is a fire.

♦ Fit lockable grilles to French windows and ground-floor windows. These can be opened or removed when you are in your home and allow you to escape through the window in case of fire.

◆ Fit bars across basement windows to protect them.

Sash windows

◆ Fit a pair of screw stops to each sash window. Fit them so that the window can be locked partly open (although not more than 12cm/5in for good security).

◆ You can fit sash locks to sash windows, but they are fairly bulky as the mechanism fits to the frame and bolts to the window. They, too, allow the window to be locked while slightly open.

◆ Don't use dual screws for sash windows because they do not allow you to lock a window while it is partly open.

◆ If you fit mortise rack bolts or locking bolts to windows, fit them so that they cannot be seen from the outside.

Casement windows

◆ Fit screws and stops to the stays of casement windows, although they are not adequate where the fasteners themselves can be unscrewed if the window is broken.

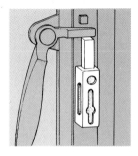

Locking a cockspur handle *Fit a locking stud to the handle, which prevents the handle from being levered to the open position. This lock is effective only as long as the handle itself cannot be unscrewed or easily removed.*

◆ For metal casement windows use a sliding wedge lock. The lock expands on a sliding wedge when the key is turned, so that the window cannot be forced open, and fits inside the frame so that only the small keyhole of the fixing bolt shows.

Sliding windows

◆ For sliding windows fit bolts with a key-operated lock, as for sliding patio doors.

Louvred windows

◆ Avoid louvred windows because these are the easiest windows to open. If your home already has them, consider getting them changed as soon as possible.

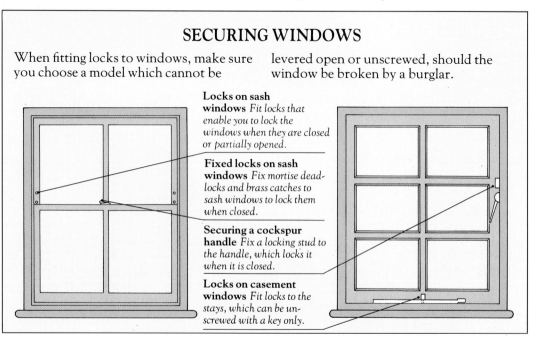

SECURING WINDOWS

When fitting locks to windows, make sure you choose a model which cannot be levered open or unscrewed, should the window be broken by a burglar.

Locks on sash windows *Fit locks that enable you to lock the windows when they are closed or partially opened.*

Fixed locks on sash windows *Fix mortise dead-locks and brass catches to sash windows to lock them when closed.*

Securing a cockspur handle *Fix a locking stud to the handle, which locks it when it is closed.*

Locks on casement windows *Fit locks to the stays, which can be unscrewed with a key only.*

Home Sewing

SEWING EQUIPMENT

If possible, keep your materials and sewing equipment in an area where they don't have to be constantly cleared away, so that you can pick up a job at the point where you left *off. If you have very young children, keep everything in a lockable room or cupboard, and don't leave needles, pins and scissors lying around.*

BASIC SEWING KIT

There are basic items that you will find useful for general sewing and repairs – these are listed below. When you buy a pattern, read the back to find out the equipment and materials you will need.

Cutting tools

◇ **Dressmaking shears** For cutting fabric; the angle of the lower blade allows the fabric to lie flat while you cut it. You can get left-handed and special dressmaking shears for sheer fabrics and synthetics.

BASIC ESSENTIALS

◆ Keep the following selection of essential materials and equipment in one place, such as a sewing box or basket, for general running repairs and emergencies.

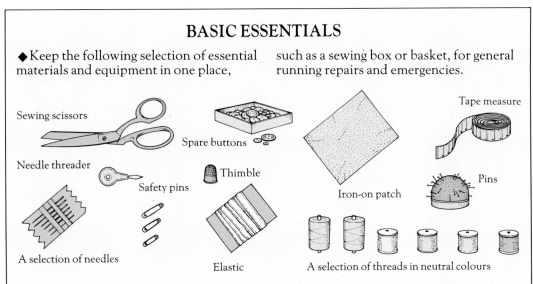

Sewing scissors

Spare buttons

Tape measure

Needle threader

Safety pins

Thimble

Iron-on patch

Pins

A selection of needles

Elastic

A selection of threads in neutral colours

◇ **Pinking shears** For cutting a zig-zag, fray-resistant edge. Good for finishing seams and raw edges on many fabrics but not to be used for cutting out paper patterns because the paper will blunt the blades, which can't be sharpened.

◇ **Small sewing scissors** For snipping the ends of thread.

◇ **Seam ripper** For cutting seams open, picking out threads, and slashing machine-made buttonholes. Use this tool carefully because it is very sharp and can quickly cut more than you intend to. Keep it in its protective case when not in use.

Measuring tools

◇ **Flexible tape measure** Buy one that is about 1.5m (5ft) long – this is the most useful length to have.

◇ **Sewing gauge** Get one with a marker that you can fix at any point, for measuring hems and pleats.

◇ **Metre stick** For long straight measurements of curtains, checking the direction of the material's grain, and marking hems.

Tracing equipment

◇ **Tailor's chalk** For transferring pattern markings onto fabric.

◇ **Chalk pencil** For making a thin accurate line. Good for pleats, buttonholes, pocket positioning, etc.

◇ **Tracing wheel** Used with dressmaker's carbon paper to transfer pattern markings to the wrong side of fabric.

Pins and needles

◇ **Pins with coloured heads** These are good as markers because you can see them easily.

◇ **Stainless steel pins** For ordinary pinning to hold fabric together before you tack or sew a seam.

◇ **Sharp needles** Keep a set with rounded eyes for most fabric weights.

◇ **Crewel needles** Keep a set with long, narrow eyes for embroidery; the long eye allows several strands of thread through.

◇ **Bodkin** Similar to a blunt needle, used for threading elastic or piping. Can be used to turn bias binding right side out.

◇ **Pincushion** This is the safest and most convenient way to store pins. Some have a needle sharpener attached for cleaning pins and needles.

◇ **Needle threader** For easy threading of needles, particularly if you have failing eyesight or shaky fingers.

Sewing threads and "notions"

◇ **Threads** Keep a variety of threads in your workbasket, of the kind and colour you might need at a moment's notice: buttonhole or strong thread, tacking cotton, general-purpose polyester thread (about size 50) for hand- and machine-sewing most fabrics, especially woven synthetics, knits and stretch fabrics, and a selection of embroidery threads for repairs to embroidered garments.

◇ **Elastic thread and knicker elastic** For emergency repairs.

◇ **Bias binding** For hemming and binding the edges of fabric.

◇ **Fasteners** Keep a selection of hooks and eyes, press studs, buttons, safety pins, etc.

Furniture

◇ **Work lamp** Get one that you can set at any angle you want, so that you can shine it on your work at the sewing table or on any part of your storage arrangement.

◇ **Full-length mirror** For checking hems and fitting clothes. Make sure there is room for you to stand back and see yourself in it.

◇ **Work table** This can be any table conveniently near the sewing area, even the dining table, but it is better if it can be a permanent table, which you don't have to clear of work until you have finished. A work table for a sewing machine needs to be stable, because the machine vibrates. If you don't have a suitable work table, a wide shelf at the right height can make a very satisfactory alternative.

STORAGE

If you do a lot of sewing, the first essential is to choose an area in the house which can be turned into a well-organized work space, where everything is to hand.

◆ Use a wardrobe, chest of drawers or shelves for large items, lengths of fabrics, clothes in the process of being made, etc., and for patterns and sewing books.

◆ Arrange separate storage for smaller items so that they don't get mixed up. Tiny chests of drawers, glass jars and small boxes are ideal.

Storing small items Use glass jars or small wooden boxes or keep a selection of baskets of various shapes and sizes.

Work box Keep your basic kit for running repairs in a plastic tool box so that you can take it into another room.

Fabric bags Use these for storing off-cuts, lace and other special bits and pieces such as ribbons and trimmings.

Storing cotton reels Divide up a desk drawer into compartments or fit a cutlery tray into it to hold cotton reels and prevent them from unravelling.

Ironing equipment Mount wall brackets for the iron, the ironing board and sleeve board if you have one so that they are nearby.

Locks Put child-proof locks on any cupboard doors if you have young children.

Spare fabric Use an old trunk for unused lengths of fabric.

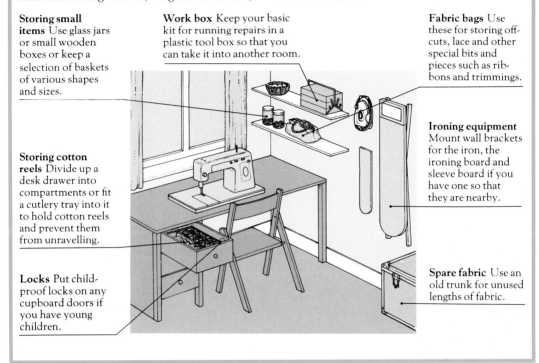

SEWING MACHINES

Sewing machines are useful for large jobs and are faster and often neater than hand sewing. All sewing machines work on basically the same principle, the main difference being the range of jobs that they can do. All modern electric machines will stitch fowards and backwards and most will also do a zig-zag stitch and a stretch stitch.

Choosing a sewing machine

Before buying a sewing machine, have a good look at the machine instruction booklet to see what the machine actually offers.

◆ If you do a lot of sewing, and especially if you use heavy fabrics or make large items, choose a robust machine which can tackle double fabrics and keep its tension constant.

◆ Check that the tension can be adjusted easily; some machines have a separate dial for this, which makes it easier.

◆ Buy a machine in which the bobbin is easy to take out and put back again. Bobbins are easier to manipulate if the bobbin case comes out too, as it does in newer machines.

◆ Look for a convenient little box attached to the machine to keep bobbins in and other machine accessories such as hemming and buttonholing feet.

◆ Check that you can control the movement of the feed, so that you can stop it for sewing on buttons and for free-motion sewing – a facility which allows you to control the movement of the fabric under the needle and is therefore particularly useful for embroidering.

◆If you want to do free-motion sewing, make sure that the machine has a hoop that will hold the fabric taut.

◆Look for a roller foot which grasps and rolls along with the top layer of fabric so that it will feed at the same rate as the bottom. An even-feed foot attachment does the same thing.

◆Make sure the machine has a seam gauge attached to it, which keeps the seam a specific distance from the edge.

Maintaining a sewing machine

New machines will have a comprehensive handbook giving full instructions for that particular machine. Handbooks for older models can usually be obtained from the manufacturers.

◆Every time you use your machine, remove dust and fluff from the bobbin and its holder, and from under the needle plate, with a small firm-bristled paint brush (this sometimes comes with the machine). If you don't do this, the mechanism may get clogged up.

◆Tighten sewing plates and other fittings regularly, using a small screwdriver. Most machines are provided with one. If your machine has not got one, get a replacement from a sewing machine shop or use the smallest standard screwdriver you can get hold of.

◆If you have constant difficulty with the tension and stitch size, take the machine to be

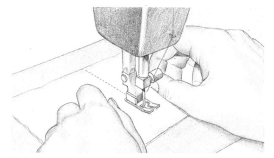

Removing excess oil from your sewing machine *Stitch through a folded scrap of fabric after oiling to remove any excess and prevent it from getting onto your sewing.*

EASY MACHINE SEWING

◆Guide the fabric evenly, without pulling or pushing it.

◆To get a straight seam, watch the presser foot, not the needle.

◆If you are a beginner, practise stitching several rows on a double piece of fabric, and practise turning corners. Practise with different types and weights of fabric, changing the needle if necessary.

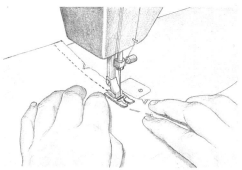

Stitching around shapes *Always stitch points, curves and scallops before the actual shape is cut out, otherwise you might distort the shape during stitching. Move the fabric gently while stitching so that you follow the curved line exactly.*

Securing the ends of seams
Reverse the stitch back over the previous stitching for about 15mm ($\frac{1}{2}$in) to secure the threads.

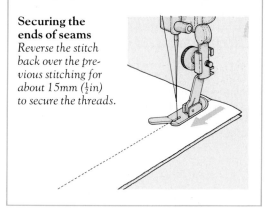

serviced professionally; there is probably something wrong with it.

◆Service and oil your machine regularly according to the manufacturer's instructions, to keep it running smoothly.

SOLVING COMMON MACHINE PROBLEMS

Try to fix a fault with your machine yourself; most problems can be fixed quite easily without having to take the machine to be repaired. The handbook for your machine will probably describe the most common faults and how to correct them.

GETTING THE TENSION RIGHT

◆ Don't alter the tension once it is set correctly, except when you are gathering or applying decorative top stitching, because the fabric will pucker.

◆ Uneven stitches or "looping" and puckering of the fabric are caused by faulty tension. If the loops are on the top, the lower tension is wrong. If the loops are on the bottom, the top tension is wrong.

◆ When making any tension adjustments, first use the upper tension-adjusting screw, which is above the needle on most machines. Adjust the lower tension only as a last resort because it is difficult to do and easy to get wrong. To adjust the tension, follow the instructions in your handbook.

◆ If you still have problems with the tension, check that you have the right thread for the fabric, that the needle has been inserted correctly, is not blunt or damaged, that the tension marking is set correctly and that the bobbin tension is right.

Positioning the needle correctly
Sewing machine needles are rounded on one side. Fit the needle into the machine with the rounded face towards you.

Side view

Front view

THE UPPER THREAD BREAKS

◆ Check that you have inserted the needle correctly.

◆ Check that you have threaded the machine properly.

◆ Look carefully at all the parts that the thread has to go through; if any part is rough or damaged it may break the thread. Replace any damaged part if necessary.

◆ Make sure that the needle is not blunt or broken.

◆ Check that the needle is not too fine for the thread.

◆ The thread may be brittle with age; use new thread.

◆ There may be a knot in the thread – pull extra thread through the needle until you are sure the knot is clear.

THE LOWER THREAD BREAKS

◆ You may have inserted the bobbin case incorrectly. Check that it is the right way around and is not loose.

◆ The bobbin may be too full. Unwind and remove some of the thread.

◆ The hole in the needle plate may be damaged or rough. Replace the needle plate if necessary.

◆ The bobbin tension may be too tight; try adjusting it.

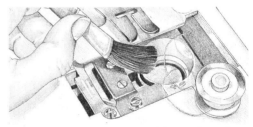

Cleaning the bobbin case *If there is dirt or lint in the bobbin case, this may affect the tension of the lower thread. Clean the case regularly with a small stiff-bristled brush.*

THE BOBBIN THREAD WON'T FEED THROUGH

◆ The bobbin case may be wrongly threaded; check in your handbook.

◆ You may not have allowed enough thread to come out of the bobbin. Always allow about 7.5cm (3in).

◆ Check that the needle is correctly threaded – consult your handbook to make sure.

Continued ▷

SOLVING COMMON MACHINE PROBLEMS

SNARLS AND LONG LOOPS IN THE STITCHES

◆ Clean the bobbin area – there may be dust or lint blocking the passage of the thread.
◆ Check that the bobbin has enough thread – it may need refilling.
◆ Make sure the tension is set correctly.
◆ The thread may have been inserted incorrectly in the bobbin case, which will affect the tension. Check the handbook.
◆ The needle may be the wrong size for the fabric – check the pattern or your handbook. Use fine needles, or the lower numbers, for sheer fabrics, and thicker needles, or the higher numbers, for more robust fabrics.
◆ You may be using the wrong needle plate – check your handbook to make sure.
◆ The timing between the needle and shuttle hook may need adjusting – consult your handbook.

THE NEEDLE BREAKS

◆ You may be pulling the fabric with your hand so that it is bending the needle, causing it to hit the needle plate and break.
◆ The fabric may be too thick for the needle; try using a thicker needle.
◆ Check the needle – it may not be inserted the right way around or it may be bent or blunt.

SKIPPED STITCHES

◆ The wrong type or size of needle may have been inserted.
◆ Check that the needle is not blunt or bent, or has not picked up lint from synthetic materials. Clean it or change it.

THE THREAD BREAKS ON KNITS OR OTHER STRETCH FABRICS

◆ You may be using the wrong thread. Stretch fabrics require stretchable threads. Use silk or polyester thread.
◆ Try stretching the fabric slightly as you stitch it.
◆ The stitch length and/or tension may be wrong. Adjust it following the instructions in your handbook.

THE FABRIC PUCKERS WHEN STITCHED

◆ If the fabric is lightweight or sheer, the stitches may be too large; keep them small.
◆ Reduce pressure on the pressure foot. You may be causing the needle to go too fast for the feed, which will affect the tension.
◆ If the fabric is tightly woven, the stitch may be too short; lengthen it.
◆ The needle may be too coarse for the fabric; change to a needle of a lower number.
◆ Check the bobbin – it may be unevenly wound. Rewind it if necessary.
◆ Check the stitch tension – it may be unbalanced.

THE MATERIAL DOES NOT FEED IN A STRAIGHT LINE

◆ The presser foot may be loose or bent.
◆ The needle may be bent.
◆ You may be pulling or pushing the fabric without realizing it.

THE MACHINE TURNS HEAVILY

◆ The machine may be dirty or not lubricated, or lubricated with unsuitable oil. Check, and clean and lubricate with sewing machine oil if necessary.

THE MOTOR TURNS TOO RAPIDLY

◆ The voltage may be higher than that indicated on the rating plate of the machine. Check the plug against the machine and replace the plug if necessary.
◆ The speed regulator may be positioned wrongly – consult your handbook.

THE MOTOR TURNS TOO SLOWLY

◆ The motor belt may be too tight.
◆ The voltage may be lower than that indicated on the rating plate of the machine. Check the plug against the machine and replace it if necessary.
◆ The speed regulator may be positioned wrongly – consult your handbook.

SEWING TECHNIQUES

Most basic sewing involves only a few standard seams and stitches. Once you have mastered these you can make or alter almost any garment and tackle almost any other sewing job. If you are a beginner and intend to sew clothes for yourself and your family, or to tackle upholstery and curtains, you may find it worth while attending evening classes which can teach basic techniques and short-cuts and give you confidence.

BASIC SEAMS

For general-purpose sewing there are just three basic seams you need to know how to put together.

Flat seam

This is the most basic seam and the simplest one to sew.

◆ Sew down the edge of two pieces of material, 16mm ($\frac{5}{8}$in) away from the edge, with the right sides of the fabric together. Press the seam edges open to flatten them.

◆ Oversew the edges by hand, or machine stitch them with a zig-zag stitch, to prevent them from fraying.

Flat fell seam

A strong seam which is used for jeans and sportswear.

1 Make a flat seam with the wrong sides together.

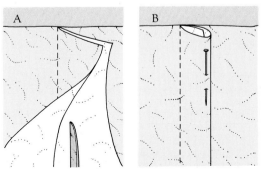

2 Trim one seam edge to 3mm ($\frac{1}{8}$in) from the stitching (A – *above*). Press a 3mm ($\frac{1}{8}$in)

fold on the wider edge and turn it over the narrower one so that it lies flat. Pin or tack the folded edge to the garment along the turned-in edge (B – *below left*).

3 Machine stitch along the tacked edge and press the seam flat.

French seam

This narrow seam can be used to strengthen fine fabrics or fabrics that fray easily.

1 Tack a line 16mm ($\frac{5}{8}$in) from the fabric edge. Place the fabric wrong sides together, matching the tack lines.

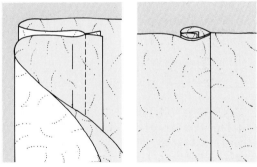

2 Machine stitch halfway between the tacking and the edge of the fabric, *above left*. Press the seam open. Fold the fabric right sides together and press it again so that the stitched line lies on the edge of the fold. Machine stitch along the tacked line to enclose the first seam, *above right*. Press flat.

HEMS

Hemming is probably the most common sewing job, for old and new garments, furnishings and bedding.

Hemming

◆Always pin, tack and try on a garment again before finally hemming it. Use hem or blind stitch for heavy to lightweight fabrics,

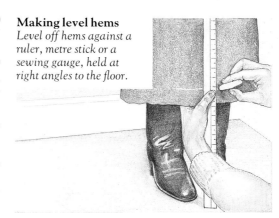

Making level hems
Level off hems against a ruler, metre stick or a sewing gauge, held at right angles to the floor.

USEFUL HAND STITCHES

TACKING (OR BASTING)
◆Use tacking to hold fabrics together while you fit and sew.
◆Make the stitches 12mm ($\frac{1}{2}$in) long. Fasten the first and last stitches with two or three back stitches, enough to keep the tacking in place, but still easy to unpick.

RUNNING STITCHES
◆Sew these in two parallel rows for gathering or as a decorative stitch.

Gathering with running stitches *Knot one end of the thread and sew two rows of stitching, making even stitches about 3mm ($\frac{1}{8}$in) long. Leave a loose end for pulling the gathers up and wind it round the head of a pin in the fabric to secure it.*

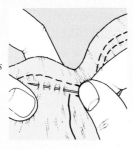

BACK STITCH
◆Use this very strong stitch for zips set in by hand or for areas which, for some reason, can't be sewn by machine.

Sewing back stitch
Sew a 3mm ($\frac{1}{8}$in) stitch, draw the needle through and take it backwards to the point where the last stitch ended. Insert the needle and repeat.

SLIP STITCH
A nearly invisible stitch made by slipping the thread under a fold of fabric.
◆Use this stitch to join a folded edge or hem to a flat surface.

1 *Fasten the thread and bring the needle out through the flat surface.*

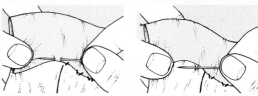

2 *Slip the needle into the fold immediately above the knot or previous stitch, and bring it out about 6mm ($\frac{1}{4}$in) along, above left. Catch up a thread of the flat surface, above right, and draw the thread through. Slip the needle into the fold again and then repeat.*

HEM STITCH
This stitch is most commonly used for hems, but can also be used for edging fabrics that fray easily.

Sewing hem stitch
Pick up a thread of the flat surface and then catch up a thread of the fold before pulling the needle through. Don't pull the thread tightly, or the fabric will pucker.

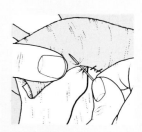

and slip stitch for fine and sheer fabrics.
◆ Make straight hems at least 5–7.5cm (2–3in) deep to give weight to the fabric and so help it to hang better.
◆ Give circular and flared garments a narrow hem to make hemming easier.
◆ For a blind-stitched hem, oversew the raw edge or stitch it with a zig-zag or blanket stitch. Then turn the fabric once, tack the hem 12mm ($\frac{1}{2}$in) from the finished edge and blind stitch it in place.
◆ For a slip-stitched hem, turn in the edge of the fabric twice to make a fold to make your slip stitches through. If the fabric is sheer,

make the turn the same depth as the hem itself, to prevent layers of fabric showing on the right side.

Pinning a hem *Place the pins at right angles to the edge of the garment so that the hem lies better when you are checking and measuring it.*

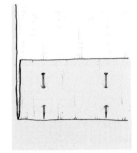

BLIND STITCH
Use this stitch to make a hem that is virtually invisible.

Sewing blind stitch
Hold the fabric with the wrong side facing you and with the bottom hem edge facing away from you. Turn up the top edge of the hem, make a small stitch just inside the hem edge and catch up a thread of the flat surface before pulling the needle through. Repeat to the end, see inset.

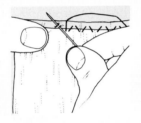

BLANKET STITCH
◆ Use this stitch to finish edges. Can also be used for buttonholes.

Sewing blanket stitch *With the fabric edge facing away from you, insert the needle 3mm ($\frac{1}{8}$in) away from the edge. Bring it over the edge and insert it 3mm ($\frac{1}{8}$in) away from the last stitch, but before you draw the needle through, pass it through the loop of thread. Continue like this to form a chain of stitches on the fabric edge.*

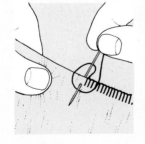

OVERSEWING
◆ Use this stitch to finish raw edges.

Finishing with oversewing *With the edge facing away from you, push the needle in 3–6mm ($\frac{1}{8}$–$\frac{1}{4}$in) from the edge, bring the thread over the edge, and insert the needle again, 6mm ($\frac{1}{4}$in) away from the last stitch. Repeat.*

HERRINGBONE STITCH
◆ Use this stitch for hemming a raw edge, but only for tightly woven fabrics.

1 *Turn in the hem edge once and tack it in place. Fasten the thread on the left of the fabric and work from left to right.*

2 *Take the needle diagonally across onto the hem fold. Insert it, pointing backwards 10mm ($\frac{3}{8}$in) from the knot or last upper stitch, catch up a couple of threads of fabric, and bring the needle through.*

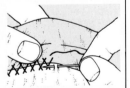

3 *Take the needle diagonally across the fabric and insert it, pointing backwards, 10mm ($\frac{3}{8}$in) from the last lower stitch. Pick up a couple of threads and pull it through. Repeat steps 2 and 3 along the row.*

FABRICS

When choosing fabrics, think about whether they will stand up to the wear that they will receive, and how easy they will be to care for and to sew. Sheer fabrics are extremely difficult to work with because they slip and pucker easily. Some fine fabrics, such as crêpe, stretch while you handle them, making it difficult to cut them accurately

and control the stitching. Heavy fabrics are hard to sew without making them look bulky, and checked fabrics and those with large patterns are difficult to match up.

For small items such as cushion covers and simple blouses, you can often find offcuts or "roll overs" at bargain prices in department stores.

CHOOSING FABRICS

◆When buying fabrics for clothes, choose those that are lightweight or mediumweight and don't slip, such as cotton, Viyella, polyester, fine wool and brushed rayon. These are easier to cut and sew than heavy-weight or slippery fabrics.

◆Try to avoid velvet or a similar fabric where the nap runs in one direction only, because every piece has to be cut and put together with the nap running in the same direction, and it is easy to get this wrong.

◆Buy fabrics that are easily washable for clothes, particularly if they are for children's clothes, cushions, duvet and quilt covers and kitchen curtains.

◆When choosing heavy curtain material, make sure that the stiffness of the material doesn't come from a surface finish that will wash out. Try rubbing the fabric between your fingers to see if the finish comes off, or ask the shop assistant if you are not sure.

◆If you are going to gather or pleat the material, make sure before you buy it that it is not too stiff to hang well.

◆Don't use knitted or stretchy fabrics for circular shapes, because when they hang they will distort.

SEWING SPECIAL FABRICS

Certain fabrics need special care when you are stitching and pressing them, because they may be quite heavy, or very delicate, or have special finishes.

Crêpe

◆Adjust stitch length and tension carefully to prevent the fabric from puckering; a longer stitch and less tension are usually best.

◆Place tissue strips between the fabric and the feed to help the grip.

◆Face the shoulders and neckline with a firmer fabric to stop the crêpe stretching.

◆To press crêpe, test a piece of offcut fabric first to see if it shrinks or puckers. Touch it lightly to avoid over-pressing.

Deep pile

◆Adjust the stitch length and tension care-fully; consult your handbook.

◆Increase the pressure on the foot because the needle has to get through the pile.

◆Stitch seams in the direction of the pile, or they will be visible.

◆Trim all the seam allowances, or the fin-ished garment will be very bulky.

◆Press on the wrong side and with little pressure, or you will flatten the pile.

◆Use the tip of the iron or your fingers to press seams open.

Double-faced fabric

This is a woven fabric which is reversible.
◆ Use flat fell seams, to take advantage of the reversible quality.
◆ Finish garment edges with fold-over braid or similar trim, again to make use of its reversibility.
◆ Press the seams with a heavy cloth to flatten them.

Lace

◆ Finish all the seams neatly because they will be highly visible, or line the fabric to conceal them. Seams can be virtually hidden with an appliqué trim.

Hemming lace

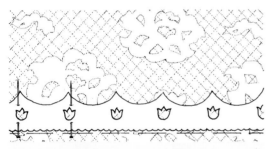

1 Mark the hemline by tacking along it, then place the trim on the right side of the garment, aligning the lower edge with the hemline, or centre trim to centre seam if you are hiding a seam, and pin it in position.

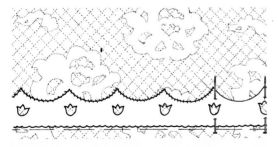

2 Stitch the trim to the garment by oversewing along the inner edge of the trim with small, close, slanting stitches, or use a narrow machine zig-zag.

3 Press gently and take care not to snag the threads of the lace.

Leather

◆ Rub chalk or put masking tape over the area to be stitched so that you can sew it accurately, but test a small piece first to make sure that the chalk marks or tape will come off without damaging the fabric. If the leather has marked, remove the marks by rubbing gently with leather soap.
◆ Use wedge-pointed needles because they go into the leather easily and are less likely to tear it.
◆ Sew carefully, because stitches make holes, which will show if you have to unpick the stitches.
◆ Press seams open using your fingers or a dry iron set at a low temperature.
◆ Use an impact adhesive to hold the seam allowances flat, if necessary.

Sheer fabrics

◆ Sew very carefully and neatly because every stitch shows up on the right side.
◆ Soft sheers such as chiffon are inclined to slip during machine stitching, so use tissue strips between the fabric and the feed to provide a grip.
◆ Handle these fabrics as for crêpe, opposite and press gently.

Stretch knit

◆ Use a stretch stitch or stretch thread, or both, to prevent the fabric puckering.
◆ Where you don't want the garment to stretch (for instance, at the shoulders), stitch 6mm ($\frac{1}{4}$in) twill tape (not bias) over the seams.
◆ If the fabric tends to curl over at the edges, overedge seams may be necessary. These are very narrow, never more than 6mm ($\frac{1}{4}$in) wide. Sew the seams with a narrow zig-zag and then trim them close to the stitching so that no seam allowances show through.

ALTERING AND RENOVATING

In many ways, altering and renovating clothes is more complicated and needs more care than making a new garment. The first rule is to take your time. Try the garment on and make sure that you know where the alteration is needed. Take the greatest care in unpicking threads; if you damage the fabric you can't make good the damage. Pin and tack at all stages and keep testing the fit by trying the garment on.

MARKING

Marking is a very important part of sewing because it allows a greater degree of accuracy; don't skimp on it.

◆ Mark fabric after you cut the pattern pieces out and before you remove the paper patterns. Mark all the symbols which show you how and where the garment pieces are joined together, and shaped, and mark the position of the darts, pockets, pleats, gathering lines, centre front and back.

◆ Mark all seamlines if you are inexperienced and intricate seamlines whether you are experienced or not.

Tailor's chalk

This is one of the quickest marking methods. However, don't use it on sheer fabrics because the chalk is hard to see.

1 Push a pin through each symbol on the pattern and both fabric layers.

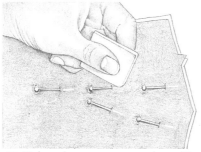

2 Take the paper pattern off and make chalk dot marks at each pin on the wrong side of each fabric layer.

Thread markings (tailor's tacks)

These must be used on fabrics on which other marks would not show up.

1 Use a long length of double thread, and make a small stitch on the pattern line through both pattern and fabric.

2 Pull the needle through, leaving at least 2.5cm (1in) of thread behind.

3 Make three or four stitches at the same point, leaving the thread very slack.

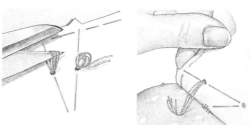

4 Cut the threads at their centre point, *above left*, and lift the pattern off the fabric, taking care not to pull out the thread markings, *above right*.

◇ *If you are working on two layers of material, open the material up very gently and cut the threads between the layers.*

Tracing wheel

The wheel is used with dressmaker's carbon paper. It is probably the fastest marking method, but it is not very clear on patterned or transparent fabrics.

◆ Place the waxed side of the paper on the wrong side of the fabric and trace the markings with the wheel with short strokes.

MEASURING FOR DRESSMAKING

Take your own and your family's measurements now and again (get someone to help you if necessary), to make sure you are buying patterns of the right size and to note any differences between your measurements and those of standard patterns.

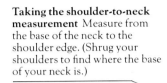

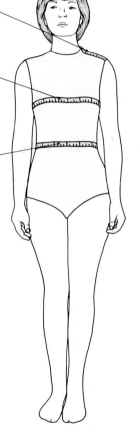

Taking the shoulder-to-neck measurement Measure from the base of the neck to the shoulder edge. (Shrug your shoulders to find where the base of your neck is.)

Taking your bust measurement Measure across the widest part of the back, under the arms, then across the full bustline.

Measuring your waist First tie a string snugly around your waist – it will roll to your natural waistline. Then measure round your waist at this point.

Measuring sleeve length Put your hand on your hip, take the tape measure along the outside of your arm from the shoulder joint round the elbow and down to the wrist.

Taking your hip measurement Measure your hips around the fullest part below the waist.

Measuring dress length Measure from the base of the neck down the centre back.

Measuring trouser length Measure from the waist down the side of each leg to the ankle, and from the crotch down the inner side of each leg to the ankle.

Measuring crotch depth *Sit on a firm chair, feet flat on the floor, and measure from your waist down to the chair seat.*

Measuring crotch length *Measure from the back waist through the legs to the front waist. Divide this into front and back crotch lengths at the midpoint between your legs.*

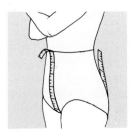

UNPICKING SEAMS

◆A seam ripper makes unpicking much quicker and is easier to control than a razor blade or scissors.

▼▼If you do use a razor blade, take care
◆ ◆ not to cut the fabric.

◆If the thread is tight, you will find it easier to cut a stitch in the middle and work towards the ends, instead of from the ends to the middle. By cutting the stitching in the middle you release some of the tension.

◆If you use a pair of scissors for unpicking, use sharp pointed ones because these will enable you to ease out the thread in a loop before you cut it.

Cutting stitches *Cut a few stitches and then pull the seam apart gently so that you can see the stitches clearly before cutting the next section.*

Unpicking with a pin *Pull up very small stitches with the point of a pin. This is the easiest method and prevents you from accidentally snipping the material.*

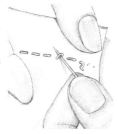

RENEWING AND REPAIRING

If a garment wears through in one part and the rest of the garment is perfectly alright, don't throw it away, because it may be possible to replace the worn part.

Collars and cuffs are often the first area of a garment to wear through. If you can catch them before they've gone too far, just stitch a piece of cotton tape over the bit about to fray. This is perfectly acceptable for school shirts and old workshirts.

Making a new collar

1 Unpick the old collar and its "stand" (the upright base piece).

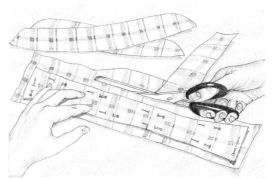

2 Using the old collar and stand as your pattern, cut two collar sections and two stand sections. Make these pieces 12mm ($\frac{1}{2}$in) larger than the area of the original stitching, to allow for seams. Cut interfacing for the collar and its stand in the same way.

3 Tack the interfacing to the wrong wide of the underpiece of the collar and lay both collar sections right sides together. Tack and stitch the three outside edges.

4 Trim the seam allowance, turn the collar right side out, and press.

5 Attach the interfacing to the wrong side of one stand piece.

6 Sandwich the collar between the two stand pieces, right sides together, with the interfacing at the bottom.

7 Match the top edge of the stand with the bottom edge of the collar. Tack it in place on the collar, then stitch the entire stand seam, securing it to the collar.

8 Trim the seam and then cut notches in the curves. Turn the collar stand down so that the right sides are showing, then press the seam allowance inwards along the inside edge of the stand.

9 Pin the unpressed edge to the outside of the shirt neck, right sides together. Tack and stitch.

10 Fold over the pressed edge of the stand to the inside neck edge to enclose the neck edge with the stand. Tack and hand stitch it onto the shirt.

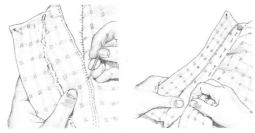

Turning a collar *As an alternative to renewing a collar, you can "turn" it. Unpick the collar from its "stand", above left, turn it around so that it is back to front, and sew it on again with the frayed edge on the underside of the collar, above right.*

Cuffs

1 Unpick the cuffs and use them as a pattern for the new cuffs.

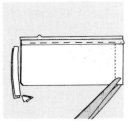

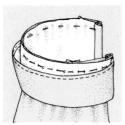

2 Pin, tack and stitch interfacing to the wrong side of the new fabric. Trim the seam allowances, *above left*, then turn to the right side, and press. Press in the seam along one edge and lay the unpressed edge on the main part of the sleeve, right sides together, *above right*. Adjust the sleeve fullness carefully, or press the tucks and pin and/or tack the cuff in place.

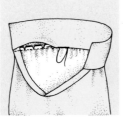

3 Stitch the seam and trim the seam allowance, *above left*. Notch the edge of the sleeve fabric. Turn the pressed edge of the cuff over to the inside of the sleeve and hand stitch it to the seam line, *above right*.

4 Press seams flat, then make buttonholes, if necessary.

Replacing a coat lining

1 Use a seam ripper to take out the old lining, leaving some of markings on the sleeves, collar and body of the coat to tell you where the lining was attached. Notice whether the lining is attached at the bottom or is loose all the way along the hem.

2 Unpick each separate piece of lining, then iron it to get it absolutely flat. Cut a new pattern from it.

3 Sew the new pieces of lining together as for any garment.

4 Pin the lining into the coat, right side out, centre back to centre back, side seams to side seams, and stitch in place.

5 Hem the bottom of the lining as on the original lining so that it hangs in the same way. Turn the sleeve hems under and slip stitch them loosely to the coat.

Replacing pockets

◆ If you are going to give a coat new pockets as well as a lining, do this before lining it.

◆ Take out the old pockets, making note of which way round they go and exactly how they were attached. Then use the old pockets as a pattern for the new ones.

Hems

The easiest way to repair a torn hem is simply to raise the hem so that the tear is hidden.

◆ Make a temporary repair with a strip of adhesive tape.

◆ Use iron-on hem tape for more permanent repairs. Slip stitch it into place if the garment is going to be washed a lot, and especially if you want to machine wash it.

EMERGENCY REPAIRS

ZIP FASTENERS

Once one of the teeth breaks at the top of a zip, you may be able to get the zip to work, but don't rely on it.

◆ If the zip is broken and undone, cut away one or two teeth, thread the tag back on, then sew the broken part together.

◆ If the zip is sticking but not broken, rub a piece of candle wax over it.

◆ If the tag of a zip is too small to get hold of easily, put a safety pin or a piece of string or leather through the tag.

Fixing a broken zip *If a tooth breaks right down at the bottom, do the zip up, then oversew the teeth just above the gap so that the zip can't open that far. You should be able to go on using it for some time after that.*

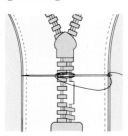

ELASTIC

If the elastic in pyjama bottoms, children's trousers, or cuffs breaks or perishes, you can renew it.

1 *Unpick part of the seam so that you can pull the old elastic out.*

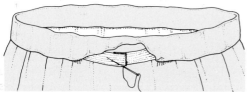

2 *Cut the new elastic to the right length. Attach a plastic threader, bodkin or safety pin to one end of the elastic and push it through the channel. Fix the other end of the elastic to the material with a safety pin so that you can't pull it right through.*

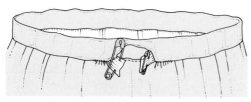

3 *Overlap the ends of the elastic and slip stitch them together, then slip stitch the seam opening.*

BUTTONS

◆ Use strong button or crochet thread when replacing buttons on children's clothes and work clothes; it doesn't wear out as quickly as ordinary thread.

Strengthening buttons *Reinforce buttons which are under strain by stitching through a square of tape at the back, or by sewing on a "keeper" button at the back.*

PATCHING

◆ For an instant repair, to patch up knees for example, glue on a patch, using an impact adhesive patch. This is strong enough even for jeans.

◆ If you are turning clothes inside out to repair them put polythene under the hole to protect the right side.

1 *Trim the edges of the hole. Cut a patch 2.5cm (1in) larger all round than the hole.*

2 *Turn the garment inside out, glue lightly round the hole and similarly glue the patch.*

3 *Leave for about 15 to 20 minutes until just tacky, then stick the patch carefully onto the hole. Do this carefully because it sticks instantly and you can't move it around afterwards.*

◆ An alternative method is to use an iron-on adhesive patch and hand stitch or zig-zag stitch it afterwards for extra strength.

ALTERING GARMENTS

◆For a better result, unpick a whole seam and re-stitch it rather than alter just the bit where the garment doesn't fit.

◆Always try on the garment at the pinning stages – don't rely on optimism.

◆Try to make a point of never ironing the bottom edge of a garment; otherwise when you let it down the crease of the original hem will show.

◆When measuring a new hemline, wear the shoes you would normally expect to wear with the garment.

Shortening a skirt or dress

1 Unpick the hem and press the garment so that it lies as flat as possible.

2 Measure and mark the new length, see page 270. Cut off the surplus material, but leave a hem allowance of at least 4–5cm ($1\frac{3}{4}$–2in).

◇ *If the skirt is flared, leave a hem allowance of about 2cm ($\frac{3}{4}$in).*

Lengthening a skirt or dress

1 Unpick the hem, pull out the threads and press to flatten the material.

2 Measure and mark the new hemline, see page 270, pin or tack it, then stitch it.

3 Camouflage the original hem crease with topstitching.

◇ *Camouflage permanent creases or stitch marks by machine stitching plain or zig-zag rows in the same or a contrasting colour along the marks, or sew braid, ribbon, rick-rack, lace or a flounce along the mark.*

False hem

If there is not enough hem allowance to lengthen a garment, make a false hem using binding made from matching fabric or with ready-made hem binding.

1 To make the binding, cut strips of the fabric on the bias and sew them together. Press a narrow fold along one edge.

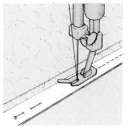
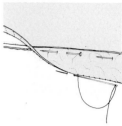

2 Lay the binding against the edge of the fabric, right sides together, and pin it. Machine stitch about 6mm ($\frac{1}{4}$in) from the edge, *above left*. Trim the seam allowance. Turn the binding up to the inside, and press along the seam. Slip stitch the false hem to the wrong side of the fabric, *above right*.

Altering skirts

◆If the side seam of a skirt or dress veers to the back, lift the waist at the centre front. Unpick the waist seam or waistband and re-stitch it, gradually tapering it from the centre front of the side seams. If the side seam veers to the front, lift the waist at the centre back.

◆If the skirt becomes too wide at the top because of your alterations, make the darts deeper, see below.

◆If a child's skirt is too big, make a series of decorative tucks in the waistband, which can be undone for the next child or as the child grows. Don't do this to fabrics such as velvet and corduroy, because the stitching may leave permanent marks.

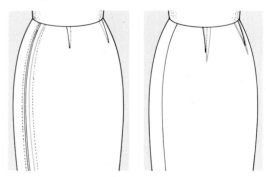

Letting out a tight skirt *Remove the waistband, and unpick the side seams. Mark a new seam, above left, and machine stitch it. If moving the seam enlarges the waistband too much, then take in darts, above right. Make a new waistband, or extend the old one and stitch it to the skirt.*

ADJUSTING PATTERNS

Compare your measurements with the pattern's to discover the places that need alteration.

◆ It is usually best to choose a pattern according to your bust measurement and alter the other parts if necessary. But if you are very full busted, you may find it better to buy according to hip measurements and alter the bust as necessary.

◆ Keep grain lines and "place on fold" lines straight when altering a pattern, or the fabric will not hang properly.

◆ Quite often when you alter something in one pattern piece, you will need to make a corresponding alteration to another piece. For example, if you add to the side seam of a bodice, be aware of the effect on the sleeve seam.

◆ If a large amount is being removed, alter skirts and trousers at both the alteration line marked on the pattern and the lower edge. Doing a bit here and a bit there like this allows the garment to retain its shape.

◆ When altering the back waist length, alter the front length to match.

▼▼ If you are altering a pattern, do so
◆ ◆ before putting it on the fabric so that you don't mark, or cut, the fabric.

BUST

◆ To raise bust darts slightly, mark the position of the new dart point above the original. Draw new stitching lines to the new point and taper them onto the original stitching lines.

Raising a bust dart substantially *Cut an "L"-shape in the pattern, below and beside the dart. Take a tuck above the dart deep enough to raise it to where you want it to be.*

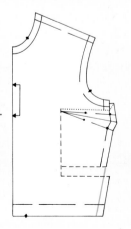

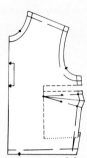

Lowering a bust dart *Mark the position of the new dart point on the pattern below the original one. Draw new stitching lines, to the new point, tapering them into the original stitching lines, above left. Alternatively, cut an "L"-shape in the pattern above and beside the dart and take a tuck below the dart deep enough to lower it to where you want it to be, above right.*

WAIST

◆ If you have to add a large amount to a skirt waist, distribute the additions between all darts and seams.

◆ When decreasing the waist of trousers by a large amount, alter the front and back crotch seams and taper them smoothly into the original cutting line.

Adjusting the waist of a circular skirt *Lower the cutting line at the waist by one-quarter of the needed increase. But be careful – it is easy to cut away too much. Lower the seamline by the same amount.*

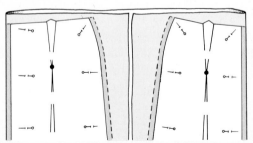

Increasing the waist *Add one-quarter of the total amount to each side of both pattern pieces. If increasing the waist of a skirt with four pattern pieces, add one-eighth to the side of each piece.*

Shortening trousers

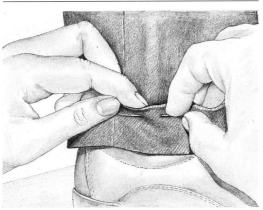

1 Pin a tuck in the leg just above the old hem to mark the desired length.

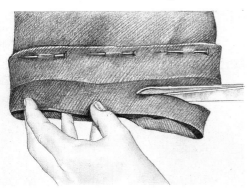

2 Measure the surplus fabric in the tuck, which will be twice the depth of the tuck. Measure the depth of the old hems or turn-ups, then unpick them. Cut the measured amount of tuck off the bottom.

3 Finish the raw edges, then pin and stitch the new hem or turn-ups to the same depth as the original ones.

Straightening trouser legs

1 Unpick the hem or turn-up. Turn the trousers inside out and lay them flat.

2 Mark a straight line from the knee to the hem on both sides of each leg and stitch along the marked lines.

3 Trim the seam allowances and press open. Re-stitch the hems or turn-ups.

Expanding a trouser waist

1 Unpick the waistband at centre back and unpick the centre seam. Undo any darts or gathers.

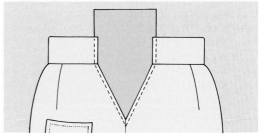

2 Cut a wedge-shaped insert from the same or similar weight fabric. Make the insert as wide as you need plus seam allowances and taper it to a point.

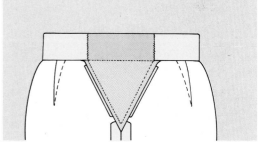

3 Turn the trousers inside out, and machine the insert (point down) into the waistband and the unpicked seam.

4 Re-stitch any darts and gathers if necessary.

Taking in a trouser waist

1 Unpick the waistband and centre seam. Cut out the excess fabric.

2 Pin the tuck at the centre back and taper the material from the waist down. Re-stitch the seam. Press the seam open and trim the excess seam allowance.

3 Re-stitch one of the bottom edges of the waistband to the trousers, right sides of the fabric together.

4 Turn under a hem on the other edge of the waistband and stitch it to the inside of the trouser waist.

FUR AND LEATHER

◆ Get valuable furs remodelled by a professional furrier; cheaper furs or odd pieces can be mended at home.

◆ Take care with your measuring and cutting and make sure there is enough fabric for what you intend to do because once the fur is cut, you can't alter it.

◆ When cutting fur, cut only the skin itself and use a razor blade or scalpel for cutting, never scissors or pinking shears – scissors and shears will leave bald bits through which you will see the seams.

◆ Use a furrier's needle, which is three-sided, to sew the fur, and use a very fine one so that you don't damage the pelt.

▼▼ Don't draw the stitches too tightly or the
◆◆ fur will pucker. You may find it helpful to put a strip of cardboard between the seam to hold the work taut.

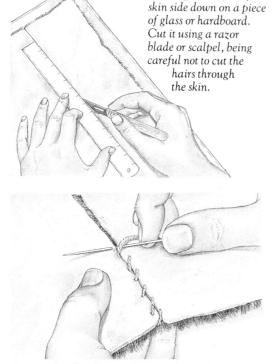

Cutting fur *Lay the fur skin side down on a piece of glass or hardboard. Cut it using a razor blade or scalpel, being careful not to cut the hairs through the skin.*

Sewing fur *Put the cut edges together so they just meet and make sure that the hairs all run downwards. Overstitch the pieces, using waxed, heavy linen or cotton thread, being careful to take up only the edge of the skin.*

◆ Mend leather bags with patches of leather, using an impact adhesive. Other leather goods should be mended professionally.

Shortening a fur coat

1 Unpick and turn back the lining of the hem. On the skin side of the fur, chalk a new length and cut it carefully with a scalpel or razor blade.

2 Place tape or a wide binding against the edge of the fur side, *above left*. Hand stitch it to the edge of the skin side with very small oversewing stitches. Tack a narrow strip of soft fabric (flannel, for instance) around the skin side of the fur, *above right*.

3 Turn the tape to the inside and herringbone stitch it down.

4 Cut the lining to length and slip stitch it into place.

REPAIRING LEATHER GLOVES

◆ Mend skin gloves using a glover's needle made for leatherwork.

◆ Repair splits between fingers with rows of blanket stitch but work lengthways instead of in a circle.

Repairing worn fingers *Using silk thread, blanket stitch around the worn part. Then work around it in narrowing circles until you have filled the hole with closely worked stitches.*

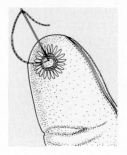

PATCHING FUR

◆ To patch fur, use a piece taken from the inside of either the facings or the sleeves so that it matches.

◆ If the worn part is near the hem, you will probably have to shorten the garment slightly.

1 *Check that the patch matches in colour and that the pile runs downwards.*

2 *Cut away the worn part of the garment. Then cut out a patch exactly the same size as the worn part and place it in the hole.*

3 *Oversew the edges of the patch and the garment together, with small stitches.*

4 *Use a fine brush to groom the hairs around the patch, working in the direction of the fur.*

WOOLLENS

Favourite jumpers and sweaters are often perfectly good except for one ladder or slightly worn cuffs. These can be repaired quite easily.

◆ When mending wool sweaters always use wool yarn and try to match both colour and weight. This should produce an almost invisible mend.

◆ Use a crochet hook to catch a dropped stitch. Then hold it with a temporary stitch or safety pin until you have time to pick up the whole ladder.

Darning

The idea of darning is to substitute your own bit of weaving for a bit that has become damaged or worn.

◆ You can save yourself a lot of trouble by darning thin patches before they actually turn into holes.

◆ Nylon socks are probably not worth darning; throw them away and get a new pair. Both cotton and wool are worth darning because they are harder wearing.

◆ Darn like with like: cotton with cotton, wool with wool, etc., and use the same thickness of thread as in the garment. If the yarn is too heavy, it will pull the fabric and make more holes; if it is too fine, it will take you twice as long to darn and the repair won't last very long.

◆ Use a darning mushroom when darning, to keep the wool taut and easier to manipulate.

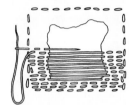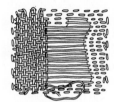

Darning a garment *Start well outside the edges of the damage, running the needle in and out of the fabric in a straight line and then back, parallel with, and as close as possible to, the last line, above left. Leave a tiny loop with each thread so that the work has some "give" and won't pull. When you have covered the entire damaged part, repeat, working at right angles, weaving in and out of the woven lines, above right.*

Darning gloves *Darn gloves while wearing them to keep the work taut. Wear the right glove on the left hand if you are right-handed and vice versa. "Weave" the repair as described above.*

SOFT FURNISHINGS

It is much more economical to make your own furnishings than to buy them. Even if you decide to have them made, measuring them up yourself will cut down on the cost.

Try to keep your furnishings in good repair. There are ways of dealing with worn patches or with holes and tears, without having to buy new furnishings.

ESTIMATING THE FABRIC

◆ Be generous rather than exact in your measurements in case the fabric shrinks in the first wash. If you want to include a tuck, for example, allow extra fabric for this.

◆ When choosing a fabric, remember that you get less wastage with a small pattern, or one with a small repeat, than with a large one, because it is easier to match up.

Cross-over net curtains

These are usually made from already flounced material and can be made up in pairs so that the two curtains overlap at the top with a single heading and the same rod.

◆ To measure the width, you need two to two-and-a-half times the window's width for cotton or polyester, and up to three times the width for muslin.

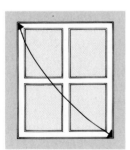

Measuring for cross-over curtains *Measure from the top left-hand corner of the window in a loose curve to the bottom right-hand corner. Add 15cm (6in) for the tail, plus 15–20cm (6–8in) for the hems and shrinkage. Multiply the total by two.*

Roller blind

The amount of fabric you need depends on whether the blind will be set into the window recess or fixed in front of it.

Measuring for a recessed roller blind *Measure the width of the glazed area and add 5cm (2in) to determine the width of the fabric. Measure from the top to the bottom of the window frame and add 16cm (6¼in) for the length.*

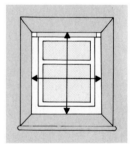

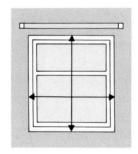

Measuring for a roller blind in front of a window *Measure the width of the window and add 15cm (6in) for overlap to establish the width of the fabric. For the fabric length, measure the length of the window and add 26cm (10¼in).*

Roman blinds

These fit into a window recess and hang as a pelmet when they are drawn up.

Measuring for Roman blinds *Measure the width of the recess and add 10cm (4in). Measure the depth of the recess and add 25cm (10in). You will need the same amount of material for the lining.*

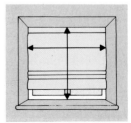

CURTAINS

◆ For the most accurate results when measuring curtains, use a steel tape or a folding ruler.

◆ Measure each window for its curtain. Even if all the windows look the same, they rarely are.

WIDTH AND LENGTH

◆ Measure the length, or proposed length, of the rail.

◇ **For velvet, velour tweed, and other heavy fabrics** Add half as much again to the measurement.

◇ **For cotton, linen, fine viscose and mixtures** Add three-quarters to the measurement.

◇ **For sheer fabrics, such as muslins, nets, ninon, etc.** Add up to twice the width, depending on the fullness you want.

◆ If there is an overlap rail, add 12.5cm (5in) to the width.

◆ To calculate the amount of fabric needed, divide the total curtain width by the width of the fabric you have chosen and adjust the figure up to the nearest whole number (the number of panels). Multiply the length for each panel by the number of panels needed for each window. When using

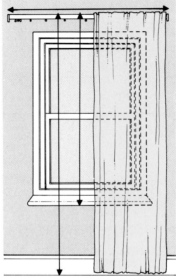

a patterned design, add one extra motif for each length.

◇ Add 30cm (12in) to the final measurement for hem, side hem, seam and heading allowances.

PLEATED HEADINGS

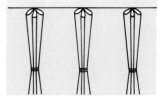

Pinch pleats *Add an extra allowance of 10cm (4in) per curtain length. Place the rail high enough so that the curtains fall in long graceful folds.*

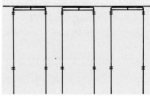

Box pleats *For a plain fabric, you'll need two-and-a-half times the length of the rail. For a printed fabric increase the width to allow for matching.*

PELMETS

When measuring the width of fabric for a pelmet, allow for the "returns" – the two sections of a valance or pelmet rail that bend back at each end to meet the wall.

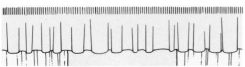

Box pelmet *You'll need a length of fabric about 10cm (5in) longer than the rail, including returns, and about 5cm (2in) deeper than the box.*

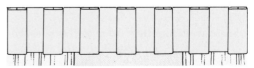

French-pleated pelmet *Double the width of the rail to get the width, and multiply by the depth allowing for hems.*

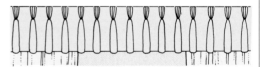

Valance frills *Measure the valance rail including the two "returns". Add half the width to the measurement for fullness and multiply by 15cm (6in) for the depth.*

Box-pleated pelmet *You'll need two-and-a-half times the rail length, multiplied by 15cm (6in) – 50cm (20in) for printed fabric – for a valance of 20cm (8in) with turnings.*

Festoon blinds

This blind fits just under the top lip of the window recess and should hang flush with the wall to look neat. Because it uses a lot of fabric, you will need to join several lengths, preferably along the lines of the vertical tapes so that you can't see the joins.

◆ To measure for a festoon blind, measure the width of the window recess and double it, adding 4cm (1½in) for side hems. For the length of each panel, measure the height of the window, and multiply it two-and-a-half times, adding 20cm (8in) for the hem.

Loose covers

When making a loose cover, use the covers already on the piece of furniture as a guide for the new pattern. Adapt these basic instructions for your particular piece.

◆ To measure the length you need, follow these instructions:

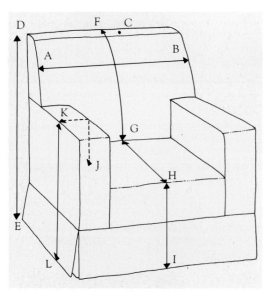

1 Measure from left to right across the chair back (A–B) to give you the width of the fabric. Find the centre back at the highest point where the front covering fabric joins the back over the top of the chair (C), and mark it with a pin or chalk.

2 Now measure the outside back down to floor level (D–E) and then the inside back

to the junction of the back and seat (F–G). Add 12.5cm (5in) for tuck-in.

3 Measure the seat from back to front (G–H), plus 12cm (5in) for tuck-in. Measure from the seat down to the floor (H–I).

4 Take the measurement of the inside arm, from the outside seam over the curve to the seat (J–K), plus 12cm (5in) for tuck-in. Multiply by two to allow for both arms. Measure the outside arm from outside seam to the floor (K–L) and multiply by two.

5 Measure the front facing of the arms or scroll, and multiply by two.

6 If you have any loose cushions, measure them right round. Add to the overall estimate an amount for self piping, say one metre (3ft).

Bedspreads and valances

◆ Make the bed before you measure it, to allow for the thickness of the bedding.

◆ Use a flexible tape measure; where it is not long enough for the whole distance, pin at the place where the tape ends and go on measuring from the pin.

◆ Allow 5cm (2in) for seam allowances, and add 12.5cm (5in) to the length and width for hem allowances.

◆ Measure the length of the bed from head to foot, allowing 35cm (14in) for pillow tuck-in. Now measure the top width from edge to edge. Measure the drop.

◇ **For a full spread** *Measure from the edge of the top to 12mm (½in) from the floor.*

◇ **For a coverlet** *Measure from the top edge to 7.5cm (3in) below the mattress.*

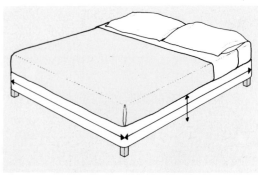

Measuring for a valance *Measure the length and width of the box spring for the top and from the top edge of the box spring to 12mm (½in) from the floor to allow for the drop.*

REPAIRING FURNISHINGS

▼▼ Don't use polyurethane foam mixtures
◆◆ to fill cushions, eiderdowns or quilts; if
they catch fire, fatal fumes will be given off in
a matter of minutes.

**Mending a torn
sheet** *Lay wide cotton
tape over the tear, turn
the ragged edges under,
and machine stitch over
the tape several times.*

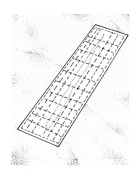

Sheets

◆ Mend tears by stitching cotton tape to the
damaged area, see above right.
◆ Putting worn sheets "sides to middle" is a
good old-fashioned way to get them to last
almost twice as long. Although you end up
with slightly narrower sheets, which have a
seam down the middle, they are useful for
children's beds (because children don't mind
the slight discomfort) or for making linings
for sleeping bags, in which the seam can be
positioned to one side. Don't wait until the
middle of the sheet is about to give up
completely, catch it when it begins to look a
bit worn. Otherwise you will have to cut
away more of the sheet when you repair it.

1 Make a small cut in the middle of the
sheet at the hem, and then tear it right
down to the bottom. This will give you a
straighter line than cutting.

2 Trim away any bit that looks really worn,
and turn the sides to the middle. Make a
French seam up the middle, see page 269, and
hem the outside edges.

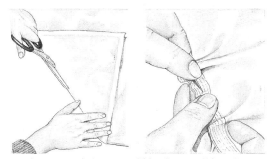

Making fitted sheets *Fold back a small bit of each
corner of a flat sheet (about 30cm/12in), and cut off
the triangular piece,* above left. *Turn up the hem
and stitch a length of elastic onto the inside edge,*
above right, *so that you don't have to hem it. Stitch
the elastic securely at each end of the fold.*

Blankets

◆ To mend a blanket, darn it as though it
were a sock, see page 283, using wool of the
same thickness as the blanket yarn.
◆ When you've finished darning, brush the
blanket very gently round the hole with a
wire brush to bring up the pile and hide the
damaged area.
◆ Blanket stitch fraying edges, see page 271.

Tablecloths

◆ To prevent tablecloths from wearing
through along fold lines, as.soon as they start
to look thin, cut 5cm (2in) off one edge of the
cloth, and hem it. Then, when you fold it, the
folds will form in unworn parts of the cloth.
◆ Cover holes or marks on a tablecloth with
appliqué or embroidery.

Towels

◆ Strengthen a fraying edge with binding or
cotton tape. Trim the edge first and then slip
stitch tape of a matching or contrasting
colour to the edge.
◆ Repair a hole with an appliquéd motif.

Re-covering an eiderdown or quilt

◆ Use sheeting material so that you don't
have to make joins in the fabric. Rub the
inside of the material thoroughly and systematically with beeswax or hard soap to
stop the features from poking through.

1 Measure the quilt, allowing extra for side, top and bottom seams, and any joins you may have to make.

2 Measure around the outside of the quilt or eiderdown and prepare any pleated trimmings and piping that you need.

3 Tack the sides of the fabric right sides together, with the trimming between them turned to the inside. Then machine all around, but leave an opening big enough to get the quilt into (most of one end).

4 If you are going to quilt the cover to the eiderdown, sew up the gap with neat stitches. If not, attach press studs or a strip of Velcro to the open edges.

5 For the quilt stitching, lay the quilt flat on the floor or on a big table, arranging it

inside the cover as evenly as you can and pin it at the corners, sides and middle. Tack along the old stitching, which you should be able to feel with your fingertips through the fabric, starting at the centre. Do the stitching by machine if you can get the material under the foot, otherwise do it by hand. Make sure the stitches go right through the fabric.

Re-filling an eiderdown

New down is expensive; you may be able to add some of the filling from another old eiderdown or from an old pillow or cushion.

1 Put the new down into a pillow case to contain it. It is best to use an old pillow case because in the re-filling process you are going to have to stitch up the pillow case, which may damage the fabric.

2 Using a seam ripper, undo the quilting and the stitching in the middle of the seam at one end of the quilt.

3 Sew the top of the down-filled pillow case to the opening you have made in the quilt, using fine neat stitches.

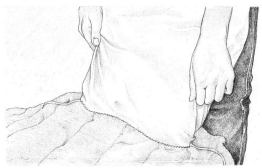

4 Gently shake the feathers from the pillow case into the quilt. Unstitch the pillow case from the quilt and close the opening in the quilt, using very close, even, small stitches. Shake the down evenly throughout the eiderdown and then lay the eiderdown flat on the floor and quilt stitch it as for the re-covered eiderdown above.

DECORATIVE PIPING

◆ Use piping to decorate the main seams of a loose cover and to strengthen the cover at its weakest points or to finish off the edges of an eiderdown.

◆ If you are using covered piping, it is less time-consuming to make a continuous length and cut as required. One metre (3ft) of narrow material will make about 24m (73ft) of 4cm ($1\frac{1}{2}$in) piping.

◆ Wash the piping cord before covering it if it is not pre-shrunk, and allow it to dry; otherwise it will shrink when you wash the loose cover.

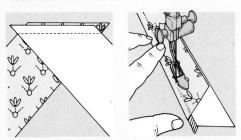

Making piping *Cut the material into strips on the bias. Join the strips together with stitching on the lengthwise grain, above left, and press the seams open. Fold the material in half lengthwise, then lay the cord in the fold. Stitch close to the cord, using the piping foot on your sewing machine and stretching the bias material slightly as you work, above right. Roll the finished piping in hanks or round a wide piece of cardboard, to stop it from tangling.*

Child Care

DAY-TO-DAY CARE

When the children are very young, they will take up a lot of your time and energy. Don't attempt the impossible, let your standards slip if necessary and do only as much as you really have to; the children are far more important than the housework. If you are out at work all day, make the most of the time you have with them; play with them until they go to bed and have your supper or do any chores later on.

HOW TO GET HELP

◆ If you are out at work and you can't afford a full-time nanny, look into sharing one with a friend who lives nearby; you can always alternate so that the children are at your house one week and your friend's the next. Alternatively, find out if anyone in your area offers a child-minding service.

◆ If you have several friends in the neighbourhood you could organize a baby-sitting rota, so that you babysit for each other as necessary.

◆ Ask friendly neighbouring teenagers to babysit occasionally in the evening; they will welcome the extra pocket money. Choose those whom you know to be trustworthy and whom your children know and like, then the children won't mind waking up when you are out.

◆ Look out for babysitting agencies who will provide responsible and vetted people to look after your children; these agencies often provide a daytime service as well as an evening one.

BATHING

Make bath times happy and relaxing and include plenty of play time – your child is less likely to develop a fear of water.

◆ Very young babies don't need bathing every day as long as you clean their faces, hands and bottom at least once a day. So save yourself some work.

Bathing a young baby

◆ To help your back, wash the baby in a baby's bath, placed on a special stand, kitchen worktop or a table. The best baby's baths are made of sculpted plastic with a non-slip surface and a sloping back. You can bath a very small baby in a plastic household basin on the draining board or in the kitchen or bathroom sink. If you use the sink, keep the baby's legs away from the taps – he could injure himself.

◆ Only fill the bath with a small amount of water until you get used to bathing a new baby; it's much easier to handle him in shallow water.

WASHING A VERY YOUNG BABY

TOPPING AND TAILING

Do this if you don't want to bath a young baby every day. Lay the baby on a firm padded surface undressed to his vest and nappy. Using moistened cotton wool, clean the face (use a new piece of cotton wool for each eye to prevent infection passing from one eye to the other), around the ears, then hands. Remove the nappy and wipe the area with damp cotton wool if he is just wet or with baby lotion or a squirt of bath liquid if he is soiled.

GIVING A BATH

You need:
◇ A large, soft towel
◇ Mild baby soap or baby bath liquid
◇ Face cloth or sponge (or you can use your hand if you prefer)
◇ Cotton wool
◇ Baby lotion
◇ Zinc and castor oil ointment
◇ New disposable nappy or clean fabric nappy and liner
◇ Clean clothes

1 Fill the bath. The temperature should be the same as the baby's body temperature (85°F/29°C). Test the temperature by putting your elbow in the water; it should feel just warm.

2 Lay your baby on a flat surface to undress him, but leave a vest on to keep him warm. Wipe the nappy area with cotton wool, moistened with a little baby lotion.

3 Remove the vest and wrap your baby in a towel while you clean his eyes, ears and nose with moistened cotton wool as for topping and tailing.

4 Hold your baby's head over the bath and wash his hair. The best way to hold him is to support his head and body on your forearm with his legs in your armpit. Rinse and pat gently dry with a towel.

5 Remove the towel. Support your baby's shoulders with your forearm and tuck your hand under his arm. Cradle your baby's legs with the other arm and gently lower him into the bath. Keep the baby semi-upright so that his head and shoulders are clear of the water.

6 Gently sponge the baby, or just wash him with your hand. When the baby is clean and rinsed, place your hand under his bottom and lift him gently out of the bath.

7 Lay him diagonally across the towel. Fold the bottom corner of the towel up and the two side corners across, making a little cocoon. Be particularly careful to dry all the folds and creases to prevent rashes or cracked skin.

▼▼ Don't leave a very young baby undres-
◆ ◆ sed for more than a couple of minutes because a baby can't regulate his own body temperature very well.
◆ Don't use baby powders – they make a baby's skin too dry.

Bathing an older baby or toddler

◆ Cover the hot tap with a flannel so that your baby won't hurt himself if he grabs it.
◆ Introduce your baby to a bigger bath gently; if you do it too quickly it may frighten him. Place the old, small bath in the big one to bath him. After a few baths, remove the little bath and fill the big one with a small amount of water. Fill the big bath a little higher than before each time you bath him; your baby will soon become used to the large bath and forget about the small one.
◆ Make bath time a treat by having a special set of toys. Household items such as plastic colanders or funnels, measuring spoons or ice-cube trays all make good toys.
◆ Let the water out of the bath after you take the baby out; the sound of the water going down the drain might frighten him.
▼▼ Don't let a baby stand in the bath with-
◆ ◆ out your support; he could fall in.

Supporting an older baby *Even if a baby can sit upright, put your arm around him and hold onto the thigh furthest from you. Put a non-slip mat in the bath for the baby to sit on.*

> ## TIPS FOR SAFE BATHING
>
> ◆ Use a rubber safety mat. Don't let your baby slip down under the water or try to see if he can sit unsupported – he might tumble in. A bad fright could put a baby off baths for a long time.
>
> ▼▼ Never leave a baby or young child ◆◆ alone in the bath; he could slip and hurt himself or even drown. A baby can drown in very shallow water.
>
> ◆ Put cold water into the bath first, then the hot, so that the surface of the bath doesn't get too hot.
>
> ◆ Don't add hot water to the bath while the baby is in it; you could hurt him if the water is hotter than you expect.

Fear of baths

If a child is frightened of baths, try to find out the reason, then change the circumstances if necessary. Fear could be caused by: a large bath; too much water in the bath; memory of a past incident of slipping under the water. Don't force your baby to have a bath: give him sponge baths until the fear subsides.

◆ Re-introduce a baby to the idea of water and being undressed gently. Put his favourite toys in a bowl of water on the floor for him to play with. Or undress your baby and lay him on a large towel on the bathroom floor with the bowl of water and the toys. He will soon

Overcoming fear of water *Fill the kitchen sink with a couple of inches of warm water. Put a towel on the draining board and some of your baby's favourite toys in the sink. Sit him on the towel on the draining board and let him paddle in the water for a while.*

get used to being near water and you can then introduce him to shallow baths – feet first, making it a game. The desire to play with the toys will eventually overcome the fear of water. If this doesn't work, try the same method in another room, say the kitchen, but make sure that it's warm.

Hair washing

Try to make hair washing as pleasant as possible, particularly for older babies because they often develop a hatred of hair washing, which could develop into being frightened of water in general.

◆ To prevent a dry skin condition called cradle cap, wash a new baby's hair every day with a mild baby shampoo, then brush it with a soft bristle brush.

◆ Keep the baby's face and eyes as dry as possible; shampoo can sting the eyes. Use a hair shield if necessary, see overleaf. If the child is old enough, encourage him to hold a face flannel over his eyes while you are washing his hair.

◆ Don't pour water directly over a child's head – children nearly always hate this; use the shower head, directed carefully away from his face.

◆ If your baby really hates having his hair washed, give it up for a few weeks; it won't hurt the hair to miss a few washes. Clean sticky bits out of dirty hair by brushing with a soft damp brush or a sponge. At any rate dissociate hair washing from bath time, which should always be a happy time.

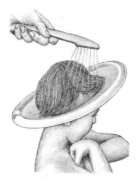

Using a hair washing shield *Fit the shield over your child's head, at the hairline, to stop the water running down his forehead into his eyes.*

NAPPY CHANGING

◆ If you live in a large house, keep a duplicate set of nappy changing equipment downstairs to save running up and down stairs whenever you need to change a nappy.

◆ Make sure the new nappy is not too tight by running your fingers around the legs; if it is too tight, it will rub your baby's legs and cause a rash.

◆ Run your fingers around the baby's waist to make sure the nappy is tight enough; if it's too loose, it will slide off.

◆ Hang a mobile above the nappy changing area to distract the baby while you change him. Placate a very wriggly or kicking baby with a favourite toy or letting him hold the cream (provided the lid is screwed on firmly). If you have an older child, enrol him as a means of distraction.

◆ Change the nappy on the floor or on a work surface at waist level. Don't bend down

Changing a boy's nappy *Lay a clean nappy over a boy's penis as soon as you take the old nappy off because boys often urinate into the air when changed.*

to change a nappy on a bed, you'll give yourself backache.

Using disposable nappies

◆ Keep a safety pin or roll of masking tape handy in case you tear the adhesive strip, or in case it won't stick.

◆ ECONOMY TIP: Use disposable pads in separate tie-on pants when the baby is ill with a bad stomach – frequent changes will work out cheaper this way.

◆ Put a paper liner in a disposable nappy to make faeces easier to dispose of.

◆ Keep a supply of fabric nappies in case you run out of disposables.

◆ At night a standard pad inside an all-in-one nappy will give extra absorbency. Alternatively, a pair of tie-on plastic pants over an all-in-one nappy will hold even the worst leaks for a while.

CHANGING A NAPPY

◆ Assemble all the paraphernalia for nappy changing before you start, in order to minimize fuss. You need:
◇ *Changing mat*
◇ *New disposable nappy or a clean fabric nappy, nappy liner, safety pins and a pair of plastic pants*
◇ *Cotton wool*
◇ *Baby lotion, baby oil or water containing a squirt of baby bath liquid*
◇ *Tissues or baby wipes*
◇ *Zinc and castor oil cream*
◇ *Clean clothes*
◇ *Distracting toy*

1 *Take off the dirty nappy, using the front of it to wipe off any faeces. Fold the dirty nappy in two and slide it underneath his bottom.*
2 *Clean the baby's legs, top and bottom, and clean the genital area. With a boy, wipe across the lower abdomen up to his navel to remove all trace of urine and prevent nappy rash in this area.*
3 *Put the clean nappy on and dress the baby again. Put the baby somewhere safe (in the baby bouncer, on a mat or in the cot) while you rinse the dirty nappy and put it to soak (or if disposable, dispose of it), then wash your hands.*

Using fabric nappies

◆Always buy the best quality you can afford; they will last longer. You need to buy at least 24; the more you have, the less often you will have to do the washing.

◆Keep your fingers between the nappy and your baby's skin when putting the pin into the fabric so that you don't stab him.

◆Keep a pile of ready-folded nappies with their nappy liners in place. It will save you a lot of time when you are changing the baby's nappy.

Washing fabric nappies

◆Use beer-making bins as nappy buckets because they have lids, are bigger than normal buckets and are quite cheap.

◆Change the nappy sterilizing solution once a day to minimize germs.

◆Keep a plastic bag near the cot for changing nappies at night, to save you searching for the bucket in the dark.

◆To stop the soaking buckets smelling, hook an air freshener to the side of the buckets, just above the waterline.

◆If there's no time to soak wet nappies before washing them, rinse them thoroughly then wash. Soiled nappies must be soaked for at least 12 hours before being washed to kill the bacteria in the faeces.

◆Use plastic tongs or rubber gloves for lifting nappies out of the sterilizing solution, because it contains bleach. Don't splash your clothes.

◆Dry nappies in a tumble dryer or in the open air to keep the fabric soft. If neither of these is possible, get a rack to put over the bath or fit a pull-out line.

▼▼Don't dry terry nappies on radiators; it ◆◆hardens the fabric, which rubs the baby's skin, causing a rash.

▼▼Don't use a fabric conditioner in the ◆◆nappy wash, the residue can irritate the baby's skin.

CLOTHES

◆Keep your child's measurements in your diary and update them regularly; then you are less likely to buy clothes that are too small for him.

◆Buy unisex clothes, particularly when the children are young, so you can use them for the next child; children always grow out of the clothes before they wear out.

◆Buy machine-washable easy-care clothing; you'll never have enough time to hand wash your baby's clothes.

◆Buy T-shirts and vests with envelope necks, they are easier to get over the baby's head. Vests with poppers that do up in the crotch are good in winter as they don't creep up and leave a cold gap around the baby's stomach.

◆Clothes that do up down the front are easier: you don't have to turn the baby over to dress him.

◆Buy clothes with popper neck fastenings; they will fit the baby for longer because you

---

CLOTHING A NEW BABY

Buy the minimum; when the baby is born you'll find out which clothes are the most useful and can then get more.

CLOTHES FOR A SUMMER BABY
◇4 vests or T-shirts
◇4 summer-weight all-in-one stretch suits
◇2 cardigans – don't get ones with big lacy holes, fingers get caught in them.
◇2 pairs cotton socks
◇2 nightdresses – get the type with drawstring bottoms to prevent draughts

CLOTHES FOR A WINTER BABY
◇4 vests
◇4 all-in-one stretch suits
◇2 nightdresses
◇2 pairs woollen socks – buy the type with ribbons round the ankle part or they will fall off all the time
◇2 pairs mittens
◇4 cardigans or jackets
◇1 woollen hat

can leave the neck fastening undone to accommodate his head.

◆ Buy outdoor clothes at least one size too big, they'll last longer. Buy a hat that fastens under the chin so that the baby can't pull it off. Allow room for thick socks inside wellington boots.

Dressing and undressing

◆ If your child won't make a fist when you are putting on his pullover, give him a treat such as a raisin; he will grasp at it, making a fist, so you can dress him easily. Don't do this too often, though, or he will start to expect it every time you dress him.

◆ To stop shoe laces coming undone, wet them before doing them up.

◆ Fit Velcro fastening to a toddler's clothes while he is learning to dress himself; it is much easier for him than a button or zip. Avoid using Velcro as a neck fastening because it can rub his skin and cause a rash.

◆ Buy trousers with elasticated waists, they are easier for a child to put on himself, or pull down when going to the toilet. Don't buy zip trousers for a young boy, he could catch his penis in the zip.

◆ Put a keyring on a zip fastener so that small hands can hold onto it more easily.

◆ Buy machine-washable trainer pants for potty training, with towelling inside and plastic outside; if they are not machine-washable, the plastic goes hard after a few washes, and feels very uncomfortable against the skin.

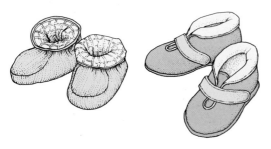

Babies' and toddlers' shoes *Washable fabric shoes with elastic around the ankles are ideal indoor shoes for babies and toddlers because they don't fall off, above left. For older toddlers who are learning to dress themselves, look for shoes with Velcro fastenings so that they can dress themselves, above right.*

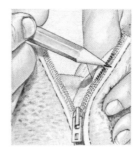

Easing a sticking zipper *To ease a sticking zipper, rub pencil lead or soap over it so that it runs properly.*

CRYING

Hunger is the most common cause of crying in very young babies, but anything from bright lights, a hard surface or a sudden loud noise, to pain, boredom and the need for physical comfort can upset a baby and make him cry.

◆ Comfort your baby promptly when he is crying; it will prevent problems of insecurity when he is older.

◆ Don't feed by the clock – feed when the baby lets you know that he wants to be fed. A full stomach is the most comforting thing of all for a young baby and it won't harm to feed him a little earlier than you'd expected.

◆ Babies sometimes cry if they get too cold. If a nappy is wet and cold, your baby will feel this as discomfort. Put an extra pad in the night nappy so that he won't be woken up by the discomfort of a wet nappy. If he gets cold in bed because his blanket or quilt falls off, secure the blanket or quilt to the side of the cot so that he can't kick it off, see opposite, or put him to bed in a sleep suit.

◆ If your baby cries whenever you put him to bed, he probably instinctively feels happier with physical contact. Try rubbing his back, or even his earlobe, gently. If he doesn't settle reasonably quickly, pick him up and carry him in a sling or shawl or against your shoulder close to your heartbeat. Try wrapping a very young baby firmly in a shawl before putting him down; this can make him feel more secure.

◆ Many quite small babies cry when they are bored. Hang a mobile above the cot or a pram toy across it; tie toys to the bars, or put pictures or a baby safety mirror on the side of the cot beside his head so that he has something to look at, see page 296.

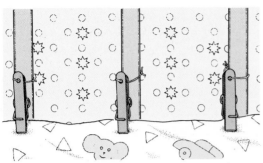

Keeping a baby warm *Tie clothes pegs or bulldog clips to the side of the cot and attach them to the blanket or quilt to hold it in place.*

SLEEP

A newborn baby should fall asleep the moment he is tired. To help him settle:

◇ *See that the room is comfortably warm*
◇ *Darken the room at night*
◇ *Rock the baby gently or just place your hand on his cheek or shoulder. Babies find this soothing.*

◆ Make bedtime as happy and relaxing as possible; your baby will be more likely to sleep through the night if he is relaxed and feels secure. With an older baby of about six months or so, develop a routine that helps him to unwind at the end of the day – bath, drink, put him into bed and have a chat about the day, read a story and/or sing a song.

◆ Put your baby to bed on a special lambskin, he will find it warm and very comforting to sleep on.

◆ Don't put your child to bed immediately after a rough game, he will be wide awake and won't be able to go to sleep.

◆ If an older baby, say, over nine months is determined to stay awake even when quite sleepy, let him stay up a little longer, give him a drink and another story; he may forget about trying to stay awake. Overtiredness causes tension, which makes getting to sleep difficult. If your child is going through a bad phase, don't take him out with you in the evening; it will disrupt the routine and he is more likely to be difficult about going to bed when you are at home.

◆ Allow your baby to take up a security habit such as thumb sucking or holding a favourite blanket or teddy; it will make him feel better and help him to fall asleep more easily. He will grow out of it after a while.

◆ Put musical mobiles above the cot; babies are fascinated by them, and can be lulled to sleep by them.

◆ If your baby resists bed night after night, say goodnight firmly and leave him to cry for about 10 minutes; then, and only then, go back to him or pick him up. If he still won't settle, put him in the car and go for a drive; the motion will probably send him to sleep.

Coping with night wakers

◆ If your baby is very young, always respond when he cries to forestall problems of insecurity later. Take it in turns with your partner so that you both get some sleep. Both of you should try to get early nights at least twice a week.

◆ Make night feeds as brief as possible by having everything prepared beforehand, keeping the lights low and not making this a play time. That way the baby won't wake up properly and is more likely to go back to sleep. Don't change his nappy unless it is really wet because changing him may wake him up and stop him getting back to sleep.

◆ Make sure the child is the right temperature. If he is too hot, remove a blanket if necessary. If the baby seems cold, or gets cold easily, put a safety heater with a thermostat in the bedroom to keep the temperature constant.

◆ If your child wakes up because he is afraid of the dark, put a low-wattage nightlight in the room or install a dimmer switch and leave a light on low all night.

◆ If your child has a nightmare, comfort him and don't leave him until he is calm. Recurrent nightmares may be from external causes – a new baby minder, for instance, or your prolonged absence. Try to find out the cause and talk to your child about it.

◆ Don't keep checking on a sleeping baby, you may end up disturbing him. Keep such checking to a minimum (say, just before your own bedtime).

◆ Check for nappy rash – a common cause of discomfort, which may wake a baby up.

◆ If you are exhausted after a bad night, have an afternoon nap when the baby has his. If you are out at work during the day, go to bed as soon as the baby is asleep; if you leave the chores until the next day, you'll have more energy to cope with them. Try to fit in naps at the weekend as well.

Early wakers

◆ Leave some toys or a play centre in the cot so your baby has something to play with when he wakes up. Make sure that the room is not too dark in the morning so that he has enough light to play by.

◆ Don't leap out of bed at the first murmur, he'll start to expect it – leave him to play for a while. Get up only if he sounds fretful.

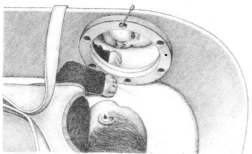

Alleviating boredom *Tie a little safety mirror to the side of the basket or cot, so that the baby can gaze at it if he wakes up.*

PLAY

Buy machine-washable soft toys, especially for very young babies, they are easier to clean. You can wash non-machine-washable soft toys with carpet or upholstery shampoo, but rinse thoroughly.

Minimizing mess

◆ Make a tray for paint pots by gouging holes in a block of polystyrene. This will prevent the paints from tipping over. Alternatively, buy paint pots with non-spill lids. Store paint brushes and pots in cutlery trays.

◆ Whenever your child is doing any gluing, painting or other "wet" activity, cover the table and surrounding floor with newspaper and put a plastic apron or overall on him so that his clothes don't get covered in paint.

◆ Encourage children to put things away. Keep your shoe boxes – dolls can be "put to bed" or farm animals "into the barn". Shoe

Storing small objects
Plastic margarine or ice-cream containers are ideal for storing little dolls, marbles and small bricks.

boxes also make good dolls' wardrobes and containers for tiny "found" objects.

◆ Put small items into large clear plastic jars with lids so that you can see at a glance which toys are inside.

◆ Label boxes and jars with brightly coloured labels (from stationery shops) so that you know where everything is.

◆ Keep a basket in each room for collecting up strewn toys for an easy tidy up – one per child if you have room, then you won't muddle up precious possessions.

SAFETY TIPS FOR TOYS

▼▼ Never let your baby have anything
◆◆ small enough to swallow: no marbles, small shells, counters, chess men. Babies love putting things in their mouths and all these items will choke them if swallowed accidentally.

◆ Make sure painted toys are lead free, because lead is poisonous. Imported toys bought in street markets are the ones to watch for particularly.

◆ Don't give a child toys with sharp edges because he could injure himself. Metal toys can be very dangerous.

◆ Never leave a young baby alone while he is playing; he could swallow something or cut himself.

◆ Buy soft toys displaying a safety label because they have to be made to a particular standard. Don't buy toys with loose eyes, eyes held in place with wire or seams that look weak; your child could choke or hurt himself on the eyes or bits of stuffing.

◆ Always buy non-toxic paint for children – they may suck the brushes or lick their fingers.

Protecting clothes
If your child is painting, protect his clothes with a plastic overall with elasticated sleeves. These overalls are also useful if he is "helping with the washing up".

Cleaning toys

◆ Wash sturdy plastic toys in the dishwasher; don't do this to thin plastic toys or they'll melt; wash them by hand.

GREEN TIP: Shake non-washable soft toys in a bag with baking powder, and then brush clean. Sponge smelly toys with a cloth wrung out in a solution of 10g (2tsp) baking soda to 600ml (1pt) water to get rid of any unpleasant smells.

IMPROVISED TOYS

YOUNG BABIES

Everything is interesting at this age. Here is a list of safe and entertaining objects you can find around the house:

◇ *Rolling things like cardboard tubes and empty cotton reels*

◇ *Round objects such as oranges or grapefruit, balls of string or wool*

◇ *Flat things and hard things such as a table mat, a ruler, wooden spoons*

◇ *Light things made of foam rubber, a shaped bath sponge for instance. Don't give him a sponge if he has teeth because he could pull bits off and swallow them*

◇ *Things with holes big enough for a little hand or finger – napkin rings, rolls of sticky tape and so on*

◇ *Rattly things – a plastic jar with beans or beads in (but only if the lid can be tightly screwed on and taped)*

◇ *Large and fairly heavy (but safe) things – a football or a cushion*

◇ *Things with interesting textures – strips of felt or other material, a fir cone*

◇ *Kitchen utensils such as a plastic sieve, or measuring spoons for playing in the bath*

Suitable toys for young babies

OLDER BABIES AND TODDLERS

◆ Start a dressing-up box. Old shoes, shirts, skirts, dresses, hats and scarves will provide endless entertainment. Real uniforms (you can sometimes get them from second-hand shops) are good too.

◆ Make your own finger paints by mixing 50ml (2fl oz) liquid starch with four drops of food colouring.

◆ Make modelling dough by combining flour and salt (three parts flour to one part salt) and add this to one part water. The dough can be coloured with food colouring or powder paints and will keep for a week or so in an airtight container.

◆ Make an innocuous glue from 1 part flour and 2 parts water with a teaspoon of salt. Put the flour and salt into a saucepan and stir the water into the flour slowly until it is absorbed. Simmer the paste for five minutes and allow to cool before use. (This is a good paste for making papier mâché, see page 220.)

◆ Keep rolls of drawing paper on a kitchen towel dispenser so that it is always close at hand when you need it.

Hand puppets *Make puppets out of brown paper bags with faces drawn on them, or out of old socks with faces sewn onto them.*

FEEDING BABIES AND TODDLERS

How you feed babies or young children can influence not only their present state of health but also their health in the future. Breast feeding is best for a baby and simplest for you but bottle feeding can be perfectly satisfactory if for any reason you are not going to, or can't, breast feed. Once you have weaned your child and established her on solid food, it is important to vary her diet so that she doesn't get bored with her food, as well as to make sure that she gets the variety of nutrients that she needs.

BREAST FEEDING

The advantages of breast feeding are that the milk is there all the time, at the right temperature and you don't have to spend hours sterilizing all of the equipment and making up formula milk.

◆ Start your baby suckling at your breast as soon as possible after the birth to establish a bond between you and your child. Ask for her to be put to your breast as soon as she is born – while you are still in the delivery room if possible.

◆ Put your baby to the breast regularly in the first days after birth (every time she cries) only for a few minutes each time, alternating breasts. This will make her feel more secure.

◆ Use a pillow to bring her a bit nearer to the breast if she is too far away. Don't bend or strain down to bring the nipple to the baby's mouth; you won't be able to hold the position for long and she may pull on the nipple, which will hurt you.

◆ Get your nipple well inside the baby's mouth so that she can suck properly and also so that you don't develop sore nipples.

◆ If your breast is very full, press it down so that the baby's nose is not buried in it, making it difficult for her to breathe.

◆ If your milk is pouring out too quickly, choking the baby, you can slow it down by expressing milk before you start feeding.

◆ If milk gushes from the breast not being fed from, press the palm of your hand over the areola to stop the flow.

▼▼ Don't pull the baby off the breast. This
◆ ◆ will hurt your nipple. Loosen her mouth by pressing gently on her chin or inserting your little finger into her mouth to get her to open it.

◆ Buy a nursing bra with wide straps so that the straps don't dig into your shoulders. For easier feeding, choose a front-fastening bra with individual flaps.

◆ It is worth buying equipment for bottle feeding in case you have trouble breast feeding – you are more likely to relax, knowing that you have an alternative.

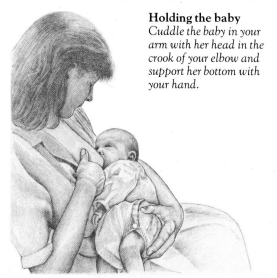

Holding the baby
Cuddle the baby in your arm with her head in the crook of your elbow and support her bottom with your hand.

Expressing milk

◆ Keep all equipment sterilized because babies are prone to gastric infections.

◆ If the squeezing hurts, you are doing something wrong. Stop and try again.

◆ Store expressed milk in a sterilized container; it will keep in the fridge for 48 hours or it can be frozen for six months.

TIPS FOR ENSURING A GOOD MILK SUPPLY

◆ Get as much rest as possible, particularly when the baby is very young. Go to bed early whenever you can. Your sleeping patterns will be broken up anyway. Behave like a cat and take small naps during the day, or curl up on the sofa with a book, while the baby is sleeping. Don't bother too much with the housework. Leave all but the most urgent things until the baby is weaned – the baby is more important.

◆ Drink at least 3.5 litres (6pt) of fluid a day while you are breast feeding and make sure you have a well-balanced diet. Don't eat a lot of refined foods, because they contain empty calories.

◆ Give yourself the odd treat when you have a moment to yourself to make you feel more relaxed – a glass of wine at the end of the day, say, or a hot bath. Don't drink spirits because they can harm the baby; don't have a heavily scented bath because the baby can be put off by the smell of your nipple.

BOTTLE FEEDING

The advantage of bottle feeding is that you can share the feeding with your partner.

◆ Buy sterilizing equipment and bottles before the baby is born so you can become used to it beforehand.

◆ Keep the equipment in the kitchen near a tap, so that you don't have to carry a full sterilizing bath about.

◆ Sterilize everything you use to prepare the feeds as well as the bottles, following the manufacturer's instructions exactly. Young babies are very prone to gastric infections. Continue to sterilize all feeding equipment until your baby is at least four months old, to prevent an upset stomach.

◆ Look out for the steam sterilizing units; they are easier to use than conventional units – they sterilize up to four bottles and teats in only five minutes and the bottles don't need rinsing afterwards.

Sterilizing bottles

For conventional sterilizing you need:
◇ *A sterilizing bath*
◇ *Sterilizing tablets*
◇ *A bottle brush*
◇ *Salt*
◇ *6–8 bottles and 12 teats*
◇ *A measuring jug*
◇ *A long-handled spoon and a knife*

1 Put the bottles into warm, soapy water and remove all traces of milk using the bottle brush. Remove any traces of milk inside the teats by rubbing them with salt.

2 Thoroughly rinse the bottles and teats in fresh warm water. Half fill the sterilizing bath with cold water and dissolve a sterilizing tablet in it.

3 Put all the bottles, teats, the measuring jug and the spoon into the sterilizing bath. Fill the bottles as you put them in so that they sink to the bottom. Then fill the bath with cold water.

4 Fit the lid and leave for the required time or until you need the first bottle. Rinse everything with boiled water before using it to get rid of the smell.

Preparing formula milk

◆ Always wash your hands before sterilizing the feeding equipment or preparing and giving feeds, to minimize the risk of passing infection to your baby.

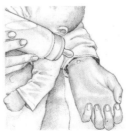

Getting a bottle to the right temperature *Stand the bottle in a bowl of hot water to warm it. Test the temperature of the milk on your wrist before you give it to the baby, above left. If it is too hot, run it under the cold tap, above right.*

How to hold the bottle *Keep the bottle at an angle so that the teat will always be full of milk, otherwise the baby will take in air with the milk, which will give her wind.*

◆ Make up a full day's batch of bottles each time; it's just as easy to make up six bottles as it is to make one bottle. Store the made-up bottles and any opened packets or tins of formula milk in the refrigerator.

◆ Make up the feeds precisely to the instructions so that the baby gets a balanced diet – level off the scoops of powder with the back of the knife. Too little will leave her unsatisfied; too much may be too rich for her, and could make her sick.

◆ Take a bottle out of the fridge half an hour before feeding and allow it to come to room temperature (like a bottle of wine, but don't take the top off).

▼▼ Once warmed, give milk to the baby
◆ ◆ straight away; the warmth encourages germs to multiply. For the same reason, never store warm milk in a thermos flask; throw left-over milk away – don't be tempted to keep it for later.

◆ Check the milk flow before feeding your baby by inverting the bottle – the milk should come out at several drops per second. A steady flow is too fast and means the hole in the teat is too big. If the milk comes out too quickly, it can choke the baby.

TIPS FOR BOTTLE FEEDING

◆ Hold the baby in a slightly sloping position – head higher than feet; otherwise she may gag or be sick.

◆ Don't force the baby to finish a bottle, she will know when she has had enough milk to satisfy her needs.

▼▼ Never leave the bottle propped up
◆ ◆ on a cushion when feeding. The wrong angle may cause the baby to take in too much air, making her uncomfortable or, worse still, she could choke.

STARTING SOLID FOOD

◆ Start introducing your baby to solids when she is about four months old, or sooner if she appears very unsatisfied after a bottle, or wants an extra feed every day.

◆ Start with bland semi-liquids like purées, which have a creamy consistency, to get her used to the change. Mix a couple of spoonfuls of solid with the normal milk feed or boiled water at first, then gradually reduce the milk content. Try one type of food at a time and stick with it for a few meals to see if she likes it.

◆ It is cheaper and probably healthier to prepare the baby's food yourself, see below.

◆ If you use branded baby food, buy one for the correct age group and check the contents label carefully.

◆ Give your child plenty of fluid. Drinks are important. Fresh fruit juice is most nutritious and won't decay the teeth like heavily sugared squash.

Helping your baby to eat solids *If your baby won't eat from a spoon, feed her with the tip of your finger.*

Preparing and cooking food

◆ Keep food simple; if you spend hours making something, you'll feel resentful towards your child if she doesn't eat it.

◆ Always peel fruit and chop it into tiny pieces before cooking, to make sure there are no lumps that could cause the baby to choke. Cook the fruit in a little water until soft, then sieve or purée it.

◆ The quickest and easiest way to purée foods for a baby is with a blender or food processor. Hand-held blenders in particular are good for small quantities.

IDEAS FOR HEALTHY SNACKS

Plan snacks carefully and consider them as a complement to the whole day's nutrition. Serve different foods in snacks and at mealtimes so that your child doesn't lose interest in meals.

◆ Try freezing yogurt, it looks like ice cream and is much healthier.

◆ If your child has a few teeth, peel a whole apple and give it to her to bite on. She won't choke because she won't be able to chew off large enough bits.

◆ Cubes of cheese, chunks of celery or carrot and bread are all good standbys.

Making snacks inviting *Cut pieces of cheese into unusual shapes or lay pieces of fruit out in a pattern or to look like a train or an animal.*

FOOD NOT TO GIVE BABIES OR TODDLERS

BABIES

◇ *Spicy foods or foods containing salt – a baby's kidneys can't process them*

◇ *Sugary foods and drinks – the sugar causes tooth decay*

◇ *Unripe fruit – it causes diarrhoea*

◇ *Oily or smoked fish or meat, salt beef or pastrami because of the saturated fat and salt content*

◇ *Shellfish – it contains saturated fats*

◇ *Alcohol, coffee or tea – they are stimulants*

◇ *Yeast extract – it's too salty*

◇ *Raisins, currants, sultanas, whole nuts, fruit with seeds or chunky peanut butter – the pips or nuts could choke a baby.*

TODDLERS

◇ *Whole nuts*

◇ *Sugary drinks*

◇ *Alcohol, tea or coffee*

◇ *Salty dishes*

◇ *Rough wholemeal bread with whole grains of wheat*

◇ *Unpeeled, thick-skinned fruit*

◇ *Fruits with whole stones or pips*

◇ *Small chunks of raw fruit or vegetables.*

Freezing purée *If you prepare too much purée, freeze it in ice-cube trays. You can thaw the blocks in the microwave, if you have one.*

◆ Cool hot food quickly: put it in a bowl of cold water or put it straight into the fridge; germs multiply fast in tepid food.

◆ Don't soak vegetables before cooking because soaking destroys some vitamins.

◆ Cook fruit and vegetables with just a little water and with a tightly fitting lid to preserve nutrients, or, better still, steam them.

◆ Leave soft edible skins on fruit because they help to retain the vitamins – light destroys some vitamins, see page 46.

◆ Don't use unlined copper pans because the copper breaks down vitamin C. Using cast-iron pans can help top up your child's iron intake because a small amount of iron will be absorbed into the food.

Children who won't eat

◆ Don't force a child to eat or meals will become a battleground. Leave her and try again later when she is hungry. Don't give her any snacks between meals for a while, until her appetite returns.

◆ Try making a game out of eating. Put vegetables on a piece of bread to form a face, serve food on a doll's plate or give her some blunt plastic "grown up" cutlery.

◆ Let your child help you prepare snacks or meals because it may make her become more interested in the food.

TIPS FOR HEALTHY EATING

◆ Give your child at least one protein dish at each meal – protein is needed for growth. Foods with high protein content are: chicken, lamb, beef, pork, fish, eggs, cheese, nuts, legumes.

◆ Offer plenty of milk and dairy products (milk, cream, yogurt, cheese) because they are high in protein. Don't give children skimmed milk because some of the protein, vitamins and other nutrients that your child needs are removed during the skimming process.

◆ Give your children fish and chicken rather than red meats because they don't contain saturated fats, see page 46.

◆ Don't give your children crushed or bruised fruit and vegetables because the bruising destroys vitamin C.

◆ See that your child has at least four servings of fruit and vegetables a day, either at meal times or as a snack, so that she gets an adequate supply of vitamins and minerals, see page 46.

◆ Give your child cereal foods (particularly wholemeal bread and noodles) for their fibre content, see page 45.

◆ Serve fruit and sugar-free yogurts rather than sweet puddings, carob rather than chocolate, and use fruit concentrate rather than sugar to sweeten things; sugar encourages tooth decay. Avoid "empty" calories in the form of cakes, biscuits and sweets – they satisfy only temporarily and leave the child craving for more. Ration sweets, perhaps as a reward for good behaviour or as a special treat.

◆ Serve small amounts and keep some in reserve for second helpings, instead of giving her large portions.

Minimizing mess

◆ Confine eating to one room so that mess is concentrated in one part of the home.

◆ Begin using a bib when the baby starts on solids to keep the baby's clothes clean.

◆ Put a pile of tissues under the neckline of the bib to stop any drink running down the baby's neck when she's learning to drink.

◆ Put a newspaper or plastic sheet under the high chair or table to protect the floor.

◆ Keep the baby well away from walls with expensive coverings when she is eating. It is great fun to see how far food will fly.

◆ Fit a paper towel holder to the wall near the high chair or to the back of a high chair so that you always have a cloth at the ready.

◆ When your baby decides it is time to feed herself, let her. As well as letting her use the spoon, prepare some foods that she can eat without one, which makes for less messy and less frustrating feeding. Fruit and vegetables can be cut into chunks or slices minus the skin and pips; shape mashed potato or rice into little grasp-sized balls or cut bread into small cubes.

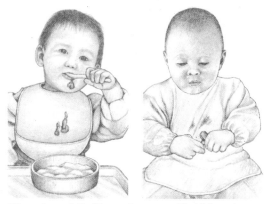

Choosing a bib *Use a plastic moulded bib with a crumb catcher, above left, for a baby who is learning to feed himself or a toddler; it's easier to contain the mess. Use machine-washable towelling ones for babies, the plastic ones can rub the neck – the best are the towelling ones with sleeves and with a plastic backing, above right.*

◆ Buy bowls with rubber suction pads on the bottom, which help to prevent the bowl being hurled onto the floor. Look for training beakers with a weighted base, which helps reduce spills.

TRAVEL AND OUTINGS

The best time to set out on any trip with a small baby is immediately after he has been fed and changed; the motion of the car or the pushchair will probably send him straight to sleep.

Find out what facilities are available at the shops and other public places you are going to visit. Some places have a special room for feeding, which is useful if you are going to be out for some time. Some supermarkets have trolleys with a basket/cradle for very young babies, which makes shopping much easier. Other places have no lifts or don't allow prams at all.

TAKING CHILDREN SHOPPING

♦ If you are breast feeding, wear the right clothes (two piece outfits or dresses that open down the front are best) and have a shawl or scarf to throw over your shoulder. Find a quiet place and try to face the wall so that you can get some privacy.

▼▼ Never put loaded shopping bags on the
♦ ♦ handles of a pram or pushchair – you might tip it backwards. Use a pram or pushchair with a basket underneath.

▼▼ Never tie a dog to a pram; it may decide
♦ ♦ it likes something on the other side of a road, and pull the pram over.

BUYING A PRAM OR PUSHCHAIR

♦ Choose a pram or pushchair with a wide base so that it is stable and won't tip up.
♦ Look for good, solid brakes that won't slip easily and that are easy to apply.
♦ Make sure there is a safety lock to prevent accidental collapse of a collapsible pram base or pushchair.
♦ Get a pushchair with an adjustable seat back so that your child can lie down if he wants to sleep.

♦ For safety buy a harness that clips onto the inside of a pram – get a harness with walking reins so that you can use it when your child starts to walk. Pushchairs or strollers are safer if they have a harness that can be adjusted for a baby or a toddler, or rings so that you can use a small harness.
♦ Buy a weatherproof cover and hood for a pushchair to keep your baby dry.

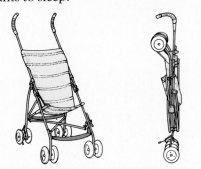

Stroller *If you travel on public transport a lot, it's worth buying a stroller because it folds up to the size of a large umbrella for easy carrying.*

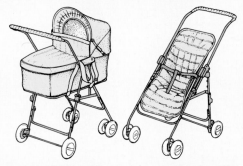

Pram/pushchair *If you want a pram, it is much cheaper to buy a carry cot and frame that can be converted into a pushchair when your baby grows out of the carry cot.*

Baby slings *Use fabric slings to carry a young baby against your chest; make sure that his head is well supported, above left. Once a baby can support his head he can be carried in a special carrying frame on your back, above right. Make sure the shoulder straps are well padded or they will dig into your shoulders, which is uncomfortable.*

◆ If you leave a pram, park it so that it won't roll into the road, even if the brakes fail. Never leave a child unattended in a pushchair or a pram.

▼▼ Never push a pram or pushchair out into
◆◆ the road until you know there is nothing coming. Never push it into the road in order to get a clearer view of the traffic.

◆ If you are walking or going on public transport, carry your baby or toddler in a sling or backpack, to leave your hands free for paying for, or carrying, things.

Crossing the road with toddlers

Teach your child good road sense from an early age. Always use the green cross code when crossing the road with your children.

1 Use subways where possible. Otherwise find a safe place to cross, such as a pedestrian crossing or controlled lights.

2 Stop at the kerb, look in both directions and listen for the traffic.

3 If traffic is coming, let it pass. Look in both directions again and, when nothing is coming, walk across the road. Keep looking and listening while you cross.

CAR JOURNEYS

◆ Never allow a child under ten to travel in the front passenger seat – even with a seat belt on – it is illegal in many countries anyway. Adult seat belts don't protect children, they are too high; they could in fact hurt them.

◆ Secure babies and toddlers in special seats (choose the correct one for the child's weight to provide adequate protection). Put a child in a child's safety belt.

◆ Always check that children's fingers will not be trapped when you close the door – they so often leave them in the way.

◆ Never turn round to talk to a child when you are driving. If the children are fighting, pull in, stop the car and sort it out. If you are on a motorway, leave at the nearest exit.

◆ Always use child locks on rear doors, then you can get the door open from the outside but the children can't open the door accidentally. If your car doesn't have them, get some fitted.

▼▼ Never let your child out of the car on the
◆◆ traffic side – teach him always to use the pavement side.

▼▼ Never let your child open a window
◆◆ more than a quarter of the way and make sure he never leans out or puts his hand or arm outside, even when the car is stationary.

▼▼ Don't put a child in the same safety belt
◆◆ as you. If there is an accident, your weight will crush the child.

▼▼ Don't, even briefly, leave your child
◆◆ unattended in the car; there are too many things in a car with which he could injure himself.

▼▼ Don't leave hard or sharp things lying
◆◆ about. These will become missiles if the car stops suddenly. Equally don't give the children pens, pencils or lollipops while the car is moving.

◆ Encourage the children to play quiet games; constant screaming is a dangerous distraction for a driver.

Long car journeys

◆ Take something to drink in a jug or vacuum flask and some paper cups. Bring small cartons of fruit juice with straws for the children, so that you don't end up with fruit juice all over the car. Drinks can help prevent travel sickness.

◆ Take some apples, dried fruit or cubes of cheese for nibbling instead of endless boiled sweets or sticky chocolate; if you have young children, peel a couple of apples before you leave and wrap them in plastic film to stop them going brown.

◆ Stop every hour or so for a few minutes and let the children stretch their legs, it'll relieve the boredom and use up energy.

◆ Keep a roll-up changing mat in the car for quick nappy changing, or a potty if you are in the middle of potty training.

◆ Keep a rubbish bag in the car for any litter that accumulates and a roll of paper towels and packet of wet wipes for wiping sticky fingers/faces.

◆ Take some soft and light toys and some books to read (provided neither you nor the children suffer from travel sickness).

CAR SEATS

Children are very vulnerable in cars because they are small and light, so they must be strapped into the car securely in case of accident.

◆ Put young or small babies – under 10kg (22lbs) – who cannot support their heads in a carry cot secured with restraining straps bolted to the car body or in a back-facing baby seat which is buckled into a safety belt.

◆ Put older babies who can support their own heads – and weigh more than 10kg (22lb) – and toddlers in an adjustable car seat secured to the rear seats either by a safety belt or by a strap which is bolted to the car frame.

◆ Get adjustable child safety belts fitted into the car for older children, say from three onwards. Use them in conjunction with a booster seat to begin with, until the child is tall enough to see out of the window, see below.

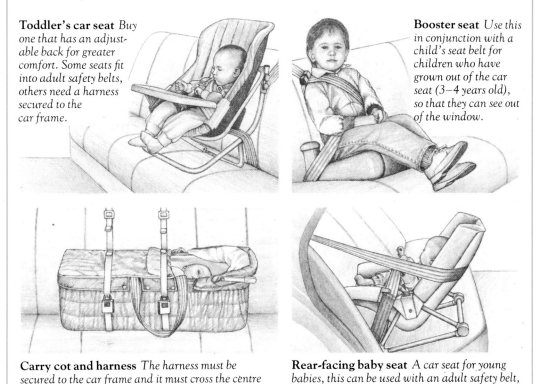

Toddler's car seat *Buy one that has an adjustable back for greater comfort. Some seats fit into adult safety belts, others need a harness secured to the car frame.*

Booster seat *Use this in conjunction with a child's seat belt for children who have grown out of the car seat (3–4 years old), so that they can see out of the window.*

Carry cot and harness *The harness must be secured to the car frame and it must cross the centre of the cot.*

Rear-facing baby seat *A car seat for young babies, this can be used with an adult safety belt, on the front or back seat of the car.*

KEEPING THE CHILDREN OCCUPIED

◆ Tie a rattle across or along the side of the car seat or carry cot to amuse the baby when he is awake. The movement of the car itself is often enough to send a small baby straight to sleep.

◆ Tune the car radio into a music station and keep a selection of tapes in the car. Story or nursery rhyme tapes keep children quiet for a long time. Take a variety though or you may end up listening to the same one time after time.

◆ Play some games, for example:

◇ *I spy with my little eye – try spotting colours, e.g. white cows or green trees, for children who can't read.*

◇ *The geography game: one person says "Paris", the next has to think of a place name beginning with "S" and so on.*

◇ *See who can form the shortest word possible using the three letters in the order in which they appear on the number plate of the car in front – e.g., for AMP – camp.*

◇ *See who can spot the most red cars, the most articulated trucks, or the most caravans on a journey.*

How to stave off travel sickness

Travel sickness is perfectly real and very inconvenient and unpleasant for everyone, although it's not serious.

◆ If your child suffers from travel sickness regularly, try giving him some travel sickness medicine before you set out.

◆ Give your child a small snack before setting out – nothing too rich or oily though.

◆ Take plenty of drinks. Sucking sweets or crystallized ginger can also help to prevent the feeling of sickness.

◆ Keep strong brown paper bags at hand to be used as sick bags if the worst comes to the worst.

◆ Keep a window open – fresh air usually helps. Keep the heater as low as possible; a stuffy car results in travel sickness.

TRAIN, BUS, AIR OR BOAT JOURNEYS

◆ Try to bring enough entertainment with you so that your children won't make everyone else's journey a misery by bawling or whining all the time. Take rattles or soft toys for young babies, books or games for toddlers and a pack of cards or a magnetic game, such as chess, for older children.

◆ Choose a window seat if you are breast feeding; you'll have more privacy.

Train and bus

◆ Buy your tickets ahead of time so you won't have to spend hours in a queue at the station. Book a seat when you get your tickets if you think the train is likely to be crowded, or get to the station early.

◆ Check whether there are special fares for families or on special trains or on special days. Get your facts right BEFORE the day because the ticket office may not always know all the available special deals.

◆ Take with you food, drink, wet wipes, etc. as you would in the car, because there may not be a buffet car on the train and there will almost certainly be a queue if there is.

Air travel

Take disposable nappies, wipes, lotions etc. in your hand luggage, NOT in your luggage. And carry several carrier bags with you as well to take dirty nappies, and other rubbish acquired on the way.

◆ Telephone the airline before booking your ticket to find out what facilities are available for children. Get a direct flight if possible, which means you won't have to change planes. Book a bulkhead seat, preferably near a window. These are the seats at the front of each compartment and they have more room for changing and stowing bags and bits and pieces. If you are flying overnight, ask for a special carry cot called a "sky cot" so the baby can sleep in it during the flight.

Pet Care

CHOOSING A PET

All pets need constant care and attention, so if you don't have the time to look after a pet, don't get one. When choosing a pet, think of the conditions and space you have available and the characteristics of the pet: dogs can be boisterous and noisy and need to be walked several times a day, whereas cats are more discreet and relatively self-sufficient; both will leave their hairs on the furniture.

Of the smaller pets, hamsters usually come out and play at night but sleep during the day, and so are not much fun for children. Guinea pigs are very friendly but are liable to catch chills.

A word of warning that applies to all pets – steer clear of any animal which shows signs of aggression towards other animals or towards you.

DOGS AND CATS

◆It is usually best to buy a dog or cat from a breeder so that you know the animal's antecedents. Reputable breeders are listed in dog and cat magazines.

◆Don't buy puppies or kittens over the telephone; go and see them before making your choice because you may not like them.

◆If you take your children to see the puppy or kitten before buying it, don't let the sight of their eager little faces make you forget to examine the animal carefully.

◆Ask the owner to provide documentation for the puppy or kitten. This should include the vaccination certificate signed by a vet, if the animal is of an age where it should have had any injections. If the animal is a pedigree, you should also be given a pedigree form and registration transfer form.

◆If any vaccinations have yet to be given, find out when they are due.

◆A puppy or kitten must be at least six weeks old before it is taken from its mother because it needs to be fed by its mother until at least that age, and can suffer psychological problems if separated from her any earlier.

Choosing a dog

Dogs are devoted and offer protection and companionship but should never be left alone for longer than half a day, because they get lonely and can become uncontrollable. They are ideal pets for families where someone is at home most of the day and regular walk times and feeding times can be kept.

◆Take your time in choosing a dog which suits your own life style, personality and environment. Large dogs are expensive in food and need a lot of exercise; small dogs take up less space but may be yappy; medium-sized dogs are usually affable and good with children. Remember that a dog will be with you for around eight to 15 years.

◆Ask yourself if you want a dog or bitch. Males are more outward-going but more likely to wander; females are somewhat more home-loving but will come into season and are very likely to become pregnant unless you take precautions, such as walking them on a lead whenever they are in season, or have them spayed.

◆A cross between two breeds of dog will usually be healthy and stable; pedigree dogs may be inbred and more highly strung.

◆If you want a pedigree dog, consider several breeds. Read books or dog magazines to find out how much a particular breed will eat, how much exercise it will need and any particular idiosyncrasies related to the breed. Talk to friends who have dogs about their characteristics. Go to a dog show to get a view of various different breeds and how well behaved or temperamental they are.

SPOTTING A HEALTHY PUPPY AND KITTEN

◆A healthy puppy should be plump without being fat.

◆The coat of a puppy is quite likely to look dull; this is not a sign of bad health, but check that there are no patches of skin irritation.

◆Inspect the eyes, ears and the inside of the mouth – they should all be clean. Comparison and experience will teach you to distinguish a healthy animal from an unhealthy one.

◆Avoid an animal which cowers and which is pushed around continually by the others. However, forward and boisterous behaviour is not necessarily a sign of good health and you can safely choose a more timid puppy.

◆When buying a kitten, look for a healthy, good-natured one. It should be forward, playful, have a smooth coat, clean ears, eyes, nose and abdomen, and a healthy pink mouth.

Clean, pink mouth
Clean ears
Clean eyes
Clean nose
Smooth coat
Clean abdomen
Clean ears
Clean eyes
Cold, clean nose
Smooth coat
Plump abdomen

Buying a dog

◆If you go to a kennel to buy a dog, look at the other animals there to make sure they seem happy and healthy. They should bark when you arrive but quieten down once you've been introduced to the owner.

◆Ask the prices of all the puppies on sale – the cheaper ones probably have something wrong with them – and check if vaccination is included in the price.

◆Ask to see the parents – their temperament is likely to give you a hint as to how the puppy will turn out.

◆The puppy should sell itself. Don't let the owner persuade you into buying a puppy you don't want.

◆Get a vet to examine any puppy you are thinking of buying. He or she will be able to confirm that the dog is old enough to be taken from its mother, that it has not got worms and is generally healthy.

◆Puppies must be vaccinated against canine distemper, canine parvovirus, canine leptospirosis, canine viral hepatitis and, in some countries, rabies. Ask your vet about any local diseases that your puppy should be immunized against. A puppy must not be allowed out for two weeks after each vaccination, because it will not be protected against disease. The first injection is normally given at six to eight weeks, the second at twelve weeks, see page 315.

◆Before collecting a new puppy, have food, water and bedding waiting for it at home.

Buying a cat

A cat will develop a strong bond with its owner, but remains far more independent than any other type of pet. Cats don't need much space, they are fairly cheap to keep, not as noisy as dogs, relatively undemanding, and exercise and clean themselves. If provided with adequate facilities, they tidy up and bury their faeces and urine scrupulously. Cats live for ten to twelve years or longer.

◆ You can get your cat from a friend or neighbour whose cat has just produced a litter, from a pet shop, animal welfare society or veterinary practice, or occasionally one may turn up out of the blue, looking for a sympathetic home.

◆ Kittens should be vaccinated against feline enteritis and influenza; these injections are normally given at nine and 12 weeks, see page 315. They will need boosters against these diseases every year,

◆ Make new cats feel at home by putting butter on their paws; they will associate the delicious taste with you and their new home and will be less likely to run away looking for their previous home.

Providing for a new cat *Make sure you have a litter tray and bed waiting for your kitten or cat, and its own food and water bowls.*

SMALL ANIMALS

These are normally fairly trouble-free, provided you give them plenty of scope for exercise within their cages, enough food and water (very important) and clean out the cages regularly.

Rabbits, hamsters, gerbils, guinea pigs, mice and rats

◆ It is best to get all these from a specialist breeder, then you can be reasonably sure that they are healthy. The breeder will also be able to give you advice on feeding habits and looking after them.

◆ If you are thinking of buying these animals from a pet shop, ask the owner how long they have been there; the longer they have been cooped up with animals of the same species, the more likely it is that the females are going to be pregnant.

◆ When buying one of these animals look for shiny fur, bright eyes, healthy skin and liveliness.

◆ Most of these animals need exercise equipment in their cages; this is available from most pet shops.

◆ Don't get more than one hamster for a cage because hamsters are solitary and very territorial, and will fight with each other. Rabbits, gerbils, guinea pigs, mice and rats, however, like company – get two females unless you want them to reproduce.

◆ Rabbits are suitable only for a home with a garden because they need a large run in which they can play.

Birds

◆ Buy all birds from a specialist breeder if possible; they are more likely to be healthier than birds in a pet shop. If you are buying specialist birds, the breeder will be able to tell you about their needs and how best to look after them.

◇ Parrots and other large birds are expensive; they also live for a long time (about 70 years). A few breeds will mimic human speech perfectly.

◇ Budgerigars are relatively cheap to buy and keep, are lively and colourful and sometimes learn to mimic human speech. They will live to about seven or eight years and some for more than ten years. Colours include blue, green, yellow and white.

◇ Canaries, like budgerigars, are lively and attractive, and they have a pretty song. They are less rumbustious in their behaviour and do not live quite as long.

◆ If you want more than one budgerigar or canary, and don't want eggs, get two cocks; hens tend to squabble. For other types of bird, check with the breeder.

◆ Most pet shops sell bird cages and food, exercise equipment, etc.

FEEDING

Animals should be fed regularly – two or three times a day when they are very young, and about once a day when they mature. They enjoy a change or a treat, just as people do, so provide some variety in the diet. It is also very important that they always have a supply of clean drinking water; change it every day.

DOGS AND CATS

▼▼ Keep cat and dog bowls separate from
♦ ♦ each other and wash them carefully every day; dog diseases can be fatal to cats.
♦ Don't feed cats on dog food, because they need more vitamins and proteins than dogs and will not get sufficient nutrients from dog food alone.

Giving your pets a treat Give dogs and cats a raw egg once a week; it is very good for their coats.

Giving your dog the right bone Give a dog a bone to chew, to exercise its jaw and strengthen its teeth. Large beef bones, marrow bones, shoulder blade or pelvis bones are all good bones and can be obtained from most butchers. If you cook the bones, don't cook them for longer than five minutes; cooked bones can cause constipation.

▼▼ Never give a dog pieces of backbone, fish
♦ ♦ bones, poultry bones and any very well-cooked bones; they can be very sharp or may splinter and become lodged in a dog's throat.

Feeding dogs

♦ Tinned meat with an added "mixer" such as dog biscuit or meal for roughage, or special dried complete dog food, provides a balanced diet. If you feed a dog dried food, soak the food thoroughly in water before giving it to the dog, and always provide extra water in a bowl.
♦ One meal a day should be enough for most dogs but individual dogs vary. Dogs are greedy and will go on eating long after they are full, so keep treats to a minimum.
♦ If a dog is fed correctly, you should be able to feel its ribs along its chest without them standing out or being buried in fat. It should also have a smooth, shiny coat.

Feeding cats

♦ Cats are fussy and may starve themselves rather than eat what they don't like. Get your cat used to variety before it becomes set in its ways and starts refusing to eat things.
♦ Good-quality tinned cat foods are carefully formulated to contain most of what a cat needs; give a cat fresh food, such as cooked chicken or boiled fish, twice a week and canned food the rest of the time. Poor-quality cat foods make a cat's breath smell.
♦ Don't give cats dried food on its own; it can have a harmful effect on the kidneys. It is best if you mix it with the tinned food and give it to them only occasionally.
♦ Keep regular feeding times, and give cats either two small meals or one larger one.
♦ Provide milk only if your cat will drink it; many don't like milk and prefer water.

SMALL ANIMALS

Most small animals need their diet supplemented with fresh fruit and vegetables to provide them with the extra vitamins and nutrients they need.

Water dispensers for caged pets *Make sure your pets always have water available, in a dispenser which cannot be tipped over.*

Feeding birds

◆ Give birds seeds with husks as the basis of their diet. Millet and canary seed are good staples for budgerigars and canaries, and sunflower seeds for parrots, but speak to specialist breeders about seed mixtures for other types of birds. ·

◆ Avoid coloured millet "treats" because the colouring can be harmful in large quantities.

◆ As a treat, soak the seed in water for 24 hours and then give it to the bird, or mix cod liver oil with the seed.

◆ Supplement seed with fruit, such as apples, bananas and grapes, and green vegetables, such as spinach, to give them extra vitamins.

◆ Provide grit (available from pet shops) to aid the bird's digestion.

Trimming your bird's beak *Wedge a piece of cuttlefish into the side of the bird's cage every so often, so that it can keep its beak and claws in trim.*

Feeding rabbits

◆ Give rabbits proprietary pellets and supplement them daily with carrots, grass, lettuce and dandelion leaves for extra nutrients.

◆ Make sure they have enough drinking water, because the pellets are dry and absorb water when they are swallowed.

Feeding hamsters and gerbils

◆ Give them about a tablespoon of hamster mix per day. You can buy this ready-mixed from a pet shop or mix it up yourself.

◆ Hamsters need some green food every day: chickweed, clover, cow parsley, dandelion leaves and grass are good. Avoid cabbage, because it makes their urine smell, and carrots, which stain their fur.

Feeding guinea pigs

◆ Feed them on pellets or a special mix, available from a pet shop. You must provide adequate drinking water with these dry foods because they get very thirsty.

Giving guinea pigs a treat *Supplement the diet of your guinea pigs with vegetables, such as cabbage and cauliflower leaves, grass or fresh hay to help digestion.*

Feeding mice and rats

◆ Feed them stale bread and dried oats soaked in milk. Supplement this with fruit and tomatoes, and hamster mix. Once a week give them dog or cat biscuits to gnaw at and strengthen their teeth.

EVERYDAY HEALTH CARE

Prevention is better than cure with most animals, and if you make sure that your pet has a well-balanced diet, provide clean surroundings and inspect it regularly for infection, you will avoid much heartache and save on vet's bills.

GENERAL HEALTH AND HYGIENE TIPS

◆ To keep your pet happy and satisfy its territorial instincts, give it an area of its own for its basket as bedding, perching or scratching its claws.

◆ All bedding and cages must be kept clean, warm and dry. Clean bird cages twice a week and rodent cages once a week. Clean out cat litter trays daily.

◆ When disposing of droppings and soiled material, wear rubber gloves.

◆ Inspect your animals regularly and deal with any illness immediately.

◆ Make sure dogs and cats have any necessary annual boosters against disease: dogs must be kept immunized against distemper, and cats against cat flu. Ask your vet about any local diseases which your pet should be immunized against.

◆ De-flea and de-worm pets every six months or so. Never use skin preparations for dogs on cats, which can absorb poisons through their pores.

◆ Keep all dishes for animals separate from the family's.

GENERAL CARE

◆ Groom all furry animals regularly to remove dead hair and clean the skin. Regular grooming also helps to strengthen the bond between an animal and its owner.

◆ Long-haired cats and dogs need to be groomed more often than short-haired ones.

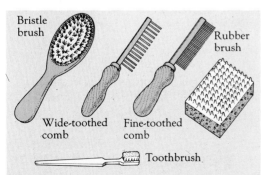

Bristle brush

Rubber brush

Wide-toothed comb

Fine-toothed comb

Toothbrush

Grooming kits *Use a wide-toothed comb first to break up long, matted fur, and then a fine-toothed comb. Brush with a bristle brush, following the direction of the hair growth. Brush the hairs around a cat's face with a toothbrush. To groom a short-haired cat, use a fine-toothed comb and a rubber brush.*

Dogs

◆ While a dog is moulting, brush it daily.

◆ Bathe your dog regularly, and always when it gets dirty, or if it seems to have a lot of dandruff. Clean dogs have fewer skin and coat problems. Washing a dog is easiest under a hand-held shower.

◆ Brush a long-haired dog before washing to reduce the tangling of its fur.

◆ Dry dogs with a large bath towel, or a hair dryer if the dog will accept it. Be warned, even short-haired coats take ages to dry.

◆ Check the inside of the animal's mouth every so often, say once a month. Foul breath and eating difficulties may indicate something wrong with the teeth. Get the teeth checked once a year by the vet.

Clipping a dog's claws *Trim your dog's claws so that they are just clear of, or just touching, the ground. Use guillotine clippers and don't overclip, or you will cut the nail bed.*

HANDLING AN INJURED ANIMAL

DOG
◆ Approach an injured dog cautiously, and talk to it reassuringly. Try to put an improvised muzzle, made from a tie or a bandage, around its snout to stop it from biting, unless it has a chest injury or trouble breathing.

◆ To carry a dog, slide a blanket under it, if possible, with the help of two other people, and lift it.

CAT
◆ Don't move an injured cat unless it is in danger, and don't raise its head because its airway may become blocked and it won't be able to breathe. If you do have to move it, slide a blanket or sheet under it and carry it to a quiet, warm place.

◆ To restrain a frightened cat, hold it by the scruff of the neck and apply firm but gentle pressure, with the other hand placed over its chest.

BIRD
◆ Approach an injured bird slowly, so as not to frighten it. Once you have it in your hands, place it in a dark, warm, quiet place, preferably an enclosed box.

Picking up an injured bird *Gently scoop it up with both hands, with the index and middle fingers on either side of its head.*

Cats

◆ Brush talcum powder or fuller's earth into the fur of a very long-haired cat, to prevent it from matting.

◆ To prevent build-up of tartar on a cat's teeth, clean them occasionally with a soft toothbrush dipped in a salt solution. You will probably need someone to help you to do this and you must wear gardening gloves to protect your hands.

◆ If your cat continually scratches its ears, clean them out with a cotton bud dipped in olive oil. Massage the outside of the ear to loosen any wax that may be causing the irritation. If the scratching continues, take the cat to the vet.

◆ Some cats have tears which discolour the fur on their face. Remove the marks with cotton wool dipped in a weak salt solution.

◆ If a cat is old or is confined indoors, provide a scratching post to keep its claws under control. If the claws get too long take the cat to a vet. Do not clip them yourself because the cat will probably struggle and hurt you; get the vet to do it.

◆ Wear gardening gloves when trying to de-flea a cat because it may scratch you.

Making a scratching post *Nail a piece of hardwood vertically to a base to make a scratching post. Encourage your cat to sharpen its claws on this rather than on your furniture or carpet.*

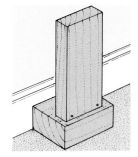

Birds

◆ Get a budgerigar's beak or claws trimmed by the vet if they are becoming too long. If the beak is not cut, it will curl around and eventually prevent the bird from feeding. If the claws are not cut, the bird may not be able to perch or walk properly.

Small animals

◆ Most small animals such as hamsters and mice will groom themselves. If you want to groom them, use a soft babies' brush. Guinea pigs in particular may need brushing because they have longer fur.

COMMON DISEASES

ABSCESSES

Common in cats, especially unneutered males; can also occur in hamsters and gerbils.

Symptoms

Painful swelling with foul-smelling, cream-like or blood-coloured discharge.

Treatment

Take a cat to the vet, who will probably prescribe antibiotics and may lance or surgically drain the abscess. For hamsters and gerbils, bathe the area with water and a mild antiseptic. When the abscess breaks, gently squeeze it to drain it.

ALLERGY

Common in dogs.

Symptoms

Itchy and inflamed paws, armpits, abdomen and thighs, or large raised blotches on the animal's skin.

Treatment

Take the dog to the vet, to identify the cause.

ANAEMIA

Common in cats, especially pedigree ones.

Symptoms

Poor appetite, weakness, high temperature, pale eye colour.

Treatment

Take the animal to the vet, who may give it antibiotics and a blood transfusion.

ASTHMA

Affects dogs and cats, mice and rats.

Symptoms

Harsh breathing and coughing.

Treatment

Take dogs and cats to the vet for advice and treatment. For mice and rats, place them in a dust-free environment for ten days and reduce the amount of dry foods. Don't give them any milk.

CANCER

This can affect any animal.

Symptoms

Small painless swellings.

Treatment

Go to the vet, never wait for swellings to grow large. Small cancers may be successfully treated.

COLDS AND CHILLS

Can affect most animals.

Symptoms

Lethargy, sneezing and shivering, loss of appetite and wet discharge from nose and eyes. Persistent coughing may be diagnosed as bronchitis. In addition, birds with colds puff out their feathers.

Treatment

Take a cat, dog or bird to the vet, who will probably give the animal antibiotics. For a guinea pig, isolate the sick animal and keep it warm; feed it bread soaked in warm milk. If it doesn't improve within three days, take it to the vet. For mice, rats, hamsters and gerbils, isolate the sick animal in a box smeared with a vapour inhalant and keep it warm. Feed it small pieces of food mixed with cod liver oil.

CONSTIPATION

Affects dogs, cats and birds.

Symptoms

In dogs and cats, constant straining and squatting to no effect. In constipated birds the droppings are white.

Treatment

Treat early with some medicinal liquid paraffin. If persistent, refer to the vet.

DERMATITIS (Eczema)

Common in dogs and cats.

Symptoms

Itching and scratching; licking or even biting the skin, and loss of hair.

Treatment

Take the animal to the vet, who will have to find the cause; this may be mites, an allergy, or germs lodged and growing in the skin.

DIARRHOEA

Can affect any animal.

Symptoms

Frequent liquid bowel movements and soiled fur or feathers.

Treatment

For dogs and cats, stop all food for 24 hours, but provide them with a little water. If it persists, take the animal to the vet. Feed hamsters and gerbils, guinea pigs, mice and rats, and birds on dry foods only until the problem clears up.

DISTEMPER (Hardpad)

Affects dogs only.

Symptoms

Clear or crusty discharges from nose and eyes; prominent blood vessels in whites of eyes; severe diarrhoea and sometimes vomiting; frothing at the mouth and violent fits.

Treatment

Immediate treatment by a vet. This is a serious disease, so prevention is better than cure. Get your dog vaccinated and don't forget the boosters.

EAR INFECTION (Canker)

Inflammation of the ear in cats and dogs, although guinea pigs can get it from seed husks which get stuck in their ears.

Symptoms
Head shaking, scratching, and a foul-smelling discharge from the ear.

Treatment
Depends on the cause, so take the animal to the vet. With a guinea pig, you can sometimes dislodge a husk with a cotton swab.

FLEAS AND LICE

These affect most animals.

Symptoms
Scratching and excessive grooming; these parasites are visible if you inspect the animal's fur.

Treatment
Don't apply flea powder for dogs to cats because they absorb the toxins into their skin. Apply flea powder for cats to hamsters and gerbils, guinea pigs, mice and rats.

HEATSTROKE

Usually occurs to animals locked in a car directly in the sun on a warm day.

Symptoms
Distress, gasping, unconsciousness, convulsions.

Treatment
This is an emergency; use cold towels and, with large dogs, water hosing, to bring down the temperature. Ring the vet.

INJURIES

Treat as soon as possible to prevent infection.

Treatment
Cuts or bites can be treated by washing in warm water and a mild antiseptic. More serious injuries must be treated by a vet who will advise on care after treatment.

SCALY FACE

Common in budgerigars

Symptoms
Horny, yellow crusts on either side of the beak and sometimes on the legs.

Treatment
Liquids or lotions are available from pet shops to treat it; disinfect the cage.

WORMS

Affects dogs and cats.

Symptoms
Poor growth, anaemia and general unfitness are symptomatic of roundworm; small segments of worm found sticking to the fur under the animal's tail are symptomatic of tapeworm (this usually affects adult animals only).

Treatment
Use anti-worm treatments approved by your vet, usually in pills or liquid form. All puppies and kittens should be routinely dewormed.
▼▼ Tapeworms and round-
♦♦ worms found in cats are of different species from those in dogs. Do not give cats tablets or medicines prescribed for dogs (or vice versa). Treatment should be discussed with the vet.

VETERINARY CARE FOR DOGS AND CATS

DOGS

VACCINATION	WORMING	SPAYING/NEUTERING
First vaccination 5–6 weeks in high-risk areas.	3 weeks old. Then every 2–3 weeks until the puppy is 16 weeks old.	Spay a bitch at 6 months, or later.
First vaccination 8–10 weeks in normal areas.	Six months later.	Neuter a dog from 6 months to a year, but only if there is a problem – aggression, mounting a bitch, etc.
Second vaccination 12 weeks.	Every 12 months.	
Third vaccination (canine parvovirus only) 4–5 months.		

CATS

VACCINATION	WORMING	SPAYING/NEUTERING
First vaccination 9 weeks.	At 5–6 weeks old.	Spay a queen at 16 weeks or later.
Second vaccination 12–14 weeks.	Every 4 months for tapeworm.	Neuter a tom at 36 weeks or later.
Boosters every 12 months.	Every 6 months for roundworm.	

PET CARE WHILE YOU GO ON HOLIDAY

◆ Get a good friend or neighbour to feed and exercise your cat or dog every day and clean out litter trays. Failing this, you will have to board your animals in kennels.

◆ Leave small pets with a friend or neighbour; they are easier to look after than dogs or cats so people are less reluctant to take care of them.

◆ If you are leaving a cat alone over the weekend, buy double bowls with a lid and a timing device. Fill both bowls before you leave, then set the lid to open at the normal feeding time.

TIPS FOR BOARDING PETS

◆ If you are going to have to board your animals, try to get them used to being away from home for a week or two every year from a young age.

◆ Choose a kennel or cattery which seems reasonably clean and has an air of competence and efficiency. Always look around it first to make sure that the animals there look happy and healthy and that they can't escape.

◆ Book a place in the kennel as soon as your holiday is arranged. If you are going away during the summer, book before your holiday because this is a popular season and kennels get booked up very early for it.

◆ When you take your animal to the kennel, take its own bedding and one or two familiar toys, to comfort it while you are away.

TRAVELLING WITH PETS

◆ Check beforehand that animals may travel on public transport; it may be up to the guard, driver or conductor to allow your pet to travel with you or not.

◆ Always carry a cat in a ventilated box or basket, and a bird and other small animals in cages or gnaw-proof boxes, when travelling on public transport or in a car.

Car travel

◆ Acclimatize a dog to car travel gradually. Sit with it in a stationary car at first. Then start with a few short journeys, gradually getting longer.

◆ Keep a dog blanket on the back seat of a car, with a waterproof sheet underneath. If you have a hatchback car, put the dog in the back behind a barrier. This will prevent the dog from disturbing the driver and covering your car and clothes with hairs.

◆ Before a journey, take the dog for a walk so that it can relieve itself.

◆ Don't hold a cat in your arms when travelling. If it gets frightened or upset, it may hurt you, and if a window is open, it may escape.

◆ Make sure the container for your cat has a window or holes that it can see through, and line the floor with a blanket to make the cat more comfortable. If the weather is very hot, place a dampened cloth over the basket to keep the temperature down inside.

◆ Keep the car window open slightly to give animals inside some air.

▼▼ Never leave animals in a car on a hot day; ◆ ◆ if they have to be left unattended for a short while, leave the window open so that they can get some fresh air.

Putting a cat in a basket *Don't chase the cat about the house. Close the doors and windows and leave the box lying open. Wait for a quiet moment, then lift the cat up with one hand under its chest, using the other to stroke its back gently. Put it in bottom first and keep your hand on its back while you close the lid.*

TRAINING CATS AND DOGS

It is essential to toilet train your dogs and cats. If you also train them to obey certain commands, you will also find that they are more controllable and behave better. This is particularly important with large dogs, which can be extremely boisterous.

Dogs and cats should wear collars permanently, with a tag with your name and phone number on it in case the animal gets lost. A cat's collar must have an elasticated strip so that it will not be choked should the collar get caught on something.

OBEDIENCE AND HOUSE-TRAINING

◆ Give your dog or cat a name as soon as you get it and use the name frequently, so that it becomes used to it. A short name is best because it has more immediacy when it is called, and animals respond to it better.

◆ Begin toilet training puppies and kittens as soon as you get them. The younger they are, the quicker they learn.

◆ Discourage bad habits early by praising good behaviour generously, with a stroke or pat and encouraging sounds, and giving the animal a firm telling-off when it behaves badly. Teach your dog or cat the meaning of "No" (i.e. stop what you're doing at once). Say it firmly but not aggressively. If necessary, restrain the animal physically from doing what it is not supposed to, until it understands.

◆ Never punish an animal for not doing something right, because the punishment will be associated with the command.

▼▼ Don't hit your dog or cat. You may
◆◆ injure it, or it may grow to fear you and become difficult to approach.

◆ Don't feed a dog or cat from your table; it will start to expect it and beg. Also, this is not very hygienic.

House-training dogs

◆ At night keep the puppy penned in a room with newspaper on the floor. Gradually move the newspaper towards the door. Regard this as an alternative to the outside for

Toilet training a puppy *To begin with, confine the puppy to one room and spread newspapers over the floor. The puppy will soon restrict itself to one area and you can remove the surrounding paper.*

the time being. Then move the paper outside, and finally remove it altogether. When there is no paper, the puppy will know that the only place it can relieve itself is outside.

◆ Take the puppy out when it wakes, after a meal and after a period of activity. Watch it closely and try to catch it before it urinates. If it looks anxious or uncomfortable, whines or barks, act promptly; take it outside and stay with it until it relieves itself, and then praise it immediately.

◆ Never punish a puppy for accidents. Ignore it (this is punishment enough) when it goes where you don't want it to, and praise it when it gets it right.

◆ Once you start taking your dog for walks, encourage it to pass motions in the gutter, not on the pavement or in parks. (In some places you must sweep up the faeces and put them in the rubbish bin).

Behavioural training for dogs

Dogs are pack animals. You are your dog's pack leader and you should develop a firm control so that it knows where it stands.

◆ Only one member of the household should train a dog, otherwise it will get

FOUR FUNDAMENTAL COMMANDS FOR A DOG

"HEEL": The dog must walk at the same pace as you on your left side. Repeat "Heel" regularly and point to your leg. Give a sharp jerk on the lead if it veers off, and leave the lead slack when the dog keeps close. Teaching this command needs patience and time.

"SIT": Hold the dog by the collar with one hand and press gently but firmly on its rump with the other, while giving the command to sit in a quiet but firm voice. When the dog sits, stroke it and praise it.

"COME": Pick up the lead and say "Come" while gently pulling the lead: Praise the dog every time it waits for the command before springing up.

"STAY": Teach this after you get the dog to sit. This takes patience. The dog will at first walk after you when you walk away. Gently take it back each time and tell it to sit. Eventually it will get the idea and you should be able to walk right out of its sight. The dog should remain in place until you come back or invite it to "come".

confused. Once it has learned the commands, other members of the family can use them, but not all at once.

◆ Keep the lessons short and make them fun so that the dog doesn't get bored. Develop a bond of affection with the dog and make it feel pride in its achievements.

◆ Attend dog-training classes with your dog if you can – you may find them useful.

◆ Train the dog to accept collar and lead early on. Use the lead while you train the dog to obey commands; in time, you will find that the lead won't be necessary.

◆ Discourage your dog from jumping up to greet you, however tempting it is to invite it to do so when it is a puppy. If it grows into a large dog you will soon regret it jumping up. A firm "No" and a definite push down will help to stop the habit.

◆ Persistent bad habits can be cured eventually if you are consistent about diverting the dog's attention.

◆ Allow your dog to bark at strangers – a barking dog is a very effective burglar deterrent. But teach it to stop when you say "No".

◆ When teething, or if left alone too much, puppies and young dogs often chew up shoes, clothes, books and furniture. Keep all chewable temptations out of reach and give plenty of bones, see page 310, and other legitimate chewy things. Don't give a dog an old shoe because it will think that it is allowed to chew all shoes, old and new.

House-training cats

Cats are instinctively clean and prefer not only to relieve themselves in private but also to bury their motions.

◆ Provide a litter tray for an indoor cat or new kitten. Keep the tray in a quiet area. A kitten may have to be confined to the area around the tray but will soon learn. Remove solid litter from the tray at least once a day.

◆ To train a kitten to use the garden, put the tray outside and take the kitten to it after it has had a meal. Eventually remove the tray and place the kitten on a suitable spot for scratching a hole.

GREEN TIP: Scatter orange peel over areas of the garden where you don't want cats to defecate. They don't like the smell and will stay away.

Protecting wooden furniture from puppies *To stop a puppy chewing on wooden furniture, dab oil of cloves on the wood.*

Using a cat flap *If you have a garden, allow a ready means of access to it, such as a cat flap. Some cat flaps are simply a swing door, others are more sophisticated and are activated by a device on the cat's collar.*

Health and Safety

SAFETY IN THE HOME

It is important to make your home as safe as possible to prevent unnecessary accidents. If you have young children or elderly people in the house you have an even greater responsibility for providing a safe home.

Young children are very inquisitive and will grab at anything; elderly people are slower to react, less nimble on their feet and may suffer from poor sight, so they can easily trip up, which can result in serious injury.

ROOM-BY-ROOM SAFETY

◆Don't leave rugs on the floor if they are worn or lifting at the corners. Elderly people and toddlers are particularly likely to trip over them. For the same reason, broken or cracked vinyl, lino flooring or ceramic tiles should be replaced at once.
◆Opt for solid furniture so that a child can't pull it over onto himself.
◆Don't leave polythene bags lying around.

Heating and fires

◆Cover radiators and hot pipes with towels or put a piece of furniture in front of them, so that your child or an unsteady elderly person can't bump into them by accident.

◆Use fireguards in front of fires. If you have children, attach the guard to the wall on both sides, so that they can't pull it over.
▼▼Don't use a portable paraffin or gas ◆◆ cylinder heater in a sick person's bedroom, particularly if the person is elderly and confused, because he could get out of bed and trip over it. Never use them in a child's room or leave children alone in the room with one.
◆Don't carry a paraffin heater while it is alight, you could set fire to your clothes.
◆Don't air clothes in front of a radiant fire or a fan heater or fire with a label that warns you not to do so, nor over gas or paraffin heaters; clothes could catch fire.
◆Buy children's clothes that are made of flame-resistant fabric.
▼▼Don't buy furniture (generally uphol- ◆◆ stered furniture and beds) that is made of polyurethane foam because the foam gives off lethal fumes if it catches fire.

Electricity

◆Cover empty sockets with socket covers so that children can't poke things into them.
◆Don't leave flexes where children can reach them or let them trail across a room, where someone could trip over them.
▼▼Don't touch any electrical appliance,
◆ ◆ socket or switch with wet hands; you could electrocute yourself.
◆Buy only electrical equipment with an official safety-approved label on it, which shows that it has been checked and has passed certain safety regulations. If using foreign equipment, check that it is suitable for use with the voltage of the country you are living in.
◆To prevent an accident, switch off any electrical appliance and unplug it before checking or repairing any piece of equipment. Switch the electricity off at the mains before checking a socket or light fitting, or changing a fuse in the fuse box.
◆Replace damaged plugs immediately; they are dangerous. Replace worn flexes; bandaging them up is not good enough. Use smash-proof plugs for appliances that you plug and unplug frequently (the vacuum cleaner for instance).
◆Check an appliance (or get it checked) if a plug feels warm to the touch or has scorch marks, see page 236.

Medicines and household chemicals

◆Buy chemicals and medicines with child-proof tops and always keep them in a locked cupboard (and don't leave the key lying about where a child could find it).
▼▼Leave chemicals in their original bottles;
◆ ◆ never put a poisonous substance in a container that previously held a harmless substance because your child may try to drink it.
◆Keep medicines and chemicals in clearly marked containers; take out-of-date medicines back to the pharmacist, some are not safe to throw away or pour down the toilet because they can be poisonous.

◆Don't leave aerosol cans where a child can reach them; the nozzle is easily depressed and the force of the spray could damage his eyes.

Fire safety

◆Work out escape routes in case of fire. Make sure you can get out of top windows, and leave a rope or ladder on the top floor.
◆Install smoke detectors in prominent places; get a safety expert to advise you.
◆Keep plenty of fire extinguishers: put one in the kitchen near the cooker, and at least one on each floor of the house.
◆Check that you know where (and how) to turn the water, electricity and gas off at the mains in the event of an accident.
◆Most adhesives are highly flammable. When working with adhesives, see that there is no naked flame nearby (don't forget the gas pilot light) and keep the windows open to clear away the fumes.

TYPES OF FIRE EXTINGUISHER

◇Multi-purpose, or universal, fire extinguishers can be used on any fire.
◇Foam fire extinguishers can be used for fires caused by flammable liquids, oils, spirits and fats.
◇Dry powder fire extinguishers are best for fires caused by spilled flammable liquids.
◇Use carbon dioxide or vapourizing liquid fire extinguishers for electrical fires because they are non-conductive.
◆You can use water to extinguish all but oil or electrical fires. Water will fan the flames of a fat fire and will ruin an electrical appliance. Water also conducts electricity and can give you an electric shock if used on an electrical fire; it can also blow a circuit fuse.
▼▼On an electric fire, it is very danger-
◆ ◆ ous to use anything apart from a multi-purpose fire extinguisher or one specially designed for electrical fires.
◆Keep a fire blanket near to the cooker in the kitchen so that it is immediately to hand in case of fire.

Bathroom

◆ Instant gas water heaters in the bathroom must be fitted with a flue and the room must be well ventilated to prevent carbon-monoxide poisoning. Check regularly that pilot lights are functioning; get them checked if necessary.

◆ If you have an elderly person living in the house, it may be useful to have handrails near the toilet and the bath.

◆ Install light switches outside the bathroom or on pull switches in the bathroom, likewise switches for bathroom heaters.

▼▼ Don't have electrical switches, sockets ◆◆ or equipment where you can touch them from the bath, it's extremely dangerous.

◆ Use non-slip mats in the bath or shower for children or the elderly, to prevent them from slipping. If you are installing a new bath or shower, get one with a non-slip surface.

◆ Label all medicines and follow the instructions. Never give prescribed medicines to those they were not prescribed for.

Medicine cupboard This must be lockable. Buy medicines with childproof tops. Don't put the cupboard above the toilet because your child could easily climb up to it.

Shower door This should be plastic, or glass covered in safety film, so that it doesn't splinter if it breaks.

Heater Bathroom heaters should be wall-mounted and the switches should not be reachable from the bath.

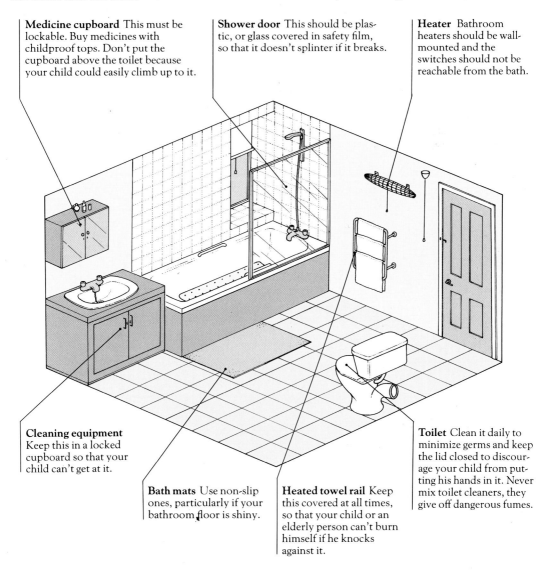

Cleaning equipment Keep this in a locked cupboard so that your child can't get at it.

Bath mats Use non-slip ones, particularly if your bathroom floor is shiny.

Heated towel rail Keep this covered at all times, so that your child or an elderly person can't burn himself if he knocks against it.

Toilet Clean it daily to minimize germs and keep the lid closed to discourage your child from putting his hands in it. Never mix toilet cleaners, they give off dangerous fumes.

Kitchen

◆It is essential to have a non-slip floor: vinyl, rubberized textured flooring, cork, non-slip ceramic tiles, quarry tiles, sanded and sealed boards and linoleum are all suitable materials.

▼▼Don't over-polish vinyl floors. Too
◆ ◆ much polish builds up a slippery surface, which is difficult to remove.

◆If you are buying a new oven, get one with an insulated door, ordinary doors can get very hot.

▼▼Never leave a fat pan unattended even
◆ ◆ for a minute. Fat will ignite spontaneously when it reaches 204°C (400°F) and is

Electric appliances
Use a curly flex for the kettle or the coffee jug to avoid trailing flexes across the worktop. Unplug appliances when they are not in use so that your child can't turn them on by accident.

Bottle sterilizing bath
Keep this near the sink, so that filling it is easier, but keep the area around it very clean.

Cleaning equipment
Keep household cleaning materials, whether soap powder or bleach, out of the reach of children; most of them are dangerous if swallowed.

Pets' bowls Either feed the animals outside or keep the bowls out of a child's reach, and where no one else can trip over them. Clean them out after use.

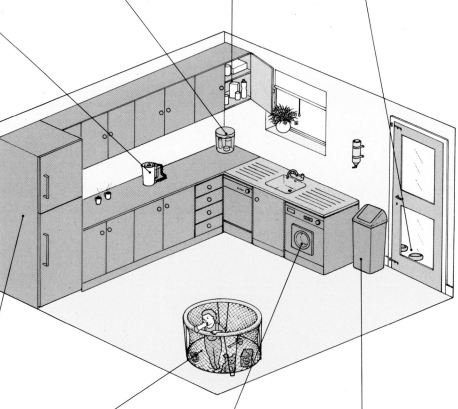

Fridge and freezer Put safety locks onto the doors so that children can't open them.

Play area Put a playpen in the kitchen to keep a young child away from your work areas. Alternatively, use a safety gate to keep children either in or out of part of the kitchen.

Washing machine and dishwasher Don't leave doors open if you have a child around. Get special child locks put on them, so that a child can't open them.

Rubbish bin Tall bins are easier to use and more difficult for a child to rummage in. Don't put anything very sharp in the kitchen bin; wrap it up and put it straight into the outdoor bin.

the cause of most kitchen fires. The danger sign is when the fat starts to smoke.

◆ Keep knives sharpened: the sharper the knife, the safer it is, because you don't have to press on it.

◆ Keep cloths away from the stove, they could catch fire.

◆ See that there are at least four to six electric sockets to avoid overloading the circuit and blowing a fuse or tripping an MCB.

◆ Get sockets installed at worktop height, where they are easy to use and not easily reached by the very young.

◆ Never leave the room with the iron on, particularly if there are children around.

◆ Keep hot drinks away from the edge of the worktop so that they can't be grabbed by a child or knocked by your elbow.

Cookers Turn pan handles inwards so that your child can't reach them and you don't knock them accidentally. Put a guard around the hob or cooker.

Fire precautions Keep a fire blanket next to the cooker and a fire extinguisher somewhere in the kitchen.

Sharp knives Keep knives out of the reach of children. The best place for them is on a knife rack; they keep their edges for longer – you could put a rack on the inside of one of the cupboard doors. Never leave knives lying on the worktop.

Storage Don't keep everyday items above shoulder height; they'll be awkward to reach. Don't put heavy things too low, you could hurt your back trying to get them out.

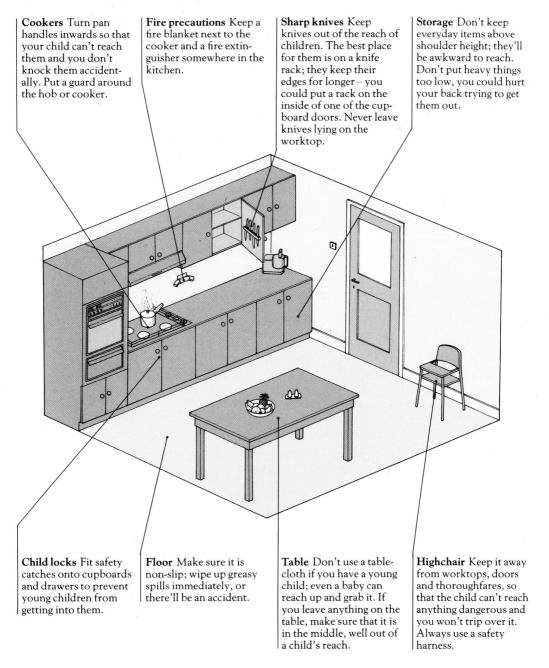

Child locks Fit safety catches onto cupboards and drawers to prevent young children from getting into them.

Floor Make sure it is non-slip; wipe up greasy spills immediately, or there'll be an accident.

Table Don't use a tablecloth if you have a young child; even a baby can reach up and grab it. If you leave anything on the table, make sure that it is in the middle, well out of a child's reach.

Highchair Keep it away from worktops, doors and thoroughfares, so that the child can't reach anything dangerous and you won't trip over it. Always use a safety harness.

Living room

◆Don't leave electric flexes and telephone leads trailing all over the floor and across doorways where you could trip over them.

◆Always switch the television set off and unplug it at night. Never take the back off to have a look, even if the set is switched off and unplugged. A colour television set generates at least 20,000 volts and some of these remain in the set for a long time after you have switched it off.

◆Don't put anything holding water (a vase or pot plant, for instance) on the television set; if the vase fell over into the set, it could cause an electrical fire.

◆See that you have a sensible fireguard in front of any fire or heater.

Drinks cupboard
Always lock away alcohol when you are out of the room. Even a small amount of alcohol can seriously harm a child.

Television and stereo
Keep these out of reach of children and, for safety, unplug them when they are not in use. Fix permanent flexes to the wall so that your child can't pull on them.

Houseplants and flowers
Don't keep houseplants that are poisonous. Keep flowers out of a child's reach.

Breakable objects Move anything you value out of a toddler's reach; nothing is safe.

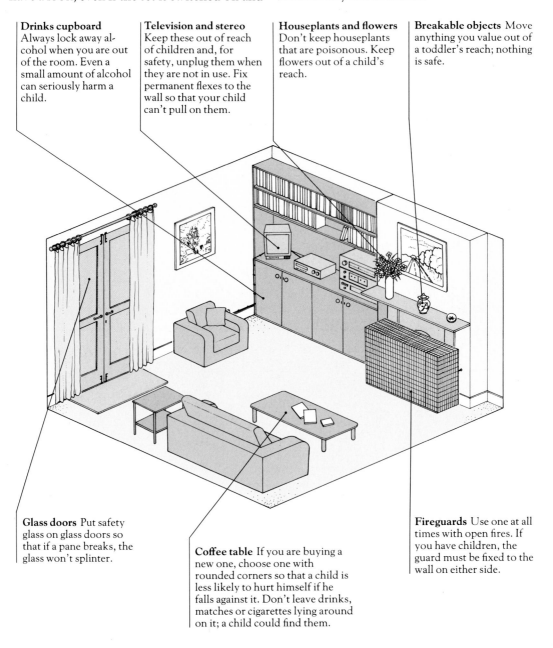

Glass doors Put safety glass on glass doors so that if a pane breaks, the glass won't splinter.

Coffee table If you are buying a new one, choose one with rounded corners so that a child is less likely to hurt himself if he falls against it. Don't leave drinks, matches or cigarettes lying around on it; a child could find them.

Fireguards Use one at all times with open fires. If you have children, the guard must be fixed to the wall on either side.

Bedrooms and children's rooms

◆ If you have young children, unplug any appliances in your bedroom during the day and put safety plugs into the sockets, in case the children get into the room when you are not looking.

◆ Install safety locks, bars or safety glass in the windows of children's rooms if they are above the ground floor. The bars must be vertical so that a child can't climb them and should only come half way up the window if they are not removable; full-height permanent bars are a fire risk.

◆ Put a child's bed against a wall and get a bedguard for the other side of the bed when you move your child from a cot to a bed, to stop him falling out.

◆ Always read the manufacturers' instructions before using a new electric blanket. At the end of winter, check for signs of wear and tear in blanket and flex and get it serviced every two years.

▼▼ Never plug an electric blanket into a
◆ ◆ light fitting or switch a blanket on if it is wet; you could cause a fire.

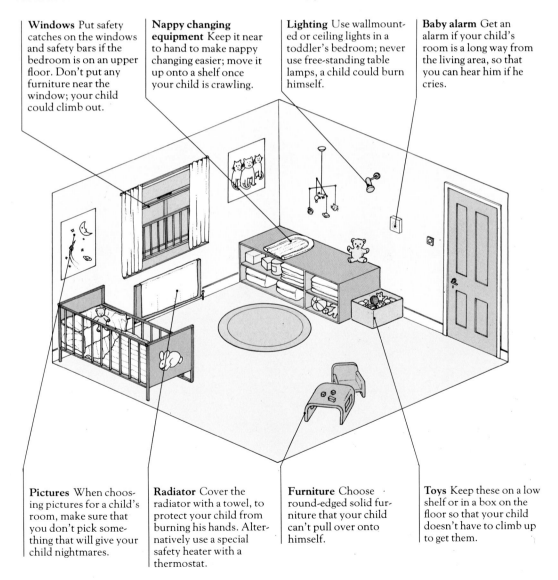

Windows Put safety catches on the windows and safety bars if the bedroom is on an upper floor. Don't put any furniture near the window; your child could climb out.

Nappy changing equipment Keep it near to hand to make nappy changing easier; move it up onto a shelf once your child is crawling.

Lighting Use wallmounted or ceiling lights in a toddler's bedroom; never use free-standing table lamps, a child could burn himself.

Baby alarm Get an alarm if your child's room is a long way from the living area, so that you can hear him if he cries.

Pictures When choosing pictures for a child's room, make sure that you don't pick something that will give your child nightmares.

Radiator Cover the radiator with a towel, to protect your child from burning his hands. Alternatively use a special safety heater with a thermostat.

Furniture Choose round-edged solid furniture that your child can't pull over onto himself.

Toys Keep these on a low shelf or in a box on the floor so that your child doesn't have to climb up to get them.

Hall and stairway

◆Make sure lighting is adequate on stairways and in passages. See that it does not cast confusing shadows over the stair treads and cause an accident. Install two-way light switches for safety.

◆Mend loose stair rods or banister rods as soon as they require it; there'll be an accident if you don't.

◆Don't keep mats at the foot of the stairs, particularly if the floor is polished.

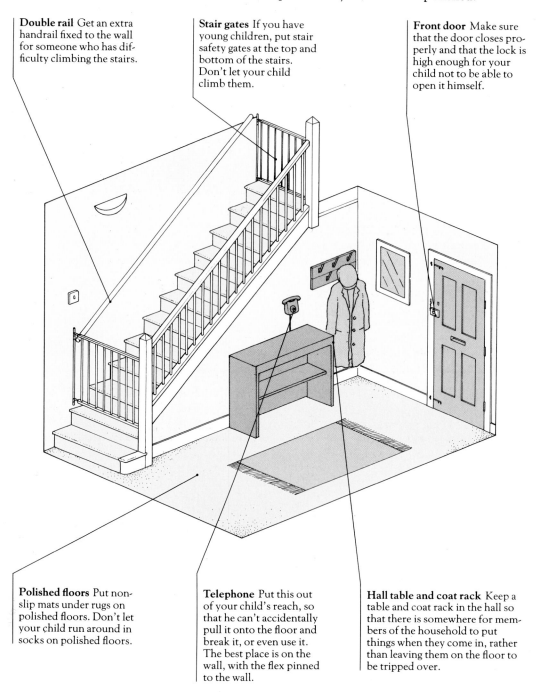

Double rail Get an extra handrail fixed to the wall for someone who has difficulty climbing the stairs.

Stair gates If you have young children, put stair safety gates at the top and bottom of the stairs. Don't let your child climb them.

Front door Make sure that the door closes properly and that the lock is high enough for your child not to be able to open it himself.

Polished floors Put non-slip mats under rugs on polished floors. Don't let your child run around in socks on polished floors.

Telephone Put this out of your child's reach, so that he can't accidentally pull it onto the floor and break it, or even use it. The best place is on the wall, with the flex pinned to the wall.

Hall table and coat rack Keep a table and coat rack in the hall so that there is somewhere for members of the household to put things when they come in, rather than leaving them on the floor to be tripped over.

HOME NURSING

When a person is really ill, rest and quiet are what is wanted most and the very sick may simply want to sleep all the time. But all ill people, particularly the very young and the very old, do need comfort and reassurance. Short, frequent visits are best. Use them to straighten the bed, bring a drink, wash the face and hands and so on.

As the patient begins to recover, boredom is the great difficulty. Keep the patient supplied with a wide variety of things; most convalescents have a short attention span.

SURROUNDINGS AND GENERAL COMFORT

If someone is likely to be ill for a time, try to position the bed so that the patient has a view, either out of the window or of something interesting in the room. Put a table by the bed for books, radio, flowers, drinks, fruit, bedside light.

◆ To keep the patient as comfortable as possible, plump up the pillows throughout the day and straighten out the sheets at least twice a day, say in the morning and evening, particularly if the patient has a fever. Offer frequent opportunities to wipe face and hands with a warm damp cloth.

◆ Use cotton sheets; they are more comfortable if a patient has a temperature. Change the sheets if they get wet.

◆ To make bedmaking easier, use fitted sheets and a duvet. Shake the duvet every day to keep the filling evenly distributed.

Sitting up in bed *If a patient wants to sit up in bed, bank about five pillows: one at the base of the bed-head, parallel to the bed, two leaning inwards, one from each side, then two higher across the top.*

Temporary backrest *Use an upturned chair, and tie padding onto the legs to protect the wall or bedhead.*

◆ If the patient wants to sit up in bed, arrange the pillows so that they provide enough support, see below. If she is going to be in bed for a while, it may be worth investing in an adjustable backrest.

Children

◆ If a child doesn't want to stay in bed, don't force her to. Wrap her up in warm clothes and let her lie down on the sofa in the living room, or make up a bed wherever you are working. Leave your child's bed straightened so that she can go back if she wants too.

◆ Babies often become more clingy and need more attention when they are unwell. Spend more time with your baby if she needs it; she won't understand what's happening.

◆ If children require constant attention, give it to them while they are very ill and forget the house and its needs.

Long-term patients

◆ Arrange the bed so that there is enough room on both sides for you to move around it easily to make the bed while the patient is in it or move her up the bed, for example. It is much easier to nurse someone in a single rather than a double bed.

◆ Leave a handbell beside the bed if you are in another part of the house, or get a portable baby alarm.

◆ If the patient is very confused, get a bed guard to prevent her from falling out.

◆ Make comfortable provision for visitors so that they will be encouraged to visit and not put off; people in bed for a long time get very bored and lonely.

◆ If the patient will be in bed for some time, remove some of the clutter and make room for some flowers, coloured pictures and posters or wall hangings. Change the pictures every so often, so that she doesn't become bored. Don't do this if the patient is easily disoriented.

◆ If the patient is feeling strong enough, it can be quite a relief to get out of bed and be able to sit up in a chair for a little while each day, say while you attend to the bed or for meal times.

◆ Even if you are worried and harassed, try to act cheerfully. This will make you feel better as well as the patient.

WHEN TO CALL THE DOCTOR

The following may be signs of serious illness. Go to see the doctor just in case.

◇ *Persistent coughing and hoarseness*
◇ *Unexplained dizziness*
◇ *Excessive indigestion or any mild but persistent indigestion after meals, especially if it prevents sleep at night*
◇ *Any persistent difficulty in swallowing*
◇ *Chronic sleeplessness*
◇ *Any chronic or prolonged tiredness without an obvious cause*
◇ *Any persistent and recurrent pain anywhere in the body*
◇ *Any persistent loss of appetite or weight*
◇ *A skin rash, an unhealing sore or unexplained change in the colour of skin or complexion*
◇ *An unexplained swelling, especially in the abdomen, joints or legs*
◇ *Lumps or growths, which are usually painless or under the skin, especially if they keep growing*
◇ *An unaccustomed breathlessness after exertion*
◇ *Persistent and excessive thirst*
◇ *Any problems with vision such as seeing double*

FOR CHILDREN

It is important that you call your doctor if you notice any of the following symptoms in your child:

◇ *A raised temperature (over 39°C/102°F), or a temperature of 38°C (100.4F) and any obvious sign of illness if it lasts more than three days*

◇ *A raised temperature accompanied by convulsions*
◇ *A low temperature which is accompanied by cold skin, drowsiness, quietness and listlessness*
◇ *If your baby has been vomiting or suffering from diarrhoea for more than six hours*
◇ *If vomiting or diarrhoea is accompanied by severe abdominal pain*
◇ *If a baby which is less than six months old goes off her food suddenly for no apparent reason*
◇ *If your child appears very listless for no apparent reason*
◇ *Dizziness, particularly if she has recently had a bump on the head*
◇ *Severe right-sided abdominal pain*
◇ *Headache accompanied by dizziness or blurred vision*

EMERGENCIES

Get medical help immediately if you notice that an adult or child:

◇ *Stops breathing or breathing is difficult and the patient starts to go blue*
◇ *Is unconscious*
◇ *Has a deep wound and is bleeding badly, or has a serious ear or eye injury*
◇ *Has a serious burn*
◇ *Has a suspected broken bone*
◇ *Has taken an overdose*
◇ *Is bitten by a poisonous insect, an animal or a snake*

Entertainment

◆Keep the patient supplied with plenty of books, newspapers and writing materials, particularly as she starts to recover. If she likes books but is unable to read, get some talking book tapes. These are good for children as well.

◆A television can be a great companion for someone alone in bed a good deal; one with a remote control switch saves having to get out of bed to change channels. A radio/cassette player and a good selection of tapes are essential.

◆Let your child play with things she is not normally allowed to have in bed, such as felt-tip pens or paints and paper (provided you cover the bed with polythene), jigsaws (on a tray), dolls to dress or books of easy word puzzles are also good forms of amusement; she could also watch television while you get on with other things.

CHANGING THE SHEETS FOR A PATIENT IN BED

1 *Remove the top bed coverings. Turn the patient onto one side and move her as near to the edge of the bed as you safely can.*

2 *Roll the old sheet lengthwise until it is against her back. Roll the new sheet in half along its length and put it on the bed beside the old one. Tuck it in on one side.*

3 *Roll the patient over the two rolls and onto the new sheet. Remove the old one and tuck the new one in on the other side.*

NURSING

◆Always carry out the doctor's instructions exactly. Keep a note of how much sleep the patient has had, how much has been eaten and drunk, whether there has been much pain. All these things will help the doctor in her diagnosis or treatment.

Temperature

The normal body temperature is 37°C (98.6°F). A raised temperature that accompanies an illness is the body's way of responding to illness.

◆Use a plastic strip or disc thermometer to take a baby's temperature, it's safer than a mercury one (although less accurate).

◆Battery-operated digital mercury thermometers are the easiest thermometers to read. Buy the type that records the previous temperature.

◆The most convenient way to take a temperature is by mouth, by placing a mercury or digital thermometer under a patient's tongue. Alternatively, take it under the patient's armpit.

▼▼ Don't use the tongue method for a
◆ ◆ young child, say under 7, or a confused elderly patient – they could easily bite off the end of the thermometer by mistake. Don't use it for a patient who can't breathe easily through her nose. Take the temperature under the arm instead. The normal reading for under the arm will be about 0.6°C (1°F)

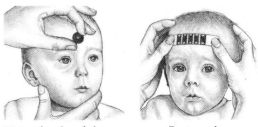

Using forehead thermometers *Put it on the centre of your child's forehead for 15 seconds; numbers will light up in sequence, before coming to rest at the correct reading. Hold the disc type with your finger and thumb, above left, and the strip with both hands, keeping them clear of the black panels, above right.*

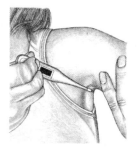

Taking a child's temperature under the arm *Sit your child on your knee, put the thermometer into his armpit and lower his arm over it; leave for two minutes.*

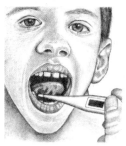

Taking the temperature by mouth *Place the bulb of the thermometer under the tongue and tell the patient to close his mouth; leave for two minutes.*

running about or been very active.
◆ To be sure of a correct reading with a mercury thermometer, shake it until the mercury has gone down into the bulb.

Pulse and breathing

The rate, regularity and strength of the pulse and breathing are an indication of a patient's health. The average pulse rate for a healthy adult should be between 72 and 80 beats per minute; for a baby the rate is 120 to 140 times a minute. An increase of the rate may be due to fever or anxiety. A healthy newborn baby breathes 30 to 50 times a minute but an adult breathes only 16 to 20 times.
◆ Take the pulse at the same time as the temperature; the patient won't notice what you are doing and the reading is more likely to be normal. You can feel the pulse at any point where an artery is close to the surface of the body; the most convenient place for taking the pulse is at the wrist (the radial pulse). It is very difficult to find a surface

lower than a reading taken under the tongue.
◆ Sit or lay the patient down quietly before the temperature is taken. Allow at least 20 minutes after a meal, hot or cold drink or a bath before taking the temperature to get an accurate reading. Likewise, don't take a child's temperature just after she has been

LOWERING A TEMPERATURE

◆ For slight fevers, the doctor may advise taking paracetamol or aspirin several times a day to help bring the temperature down. Children should only be given junior paracetamol; adult's paracetamol is too powerful and aspirin can be dangerous.

▼ ▼ Never give aspirin to a child, because
◆ ◆ it is a stomach irritant and can cause vomiting, which results in further fluid loss. Also, if the child has influenza or chickenpox, there is a risk of her developing a serious condition known as Reye's syndrome if she is given aspirin.

▼ ▼ A pregnant woman should never take
◆ ◆ aspirin; it can harm the foetus.
◆ Drinking a lot of fluid can help to bring the temperature down because it replaces the fluid lost during sweating (the body's natural way of losing heat) as a result of having a temperature.
◆ If the patient has a high fever, sponge the forehead with a tepid sponge. Never use cold water because it causes the surface blood vessels to contract and retain heat,

whereas tepid water helps them to dilate and lose heat.
◆ If a patient has a very high temperature, take her clothes off and cover her with a sheet, preferably cotton because it is cooling and absorbent, but don't let her get too cold or she could get a chill.

TEPID SPONGING

1 *If your child's temperature has been above 40°C (104°F) for over half an hour, and undressing her hasn't reduced it, sponge her all over with tepid water until her temperature is below 38°C (100°F). Take her temperature every five minutes until it drops, then stop.*

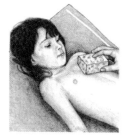

2 *Cover her with a cotton sheet but don't let her get too cold. Sponge her again if she starts to get hot again. Call the doctor.*

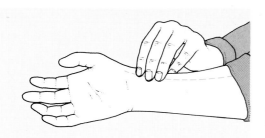

Giving eye drops *Tilt the patient's head back and to one side, so that drops can't run from an infected eye into a clear one. Pull down the lower lid and let the drops fall between the eye and the eyelid.*

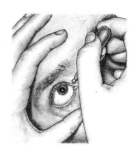

Taking the pulse *Put three fingers on the patient's wrist, just above the wrist crease on the thumb side. Do not take a pulse with your thumb or fingertips because they have a pulse of their own. Count the number of beats in 15 seconds and multiply by four to get the number of beats in a minute.*

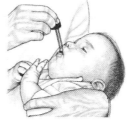

artery in a baby, instead lay your hand on her chest and feel her heartbeat.

◆Count the respiration rate after the pulse rate but before you let go of the hand, or do it while the patient is sleeping; she'll be unaware of what you are doing and you will get a better reading.

Giving medicine to a baby *Pick up the required dose with a dropper, above left, or pour it into a medicine spoon, above right. Wrap your baby in a shawl to keep her arms down if she is difficult.*

Giving medicine

◆Give the right amount of medicine at the right times. Read the label on the bottle each time, to check the contents, especially if you are giving several medicines a day, to make sure you give the correct dose.

▼▼Keep medicines out of the reach of
◆ ◆ children at all times.

◆If a baby won't take medicine on a spoon, get a medicine tube spoon or use a dropper. If none of these methods works, dip a clean finger into the baby's medicine and let her suck off that.

◆Children often hate being given ear or eye drops, especially if the drops are cold, so warm them by sitting them in a bowl of warm water for a few minutes.

▼▼Don't let the tip of a dropper touch the
◆ ◆ skin or you'll transfer the germs to the bottle. If the dropper does touch the skin, wash it before replacing it.

◆Don't punish a child for not wanting her medicine, you'll create more problems when the next dose is due; bribe her to take it if necessary, it's worth it.

Dealing with vomiting

◆Consult the doctor if the vomiting continues over a six hour period or if it is accompanied by diarrhoea or a high fever.

◆Put the patient to bed and place a bowl within easy reach for her to vomit into.

◆Give frequent small amounts of liquid, preferably cold water with a pinch of salt and 5ml (1 tsp) of glucose added, every 10 to 15 minutes to replace the lost fluids.

▼▼Don't give milk, and preferably not fruit
◆ ◆ juices, until the nausea has passed; they can induce vomiting.

◆Reintroduce solid foods slowly; if you do it too fast, the patient may be sick again.

◆After a patient has vomited, wipe her face with a cool damp cloth. Give her a toothbrush to brush her teeth to take away the taste. Give her a mint, a strongly flavoured sweet or some peppermint tea.

Food and drink

Anyone who is ill can survive without food for a time but they must drink fluids, to replace fluids lost through sweating, diarrhoea or vomiting to prevent dehydration.

GIVING A BED BATH

If a patient cannot get out of bed, give her a bed bath every day, particularly if she has a fever; she'll feel more comfortable and it will help to prevent bedsores from forming. You'll need:

◇ *A bowl of warm water and some soap*

◇ *2 flannels (one for the face and hands and one for the rest of the body)*

◇ *2 large towels*

◇ *Toothbrush, toothpaste and a mug of rinsing water*

◇ *Clean pyjamas or nightdress*

◇ *Cosmetics, talcum powder or skin cream as required. (Ask the patient if she has any particular likes or dislikes.)*

1 *Help the patient to take off her clothes, but leave her covered with a blanket or duvet.*

2 *Half roll one of the towels up lengthwise. Roll the patient towards you onto her side and place the rolled towel against her back. Roll the patient gently back over the towel and unroll it across the bed (see page 329).*

3 *Then let her wash her face and hands with a damp flannel, or do it for her.*

4 *Remove the blanket or duvet and cover her with another towel, then uncover each part in turn for washing. Start from the feet and work upwards; change the water after washing the groin and genital area.*

5 *Help the patient to brush her teeth. Remove the towels, then help her into clean clothes.*

◆Encourage a child to drink by making the drinks more interesting: allow her to drink out of an adult's glass; use a curly straw or a mug incorporating a colourful straw. Vary drinks as much as possible to prevent boredom. Give a child milkshake drinks if she doesn't like milk; freeze fruit juice to make iced lollies. Fruit juice lollies are also good for sore throats.

◆Make the meal as attractive as you can, particularly for an adult patient. A nicely laid out tray with a pretty, ironed cloth and food in pretty bowls, even with a tiny bunch of flowers is not only appetizing but shows that you've put some care and thought into it. Lay a child's food out to make interesting shapes and give her some of her favourite things.

◆Serve one course at a time, and keep the portions small; don't be impatient if the patient eats slowly or if she doesn't eat it all.

◆Don't deny a person alcohol if she wants some, unless the doctor has advised against it. A glass of stout or wine could do her good; don't give her spirits though.

Giving fluids *If a patient cannot sit up easily or finds it difficult to drink comfortably, use a beaker with a lid and a spout or a bendy straw.*

Lifting and moving a patient

◆Turn a bedridden patient regularly (or encourage her to move) to prevent bedsores.

▼▼ Never try to lift an adult patient on your
◆◆ own; you'll hurt your back.

Lifting a patient *Stand facing each other, one on each side of the patient, and grasp each other's wrists, under her thighs; join hands around the back. Ask the patient to put her arms around your shoulders, then lift her up; the patient should sit in the well formed by the two pairs of arms.*

MOVING A PATIENT UP THE BED

1 Sit the patient up. Sit on the bed, one person on each side of the patient, with one knee on the bed (your knees should be level with the patient's hip). Ask the patient to put his arms over your shoulders.

BEDSORES

Bedsores, or pressure sores, occur at the bony parts of the body such as the heels, toes, knees, buttocks, elbows and shoulders where the weight of the body pressing down on the area cuts off the blood supply to it causing ulceration. Once there, bedsores are difficult to cure. Elderly and bedridden patients are particularly susceptible.

◆ Adjust the position of a bedridden patient every two hours.

◆ Keep the skin clean and dry with talcum powder or dab any tender spots with surgical spirit.

◆ Get foam or sheepskin pads to put around the sensitive areas to relieve pressure. Look out for special sheepskins that can be put over the whole bed. Don't use these if the patient is incontinent because although they are washable, they take a long time to dry.

◆ Place an inflated air ring, enclosed in a pillowcase, under the buttocks.

2 Grasp each other's wrists under the patient's legs, and put your other hands at the level you want to move the patient to. Lean in towards the patient to support his armpits and stand up, using your knees to push yourselves forward.

NURSING THE ELDERLY

Elderly people often become timid and apologetic with the loss of their strength and vigour. Be patient and listen to what they are trying to tell you.

◆ A fluorescent light is often easier for the elderly to see by than an ordinary bulb.

◆ Keep the room at least 16°–19°C (61°–66°F) because the elderly can't regulate their own body temperature very well. See that the room is well insulated, with enough ventilation for comfortable breathing. Central heating, gas and electric fires make the atmosphere extremely dry, which can exacerbate chest infections.

◆ Put an electric overblanket on the bed; these are better than electric underblankets as they can be left on while the person is in bed. Don't leave the blanket on if she is very confused or incontinent.

◆ Get extra handrails put on the stairs or by the toilet or bath if an elderly person finds it difficult to get about.

◆ Get a shower installed if possible; they are easier to get in and out of than a bath. Get one with a non-slip tray or use a special mat and put a shower seat in it so that an elderly person can sit down to wash.

◆ Provide a bedpan or urinal for a bedridden person to minimize accidents. If an elderly person can get out of bed, but can't get to the bathroom, you may be able to get a commode (movable toilet).

◆ Find out if your local authority can provide nursing help, say a daily or weekly visit from a district nurse.

◆ Put a waterproof cover on the bed to protect the mattress if the person is incontinent.

◆ Ring your local authority to see if they can arrange to collect, launder and return linen if you are looking after an incontinent person.

◆ Ask the doctor for some incontinence pads; they are available on prescription.

▼▼ Don't stop someone drinking if he is
◆ ◆ incontinent; fluids are essential to the correct functioning of the body. Try to discourage drinking too much just before bedtime to minimize bedwetting at night.

COMMON INFECTIOUS DISEASES

◆Consult your doctor as soon as possible to get the diagnosis confirmed for any of the following conditions.
◆If a patient starts to deteriorate by the time she should be getting better, of if she develops any new symptoms, call your doctor immediately; there could be a complication.

DISEASE	SYMPTOMS	TREATMENT
CHICKENPOX Virus disease that in very rare cases may lead to complications such as encephalitis or Reye's syndrome. **Incubation period:** 17 to 21 days ◆ Your child will be infectious until all the scabs have dropped off.	Headache, fever, and itchy spots over the whole body, which develop into tiny blisters leaving a scab. The fever dies down when the spots appear. Eventually the scabs will drop off.	◆Soothe spots with calamine lotion and give warm baths containing a handful of bicarbonate of soda. ◆Keep fingernails short and clean; discourage scratching. If your child is still in nappies, change them frequently and leave them off when you can. ◆Your doctor may prescribe anti-infective cream if spots are infected, and a sedative. ◆Consult your doctor immediately if your child has neckache or is feverish after the spots go.
GASTROENTERITIS Virus that causes inflammation of the intestines. It can be very serious in children, especially babies, because it can rapidly lead to dehydration.	Nausea and vomiting, possible diarrhoea, loss of appetite and abdominal cramps, raised temperature.	◆Stop solid foods and give water only. Consult your doctor if vomiting continues for longer than six hours; he may hospitalize the baby. ◆Reintroduce food slowly, giving bland, non-fatty foods.
GLANDULAR FEVER (MONONUCLEOSIS) A fairly common infectious virus disease that affects teenagers and young adults. It is debilitating and can last for six months. The virus may reappear during the two years after the first attack, so keep your eyes open for symptoms.	Similar to influenza: runny nose, sore throat, aches, pains and tiredness, perhaps a rash behind the ears, spreading to the forehead. The neck glands may be swollen and there may be fever.	◆Consult your doctor; the diagnosis has to be confirmed by blood test. ◆Make sure the patient gets plenty of rest. Your doctor may recommend paracetamol to reduce the fever. Offer plenty of fluids. ◆Keep the patient occupied because depression is very common with this illness.
MEASLES A contagious virus disease usually of childhood. One attack usually gives immunity for life. Rarely it leads to complications such as middle ear infection or Reye's syndrome. Immunization against measles is available. **Incubation period:** eight to 14 days	Sore eyes, intolerance of bright light, sneezing, coughing, runny nose and a high fever, and sometimes white spots inside the mouth. The fever begins to subside by the fourth day, when a rash appears behind the ears and on the forehead and spreads over the entire body.	◆Control the fever with tepid sponging. Give plenty of fluid to prevent dehydration. ◆Bathe sore eyes with water; your doctor may prescribe drops. Darken the room. ◆Don't send a child back to school until the rash goes. ◆If the child gets worse after seeming to get better, call the doctor immediately.

DISEASE	SYMPTOMS	TREATMENT
MUMPS An acute virus disease transmitted in the saliva of an infected person. One attack usually brings immunity for life. Rarely it results in complications such as meningitis or encephalitis. **Incubation period:** 17 to 28 days	Swelling of face and neck (just below the ears and beneath the chin), usually beginning on one side and sometimes appearing on the other side in a day or two. It can cause swollen, painful testicles in males or lower abdominal pain in females. Other symptoms include headache, dry throat, painful swallowing and fever, sometimes vomiting.	◆ Treat fever with tepid sponging. ◆ Liquidize food if eating is difficult. Give plenty to drink and encourage rinsing of the mouth to alleviate dryness. ◆ Give the patient a hot water bottle wrapped in a towel to hold against the swollen area. ◆ Consult the doctor immediately if after 10 days the patient has a bad headache and a stiff neck.
RUBELLA (GERMAN MEASLES) A highly contagious virus disease. The illness is mild but if contracted by a woman during the first three months of pregnancy, it may affect her baby. One attack usually gives immunity for life. Girls should be immunized at puberty if they have not had the disease. **Incubation period:** 14 to 21 days	Slight fever and pink rash on face, neck and body. The rash disappears after one to three days.	◆ Consult your doctor by telephone first, so that he is not exposed to the disease. ◆ Keep the patient away from: anyone who might be pregnant, from school and public places. ◆ Bed rest if necessary.
SCARLET FEVER One of the less common infectious diseases caused by the *streptococcus* bacterium. Rarely there may be complications involving the kidneys, joints and heart. One attack usually gives immunity for life. **Incubation period:** one to five days	Sore throat, nausea, vomiting, headache, high fever with hot, dry skin. Rash appears over the body and tongue, which turns brilliant red. After a week the rash fades, the skin starts to peel and the disease is no longer infectious.	◆ Consult a doctor who will prescribe antibiotics. ◆ Bed rest if the patient feels ill. Otherwise keep her warm and quiet. ◆ Treat fever with tepid sponging if necessary. Give plenty of fluids. ◆ Liquidize foods and give soups and ice cream if swallowing is painful.
WHOOPING COUGH An acute, very contagious disease of the bronchial tubes and upper respiratory passages. Usually attacks children under ten years old. This disease is very dangerous in young children, particularly babies under one year. A vaccine is available for young babies. This disease is contagious throughout its duration. **Incubation period:** seven to 14 days	◇ Early stage, which lasts a week or two, is like a heavy cold with some fever and a persistent cough. ◇ Second stage, the cough grows worse and the patient begins to "whoop" or "bark". This stage can last from two to 10 weeks, then subsides.	◆ Consult your doctor immediately; antibiotics can shorten the duration of the illness if given early. ◆ Bed rest until the fever has gone. Keep the room well-ventilated. Stay with a child when she is coughing, give her a bowl to spit the phlegm into. ◆ A well-balanced diet is important to prevent loss of weight. If vomiting occurs after coughing, give small amounts of food frequently.

TRADITIONAL REMEDIES

Many herbs and spices contain beneficial volatile oils, minerals and other substances which can promote good health. They are available in many different forms: dried or fresh herbs, herb teas, alcoholic tinctures of herbs, fluid extracts, essential oils, syrups, vinegars, capsules, pills and tablets.

▼▼ *Home-prescribed remedies are only for* ♦♦ *mild conditions. If in doubt, consult your doctor or a medical herbalist. You should never exceed the stated dose.*

♦ Always buy from a reputable supplier so that you know the remedies are fresh and unadulterated.

♦ It can be cheaper to make your own herbal remedies. Buy the different dried or fresh herbs, or you can dry your own (see pages 19 and 167) and make a herbal tea by infusion or decoction. Dry only organically grown herbs.

▼▼ Essential oils are very concentrated ♦♦ and must not be used neat or taken internally because they can be toxic; use them mixed with a carrier oil (oils sold as aromatherapy oils are combined with a carrier oil), for inhaling or as a bath oil.

♦ To dry herbs quickly, you can dry them in a microwave oven. Put them on kitchen paper and dry for 30 seconds to 1½ minutes depending on the herbs and your appliance. Crumble the dried herbs into jars.

HERB TEAS

Buy them from a reputable supplier or make your own. Make an infusion if you are using soft leaves and flowers; make a

REMEDIES

ABSCESS
♦ Soak raspberry or comfrey (*Symphytum officinale*) leaves in hot water for a few minutes and apply directly to the affected area.
♦ Drink an infusion of chickweed (*Stellaria media*).

ANXIETY, STRESS
♦ Drink an infusion of valerian (*Valeriana officinalis*) chamomile (*Matricaria recutita*) flower tea or a mug of hot milk containing honey and a pinch of nutmeg or cinnamon.

ALLERGIES
♦ Drink an infusion of wild thyme (*Thymus vulgaris*), which is a powerful anti-bacterial agent.
♦ Chew peeled cloves of garlic or take garlic capsules.
♦ Drink nettle (*Urtica dioica*) or sage (*Salvia officinalis*) tea; they contain mineral salts.

ARTHRITIS
♦ Drink an infusion of wild thyme (*Thymus vulgaris*), which is a powerful anti-

bacterial agent and aids healing, or a decoction of celery (*Apium graveolens*) seeds, they are anti-rheumatic.
♦ Chew peeled garlic cloves or take garlic capsules (the capsules are odourless).
♦ Shred primrose (*Primula*) leaves into salads.
♦ Drink an infusion of honeysuckle flowers (*Lonicera caprifolium*), 225g (8oz) to 600ml (1pt) of water.

COLDS, COUGHS, FLU, CATARRH
♦ Make an infusion of any or all the following: 25g (1oz) coltsfoot (*Tussilago farfara*), 25g (1oz) elder flowers (*Sambucus nigra*), 25g (1oz) white horehound (*Marrubium vulgare*) in 1.2 litres (2pt) water and simmer until reduced by half. When cool add half a teaspoonful of cinnamon.
♦ Drink slippery elm (*Ulmus rubra*) tea (usually bought as a powder) mixed with cayenne pepper, honey and a little warm water twice a day.

♦ Grated horseradish (*Amoracia rusticana*) is a good decongestant.

CONSTIPATION
♦ Drink slippery elm (*Ulmus rubra*) tea mixed with equal parts of warm water and honey before breakfast and at bed time.
♦ Drink dandelion (*Taraxacum officinale*) coffee.
♦ Eat watercress, parsley or dandelion leaves.

CRAMP
♦ Massage a half-and-half mixture of olive oil and clove oil into the muscle.

DIGESTIVE UPSETS
♦ Drink peppermint (*Mentha piperita*) tea. Alternatively, drink tea made from the seeds and leaves of dill (*Anethum graveolens*) or chamomile (*Matricaria recutita*) or rosemary (*Rosmarinus officinalis*) tea.
♦ Chew raw carrots to prevent indigestion. Eat fresh pineapple at the end of a meal.
♦ Eat apples and cucumber with their peel on. The rinds and peel contain mineral salts which help digestion.

decoction if using tough, woody or very fluffy herbs or when the roots are used.
◆ **Adults** Aim to take about 150 ml ($\frac{1}{4}$pt) three times a day. Start off with smaller quantities; if the tea disagrees with you try

a weaker solution or use another remedy.
◆ Flavour herb tea with mint and thyme or a little honey or apple juice.
◆ **Children** Make smaller quantities and try 5ml (1tsp) at a time for small children.

MAKING AN INFUSION

◇ Unless specified in the recipe, use 25g (1oz) of the dried herb or 75g (3oz) of the fresh herb to 600ml (1pt) of boiling water. For a small amount use 5–10g ($\frac{1}{4}$–$\frac{1}{2}$oz) of dried herb to a cup of boiling water.

1 *Put the herbs into a warmed teapot or other china (not metal) container and pour the water over them.*

2 *Allow the herbs to steep for ten minutes then strain off the herbs and use immediately unless otherwise specified.*

MAKING A DECOCTION

◇ Use 25g (1oz) of the dried herb, torn or cut into pieces, to 900ml (1$\frac{1}{2}$pt) water. For a small amount use 5g ($\frac{1}{4}$oz) of the dried herb to a large cup of water.

1 *Put the herbs into an enamel, glass or stainless steel pan, then add the water. (Don't use any other container because it could affect the herbs.)*

2 *Bring to the boil and simmer for about 10–20 minutes or until the liquid is reduced by one third or as recommended below, then strain. Use while it is still hot, unless specified.*

REMEDIES

◆ Eat parsley or watercress.
◆ Make a digestive tonic by leaving a handful of basil (*Ocimum basilicum*) leaves for several hours in a bottle of wine.
◆ Grated horseradish (*Armoracia rusticana*) stimulates digestion.

FEET, TIRED, COLD OR ACHING
◆ Rub lemon peel, onion or garlic over the feet.
◆ Bathe the feet in hot water containing birch leaves, pine needles or mustard powder. Use a handful of birch leaves or pine needles or a teaspoonful of mustard to a washing up bowl of water.

FEVER, MILD
◆ Drink yarrow tea (*Achillea millefolium*), apple cider vinegar and honey, marigold flower (*Calendula*) tea or borage (*Borago officinalis*) tea made with fresh, young leaves, stems and flowers.

HEADACHES
◆ Drink basil (*Ocimum basilicum*) tea, Bergamot, or Oswego (*Monarda didyma*) tea, lemon balm (*Melissa*

officinalis) tea or tea made with lovage leaves (*Ligusticum officinalis*) at the onset of a headache.

INSOMNIA
◆ Rub a sliced clove of garlic onto the feet at bedtime.
◆ See also ANXIETY, STRESS

KIDNEY AND BLADDER TROUBLES
◆ Drink an infusion of golden rod (*Solidago virgaurea*) or borage (*Borago officinalis*), made using young leaves and flowers.
◆ Eat sorrel (*Rumex acetosa*) soup.

RHEUMATISM
◆ Drink infusion of lovage (*Levisticum officinale*). Don't take this if you are pregnant.
◆ See also ARTHRITIS

SINUSITIS
◆ See COLDS, COUGHS

SORE EYES
◆ Bathe them with cotton wool soaked in fennel tea.

SORE THROATS, MOUTH ULCERS
◆ Apply a drop of clary sage (*Salvia sclarea*) extract, which you can buy in chemists or health stores.
◆ Soak a handkerchief in apple cider vinegar or malt vinegar and hold it against the neck.
◆ Make a gargle with 5g ($\frac{1}{4}$oz) cayenne pepper, 10g ($\frac{1}{2}$oz) salt, 10ml (2tsp) vinegar (any vinegar). Add to 300ml ($\frac{1}{2}$pt) warm water and gargle. Use twice a day, or as necessary.
◆ Chew garlic cloves, onions or leeks every two hours.
◆ Drink sage (*Salvia officinalis*) tea, nettle (*Urtica dioica*) tea with a little wild thyme (*Thymus vulgaris*) or lemon thyme (*Thymus citriodorus*) to soothe the throat, several times a day.

MEDICINES

Keep a well-stocked medicine cupboard and first aid kit in the house; you never know when a member of the household will fall ill or have an accident. Although you can improvise quite adequately for first aid, it is much better to have the real thing at hand.

Check the first aid box and medicine cupboard every so often to make sure it is well stocked; replace items as necessary, don't wait until they have run out.

MEDICINE CUPBOARD

▼▼ Keep the medicine cupboard locked at
♦ ♦ all times; most medicines are poisonous. Never mix different pills in the same container; you may give someone the wrong one. Don't mix medicines either.

◆ Never keep old prescription medicines in the cupboard. Destroy them or take them back to the pharmacist; some are not safe to be thrown away.

◆ Use a lockable medicine cabinet, out of the reach of children, and hide the key.

WHAT TO KEEP IN THE MEDICINE CUPBOARD

◇ *Two mercury thermometers (in case one breaks). The digital type is easier to read*
◇ *Forehead thermometer for a baby*
◇ *Paracetamol and junior paracetamol elixir to help reduce fevers*
◇ *Calamine lotion for soothing bites and stings. Arnica ointment for bruises (don't use if the skin is broken)*
◇ *Currently prescribed medicines*
◇ *Syrup of Ipecac, to induce vomiting*
▼▼ Don't keep proprietary products
♦ ♦ containing local anaesthetic or skin creams containing anti-histamines (unless prescribed by your doctor) because they cause allergies.
▼▼ Don't keep mouth washes, gargles,
♦ ♦ eye drops, nose drops, ear drops, unless recommended by your doctor because they can be harmful.
▼▼ Don't keep proprietary children's
♦ ♦ medicines containing aspirin.

FIRST AID KIT

◆ Keep equipment in a clean, dry, airtight container so that it will remain sterile.
◆ Label the box clearly and put it somewhere easily accessible but not in the bathroom because the equipment can get damp.
◆ Check the packet when buying dressings; the seals on sterile dressings must be intact.

WHAT TO KEEP IN A FIRST AID BOX

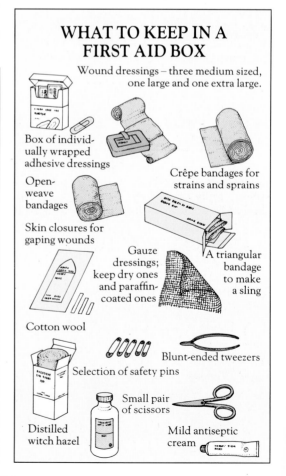

Wound dressings – three medium sized, one large and one extra large.

Box of individually wrapped adhesive dressings

Crêpe bandages for strains and sprains

Open-weave bandages

Skin closures for gaping wounds

Gauze dressings; keep dry ones and paraffin-coated ones

A triangular bandage to make a sling

Cotton wool

Blunt-ended tweezers

Selection of safety pins

Small pair of scissors

Distilled witch hazel

Mild antiseptic cream

USEFUL HOUSEHOLD ITEMS

◇ Packets of frozen peas or ice cubes in plastic bags make good cold compresses because they can be moulded to the shape of the injured part of the body.
◇ An elastic belt can be used to make an adequate support for strains and sprains. A leather belt can support a broken arm.
◇ Bicarbonate of soda – it can be added to a bath to relieve itching or added to warm water to soothe bee stings.
◇ Salt – a handful in the bath helps to cleanse a wound.
◇ Vinegar – dab it neat, or mixed half-and-half with water onto wasp or jellyfish stings to soothe them.
◇ Make a temporary splint for a broken limb out of rolled-up newspapers or a broom handle.

FIRST AID TECHNIQUES

No home is completely safe from accidents; however, knowing the correct procedures can help you to act quickly, and prevent a situation from becoming any worse. There are a few points that are worth remembering. If possible, look after the casualty and get someone else to call for the ambulance or doctor. If not, make the casualty comfortable, then summon help. If there is more than one casualty, deal with the most seriously injured first; equally, if a casualty has several injuries, treat the most serious one first, because the correct treatment of one may interfere with the treatment of another.

LIFE-SAVING TECHNIQUES

In order to survive, everyone needs a constant supply of oxygen to every part of the body. To achieve this, you must be able to breathe in order to take air containing oxygen into the body, and the blood must be circulating to carry the oxygen around the body. A casualty's vital needs are commonly abbreviated as A B C:
A An open AIRWAY
B Adequate BREATHING
C Sufficient blood CIRCULATION

EMERGENCY ACTION FOR A SERIOUSLY INJURED CASUALTY

This is a summary of the treatment, the techniques are described in more detail on the following pages.

1 *Send someone to telephone for an ambulance.*

2 *Open the casualty's airway, see page 340. Check to see if he is breathing, see page 340.*

3 *If he is breathing, turn him into the recovery position, see page 342.*

4 *If he is not breathing, try clearing his airway, see page 340, then check his breathing again.*

5 *If he is still not breathing after you have cleared the airway, give him two breaths of mouth-to-mouth ventilation, see page 341. Then check his heartbeat, see page 341.*

6 *If the casualty's heart has stopped beating, begin external chest compression, see page 342. Continue mouth-to-mouth and chest compression until heartbeat is restored, then mouth-to-mouth on its own.*

7 *If the heart is beating, continue mouth-to-mouth until breathing is restored, then turn the casualty into the recovery position.*

◆It is always worth starting resuscitation; even if the person's breathing or heart doesn't start, you may keep his system going long enough for a doctor to be able to take over. Brain cells will start to die after only three minutes without oxygen.

Opening the airway

◆Tilt the casualty's head back to allow him to breathe, because when a person is unconscious, particularly if he is lying on his back, the airway can be blocked by the tongue falling back across the top of the windpipe. It can also be blocked by vomit collecting in the back of the throat or the muscles in the throat relaxing and closing off the windpipe.

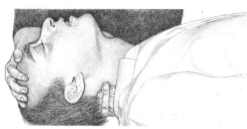

1 Put one hand under the casualty's neck and the other on his forehead, and tilt the head backwards. This will extend the neck to open the air passage.

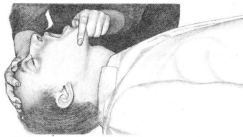

2 Take your hand from the neck and push the chin upwards to lift the tongue forwards, away from the airway.

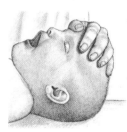

Opening a baby's airway *Lay him on a firm surface and press very gently on his forehead to tilt the head slightly. Don't press it back too far; you'll block the airway.*

Checking breathing

◆To find out if a casualty is breathing, kneel down beside him and put your ear as close as possible to his mouth. Look along the chest to see if you can detect any movement, and listen carefully and feel for any breaths against your face.

Clearing the airway

◆If the casualty isn't breathing, clear the mouth of any debris.

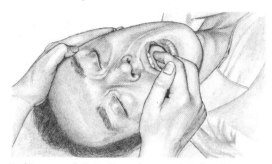

Lifting out debris *Turn the casualty's head to one side and sweep around his mouth with your forefingers, removing any foreign bodies that can be seen or felt. Do not waste time searching for a hidden blockage; the casualty could choke before you find it.*

Mouth-to-mouth ventilation

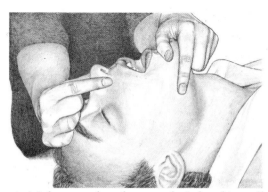

1 Make sure that the casualty's head is well back. Support his chin with one hand and pinch his nostrils together with the other one. Take a deep breath, then seal your lips around the casualty's mouth and blow.

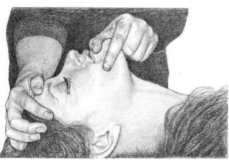

◇ *If the casualty has a poisonous substance around her mouth, give mouth-to-nose ventilation to prevent poisoning yourself. Put your thumb against the casualty's lower lip and push it against her upper lip to seal the mouth, then put your mouth over her nose.*

2 Look along the chest and blow into the mouth (or nose) until the chest has risen as far as it can.

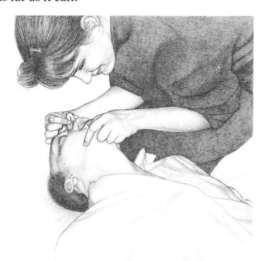

3 Move your mouth well away from the casualty's and breathe in fresh air as you watch the chest fall.

4 Check the casualty's pulse to find out if the heart is beating, see right.

5 If the heart is not beating, begin External chest compression immediately, see overleaf.

6 If the casualty's heart is beating, continue mouth-to-mouth at a rate of about 16–18 times per minute until he starts breathing for himself.

7 When he does start breathing, turn him into the recovery position to keep his airway clear and watch him carefully in case he stops breathing again.

TIPS FOR GIVING MOUTH-TO-MOUTH VENTILATION

◆ If the chest does not rise, adjust the position of the head as the airway may not be open properly. Then check that you are holding the nostrils shut and that your mouth is forming a tight seal around the casualty's.

◆ If, after you have adjusted the head, the chest still doesn't rise, try treating the casualty as for choking, see page 349.

Giving mouth-to-nose-and-mouth *If you are resuscitating a baby or young child, it may be easier to put your mouth around his mouth and nose.*

Checking for heartbeat

◆ **For an adult** Check the pulse in the arteries in the neck (the carotid arteries) – these are the easiest arteries to find.

◆ **For a child** Place your hand over the child's heart; the neck is too short for you to be able to find the arteries easily.

Finding the pulse *Find the front of the windpipe and slide your fingers across into the groove between it and the large muscle in the neck.*

External chest compression

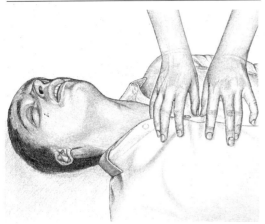

5 Carry on with 15 compressions, then two ventilations, and repeat the heart check after a minute. Then check the heartbeat again after every 12 cycles.

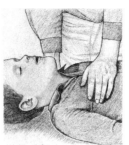
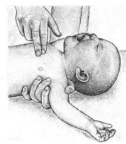

For children *Perform external chest compression with light pressure, using only one hand to a depth of 1.5–2.5cm (½–1in) at a rate of 80 times per minute.*

For babies *Use just two fingers, pressing at a rate of 100 times per minute to a depth of 1.5 to 2.5cm (½–1in).*

1 With the casualty on a firm surface, kneel alongside him level with his chest and in line with his heart. Find the lower part of the breastbone: feel for the notch at the top and the intersection of the rib margins at the bottom. Place your thumbs between these two "landmarks" to locate the centre.

The recovery position

◆ When an unconscious person is breathing and the heart is beating, put him into the recovery position. This ensures an open airway, keeps the tongue from falling into the back of the throat, keeps the head and neck extended and allows any vomit or other debris to drain freely. The steps below are for a casualty lying on his back; they won't all be necessary if the casualty is already on his side or front.

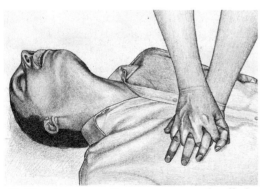

2 Keeping your fingers open and off the ribs, place the heel of one hand over the centre of the lower half of the breastbone. Cover this hand with the heel of the other one and lock your fingers together.

3 Keep your arms straight and move forward until they are vertical. Press down on the lower half of the breastbone about 4–5cm (1½–2in). Move backward to release pressure. Complete 15 compressions at the rate of 80 a minute (count "One-and-two-and-three" etc.).

4 Move back to the head, re-open the airway and give two breaths of mouth-to-mouth ventilation.

1 Kneel alongside the casualty level with the chest. Turn his head towards you, keeping the neck extended with the jaw forward to keep the airway open.

2 Place the arm nearest to you by the casualty's side and put the hand, palm up, under his buttock. Cross the far leg over the near leg at the ankle, then lay the arm furthest from you across his chest, pointing towards his shoulder.

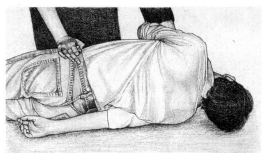

3 With one hand protecting and supporting the casualty's head, use the other to grasp the clothing by the far hip and quickly pull the casualty toward you until he is against your knees.

4 Readjust the head so that the airway is open. Bend the casualty's arm so that it supports the upper body and bend the uppermost leg at the knee so that the thigh comes forward to support the lower body.

5 Pull the other arm from under the casualty from the shoulder down and leave it lying parallel to his body to prevent him rolling onto his back.

WOUNDS AND BLEEDING

◆ If the injury is a small cut or graze, clean and dress it to prevent infection.

✴ EMERGENCY: If the wound is serious, control bleeding immediately and call an ambulance, or take the casualty to hospital, whichever is easier and quicker. If the casualty loses a lot of blood, there won't be enough to keep the internal organs supplied.

Foreign body in a wound

◆ Apply pressure above and below the object, to compress the blood vessels supplying blood to the area, then apply a dressing and

EMERGENCY ACTION FOR SEVERE BLEEDING

1 *Act quickly to stop any bleeding. Place a pad or dressing over the wound and press hard against it.*

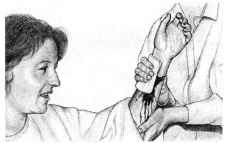

2 *Raise the injured part above the casualty's heart; this will slow down the flow of blood to the injury. Help the casualty to lie down, keeping the injured part raised. Support it on a cushion or rolled-up coat, if necessary.*

3 *Place a wound dressing over the wound, large enough to extend well beyond the edges. Secure it with a bandage tied firmly enough to maintain pressure but not so tight as to cut off circulation, see page 355.*

4 *If blood begins to show through the first dressing, put another one on top. Don't remove the original dressing, you'll disturb any clot that is forming.*

bandage that maintain the pressure but protect the object, see below, and take the casualty to hospital.

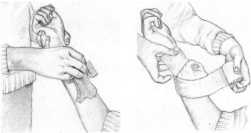

Applying a dressing around a foreign body
Drape a piece of gauze over the wound and the object, then place crescent-shaped pads of cotton wool around it, above left. Build up the pads until they are higher than the object. Pass the bandage under the limb and make two straight turns below the injury and over the bottom edge of the padding. Carry the bandage under the limb, then up over the outer edge of the padding, above right. Continue these turns above and below the wound to secure the dressing.

Small cuts and grazes

Trivial wounds which involve only slight bleeding will stop bleeding quite quickly even if blood oozes from all parts of them.

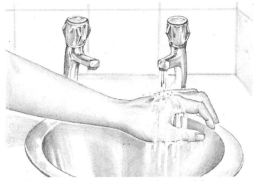

1 Rinse the injury under cold running water; the cold water will slow down the blood flow and clean the wound. If there is no water, use moistened cotton wool.
◇*If bleeding persists, press a clean pad of material over the wound.*

2 Clean the surrounding skin with soap and water, using a cotton wool swab. Use another part of the swab for each stroke to prevent infection. Don't wipe away blood clots because you may restart the bleeding.

◇*Remove any grit or other foreign matter on or near the surface with damp cotton wool or tweezers; don't dig into the wound, you could worsen it.*

3 Dress a small wound with an adhesive dressing ("plaster") to protect it; put a wound dressing on a larger wound.

GREEN TIP: Distilled witch hazel can be used to clean and soothe the wound.

GREEN TIP: Put calendula cream on a wound to speed up healing.

◆If you have any doubts about a wound, or if it starts to look red and "angry" after a few days, consult your doctor, it may be infected.
◆Ask the person if he has had a tetanus inoculation recently, particularly if the wound is very dirty. If he has not, consult his doctor.

Bruises

◆Raise the injured part and hold it under cold water for 5–10 minutes to slow down the flow of blood.
◇*If the site of the injury makes this difficult, place a cold pack on the area, see page 349.*

GREEN TIP: Break off a piece of aloe vera leaf and rub the sap onto the injury. Alternatively, if you are certain the skin is not broken, rub some arnica ointment onto the injury.
◆Get medical help if you are worried about the injury; a heavy blow can cause serious internal bleeding or even injury to an underlying bone.

SHOCK

"Traumatic" or injury shock is the effect of some form of injury or illness that has reduced the volume of blood or fluid in the body. Shock can be caused by excessive bleeding, severe burns, loss of water due to intestinal obstruction, recurrent vomiting or severe diarrhoea, extreme pain or fear. The body responds by directing most of the available blood to the vital organs of the body such as the heart.

★ Shock is an emergency; treat as described below and get the person to hospital as soon as possible if you notice any of the following symptoms:

◇ *Weakness, faintness, giddiness, anxiousness and restlessness*
◇ *Sickness and vomiting*
◇ *Thirst*
◇ *Pale, cold, clammy skin, perhaps sweating*
◇ *Shallow and rapid breathing with yawning and sighing*
◇ *Increased pulse rate but becoming weaker and sometimes irregular*
◇ *Possible unconsciousness – this is very serious.*

EMERGENCY ACTION FOR SHOCK

1 *Send someone for medical help.*

2 *Reassure and comfort the casualty. Lay him down, preferably on a blanket. Keep his head low and turn it to one side so that fluid in his mouth can drain. Raise his legs (unless you suspect a fracture) to keep the circulating blood in the centre of the body where it is most needed. Loosen tight clothing.*

3 *Keep the casualty comfortable, cover him with a blanket or similar if it is cold.*

4 *Call for an ambulance if someone has not already done so.*

5 *Check breathing and pulse and levels of consciousness every 10 minutes. Place the casualty in the recovery position, see page 342, if breathing is or becomes difficult.*

6 *Look for and treat the cause of the shock (e.g. severe bleeding) if you can.*

7 *If breathing or heartbeat stops, begin mouth-to-mouth ventilation and external chest compression as necessary, see pages 340–42.*

‼ *Don't give the casualty anything to drink or eat because he may need a general anaesthetic later; just moisten the lips with water if asked.*
‼ *Never warm the casualty with a hot water bottle or an electric blanket because it will dilate the blood vessels in the skin and encourage blood flow to it, away from the centre of the body.*
‼ *Don't move the casualty unnecessarily and don't let him smoke.*

Nose bleeds

◆Give the casualty a bowl into which he can spit out any blood that gets into his mouth; if he swallows too much of the blood, he may be sick.
◆Clean around the nose and mouth with lukewarm water; don't use hot water as you may disturb the clot.

Stopping a nose bleed
Tell the casualty to breathe through her mouth, pinch the soft part of her nose and lean forward to help the clots form; you may have to help a child do this.

▼▼ Don't give the casualty a hot drink for a
♦ ♦ few hours after the nose bleed; the heat
could disturb the blood clot. Likewise, advise him not to blow his nose; the action
could restart the bleeding.

◆ If the bleeding hasn't stopped after 10
minutes, carry on for another 10 minutes.
Call the doctor if it hasn't stopped after
about 30 minutes.

Mouth and gum wounds

1 Sit the casualty down and tell her to lean
her head to the injured side. Put a small
pad of gauze against the gum wound or on
(not INTO) the empty tooth socket so that it
projects above the remaining teeth. (If you
put the pad into the tooth socket, you could
worsen the injury.) Get the casualty to bite
on the pad for 10–20 minutes.

2 If the bleeding continues, gently remove
the pad and replace it with another clean
one. Maintain the pressure on the new pad
for another 10 minutes.

3 If the bleeding persists after that, call the
doctor or take her to hospital.

DISPLACED TOOTH

If a casualty has knocked out a tooth,
keep the tooth, it may be possible for it
to be replaced.

▼▼ Don't wash a broken tooth, put it in
♦ ♦ a clean polythene bag or get the
casualty to suck it. Take the casualty
(with the tooth) to the dentist or hospital
as soon as possible. Washing the tooth
reduces the likelihood of being able to
replace it because it can destroy the bacteria in it.

UNCONSCIOUSNESS

This is a dangerous condition because the
body's normal reflexes which allow you to
breathe while asleep, for example, stop
working properly.

◆ If a person has been unconscious, even for
a short time, take him to your doctor or to
hospital; there may be an underlying injury
or condition that needs treatment.

▼▼ Don't give an unconscious person any-
♦ ♦ thing by mouth; he could easily choke.

EMERGENCY ACTION FOR
UNCONSCIOUSNESS

1 *Shake the person by the shoulders or pinch her
earlobe and ask her a question such as "Are
you alright?" Give her 10 seconds to respond.*
For a baby *Tap the sole of her foot – she should
respond immediately if she is conscious.*

2 *If there is no response, tilt the head back to
open the airway then check breathing, see
page 340. If she is breathing but is making gurgling sounds, try clearing the airway, there may
be something blocking it.*

3 *If she is breathing normally, turn her into the
recovery position, see page 342. Keep an eye
on her while you are waiting for the doctor and
note down any changes in her condition.*

4 *If she is not breathing, begin mouth-to-mouth
ventilation and external chest compression,
see pages 340–42, as necessary.*

5 *Examine her body for any signs of injury, or if
you don't know her, for any lockets or cards
indicating that she has a condition that can result
in unconsciousness. If you notice fluid coming
from an ear, turn her so that she is lying on the
affected side to let it drain.*

▼▼ Don't leave an unconscious casualty un-
◆ ◆ attended because his condition could worsen at any time.

Fainting

Fainting is a short spell of unconsciousness and recovery is usually quick and complete.

1 Sit the casualty down, and help her to lean forward with her head down between her knees and take deep breaths.

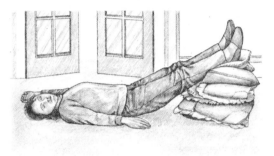

◇ If the casualty collapses and is unconscious, turn her onto her back and raise her legs to get the blood flowing back to the heart. She should recover very quickly. If she doesn't recover, treat as described opposite.

2 Loosen tight clothes at the neck, chest and waist. Provide plenty of fresh air, fanning it onto the face if necessary. Gently raise the casualty into a sitting position and let her sit quietly for a while.

BONE, JOINT AND MUSCLE INJURIES

These include broken bones, or fractures, sprained or torn ligaments (ligaments are the bands of tissue that hold joints together) and strained muscles. In some cases it's difficult to differentiate between a broken bone and a sprain or a dislocated joint, as they can all be extremely painful. If in doubt, treat the injury as a break, then at least you won't worsen it.

Broken bones

◆ Treat breathing difficulties, severe bleeding or unconsciousness before treating a broken bone, because these conditions can be life-threatening.

▼▼ If you have to move a casualty because
◆ ◆ his life is in danger, for example, temporarily immobilize the broken limb first; broken bone ends can be sharp and cause serious internal injury.

◆ Note any symptoms, but don't move any part unnecessarily as you could make the injury worse. Compare injured with uninjured limbs to help you establish the site of the injury. Possible symptoms are:
◇ The casualty may have heard and/or felt the bone snap
◇ Movement of the part may be difficult or impossible and attempts to move increase pain at or near the injury
◇ Tenderness when pressure is applied
◇ Swelling, and later, bruising
◇ The limb may look deformed – shortened or rotated or sticking out at an unnatural angle; this will be particularly noticeable if the top of the thighbone or both bones in the lower leg are broken
◇ The casualty may be in Shock, especially if the thigh or pelvis is broken, because both injuries are often accompanied by severe blood loss, see page 345.

◆ Get medical help as soon as possible. You can take a casualty with a broken arm to hospital yourself if you have a car; a casualty with a broken leg will need an ambulance because he will probably need to be carried on a stretcher.

1 Steady and support the injured limb with your hands. The casualty may be able to support his own arm.

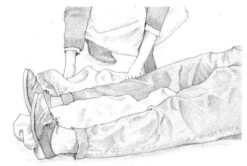

2 If transport to hospital is on the way, keep the injured part supported by hand and by placing rolled-up blankets or coats along either side of it. Make the casualty as comfortable as possible.

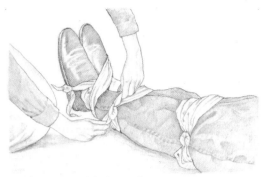

3 If you are likely to have to wait half an hour or more for transport, secure the injured part to a sound part of the body with padding and a sling and/or wide bandages. Tie the bandages so that they are firm enough to stop movement but not so tight that they will cut off blood circulation or cause pain, see page 355.

4 Raise the injured part after immobilizing it to slow down blood flow to it, so minimizing swelling and discomfort.

Sprained joint

A sprain is caused when one or more of the ligaments and tissues around a joint is wrenched and torn (when a foot turns over while running, for instance).
◆ Suspect a sprain if after a fall:
◇ *The casualty complains of pain and tenderness around the joint, made worse by movement*
◇ *You notice swelling, or later, bruising.*
◆ If in doubt treat as a fracture; it can be difficult to differentiate between a bad sprain and a fracture anyway.

1 Raise the injured limb and support in a comfortable position. Apply a cold compress to reduce swelling and pain (a bag of frozen peas wrapped in a thin towel is ideal because it moulds to the shape of the limb.

2 Support the joint with a thick layer of cotton wool secured with a bandage. Don't apply a tight bandage because the joint will probably swell quickly. Take the casualty to hospital or to your doctor.

Supporting a sprained ankle *If the casualty has a tight shoe or boot, on, don't remove it because it will be supporting the injury. Tie a bandage in a figure-of-eight around the ankle and over the shoe and take the casualty to hospital or to your doctor.*

Dislocated joint

This occurs when the ligaments that hold a joint together are torn – shoulders, elbows, thumbs, fingers and jaws can all be dislocated. Sometimes it is hard to tell the difference between a dislocated joint and a broken bone because they are both extremely painful. If in doubt, treat as a fracture.
◆ Suspect dislocation if you notice deformity at a joint as well as any signs of a sprain.
◆ Support the part in the position the casualty finds most comfortable and, if possible, immobilize it with padding and bandages or a sling. Get the casualty to hospital.
▼▼ Don't attempt to replace dislocated
◆◆ bones or you may do more damage.

Strained or "pulled" muscle

◆ A cold compress, see opposite, may help to ease the pain, particularly if the muscle is stiff as a result of sitting or lying still for a while. Put a wrapped hot water bottle on an old injury.

Supporting the injury *Rest the injured part on a cushion, and place a compress on it. Apply a soft, preferably crêpe, bandage to support it if necessary.*

COOLING FOR PAIN RELIEF

Cooling an injury slows down the blood flow to it, minimizing swelling and therefore easing pain. This works particularly well for sprains, strained muscles, dislocated joints, or bruising and small cuts and grazes, see page 344.

◆ Hold the injury under cold running water for up to half an hour to cool it. Don't do this for too long with a baby or young child, though, because he could get too cold.

◆ If the site of the injury makes it difficult to put the injury under cold water, make a cold water or ice compress, see below, or wrap a packet of frozen peas in a thin towel and use that. Leave the compress on for up to half an hour.

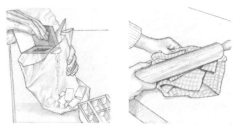

Making an ice compress *Put some crushed ice or ice cubes in a polythene bag. Pour some salt into the bag to lower the melting temperature of the ice, above left. Exclude any air from the bag, seal it, and wrap it in a thin towel. Crush the ice blocks by hitting the bag with a rolling pin, above right, so that the compress will mould to the shape of the injured area, then place it on the injury as required.*

Making a cold water compress *Soak a large pad of cotton wool or small towel in cold water, preferably iced water, above left. Wring it out so that it is just damp, above right, and place it on the injury; replace it when it starts to feel warm, or drip more iced water onto it.*

CHOKING

Young children are particularly at risk of choking because of their tendency to put things into their mouths.

◆ Suspect choking and act quickly if you notice that a person:

◇ *Is trying to cough, gripping his throat and is unable to speak or breathe*

◇ *Looks blue around the face and lips and may have prominent veins in the neck and face.*

✳ EMERGENCY: If the casualty becomes unconscious, treat as described on page 346 and get medical help.

EMERGENCY ACTION FOR CHOKING

1 *If the person is coughing, encourage him to do so; this may be enough.*

2 *If he is not coughing, help him to bend over until his head is lower than his lungs. Give a smart slap with the heel of your hand between the shoulder blades. Repeat up to four times.*

For a child *Lay him across your lap with his head lower than his chest and slap his back hard between his shoulder blades.*

For a baby *Pick him up and lay him face down, with his head lower than his chest, along your forearm and slap his back.*

3 *Check the mouth to see if the obstruction has been dislodged. If it's still there and visible, try to hook it out with your forefinger. If you can't see anything, slap the casualty's back until the object is free.*

▼▼ *Be very careful not to push the object back down the throat again. Never probe too far back if you can't see it; you could damage the tissues lining the throat.*

OTHER INJURIES

Most small injuries can be treated easily at home. If you are ever in any doubt though, call your doctor, or take the person to the nearest casualty department.

Burns and scalds

◆If the casualty is an infant or sick elderly person, always get medical help.

EMERGENCY ACTION FOR SEVERE BURNS

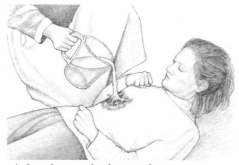

1 Lay the casualty down and get someone to call an ambulance while you cool the injury by carefully pouring jugs of cold water over it. Remove any constricting clothing or jewellery that is not sticking to the injury.

2 Cover the injury with a dressing or clean non-fluffy material (a pillow case is ideal) to minimize infection.

3 Treat as described for shock, see page 345; there can be severe fluid loss.

BURNS TO THE MOUTH AND THROAT

1 Give frequent sips of cold water to cool the throat (the tissues in the throat swell very quickly). Remove constricting clothing or jewellery from around the neck and chest. Call an ambulance.

2 If the casualty loses consciousness, place him in the recovery position, see page 342. Check breathing and heartbeat and start mouth-to-mouth and external chest compression as necessary, see pages 340–42.

◆Cool a burn to minimize the damage. Use cold water if possible, but if there isn't any clean water available, use any cold liquid like milk or beer.

▼▼ Don't put fats or ointments onto a burn, ◆ ◆ the residual heat can heat up the cream and make the injury worse.

▼▼ Don't break blisters, remove loose skin, ◆ ◆ or anything that is sticking to a burn, or otherwise interfere with a burn; burns are easily infected.

Treating a minor burn Hold the injured area under cold running water or immerse it in cold water for at least 10 minutes to cool it down, above left. Gently remove any constricting clothing, rings, watches, belts, shoes etc. from the injured area, above right. Do this before it starts to swell. Cover the burn with a dressing that is larger than the wound.

Electric shock

▼▼ Don't approach the casualty until you ◆ ◆ are sure you are in no danger yourself. Either switch off the power supply at the mains or knock the casualty clear of the electrical contact, see below. If he is unconscious, see EMERGENCY ACTION FOR UNCONSCIOUSNESS, page 347.

Breaking electrical contact If you are some distance from the power switch, wear wellington boots or stand on a wad of newspaper and knock the casualty away from the electrical source with a non-conductive object such as a wooden broomstick.

Head injuries

◆Cover a scalp wound with a dressing, secured with a bandage. Take the casualty to hospital if the wound is large because it may need stitches. Scalp wounds often look worse than they actually are; the skin is so tightly stretched across the scalp that, if damaged, it bleeds profusely. Keep an eye on the casualty for a few days after the incident and take him to the doctor immediately if you notice any changes; there may be an underlying injury.

◆If your child suffers a blow to the head, take him to your doctor or the hospital immediately because a child's skull is not very tough and there may be a fracture.

◆If, after a casualty has suffered a blow to the head, you notice him losing consciousness, becoming vague or vomiting while recovering consciousness, or if you notice that when he is conscious again he can't remember anything that has happened, he may have concussion. Take him to hospital by car or call an ambulance.

For an unconscious casualty *If a person is unconscious after a head injury, place her in the recovery position, see page 343, and call an ambulance. If you see any fluid coming from her ear, put a pad of material against the ear and position her so that she is lying on that ear. This is to allow fluid to drain and prevent a build-up of pressure within the skull.*

Poisoning

◆Suspect poisoning if you find a person collapsed with a container nearby that you know contained a poisonous substance or with some poisonous berries or leaves in his hand or near him.

EMERGENCY ACTION FOR POISONING

CONSCIOUS CASUALTY

1 *If the casualty is conscious, quickly ask him to tell you, or point to, what he has taken because he could lose consciousness at any moment. Call an ambulance.*

2 *If the casualty's lips or mouth show signs of burning, cool them by dabbing milk or water onto them.*

▼▼ *If the casualty has swallowed a corrosive*
◆◆ *poison, don't try to make him vomit; anything that burns going to the stomach will burn again on its way up.*

3 *If you are certain that the casualty has not taken a corrosive poison, he is fully conscious and not having a convulsion, try to make him sick by giving him some syrup of Ipecac or a glass of salty water.*

UNCONSCIOUS CASUALTY

1 *If the casualty is unconscious, call an ambulance immediately or get someone to drive you and the casualty to hospital, while you give first aid in the back of the car.*

2 *Place him in the recovery position, see page 342. If breathing or heartbeat stops, begin mouth-to-mouth and external chest compression as necessary, see pages 340–42.*

▼▼ *If you think that there is poison around the*
◆◆ *casualty's mouth, use mouth-to-nose ventilation so that you don't burn your lips.*

◆Act quickly if you notice any of the following symptoms and signs:

◇*Burns around lips and mouth, intense stomach pains; these may indicate that the casualty has taken a corrosive substance such as bleach, caustic soda, toilet cleaner or oven cleaner*

◇*Convulsions*

◇*Vomiting and, later on, diarrhoea.*

✹ EMERGENCY: Get the casualty to hospital as soon as possible, taking samples of vomit, and any bottles, pillboxes, plants etc., found near him or that he is known to have eaten, because they will help the doctor decide on the best treatment.

◆Ring your local poison advice centre if you have one.

Sunburn

◆ Get the casualty into the shade and soothe the skin with calamine lotion or tepid water. Advise him not to expose the skin to direct sun for at least 48 hours.

◆ If there is extensive blistering, get medical help at once; don't break the blisters.

✸ EMERGENCY: If the person has a fever and hot dry skin, he may be suffering from the early stages of heatstroke, see below; call the doctor immediately.

Heat exhaustion

Caused by loss of salt and water from the body through profuse sweating. It can be aggravated by extra fluid loss as a result of a stomach upset.

◆ Suspect heat exhaustion if during hot weather a person starts to feel exhausted and restless or faint, with a possible headache, or if he feels sick and has cramp-like pains in the calf muscles. The skin will be clammy but pale and his pulse may be rapid.

◆ Lay the casualty down in a cool place and give him sips of cold water. If symptoms persist, call the doctor.

◇ *If there are cramps, diarrhoea and vomiting, put 2.5g (½ tsp) salt into each 600ml (1pt) water.*

EMERGENCY ACTION FOR HEATSTROKE

If, in very hot weather, a person has a high fever and hot DRY skin, he may have heatstroke, which needs urgent treatment by a doctor.

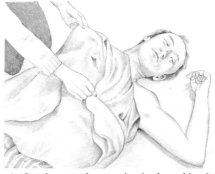

1 *Get the casualty into the shade and lay him down. Cool him down as quickly as you can: remove his clothes and wrap him in a cold wet sheet or towel. Call the doctor immediately.*

2 *Once the skin has cooled down, replace the wet towel with a dry one and stay with the casualty. If he loses consciousness, treat as necessary, see page 346.*

Hypothermia

If the body gets very cold, the body's systems slow down, and less blood is supplied to the limbs and skin in order to keep the vital organs, such as the heart, supplied with blood. Elderly people and babies are particularly susceptible to hypothermia in cold weather because their body temperature control is not very efficient.

◆ Suspect hypothermia and act quickly if a person is shivering, his skin feels very cold, and looks pale, if he becomes irrational, has very slow breathing and pulse rate. If left, he may become unconscious.

◇ **In a baby** *The skin will feel cold but he may look very pink and healthy; he will probably be very quiet, drowsy and limp.*

1 Wrap the casualty in a sleeping bag, duvet or eiderdown, covering everything except the face. You can sit under the duvet or in the sleeping bag as well so that your body heat helps to warm him, or put a well-wrapped hot-water bottle against his body (not his limbs). Call the doctor.

◇ *If he is unconscious, lay him in the recovery position, see page 342.*

2 Put a conscious adult in a warm bath, warm enough to be comfortable to your elbow. Top it up with hot water as necessary.

When his skin feels warm, put him in a warm bed and give hot, sweet drinks.

3 If breathing or heartbeat stops, begin mouth-to-mouth or external chest compression as necessary.

▼▼ Don't rub or massage limbs or warm
♦ ♦ them with a hot-water bottle because it will increase the blood flow to them and away from the centre of the body. Don't give alcohol as it dilates the blood vessels, encouraging blood to flow all over the body and not remain in the centre of the body where it is needed most.

Insect bites and stings

Stings from insects such as bees, wasps and hornets are not normally dangerous, although they are both painful and alarming. Spiders in some countries are poisonous; if in doubt, treat as for snake bites, see right.

✸ EMERGENCY: Get the casualty to hospital as soon as possible if:

◇ *He is known to be allergic to stings (the effect of stings is accumulative and there can be a severe reaction)*

◇ *He is stung in the mouth or throat, because the tissues swell quickly and can block the airway and prevent breathing*

◇ *He has several stings, because he has disturbed a nest, for example.*

♦ If the sting is still in the skin, use tweezers to get it out, see above right.

🌿 GREEN TIP: Soothe a wasp sting with vinegar (wasp stings are alkaline and neutralized by acid); dab a bee sting with cotton wool soaked in a cup of warm water containing 5g (1tsp) bicarbonate of soda (bee stings are acidic).

♦ If pain or swelling persists for longer than 24 hours, go to your doctor.

🌿 GREEN TIP: Apply a drop of essential oil of lavender or eucalyptus to soothe the area and reduce the swelling.

For a sting in the throat *Wrap a cold pack around the casualty's neck and give him an ice cube to suck to keep the swelling down. Get him to hospital quickly.*

Removing a bee sting *Grasp the base of the sting as close to the skin as possible with a pair of tweezers, but don't squeeze the poison sac (you will force more poison into the skin).*

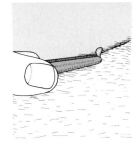

Jellyfish sting

♦ Lay the casualty down and flood the area of the sting and remaining tentacles with vinegar to neutralize them, then immobilize with bandages as for snake bites, see below, and get medical help.

Snake bites

♦ Lay the casualty down so that the site of the bite is lower than his heart, and advise him not to move. This is to slow down the flow of blood containing poison back to the heart. Immobilize the area with bandages and get the casualty to hospital.

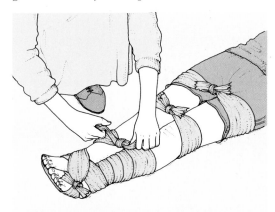

Treating a snake bite *Keep the casualty as still as possible. Bandage the affected area, then immobilize it. If the bite is on the casualty's arm, put it in a sling, then tie a bandage around the body and affected arm; if the bite is on the leg, tie both legs together at the ankles, knees and thighs.*

Splinters

1 Sterilize a pair of tweezers by holding them in a naked flame; don't wipe the soot off, you'll have to sterilize them again.

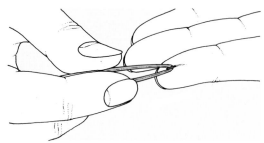

2 Hold the tweezers as near to the skin as possible and grasp the splinter. Gently pull it out in the opposite direction to which it entered the skin.

▼▼ DON'T probe the area to get to the
◆ ◆ splinter, you may break it. If the splinter is deeply embedded, get your doctor to remove it.

◆ If the splinter is very dirty, the casualty may need a tetanus injection.

Foreign body in the nose

▼▼ DON'T attempt to remove a foreign
◆ ◆ body lodged in the nose. A sharp object may easily damage the tender nose tissues.

◆ Keep the casualty quiet and advise him to breathe through his mouth. Get medical help as soon as possible.

Foreign body in the ear

Children are particularly prone to this type of injury.

◆ Tilt the head so that the affected ear is downwards; this may help the object to drop out. If it doesn't, take the casualty to the doctor.

▼▼ DON'T try to dislodge any object your-
◆ ◆ self even if you can see it clearly. You may perforate the eardrum.

◆ If the casualty can hear an insect buzzing in his ear, try "floating" it out with tepid water, see above right, or take him to the doctor as soon as possible.

Removing an insect from an ear *Tilt the person's head so that the affected ear is uppermost and gently flood the ear with tepid water; it must not be too hot or too cold, you could damage the eardrum.*

Foreign body in the eye

▼▼ DON'T let the casualty rub the eye, the
◆ ◆ object could become embedded.

◆ Sit the casualty down facing a bright light. Separate the eyelids, then ask him to look left, right, up and down so that you can look at the whole eye. If you can see the object, remove it as shown below. If it is under the upper lid, pull the upper lid downwards and outwards over the lower lid and ask the casualty to blink; the lashes may lift it. If it is on the eye under the upper lid, expose the area by pulling the lid back over a match-stick, then use a moistened handkerchief to get the object out.

◆ **If the object is embedded or on the coloured part of the eye** Tell the casualty to keep the eye closed. Cover it with a pad or clean handkerchief, taped in position, tell him to keep both eyes still (cover up the other eye if necessary). Take him to hospital immediately.

Removing dust from an eye *Remove it with the dampened corner of a clean tissue, handkerchief or cotton wool swab.*

BANDAGING TECHNIQUES

◆ When you have finished securing a bandage or sling, check the limb to make sure the blood is circulating. Press one of the exposed fingernails or toenails until it goes white, then release the pressure. If the nail goes pink again immediately, blood is circulating through the area; if not, remove the bandage and start again.

SLING

◆ Make an improvised sling by folding the bottom of the casualty's jacket up over the arm and pinning it to the top of the jacket.

◆ Use a triangular bandage or a piece of material about 1m/yd square folded in half to make a sling.

1 *Place the arm across the casualty's chest, with his hand slightly higher than his elbow and tell him to support it.*

2 *Fold the long edge of the bandage to make a hem and slide it through the gap between the casualty's elbow and body, leaving the long edge parallel to the other arm; take the top corner around the casualty's neck to the front.*

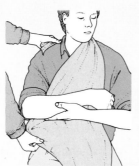

3 *Carry the lower end of the bandage up over the arm and tie a reef knot in the hollow below his shoulder.*

4 *Fold the corner of the bandage at the elbow back, then bring the point forward and pin it to the front.*

STRAIGHT BANDAGE

Use to secure a dressing to a leg or arm or to support strained muscles.

1 *Unroll the bandage slightly and, holding it with the rolled part uppermost, place the end of the bandage on the limb and make a straight turn.*

2 *Work up the limb, making spiral turns so that each layer covers two thirds of the previous one. Finish off with a straight turn and secure with a safety pin.*

ANKLE/HAND BANDAGE

1 *Holding the bandage with the roll uppermost, and working from the inner side of the leg outwards, make one straight turn.*

2 *Take the bandage across the top of the foot to the little toe, around under the foot and up at the base of the big toe. Make two complete turns around the foot.*

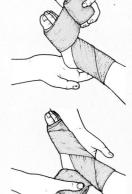

3 *Take the bandage across the top of the foot to the ankle. Continue figure-of-eight turns around the foot and ankle until the foot is covered – overlapping each turn.*

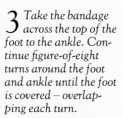

4 *Finish off with two turns at the ankle and secure the bandage.*

ACTION FOR EMERGENCIES

In any emergency speed is of paramount importance: seconds can mean the difference between life or serious injury and even death, or minor and major damage to property. Make sure that you are safe, and stay as calm as you can; the calmer you are the more you can help and comfort others. Deal with the incident as quickly as you can. If possible, get everyone to safety while someone else summons help.

INJURIES

This is meant as a summary of immediate action in the case of someone being injured in the home. For more detailed advice, see pages 339–55.

Serious bleeding

1 Lay the person down and *raise the injured area* higher than the chest.

2 Apply *pressure* to the wound, through a clean pad or dressing.

3 Send someone to call for an ambulance.

Unconsciousness

1 Tilt the person's head back to *open the airway*, see page 340, and *check breathing*, page 340.

2 If he is breathing, turn him into the *recovery position*, see page 342.

3 If breathing stops, begin *mouth to mouth ventilation* and *external chest compression* as necessary, see pages 340–42.

4 Ring for an ambulance if someone has not already done so for you.

Choking

1 Get the casualty's head lower than her chest and *slap her back hard.*

◇ **For a baby** *Hold her upside down and slap her back.*

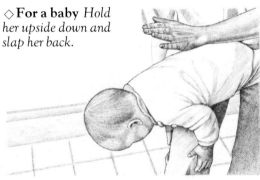

◇ **For a child** *Quickly lay him head down, across your lap and slap his back.*

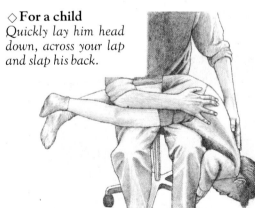

2 If breathing stops, start *mouth-to-mouth ventilation*, see page 340, and get someone to call an ambulance.

GAS LEAK

▼▼ Don't try to mend a gas leak yourself,
♦ ♦ you could cause an explosion.

Small gas leak

1 Search for the leak by checking all switches on a gas stove, *above left*, the gas taps and pipes for leaks *above right*, and making sure the pilot lights are alight.

◇ *Put out any naked flames and cigarettes while searching for the leak.*

▼▼ If in the dark, use a torch and NOT a
♦ ♦ match or candle to search for the leak. Don't turn on a light; the spark could ignite the gas.

2 If the smell lingers and you can't find the source, telephone the gas service.

Serious gas leak

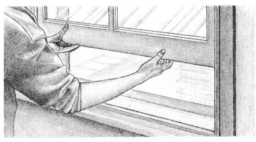

1 If there is a very strong smell of gas, open all doors and windows and put out all naked flames.

▼▼ Don't switch electric switches either on
♦ ♦ or off; you could cause an explosion.

2 Telephone the gas service immediately. Turn off the gas at the mains if you can.

FIRE

◆ Get everyone out of a building before treating any injuries.

Major fire

1 Get everybody out of the building. Don't stop to gather up possessions.

2 Ring the fire service from a neighbour's home or a telephone box.

IF TRAPPED ON AN UPPER FLOOR

1 Go into a room, close the door, and block the gap under it with garments, bedding or rugs to stop smoke coming underneath it, *above left*. Open the window and shout for help, *above right*.

2 If the room fills with smoke, lean out of the window or lie down on the floor and get below the level of the smoke.

3 If possible, tie a wet rag around your mouth and nose to keep some of the fumes out. Make a rope of bed clothes, belts etc. to use only as a last resort.

Small fire

1 Get out of the room, and close the door so that draughts cannot fan the flames. (A fire can take half an hour to burn through a solid door.)

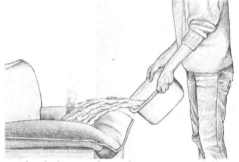

◇ If upholstery is burnt by a cigarette falling on it and is only beginning to smoulder, pour water over it.

◇ If the fire is smouldering seriously or is already burning, get out of the room and the house; the foam used in some upholstered furniture gives off lethal fumes.

2 Ring the emergency services and ask for the fire brigade.

Clothes on fire

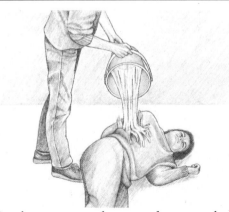

Get the person on the ground, to stop the flames rising up towards her face; douse the flames with water. Alternatively, wrap her with a blanket or coat to smother the flames; the heavier the material the better.

▼▼ Don't roll him on the ground because
◆ ◆ the hot clothes could burn him or the
flames could spread to a previously
undamaged area.

▼▼ Don't use flammable material to
◆ ◆ smother the flames; it will melt and
could cause severe burns.

Fat fire

1 Turn off the heat under the pan (or turn off at the mains).

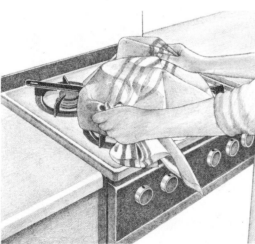

2 Smother the flames with a lid, a large plate, a tin tray or a damp (not wet) tea towel or a fire blanket if you have one.

◇ *Don't move the pan or pour water over it, you'll fan the flames.*

▼▼ If your chip pan begins to smoke, turn
◆ ◆ off the heat because it could ignite.

Electric fire

1 Switch off electricity at the mains.

2 Extinguish the fire with an all-purpose fire extinguisher or one that is designed for use on electrical fires.

◇ *If you haven't got a suitable fire extinguisher, smother a burning appliance with a heavy rug or blanket; the heavier the better.*

▼▼ Don't use water unless you know that
◆ ◆ the current is switched off.

3 If you can't control the fire quickly, shut the door into the affected room and get everyone out of the house; ring the fire brigade from a neighbour's home.

▼▼ Never use water to put out a fire in a
◆ ◆ television or computer even if it is
switched off, because there may be residual
current in the machine and you will get an
electric shock.

FLOOD

◆ Act quickly to minimize the structural damage; water travels quickly and a little goes a long way.

Burst tank or pipe

1 Stop the source of water: turn off water at the mains if necessary.

2 If this doesn't stop the water, turn on all the taps to drain the water tank.

3 If water is coming down a light fitting, remove the relevant fuse from the mains fuse box. Don't replace the fuse until the area is completely dry.

4 If there is a bulge in the ceiling, pierce it with a screwdriver, to minimize the damage to the ceiling.

5 Tie up the ball float in the cold water tank to stop it filling up, then turn on the mains tap so that you can at least have some water in the kitchen.

6 Do emergency repairs if you can, see pages 230–31, and call the plumber.

7 Mop up the water with towels as quickly as you can and, if it is safe, put a fan heater in the room to speed up the drying time. (Use a long extension lead if necessary from another part of the home.) Lift up all floor coverings to let air circulate around them; they'll dry faster.

Floods from outside

1 Turn off the electricity, gas and water, to prevent a fire.

2 Put polythene bags full of soil or rolled-up blankets on the outside of all the exterior doors. If the water keeps rising, put more bags along the sills of the ground floor windows to keep as much water out of the house as possible.

3 If you have time, put valuables on an upper floor and lift the carpets, or at least any rugs and move them to a safer place.

4 If the water continues to rise, take any food you have in the house to an upper floor and wait for the emergency services, or if advised to, evacuate the building before access routes are cut off.

Appendix

HOUSEHOLD CHEMICALS

Most households contain a startlingly large number of potentially dangerous chemicals that are in weekly if not daily use. The majority of these products are advertised as performing specific jobs in the home quickly and efficiently. If you do use these chemicals, use them sparingly: some of them pollute the environment; others can harm you. If you can avoid them, don't use those sold in aerosols; they explode and release dangerous gases if incinerated. Some aerosols contain chlorofluorocarbons which damage the protective ozone layer around our planet.

It is possible to substitute less dangerous chemicals for a great many of these products and better still, in many cases there are completely safe and ecologically sound alternatives. On the following pages the dangers of some of the chemicals most commonly used are described, together with guidelines for their safe use and an ecological alternative if it exists. If you are using hazardous chemicals, such as white spirit or paint stripper, it is important to dispose of them safely and not pour them down the drain, because they can pollute the water.

KEY TO SYMBOLS

With the descriptions of the chemicals on the following pages are symbols that indicate their possible problems or dangers, and the alternative if there is one.

 Poisonous

 Can cause respiratory problems

 Can cause rashes

 Potentially carcinogenic

 Inflammable

 Corrosive

Pollutes the water supply

 Ecologically sound

HOUSEHOLD CLEANING PRODUCTS

AMMONIA

An alkali that can remove fruit juice or blood stains from clothing and dirt from floors and walls, ammonia is often added to household cleaners. Ammonia can cause allergic rashes so you should protect your hands; use it only in a well-ventilated room.

 ALTERNATIVE
For cleaning surfaces, use a solution of borax, diluted as recommended, or a teaspoonful of bicarbonate of soda or vinegar in a cup of water.

BLEACH

See CLOTHES CARE PRODUCTS, page 364.

CARPET AND UPHOLSTERY SHAMPOOS

These contain detergents and alkalis. Many need to be mixed with water, so must be applied very sparingly to avoid saturating the carpet backing or the fabric, which could ruin it. Any remaining soapy water poured down the drain becomes a pollutant.

ALTERNATIVE
Use dry foam shampoos which neither saturate the fabric nor pollute the water.

CAUSTIC SODA

Sometimes known by its chemical name sodium hydroxide, this is a strong and highly poisonous and corrosive alkali often recommended for cleaning blocked drains. Caustic soda is sometimes a constituent of oven and toilet cleaners. Don't use caustic soda to clear a kitchen sink: it combines with grease to form a hard soap which blocks the drain. Never keep it in the house because it is so potent and potentially lethal. If you get it on your skin, flush with cold running water for at least 10 minutes.

ALTERNATIVE
Pour vinegar or washing soda and boiling water down a blocked drain. If that doesn't work, undo the bolt on the drainage pipe and clear the pipe with a wire coat hanger.

CREAM CLEANERS

Most proprietary household cleaners contain any number of powerful chemicals, such as ethanol, ammonia, formaldehyde and chlorine. They are all bad for the environment and lethal if swallowed. If you use such cleaning products use them only rarely

and sparingly. Keep them on a high shelf or in a locked cupboard.

ALTERNATIVE
Wipe surfaces and floors regularly with very dilute soap and water. To clean the bathroom, use vinegar, diluted in warm water. To get rid of hard-water lines, neutralize the alkalinity of the lime-scale with an acid such as neat vinegar or lemon juice.

DESCALING PRODUCTS

Most descaling products, used to remove hard-water deposits from kettles, coffee machines, baths, toilets, taps, etc., contain ammonia and caustic ingredients.

ALTERNATIVE
Soften deposits in the kettle by adding 15g (1tbsp) of borax (a water softener) to a kettleful of cold water and bringing it to the boil. Leave the water to cool, then rub off the softened deposits with a rough cloth. Or cover the element with vinegar, bring the vinegar to the boil, leave to cool then empty and rinse the kettle several times. Prevent further scale from forming by keeping a marble or a small piece of loofah in the kettle. If you live in a hard-water area, it may be worth using a water softener, such as sodium sesquicarbonate, in your water tank.

DISINFECTANTS

Many household disinfectants contain bleaches such as chlorine or may be based on phenol, cresol or chloroxylenol: all of these are poisonous and corrosive. Others contain bactericides (ammonium compounds), which are non-toxic but can disrupt the balance of micro-organisms in the sewage. They can be used on clothes, bedclothes and dishes. Triethylene glycol is added to some antiseptic air sprays or purifiers; it is unnecessary and adds to the pollution.

ALTERNATIVE
Clean in and around the toilet with a solution of vinegar or lemon and hot water. Pour washing soda crystals and boiling water down the drains to keep them clear.

FURNITURE POLISHES

FOR KEY TO SYMBOLS, SEE PAGE 361

Most furniture polishes sold in spray cans or applicators are based on synthetic ingredients such as silicones and solvents and often contain artificial perfumes, which are unnecessary and unhealthy. The spray from aerosols can emerge with such force that it can actually damage the furniture, leaving cloudy marks on it. The only way to remove these marks is to strip the surface completely and repolish or varnish.

 **ALTERNATIVE**
Many modern surfaces don't need polishing. Laminates, varnishes and seals only need a wipe over with a damp cloth. Natural wood does benefit from occasional polishing (two or three times a year) to fill the cracks and marks, since it is a "living" substance and can dry out, particularly in centrally heated homes. Furniture polishes made of natural oils and beeswax are available or you can make your own by mixing two parts olive oil or vegetable oil with one part lemon juice; use beeswax instead of the oil if you can get it because it smells delicious.

METAL POLISHES

Proprietary metal polishes may contain ammonia, which can burn the skin, and petroleum distillates, which are poisonous. They may also give off unpleasant fumes while being used. Keep proprietary silver polishes away from other metals, as they may cause tarnishing.

 ALTERNATIVE
Clean brass with a lemon dipped in salt or with a paste made of equal parts vinegar or lemon juice and salt. For copper, use a paste made of equal parts vinegar, salt and flour. Apple cider vinegar gives a shine to chrome, or you can simply wipe it with a soft damp cloth and buff it up with a dry cloth. Put silver in a bowl containing a handful of washing soda and some aluminium foil. Add enough water to cover the silver. Rinse in hot water and dry thoroughly. Soak stainless steel in warm water, then rub with lemon juice or vinegar before rinsing thoroughly.

OVEN CLEANERS

Many are based on caustic soda (sodium hydroxide), which is extremely poisonous and corrosive. Non-caustic cream cleaners contain other harmful chemicals, such as strong alkalis, which can cause skin complaints.

 ALTERNATIVE
If you haven't got an oven with a self-cleaning lining, roast meat at lower temperatures which won't make the fat splash or spit. Cover the food with a lid or foil. Wipe the oven while it is still warm with a damp cloth to prevent a build-up of grease. If it gets dirty, sprinkle bicarbonate of soda around the oven while it is still warm. Leave for an hour, then wipe clean.

RUST REMOVERS

Proprietary rust removers may contain phosphoric acid and oxalic acid, which are poisonous and corrosive, as well as solvents, which are flammable. Do not use on silk, wool or rayon; you'll rot the fabric.

 ALTERNATIVE
Treat rust stains on clothes with lemon juice and then rinse. Use neat vinegar on baths and basins. Rust can be removed from cast-iron furniture by rubbing it with wire wool dipped in paraffin. Remove the paraffin by wiping it with cotton wool soaked in white spirit. Dry thoroughly, then paint with an oil-based paint to prevent the piece from going rusty again.

SCOURING POWDERS

These usually contain whiting or pumice and/or silver sand with bleaches, detergents and perfumes. There are very few items in the home that need to be so roughly treated. Scouring can damage the surface of baths, basins, sinks, enamel finishes and cooking pans irreparably.

ALTERNATIVE
Wipe surfaces such as baths, showers and basins frequently with a damp cloth so that they don't need scouring. Soak pans in water before you wash them. Use vinegar to break down the grease.

TOILET CLEANERS

Chemical toilet cleaners often contain highly caustic sodium hypochlorite (chlorine), which is found in most bleaches. This pollutes rivers and ponds and destroys bacterial balance in sewage. It is poisonous to human beings and should not be breathed in. Always keep it in a locked cupboard. DO NOT mix toilet cleaners, as a dangerous gas will form.

ALTERNATIVE
Use vinegar to remove lime-scale and as a disinfectant. Clean the toilet with a lavatory brush and cloth and wipe down the surrounds with vinegar and hot water.

WASHING-UP DETERGENTS

Detergents are man-made degreasing agents. Many washing-up detergents also contain phosphates, which are very damaging to the life in ponds and rivers – phosphates prevent bacteria breaking down the effluents and returning them to the soil in a useful form. Washing-up detergents can dry up the skin and cause vomiting and diarrhoea if swallowed neat. Washing-up detergents also contain a drying agent, which may increase the body's absorption of the pesticide residues that are present in a great many foods.

ALTERNATIVE
Washing soda crystals with a little soap dissolved in very hot water will get dishes clean with much less damage to the environment. In soft-water areas you will not need the soda crystals, and perhaps not even the soap, except for greasy items.

If you do want to use a washing-up liquid, buy one that is "phosphate-free" and use much less than you do at present; rinse everything with hot water after washing.

CLOTHES CARE PRODUCTS

ACETONE

A powerful solvent, derived from petroleum, used to remove nail varnish and grease stains and to thin varnishes. Never use it on acetate fabrics as they dissolve. Nail varnish remover has oil added to it, which may leave a mark on clothes if it is used as a stain remover. Use in a well-ventilated room if thinning varnish.

ALTERNATIVE
Use acetic acid (white vinegar) or citric acid (lemon juice) for stain removal.

AMYL ACETATE

A highly flammable and toxic solvent which can be used, in a well-ventilated room, to remove cellulose paint or adhesives from clothing. There is no alternative; it should be used with great care.

BLEACH

Sodium hypochlorite, a chlorine compound, is used in most household bleaches. Its strength varies according to the manufacturer. Don't use sodium hypochlorite in a hot wash, as it gives off dangerous fumes in boiling water. Because chlorine can damage or destroy silk, wool, leather, elastane or resin-treated fabrics, a bleaching agent with similar properties, such as hydrogen peroxide or sulphur dioxide, should be used.

ALTERNATIVE
Don't overlook the natural bleaching effect of the sun on white or pale garments hung outdoors to dry. Unfortunately sunlight is not a practical solution for stained nylon or silk, which turn yellow and rot in the sun.

Use sodium perborate bleach on silk and wool or sodium hydrosulphite bleach, which is a mild bleach and safe on wool and nylon as well as on cotton and linen. Sodium hydrosulphite will also remove many stains of vegetable and animal origin. A mild bleach for removing stains from delicate fabrics can be obtained by diluting one part hydrogen peroxide with four parts water.

DRY-CLEANING SOLVENTS

These are flammable and toxic in varying degrees. Most proprietary grease stain removers contain a solvent called trichloroethane, which is non-flammable and less toxic than other solvents. Spot-removers are usually based on perchloroethylene, a non-flammable solvent which should be applied in a well-ventilated room or out of doors. Used near heat, it gives off dangerous vapours. The symbol $\underline{P}$ on a clothes-care label means that the garment should be cleaned with a perchloroethylene based dry-cleaning solvent.

 ALTERNATIVE
Acetic acid (white vinegar) and citric acid (lemon juice) can be used to take out some stains. Try softening tar and oil with mayonnaise or butter. Fuller's earth, a clay mineral, will absorb grease from unwashable items such as felt, suede and fur.

FABRIC CONDITIONERS

These work by coating fibres with a substance to make the clothes feel soft. They contain perfumes that are harmful to sensitive skins, and many people find the smell intrusive. They also include other chemicals that irritate some skins, especially those of young babies.

 ALTERNATIVE
Rinse clothes well. If possible, dry clothes out of doors; if not, tumble dry carefully, according to instructions. Don't dry clothes on radiators, as this type of drying hardens the fabric.

FOR KEY TO SYMBOLS, SEE PAGE 361

LAUNDRY DETERGENTS

Most laundry powders contain bleaches, phosphates, perfumes, synthetic detergents and often enzymes too. Between them they can seriously pollute fresh water and aggravate or cause eczema and other skin complaints. Many only work well when used with hot water, which is a waste of energy.
ALTERNATIVE
There are proprietary powders and liquids on the market which use little or none of these harmful ingredients. Read the labels carefully. The fewer ingredients the better, and if the products are formulated for cold-water washes and enzyme-free, better still. For hand washing, use pure soap dissolved in very hot water; add washing soda crystals if you live in a hard-water area. Some liquid laundry cleaners can be used for hand washing too. If you use washing powders, try to buy phosphate-free products and use half the recommended amount.

METHYLATED SPIRITS

Basically ethanol with additives including dye, methylated spirits dissolves essential oils, castor oil, shellac, ball point ink, iodine, grass stains and some medicines. It is also useful for cleaning mirrors and glass as well as paint brushes. Highly flammable, it should not be used near a naked flame. Methylated spirits contains methyl alcohol, which is toxic and can cause blindness if drunk. Always use it in a well-ventilated room and never pour it down the drain.

 ALTERNATIVE
Use vinegar to clean glass, glycerine to remove grass stains.

MOTH PROOFERS

There are several chemicals that will protect temporarily against moths. These may contain DDT or naphthalene, which can have a cumulative toxic effect if swallowed. Para-dichlorobenzene crystals are preferable because they are less pungent.

 **ALTERNATIVE**
Camphor deters moths, as does lavender oil or orange peel sprinkled over the clothes. Another traditional deterrent is a mixture of ground cloves, cinnamon, black pepper and orris root in a muslin bag placed among the clothes. Always clean clothes before storing them and re-treat them every six months.

NAPHTHALENE

This volatile liquid made from coal tar is an ingredient in some paints, varnishes and wax polishes as well as in methylated spirits. It can be used as a solvent for rubber and some greasy stains. It is unsafe to store naphthalene at home, as it is highly flammable.

ALTERNATIVE
It is safer to use a proprietary dry-cleaning solvent, following instructions, or a liquid detergent solution or soap and water.

RUST REMOVERS
See HOUSEHOLD CLEANING PRODUCTS page 363.

WHITE SPIRIT
See HOME DECORATING PRODUCTS, opposite.

YELLOW LAUNDRY SOAP

This is manufactured from animal fats, olive or palm-kernel oils and caustic soda. "Builders", which include borax, sodium carbonate, waterglass and sodium phosphates, are often added. Laundry soap will pollute the water and can cause allergies. Never use it for washing the body.

ALTERNATIVE
Soap flakes are also good for hand washing, particularly in soft water. They are preferable for delicate articles.

HOME DECORATING PRODUCTS

ACETONE
See CLOTHES CARE PRODUCTS page 364.

AMYL ACETATE
See CLOTHES CARE PRODUCTS page 364.

METHYLATED SPIRITS
See CLOTHES CARE PRODUCTS page 364.

PAINT STRIPPERS

All paint solvents are flammable and carry a risk of brain damage if inhaled excessively. Use only in a well-ventilated room. Use all solvents as sparingly as possible and with extreme caution. Wear a mask and gloves. Contact with the skin can cause dermatitis. If you get paint stripper on your skin, wash your hand under cold running water for at least 10 minutes. Many chemical strippers are caustic, so it may even be advisable to wear goggles.

ALTERNATIVE
Whenever possible, strip paint using a gas or paraffin blowtorch or heat gun.

PAINTS AND WOOD STAINS

Paints made after 1986 are lead-free, but left-over paint may not be. Throw old paints away rather than risk lead-poisoning. Modern paints and wood stains may contain cadmium or titanium oxide, which are both poisonous. Avoid metallic paints, or those with a high metal content, as they are poisonous. Don't use fungicidal paints in kitchens because the fungicide may get into the food.

ALTERNATIVE
Use water-based paints where possible. These are less toxic than oil-based paints.

WHITE SPIRIT

A colourless solvent made of a mixture of mineral salts. Among its many uses, it is a paint thinner and general-purpose grease remover. White spirit can sometimes be used instead of turpentine and is much cheaper. Flammable and toxic, it dries out the skin's natural oils and may cause an allergy.

 ALTERNATIVE
Use white vinegar or lemon juice instead of solvents to remove grease stains. There is no alternative for thinning paint.

HOME MAINTENANCE PRODUCTS

ADHESIVES

Solvent-based, general-purpose adhesives are highly flammable, toxic and may be addictive when "sniffed". Chemical-based adhesives (epoxy resins) are often stronger than the materials to be bonded and can be corrosive, poisonous and flammable. Many adhesives contain cyclic hydrocarbons, which have been linked with cancer.

ALTERNATIVE
Water-based adhesives are taking the place of some traditionally solvent-based adhesives. Choose these where possible; not only are they safer, but they are also reversible.

 GREEN TIP: Make a non-toxic adhesive for children with flour and water. Use one part flour to two parts water, combine them in a saucepan, then simmer, stirring all the time, for five minutes. Allow to cool before using.

FOR KEY TO SYMBOLS, SEE PAGE 361

BLACKLEAD

A black mineral form of carbon, also known as graphite or plumbago, that actually contains no lead. It is used for giving a metallic black sheen to grates. Available in tubes, blacklead is flammable and should not be applied near a naked flame. Wear rubber gloves and reserve a polishing cloth especially for blackleading, as it stains easily.

ALTERNATIVE
If you don't want to polish your grate regularly, paint it with heat-resistant paint.

CAUSTIC SODA

See HOUSEHOLD CLEANING PRODUCTS page 362.

INSECTICIDES AND PESTICIDES

All insecticides and pesticides are poisonous to human beings as well as to pests. It may be better to live with certain creatures than to risk being poisoned yourself. Remember that some poisons can accumulate in the body. Use all pesticides with extreme caution. Do not spray over or near food, pets or elderly or very young people. Leave the room for some time after spraying.

ALTERNATIVE
You can get ultra-violet products which will electrocute flies – though they will also kill moths and other harmless flyers. Pyrethrum powder (a product derived from the pyrethrum plant) will get rid of cockroaches and mosquitoes; wormwood and fleabane will get rid of fleas. Get a cat to keep mice away.

GLOSSARY OF COOKERY TERMS

A la grecque: Vegetables cooked in olive oil with coriander seeds and other seasonings, served cold.

Aspic: Savoury meat jelly to cover or glaze cold foods.

Au gratin: Usually a precooked dish topped with a sauce and breadcrumbs or grated cheese, then browned in the oven or under the grill.

Baste: Spoon juices over food while it is cooking to keep it from becoming dry.

Béarnaise sauce: Sauce made with egg yolks, butter, vinegar and spice mixture, reduced by boiling and served with herbs.

Béchamel sauce: Basic white sauce made with flour, milk and fat.

Bind: Add egg or liquid to a mixture to hold it together.

Blanch: Immerse food in boiling water for a very short time to soften it, to remove the skin or to prepare it for freezing.

Bonne femme: Any dish with the addition of potatoes, peas and carrots.

Bortsch: Russian beetroot soup.

Bouillabaisse: French Provençale fish soup.

Bouquet garni: Bunch of herbs, normally wrapped in muslin and added to casseroles and stocks. Remove before serving.

Braise: Cook food slowly, in a very little liquid in a tightly covered pan, after it has been browned.

Brine: Salt water solution used to preserve fish, meat or vegetables.

Brûlée: Burned (of sugar) as in CARAMEL.

Caramel: Concentrated sugar syrup boiled until thick and brown.

Carbonnade: Beef stew made with beer.

Cassoulet: French stew made with haricot beans, pork, ham sausages, and duck or goose.

Clarify: Take the impurities out of fats, stocks and consommés by melting them slowly, letting them cool down and skimming.

Compôte: Fruit cooked in sugar syrup, seasoned with spices (e.g. cinnamon and cloves).

Consommé: Clear meat stock (bouillon).

Court bouillon: Liquid used for poaching fish, made from water and wine or vinegar with herbs and vegetables.

Cream: To beat butter or butter and sugar until it is a light consistency and nearly white.

Dal or Dhal: Indian term for dried beans and lentils.

Deglaze: Add wine, brandy or stock to the roasting pan and scrape browned, solidified cooking juices off the bottom to make stock or gravy.

Degorge: Soak foods in water to remove excess liquid or strong or bitter flavours, or to improve colour. Some are sprinkled with salt while soaking.

Devil: Season with spicy ingredients such as mustard, cayenne, Worcestershire sauce.

Dolmas: Stuffed vine leaves, most commonly Turkish or Greek.

Dredge: Sprinkle foods lightly with flour, icing sugar or other fine powder.

Dress: Mix salad with a dressing; pluck clean and trim (game and poultry).

En croûte Cooked in a case of pastry.

Fry, deep: Immerse food, usually coated in batter and breadcrumbs, in very hot, deep fat.

Fry, shallow: Cook food in a little fat in a shallow pan.

Frying, stir: Chinese method of cooking quickly, stirring constantly, in a little fat in a wok or frying pan, to preserve nutrients.

Garam masala: Indian cooking term meaning "hot spices". A variable aromatic mixture used sparingly, normally added towards the end of the cooking time.

Glaze: Give food a glossy appearance by coating it, for example, with a sugar syrup, aspic, beaten egg or milk.

Gnocchi: Italian dish of potato or semolina shaped into small rounds or squares.

Goulash: Hungarian meat stew with paprika.

Hang: Suspend meat, particularly game, from hooks for a period to make it tender and allow the flavour to mature.

Infuse: Extract flavour by steeping food in hot liquid.

Liaison: Thickening for sauces or soups.

Macerate: Steep in sugar or liqueurs.

Marinate: Soak raw food in spicy or herby liquid to make it more tender and tasty, often used for grilled or barbecued food.

Mirepoix: Diced vegetables, usually carrots, onion and celery, used as a basis for a braised dish.

Paella: Spanish rice dish with fish and shellfish or meat.

Petits fours: Small, rich, sweet cakes and biscuits.

Poach: Cook gently by immersing food in simmering liquid such as a court bouillon.

Pot au feu: Classic French provincial dish of meat cooked in water. The resulting soup is eaten as the first course, the meat as the second.

Pressure cook: Cook quickly in pressurized pan at very high temperatures to save energy and retain vitamins.

Provençale: Food cooked with tomatoes and garlic.

Purée: Mash and sieve food or process it in a blender.

Quiche: Baked pastry shell with savoury filling, generally made with egg.

Ragoût: French stew of meat and vegetables.

Ragu: Italian meat stew or sauce.

Reduce: Thicken and concentrate a liquid by rapid boiling with the lid off.

Render: Melt animal fat slowly to a liquid and then strain.

Risotto: Italian round grain rice dish, traditionally made with an absorbent rice.

Roux: Butter and flour cooked together as a basis for sauces.

Rub in: Use fingertips to mix flour and other dry ingredients with butter or lard to give a crumbly texture.

Sambals: Spicy side dishes served with Indian or Indonesian food.

Sauerkraut: German pickled white cabbage.

Sauté: Brisk cooking in a small amount of fat in a shallow pan until just browned or cooked through.

Scald: Heat milk or cream to just below boiling point, when bubbles form in pan. Fruit and vegetables may be scalded (blanched) in water to make skins easier to remove.

Score: Make shallow cuts over surface of food to allow marinades to penetrate and to speed up cooking time.

Slow cooker: Electric pot which cooks food slowly at very low temperatures, using very little power.

Souse: Pickle with vinegar or brine, most commonly used for oily fish such as herrings.

Steam: Cook food in steam in perforated container set above boiling water, to preserve nutrients.

Stufato: Italian meat stew with wine.

Sweat: Soften food such as onions or root vegetables by cooking gently in melted fat until it releases its juices.

Tapas: Snacks served with drinks before a meal in Spain.

Terrine: Oblong pot used for cooking pâté.

Timbale: Cup-shaped earthenware or metal mould, for savoury preparations.

Tofu: Made from pressed soya bean curd, with the consistency of soft cheese.

Vol au vent: Puff pastry case, filled with diced meat, vegetables or fish in a sauce.

Whey: Watery liquid which separates out from curdled milk, cream, junket or yogurt.

Wok: Traditional Chinese rounded pan for stir frying. (Flat-bottomed ones are available for electric cookers.)

Zest: Thin shavings of orange or lemon peel used as flavouring.

COOKING TIMES

SOAKING AND COOKING TIMES FOR PULSES

Boil all pulses (except lentils and soya beans) fast for the first 10 minutes of cooking time to get rid of toxins, then simmer. Lentils don't need a fast boil; soya beans must be boiled hard for an hour, then simmered for the rest of the cooking time.

PULSE	SOAKING TIME	COOKING TIME
Whole lentils	Don't need soaking	30–45 mins
Split lentils	Don't need soaking	15–30 mins
Whole peas	8–12 hours	60–90 mins
Split peas	Don't need soaking	40–45 mins
Beans (large)	8–12 hours	50–90 mins
(small)	8–12 hours	45–50 mins

ROASTING TIME FOR MEAT

◆ Never undercook veal and pork, you could give yourself food poisoning.

TYPE OF ROAST	HIGH-TEMPERATURE ROAST	COOKING TIME
Beef and lamb	30 mins at 220°C/425°F/gas mark 7, then lower temperature to 200°C/400°F/gas mark 6	Thin joints: 15 mins per 450g (1lb) + 15 mins
		Thick joints: 20–25 mins per 450g (1lb) + 20–25 mins
Veal and pork	30 mins at 220°C/425°F/gas mark 7, then lower temperature to 190–200°C/375–400°F/gas mark 6	30 mins per 450g (1lb) + 30 mins
TYPE OF ROAST	LOW-TEMPERATURE ROAST	COOKING TIME
Beef and lamb	190°C/375°F/gas mark 5	Thin joints: 20 mins per 450g (1lb) + 20 mins
		Thick joints: 33 mins per 450g (1lb) + 33 mins
Veal and pork	190°C/375°F/gas mark 5	35 mins per 450g (1lb) + 35 mins

ROASTING TIME FOR POULTRY

TYPE OF ROAST	HIGH-TEMPERATURE ROAST	COOKING TIME
Chicken	200°C/400°F/gas mark 6	20 mins per 450g (1lb) + 20 mins
Goose	200°C/400°F/gas mark 6	15 mins per 450g (1lb) + 15mins
Turkey (stuffed)	230°C/450°F/gas mark 8	2.7–5.4kg (6–12lb) bird: $2\frac{1}{2}$–3 hrs
		5.4–8.2kg (12–18lb) bird: 3–$3\frac{1}{2}$ hrs
	LOW-TEMPERATURE ROAST	COOKING TIME
Duck	190°C/375°F/gas mark 5	20 mins per 450g (1lb)
Goose	180°C/350°F/gas mark 4	25–30 mins per 450g (1lb)
Guinea fowl	190°C/375°F/gas mark 5	40 mins per 450g (1lb)
Turkey (stuffed)	170°C/325°F/gas mark 3	2.7–5.4kg (6–12lb) bird: $3\frac{1}{2}$–4 hrs
		5.4–8.2kg (12–18lb) bird: 4–$4\frac{3}{4}$ hrs

ROASTING TIME FOR GAME BIRDS

AVERAGE-SIZED BIRD	COOKING TIME AT 220–230°C/425–450°F/gas mark 7–8
Pheasant	45 mins to 1 hr
Partridge Grouse Ptarmigan	30 mins
Snipe Plover Woodcock Quail Wild duck	20–30 mins

CONVERSION TABLES

It is rarely possible to make an exact comparison between the different measuring systems. All of the following figures have been rounded up slightly to make it easier to read off equivalents quickly. If you need a more precise conversion for any reason, calculate it using the formula that is given below each table.

TEMPERATURES

FAHRENHEIT		CENTIGRADE
0°		− 18°
10		− 10
20		
32		0
40		
50		10
60		
70		20
80		
90		30
100		
110		40
120		50
130		
140		60
150		
160		70
170		
180		80
190		
200		90
212		100

To convert Fahrenheit to centigrade, subtract 32, then multiply by 0.5555

To convert centigrade to Fahrenheit, multiply by 1.8, and add 32

OVEN TEMPERATURES

ELECTRIC		GAS	SOLID FUEL
°C	°F		
70	150		
80	175		
100	200	Low	
110	225	$\frac{1}{4}$	
120	250	$\frac{1}{2}$	Very cool
140	275	1	Cool
150	300	2	
160	325	3	Slow
180	350	4	Moderate
190	375	5	
200	400	6	Moderately hot
220	425	7	Hot
230	450	8	Very hot
240	475	9	Very hot

SOLIDS

When cooking always use one system of measurements throughout; never mix them because you may get the proportions wrong and ruin the dish.

METRIC	IMPERIAL
5g	$\frac{1}{4}$oz (1tsp)
15g	$\frac{1}{2}$oz (1tbsp)
25g	1oz
50g	2oz
85g	3oz
110g	4oz
140g	5oz
180g	6oz
200g	7oz
225g	8oz

METRIC	IMPERIAL
250g	9oz
280g	10oz
300g	11oz
340g	12oz
375g	13oz
400g	14oz
425g	15oz
450g	16oz (1lb)
1 kilogramme	2·2lbs

To convert pounds to kilogrammes multiply by 0.4536

To convert kilogrammes to pounds divide by 0.4536

To convert ounces to grammes, multiply by 28.3495

To convert grammes to ounces, divide by 28.3495

AMERICAN SOLID WEIGHT CONVERSIONS

These vary slightly depending on the density of the ingredients in the recipe.

Butter or fat		1 cup	225g (8oz)
Sugar,	brown,	1 cup	200g (7oz)
	castor or powdered	1 cup	100g (4oz)
Flour,	plain sieved,	1 cup	100g (4oz)
	self-raising, wholewheat	1 cup	150g (5oz)
Cheese,	grated,	1 cup	100g (4oz)
	cottage	1 cup	225g (8oz)
Nuts,	ground,	1 cup	100g (4oz)
	chopped	1 cup	175g (6oz)
Currants		1 cup	150g (5oz)
Breadcrumbs		1 cup	100g (40z)
Onions, chopped,		1 cup	175g (6oz)
	sliced	1 cup	100g (4oz)
Beans,	dried	1 cup	175g (6oz)
Rice		1 cup	175g (6oz)

LIQUIDS

METRIC	IMPERIAL	USA
5ml	$\frac{1}{8}$fl oz	1tsp
15ml	$\frac{1}{2}$fl oz	1tbsp
25ml	1fl oz	$\frac{1}{8}$ cup
50ml	2fl oz	$\frac{1}{4}$ cup
65ml	$2\frac{1}{2}$fl oz	$\frac{1}{3}$ cup
100ml	4fl oz	$\frac{1}{2}$ cup
150ml	5fl oz	$\frac{2}{3}$ cup
175ml	6fl oz	$\frac{3}{4}$ cup
225ml	8fl oz	1 cup ($\frac{1}{2}$ USA pt)
300ml	10fl oz ($\frac{1}{2}$ UK pt)	$1\frac{1}{4}$ cups
350ml	12fl oz	$1\frac{1}{2}$ cups
400ml	14fl oz	$1\frac{3}{4}$ cups
475ml	16fl oz	2 cups (1 USA pt)
600ml	20fl oz (1 UK pt)	$2\frac{1}{2}$ cups
750ml	24fl oz	3 cups
900ml	32fl oz	4 cups (2 USA pt)
1 litre	35 fl oz	$4\frac{1}{4}$ cups
1.14 litres	40fl oz (2 UK pt)	5 cups

To convert UK pints to litres multiply by 0.568
To convert USA pints to litres multiply by 0.473
To convert litres to UK pints divide by 0.568
To convert litres to USA pints divide by 0.473

LENGTH

METRIC	IMPERIAL
5mm	$\frac{1}{4}$in
1cm	$\frac{1}{2}$in
2.5cm	1in
5cm	2in
7cm	3in
10cm	4in
12cm	5in
15cm	6in
18cm	7in
20cm	8in
23cm	9in
25cm	10in
28cm	11in
30cm	12in (1ft)
91cm	36in (1 yard)
1m	39in
3.05m	10ft

To convert feet to centimetres multiply by 30.48
To convert centimetres to feet divide by 30.48
To convert yards to metres multiply by 0.9144
To convert metres to yards divide by 0.9144

CLOTHING SIZES

CHILDRENS' CLOTHES

These are measured according to a child's length or height. For babies up to one year, the size is based mainly on their weight, but the length will be given. Some clothes are marked with ages, but this should only be taken as a rough guide.

AGE	HEIGHT/LENGTH	WEIGHT
Newborn	55cm (22in)	up to 4.5kg (10lbs)
3 months	60cm (24in)	5.5kg (12lb)
6 months	68cm (27in)	8kg (18lb)
9 months	74cm (29in)	9.5kg (21lb)
12 months	80cm (31½in)	11kg (24lb)
18 months	86cm (34in)	
2 years	92cm (3ft)	
3 years	1m (3ft 3in)	
4–5 years	1.1m (3ft 6in)	
6–7 years	1.2m (3ft 11in)	
8–9 years	1.4m (4ft 7in)	
10–11 years	1.5m (4ft 11in)	

ADULTS' CLOTHES

The following is an approximate guide to clothing sizes. Hat sizes are normally given in centimetres or inches, according to the circumference of the head.

MENS' CLOTHES

SUITS AND OVERCOATS
(chest measurement)

UK	USA	CONTINENTAL
36	36	46
38	38	48
40	40	50/52
42	42	54
44	44	56
46	46	58/60
48	48	62
50	50	64

TROUSERS (waist measurement)

UK	USA	CONTINENTAL
30	30	40
32	32	42
34	34	44
36	36	46
38	38	48
40	40	50
42	42	52
44	44	54

SHIRTS (collar sizes)

UK	USA	CONTINENTAL
14	14	35
$14\frac{1}{2}$	$14\frac{1}{2}$	36/37
15	15	38
$15\frac{1}{2}$	$15\frac{1}{2}$	39/40
16	16	41
$16\frac{1}{2}$	$16\frac{1}{2}$	42/43
17	17	44
$17\frac{1}{2}$	$17\frac{1}{2}$	45

WOMENS' CLOTHES

UK	USA	CONTINENTAL
8	6	38
10	8	40
12	10	42
14	12	44
16	14	46
18	16	48
20	18	50

SHOE SIZES

The following should be taken as an approximate guide to international shoe sizes. Continental sizes, in particular, vary from one country to another and the half sizes are not always available. When buying children's shoes always check the width of the shoe as well as the length; the wrong size can damage a child's foot.

CHILDRENS' SHOES

UK	USA	CONTINENTAL
3	4	19
$3\frac{1}{2}$	$4\frac{1}{2}$	$19\frac{1}{2}$
4	5	20
$4\frac{1}{2}$	$5\frac{1}{2}$	$20\frac{1}{2}$
5	6	21
$5\frac{1}{2}$	$6\frac{1}{2}$	22
6	7	$22\frac{1}{2}$
$6\frac{1}{2}$	$7\frac{1}{2}$	23
7	8	24
$7\frac{1}{2}$	$8\frac{1}{2}$	$24\frac{1}{2}$
8	9	25
$8\frac{1}{2}$	$9\frac{1}{2}$	26
9	10	$26\frac{1}{2}$
$9\frac{1}{2}$	$10\frac{1}{2}$	27
10	11	$27\frac{1}{2}$
$10\frac{1}{2}$	$11\frac{1}{2}$	28
11	12	29
$11\frac{1}{2}$	$12\frac{1}{2}$	$29\frac{1}{2}$
12	13	30
$12\frac{1}{2}$	$13\frac{1}{2}$	31
13	1	$31\frac{1}{2}$
$13\frac{1}{2}$	$1\frac{1}{2}$	32
1	$1\frac{1}{2}$	33

ADULTS' SHOES

UK	USA	CONTINENTAL
2	3	34
$2\frac{1}{2}$	$3\frac{1}{2}$	$34\frac{1}{2}$
3	$4\frac{1}{2}$	35
$3\frac{1}{2}$	5	36
4	$5\frac{1}{2}$	$36\frac{1}{2}$
$4\frac{1}{2}$	6	37
5	$6\frac{1}{2}$	38
$5\frac{1}{2}$	7	$38\frac{1}{2}$
6	$7\frac{1}{2}$	39
$6\frac{1}{2}$	8	$39\frac{1}{2}$
7	$8\frac{1}{2}$	40
$7\frac{1}{2}$	9	41
8	$9\frac{1}{2}$	$41\frac{1}{2}$
$8\frac{1}{2}$	10	42
9	$10\frac{1}{2}$	43
$9\frac{1}{2}$	11	$43\frac{1}{2}$
10	$11\frac{1}{2}$	44
$10\frac{1}{2}$	12	45
11	$12\frac{1}{2}$	$45\frac{1}{2}$
$11\frac{1}{2}$	13	46
12	$13\frac{1}{2}$	$46\frac{1}{2}$
$12\frac{1}{2}$	14	47

FAMILY HEALTH RECORDS

Name	
Date of birth	
Blood group	

IMMUNIZATIONS	Date
DPT (Diphtheria, pertussis/ whooping cough, tetanus) plus polio drops	1 2 3
Measles	
Diphtheria, tetanus plus polio drops pre-school booster	
Rubella (German measles)	
BCG (tuberculosis)	
Tetanus boosters	
Polio boosters	
Other immunizations	

IMPORTANT ILLNESSES (and treatments)	Date
ALLERGIES	

OTHER INFORMATION

Name	
Date of birth	
Blood group	

IMMUNIZATIONS	Date
DPT (Diphtheria, pertussis/ whooping cough, tetanus) plus polio drops	1 2 3
Measles	
Diphtheria, tetanus plus polio drops pre-school booster	
Rubella (German measles)	
BCG (tuberculosis)	
Tetanus boosters	
Polio boosters	
Other immunizations	

IMPORTANT ILLNESSES (and treatments)	Date
ALLERGIES	

OTHER INFORMATION

Name

Date of birth

Blood group

IMMUNIZATIONS	Date
DPT (Diphtheria, pertussis/ whooping cough, tetanus) plus polio drops	1 2 3
Measles	
Diphtheria, tetanus plus polio drops pre-school booster	
Rubella (German measles)	
BCG (tuberculosis)	
Tetanus boosters	
Polio boosters	
Other immunizations	

IMPORTANT ILLNESSES (and treatments)	Date

ALLERGIES	

OTHER INFORMATION

Name

Date of birth

Blood group

IMMUNIZATIONS	Date
DPT (Diphtheria, pertussis/ whooping cough, tetanus) plus polio drops	1 2 3
Measles	
Diphtheria, tetanus plus polio drops pre-school booster	
Rubella (German measles)	
BCG (tuberculosis)	
Tetanus boosters	
Polio boosters	
Other immunizations	

IMPORTANT ILLNESSES (and treatments)	Date

ALLERGIES	

OTHER INFORMATION

BIRTH RECORD

NAME

Date of
birth

Time of
birth

Born at

Duration of
pregnancy

MOTHER'S HEALTH DURING PREGNANCY

Illness

Medication

Problems

DELIVERY

Type

Monitoring

Drugs

Problems

Special care

Consultant

Hospital

Length of stay

BABY

Height

Weight

Blood type

Head
circumference

Type of feeding:

Breast

Bottle

DEVELOPMENT RECORD

ACTIVITY	AGE
Holds head up for a few seconds	
Smiles	
Laughs	
Sleeps through night	
Rolls over	
Sits unsupported	
Crawls/shuffles	
Cruises	
Walks	
First tooth	
Starts solids	
Is weaned	
Feeds self	
Looks for hidden toy	
First words	
Points to parts of the body	
Makes simple statements	
Pedals tricycle	
Stays dry throughout nap	
Gains bladder control	
Gains bowel control	
Can do up buttons	
Draws a circle	
Starts playgroup/nursery school	
First visit to the dentist	

BIRTH RECORD

NAME

Date of birth

Time of birth

Born at

Duration of pregnancy

MOTHER'S HEALTH DURING PREGNANCY

Illness

Medication

Problems

DELIVERY

Type

Monitoring

Drugs

Problems

Special care

Consultant

Hospital

Length of stay

BABY

Height

Weight

Blood type

Head circumference

Type of feeding:

Breast

Bottle

DEVELOPMENT RECORD

ACTIVITY	AGE
Holds head up for a few seconds	
Smiles	
Laughs	
Sleeps through night	
Rolls over	
Sits unsupported	
Crawls/shuffles	
Cruises	
Walks	
First tooth	
Starts solids	
Is weaned	
Feeds self	
Looks for hidden toy	
First words	
Points to parts of the body	
Makes simple statements	
Pedals tricycle	
Stays dry throughout nap	
Gains bladder control	
Gains bowel control	
Can do up buttons	
Draws a circle	
Starts playgroup/nursery school	
First visit to the dentist	

USEFUL ADDRESSES

GENERAL

Consumers' Association
2 Marylebone Road
London NW1 4DX
01-486 5544
Campaigns for improvements to products, conducts surveys and publishes reports on products, publishes the monthly magazine Which?

British Standards Institution
2 Park Street
London W1A 2BS
01-629 9000
Helps to establish standards for consumer goods. The Kitemark indicates that goods conform to these standards

National Association of Citizens' Advice Bureaux
26 Bedford Square
London WC1B 3HU
01-636 4066
For information and advice on legal and consumer problems

Good Housekeeping Institute
72 Broadwick Street
London W1
01-439 7144
For advice on household, cookery and consumer problems

The Building Societies' Association
3 Savile Row
London W1
01-437 0655
Can give advice on obtaining a mortgage, and can investigate complaints

ENVIRONMENTAL GROUPS

Greenpeace
30–31 Islington Green
London N1 8XE
01-354 5100
International organization committed to preventing the destruction of wildlife and the environment

Friends of the Earth
26–28 Underwood Street
London N1 7JQ
01-490 1555
Organization with a network of local groups that campaigns on all environmental matters

●The following councils give information and advice on preserving the countryside

Council for the Protection of Rural England
40 Hobart Place
London SW1W 0HY
01-235 9481

Council for the Protection of Rural Scotland
14a Napier Road
Edinburgh EH10 5AY
031-229 1898

Council for the Protection of Rural Wales
31 High Street
Welshpool
Powys
0938 2525

Centre for Alternative Technology
Llwyngwern Quarry
Machynlleth
Powys
0654 2400
Tests and demonstrates alternative technology, runs courses in home energy use

Energy Efficiency Office
Thames House South
Millbank
London SW1P 4QJ
01-211 6326
Aims to promote the efficient use of energy in industry, commerce and the home. Will give information on home insulation

FOOD AND DRINK

British Nutrition Foundation
15 Belgrave Square
London SW1X 8PS
01-235 4904
Organization concerned with information, education and research into all aspects of nutrition. Will give advice on nutrition and food labelling

Food and Drinks Federation
6 Catherine Street
London WC2B 5JJ
01-836 2460
Trade association for British food manufacturers; can answer some consumer queries

Health Food Manufacturers' Association
The Old Coach House
Southborough Road
Surbiton
Surrey KT6 6JN
01-399 6693
For information on health foods

Caterer and Hotel Keeper
Quadrant House
The Quadrant
Sutton
Surrey SM2 5AS
01-661 3064
Magazine with an information service on catering; can supply a list of local caterers

CLEANING AND LAUNDERING

British Cleaning Council
8 Leicester Street
London WC2H 7BN
01-437 0678
Co-ordinating council for the British cleaning industry, information on all aspects of cleaning

Home Laundering Consultative Council
24 Buckingham Gate
London SW1E 6LB
01-493 7446
Information on the International Textile Care Labelling Code which explains how to wash garments

London Suede Cleaning Company
11–14 Broadwalk Lane
London NW11
01-458 7373
Cleaning service by post

Carpet Cleaners Association
47 Knighton Fields Road West
Leicester
0533 554352
Has established a code of practice for members, can supply a list of members

International Wool Secretariat
6 Carlton Gardens
London SW1
01-930 7300
Information on caring for wool, including wool carpets, list of suppliers of woollen upholstery

WIRE Technology Group Ltd
WIRE House
West Park Ring Road
Leeds LS16 6QL
0532 781381
Information on caring for and cleaning wool

Dylon International Ltd
Consumer Advice Bureau
Worsley Bridge Road
Lower Sydenham
London SE26 5HD
01-650 4801
For information on all aspects of dyeing, including free test to establish whether fabric is suitable

PAINTING AND DECORATING

The Design Council
28 Haymarket
London SW1
01-839 8000
Glasgow: 041-221 6121
Promotes good design; approves products – marked with Design Council label – for safety, design and value for money; displays well-designed products, and publishes a monthly magazine, Design

Royal Institute of British Architects
66 Portland Place
London W1
01-637 8991
Professional body of architects, can supply a list of qualified architects

British Decorators' Association
6 Haywra Street
Harrogate
N. Yorks HG1 5BL
0423 67292
Members conform to a code of practice; the Association will investigate a complaint against a member

Wallpaper Manufacturers' Association
6th Floor
Alembic House
93 Albert Embankment
London SE1
01-582 1185
Can identify the manufacturer of a wallpaper, and may be able to help with a complaint

BUILDING AND HOME IMPROVEMENTS

National Home Improvements Council
19 Store Street
London WC1E 7BT
01-636 2562
Displays a range of household units and appliances at about 500 centres in Britain; can give information on home improvements and grants

National Association of Building Centres
26 Store Street
London WC1E 7BT
01-637 1022
Several centres in Britain offering information and displays of building materials, products and heating systems

National Association of Builders and Plumbers Merchants
15 Soho Square
London W1V 5FB
01-439 1753
Will give addresses of improvement centres throughout Britain

Institute of Plumbing
64 Station Lane
Hornchurch
Essex RM12 6NB
04024 72791
List of qualified members, will take up a complaint against a member

Federation of Master Builders
33 John Street
London WC1N 2BB
01-242 7583
For a list of local, qualified, experienced builders

Building Employers Federation
82 New Cavendish Street
London W1M 8AD
01-580 5588
Will recommend members

Hire Service Shops Ltd
Head Office
25 Willow Lane
Mitcham
Surrey CR4 4TS
01-685 9900
*Network of shops throughout
Britain for hiring almost anything
– ladders, wheelbarrows, tools and
machines*

PEST CONTROL

◆ Your local council will have a
pest control officer

**British Pest Control
Association**
Kings Buildings
Smith Square
London SW1P 3JJ
01-828 2638
*Will provide a list of members who
conform to its code of practice, and
will investigate a complaint
against a member*

HEATING

National Heating Consultancy
73 New Bond Street
London W1Y 9DD
01-859 5543
*Gives information and advice on
installing a heating system, can
design a heating system and can
take up a complaint on your behalf*

Solid Fuel Advisory Service
Hobart House
Grosvenor Place
London SW1
01-235 2020
*For information leaflets and ad-
vice on using solid fuel*

Institute of Gas Engineers
17 Grosvenor Crescent
London SW1X 7ES
01-245 9811
*Can supply a list of qualified
members who conform to a standard code of practice*

British Gas Corporation
Head Office
152 Grosvenor Road
London SW1V 3JL
01-723 7030
*Showrooms throughout Britain sell
gas appliances, provide information leaflets, offer planning advice, supply a list of registered in-
stallers of gas heating; appliances
approved by BGC carry a label*

The Electricity Council
30 Millbank
London SW1P 4RD
01-834 2333 (ext 387)
*Promotes and protects the interests
of all consumers, investigates
complaints*

**British Electrotechnical
Approvals Board for
Household Equipment**
2 Park Street
London W1A 2BS
01-629 9000
*Tests and approves household
electrical equipment for durability
and safety. Its Mark of Safety is
given to approved equipment*

**Electrical Contractors
Association**
34 Palace Court
London W2 4HY
01-229 1266
Edinburgh: 031-225 7221/3
*Will supply a list of members,
guarantees the installation work of
its members and completion of the
job at quoted price if firm goes out
of business*

CHILDCARE

**Pre-school Playgroups
Association**
61–63 Kings Cross Road
London WC1X 9LL
01-582 8871
Glasgow: 041-331 1340
*Network of independent play-
groups for children under five*

**British Association for Early
Childhood Education**
Studio 2:3
140 Tabernacle Road
London EC2A 4SD
01-250 1768
*Will answer queries about the
education of children up to eight*

**National Council for One-
Parent Families**
255 Kentish Town Road
London NW5 2LX
01-267 1361
*Gives information and advice to
single parents*

Gingerbread
35 Wellington Street
London WC2E 7BN
01-240 0953
*Selp-help organization for single-
parent families*

PETS

RSPCA
The Causeway
Horsham
West Sussex RH12 1HG
0403 64181
*Aims to prevent cruelty to animals;
runs two animal hospitals in London, 71 clinics, 60 homes, a hostel
at Heathrow airport and 200
branches throughout the country*

**Peoples' Dispensary for Sick
Animals**
PDSA House
South Street
Dorking
Surrey RH4 2LB
0306 888291
*Charitable trust offering free treat-
ment to animals if their owners
can't pay*

Blue Cross
1 Hugh Street
London SW1
01-834 4224/5556
*Treats animals whose owners can't
pay; runs two hospitals in London,
one in Grimsby, and clinics all
over Britain*

Royal College of Veterinary Surgeons
35 Belgrave Square
London SW1
01-235 4971
Will supply a register of qualified vets for a fee

HEALTH

Family Practitioner Committee
See your local telephone directory
Supplies lists of local General Practitioners

Health Education Council
78 New Oxford Street
London WC1A 1AH
01-631 0930
Gives information and advice, publishes leaflets

Scottish Health Education Group
Woodburn House
Canaan Lane
Edinburgh EH10 4SG
031-447 8044
Publishes information

Institute for Complementary Medicine
21 Portland Place
London W1N 3AF
01-636 9543
Publishes information on alternative therapies available

British Holistic Medical Association
179 Gloucester Place
London NW1
01-262 5299
Publishes information

Age Concern
Bernard Sunley House
60 Pitcairn Road
Mitcham
Surrey CR4 3LL
01-640 5431
Advice and information on the welfare of elderly people; 1100 local volunteer groups

Disabled Living Foundation
380–384 Harrow Road
London W9 2HU
01-289 6111
Advice for the disabled, showroom for aids for disabled and elderly people

Royal Association for Disability and Rehabilitation
25 Mortimer Street
London W1N 8AB
01-637 5400
Publishes information and offers advice on social and legal aspects of disability

Family Planning Association
27–35 Mortimer Street
London W1
01-636 7866
Birth control services and information

Pregnancy Advisory Service
11–13 Charlotte Street
London W1
01-637 8962
Advice on contraception, sterility, pregnancy, unwanted pregnancy and abortion

British Red Cross Society
9 Grosvenor Cresent
London SW1X 7EJ
01-235 5454
Concerned with first aid, nursing and welfare; runs first aid courses

St. John Ambulance Association
1 Grosvenor Crescent
London SW1X 7EF
01-235 5231
Trains people in first aid, volunteers help at public functions to provide first aid

St. Andrew's Ambulance Association
St Andrew's House
Milton Street
Glasgow G4 OHR
041-331 4031
Runs first aid courses

Samaritans
Head Office
39 Walbrook Street
London EC4
01-283 3400/629 9000
Confidential service offering advice and support to anyone in distress

For your local branch, look in the telephone directory, either on the emergency numbers page inside the front cover, or in the alphabetical listing.

HOME SAFETY

◆ Your local fire brigade will also give advice and information on preventing fires. See your telephone directory.

Royal Society for the Prevention of Accidents
Cannon House
The Priory
Queensway
Birmingham B4 6BS
021-200 2461
Information on all aspects of safety in the home

Fire Protection Association
140 Aldersgate Street
London EC1A 4HX
01-606 3757
Information on fire and its prevention

Index

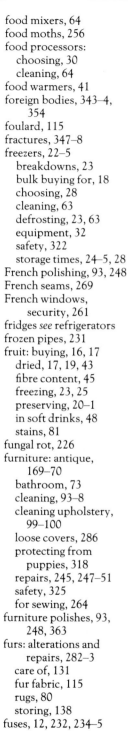

Acknowledgments

Author's Acknowledgments

This book is the result of many years of writing about all aspects of running a home. I could never have achieved it without help over those years of innumerable friends, especially Laurie Purden and Charlotte Lessing at *Good Housekeeping* and George Seddon at *The Observer*, without whom I would never have made it in journalism at all. I have received invaluable help and advice from The Consumers' Association, The Building Centre, The Design Centre, The Royal Institute of British Architects, British Standards Institution, Disabled Living Foundation, ICI Ltd., The Home Laundering Consultative Council, Dylon Ltd., Shirley Barnett of Copydex Ltd., Evode Ltd., The Royal Society for the Prevention of Accidents, The Glass and Glazing Federation, The Royal Society for Protection of Animals, Rentokil Ltd., Concorde Lighting International, Christopher Wray, The Department of Energy, The Heating and Ventilating Contractors Association, The Department of the Environment, The National Trust, The Electricity Council, The Electrical Association for Women, The British Gas Corporation, The Good Housekeeping Institute, The Council of British Ceramic Sanitaryware Manufacturers, The London Fire Brigade, The Solid Fuel Advisory Service, Afia Carpets. I'd like also to thank all my friends, family and neighbours who between them gave me hundreds of tips I hadn't thought of, including Rosamund and Eion Downs, Jane and Phil Glynn, Kathleen le Mare, Pauline Adams, Sue Donovan, Tessa Lippa, Maggie Phillips and specially to John Phillips who researched and coordinated it all with me.

Dorling Kindersley would like to thank Judy Sandeman and Simonne Waud for production, Lindy Newton and Sarah Bevan for editorial help, Mike Snaith and everyone at MS for the typesetting, Diane Burston for proofreading and Hilary Bird for the index.

Illustrators
Nick Hall
Chris Forsey
Will Giles
Sandra Pond
Kuo Chang Chen
Andrew MacDonald

Typesetting Typeset in 10½/11pt Goudy by MS Filmsetting Limited, Frome, Somerset
Reproduction Colourscan, Hong Kong